ENCYCLOPEDIA OF
BUSINE$$
AND
FINANCE

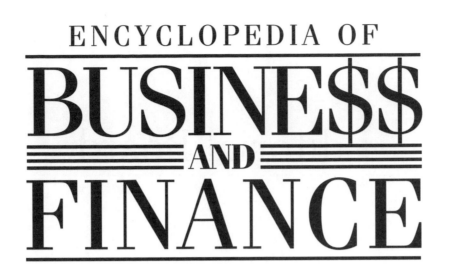

Editorial Board

ENCYCLOPEDIA OF

BUSINE$$

AND

FINANCE

VOLUME 2

BURTON S. KALISKI,
Editor-in-Chief

Macmillan Reference USA
an imprint of the Gale Group
New York • Detroit • San Francisco • London • Boston • Woodbridge, CT

Encyclopedia of Business and Finance

Macmillan Reference USA
An imprint of the Gale Group
27500 Drake Rd.
Farmington Hills, MI 48331-3535

Macmillan Reference USA
An imprint of the Gale Group
1633 Broadway
New York, NY 10019

Library of Congress Catalog Card No.: 00-107932

Printing number
2 3 4 5 6 7 8 9 10

ISBN 0-02-865065-4 (set).—ISBN 0-02-865066-2 (v. 1).—ISBN 0-02-865067-0 (v. 2)

Printed in the United States of America by the Gale Group

Gale Group and Design is a trademark used herein under license.

I

IDEA SELLING

(SEE: *Advertising*)

IMPORTS

(SEE: *International Trade*)

IMPULSE ITEMS

(SEE: *Shopping*)

INCOME

By working and being productive, households earn an income and businesses make a profit. The total amount that households and businesses receive *before* taxes and other expenses are deducted is called aggregate income. The amount of money that is left *after* taxes and other expenses have been deducted from one's pay is called disposable income. Discretionary income is what consumers (households) have to pay for the goods and services they desire. We shall focus only on households and how they consume their income. Households spend most of their discretionary income on consumption. Some consumers spend even more than their current discretionary income on consumption by borrowing. Consumption consists of almost everything that consumers purchase, from durable to nondurable goods as well as all types of services. The only exception to this rule is the purchase of a new home: It is counted as an investment because homes tend to appreciate in value.

Households (individuals) cannot spend all their earnings on consumer goods and services. Part of the income each household receives must be used to pay different kinds of taxes, such as income taxes to federal, state, and local governments. Most state and local governments also impose sales taxes. In addition to paying income and sales taxes, households may also have to pay property taxes to local governments. After paying taxes and spending income on consumables, some households put aside money as savings to be used for consumption at a later time.

Earnings differ among individuals and households because of several factors: (1) inborn differences, (2) human-capital differences, (3) work and job performance, (4) discrimination, (5) age, (6) labor mobility, (7) government programs and policies, and (8) luck.

Inborn differences are those characteristics that one is blessed with, such as strength, energy, stamina, mental capacity, natural ability, and motivation.

Human-capital differences reflect how people invest various amounts of both their physical and mental capacities toward the achievement of specific goals.

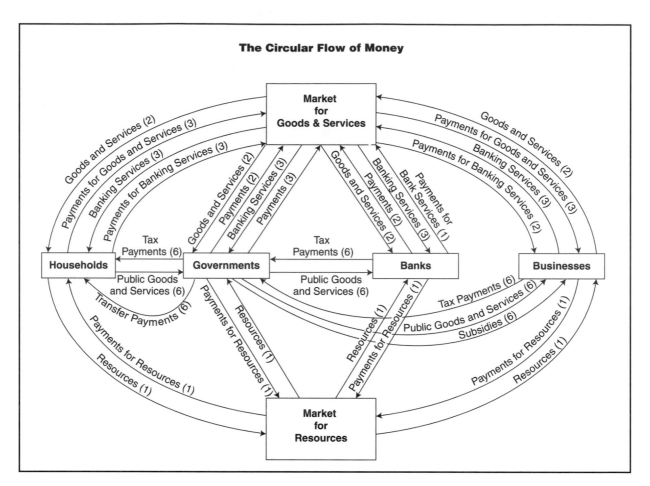

The Circular Flow of Money

Figure 1

SOURCE: Federal Reserve Bank of St. Louis, Missouri, Council on Economic Education. *The Money Tree*. University of Missouri-St. Louis: June 1989.

Work and job performance indicates how individuals differ in their preferences regarding the trade-off between work and leisure. Those who wish to work more usually receive a higher income; others prefer more leisure at the cost of earning a lower income. People also prefer different types of jobs. These specific job choices will affect the distribution of income.

Discrimination is treating people differently solely on the basis of factors unrelated to productivity.

Age affects earnings significantly. Most individuals earn little before the age of eighteen. Earnings tend to increase as workers gain experience and their productivity increases.

Labor mobility—the willingness to go where the jobs are or to move wherever the company has a need—enhances an individual's income potential. Immobility limits workers' response to changes in wage rates and can contribute to an unequal distribution of income.

Government policies and programs, such as benefit programs and the progressive income tax, reduce income inequality. The minimum wage may also increase income inequality.

Luck plays a role in determining the distribution of income, but choices are perhaps the most important factor.

BIBLIOGRAPHY

Mings, Turley. (2000). *The Study of Economics: Principles, Concepts, and Applications*, 6th ed. Guilford, CT: Dushkin Publishing Group.

GREGORY P. VALENTINE

INCOME TAX, HISTORY OF

A tax consists of a rate and a base. Because income is the base for the income tax, a central question is: What constitutes income? Different theoretical concepts of income exist in economics, accounting, and taxation. The base of income to which the federal income tax rate structure applies is taxable income as constitutionally and statutorily defined. Thus, the concept of taxable income is grounded in theory and modified by political dynamics and administrative concerns.

From its modern introduction in 1913, the rate structure for the individual income tax has been progressive, meaning that tax rates graduate upward as the base of taxable income increases. Different tax rates apply to ranges of income, called brackets. Over time, the number of brackets and tax rates that apply to them have varied greatly. The tax rate applied to the last dollar of taxable income earned by a taxpayer is called the marginal tax rate. Total income tax as a percentage of total taxable income is the average tax rate, whereas total income tax as a percentage of total economic income is the effective tax rate.

ADOPTION AND EARLY IMPLEMENTATION OF FEDERAL INCOME TAX

Until the Civil War, federal revenues came from relatively low tariff rates imposed on a broad base of imported goods and from excise taxes. However, tariffs and excise taxes could not support escalations in government spending caused by the Civil War. Drawing on the example of the British Parliament's adoption of an income tax in 1799 to help finance the Napoleonic Wars, the U.S. Congress adopted the first federal income tax in 1861 to partially finance the Civil War. Legislators regarded the war-motivated income tax as an indirect tax because neither real nor

A tax collector in his office.

personal properties were taxed directly. The constitutionality of the tax was not challenged, and it expired in 1872.

During the post-Civil War years, high tariffs, often established to protect selected industries from foreign competition, and excise taxes were the major sources of revenues. By the early 1890s, tax structure was a political issue, with debate centering on the equity of the tax burden. In

1894, with strong Democratic support, a modest income tax was adopted. The first $4000 of income was exempt from taxation, and the initial tax rate was 2 percent. The prevailing view was that this tax would apply to high-income taxpayers and corporations without extending to the wages and salaries of working people.

In 1895, the U.S. Supreme Court declared the income tax unconstitutional in the case of *Pollock v. Farmers' Loan and Trust Co.* on the basis that it was a direct tax. Article I, Section 9 of the original U.S. Constitution provided that "No capitation, or other direct tax shall be laid, unless in proportion to the census." After the income tax was declared unconstitutional, Democrats began to introduce constitutional amendments to permit it. By the early 1900s, political support had broadened to include progressive Republicans. The Sixteenth Amendment, which legalized an income tax, was submitted to the states in 1909 and ratified in 1913. At this time, roughly 2 percent of American households paid the new tax.

MODIFICATIONS TO FEDERAL INCOME TAX OVER TIME

Various aspects of the federal income tax have changed since its inception.

World War I and Depression Years. During World War I, the Democrats altered the tax by adopting highly progressive rates and structuring the base to consist of the incomes of corporations and upper-income individuals. Additionally, an excess profits tax was imposed. This was a progressive tax on above-normal profits, and it generated most of the new tax revenue raised during World War I. Together the income tax and excess profits tax became an explicit means for the redistribution of income. To administer these taxes, the Bureau of Internal Revenue reorganized along functional lines, expanded in size, and employed such experts as accountants, lawyers, and economists. In 1916, "reporting at the source" was adopted, which required corporations to report salaries, dividends, and wages to the Treasury Department.

When the Republicans took control of the presidency and Congress in 1921, taxes on corporations and upper-income taxpayers were reduced, the excess profits tax was repealed, and the tax rate structure was adjusted to be less progressive. Many preferences were incorporated into tax law in the form of deductions, and the preferential taxation of capital gains was adopted. A capital gain is a gain that results from the sale of a capital asset, such as shares of stock in a corporation. In 1932 under President Hoover and in 1935 and 1937 under President Roosevelt, tax rates increased and the tax base expanded. However, the income tax was not a dominant policy focus during the 1930s, partially because the federal government relied heavily on excise taxes and debt to obtain funds to support government activities.

World War II. The most significant impact of World War II on the individual income tax was to transform it to a mass tax that was broadly based and progressive. In 1941, changes were made to both rates and base. Higher tax rates were adopted and lower exemptions were allowed, thus expanding the base. Higher tax rates were adopted again in 1942. With the inclusion of a surtax, tax rates ranged from 13 percent on the first $2000 of taxable income to 82 percent on taxable income in excess of $200,000. The number of taxpayers increased from 3.9 million in 1939 to 42.6 million in 1945. At the end of the war, 60 percent of households paid the income tax. The efficiency of collection was enhanced by the adoption of payroll withholding in 1943. By 1944, the individual income tax generated about 40 percent of federal revenues.

For corporations, progressive tax rates, also called graduated tax rates, were introduced in 1935, repealed in 1938, and remained flat during World War II. However, wartime corporations were subject to a graduated tax on excess profits, with the maximum rate of 50 percent after an allowance for a substantial credit.

During the World War II years, there was a major shift in the taxing power of the federal government relative to state and local governments. Federal revenues, as a percent of total taxes collected by all levels of government, increased from 16 percent in 1940 to 51 percent in 1950.

With some modifications, the basic structure of the income tax remained in place during the post-World War II years and continues to the present. Individual tax rates were reduced from wartime highs, and the tax base began to narrow with the adoption of exemptions, deductions, and credits. Inflation in the 1960s and 1970s created a condition called "bracket creep." Taxpayers whose monetary incomes were increasing because of inflation, but with no equivalent increase in purchasing power, were pushed into higher tax brackets and thus subject to higher marginal tax rates. Because the corporate rate structure was not progressive, bracket creep did not apply to corporations. Although the corporate and individual income taxes had generated roughly the same revenue in 1950, by 1980, partially as a result of bracket creep, the individual income tax generated four times the revenue of the corporate tax.

After World War II. During the post-World War II years, the tax system was used increasingly as a means of financing. A government may deliver services by direct payment or indirectly by subsidy through a reduction in tax. For example, the deduction for home mortgage interest provides a tax subsidy for investing in housing. The term *tax expenditure* is used to describe subsidies for various purposes achieved by use of exemptions, deductions, and credits. Exempt income is not subject to tax. A deduction reduces the amount of income that is subject to tax, and a credit represents a direct reduction in the amount of tax liability. From 1967 to 1982, tax expenditure increased from 38 percent to 73.5 percent of tax receipts. Tax expenditure provisions complicate the determination of taxable income, the base for the income tax.

The sophisticated study of tax policy, which continues to the present, began on a widespread basis during the post-World War II period. Central questions concerned the impact of tax policy on the amount of investment, the movement of capital, and labor-force participation.

From 1980 until 2000. The 1980s began with the adoption of the Economic Recovery Tax Act (ERTA) during President Reagan's term. A key provision of this act was the indexing of tax rates for inflation to eliminate bracket creep. ERTA provided for significant reductions in tax rates and began to reduce the role of the income tax in the nation's revenue system. During the 1980s, interest in tax reform grew, culminating in passage of the Tax Reform Act of 1986. The goal of this act was to be revenue-neutral, neither increasing nor decreasing revenues. It provided for a reduction in tax rates by expanding the tax base through the elimination of some tax expenditures.

After passage of the 1986 Tax Reform Act, attention shifted to the taxation of capital gains and replacement of the income tax. Beginning in 1987, capital gains and ordinary income were taxed in the same manner. Then preferential treatment was reintroduced for capital gains. Commonly proposed alternatives to the income tax include the value-added tax and national sales taxes, two taxes for which the tax base would be consumption rather than income. Another alternative is the flat tax on income. In theory, with one single tax rate—a flat tax—all taxpayers would pay the same proportion of taxable income in taxes. If the base of taxable income were defined as earned income, taxpayers receiving only interest and dividends would be excluded from the payment of taxes. Currently interest and dividends are subject to a double tax. Corporations pay income tax on the earnings from which dividends and interest are paid, and individuals pay income tax on dividend and interest income that they receive. Most flat tax proposals eliminate double taxation.

ADMINISTRATION OF FEDERAL INCOME TAX

The Internal Revenue Service (IRS), which administers the income tax, is part of the U.S. Department of Treasury. Adapting to changes in technology to achieve the most efficient processing of information is a major challenge for the IRS. For many years the IRS was organized on a geographical basis, but in 1998 it was reorganized into four functional divisions differentiated by type of taxpayer.

For corporate and individual taxpayers that report on a calendar-year basis, annual tax returns are due on or before March 15 and April 15, respectively, following the close of the calendar year. Providing that the tax due is paid, time extensions for filing returns may be obtained. Although the closing dates for the quarters differ, both individuals and corporations are subject to the payment of estimated tax in quarterly installments. Taxpayers who fail to file tax returns or fail to pay taxes are subject to monetary penalties, fines, and possibly prison sentences.

EXTENSION OF INCOME TAX TO THE STATE LEVEL

Wisconsin was the first state to adopt an income tax—in 1911. Massachusetts and New York soon followed by adopting income taxes when faced with problems related to World War I. Most other states adopted the income tax as a response to revenue crises created by the Great Depression. At the state level, definitions of taxable income differ from the federal definition and differ among states. Exemptions, deductions, and rates of taxation vary among states. As of January 2000, Nevada, South Dakota, Washington, and Wyoming did not impose individual or corporate income taxes; Alaska, Florida, New Hampshire, and Texas did not impose an individual income tax; and Michigan did not impose a corporate income tax. Formulas are used to allocate the income of multistate corporations among the states in which they operate.

(SEE ALSO: *Taxation*)

BIBLIOGRAPHY

Brownlee, W. Elliot. (1996). *Federal Taxation in America.* New York: Cambridge University Press.

Witte, John F. (1985). *The Politics and Development of the Federal Income Tax.* Madison: University of Wisconsin Press.

JEAN E. HARRIS

INDEPENDENCE STANDARDS BOARD

The Independence Standards Board (ISB) was established in May 1997 as a result of discussions between the American Institute of Certified Public Accountants (AICPA) and the U.S. Securities and Exchange Commission (SEC). The various securities laws enacted by Congress and administered by the SEC recognize that the integrity and credibility of the financial reporting process for public companies depends, in large part, on auditors remaining independent from their audit clients. The operating policies of the ISB are designed to permit timely, thorough, and open study of issues involving auditor independence and to encourage broad public participation in the process of establishing and improving independence standards. The mission of the ISB is to establish independence standards applicable to audits of public entities in order to serve the public interest and to protect and promote investors' confidence in the securities markets.

ISB STRUCTURE

The ISB is a board of eight members, supported by an Independence Issues Committee, an executive director, and other support staff. The ISB operates as an independent body, funded by the AICPA SEC Practice Section of its Division of CPA Firms (SECPS). Accordingly, the ISB has authority to make public statements on matters relating to the subject of auditor independence in connection with audits of public entities without clearance from the SECPS or the AICPA board of directors. ISB board members serve on a part-time basis. Four are public members, three are senior partners of SECPS member firms, and one is the president of the AICPA or the president's designee. Public members are supposed to be prominent individuals of high integrity and reputation who understand the importance of investor protection, the U.S. capital markets, and the accounting profession. The appointment of the initial board was made by the SECPS Executive Committee after consultation with the SEC and the president of the AICPA. The terms of the board members are staggered and may be of varied lengths. Following the appointment of the initial board, successor public members will be nominated for three-year terms by the existing public members of the board. New members from SECPS member firms will be nominated for three-year terms by the SECPS Executive Committee subject to the approval of the AICPA's board of directors. The entire board will elect replacement members from those slates of nominees. The board selects its own chairperson from among the four public members.

ROLE OF CHAIR

The chair of the ISB serves a three-year term. The chair has powers and responsibilities relating to the appointment and supervision of personnel at the ISB, the distribution of work among such personnel, and the use and expenditure of funds by the ISB within the budget constraints approved by the ISB. The chair also has the authority to establish and appoint persons to task forces following approval by the ISB and after consultation with the executive director and others. The chair provides the leadership in identifying the pronouncements the ISB will issue, including, if necessary and appropriate, the authority, hierarchy, and exposure process for each pronouncement. All proposed standards will be exposed for public comment for a minimum of thirty days.

ISB STAFF

The ISB has a full-time executive director and, as necessary or appropriate, other full-time professional and administrative staff. The ISB staff fields telephone and other inquiries concerning independence issues in the manner that the board directs and pursuant to policies established by the board. In responding to inquiries, the ISB staff provides informal interpretations or guidance to the inquiring parties. As appropriate, the ISB staff informs the board regarding issues raised in such inquiries that might benefit from more comprehensive consideration by the board and, to the extent delegated or assigned by the board, the Independence Issues Committee (IIC). The ISB and its staff address independence

inquiries that arise, and the ISB understands that the SEC will encourage registrants and auditors to look to the ISB and its staff to address such matters. Further, the ISB understands that the SEC staff expects to refer specific independence-related issues that may arise to the ISB. Absent express ratification by the board, ISB staff interpretations will be considered as applying only to the particular parties directly affected by the interpretation, who may rely on such interpretation. The executive director advises and consults with the AICPA, including its Professional Ethics Executive Committee, as appropriate, on independence issues of interest to the AICPA. A public file on all ISB meetings is kept for public reference and inspection for a reasonable period of time consistent with the public interest in the AICPA library.

THE INDEPENDENCE ISSUES COMMITTEE

The Independence Issues Committee (IIC) assists the ISB in establishing independence standards through the timely identification and discussion of emerging independence issues within the framework of existing authoritative literature. The IIC also addresses broader interpretative issues, including those that emerge from inquiries fielded by the ISB staff, and communicates its consensus on such issues to the board. The IIC makes publicly available its consensuses and the rationales or bases for such conclusions.

The IIC is comprised of nine certified public accountants (CPAs), drawn from SECPS member firms that audit SEC registrants, who are knowledgeable about the existing independence literature and are in positions to be aware of emerging practice issues as they develop. The SECPS Executive Committee nominates the nine members of the IIC, in consultation with and subject to the approval of the ISB. The ISB specifies the terms of the IIC members. The ISB names the chair from the nine members of the IIC.

The meetings of the IIC are usually open to the public, but sessions or portions of sessions may be closed to the public if they deal with (1) administrative matters, (2) matters that may cause substantial harm or injury (a rare occurrence), or (3) matters involving or relating to advice of counsel; all such closed sessions must be authorized by the chair or his or her designee, and in no instance can the SEC staff be excluded from these sessions. For the IIC to reach a consensus, at least six IIC members must approve the judgment or determination and no more than two IIC members may oppose it. On reaching a consensus, the IIC will promptly forward the matter to the ISB for ratification. If a majority of the ISB ratifies the consensus, the ISB understands that the SEC will consider such consensus as having substantial authoritative support.

PUBLIC HEARINGS

The ISB may seek information about independence matters by holding a public hearing. The basis for a public hearing generally will be an exposure draft, although the ISB may also determine to hold a public hearing for any other purpose. Each public hearing will be conducted by one or more members of the ISB or IIC, the executive director, or technical staff pursuant to procedures approved by the ISB for such hearing. The ISB will publicly announce its intent to hold a public hearing at least sixty days prior to the hearing, unless a shorter period (but in no event less than thirty days) is considered appropriate by the ISB, in any manner reasonably designed to inform the public.

Any individual or organization may request to be heard at a public hearing, and, to the extent practicable, the ISB will attempt to schedule all those making timely requests. Submission of written comments, a position paper, or an outline of a proposed oral presentation will generally be a condition of being heard. Materials submitted to the ISB in this connection will constitute a part of its public file.

More information is available from Independence Standards Board, 6th floor, 1211 Avenue of the Americas, New York, NY 10036-8775; (212)596-6133 (telephone); (212)596-6137 (fax); or http://www.cpaindependence.org.

(SEE ALSO: *American Institute of Certified Public Accountants; Auditing; Securities and Exchange Commission*)

C. RICHARD BAKER

INFLATION

(SEE: *Economic Cycles*)

INFLUENCE

(SEE: *Management: Authority and Responsibility*)

INFORMATION PROCESSING

Information processing may be defined as the manipulation of data to produce useful information. Over the past several years, the explosion of sophisticated computer software has dramatically changed the way computer users create documents. When word-processing, spreadsheet, and database software packages first became available to the public in the late 1970s and early 1980s, they were very different. The user interface, menus, and procedures were quite different depending on the program. As the years passed and computer software became more sophisticated, the software programs began to share many common features. Today, computer software not only shares common features, it is extremely compatible—that is, information created in one software package can be shared with that of another.

In today's modern office, computer documents often require that a combination of software packages be used together. For example, it might be necessary to place a spreadsheet in a word-processing document or a spreadsheet graph on one of the slides in a presentation file. This ability to integrate software applications is one of the most useful features of using Microsoft Windows and other software designed to be used in the Windows environment.

Integration simply means the sharing of information among applications. Windows allows the user to use different software packages as if they were parts of a single program. Shelley, Cashman, and Vermaat (2000) explain that integrating these software programs allows the user to move quickly among applications and transfer text and graphics easily. The Windows environment offers three ways that information can be integrated: (1) the clipboard, (2) linking objects, and (3) embedding objects.

THE CLIPBOARD—COPYING, CUTTING, AND PASTING

Software running in the Windows environment makes it very easy to copy and move text from one software application to another. The user can copy or move text, graphics, or other objects from one place to another using the clipboard application. For example, a chart created in Excel could be copied and pasted into a written report created in Word. To complete this procedure successfully, the user must first select the desired text or object. Then the user may choose to copy or cut (move) the selected text from the edit menu. Shortcuts usually exist for these two commands, such as clicking a button on the toolbar. If the user copies the selected text, an exact copy of the original text will be placed on the clipboard. If the user cuts the text, however, the original text will be moved to the clipboard. Text that is placed on the clipboard will stay there until it is pasted somewhere else. To paste the information, the user selects the paste option from the edit menu. It is important to remember that only one object can be stored on the clipboard at a time. When a new object is copied or cut to the clipboard, whatever information was previously there will be removed.

Because multiple software programs (applications) can run at the same time in Windows, the user can place information on the clipboard, open another program, and paste the information in the desired location in the new program. This method is the simplest and most frequently used for sharing information among software applications.

Copying/cutting and pasting among different applications has several advantages. This proce-

dure saves time, eliminates keying errors, and allows the user to tie various applications together as if they were part of a single program.

LINKING INFORMATION BETWEEN PROGRAMS

Some limitations exist in using the clipboard to copy and move information between applications. Once the information has been pasted from the clipboard to the new location, all ties between the original source document and the pasted information cease to exist. The destination document, which contains the pasted information, will not be automatically updated if any changes are made to the original source document. This limitation creates a problem in many of today's fast-paced work environments. For example, many annual reports created in word-processing packages contain financial status information that is produced in a spreadsheet package. If the financial data are changed or updated in any way, the information that was previously pasted into the actual word-processing report would not show those changes.

To rectify many of these situations, Windows has developed Object Linking and Embedding (OLE). The first OLE method, linking, allows the user to share information among applications by creating a connection (or link) between the original source document and the destination document. If the source is altered after an OLE has been established, the destination document will automatically update and show all the changes that have been made. When data are linked between two documents in this way, the data are not actually stored in a destination file. The destination document stores only the information it needs to link back to the original source document. If changes need to be made to the linked information, the changes must be made and saved in the original source application.

Linking is very useful when there is a large group of users who need to view the source data. These users can access the source data and then view the updates if changes are made frequently. To link a selected object that has already been copied to the clipboard, the user must choose the

Paste special option on the edit menu. Within this menu, the user selects the Paste link option.

The user may find several advantages by deciding to link objects. Linking does not waste the computer's memory or storage space because it never duplicates information in two separate locations. Linking allows the user to place objects such as those created in other applications or sound and video clips into word-processing, spreadsheet, and presentation documents that have no other options for performing such procedures.

Linking can also be very beneficial when different users have to share computing tasks. For example, the accounting department might be responsible for the creation of all spreadsheets and graphs within a company. If the accounting department saves the files on the network drive, employees throughout the company can link these spreadsheet and graph files into their necessary applications. If changes need to be made to the original spreadsheet files, the accounting department would be responsible for making these updates. When other users throughout the company open their destination documents that contain the link, the changes can either be automatically updated (called an automatic link) or can be updated when the user requests it (called a manual link). Most Windows software has an Update Now feature that allows a user to decide when to update a link. A lock feature is also widely available in case the user does not want the link to be accidentally updated.

One important point to remember when linking information is that the destination document must always be able to locate the original source document. If a destination file was copied to a floppy disk and taken to another computer, all linked files must also be copied onto the floppy disk in order for the links to be able to find their connections.

EMBEDDING OBJECTS

The second type of OLE process, embedding, is another feature of Windows. When information from one application is embedded into another, the information becomes part of the destination

file. Although this process requires the use of more memory, it allows the destination file to be self-supporting. When the embedded object needs to be edited or updated, the user must double-click on the object. This double-clicking opens the source application file inside an editing window. All the necessary menus and features will be available in this window for use in editing the source information. After making the appropriate changes to the embedded object, the user simply clicks outside of the editing window and returns to the destination document. Because the user does not have to keep opening and closing the source application file, a great deal of time is saved. Another advantage of this feature is that the user can make changes in the embedded object and the destination file without touching the original source document and vice versa. In keeping with linking objects, the user must be able to access all source applications in order to make changes in any embedded objects. The user does not, however, need to have access to the original source application in order to print or view the destination document. To embed an object, the user follows the same procedures as for linking an object except that in the Paste special menu the Paste option is selected instead of the Paste Link option.

O'Leary and O'Leary (1996) explain that embedding text or objects is often favored over linking objects in the following situations: (1) The size of the file is not important; (2) users have access to source applications, but not the original source file; and (3) the embedded data is changed only occasionally. For example, if the user intends to use the shared information at a location removed from the source file, it would be necessary to embed the object in order to edit the information. When linking, however, the user must always have access to the source file via a network or an accessible fixed drive.

Unfortunately, not every software program supports OLE features. If a software package supports OLE features, it is called OLE-aware. The first version of OLE was introduced with Windows 3.x; therefore, nearly all software created to run under the Windows environment is OLE-aware.

CONCLUSION

Information processing is a broad concept covering the many aspects of manipulating data to produce useful information. This article has addressed the specific skills of integrating information by using the clipboard, linked objects, and embedded objects. With the increased sophistication of software packages, the concepts and skills used in copying/cutting and pasting to the clipboard, linking objects, and embedding objects are no longer difficult to use. Software integration allows a number of software application packages to be used as if they were a single package, thereby increasing efficiency and productivity within the work environment. Various departments within an organization are able to access files from any desktop and link them to necessary applications. Users are able to save time and eliminate keying errors. As these activities become more commonplace, it may be necessary for computer users within organizations to update their skills in these areas.

BIBLIOGRAPHY

O'Leary, Timothy J., and O'Leary, Linda I. (1996). *Microsoft Office Integration*. New York: McGraw-Hill.

Shelly, G. B., Cashman, T. J., and Vermaat, M. E. (2000). *Microsoft Office 2000: Introductory Concepts and Techniques*. Cambridge, MA: Course Technology.

J. D. THOMERSON
DONNIE MCGAHEE
MARY ALICE GRIFFIN

INFORMATION PROCESSING: AN HISTORICAL PERSPECTIVE

Throughout history humanity has tried to invent new ways to simplify the problem-solving process. With each generation, people have used various tools and methods to help them process information. Information is defined as letters, symbols, or numbers that are used to express an idea.

The history of information processing goes back five thousand years to the abacus, one of the earliest known counting devices. This first reported calculator or processor was developed in ancient Egypt and in the Far East during the thirteenth century. The abacus consisted of wires strung across a rectangular frame. The frame divides each wire into two sections: The one on the top contains two beads, and the one on the bottom contains five beads. Each top bead represents the quantity 5; each bottom bead represents the quantity 1. Each wire represents a place: units, tens, hundreds, and so on. Computations were done by moving the correct number of beads up to the top of the frame.

The invention of logarithms by John Napier was a landmark in the history of mathematics, enabling people to multiply or divide large numbers quickly and accurately. As a product of logarithms, Napier invented a tool, nicknamed "Napier's Bones," that was used to multiply, divide, and extract square and cube roots.

In 1642 a French philosopher and mathematician, Blaise Pascal, invented the first adding machine, called the Pascaline. It consisted of a series of ten-toothed wheels connected to numbers that could be added together by advancing the wheels by a correct number of teeth. The Pascaline was used until it was replaced by the electronic calculator in the 1960s.

In the 1820s, Sir Charles Babbage, an inventor and genius, developed a mechanical device that could be programmed to perform simple mathematical calculations. He called his invention the Difference Engine. In 1834, he designed the Analytical Engine, which could do more complicated calculations. It could multiply, divide, add, subtract, and even print out an answer. It included an input device, a storage facility to hold numbers for processing, a processor or number calculator, a control unit to direct tasks to be performed, and an output device. The concept used in the Analytical Engine is the concept used in today's general-purpose computer, which is why Babbage is considered to be the father of the modern computer and the field of study known today as operational research.

The Hollerith Tabulator was created at MIT in 1884.

In 1884, an American inventor at MIT, Herman Hollerith, filed his first patent for a system of encoding data on cards through a series of punched holes. His hand-fed press sensed the holes in punched cards as a wire passed through the holes into a cup of mercury beneath the card, closing the electrical circuit. This process triggered mechanical counters and sorter bins that tabulated the appropriate data. The U.S. government used Hollerith's machine to help with the 1890 census tabulation. His later machines mechanized the card-feeding process, added numbers, and sorted cards, in addition to merely counting data. In 1896, Hollerith started the Tabulating

Herman Hollerith.

Machine Company, which was the predecessor of the IBM (International Business Machines) Corporation.

Two major types of information-processing equipment were developed at the end of the nineteenth century. Christopher Sholes developed the first typewriter; it operated at a speed faster than a person could write, and its letters were always legible. Alexander Graham Bell, Charles Painter, and Chickester Bell invented the first telephone, which enhanced the processing of oral information.

Dr. John V. Atanasoff and Clifford Berry are believed to have invented the first electronic digital computer during the period 1937-1942. Their invention was called ABC, which stood for Atanasoff-Berry Computer.

In 1945, Howard Aiken, a mathematician, created the first digital computer, constructed from mechanical adding machine parts. An instruction sequence was fed into the machine on a roll of punched paper tape, rather than being stored in the computer, to solve a problem.

A research team at the University of Pennsylvania under the leadership of Dr. John W. Mauchly and J. Presper Eckert, Jr., was working with the U.S. Army in 1945 on the ENIAC (Electrical Numerical Integrator and Calculator) project. Their goal was to develop a calculating device with memory that could set firing tables for different weapons under varied conditions with target accuracy. They refined the ABC by developing five functional units—called central control, central arithmetic, input, output, and memory—to enhance these first electronic computers.

In 1946, John Presper Eckert and John Mauchly introduced the first "true computer" by unveiling the ENIAC I. It was an enormous machine covering 1800 square feet, weighing 60,000 pounds, and consuming 160 kilowatts of electrical power. This early machine had the calculating power of today's pocket calculator. With so many vacuum tubes, one of them would burn out every few minutes, which severely limited the running time of a program. They started the Eckert-Mauchly Computer Corporation, which was later bought out by Remington Rand Corporation, which changed the name to the UNIVAC division of Remington Rand.

The transistor, which was invented in the late 1940s, offered a huge advantage over vacuum tubes for building computers. Improvements in transistors led to the first integrated circuit, in which a number of transistors and other electronic devices, together with the wiring that connects them, are manufactured in one piece. Development of this technology changed the future of computers forever.

The next computer was UNIVAC I, built by Remington Rand. It introduced the use of magnetic tape as a means of input into a computer. The UNIVAC I was the first commercially available computer; the first one was installed at the Census Bureau in 1951 and the second one was installed at General Electric Appliance Park.

In the 1950s, when a computer was first used for business and engineering applications, the term *data processing* was first used, defined as the process of changing letters, numbers, and symbols into usable written information. The next attempt at data processing was the development of word-processing equipment to automate the production stage of typing documents. These machines produced high-quality documents efficiently but, unlike data-processing equipment, did not have calculating capabilities.

Until 1956, the only commercial computer was the UNIVAC I. IBM, recognizing the large potential for commercial applications, developed the IBM 650 computer system. Smaller than the UNIVAC I, it became the most successful computer system in use during the 1950s.

The 1960s saw the introduction of second-generation computers that used transistor technology. The transistor performed the same duties as the vacuum tube but was less expensive, required little power, and generated little heat. Computers became smaller in size, lower in cost, and quicker in operation when transistors replaced the vacuum tubes. Second-generation computers replaced machine language with assembly language, allowing abbreviated programming codes to replace long, difficult binary codes. Second-generation computers, however, had limited compatibility and used low-level programming languages. More than five thousand second-generation computers were installed in the United States, with the most successful machine being the IBM 1401.

Integrated circuits replaced transistors in third-generation computers. Integrated circuitry utilized extremely small chips of silicon mounted on a ceramic or glass substrate, segments of which had been metalized to form an electronic circuit similar to the transistor found on the printed circuit board. Third-generation computers had increased internal processing speed, disk-oriented systems, compatibility and multiprogramming capability, and data communications with on-line systems.

Fourth-generation computers are characterized by a microprocessor contained on a single silicon chip, called a semiconductor. These machines were smaller and more energy-efficient.

IBM's System/360 computers gave customers a choice of processors, power, speed, and memory. Intel, the leading manufacturer of microprocessor chips, introduced the Pentium processor. The microcomputer moved the computer into small businesses and homes.

The history of information processing is vast and filled with inventions. We have gone from an abacus to a graphing calculator, from Babbage's Analytical Engine to powerful computers in the home. We now have cell phones, faxes, and answering machines.

IBM, which entered the computer field in 1951, created the personal computer for business and home use and rapidly advanced the field of data processing. Its relatively low-cost desktop microcomputer, with its enhanced graphics and communications capabilities, gave birth to the huge software industry that automated the processing of information.

By the 1980s, attention had focused on other stages of the document cycle in which manual tasks other than typing might be automated. The term *word/information processing* was introduced to describe automation as it is applied to all stages of the document cycle.

In today's fast-paced business world, information must be gathered, processed, and made available at an ever-increasing speed. The computer has proven to be a fast, reliable, and economical means of processing information critical to all organizations. Effectively managed information helps an organization serve its customers better and operate more efficiently. Information processing has given us the tools that can help us to become more creative and productive in our work while eliminating many of the boring, repetitive tasks of the workplace.

BIBLIOGRAPHY

"Babbage's Calculating Engines, The Charles Babbage Institute Reprint Series for the History of Computing." (1982). www.cbi.umn.edu/charles.htm.

Bellis, Mary. (1998, 23 June). "Inventors of the Modern Computer: The UNIVAC Computer." inventors.miningco.com/library/weekly/aa062398.htm.

Bergerud, Marly, and Gonzalez, Jean. (1998). "A Calculating Man." *US News and World Report* August 17-24:

Bradbeer, Robin, DeBona, Peter, and Laurie, Peter. (1982). *The Beginner's Guide to Computers.*

Cashman, T., and Keys, W. (1980). *Essentials of Information Processing.* New York: Harper Row.

"Computers: History and Development." www.digitalcentury.com/encyclo/update/comp_hd.html.

Jennings, C. (1981). *Information Processing.* Stillwater, OK: Mid-America Vocational Curriculum Consortion.

Limback, R. (1981). *Introduction to Data Processing: Instructor's Guide.* Columbia: University of Missouri, Instructional Materials Laboratory.

Long, L. (1984). *Introduction to Computers and Information Processing.*, NJ: Prentice Hall.

Patton, Peter C. (1994). "ENIAC 1996: Celebrating the Birth of Modern Computing." *PennPrintout* 10(4) February:

Spencer, D. (1974). *Introduction to Information Processing.* OH: Charles and Merrill Publishing Company.

"System/360." www.ibm.com/ibm/history.

JAMES E. MILES

INFORMATION SYSTEMS

The term *information system* refers to information technology that is used by people to accomplish a specified organizational or individual objective. The technology may be used in the gathering, processing, storing, and/or dissemination of information, and the users are trained in the use of that technology, as well as in the procedures to be followed in doing so. The specific technologies that collectively comprise information technology are *computer technology* and *data communications technology*. Computers provide most of the storage and processing capabilities, while data communications—specifically networks—provide the means for dissemination and remote access of information.

Advances in computer hardware, software, and networking technologies have spurred an evolution in the structure, design, and use of corporate information systems.

COMPUTER HARDWARE

When computers first began moving into the business world in the late 1950s and early 1960s,
the computing environment was best described as *centralized, host-based computing.* In this environment, the typical organization had a large *mainframe computer* (the centralized host) connected to a number of "dumb" terminals scattered throughout the organization or at remote sites. These terminals were labeled "dumb" because they had no native "intelligence" (i.e., they had no built-in central processing units [CPUs] that were capable of processing data). The mainframe did all the data processing for all the user terminals connected to it.

In the mid-1960s, Digital Equipment Corporation (DEC) announced the development of the *minicomputer.* Smaller than the mainframe, the minicomputer ushered in the era of *distributed data processing* (DDP). In this new processing environment, an organization could connect one or more minicomputers to its mainframe. Typically, the minicomputers were located in an organization's regional offices, from which they were connected to the mainframe in corporate headquarters. Thus, the organization's data-processing function was no longer localized in a single, centralized computer (the mainframe) but, rather, *distributed* among all the computers.

The commercial introduction of the personal computer by IBM in the early 1980s revolutionized organizational data processing. The personal computer carried the distributed processing concept even further within organizations— it brought data processing to the desktop. Also, it eclipsed the dumb terminal as the terminal of choice by users. The commercial success of the IBM personal computer led other computer manufacturers to develop their own personal computers that were compatible with the IBM PC (these are usually described as *IBM clones* or *IBM-compatible computers*). One notable exception is Apple Computers, Inc., which developed its own line of non-IBM-compatible computers, namely the *Apple* and *Macintosh* line of computers. The all-inclusive term *microcomputer* is sometimes used to encompass all makes and models of desktop computers, including the IBM

IBM personal computer.

PC (and its clones) and the Apple/Macintosh computers.

It is important to note that, despite their proliferation and ubiquity, personal computers have *not* replaced minicomputers or mainframes. A large number of organizations still rely on these larger computers for significant aspects of their day-to-day operations.

COMPUTER SOFTWARE

Computer software is the set of programs and associated data that drive the computer hardware to do the things that it does, such as performing arithmetic calculations or generating and printing a report. Software typically comes in one of two forms: *custom-written application programs* or *off-the-shelf software packages*. Custom-written application programs are usually written by an organization's own programming team or by professional contract programmers to satisfy unique organizational requirements. Off-the-shelf software packages are produced by software development companies and made commercially available to the public. They usually fall in one of two main categories, namely *system software* or *application software.* The former includes such specialized programs as operating systems, compilers, utility programs, and device drivers. While these programs are important—and necessary—to the overall performance of an information system (especially from the "machine" perspective), they are not the primary focus of corporate information systems. Their basic functions are more machine-oriented than human-oriented.

Application software is designed to more directly help human users in the performance of their specific job responsibilities, such as business decision making, inventory tracking, and customer record keeping. From a software perspective, this is what corporate information systems are primarily concerned with.

One of the very important information systems functions is *systems analysis and design*, that is, analyzing a client's business situation (or problem), with respect to information processing, and designing and implementing an appropriate—usually computerized—solution to the problem. Information systems professionals who specialize in this area are known as *systems analysts.* The process begins with a detailed determination of the client's information requirements and business processes. The solution frequently involves some programming, as well as the use of an appropriate application software package(s), such as a database management system (DBMS) for designing and implementing a database for the client. It may also involve some networking considerations, depending on the user's requirements and goals. Some typical organizational information systems that can result from a systems analysis and design effort include the following.

Transaction processing systems: These record and track an organization's transactions, such as sales transactions or inventory items, from the moment each is first created until it leaves the system. This helps managers at the day-to-day operational level keep track of daily transactions as well as make decisions on when to place orders, make shipments, and so on.

Management information and reporting systems: These systems provide mid-level and senior managers with periodic, often summarized, reports that help them assess performance (e.g., a particular region's sales performance in a given time period) and make appropriate decisions based on that information.

Decision support systems: These systems are designed to help mid-level and senior managers make those difficult decisions about which not every relevant parameter is known. These decisions, referred to as *semistructured decisions*, are characteristic of the types of decisions made at the higher levels of management. A decision on whether or not to introduce a particular (brand-new) product into an organization's product line is an example of a semistructured decision. Another example is the decision on whether or not to open a branch in a foreign country. Some of the parameters that go into the making of these decisions are known. However, there are also many unknown factors—hence the "semistructuredness" of these decisions. The value of a decision support system (DSS) is in its ability to permit "what-if" analyses (e.g., What if interest rates rose by 2 percent? What if our main competitor lowered its price by 5 percent? What if import tariffs are imposed/increased in the foreign country in which we do, or plan to do, business?). That is, a DSS helps the user (decision maker) to model and analyze different scenarios in order to arrive at a final, reasonable decision, based on the analysis. There are decision support systems that help groups (as opposed to individuals) to make consensus-based decisions. These are known as group decision support systems (*GDSS*).

A type of decision support system that is geared primarily toward high-level senior managers is the *executive information system* (EIS) or *executive support system* (ESS). While this has the capability to do very detailed analyses, just like a regular DSS, it is designed primarily to help executives keep track of a few selected items that are critical to their day-to-day high-level decisions. Examples of such items include performance trends for selected product or customer groups, interest rate yields, and the market performance of major competitors.

Expert systems: An expert system is built by modeling into the computer the thought processes and decision-making heuristics of a recognized expert in a particular field. Thus, this type of information system is *theoretically* capable of making decisions for a user, based on input received from the user. However, due to the complex and uncertain nature of most business decision environments, expert system technology has traditionally been used in these environments primarily like decision support systems—that is, to help a human decision maker arrive at a reasonable decision, rather than to actually *make* the decision for the user.

COMPUTER NETWORKS

Together with computer technology, data communications technology has had a very significant impact on organizational information processing. There have been tremendous increases in the bandwidths (i.e., signal-carrying capacities) of all data communications media, including coaxial cables, fiber-optic cables, microwave transmission, and satellite transmission. Wide area networks (WANs) provide access to remote computers and databases, thus enabling organizations to gain access to global markets, as well as increase their information sources for decision making purposes. The Internet in particular— the worldwide network of computer networks— has greatly facilitated this globalization phenomenon by making it possible to connect any computer to virtually any other computer in any part of the world. Advances in networking technologies have also enabled organizations to connect their in-house personal computers to form local area networks (LANs). This greatly facilitates organizational communication and decision-making processes.

The combination of computer and networking technologies has also changed the way basic work is done in many organizations. For example, *telecommuting* and *virtual offices* are commonplace in several organizations. Telecommuting refers to the practice of doing office work from home (i.e., without physically being in the office). The term "virtual office" acknowledges the fact that a person's office does not necessarily have to be a physical location. A person can do productive "office work" (including the making of managerial decisions) on the go, for example, at the airport while waiting for a flight, on the airplane, or from a beach half-way around the world. These practices are made possible through modem-equipped computers that can access a remote computer (the office computer) via a data communications network.

An organization's overall performance can be greatly enhanced by strategically planning for, and implementing, information systems that optimize the inherent benefits of information technology to the benefit of the organization. This requires effective leadership and vision, as well as knowledge of both information technology and the organization's (business) environment.

BIBLIOGRAPHY

Laudon, Kenneth C., and Laudon, Jane P. (1996). *Management Information Systems: Organization and Technology*, 4th ed. Upper Saddle River, NJ: Prentice-Hall.

Oz, Effy. (1998). *Management Information Systems*. Cambridge, MA: Course Technology.

Parsons, June J., and Oja, Dan. (1998). *Computer Concepts —Comprehensive*, 3rd ed. Cambridge, MA: Course Technology.

Senn, James A. (1998). *Information Technology in Business: Principles, Practices, and Opportunities*, 2nd ed. Upper Saddle River, NJ: Prentice-Hall.

THEOPHILUS B. A. ADDO

INFORMATION TECHNOLOGY

Information technology, as defined by the Information Technology Association of America

The first commercial computer was the UNIVAC I.

(ITAA), is "the study, design, development, implementation, support or management of computer-based information systems, particularly software applications and computer hardware." Encompassing the computer and information systems industries, information technology is the capability to electronically input, process, store, output, transmit, and receive data and informa-tion, including text, graphics, sound, and video, as well as the ability to control machines of all kinds electronically.

Information technology is comprised of computers, networks, satellite communications, robotics, videotext, cable television, electronic mail ("e-mail"), electronic games, and auto-mated office equipment. The information industry consists of all computer, communications, and electronics-related organizations, including hardware, software, and services. Completing tasks using information technology results in rapid processing and information mobility, as well as improved reliability and integrity of processed information.

HISTORY OF INFORMATION TECHNOLOGY

The term "information technology" evolved in the 1970s. Its basic concept, however, can be traced to the World War II alliance of the military and industry in the development of electronics, computers, and information theory. After the 1940s, the military remained the major source of research and development funding for the expansion of automation to replace manpower with machine power.

Since the 1950s, four generations of computers have evolved. Each generation reflected a change to hardware of decreased size but increased capabilities to control computer operations. The first generation used vacuum tubes, the second used transistors, the third used integrated circuits, and the fourth used integrated circuits on a single computer chip. Advances in artificial intelligence that will minimize the need for complex programming characterize the fifth generation of computers, still in the experimental stage.

The first commercial computer was the UNIVAC I, developed by John Eckert and John W. Mauchly in 1951. It was used by the Census Bureau to predict the outcome of the 1952 presidential election. For the next twenty-five years, mainframe computers were used in large corporations to do calculations and manipulate large amounts of information stored in databases. Supercomputers were used in science and engineering, for designing aircraft and nuclear reactors, and for predicting worldwide weather patterns. Minicomputers came on to the scene in the early 1980s in small businesses, manufacturing plants, and factories.

In 1975, the Massachusetts Institute of Technology developed microcomputers. In 1976, Tandy Corporation's first Radio Shack micro-

computer followed; the Apple microcomputer was introduced in 1977. The market for microcomputers increased dramatically when IBM introduced the first personal computer in the fall of 1981. Because of dramatic improvements in computer components and manufacturing, personal computers today do more than the largest computers of the mid-1960s at about a thousandth of the cost.

Computers today are divided into four categories by size, cost, and processing ability. They are supercomputer, mainframe, minicomputer, and microcomputer, more commonly known as a personal computer. Personal computer categories include desktop, network, laptop, and handheld.

INFORMATION TECHNOLOGY'S ROLE TODAY

Every day, people use computers in new ways. Computers are increasingly affordable; they continue to be more powerful as information-processing tools as well as easier to use.

Computers in Business One of the first and largest applications of computers is keeping and managing business and financial records. Most large companies keep the employment records of all their workers in large databases that are managed by computer programs. Similar programs and databases are used in such business functions as billing customers; tracking payments received and payments to be made; and tracking supplies needed and items produced, stored, shipped, and sold. In fact, practically all the information companies need to do business involves the use of computers and information technology.

On a smaller scale, many businesses have replaced cash registers with point-of-sale (POS) terminals. These POS terminals not only print a sales receipt for the customer but also send information to a computer database when each item is sold to maintain an inventory of items on hand and items to be ordered. Computers have also become very important in modern factories. Computer-controlled robots now do tasks that are hot, heavy, or hazardous. Robots are also used to do routine, repetitive tasks in which boredom or fatigue can lead to poor quality work.

Computers in Medicine Information technology plays an important role in medicine. For example, a scanner takes a series of pictures of the body by means of computerized axial tomography (CAT) or magnetic resonance imaging (MRI). A computer then combines the pictures to produce detailed three-dimensional images of the body's organs. In addition, the MRI produces images that show changes in body chemistry and blood flow.

Computers in Science and Engineering Using supercomputers, meteorologists predict future weather by using a combination of observations of weather conditions from many sources, a mathematical representation of the behavior of the atmosphere, and geographic data.

Computer-aided design and computer-aided manufacturing programs, often called CAD/CAM, have led to improved products in many fields, especially where designs tend to be very detailed. Computer programs make it possible for engineers to analyze designs of complex structures such as power plants and space stations.

Integrated Information Systems With today's sophisticated hardware, software, and communications technologies, it is often difficult to classify a system as belonging uniquely to one specific application program. Organizations increasingly are consolidating their information needs into a single, integrated information system. One example is SAP, a German software package that runs on mainframe computers and provides an enterprise-wide solution for information technologies. It is a powerful database that enables companies to organize all their data into a single database, then choose only the program modules or tables they want. The freestanding modules are customized to fit each customer's needs.

SOFTWARE

Computer software consists of the programs, or lists of instructions, that control the operation of a computer. Application software can be used for the following purposes:

- As a productivity/business tool
- To assist with graphics and multimedia projects
- To support household activities, for personal business, or for education
- To facilitate communications

Productivity Software Productivity software is designed to make people more effective and efficient when performing daily activities. It includes applications such as word processing, spreadsheets, databases, presentation graphics, personal information management, graphics and multimedia, communications, and other related types of software. *Word-processing* software is used to create documents such as letters, memos, reports, mailing labels, and newsletters. This software is used to create attractive and professional-looking documents that are stored electronically, allowing them to be retrieved and revised. The software provides tools to correct spelling and grammatical mistakes, permits copying and moving text without rekeying, and provides tools to enhance the format of documents. Electronic *spreadsheet* software is used in business environments to perform numeric calculations rapidly and accurately. Data are keyed into rows and columns on a worksheet, and formulas and functions are used to make fast and accurate calculations. Spreadsheets are used for "what-if" analyses and for creating charts based on information in a worksheet. A *database* is a collection of data organized in a manner that allows access, retrieval, and use of that data. A database management system (DBMS) is used to create a computerized database; add, change, and delete data; sort and retrieve data from the database; and create forms and reports using the data in the database. *Presentation graphics software* is used to create presentations, which can include clip-art images, pictures, video clips, and audio clips as well as text. A *personal information manager* is a software application that includes an appointment calendar, address book, and notepad to help organize personal information such as appointments and task lists. Engineers, architects, desktop publishers, and graphic artists often use *graphics and multimedia software* such as computer-aided design, desktop publishing, video and audio entertainment, and Web page authoring. Software for *communications* includes groupware, e-mail, and Web browsers.

HARDWARE

Information processing involves four phases: input, process, output, and storage. Each of these phases and the associated devices are discussed below.

Input devices: Input devices include the keyboard, pointing devices, scanners and reading devices, digital cameras, audio and video input devices, and input devices for physically challenged users. Input devices are used to capture data at the earliest possible point in the workflow, so that the data are accurate and readily available for processing.

Processing: After data are captured, they are processed. When data are processed, they are transformed from raw facts into meaningful information. A variety of processes may be performed on the data, such as adding, subtracting, dividing, multiplying, sorting, organizing, formatting, comparing, and graphing. After processing, information is output, as a printed report, for example, or stored as files.

Output devices: Four common types of output are text, graphics, audio, and video. Once information has been processed, it can be listened to through speakers or a headset, printed onto paper, or displayed on a monitor. An output device is any computer component capable of conveying information to a user. Commonly used output devices include display devices, printers, speakers, headsets, data projectors, fax machines, and multifunction devices. A multifunction device is a single piece of equipment that looks like a copy machine but provides the functionality of a printer, scanner, copy machine, and perhaps a fax machine.

Storage devices: Storage devices retain items such as data, instructions, and information for retrieval and future use. They include floppy disks or diskettes, hard disks, compact discs (both read-only and disc-recordable), tapes, PC cards, Smart Cards, microfilm, and microfiche.

INFORMATION AND DATA PROCESSING

Data processing is the input, verification, organization, storage, retrieval, transformation, and extraction of information from data. The term is usually associated with commercial applications such as inventory control or payroll. An information system refers to business applications of computers and consists of the databases, application programs, and manual and machine procedures and computer systems that process data. Databases store the master files of the business and its transaction files. Application programs provide the data entry, updating, and query and report processing. Manual procedures document the workflow, showing how the data are obtained for input and how the system's output is distributed. Machine procedures instruct the computers how to perform batch-processing activities, in which the output of one program is automatically fed into another program. Daily processing is the interactive, real-time processing of transactions. Batch-processing programs are run at the end of the day (or some other period) to update the master files that have not been updated since the last cycle. Reports are printed for the cycle's activities. Periodic processing of an information system involves updating of the master files—adding, deleting, and changing the information about customers, employees, vendors, and products.

BIBLIOGRAPHY

Cannings, Terence, and Finkel, Leroy. (1993). *The Technology Age Classroom.* Wilsonville, OR: Franklin, Beedle, & Associates.

New Book of Knowledge, The; (1994). Danbury, CT: Grolier.

Saettler, Paul. (1990). *The Evolution of American Educational Technology.* Englewood, CO: Libraries Unlimited.

Shelly, Gary, Cashman, Thomas, Vermaat, Misty, and Walker, Tim. (1999). *Discovering Computers 2000: Concepts for a Connected World.* Cambridge, MA: Course Technology.

Swanson, Marie, Reding, Elizabeth Eisner, Beskeen, David W., and Johnson, Steven M. (1997). *Microsoft Office 97 Professional Edition—Illustrated, A First Course.* Cambridge, MA: Course Technology.

Webster, Frank, and Robins, Kevin. (1986). *Information Technology—A Luddite Analysis.* Norwood, NJ: Ablex.

LINDA J. AUSTIN
DEBBIE HUGHES

INPUT

(SEE: *Operations Management*)

INSTITUTE OF INTERNAL AUDITORS

The Institute of Internal Auditors was founded in 1941 by a small group of dedicated internal auditors who wanted an organization that would promote the role of the internal auditor and provide educational activities and standards for the professional practice of internal auditing. By 1999, the Institute had grown to include over 70,000 members representing more than one hundred countries around the world.

In 1944 the Institute began publishing its journal, *Internal Auditor.* This award-winning journal continues to present in-depth information on auditing practices and techniques and features articles written by experts from all over the world. In 1947 *the Statement of Responsibilities of Internal Auditing* was issued and became the foundation for development of internal auditing standards. The official motto "Progress Through Sharing" was adopted in 1955 and continues to guide the Institute's contributions to the profession. Institute members approved the *Code of Ethics* in 1968. Institute members, in 1972, adopted a *Common Body of Knowledge*, which identified the content for the examination offered for the first time in 1973. The examination is a requirement for attainment of the Certified Internal Auditor (CIA) designation. The IIA Research Foundation, founded in 1976, sponsors research on trends and issues in internal auditing. The *Standards for the Professional Practice of In-ternal Auditing* were approved in 1978. Awareness of the importance of university preparation for internal auditing motivated a pilot program in internal auditing at Louisiana State University. The success of this initial program effort led to establishment of similar programs in other colleges and universities. By 1999 more than 35 colleges and universities throughout the globe were participants in the *Endorsed Internal Audit Program.*

Noteworthy developments in the 1980s included the introduction of the Institute's first computer software product, audit Masterplan; establishment of the Quality Assurance Review Service; mandatory continuing professional development for CIAs; and the granting of consultative status to the Institute by the United Nations. The 1990s have seen professional certifications exceed 25,000; development of the Global Auditing Information Network that compiles and disseminates benchmarking information; and creation of two internet web sites—*www .theiia.org* and *www.itaudit.org*. The 1990s have also seen the introduction of specialty groups, services, and products to support unique membership needs. These include the Control Self Assessment Center, Certification in Control Self Assessment, Certified Governmental Auditor Program, Board of Environmental Auditors Certification, and the Chief Audit Executive Program.

In 1999 the Institute's Board of Directors approved a new *Professional Practices Framework* that will be the basis for development of comprehensive new standards for internal auditing. The board also approved a new definition that defines internal auditing as an independent, objective assurance and consulting activity designed to add value and improve an organization's operations. The internal audit function helps an organization accomplish its objectives by bringing a systematic, disciplined approach to evaluate and improve the effectiveness of risk management, control, and governance processes.

The Institute of Internal Auditors' mission is to be the primary international association, organized on a global basis, dedicated to the promotion and development of the practice of internal auditing. The Institute is organized as a non-profit association governed by a volunteer board elected by the membership. National Institutes are located around the world and usually support individual chapters on a local basis. Volunteer committees at the international, regional, district, and local levels support the local chapters, national institutes, and the international board.

The Institute offers a variety of membership options and certification programs, establishes internal auditing standards and other guidance, provides training through conferences and seminars, produces educational products which include videos, study aids, textbooks, and software, generates research publications, and promotes academic relations. The Institute publishes several periodicals, offers an employment referral service, generates benchmarking information, provides quality assurance and consulting services, maintains an electronic information resource center, and maintains partnerships with other professional organizations to monitor and report on issues affecting the profession. More information about the Institute of Internal Auditors is available at *www.theiia.org*, or by writing to the Institute at 249 Maitland Avenue, Altamonte Springs, FL 32701.

(SEE ALSO: *Certified Internal Auditor*)

BIBLIOGRAPHY

Flesher, Dale L. (1991). *The Institute of Internal Auditors 50 Years of Progress Through Sharing*. Altamonte Springs: The Institute of Internal Auditors.

STEVEN E. JAMESON

INSTITUTE OF MANAGEMENT ACCOUNTANTS

The Institute of Management Accountants (IMA) is the largest educational, nonprofit association in the world devoted exclusively to management accounting, finance, and information management. It was founded in 1919 in Buffalo, New York, as the National Association of Cost Accountants by a group of businesspeople to expand the knowledge and professionalism of people specifically interested in cost accounting.

Subsequently its name was changed to the National Association of Accountants and then in 1991 to the current name. These changes were made to reflect its broadened mission to disseminate the latest knowledge in accounting and finance to all those professionals employed in public and private companies as well as governmental and educational organizations. In its statement of mission, the IMA states that it will "provide to members personal and professional development opportunities through education, association with business professionals, and certification in management accounting and financial management skills and ensure that IMA is globally recognized by the financial community as a respected institution influencing the concepts and ethical practices of management accounting and financial management."

As an international educational organization, the IMA sponsors two certification programs: certified management accountant (CMA) and certified in financial management (CFM). [See certified management accountant (CMA)]. These certification programs are administered by an affiliate, the Institute of Certified Management Accountants, which was established in 1972.

The flagship publication of the Institute is a monthly magazine, *Strategic Finance*. The IMA also publishes *Management Accounting Quarterly* four times a year and a quarterly newsletter, *Focus*, which goes to all members. Through another affiliate, the IMA Foundation for Applied Research (FAR), it conducts research and publishes field-based research and analysis. It also publishes, in conjunction with other organizations, a series of guides called *Statements on Management Accounting*. As part of its professional responsibilities, the IMA contributes to and comments on the accounting rule-making process through a senior-level committee.

The IMA offers its 65,000 members an opportunity to join three member interest groups—the Controllers Council, Cost Management Group, and Small-Business Council. Each group publishes a newsletter ten times per year featuring information on industry trends and practices, emerging technologies, and financial and management reporting issues. Members' surveys are conducted to keep members apprised of how their colleagues in other industries and organizations are handling key issues. In addition, members can join Internet-based groups that enable them to network and exchange information on-line dealing with their particular industry or special interests.

The IMA requires certified members to obtain a certain number of Continuing Professional Education credits every year. It offers a number of methods to achieve this objective, including an annual conference, chapter/council education programs, Regional Education Assistance Programs, self-study courses (including on-line offerings), a monthly video-subscription program, and national seminars. It also offers in-house education programs for companies, focusing on current trends, industry-specific developments, and continuing skills enhancement.

The IMA is governed by a volunteer president, executive committee, and board of directors. A salaried, full-time executive director directs the day-to-day operations of the Institute based on policy guidelines promulgated by the executive committee and board of directors. Activities also are conducted by approximately three hundred local chapters and twenty-four regional councils, which hold regular technical meetings and other functions. The IMA's headquarters is located at 10 Paragon Drive, Montvale, New Jersey. Its Internet addresses are www.imanet.org and www.strategicfinancemag.com.

(SEE ALSO: *Certified Management Accountant*)

KATHY WILLIAMS
ROBERT F. RANDALL

INSURANCE

Insurance is vital to a free enterprise economy. It protects society from the consequences of financial loss from death, accidents, sicknesses, damage to property, and injury caused to others. The person seeking to transfer risk, the *insured* (*policyholder*), pays a relatively small amount, the *premium*, to an insurance company, the *insurer*, which issues an *insurance policy* in which the insurer agrees to reimburse the insured for any losses covered by the policy. Insurance is the process of *spreading the risk* of economic loss among as many as possible subject to the same kind of risk and is based on the laws of probability (chance of a given outcome happening) and large numbers (enables the laws of probability to work).There are many perils (causes of loss) that society faces, some natural (e.g., earthquakes, hurricanes, tornados, flood, drought), some human (e.g., arson, theft, fraud, vandalism, contamination, pollution, terrorism), and some economic (e.g., expropriation, inflation, obsolescence, depressions/recessions). Insurers are able to provide coverage for virtually any predictable loss.

EARLY HISTORY

Concepts of insurance evolved thousands of years ago. The Chinese, for example, divided their cargoes among many boats to reduce the severity of loss from the perils of the seas, while the biblical story of Joseph and the famine in Egypt illustrates the storing of grain during the seven good years to relieve shortages during the seven years of famine. Marine insurance emerged in London when ships sailed for the New World. Fire insurance arose from the great fire of London in 1666, in which 14,000 buildings were destroyed. In 1752 Benjamin Franklin founded the first mutual fire insurance company in the United States, the Philadelphia Contributorship for the Insurance of Houses from Loss by Fire. In 1759, he helped establish the first life insurance company, now known as the Presbyterian Ministers Fund. In 1887 the first auto-liability policy was written. Advancing technologies and a dynamic marketplace constantly change society's insurance needs. The insurance industry's goal is to respond to those needs with available and affordable insurance.

U.S. INSURANCE INDUSTRY

The U.S. insurance industry is comprised of approximately 1600 life (life/health) and 3000 non-life (property/casualty) insurance and re-insurance companies; it is the world's largest insurance market, accounting for $736 billion or 34 percent of 1998's worldwide premiums of $2.2 trillion. Insurance is sold either directly by insurers (*direct insurers*) or through the *independent agency system, exclusive agencies,* and *brokers.*

Based on the 1997 U.S. Bureau of Labor Statistics, the life and health insurance industry employed 909,000 persons and the property/casualty insurance industry, 635,000; 706,000 persons were engaged in agency or brokerage activities and in insurance service organizations.

LIFE/HEALTH INSURANCE

Life/health insurance in the United States in 1998 represented 27.6 percent of the worldwide market, second to Japan's 28.6 percent and well ahead of the United Kingdom's 9.8 percent, which ranked third. A variety of life insurance (which provides income for a beneficiary at the insured's death), annuities (provides income for life for the annuitant), and health care products are offered. In 1997 Americans purchased $1.97 trillion of new life insurance; the average new policy totaled $97,358. Term policies and ordinary/whole life policies account for virtually all of the total life insurance in-force of $13.2 trillion. At the end of 1997, 373 million policies were in-force with an average size of $165,800 per insured household. Term policies provide "pure insurance" (no cash value) and maximally cost-effective protection to growing families.

Ordinary/whole life policies provide protection as well as building up cash values (investment component), which the policyholder can either borrow on or obtain by surrendering the policy. Life/health policies are sold on an individual or group basis—(the employer or association receives the master policy and the insured members receive certificates of insurance). Annuities-fixed (predetermined amount) and variable (varies with investment returns) can be purchased by making a single payment or a series of payments. The annuity income can start immediately or at some future date. Different types of annuity contracts meet different needs. Today there is a strong demand for individual annuity products, driven by the movement of the baby boomers through the preretirement phase, increased life expectancy and the fear of outliving savings, and concerns about the long-term viability of Social Security. Health (medical, disability, long-term care) insurance plans are offered by insurance companies, managed health care organizations, and medical prepayment organizations. Long term care products provide for reimbursement for covered nursing home and home health care expenses incurred due to physical or mental disability. The top ten U.S. life insurance companies are shown in Table 1.

PROPERTY/CASUALTY (P&C) INSURANCE

The United States dominates the world in P&C insurance (also known as general insurance). In 1998 the U.S. generated 43.4 percent of worldwide P&C premiums, Japan was next with 10.3 percent and Germany third with 8.8 percent. P&C insurance is broken down into personal lines (auto/private passenger and homeowners) and commercial lines (farm, commercial auto, aviation, marine/ocean/inland, crime, surety, boiler and machinery, glass, commercial credit, workers' compensation, public liability (including environmental pollution), professional liability (directors and officers, errors and omissions), product liability, commercial multiple-line, nuclear, title, and surplus and excess lines insurance). The top ten U.S. P&C insurers are shown in Table 2.

ORGANIZATION

Insurers primarily operate as stock (owned by stockholders) or mutual (owned by policyholders) companies. Today, many mutual companies are changing to stock companies (demutualizing) to facilitate the raising of capital. Other forms of structure are pools and associa-

Top Ten U.S. Life Insurers Ranked by Life Insurance In-Force 1998

(IN MILLIONS)

Metropolitan Life Insurance	$1,545,453
Prudential Insurance Company of America	1,013,109
Connecticut General Life Insurance	543,369
Northwestern Mutual Life Insurance	536,379
Transamerica Occidental Life	498,247
New York Life Insurance	440,527
Aetna Life Insurance	385,525
RGA Reinsurance	381,634
Lincoln National Life Insurance	367,155
State Farm Life Insurance	347,430

Table 1

SOURCE: A.M. Best Company. (1999). *Best's Insurance Reports-Life/Health-United States.* 1999 ed.

tions (groups of insurers), risk retention groups, purchasing groups, and fraternal organizations (primarily life and health insurance). An insurer within a given state is classified domestic, if formed under that state, foreign, if incorporated in another state, or alien, if incorporated in another country.

FUNCTIONS

The key functions of an insurer are marketing, underwriting, claims (investigation and payment of legitimate claims as well as defending against illegitimate claims), loss control, reinsurance, actuarial, collection of premiums, drafting of insurance contracts to conform with statutory law, and the investing of funds. Underwriters are expert in identifying, understanding, evaluating, and selecting risks. Actuaries play a unique and critical role in the insurance process; they price the product (the premium) and establish the reserves.

The primary goal of an insurer is to underwrite profitably. Disciplined underwriting combined with sound investing and asset/liability management enables an insurer to meet its obligations to both policyholders and stockholders. Underwriting combines many skills—investigative, accounting, financial, psychological. While some lines of business (e.g homeowners, auto) are underwritten manually or class rated, many large commercial property and casu-

Top Ten U.S. Property/Casualty Insurers Ranked by Net Premiums Written (NPW) 1998

	NPW* (in millions)	Combined Ratio**
State Farm Group	$34,755.3	108.2
Allstate Insurance Group	19,072.1	95.5
American International Group	10,727.9	99.5
Farmers Insurance Group	10,316.4	101.7
CNA Insurance Group	10,044.0	115.2
Nationwide Group	8,494.9	108.9
Travelers Property Casualty Group	8,209.8	102.3
Berkshire Hathaway Insurance Group	7,731.8	95.7
Liberty Mutual Insurance Group	7,197.2	117.0
The Hartford Insurance Group	6,028.4	105.9

* Net premiums written includes only premiums written by domestic companies.
**A combined ratio of less than 100.0 indicates an underwriting profit.

Table 2

SOURCE: A.M. Best Company. *Best's Aggregate Averages-Property-Casualty-United States.* 1999 ed.

alty risks are judgment rated, relying on the underwriter's skill, experience and intuition.

PRODUCT AND RATINGS

The Insurance Policy varies among states and class of business; however, there are common features.

- *Declaration Page*: names the policyholder, describes the property or liability to be insured, type of coverage, and policy limits.

- *Insuring Agreement*: describes parties' responsibilities during the policy term.

- *Conditions of the Policy*: details coverage and requirements in event of a loss.

- *The Exclusions*: describes types of property and losses not covered. The states and insurers continually work together to make the policy more readable.

A. M. Best is the key rating organization of the industry. The Best's Ratings range from the excellent category (A + + and A +) to the lowest categories—E (under regulatory supervision), F (in liquidation), and S (rating suspended). Other important rating organizations are *Moody's* and *Standard and Poor's*.

ROLE OF GOVERNMENT

Federal and state governments play important roles in managing large social insurance programs, such as social security, medicare, unemployment compensation, federal deposit insurance, and pension benefit guaranty. In these areas the government acts either as a partner or competitor to the insurance industry, or as an exclusive provider. Federal and state governments also manage property and casualty programs, such as "all-risk" crop, crime, flood, and workers' compensation.

REINSURANCE

Reinsurance is critical to the insurance process; it brings capacity, stability, and financial strength to insurers. The purpose of reinsurance is to spread large risks and catastrophes over as large a base as possible. It is the assumption by one insurance company (the reinsurer) of all or part of a risk undertaken by another insurance company (the cedent). It enables an insured with a sizable risk exposure to deal with and receive coverage from one insurer, rather than dealing with a number of insurers. The portion of the risk that exceeds the primary insurer's retention level is layed-off (ceded) to a reinsurer. The reinsurer can further reinsure a part of the risk assumed; this is called retroceding. If the reinsurer agrees to share losses arising from only one risk, the agreement is known as facultative reinsurance; if the reinsurer agrees to share losses arising from more than one risk, usually a whole line or book of business, the agreement is known as treaty reinsurance. Western Europe is the largest provider of worldwide reinsurance. The Caribbean, including Bermuda, is the largest foreign supplier of reinsurance to the United States. The financial strength of the reinsurer is most impor-tant, since the direct writer is always primarily responsible for payment of losses.

REGULATION

Under the McCarran-Ferguson Act of 1945, state insurance departments bear the primary responsibility to oversee insurance companies' operations to protect policyholders from insurer insolvency and unfair treatment. In doing so, they license insurers, agents, and brokers; enforce statutory accounting requirements; and conduct examinations of the financial position and market conduct of insurers. The examination is assisted by the Insurance Regulatory Information System (IRIS) Ratios, which test insurers' overall profitability, liquidity, and reserve strength. State insurance departments work with the National Association of Insurance Commissioners (NAIC) to develop and promote laws and regulations that serve as model laws, with the state legislatures, which pass the laws and set the budgets; with the courts, which interpret insurance regulations and policy wording; with Congress and the U.S. General Accounting Office, which periodically evaluate state insurance regulation; and with professional, trade, and consumer groups.

COMPETITION

Because the insurance market has many sellers and buyers, little product differentiation, and freedom of entry and exit, it is highly competitive. This is especially true in the P&C segment, where the leading company accounts for only 12 percent of the market and the top ten companies combined comprise only 44 percent. While demand for insurance grows steadily over time, with the increase in exposures and legal requirements, the supply of insurance, because it is financial and flexible, can be easily shifted in and out of the market. This attracts capital during periods of high interest and stock market strength because of high profit expectations from investing underwriting cash flows.

This excess capacity in the insurance industry has led to consolidation and convergence with capital markets and financial service institutions. Insurance companies seek to operate more efficiently and improve their communication and distribution systems. Combining insurance with other financial products and services is perceived to provide better sources for customers.

AN INDUSTRY IN TRANSFORMATION SECURITIZATION

With population growing in coastal, as well as hurricane, and earthquake-prone areas in the United States and scientists predicting a 100 percent chance of a major earthquake in the century before 2010, the insurance industry is faced with a potential megadisaster earthquake or hurricane that could produce insured losses in the $75,000,000,000 to $100,000,000,000 range. Losses of that magnitude would wreak havoc to the industry (see Table 3 for a list of the ten largest catastrophes as of 1999). In 1996, the industry started to securitize its catastrophe risk by packaging insurance risk as securities that could be traded in the capital markets, whose combined $26 trillion is 80 times greater than the capital of the insurance industry. To date, the industry has been successful in selling more than $4 billion worth of catastrophe-linked securities; it plans to build on these successes and continue to spread catastrophe risks to the capital markets through the issuance of catastrophe securities. As the insurance industry continues to converge with the capital markets and the financial services industry, other lines of business are likely to be securitized.

GLOBALIZATION

While reinsurers have always had an international presence and brokers have moved in that direction, primary insurers, with one notable exception, have been reluctant to expand internationally. The rapid growth of computer technology, however, has transformed the world into one global economy, in which U.S. and foreign insurers must, along with all other businesses, compete.

DISTRIBUTION CHANNELS

The insurance industry continues to explore new distribution systems, including the Internet and

formation of alliances with banks and other financial services organizations in an effort to become more efficient and focused on the customer, who today places as much importance on service and convenience, as on price.

(SEE ALSO: *Personal Financial Planning*)

BIBLIOGRAPHY

"The Art of Underwriting," "Memo from MRG," Contact (New York, American International Group), 1982, p 5-9, 24.

Best's Aggregate & Averages-Property/Casualty, (Oldwick, N.J., A. M. Best Company), 1999.

Best's Insurance Reports-Life/Health, (Oldwick, N.J., A. M. Best Company), 1999, p. A87.

"Chasing the Markets," Board Member-Special Supplement (Brentwood, TN: Board Member Inc), 1998, p. 4-9.

"Convergence 101," Special Report, The Insurance Tax Review, November 1998.

"Disaster Relief," Best's Review Property/Casualty, (Oldwick, N.J., A. M. Best Company), April 2000.

Insurance Operations, Volumes I and II, (Malvern, Pennsylvania, American Institute For Chartered Property Casualty Underwriters (CPCU), First Edition, 1992.

Let the Trumpet Resound, Lawrence G. Bandon, CPCU (Malvern, Pennsylvania, CPCU-Harry J. Loman Foundation) 1996.

Life Insurance Fact Book, (Washington, D.C., American Council of Life Insurance), 1998.

"Securitization Frontierland," Best's Review Property/Casualty, (Oldwick, N.J., A. M. Best Company), July 1999.

Sharing the Risk, (New York: Insurance Information Institute), Revised, Second Edition, 1985.

Statistical Abstract of the United States, (Washington, D.C., U.S. Census Bureau), 1999, p. 515, 540, 541.

Swiss Re. sigma No.2/2000, sigma No. 7/1999 (Zurich, Swiss Reinsurance Company).

"Top 250 Property/Casualty Insurers by Net Premiums Written," Best's Review Property/Casualty, (Oldwick, N.J., A. M. Best Company), July 1999.

EDWARD J. KELLER, JR.

INTEGRATED SOFTWARE

In today's fast-paced and volatile business world, it is hard to imagine any part that is not affected by information technology. We live in a world

**Largest Ten Catastrophes in the United States
(between 1957 and 1999 in 1999 dollars)**

Year	Catastrophe	Location	Insured Losses (in billions)
1992	Hurricane Andrew	Gulf Coast U.S.	$19.1
1994	Northridge earthquake	California	14.1
1989	Hurricane Hugo	Puerto Rico/Southeast U.S.	5.7
1997	Hurricane Georges	Southeast U.S./Caribbean	3.6
1965	Hurricane Betsy	Southeast U.S.	2.5
1999	Hurricane Floyd	East Coast U.S./Bahamas	2.4
1995	Hurricane Opal	Guatemala/Gulf Coast U.S.	2.3
1993	Blizzard/tornados	East Coast/20 U.S. states	2.0
1992	Hurricane Iniki	Hawaii	1.9
1991	Fire	Oakland, California	1.8

Table 3

SOURCE: Swiss Re. Sigma No. 2/2000:33.

where worldwide markets change, technologies change, and economies and businesses need immediate access to accurate information. Integrated software has helped harness information and computing resources to maximize competitive advantage. This article focuses on the use of integrated software from an educator's point of view.

DEFINITION OF AND REASONS TO USE INTEGRATED SOFTWARE

Integrated software is a single program that contains "modules" or "tools" to complete many popular business applications. These applications include word processing, spreadsheets, database management, graphics, and communications.

These tools are sufficient for the typical tasks performed by a small business, a student, or a home user. The word processing module might be used to type a letter or report. The spreadsheet module might be used to do financial analysis or to record comparisons. The database module can be used in a variety of ways, such as to organize an inventory; to compile a list of customers' (or friends') names, street or e-mail addresses, and phone and fax numbers; and to maintain a household inventory for insurance purposes. A graphics module can give an individual or a business an edge by providing tools that will give a "professional look" to documents produced.

INTEGRATED SOFTWARE IN THE EDUCATION WORLD

One of the reasons integrated software is popular in the education world is that the user can easily switch from one type of application to another without exiting the program. In a beginning or an introductory class or curriculum, the use of integrated software is beneficial because a teacher can quickly develop an entire year's syllabus. The instructor can design applications for specific projects and without losing valuable time waiting for "new" software to be loaded onto the network. The instructor will not have to reteach "new" software basics. Once the basics of a particular module of the integrated software are known, other modules will fall into place. For instance, if the integrated software's word processing module highlights *SAVE* under the dropdown *FILE* menu, its spreadsheet module will also highlight *SAVE* under the dropdown *FILE* menu.

ADVANTAGES OF USING INTEGRATED SOFTWARE

Integrated software is invaluable to the new learner of computer software, to application typing, and to a cost-conscious small business. The first advantage is its low cost which may be as little as $200 for five programs packaged as one piece of integrated software.

A second advantage is that there is only one program to install. If you are a manager of a computer network with fifty or more computers trying to access the same information at the same time, this is a significant advantage. With only one piece of software to troubleshoot, a network manager can become familiar with the little "quirks" of the program quickly. The downtime of the network then becomes minimal. There is also only one program to learn, which, of course, simplifies the learning task.

A third advantage is the ease and consistency of the interface from one module to another. Sharing data among the applications is almost effortless. For instance, one can easily add a spreadsheet, chart, and/or other graphic to a letter created in the word-processing module. As mentioned earlier, the basic functions and commands are found in the same location throughout the entire integrated software package. This consistency allows one to use the same methods for performing basic tasks. Most integrated software packages on the market today are designed so that all the applications work together.

A fourth advantage is integrated software's ability to share information between modules. For instance, an individual can first use the word-processing module to prepare a letter. Second, using the database module, the individual can create a database. Third, the individual can use the graphics module to design letterhead stationery as well as a standard format for, say, informa-

tion on credit balances gathered from the data contained in the spreadsheet module. Finally, the database can be used to perform a mail merge, which involves individually addressing the letter created in the word processing module to each of the names in the database.

A final advantage is that usually there is only one manual to read and refer to when encountering a problem. If one had separate suites for each program, each would come with its own separate manual.

CREATING PROFESSIONAL-LOOKING DOCUMENTS

Integrated software provides the tools for creating professional-looking documents. Numerous typefaces, print sizes, and other features (such as **bold**, *italic*, and <u>underlining</u>) are usually available. Margins and tabs are easily set and changed. It requires minimal work to change line spacing, text alignment (i.e. left, right, or center align) and page size.

The word-processing module allows the user to:

- Print in columns
- Insert footnotes in a document
- Add titles, page numbers, or other information at the top and/or bottom of each page
- Add tables and/or figures to a document
- Check and correct spelling
- Replace one word with another
- Search a document for a word or phrase and replace it with something else
- Add a graphic or piece of clip art to the document

The spreadsheet module allows the user to:

- Calculate numbers automatically
- Change data within the spreadsheet (worksheet) and get immediate feedback
- Calculate and analyze mathematical and scientific data
- Enhance spreadsheets (worksheets) by adding *bold*, *italic*, and *underlining* to selected data as well as change font sizes and styles within the spreadsheet

- Make the spreadsheet into a graph or chart to aid in understanding of data

The database module allows the user to:

- Catalogue information
- Sort catalogued information by certain criteria
- Query a database to deliver only certain information (e.g. Which friends have the ZIP code 80015?)
- Do calculations in a database quickly and easily
- Merge information

The graphics module allows the user to:

- Include prepared drawings to add humor, draw attention, or illustrate a point
- Create custom-designed drawings to achieve the documents
- Shape and bend text to stylize it in titles, logos, and headlines
- Insert unique graphics into a document to give special meaning

COMMUNICATIONS

Communications is often an additional module with integrated software. With a modem, the user can use the communications module to log on to the Internet. Internet access allows use of the World Wide Web for research on, for instance, stock prices, which can then be imported into a spreadsheet. It also allows communication via e-mail.

SUMMARY

In summarizing the advantages of integrated software, *integrated* is the key word. The real power of integrated software lies in the software modules that allow you to combine two or more documents into one (word processing), insert pictures or other objects into a document (graphics), send files and/or messages electronically (e-mail), and compiling information by selecting the information from a list (database) and merging it into another document. Data from a table (spreadsheet) can also be incorporated into a document.

Virtually all parts of the business world are affected by information technology. Integrated software has helped to harness information and computing resources to maximize competitive advantage. Minimal specific skills are needed to integrate software effectively and efficiently. *Effortless, efficient, effective,* and *easy* are four summary words that explain why the use of integrated software has become so popular today.

BIBLIOGRAPHY

"Integrated Software." (2000). http://www.isspec.com/.

"Office Suites for the Millenium." http://www.CNET.com.

Walkowski, Debbie. (1997). *Using Microsoft Works 4.5.* Indianapolis, IN: Que® Corporation.

JUDITH CHIRI

INTERACTIVE TECHNOLOGY

Interactive is a new buzzword, but its sense is ancient, a lot more ancient than that of the telephone or telegraph. The interesting scientific question now is: How long have people been using words and sentences to communicate with each other? Humans are not a passive animal; they are very communicative.

The only 100% interactive (audio) technology remains today as it was at its beginning in 1875: the telephone—if interactive means truly equal two-way or multiple-way communication. Telegraphy, however, offers even more parallels with today's world than the telephone. It prefigured a major nonaudio trend in our current interactivity: computer nets which range from those used in local libraries and college classrooms to the worldwide Internet. All these, like the telegraph, use digital coding, not analog words.

The interactivity of e-mail and bulletin boards has contributed greatly to the popularity of the Internet. Mail or telephone communications are fine for a one-on-one discussion, but they are pretty expensive if one is trying to communicate with a group. It costs nearly a dollar to print and mail a letter and, on average, that much

Marshal McLuhan.

for a long-distance phone call. And to make such a call, one has to know the number and to have coordinated a time to talk. So it takes considerable time and effort to contact even a modest-size group. On a bulletin board, all one has to do is type a message once and it's available to all readers.

LINEAR VERSUS NONLINEAR TECHNOLOGY

One way to understand the benefits brought about by interactive technology is to compare linear and nonlinear multimedia. An example of linear multimedia is the typical presentation that combines video and sound, but without choices. You watch it from beginning to end. Users are reacting to, not reacting with, what they see.

Nonlinear, interactive multimedia combine the same technologies as linear ones, but with a twist. The viewer is hands-on, controlling what is viewed. Nonlinear multimedia are more complex to produce, because cogent vignettes must be worked through and likely viewer choices must

be logically mapped out before the presentation. Distribution is also then limited to technology that can be dynamic in the presentation. For this category, one must pay greater attention to the interface methodology used that will let the viewer control the experience.

USES OF INTERACTIVE TECHNOLOGY

The uses of interactive technology are varied. They are utilized in such varied circumstances as education, training, marketing, and information gathering.

Education and Training. Computers with social interfaces present information in such a way that it is customized for the particular user. Different learning rates are accommodated, because computers are able to pay individual attention to independent learners. Regardless of ability or disability, each user will be able to work at an individual pace.

The interactive network allows learners to quiz themselves anytime in a risk-free environment. A self-administered quiz is a form of self-exploration. A mistake will not call forth a reprimand; it will trigger the system to help the student overcome a particuar misunderstanding. As a result, students should be less apprehensive about formal tests and such tests should contain fewer surprises, because ongoing self-quizzing gives us all a better sense of where we stand.

Interactivity is the key to successful on-line learning. Yet a survey of on-line instructional materials reveals a surprising deficiency in educational interactive programs, for three reasons: (1) Cyber-courses are largely a combination of conventional classroom and textbook material, neither of which are conducive to interactivity; (2) instructors tend to think of interactivity primarily as a means of assessment, instead of learning; (3) the concept itself is extended to cover everything from navigational buttons to chatrooms to on-line games.

Marketing. Interactive technology has two distinct advantages over traditional means of gathering consumer data. First, it allows the information to be gathered in real time, and therefore the response to the customer can be more timely than with traditional media. The more one orders from Amazon.com, for example, the more information about that consumer's reading tastes is acquired. This information is used immediately to update that buyer's "Recommend Reading List." This is critical; many sales are lost due to the lag time between the request for information and its provision.

Second, the information gathered is more specific, since the branching of questions can be as detailed as the marketer wishes. For example, if an initial set of questions asks the viewer to input his or her age and number of children, the next set of questions derives from the answer to the first, and so on. When this information is used to enhance a marketing database, marketers are able to respond to the individual needs of viewers, taking one-to-one marketing to its limits.

Gathering information. Interactive documents add value to traditional methods. Surveys that attempt to gauge satisfaction with expectations of, and responses to, new products can be more effective when done with interactive multimedia. In the previous example, Amazon.com would have more reliable information about a consumer's selections than it would have from any paper survey it might ask the public to complete. These surveys may gather more information by being more interesting than the paper alternatives. Once you get used to this sort of system, you find that being able to look at information in different ways makes the information more valuable. The flexibility invites exploration, and the exploration is rewarded with discovery.

INTERACTIVITY IS COOL

Using Marshall McLuhan's classic distinction between "hot" and "cool" media can make both the prospects and problems of interactivity clearer. In *Understanding the Media*, McLuhan (1964) explained that "a hot medium is one that extends one single sense in 'high definition.' High definition is the state of being well-filled with data (p. 22)." A cool medium, by contrast, is one in which "little is given and so much has to be filled in (p. 23)." McLuhan was primarily interested in the media themselves, and had little to say about that process of "filling in"—what today is called interactivity.

Learning is "cool" as a measure of the individual's involvement in the medium. One can easily recognize the difference between "hot" mindlessness of channel surfing and the "cool" absorption and involvement of learning. The challenge, then, is not only to produce a "cool" digital medium in which learning can take place, but to do so despite use of a screen that may remind us of television and the uninvolved behavior patterns it induces. The key to success in this challenge is interactivity—the activity of "filling in" the knowledge presented in the medium. Strategies for interactivity can be divided into three parts: passive, hyperlinked, and interpersonal.

PASSIVE INTERACTIVITY

Synchronous learning involves the simultaneous interaction of instructor and student. The standard classroom is the traditional example of synchronous interaction where the instructor and students are in the same place at the same time. Distance learning, where the instructor and students are at different locations at the same time, frequently involves audio/visual connections and "chat rooms." Asynchronous learning, on the other hand, involves the interaction of instructor and student at different times.

"Passive interactivity" need not be a contradiction in terms, because one of the problems with digital instruction is the loss of context—both physical and psychological—that a classroom setting provides. To compensate for this, on-line training needs to create a visual "focus" for the lesson at hand—a referential map of where the student has been, and where he or she is headed, to provide a context for where he or she is now. Such a context allows a student to relate the subject matter of an individual lesson to the larger scope of the course. Passively interactive page designs are thus "interactive" because the visual mapping succeeds in making the student actively aware of its importance by providing a broader context for the current lesson.

HYPERLINKED INTERACTIVITY

The key to asynchronous learning is "hyperlinked interactivity," a feature of HTML, which makes possible the creation of multiple-choice questions, expert systems, and other such branching-informational models. Branching models approximate the way people actually work through problems. Individuals take different paths, ask diferent questions, and need different information. While books can utilize limited branching schemes in a clumsy way, only computers have complex and speedy branching capabilities. Complete interaction, combined with accessibility at our convenience, exact repeatability, and uniform quality gives asynchronous on-line learning the potential, in suitable situations, of not merely replacing the traditional learning experience, but surpassing it.

INTERPERSONAL INTERACTIVITY

Even asynchronous projects benefit from the variety of communication options now available on the Internet, including e-mail, listservs, and bulletin boards. Such communication, which can be roughly grouped under the heading of "interpersonal interactivity," helps to reproduce online some of the advantages of collaborative peer learning. When utilized effectively, such communication can give people more direct and more convenient access to others and can make individual contributions more formal, thoughtful, and precise.

SUMMARY

All learning is a function of interaction. In taking training onto the Internet, instructors have an opportunity to script levels of interactivity in ways previously unavailable. To do so, however, requires rethinking on-line activities—not merely as means of assessment, but as the primary way to involve us and make learning "cool."

BIBLIOGRAPHY

Gates, William H., III. (1999). *Business @ the Speed of Thought.* New York: Warner Books.

McLuhan, Marshall. (1964). *Understanding the Media.* Cambridge, MA: MIT Press.

Shapiro, Carl, and Varian, Hal. (1998). *Information Rules: A Strategic Guide to the Network Economy.* Campbridge, MA: Harvard Business School Press.

PHILIP D. TAYLOR

INTEREST RATES(S)

An interest rate is a standardized measure of either: (1) the cost of borrowing money or (2) the return for lending money for a specified period of time (usually one year), such as 12% annual percentage rate (APR).

First consider the term "interest" from the perspective of a borrower. In this case, "interest" is the difference between the amount of money borrowed and the amount of money repaid. Interest expense is incurred as a result of borrowing money. On the other hand, interest revenue is earned by lending money.

For example, the amount of interest expense, as a result of borrowing $1000 on January 1, 20XX, and repaying $1120 on December 31, 20XX is $120 ($1120 − $1000). The lender, on the other hand, received $1120 on December 31, 20XX in exchange for lending $1000 on January 1, 20XX, or a total of $120 in interest revenue. Thus, with regard to any particular lending event, interest revenue equals interest expense.

The formula used to calculate the amount of interest is:

$$\text{interest} = \text{principal} \times \text{interest rate} \times \text{time} \quad [1]$$

where:

principal = amount of money borrowed

interest rate = percent paid or earned per year

time = number of years

Equation (1) can be rewritten as:

$$\text{interest rate} = \text{interest} \div \text{principal} \quad [2]$$

where:

time = one year

The principal is also known as the *present value*. The interest rate in equation (2) is called the annual percentage rate or *APR*. APR is the most useful measure of interest rate. (In the remainder of this discussion, the term "interest rate" refers to the APR.)

Equations (1) and (2) are useful in situations that involve only one cash flow (a single-payment scenario). Many economic transactions, however, involve multiple cash flows. For instance, a consumer acquires a good or service and in exchange promises to make a series of payments to the supplier. This type of transaction describes an annuity. An *annuity* is a series of equally spaced payments of equal amount. The annuity formula is:

$$\text{present value of annuity} = \text{annuity payment} \times \text{annuity factor } _{i,n} \quad [3]$$

where:

present value of annuity = value of the good or service received today (when the exchange transaction is finalized)

annuity payment = amount of the payment that is made each period

annuity factor = a number obtained from an ordinary annuity table that is determined by the interest rate (i) and the number of annuity payments (n).

An analysis of the effect of changes in interest rates requires controlling (or holding constant) two of the other three variables in equation (3).

The term "future cash flow(s)" describes cash that will be received in the future. Holding the number of payments and the amount of each payment constant, the present value of future cash flows is inversely related to the interest rate. Holding the number of payments and present value of the future cash flows constant, the amount of each payment is directly related to the interest rate. Holding the present value of the future cash flows and the amount of each payment constant, the number of payments is di-

rectly related to the interest rate. In summary, everything else held constant, increases in the interest rate (1) increase the amount of each payment, or (2) increase the number of payments required, or (3) decrease the present value of the future cash flows.

In order to understand the effect of changes in interest rates from a consumer's perspective, we first examine borrowing transactions in which the present value of the future cash flows and the number of payments are fixed. Consider, for instance, a thirty-year mortgage or a four-year auto loan. In each case, the effect of an increase in interest rates is an increase in the amount of the home or auto payment. This is shown in Table 1.

Well-known lending interest rates include the prime rate, the discount rate, and consumer rates for automobiles or mortgages. The *discount rate* is the rate that the Federal Reserve bank charges to banks and other financial institutions. This rate influences the rates these financial institutions then charge to their customers. The *prime rate* is the rate banks and large commercial institutions charge to lend money to their best customers. While the prime rate is not usually available to consumers, some consumer loans (such as mortgage lines of credit) are priced at "prime + 2 percent; that is, a consumer will pay 2 percent over the prime rate to borrow money. When the Federal Reserve raises the discount rate, typically banks raise the prime rate and consumers pay higher interest rates.

Individuals lend money by investing in debt instruments, such as Treasury bills and bonds. In this scenario, the investor receives periodic payments (annuity payments) and a lump sum when the debt instrument matures. This stream of cash flows is valued as follows:

$$\text{market value} = \text{annuity payment} \times \text{annuity factor } _{i,n} + \text{maturity value} \times \text{present value factor } _{i,n} \quad [4]$$

where:

market value = value of the debt instrument

annuity payment = amount of the payment that is made each period; it is equal

Effect of Changing Interest Rates On the Amount of Monthly Payments

Borrow $100,000 for home purchase		Borrow $20,000 for auto purchase	
Interest Rate	30-Year Mortgage Payment	Interest Rate	4-Year Auto Loan
6%	$599.55	7%	$478.93
8%	$733.76	10%	$507.25

Table 1

to the interest rate stated on the debt instrument multiplied by the face value of the debt instrument

annuity factor = a number obtained from an ordinary annuity table that is determined by the interest rate (i) and the number of annuity payments (n).

maturity value = amount received by the investor when the instrument matures, also known as the face value of the debt instrument

present value factor = a number obtained from a present value table that is determined by the interest rate (i) and the number periods until maturity (n).

When an investor purchases a debt instrument, the following factors are "fixed": (1) the amount of each annuity payment, (2) the amount of the maturity value, and (3) the number of periods until maturity (this is also the number of annuity payments that will be received in the future). As interest rates increase, the market value of the investment will decrease; that is, the price of debt securities is inversely related to the market rate of interest. This is shown in Table 2.

The investors who keep the investment until the debt instrument matures will receive the market rate of interest on their investment from the date of purchase. The investor who sells their investment prior to maturity will receive the market rate of interest on the investment until it is sold. At that time, this investor

Effect of Changing Interest Rates on the Value of an Investment in Debt, Holding n constant

$20,000 Maturity Value Bonds paying 8% (stated) annual interest, Due in 25 years		$20,000 in Treasury Bills paying 0% Interest, Due in 90 Days	
Market Interest Rate	Market Value of the Bonds	Market Interest Rate	Market Value of the Treasury Bills
6%	$25,113	6%	$19,711
8%	$20,000	8%	$19,619
10%	$16,369	10%	$19,529

Table 2

will also receive either a gain or a loss due to changes in the market value of this investment. If market interest rates decrease, the investor will receive a gain. If market interest rates increase, the investor will receive a loss on the value of the investment.

HENRY H. DAVIS

INTERNAL CONTROL INTEGRATED FRAMEWORK (COSO REPORT)

(SEE: *Internal Control Systems*)

INTERNAL CONTROL SYSTEMS

Internal control can be described as any action taken by an organization to help enhance the likelihood that the objectives of the organization will be achieved. The definition of *internal control* has evolved over recent years as different internal control models have been developed. This article will describe these models, present the definitions of internal control they provide, and indicate the components of internal control. Various parties responsible for and affected by internal control will also be discussed.

THE COSO MODEL

In the United States many organizations have adopted the internal control concepts presented in the report of the Committee of Sponsoring Organizations of the Treadway Commission (COSO). Published in 1992, the COSO report defines internal control as:

a process, effected by an entity's board of directors, management and other personnel, designed to provide reasonable assurance regarding the achievement of objectives in the following categories:

- effectiveness and efficiency of operations,
- reliability of financial reporting, and
- compliance with applicable laws and regulations.

COSO describes internal control as consisting of five essential components. These components, which are subdivided into seventeen factors, include:

1. The control environment
2. Risk assessment
3. Control activities
4. Information and communication
5. Monitoring

The COSO model is depicted as a pyramid, with control environment forming a base for control activities, risk assessment, and monitoring. Information and communication link the different levels of the pyramid. As the base of the pyramid, the control environment is arguably the most important component because it sets the tone for the organization. Factors of the control environment include employees' integrity, the organization's commitment to competence, management's philosophy and operating style, and the attention and direction of the board of directors and its audit committee. The control environment provides discipline and structure for the other components.

Risk assessment refers to the identification, analysis, and management of uncertainty facing the organization. Risk assessment focuses on the uncertainties in meeting the organization's financial, compliance, and operational objectives. Changes in personnel, new product lines, or rapid expansion could affect an organization's risks.

Control activities include the policies and procedures maintained by an organization to address risk-prone areas. An example of a control activity is a policy requiring approval by the board of directors for all purchases exceeding a predetermined amount. Control activities were once thought to be the most important element of internal control, but COSO suggests that the control environment is more critical since the control environment fosters the best actions, while control activities provide safeguards to prevent wrong actions from occurring.

Information and communication encompasses the identification, capture, and exchange of financial, operational, and compliance information in a timely manner. People within an organization who have timely, reliable information are better able to conduct, manage, and control the organization's operations.

Monitoring refers to the assessment of the quality of internal control. Monitoring activities provide information about potential and actual breakdowns in a control system that could make it difficult for an organization to accomplish its goals. Informal monitoring activities might include management's checking with subordinates to see if objectives are being met. A more formal monitoring activity would be an assessment of the internal control system by the organization's internal auditors.

OTHER CONTROL MODELS

Some users of the COSO report have found it difficult to read and understand. A model that some believe overcomes this difficulty is found in a report from the Canadian Institute of Chartered Accountants, which was issued in 1995. The report, *Guidance on Control*, presents a control model referred to as Criteria of Control (CoCo). The CoCo model, which builds on COSO, is thought to be more concrete and user-friendly. CoCo describes internal control as actions that foster the best result for an organization. These actions, which contribute to the achievement of the organization's objectives, center around:

- Effectiveness and efficiency of operations
- Reliability of internal and external reporting
- Compliance with applicable laws and regulations and internal policies.

CoCo indicates that control comprises:

those elements of an organization (including its resources, systems, processes, culture, structure and tasks) that, taken together, support people in the achievement of the organization's objectives.

CoCo model recognizes four interrelated elements of internal control, including purpose, capability, commitment, and monitoring and learning. An organization that performs a task is guided by an understanding of the purpose (the objective to be achieved) of the task and supported by capability (information, resources, supplies, and skills). To perform the task well over time, the organization needs a sense of commitment. Finally, the organization must monitor task performance to improve the task process. These elements of control, which include twenty specific control criteria, are seen as the steps an organization takes to foster the right action.

In addition to the COSO and CoCo models, two other reports provide internal control models. One is the Institute of Internal Auditors Research Foundation's Systems Auditability and Control (SAC), which was issued in 1991 and revised in 1994. The other is the Information Systems Audit and Control Foundation's CobiT (Control Objectives for Information and Related Technology), which was issued in 1996.

The Institute of Internal Auditors issued SAC to provide guidance to internal auditors on internal controls related to information systems and information technology (IT). The definition of internal control included in SAC is:

a set of processes, functions, activities, sub-systems, and people who are grouped together or consciously segregated to ensure the effective achievement of objective and goals.

CobiT focuses primarily on efficiently and effectively monitoring information systems. The report emphasizes the role and impact of IT control as it relates to business processes. This control model can be used by management to develop clear policy and good practice for control of IT. The following CobiT definition of internal control was adapted from COSO:

The policies, procedures, practices, and organizational structures are designed to provide reasonable assurance that business objectives will be achieved and that undesired events will be prevented or detected and corrected.

While the specific definition of internal control differs across the various models, a number of concepts are very similar across these models. In particular, the models emphasize that internal control is not only policies and procedures to help an organization accomplish its objectives but also a process or system affected by people. In these models, people are perceived to be central to adequate internal control.

These models also stress the concept of reasonable assurance as it relates to internal control. Internal control systems cannot guarantee that an organization will meet its objectives. Instead, internal control can only be expected to provide reasonable assurance that a company's objectives will be met. The effectiveness of internal controls depends on the competency and dependability of the organization's people. Limitations of internal control include faulty human judgment, misunderstanding of instructions, errors, management override of controls, and collusion. Further, because of cost-benefit considerations, not all possible controls will be implemented. Because of these inherent limitations, internal controls cannot guarantee that an organization will meet its objectives.

PARTIES RESPONSIBLE FOR AND AFFECTED BY INTERNAL CONTROL

While all of an organization's people are an integral part of internal control, certain parties merit special mention. These include management, the board of directors (including the audit committee), internal auditors, and external auditors.

The primary responsibility for the development and maintenance of internal control rests with an organization's management. With increased significance placed on the control environment, the focus of internal control has changed from policies and procedures to an overriding philosophy and operating style within the organization. Emphasis on these intangible aspects highlights the importance of top management's involvement in the internal control system. If internal control is not a priority for management, then it will not be one for people within the organization either.

As an indication of management's responsibility, top management at a publicly owned organization will include in the organization's annual financial report to the shareholders a statement indicating that management has established a system of internal control that management believes is effective. The statement may also provide specific details about the organization's internal control system.

Internal control must be evaluated in order to provide management with some assurance regarding its effectiveness. Internal control evaluation involves everything management does to control the organization in the effort to achieve its objectives. Internal control would be judged as effective if its components are present and function effectively for operations, financial reporting, and compliance. The board of directors and its audit committee have responsibility for making sure the internal control system within the organization is adequate. This responsibility includes determining the extent to which internal controls are evaluated. Two parties involved in the evaluation of internal control are the organization's internal auditors and their external auditors.

Internal auditors' responsibilities typically include ensuring the adequacy of the system of internal control, the reliability of data, and the efficient use of the organization's resources. Internal auditors identify control problems and develop solutions for improving and strengthening internal controls. Internal auditors are concerned with the entire range of an organization's internal controls, including operational, financial, and compliance controls.

Internal control will also be evaluated by the external auditors. External auditors assess the effectiveness of internal control within an organization to plan the financial statement audit. In contrast to internal auditors, external auditors focus primarily on controls that affect financial reporting. External auditors have a responsibility to report internal control weaknesses (as well as reportable conditions about internal control) to the audit committee of the board of directors.

BIBLIOGRAPHY

Bishop, W. G., III. (1991). "Internal Control—What's That?" *Internal Auditor* June: 117-123.

Canadian Institute of Chartered Accountants. (1995). *Guidance on Control.* Toronto, Ontario, Canada: Author.

Colbert, J. L., and Bowen, P. L. (1996). "A Comparison of Internal Controls: CobiT, SAC, COSO and SAS 55/78." *IS Audit and Control Journal* 4:26-35.

Committee of Sponsoring Organizations of the Treadway Committee (COSO). (1992). *Internal Control—Integrated Framework, Executive Summary.* www.coso.org.

Galloway, D. J. (1994). "Control Models in Perspective." *Internal Auditor* December: 46-52.

Information Systems Audit and Control Foundation. (1995). CobiT: Control Objectives and Information Related Technology. Rolling Meadows, IL: Author.

Institute of Internal Auditors Research Foundation. (1994). *Systems Auditability and Control.* Altamonte Springs, FL: Author.

Price Waterhouse. (1993). *Improving Audit Committee Performance: What Works Best.* Altamonte Springs, FL: Institute of Internal Auditors Research Foundation.

Roth, J. (1997). *Control Model Implementation: Best Practices.* Altamonte Springs, FL: Institute of Internal Auditors Research Foundation.

Simmons, M. R. (1997). "COSO Based Auditing." *Internal Auditor* December: 68-73.

AUDREY A. GRAMLING

INTERNATIONAL ACCOUNTING STANDARDS

Comparable, transparent, and reliable financial information is fundamental for the smooth functioning of capital markets. In the global arena, the need for comparable standards of financial reporting has become paramount because of the dramatic growth in the number, reach, and size of multinational corporations, foreign direct investments, cross-border purchases and sales of securities, as well as the number of foreign securities listings on the stock exchanges. However, because of the social, economic, legal, and cultural differences among countries, the accounting standards and practices in different countries vary widely. The credibility of financial reports becomes questionable if similar transactions are accounted for differently in different countries.

To improve the comparability of financial statements, harmonization of accounting standards is advocated. Harmonization strives to increase comparability between accounting principles by setting limits on the alternatives allowed for similar transactions. Harmonization differs from standardization in that the latter allows no room for alternatives even in cases where economic realities differ.

The international accounting standards resulting from harmonization efforts create important benefits. Investors and analysts benefit from enhanced comparability of financial statements. Multinational corporations benefit from not having to prepare different reports for different countries in which they operate. Stock exchanges benefit from the growth in the listings and volume of securities transactions. The international standards also benefit developing or other countries that do not have a national standard-setting body or do not want to spend scarce resources to undertake the full process of preparing accounting standards.

The most important driving force in the development of international accounting standards is the International Accounting Standards Committee (IASC), an independent private-sector body formed in 1973. The broad objective of the IASC is to further harmonization of accounting practices through the formulation of accounting standards and to promote their worldwide acceptance.

One hundred and forty-three professional accounting organizations in one hundred and four countries are IASC members. The IASC Board, presently consisting of sixteen member organizations, is responsible for establishing accounting and disclosure standards. The board follows due process in setting accounting standards, thus allowing for a great deal of consultation and discussion and ensuring that all interested parties can express their views at several points in the standard-setting process. The final standard requires approval by at least twelve member organizations.

On May 24, 2000, a new structure for IASC was approved unanimously by its membership. Under the new structure, IASC will be established as an independent organization that will have two main bodies, the Trustees and the Board. The Trustees will appoint the board members, exercise oversight and raise the funds needed, whereas the board will have sole responsibility for setting accounting standards. It is expected that the new structure would come into effect on January 1, 2001.

The IASC has issued forty International Accounting Standards (IASs) to date covering a range of topics, such as inventories, depreciation, research and development costs, income taxes, segment reporting, leases, business combinations, investments, earnings per share, interim financial reporting, intangible assets, employee benefits, impairment of assets, and financial instruments. It has also issued a Framework for the Preparation and Presentation of Financial Statements that sets forth the concepts underlying the preparation and presentation of financial statements for external users.

International Accounting Standards initially tended to be too broad, allowing many alternative accounting treatments to accommodate country differences. This was a serious weakness in achieving the objective of comparability. To gain acceptability of its standards, in 1989 the IASC undertook a project (called the Comparability Project) aimed at enhancing comparability of financial statements by reducing the alternative treatments. An important part of this effort was its work plan to produce a comprehensive core set of high-quality Standards (Core Standards project). The IASC has completed its Core Standards project, and the revised standards are a significant improvement over the earlier ones.

IASC standards are not mandatory. However, the acceptability of IASs has been on the rise, with an increasing number of companies stating that they prepare financial reports in accordance with IASs. Many countries endorse IASs as their own standards with or without modifications, and many stock exchanges accept IASs for cross-border listing purposes. For example, the Arab Society of Certified Accountants, comprising twenty-two Arab nations, has signed a declaration supporting IASs as the national accounting standards in all its member countries. Some European countries are developing legislation to allow not only foreign but also domestic companies to use IASs in their consolidated financial statements.

In the United States as of mid-2000, IASs are not an acceptable basis for financial statements filed with the Securities and Exchange Commission (SEC). Although the SEC has expressed support for the IASC's objective of developing accounting standards for financial statements used in cross-border offering, it has also stated that such standards must be comprehensive, possess high quality, and be subject to rigorous interpretation and application. The SEC is under increasing pressure to make U.S. capital markets more accessible to non-U.S. issuers.

Internationally, the International Organization of Securities Commissions (IOSCO), an organization comprised of securities regulators from more than eighty countries, as of mid-2000 is considering the endorsement of IASs for cross-border capital raising and listing purposes in all global markets.

Many other organizations also play an important role in the march toward international accounting standards. Among the more important are those discussed below.

IFAC. The International Federation of Accountants is a worldwide association formed in 1977 to develop the accounting profession, harmonize its auditing practices, and reduce differences in the requirements to qualify as a professional accountant in its member countries. It currently has a membership of one hundred and forty-three national professional organizations in one hundred and four countries representing more than 2 million accountants. The IFAC issues International Standards on Auditing (ISA) aimed at harmonizing auditing practices globally. The IFAC Council also appoints country representatives on the IASC Board (thirteen in total).

UN. Several organizations within the United Nations have been involved in international accounting standards. Its Group of Experts prepared a four-part report in 1976, "International Standards of Accounting and Reporting for Transnational Corporations." The report listed financial and nonfinancial items that should be disclosed by multinational corporations to host governments. More recently, it has worked to promote the harmonization of accounting standards by discussing and supporting best practices in a variety of areas, including environmental disclosures.

OECD. The Organization for Economic Cooperation and Development formed in 1960 currently has twenty-nine of the world's developed, industrialized countries as its members. A valuable contribution of the OECD is its surveys of accounting practices in member countries and its assessment of the diversity or conformity of such practices. Its Working Group on Accounting Standards supports efforts by regional, national, and international bodies promoting accounting harmonization. In 1998, the OECD issued "Principles of Corporate Governance" that support the development of high-quality, internationally recognized standards that can serve to improve the comparability of information between countries.

EU. The European Union, the powerful regional alliance of fifteen nations, aims to bring about a common market that allows free mobility of people, capital, and goods among member countries. To promote the cross-country economic integration, the EU has made significant progress in the harmonization of laws and regulations. Its Commission (European Commission) establishes standardization and harmonization of corporate and accounting rules through the issuance of Directives. Directives incorporate uniform rules (to be implemented exactly in all member states), minimum rules (which may be strengthened by individual governments), and alternative rules (which members can choose from). Directives are mandatory in that each member country has the obligation to incorporate them into its respective national law. However, each country is free to choose the form and method of implementation and also to add or delete options.

The Fourth and Seventh Directives deal exclusively with accounting issues. The Fourth Directive, adopted in 1978, covers financial statements, their contents, method of presentation, valuation methods, and disclosure of information. The Seventh Directive, adopted in 1983, requires worldwide consolidated financial statements regardless of the location of the parent company. Given the large variety of alternatives for consolidation permitted in member countries prior to its issuance, the Seventh Directive is regarded as a major development toward harmonization. The European Commission announced in 1995 its decision to rely heavily on IASC to produce results that meet the needs of capital markets. It is also investigating the possibility of requiring all member states to require listed companies to report under IASs.

NAFTA. The North American Free Trade Agreement was formed in 1993 among Canada, Mexico, and the United States to create a common market. It will phase out duties on most goods and services and promote free movement of professionals, including accountants, among the three countries. There are projects under way to analyze the similarities and differences between financial reporting and accounting standards of the member countries of NAFTA.

Other organizations. Some regional organizations—such as the Association of Southeast Asian Nations (ASEAN), Community of Sovereign States, Economic Cooperation Organization (ECO), Baltic Council, Asia Pacific Economic Cooperation (APEC), Confederation of Asian and Pacific Accountants (CAPA), and Nordic Federation of Accountants (NFA)—have made efforts toward harmonizing accounting and disclosure standards. G4—a group of standard-setting bodies in Australia, Canada, the United Kingdom, and the United States, has also started playing an important role in the harmonization of international accounting standards.

The process of harmonizing international accounting standards has come a long way on a path that has been far from smooth. While some critics still doubt the need and feasibility of such standards, it is becoming increasingly clear that the question is not whether but when the International Accounting Standards will be required and followed by business and other entities worldwide. The likely endorsement by the IOSCO and SEC will make that time sooner rather than later.

(SEE ALSO: *International Federation of Accountants*)

BIBLIOGRAPHY

International Accounting Standards Committee (IASC). http://www.iasc.org.uk. (April 2000).

McGregor, Warren. (1999). "An Insider's View of the Current State and Future Direction of International Accounting Standard Setting." *Accounting Horizons* June: 159-168.

Pactor, Paul. (1998). "International Accounting Standards: The World's Standards by 2002." *The CPA Journal* July: 14-21.

Saudagardan, Shahrokh. (2001). *International Accounting: A User Perspective.* Cincinnati, OH: South-Western College Publishing.

Zeff, Stephen A. (1998). "The IASC's Core Standards: What Will the SEC Do?" *Journal of Financial Statement Analysis* Fall: 67-78.

MAHENDRA GUJARATHI

INTERNATIONAL FEDERATION OF ACCOUNTANTS

The International Federation of Accountants (IFAC) was officially constituted in October 1977 at the World Congress of Accountants in Munich. Its constitution was signed by sixty-three accountancy bodies in forty-nine countries. Its original terms of reference emphasized (1) the promotion of harmonized *accounting* standards, that is, measurement and disclosure standards, and (2) the development of harmonized *professional* standards, for example, auditing, education, and ethical standards. This duality of purpose placed IFAC in potential conflict with the International Accounting Standards Committee (IASC), whose mission also embraced accounting harmonization. To minimize duplication of effort, both organizations agreed in 1982 to have a uniform membership in which IASC would concentrate on promoting harmonized accounting standards while IFAC would focus on promoting harmonized professional standards.

MEMBERSHIP

Support for IFAC's quest to develop a truly international and cohesive accountancy profession is reflected in its expanded membership of one hundred twenty-three professional accountancy bodies in eighty-seven countries. As of 1999, IFAC recognizes three types of members.

1. Full membership is open to national accountancy organizations that have a professional standard-setting role and that possess rigorous credentialing standards.

2. Associate membership is confined to national accountancy organizations that do not meet full membership criteria.

3. Affiliate membership is open to international organizations that have an interest in the accountancy profession.

ORGANIZATION

IFAC's governance structure is made up of the following components:

1. An *Assembly* comprised of representative from each member accountancy organization. Meeting every two and half years, it is responsible for electing *Council* and approving changes to IFAC's constitution.

2. A *Council* consisting of elected representatives from eighteen countries serving two-and-a-half-year terms. It establishes broad policies, appoints various technical committees and task forces, and oversees IFAC's operations through an *Executive Committee*.

3. An *Executive Committee* comprised of a president, deputy president, director general, and three other members of Council. It is responsible for the implementation of Council's established policies.

4. A *Secretariat*, headquartered in New York City, that provides overall direction and administration.

5. *Technical Committees and Task Forces* that carry on the work of IFAC. Each issues professional guidelines and relevant documents.

COMMITTEE ACTIVITIES

Six standing committees make up the backbone of the IFAC:

Education Committee: issues guidelines on entry-level and continuing professional education requirements, including prequalification, formal education, tests of professional competence, practical experience requirements and continuing education

Ethics Committee: promotes a current code of ethics for accountants

Financial and Management Accounting Committee: works to increase financial and management accountants' awareness of their professional responsibilities via publications, sponsored research, and forums for the exchange of ideas

Public Sector Committee: produces guidelines and studies of international applicability to national, regional, and local governments and related agencies

Information Technology Committee: assesses and relates the impact of information technology on accountant's roles and responsibilities

Membership Committee: strives to increase IFAC's membership and maintain stringent membership criteria

IFAC's Council occasionally appoints special task forces to address important issues. Six task forces active in the mid-1990s include:

- Anti-Corruption
- General Agreement on Trade in Services
- Legal Liability
- Quality Assurance
- Small and Medium Enterprise
- Structure and Organization

IFAC has close ties with other international organizations such as IASC and the International Organization for Securities Commissions (IOSCO). The financial statements of an increasing number of companies are being audited in conformity with IFAC's International Standards on Auditing.

Further information on IFAC, its membership, activities, pronouncements and publications can be secured from the IFAC Web site, http://www.ifac.org/FactsAndFigures/index .html.

(SEE ALSO: *International Accounting Standards*)

BIBLIOGRAPHY

Choi, Frederick D. S., Frost, Carol Ann, and Meek, Gary K. (1999). *International Accounting,* 3rd ed. Upper Saddle River, NJ: Prentice-Hall.

Gruner, John W. and Salter, Stephen. (1997). "Building a Cohesive Accountancy Profession," in *International Accounting and Finance Handbook,* 2nd ed., ed. Frederick D. S. Choi. New York: John Wiley and Sons.

FREDERICK D. S. CHOI

INTERNATIONAL INVESTMENT

International business is not a new phenomenon; it extends back into history beyond the Phoenicians. Products have been traded across borders throughout recorded civilization, extending back beyond the Silk Road that once connected East with West from Xian to Rome. The Silk Road was probably the most influential international trade route of the last two millennia, literally shaping the world as we know it. For example, pasta, cheese, and ice cream, as well as the compass and explosives, among other things, were brought to the Western world from China via the Silk Road.

What is relatively new, beginning with large U.S. companies in the 1950s and 1960s and with European and Japanese companies in the 1970s and 1980s, is the large number of companies engaged in international investment with interrelated production and sales operations located around the world. At no other time in economic history have countries been more economically interdependent than they are today. Although the second half of the twentieth century saw the highest sustained growth rates of gross domestic product (GDP) in history, the growth in the international flow of goods and services has consistently surpassed the growth rate of the world economy. Simultaneously, the growth in international financial flows—including foreign direct investment, portfolio investment, and trading in currencies—has achieved a life of its own. Daily international financial flows now exceed $1 trillion.

Thanks to trade liberalization, heralded by the General Agreement on Tariffs and Trade (GATT) and its successor, the World Trade Organization (WTO), the barriers to international trade and financial flows keep getting lower. While global GDP has grown fivefold since 1950, global trade has expanded seventeenfold during the same period. For forty-nine countries, average exports as a share of GDP also increased to approximately 24 percent in 1998 from 17 percent a decade earlier. Expanding world markets are a key driving force for the twenty-first-century economy. Although the severe slump in Asia in the late 1990s points up the vulnerabilities in

Country Competitiveness Report

Human Resources			Natural Resources			Capital Resources		
Country	Score	Rank	Country	Score	Rank	Country	Score	Rank
Japan	73.2	1	Russia	74.1	1	France	97.3	1
United States	73.0	2	Australia	69.1	2	Japan	96.9	2
Indonesia	72.1	3	Canada	62.8	3	Luxembourg	96.4	3
Thailand	70.9	4	Iceland	60.3	4	Singapore	96.3	4
Singapore	70.7	5	Austria	53.7	5	United Kingdom	96.2	5
Taiwan	69.0	6	Norway	53.1	6	Norway	96.0	6
Korea	67.9	7	France	48.6	7	Denmark	95.8	7
Hong Kong	67.7	7	United States	48.5	8	Netherlands	95.6	8
Malaysia	66.5	9	Spain	47.5	9	United States	95.6	9
Austria	65.7	10	Italy	47.5	10	Hong Kong	95.4	10

Table 1

SOURCE: Dong-Sung Cho and Hwy-Chang Moon. (1998). *The New Competitive Report.* The Institute of Industrial Policy Studies. http://www.ips.ok.kr.

the global marketplace, the long-term trends of increasing trade and investment and rising world incomes continue. As a consequence, even a firm that is operating in only one domestic market is not immune to the influence of economic activities external to that market. The net result of these factors has been the increased interdependence of countries and economies, increased competitiveness, and the concomitant need for firms to keep a constant watch on the international economic environment.

INTERTWINED WORLD ECONOMY

Human, natural, and capital resources shape the nature of international business. A country's relative endowments in those resources shape its competitiveness. Although wholesale generalizations should not be made, the role of human resources has become increasingly important as a primary determinant of industry and country competitiveness. As shown in Table 1, the Institute of Industrial Policy Studies' country competitiveness report in 1998 placed the Asian Tigers—Indonesia, Thailand, Singapore, Taiwan, Korea,

Hong Kong, and Malaysia—among the world's top ten economies, along with Japan and the United States, in terms of human resources. A word of caution is in order when we use any aggregate reports. Although the rankings for human and natural resources may not vary much from year to year, the ranking for capital resources could change drastically from year to year because of their fluid nature. Once all these resources are combined, we could expect enormous complexity in country competitiveness.

The importance of international trade and investment cannot be overemphasized for any country. In general, the larger the country's domestic economy, the less dependent it tends to be on exports and imports relative to its GDP. For the United States (GDP = $7.43 trillion in 1998), international trade in goods and services (sum of exports and imports) rose from 10 percent of GDP in 1970 to about 20 percent in 1998. For Japan (GDP = $5.15 trillion), with approximately two-thirds the U.S. GDP, trade forms a little over 14 percent of GDP. For Germany (GDP = $2.37 trillion), with slightly less than

Leading Exporters and Importers in World Trade in Merchandise and Services, 1998

(IN $BILLION)

Rank	EXPORTERS	Value	Value per capita	Rank	IMPORTERS	Value	Value per capita
1	United States	911.6	3,320	1	United States	1,106.1	4,090
2	Germany	615.4	7,500	2	Germany	588.4	7,170
3	Japan	448.0	3,560	3	United Kingdom	392.2	6,650
4	France	385.6	6,560	4	Japan	390.0	3,100
5	United Kingdom	372.2	6,310	5	France	350.0	5,950
6	Italy	311.0	5,480	6	Italy	283.3	4,990
7	Netherlands	246.5	15,670	7	Canada	239.8	7,820
8	Canada	243.1	7,930	8	Netherlands	228.9	14,550
9	Hong Kong, China	208.3	31,080	9	Hong Kong, China	211.4	31,530
	Domestic exports	*24.3*			*Retained imports[a]*	*38.9*	
10	China	206.8	170	10	Belgium-Luxembourg	192.4	17,443

[a] Retained imports are defined as imports less re-exports.

Table 2

SOURCE: Computed from: *World Trade Growth Slower in 1998 After Unusually Strong Growth in 1997.* World Trade Organization, press release, April 16, 1999; *Statistical Abstract of the United States 1998.* Washington, DC: Census Bureau, 1998.

half the GDP of Japan, trade forms about 40 percent of GDP. For Taiwan (GDP = $0.27 trillion), trade forms as much as 82 percent of GDP. These trade statistics are relative to the country's GDP. In absolute dollar terms, however, a small relative trade percentage of a large economy still translates into large volumes of trade (Table 2). As shown in the last column for both exports and imports in Table 2, the per-capita amount of exports and imports is another important statistic for marketing purposes, since it represents, on average, how much each individual is involved in or dependent on international trade. For instance, individuals (consumers and companies) in the United States and Japan tend to be able to find domestic sources for their needs because their economies are diversified and extremely large. The U.S. per-capita values of exports and imports are $3320 and $4090, respectively. The numbers for Japan are very similar to those of the United States, with $3560 and $3100, respectively. On the other hand, individuals in rich but smaller economies tend to rely more heavily on international trade, as illustrated by the Netherlands, with per-capita exports and imports of $15,670 and $14,550, respectively, and by Hong Kong, with per-capita exports and imports of a whopping $31,080 and $31,530, respectively. Although China's overall exports and imports amounted to $206.8 billion and $168.8 billion (not shown in Table 2), respectively, per-capita exports and imports amounted to only $170 and $136, respectively, in 1998. One implication of these figures is that the higher the per-capita trade, the more closely intertwined is that country's economy with the rest of the world. Intertwining of economies by the process of specialization due to international trade leads to job creation in both the exporting country and the importing country.

However, beyond the simple figure of trade as a rising percentage of a nation's GDP lies the more interesting question of what rising trade does to the economy of a nation. A nation that is a successful trader—that is, it makes goods and services that other nations buy and it buys goods and services from other nations—displays a natural inclination to be competitive in the world market. The threat of a possible foreign competitor is a powerful incentive for firms and nations to invest in technology and markets in order to remain competitive. Also, apart from trade flows, foreign direct investment, portfolio investment, and daily financial flows in the international money markets profoundly influence the economies of countries that may be seemingly completely separate.

FOREIGN DIRECT INVESTMENT

Foreign direct investment—which means investment in manufacturing and service facilities in a foreign country—is another facet of the increasing integration of national economies. Between 1990 and 1997, the value of international trade grew by just under 60 percent in dollar terms, whereas foreign direct investment nearly doubled over the same period. Most of this investment went from one developed country to another, but a growing share is now going to developing countries, mainly in Asia. The overall annual world inflow of foreign direct investment reached $400 billion in 1997. Flows to developing countries in 1997 amounted to $149 billion, representing 37 percent of all global foreign direct investment, compared with $34 billion, or 17 percent of all foreign direct investment, in 1990.

In the past, foreign direct investment was considered to be an alternative to exports in order to avoid tariff barriers. However, today foreign direct investment and international trade have become complementary. For example, Dell Computer uses a factory in Ireland to supply personal computers in Europe instead of exporting from Austin, Texas. Similarly, Honda, a Japanese automaker with a major factory in Marysville, Ohio, is the largest exporter of automobiles from the United States. As firms invest in manufacturing and distribution facilities outside their home countries to expand into new markets around the world, they have added to the stock of foreign direct investment.

The increase in foreign direct investment is also promoted by the efforts of many national governments to attract multinationals and by the leverage that the governments of large potential markets, such as China and India, have in granting access to multinationals. Sometimes trade friction can also promote foreign direct investment. Investment in the United States by Japanese companies is, to some extent, a function of the trade imbalances between the two nations and of the U.S. government's consequent pressure on Japan to do something to reduce the bilateral trade deficit. Since most of the U.S. trade deficit with Japan is attributed to Japanese cars exported from Japan, Japanese automakers, such as Honda, Toyota, Nissan, and Mitsubishi, have expanded their local production by setting up production facilities in the United States. This localization strategy reduces Japanese automakers' vulnerability to retaliation by the United States under the Super 301 laws of the Omnibus Trade and Competitiveness Act of 1988.

PORTFOLIO INVESTMENT

The increasing integration of economies also derives from *portfolio investment* (or *indirect investment*) in foreign countries and from money flows in the international financial markets. Portfolio investment refers to investments in foreign countries that are withdrawable at short notice, such as investment in foreign stocks and bonds. In the international financial markets, the borders between nations have, for all practical purposes, disappeared. The enormous quantities of money that are traded on a daily basis have assumed a life of their own. When trading in foreign currencies began, it was as an adjunct to the international trade transaction in goods and services— banks and firms bought and sold currencies to complete the export or import transaction or to hedge the exposure to fluctuations in the exchange rates in the currencies of interest in the trade transaction. However, in today's international financial markets, traders usually trade currencies without an underlying trade transaction. They trade on the accounts of the banks and financial institutions they work for, mostly on the basis of daily news on inflation rates, interest rates, political events, stock and bond market movements, commodity supplies and demand, and so on. The weekly volume of international trade in currencies exceeds the annual value of the trade in goods and services.

The effect of this trend is that all nations with even partially convertible currencies are exposed to the fluctuations in the currency markets. A rise in the value of the local currency due to these daily flows vis-à-vis other currencies makes exports more expensive (at least in the short run) and can add to the trade deficit or reduce the trade surplus. A rising currency value will also deter foreign investment in the country and encourage outflow of investment. It may also encourage a decrease in the interest rates in the country if the central bank of that country wants to maintain the currency exchange rate and a decrease in the interest rate would spur local investment. An interesting example is the Mexican meltdown in early 1995 and the massive devaluation of the peso, which was exacerbated by the withdrawal of money by foreign investors. The massive depreciation of many Asian currencies in the 1997-1999 period, known as the Asian financial crisis, is also an instance of the influence of these short-term movements of money. Today, the influence of these short-term money flows is a far more powerful determinant of exchange rates than an investment by a Japanese or German automaker.

Despite its economic size, the United States continues to be relatively more insulated from the global economy than other nations. Most of what Americans consume is produced in the United States—which implies that, in the absence of a chain reaction from abroad, the United States is relatively more insulated from external shocks than, say, Germany and China.

The dominant feature of the global economy, however, is the rapid change in the relative status of various countries' economic output. In 1830,

China and India alone accounted for about 60 percent of the manufactured output of the world. However, the share of the world manufacturing output produced by the twenty or so countries that today are known as the rich industrial economies increased from about 30 percent in 1830 to almost 80 percent by 1913. In the 1980s, the U.S. economy was characterized as "floundering" or even "declining," and many pundits predicted that Asia, led by Japan, would become the leading regional economy in the twenty-first century. Then the Asian financial crisis of the late 1990s changed the economic milieu of the world; today, the U.S. economy has been growing at a faster rate than that of any other developed countries. In recent years, the United States and Western European economies have become the twin engines of the world economy, driven by increased trade and investment as a result of continued deregulation, improved technology, and transatlantic mergers, among other things. Obviously, a decade is a long time in the ever-changing world economy; and indeed, no single country has sustained its economic performance continuously.

BIBLIOGRAPHY

Statistical Abstract of the United States.(1998). Washington, DC: U.S. Census Bureau.

World Investment Report 1998.(1999). Geneva: UNCTAD.

"World Trade Growth Slower in 1998 After Unusually Strong Growth in 1997." (1999, April 16). World Trade Organization press release. http://www.wto.org/wto/intltrad/internat.htm.

MASAAKI KOTABE

INTERNATIONAL MONETARY FUND

The International Monetary Fund was established to foster international trade and currency conversion, which it does through consultation and loan activities. When created in 1946, the IMF had 39 member countries; by November 1999 the membership in the IMF had grown to 182 member countries. As of this writing, every major country is now a member, including the

Harry Dexter White.

former communist countries, as are includes numerous small countries. The only exceptions are Cuba and North Korea.

To join the IMF, a country must deposit a sum of money called a quota subscription, the amount of which is based on the wealth of the country's economy. Quotas are reconsidered every five years and can be increased or decreased based on IMF needs and the prosperity of the member country. In 1999, the United States contributed the largest percentage of the annual contributions—18 percent—because it had the largest, richest economy in the world. Voting rights are allocated in proportion to the quota subscription.

HISTORICAL DEVELOPMENT

The Depression in the 1930s devastated international trade and monetary exchange, creating a great loss of confidence on the part of those engaged in international business and finance. Because international traders lost confidence in the paper money used in international trade, there was an intense demand to convert paper money into gold—a demand beyond what the treasuries of countries could supply. Nations that defined the value of their currency in terms of a given amount of gold were unable to meet the conversion demand and had to abandon the gold standard. Valuing currencies in terms of given amounts of gold, however, had given currencies stable values that made international trade flow smoothly.

The relationship between money and the value of products became confused. Some nations hoarded gold to make their currency more valuable so that their producers could buy raw materials at lower prices. Other countries, desperate for foreign sales of their goods, engaged in competitive devaluations of their currencies. World trade became difficult. Countries restricted the exchange of currency, and even encouraged barter. In the early 1940s Harry Dexter White of the United States and John Maynard Keynes of the United Kingdom proposed the establishment of a permanent international organization to bring about the cooperation of all nations in order to achieve clear currency valuation and currency convertibility as well as to eliminate practices that undermine the world monetary system.

Finally, at an international meeting in Bretton Woods, New Hampshire, in July 1944, it was decided to create a new international monetary system and a permanent international organization to monitor it. Forty-four countries agreed to cooperate to solve international trade and investment problems, setting the following goals, for the new permanent, international organization:

- Unrestricted conversion of currencies
- Establishment of a value for each currency in relation to others
- Removal of restrictive trade practices

CREATION OF THE INTERNATIONAL MONETARY FUND

In 1946 in Washington, D.C., the international organization to monitor the new international monetary system came into existence—the International Monetary Fund (IMF). The purposes of the IMF are as follows:

To promote international monetary consultation, cooperation, and collaboration

To facilitate the expansion and balanced growth of international trade

To promote exchange stability

To assist in the establishment of a multilateral system of payments

To make its general resources temporarily available to its members experiencing balance of payments difficulties under adequate safeguards

To shorten the duration and lessen the degree of disequilibrium in the international balances of payments of members

The Bretton Woods agreement created fixed exchange rates between countries based on the value of each country's currency in relation to gold or indirectly in relation to gold by relating their currency to the U.S. dollar. The United States in turn guaranteed that the dollar could be exchanged for gold at a fixed exchange rate. The United States, however, ultimately could not maintain the dollar's promised convertibility, ending it in 1971, in large part because of inflation and a subsequent run on the U.S. gold reserve. The fixed-exchange-rate system collapsed. This led to a managed flexible-exchange-rate system with agreement among major countries that they would try to coordinate exchange rates based on price indexes. However, without operational criteria for managing currency relationships, exchange rates have been increasingly determined by volatile international capital movements rather than by trade relationships.

ORGANIZATIONAL STRUCTURE

The organization of the IMF has at its top a board of governors and alternate governors, who are usually the ministers of finance and heads of central banks of each member country. Because of their positions, they are able to speak authoritatively for their countries. The entire board of

governors and alternate governors meets once a year in Washington, D.C., to formally determine IMF policies. During the rest of the year, a twenty-four-member executive board, composed of representatives or the total board of governors, meets a number of times each week to supervise the implementation of the policies adopted by the board of governors. The IMF staff is headed by its managing director, who is appointed by the executive board. The managing director chairs meetings of the executive board after appointment. Most staff members work at IMF headquarters in Washington, D.C. A small number of staff members are assigned to offices in Geneva, Paris, and Tokyo and at the United Nations.

SURVEILLANCE AND CONSULTATIONS

At least annually, a team of IMF staff members visits each member country for two weeks. The team of four of five meets with government officials, makes inquiries, engages in discussions, and gathers information about the country's economic policies and their effectiveness. If there are currency exchange restrictions, the consultation includes inquiry as to progress toward the elimination of such restrictions. Statistics are also collected on such matters as exports and imports, tax revenues, and budgetary expenditures. The team reports the results of the visit to the IMF executive board. A summary of the discussion is transmitted to the country's government, and for countries agreeing to the release of the summary, to the public.

FINANCIAL ASSISTANCE

The IMF endeavors to stabilize the international monetary system by temporarily lending resources in the form of foreign currencies and gold to countries experiencing international payment difficulties. There are a number of reasons why a country may need such assistance. One possibility is that the country has a trade deficit, which is often offset by lending, capital investment, and possibly aid from richer countries. However, confidence in the country's economic system and its ability to repay its debts becomes diminished in such a situation. The IMF requires that the borrowing country provide a plan for reform that will ultimately result in resolving the payments problems. Reforms such as tighter fiscal and monetary policies, good government control of expenditures, elimination of corruption, and provision for greater disclosure are required.

The most immediate assistance to a member country with payments difficulty is permission to withdraw 25 percent of the quota subscription that was initially paid in the form of gold or convertible currency. If the country still cannot meet its payments obligations it can, ultimately, borrow up to three times its original quota payment. The borrowing country must produce a plan of reform that will overcome the payments problem.

The IMF has a number of additional lending plans to meet various problems experienced by its members as well as emergency lending programs. There are Stand-By Arrangements disbursed over one to two years for temporary deficits, the Compensatory and Contingency Financing Facility for sudden drops in export earnings, Emergency Assistance for natural disasters, Extended Fund Facility to correct structural problems with maturities of greater length, the Supplemental Reserve Facility to provide loans to countries experiencing short-term payments problems due to a sudden loss of market confidence in the country's currency, and the Systemic Transformation Facility for the former communist countries in Eastern Europe and Russia.

SPECIAL DRAWING RIGHTS (SDRS)

In the 1960s, during an expansion of the world economy while gold and the U.S. dollar were the reserve currencies, it appeared that reserves were insufficient to provide for international trade needs. The IMF was empowered to create a new reserve asset, called the special drawing right (SDR), which it could lend to member countries. The value assigned to the SDR is the average of the world's major currencies. Countries with strong currencies agreed to buy SDRs when needed by a country because of payment problems, and in turn sell other currencies. However,

at present SDRs are used mostly for repayment of IMF loans. Creation of SDRs is limited by the IMF constitution to times when there is a long-term global reserve shortage. The board of governors and alternate governors is empowered to make such a determination.

LOANS TO POOR, INDEBTED COUNTRIES

The IMF has created various loan facilities such as the Trust Fund to provide loans to its poorest member countries. In addition, the IMF works cooperatively with the World Bank, other international organizations, individual countries, and private lenders to assist poor, debt-ridden countries. It encourages such countries to restructure their economies to create better economic conditions and better balance of payment conditions.

There have been critics of the IMF's effectiveness. Such critics have noted, for example, instances of massive corruption on the part of recipient governments that resulted in IMF funds being stolen and/or wasted. Also, there have been a number of instances in which IMF efforts have been assessed as unsuccessful. Recommended restrictive fiscal policies have been seen as causing troublesome conditions, such as food shortages and citizen unrest. Nobel-prize-winning economist Robert Mundell, for example, has taken the position that current IMF policy options are insufficient to achieve stable international currency exchange and thereby foster international trade. He recommends that a global currency and world central bank be created to establish a stable international currency.

(SEE ALSO: *Global Economy; International Investment; International Trade*)

BIBLIOGRAPHY

Driscoll, David D. (1998). "What Is the International Monetary Fund?" www.imf.org.

Gotherstrom, Maria (1998). "Development and Financial Structure of the International Monetary Fund." *Quarterly Review—Sveriges Riksbank* (Stockholm) 4:60-74.

Hearing before the Subcommittee on General Oversight and Investigations of the Committee on Banking and Financial Services, U.S. House of Representatives. Review of the Op-

erations of the International Monetary Fund. No. 105-55. (1998). Washington, DC: U.S. Government Printing Office.

International Finance Section, Department of Economics, Princeton University, Princeton, NJ. Essays in International Finance: *A Survey of Financial Liberalization* (No. 211), November 1998; *The International Commercial System* (No. 210), September 1998; *Should the IMF Pursue Capital Account Convertibility?* (No. 207), May, 1998; *From Halifax to Lyons: What Has Been Done About Crisis Management?* (No. 200), October 1996.

International Monetary Fund. (1999). "IMF, at a Glance—Factsheet." www.imf.org.

BERNARD H. NEWMAN

INTERNATIONAL TRADE

The world has a long, rich history of international trade among nations that can be traced back to early Assyrian, Babylonian, Egyptian, and Phoenician civilizations. These and other early civilizations recognized that trade can be tied directly to an improved quality of life for the citizens of all the partners. Today, the practice of trade among nations is growing by leaps and bounds. There is hardly a person on earth who has not been influenced in some way by the growing trade among nations.

WHY INTERNATIONAL TRADE?

One of the most logical questions to ask is, why do modern countries trade with one another? There are numerous reasons that countries engage in international trade. Some countries are deficient in critical raw materials, such as lumber or oil. To make up for these various deficiencies, countries must engage in international trade to obtain the resources necessary to produce the goods and/or services desired by their citizens. In addition to trading for raw materials, nations also exchange a wide variety of processed foods and finished products. Each country has its own specialties that are based on its economy and the skills of its citizens. Three common specialty classifications are capital, labor, and land.

Capital-intensive products, such as cars and trucks, heavy construction equipment, and in-

dustrial machinery, are produced by nations that have a highly developed industrial base. Japan is an example of a highly developed industrial nation that produces large quantities of high-quality cars for export around the world. Another reason Japan has adapted to producing capital-intensive products is that it is an island nation; there is little land available for land-intensive product production. Labor-intensive commodities, such as clothing, shoes, or other consumer goods, are produced in countries that have relatively low labor costs and relatively modern production facilities. China, Indonesia, and the Philippines are examples of countries that produce many labor-intensive products. Products that require large tracts of land, such as cattle production and wheat farming, are examples of land-intensive commodities. Countries that do not have large tracts of land normally purchase land-intensive products from countries that do have vast amounts of suitable land. The United States, for example, is one of the leading exporters of wheat. The combination of advanced farming technology, skilled farmers, and large tracts of suitable farmland in the Midwest and the Great Plains makes the mass production of wheat possible.

Over time a nation's work force will change, and thus the goods and services that nation produces and exports will change. Nations that train their workers for future roles can minimize the difficulty of making a transition to a new, dominant market. The United States, for example, was the dominant world manufacturer from the end of World War II until the early 1970s. But, beginning in the 1970s, other countries started to produce finished products more cheaply and efficiently than the United States, causing U.S. manufacturing output and exports to drop significantly. However, rapid growth in computer technology began to provide a major export for the United States. Practically speaking, the United States has been slowly transformed from a manufacturing-based economy into a new Information Age-based economy that relies on exporting cutting-edge technology as high tech software and computer companies proliferate.

POLITICAL ENVIRONMENT

Each country varies regarding international trade and relocation of foreign plants on its native soil. Some countries openly court foreign companies and encourage them to invest in their country by offering reduced taxes or some other investment incentives. Other countries impose strict regulations that can cause large companies to leave and open a plant in a country that provides more favorable operating conditions. When a company decides to conduct business in another country, it should also consider the political stability of the host country's government. Unstable leadership can create significant problems in recouping profits if the government falls of the host country and/or changes its policy towards foreign trade and investment. Political instability is often caused by severe economic conditions that result in civil unrest.

Another key aspect of international trade is paying for a product in a foreign currency. This practice can create potential problems for a company, since any currency is subject to price fluctuation. A company could lose money if the value of the foreign currency is reduced before it can be exchanged into the desired currency. Another issue regarding currency is that some nations do not have the necessary cash. Instead, they engage in countertrade, which involves the direct or indirect exchange of goods for other goods instead of for cash. Countertrade follows the same principles as bartering, a practice that stretches back into prehistory. A car company might trade new cars to a foreign government in exchange for high-quality steel that would be more costly to buy on the open market. The company can then use the steel to produce new cars for sale.

In a more extreme case, some countries do not want to engage in free trade with other nations, a choice known as self-sufficiency. There are many reasons for this choice, but the most important is the existence of strong political beliefs. For example, the former Soviet Union and its communist allies traded only with each other because the Soviet Union feared that Western countries would attempt to control their governments through trade. Self-sufficiency allowed the Soviet Union and its allies to avoid that possibility. However, these self-imposed trade restrictions created a shortage of products that could not be produced among the group, making the overall quality of life within the Soviet bloc substantially lower than in the West since consumer demand could not be met. When the Berlin Wall came down, trade with the West was resumed, and the shortage of products was reduced or eliminated.

ECONOMIC ENVIRONMENT

An important factor influencing international trade is taxes. Of the different taxes that can be applied to imported goods, the most common is a tariff, which is generally defined as an excise tax imposed on imported goods. A country can have several reasons for imposing a tariff. For example, a revenue tariff may be applied to an imported product that is also produced domestically. The primary reason for this type of tariff is to generate revenue that can be used later by the government for a variety of purposes. This tariff is normally set at a low level and is usually not considered a threat to international trade. When domestic manufacturers in a particular industry are at a disadvantage, vis-à-vis imports, the government can impose what is called a protective tariff. This type of tariff is designed to make foreign products more expensive than domestic products and, as a result, protect domestic companies. A protective tariff is normally very popular with the affected domestic companies and their workers because they benefit most directly from it.

In retaliation, a country that is affected by a protective tariff will frequently enact a tariff of its own on a product from the original tariff enacting country. In 1930, for example, the U.S. Congress passed the Smoot-Hawley Tariff Act, which provided the means for placing protective tariffs on imports. The United States imposed this protective tariff on a wide variety of products in an attempt to help protect domestic producers from foreign competition. This legislation was very popular in the United States, because the Great Depression had just begun, and the tariff was seen as helping U.S. workers. However, the tariff caused immediate retaliation by other countries, which immediately imposed protective tariffs of their own on U.S. products. As a result of these protective tariffs, world trade was severely reduced for nearly all countries, causing the wealth of each affected nation to drop, and increasing unemployment in most countries. Realizing that the 1930 tariffs were a mistake, Congress took corrective action by passing the Reciprocal Trade Agreements Act of 1934, which empowered the president to reduce tariffs by 50 percent on goods from any other country that would agree to similar tariff reductions. The goal was to promote more international trade and help establish more cooperation among exporting countries.

Another form of a trade barrier that a country can employ to protect domestic companies is an import quota, which strictly limits the amount of a particular product that a foreign country can export to the quota-enacting country. For example, the United States had threatened to limit the number of cars imported from Japan. However, Japan agreed to voluntary export quotas, formally known as "voluntary export restrictions," to avoid U.S. imposed import quotas. The power of import quotas has diminished because foreign manufacturers have started building plants in the countries to which they had previously exported in order to avoid such regulations.

A government can also use a nontariff barrier to help protect domestic companies. A nontariff barrier usually refers to government requirements for licenses, permits, or significant amounts of paperwork in order to allow imports into its country. This tactic often increases the price of the imported product, slows down delivery, and creates frustration for the exporting country. The end goal is that many foreign companies will not bother to export their products to those markets because of the added cost and aggravation. Japan and several European countries have frequently used this strategy to limit the number of imported products.

CULTURAL ENVIRONMENT

Before a corporation begins exporting products to other countries, it must first examine the norms, taboos, and values of those countries. This information can be critical to the successful introduction of a product into a particular country and will influence how it is sold and/or marketed. Such information can prevent cultural blunders, such as the one General Motors committed when trying to sell its Chevy Nova in Spanish-speaking countries. *Nova*, in Spanish, means "doesn't go"—and few people would purchase a car named "doesn't go." This marketing error—resulting simply from ignorance of the Spanish language—cost General Motors millions in initial sales—as well as considerable embarrassment.

Business professionals also need to be aware of foreign customs regarding standard business practices. For example, people from some countries like to sit or stand very close when conducting business. In contrast, people from other countries want to maintain a spatial distance between them and the people with whom they are conducting business. Thus, before businesspeople travel overseas, they must be given training on how to conduct business in the country to which they are traveling.

Business professionals also run into another practice that occurs in some countries—bribery. The practice of bribery is common in several countries and is considered a normal business practice. If the bribe is not paid to a businessperson from a country where bribery is expected, a transaction is unlikely to occur. Laws in some countries prohibit businesspeople from paying or accepting bribes. As a result, navigating this legal and cultural thicket must be done very carefully in order to maintain full compliance with the law.

PHYSICAL ENVIRONMENT

Other factors that influence international trading activities are related to the physical environment. Natural physical features, such as mountains and rivers, and human-made structures, such as bridges and roads, can have an impact on international trading activities. For example, a large number of potential customers may live in a country where natural physical barriers, such as mountains and rivers, make getting the product to market nearly impossible.

WORLD TRADE ORGANIZATIONS AND AGREEMENTS

After World War II, the world's leading nations wanted to create a permanent organization that would help foster world trade. Such an organization came into being in 1947 when representatives from the United States and twenty-three other nations signed the document creating the General Agreement on Tariffs and Trade (GATT), which now includes more than one hundred countries as signatories. The threefold purpose of GATT was to (1) foster equal, nondiscriminatory treatment for all member nations; (2) promote the reduction of tariffs by multilateral negotiations; and (3) foster the elimination of import quotas. GATT nations meet periodically to review progress toward established objectives and to set new goals that member countries want to achieve. The goals and objectives of GATT vary and change over time as trade issues evolve based on domestic and world economies.

Likewise, representatives from Belgium, Denmark, France, Germany, Greece, Ireland, Italy, Luxembourg, the Netherlands, Portugal, Spain, and the United Kingdom came together to form the European Economic Community (EEC)—sometimes called the Common Market—in 1958. The purpose of the EEC was to create equal and fair tariffs for all of the nations in the organization so that trade could flourish in Europe. The EEC has generally been regarded as successful.

The United States and Canada signed the U.S. Canadian Free Trade Agreement in 1989, which provided for the removal of all trade barriers between the two countries—such as tariffs, quotas, or other trade restrictions—within a ten-year period. This act helped promote even more trade between the two countries, thus further

strengthening an already strong trade relationship.

The United States, Canada, and Mexico signed the North American Free Trade Agreement (NAFTA) in 1994 in order to create a free-trade zone among the three countries. Leaders of these three countries realized that a large North American free-trade zone could compete effectively against the EEC and other trading blocs that might develop in the future. This competitive factor was a driving force in the nations' signing of the agreement, each believing that, over the long run, all three would benefit from the agreement.

In addition to feeling the impact of trade agreements and trade organizations per se, international trade is affected more indirectly by the financial stability and general economic well-being of all countries in our increasingly interconnected world. Thus two other international organizations ultimately affect the health of world trade.

To further promote trade among countries, the Allied nations of World War II met in 1944 in Bretton Woods, New Hampshire, to help set postwar global financial policies and thereby avoid future financial crises. The International Monetary Fund (IMF) was created as a result of that conference, its mission being to provide loans to countries that are in financial trouble. The IMF dictates the terms of the loans, which may include cutting domestic subsidies, privatizing government industries, and moderating trade policies. To fund these loans, IMF members make annual contributions, with each country's contribution determined by its size, national income, population, and volume of trade. Larger contributing countries, such as Britain and the United States, have more say as to what countries get loans and the terms of the loan.

The World Bank, with approximately 157 members, is another international organization to which the United States is a major contributor. The World Bank's mission is to help less developed countries achieve economic growth through improved trade. It does so by providing loans and guaranteeing or insuring private loans to nations in need of financial assistance. The World Bank has been characterized as (1) a last-resort lender, (2) a facilitator of development projects so as to encourage the inflow of private banking funds, and (3) a provider of technical assistance for fostering long-term economic growth.

SUMMARY

The world has a long history of international trade. In fact, trading among nations can be traced back to the earliest civilizations. Trading activities are directly related to an improved quality of life for the citizens of nations involved in international trade. It is safe to say that nearly every person on earth has benefited from international trading activities.

BIBLIOGRAPHY

Boone, L., and Kurtz, D. (1992). *Contemporary Marketing.* New York: Dryden Press.

Brue, S., and McConnell, C. (1993). *Economics.* New York: McGraw-Hill.

Churchill, G., and Peter, P. (1995). *Marketing: Creating Value for Customers.* Austen Press.

Czinkota, M. R., and Ronkainen, I. A. (1995). *International Marketing.* New York: Dryden Press.

Farese, L., Kimbrell, G., and Woloszyk, C. (1991). *Marketing Essentials.* Mission Hills, CA: Glencoe/McGraw-Hill.

Kotler, P., and Armstrong, G. (1993). *Marketing: An Introduction.* Upper Saddle River, NJ: Prentice-Hall.

ALLEN D. TRUELL
MICHAEL MILBIER

INTERNET

The Internet is a technology and electronic communication system such as the world has never seen before. In fact, some people have said that the Internet is the most important innovation since the development of the printing press.

HISTORY OF THE INTERNET

The Internet was created as a result of the Cold War. In the mid 1960s it became apparent that there was a need for a bomb-proof electronic communication system. A concept was devised to link computers by cable or wire throughout the country in a distributed system so that if some parts of the country were cut off from other parts, messages could still get through. In the beginning, only the federal government and a few universities were linked because the Internet was basically an emergency military communication system, operated by the Department of Defense's Advanced Research Project Agency (ARPA). The whole operation was referred to as ARPANET.

ARPA was linked to computers at a group of top research universities receiving ARPA funding. The first four universities connected to ARPANET were the University of California-Los Angeles, Stanford University, the University of California-Santa Barbara, and the University of Utah. Thus, the Internet was born. Because of a concept developed by Larry Roberts of ARPA and Glen Kleinrock at UCLA, called packet switching, the Internet was able to become a decentralized system, which would prevent large-scale destruction of any centralized system. The system allowed different types of computers from different manufacturers to send messages to one another. Computers merely transmitted information to one another in a standardized protocol packet. The addressing information in these packets told each computer in the chain where the packet was supposed to go.

As the Internet grew, more capability was added. A program called Telnet allowed remote users to run programs and computers at other sites. The File Transfer Protocol (FTP) allowed users to transfer data files and programs. Gopher programs, developed at the University of Minnesota and named after the university's mascot, allowed menu-driven access to data resources on the Internet. Search engines such as Archie and Wide Area Index Search (WAIS) gave users the ability to search the Internet's numerous libraries and indices. By the 1980s people at universities, research laboratories, private companies, and libraries were aided by a networking revolution. There were more than thirty thousand host computers and modems on the Internet. The forerunner of the Internet was the Bitnet, which was a

Tim Berners-Lee developed protocols for the exchange of Internet information.

network of virtually every major university in the world. E-mail became routine and inexpensive, since the Internet is a parasite using the existing multibillion-dollar telephone networks of the world as its carriers.

In 1972 Ray Tomlinson invented network e-mail, which became possible with the FTP. With e-mail and FTP, the rate at which collabo- rative work could be conducted between re- searchers at participating computer science de- partments was greatly increased. Although it was not realized at the time, the Internet had begun. TCP (Transmission Control Protocol) breaks large amounts of data down into packets of a fixed size, sequentially numbers them to allow reassembly at the recipient's end, and transmits the packets over the Internet using the Internet protocol.

After the invention of e-mail, it wasn't long before mailing lists were invented. This was a technique by which an identical message could be sent automatically to large numbers of people. The Internet continues to grow. In fact, it is estimated that almost 65 million adults go online on the Internet in the United States every month. Presently, no one operates the Internet. Although there are entities that oversee the system, "no one is in charge." This allows for a free transfer and flow of information throughout the world.

In 1984 the National Science Foundation (NSF) developed NSFNET. Later NASA, the National Institutes of Health, and others became involved, and nodes on the Internet were divided into basic varieties that are still used today. The varieties are grouped by the six basic Internet domains of GOV, MIL, EDU, COM, ORG, and NET. The ARPANET itself formally expired in 1989, a victim of its own success, and the use of TCP/IP (Transfer Control Protocol/Internet Protocol) standards for computer networks is now global.

If Internet invention had stopped at this point, we would probably still be using the Internet primarily just for e-mail. However, in 1989 a second miracle occurred. Tim Berners-Lee, a software engineer at the CERN physics lab in Switzerland, developed a set of accepted protocols for the exchange of Internet information, and a consortium with users was formed—thus creating the World Wide Web, the standard language for encoding information. Hypertext Markup Language (HTML) was adopted. Berners-Lee proposed making the idea global to link all documents on the Internet using hypertext. This lets users jump from one document to another through highlighted words. Other web standards, such as URL (Universal Resource Language) addresses on the Web page and HTTP (Hypertext Transfer Protocol), are also Berners-Lee's inventions. Berners-Lee could have been exceedingly rich based on his invention, but he

left the fortune-building to others because he "wanted to do the revolution right."

As a result of Berners-Lee's invention, in 1993 a group at the University of Illinois, headed by Mark Andreesen, wrote a graphical application called Mosaic to make use of the Web easier. The next year a few students from that group, including Andreesen, co-founded Netscape after they graduated in May and released the browser for the World Wide Web in November 1994. The World Wide Web is making the Internet easier to use and has brought two giant advantages. Until the Web, the Internet communicated text only, but the Web permits exchange of uncoded graphics, color-coded graphics, color photographs and designs, even video and sound; and it formats typed copy into flexible typographic pages. The Web also permits use of hyperlinks, whereby users can click on certain words or phrases and be shown links to other information or pictures that explain the key words or phrases. As a result of the World Wide Web and Web browsers, it became easy to find information on the Internet and the Web. Various search engines have been developed to index and retrieve this information.

USING THE INTERNET

How does one use the Internet? First, one must have a computer with a connection to the outside world either by a modem connection, a fiber connection such as used in local cable television, or a wireless connection, which is becoming more important. The user is then connected to a system of linked computer networks that encircle the globe, facilitating a wide assortment of data communication services including e-mail, data and program file transfers, newsgroups and chatgroups, as well as graphic images, sound, and video of all kinds. One must choose the right tool to accomplish each task. Thus, one needs to understand the tools to travel this information superhighway.

The Internet is in cyberspace; think of it as a number of planets, each with a unique kind of data program or other type of information service. The only hitch is that each planet's communicating language is different, and one needs several communicating applications and tools. A person is responsible for selecting the proper software program or utility to access what he or she wants. Each program performs a specific task, ranging from providing basic connections, to accessing resources, to preparing e-mail. Common Internet tools include the following:

1. *Connection and log-on software.* This software provides access to log on to cyberspace. The software sets up the connections to the Internet. This software is usually provided by an Internet service provider.

2. *Web browser.* Web browsers are usually free. The most common Web browsers are Microsoft's Internet Explorer and Netscape's Navigator. These software programs can usually be downloaded free of charge; they also come with office suites such as Microsoft Office.

3. *E-mail manager and editor.* To communicate by e-mail users must have an e-mail manager and editor. This editor creates, sends, receives, stores, and organizes your e-mail. Again, many of these e-mail editors can be downloaded free from the Web. One of the most common editors is Eudora. However, office suites usually come with an e-mail manager as well.

A custom connect program starts the procedure for logging on to the Internet using TCP/IP. This is a set of standards and protocols for sharing data between computers and the Internet. Once the protocols have connected, a user must establish his or her identity and authorization to use the Internet services. The Internet service provider used has its own identity on the Internet, and this identity is known as a domain. Domain names, as mentioned previously, are all names listed to the right of the @ sign in the address with an extension such as .com or .edu. The computer then sends and receives data from a host computer over the Internet. A program such as Telnet breaks up the data into packets. The protocols specify how packets should be layered, or packaged. Different layers of packets address a variety of software and hardware needs to send information over different networks and communication links. After a user has properly logged on, he or she can begin using the Internet services.

After a user has completed an on-line work session, he or she must log off the Internet and, depending on the circumstances, disconnect from the Internet service provider. If a user is using an educational service provider such as a college or other educational institution, he or she probably logs off but does not disconnect, since the service is a virtual service provided to many others at the terminal or computer. If one is using a private commercial service provider, one must be sure that a complete disconnection has been made between the computer and provider or one may still be paying fees.

The Internet has spawned an entirely whole new industry called electronic commerce or sometimes electronic business. Businesses sell to other businesses and to consumers on the Internet using secure Web sites. The current market value of U.S. companies with substantial Internet revenue via e-commerce exceeds $3 trillion and is growing annually. It is estimated that by 2003 over 88 percent of all businesses will derive some of their revenue from e-commerce. It has also been said that the growth of the Internet and e-commerce has been one of the main causes of the robust economy in the United States.

Thus, the Internet has been one of the most productive technologies in recent history. The Internet can transport information from nearly any place on the globe to nearly any other place in seconds. The Internet has changed people's notion of how fast things happen. People say now they "did it in Internet time," meaning something was done in a fraction of the traditional or expected amount of time. The Internet is becoming a major cause of time compression.

FUTURE OF THE INTERNET

What does the future hold for the Internet? Predictions are that in the future nearly every Internet-connected device will communicate wirelessly. Low-power radio cells rather than fiber or copper wire, will connect and relay information. Before 2010, more than half of American homes will have at least one low power radio cell connected to Internet bandwidth. The future appears to hold a wireless Internet because of bandwidth problems with cable or wire.

The personal computer will continue to evolve, but there will be a lot of other Internet-smart appliances. Predictions are that there will be Internet wristwatches to match the person with the message. Televisions will, when prompted, record our favorite shows. Various kitchen appliances will start by Internet commands. The personal automobile will also be a mobile personal information store. Automobiles will have internal connectivity and easily carry a very large cache of favorite music, talk, interactive games, and pictures, while passengers will have the option of looking out the window at the real world or looking in the window of their in-car display. Like the explorers who discovered new continents, people are just beginning to discover the full impact of the Internet on information, space, and time.

BIBLIOGRAPHY

Anderson, John. "Internet History and Perspective." www2 .advisorworks.com. February 28, 2000.

Baylogic. "Net History and Statistics." www.baylogic.com. February 28, 2000.

Berners-Lee, Tim. (1996) "Passing up Fortune-Building 'To Do the Revolution Right'." *Investor's Business Daily* 13(43)(June 7):1-2.

Reidelbach, Dorothy. (1996). "The Amazing New World Wide Web." *Planning for Higher Education* 24 (Spring):1-6.

Ricart, Glenn. (2000). "Unofficial Technology Marvel of the Millennium." *Educause Review* January/February: 38-59.

Rochester, Jack B. (1996). *Using Computers and Information.* Indianapolis, IN: Macmillan.

LLOYD W. BARTHOLOME

INTERPERSONAL RELATIONS

(SEE: *Human Relations*)

INTERSTATE COMMERCE

Interstate commerce is the transportation of products and services from one state to geographic points in other states. This involves the transportation of goods and services across state lines, creating a dependency on transportation modes and making the process subject to state laws regarding the transportation of goods.

Transportation plays an important role in determining the profitability of operating both farm and nonfarm businesses in rural areas. Farms, businesses, and industries in rural areas rely on transportation services to achieve necessary production outputs and to deliver commodities and products to market.

Interstate commerce has its roots in farming. During most of the first decade after the Civil War, farmers in seven midwestern states were responsible for approximately one-half of the nation's output of corn, wheat, and oats. Illinois farms were the leaders in the production of each of these grains; farmers to the north provided large amounts of the hard varieties of wheat, while those to the south and east produced most of the corn. Based on the presence of abundant feed, these producers established locations for fattening livestock and producing meat products. Given this state of affairs, farmers were in the market for transport services to carry livestock and crops to major produce exchanges located in other states.

Chicago and St. Louis were established as collection centers, but these centers were not the sites of final consumption. By 1870, there were well-established lines of supply between states. The Great Lakes steamers and schooners provided most of the service between Chicago and the northern portions of the Great Lakes area, and the four major railroads provided ground transportation. The two railroads with independent and complete service were the New York Central system and the Pennsylvania system.

Between 1874 and 1919, many laws were enacted that imposed economic regulation on the dominant means of interstate commerce in the United States: the railroad. However, federal transportation regulations were not of a sufficient magnitude to justify forming a cabinet-level department solely for matters of interstate commerce.

Economic conditions between 1874 and 1919 vacillated. Agricultural depression was extensive during the 1870s and 1880s and constituted a factor that ultimately resulted in the economic regulation of interstate railroads in 1887. Furthermore, an international depression occurred in 1893 that sent seventy-four railroad companies into financial distress. Between 1901 and 1919, U.S. society experienced relative prosperity; it was during this period that 145,000 miles of track were constructed to carry goods between states.

Executive and legislative agencies related to transportation functions proliferated between 1874 and 1919; it was during this same period that highway transportation began to increase in importance. Financing and planning of highway development within state lines was primarily the responsibility of each individual state. However, the Bureau of Public Roads began to play a significant role. In addition, the airline industry had its beginnings during the early part of the twentieth century.

The Interstate Commerce Commission (ICC), an independent U.S. government agency established in 1887, is responsible for the economic regulation of services of specified carriers engaged in transportation between states. The first regulatory agency formed within the federal government, it was established in response to mounting public indignation against railroad malpractices and abuses. The ICC's effectiveness, however, was limited by Congress's failure to give it enforcement power, by the Supreme Court's narrow interpretation of its powers, and by the vague language of its enabling act.

Beginning with the Hepburn Act of 1906, the ICC's domain was gradually extended beyond railroads to all common carriers except airplanes by 1940. It was also given the task of consolidating railroad systems and managing labor disputes in interstate transport. In the 1950s and 1960s, the ICC enforced U.S. Supreme Court rulings that required the desegregation of passenger terminal facilities.

Part I of the Interstate Commerce Act enacted of 1935 grouped together a series of laws that were enacted in the late 1800s and early 1900s. The first of these laws required that railroad carriers publicize their rate schedules and forbade rate changes without due notice to the public. Subsequent acts increased regulation and extended the ICC's jurisdiction. Part II of the act extended federal authority to motor carriers engaged in interstate commerce. Part III gave the federal government authority to regulate common carriers operating in interstate commerce in the coastal, intercoastal, and inland waters of the United States. Part IV comprised regulations governing the operations of freight operators.

Subsequently, the ICC's jurisdiction expanded to included trucking, bus lines, water carriers, freight forwarders, pipelines (those not already regulated by other agencies) and express delivery agencies. The ICC controlled rates and enforced federal and local laws against discrimination in these areas. The safety functions of its jurisdiction were transferred to the Department of Transportation in 1967, and the deregulation of the late 1970s and the 1980s further reduced the ICC's role. Most ICC control over interstate trucking was removed in 1994, and the agency was terminated at the end of 1995. Many of its remaining functions were transferred to the National Surface Transportation Board.

Interstate commerce is currently supervised by several federal agencies. The Civil Aeronautics Board was created by the Civil Aeronautics Act of 1938, to oversee the airline industry. This act dealt with the airline industry's ability to provide efficient service at reasonable charges without unjust discrimination, undue preferences, or advantages or unfair or destructive competitive practices. Forty years later, President Jimmy Carter signed into law the Airline Deregulation Act of 1978, which would phase out the Civil Aeronautics Board and let the airlines determine their own pricing and routes. It was thought that a lack of competition had made the industry unresponsive to consumers. As a result, the industry became deregulated and the pricing wars began.

There are many other federal regulatory agencies and laws that deal with govern interstate commerce. The Federal Trade Commission was established in 1914 with investigatory powers to be used in preventing unfair methods of competition. The FTC enforces laws and guidelines regarding business practices and takes action to stop false and deceptive advertising, pricing, packaging, and labeling. It assists businesses in complying with both state and federal laws, and it evaluates new business methods used each year. It holds conferences on electronic commerce, which is the most recent form of interstate commerce. When general sets of guidelines are needed to assist businesses involved in interstate commerce, the FTC encourages firms within that industry to establish a set of trade practices voluntarily.

The Clayton Act, passed in the same year that the FTC was created (1914), prohibits specific practices such as price discrimination, exclusive dealer arrangements, and stock acquisitions whose effect may notably lessen competition or tend to create a monopoly.

In addition, the Federal Communications Commission (FCC) has evolved as a crucial regulatory component in e-commerce development. The FCC regulates communication by wire, radio, and television in interstate and foreign commerce. This agency has been undergoing rapid changes as a result of the need for e-commerce regulation.

CURRENT INTERSTATE COMMERCE ENVIRONMENT

Today's transportation environment is much different from that of previous decades. The shift from a rural to an urban economic base, policy changes, and technological and organizational innovations have changed the way in which products and services are distributed in the United States. Today, less than 10 percent of the people living in nonmetropolitan areas are employed in farming, forestry, fisheries, or mining. Present-day farms tend to be larger and

more capital-intensive. Large tractor-trailer trucks are rapidly replacing smaller vehicles in the delivery of production inputs to farms and products to market.

Nonagricultural demands for interstate commerce increased dramatically in the last quarter of the twentieth century. Manufacturing employment in nonmetropolitan areas grew at a rate three times that in metropolitan areas. Approximately 20 percent of nonmetropolitan residents were employed by manufacturing firms at the turn of the twenty-first century.

As a result of these changes, the amount and type of interstate traffic have also changed dramatically. The larger, heavier vehicles on these roads require major investments in bridges and in surfaces of paved roads. A recent Department of Transportation survey suggests that more than 50 percent of the local road mileage in the United States is structurally inadequate. This problem is one of surface type and condition and even safety deficiencies, such as inadequate lane widths or lack of shoulders.

The increased financial responsibility of local governments for construction and maintenance of rural road system is a special concern for those rural regions dependent on interstate commerce. Transportation deregulation is another major federal policy change likely to influence the cost and availability of transportation services and facilities needed for interstate commerce. Technological and organizational innovations have accompanied the new deregulated environment. Railroad mergers, for example, have resulted in reduced service on many routes, potentially affecting the relative competitiveness of regions as a location for business or industry. Developments of unit-train facilities and railroad contracts encourage consolidation and growth of processing firms.

Transportation improvements that result in lower operating costs for area enterprises aid rural communities in efforts to attract new business and industry and encourage the expansion of existing firms. Business surveys consistently find that firms rank transportation access, cost, and quality as high-priority considerations in choosing a business location. The availability of highway transportation is particularly important to a wide variety of rural businesses that depend on the ability to deliver their products to other states.

Freight carriers are dependent on the rural road systems, which are financed through a combination of local tax revenues. The shared state-highway user taxes and fees vary from state to state. A faltering local economy can severely limit a local government's ability to raise revenue for road system improvements, and the likely result of this is a cycle of decline in interstate commerce. Without additional revenues, local road systems will continue to deteriorate, thus further reducing the attractiveness of the area for business and industry and thus further eroding the area's tax base.

Interstate commerce involves the transportation of services as well as goods. Of particular importance is the transportation of people between states. Formerly, carriers were partially protected from competition in return for fulfilling public service obligations. Under this arrangement, common carriers were not free to choose customers, nor were they free to eliminate parts of their services without the consent of the public. This obligation placed liabilities for loss and damage with the interstate carriers who were responsible for transportation losses. In addition, common carriers had to serve all customers without discrimination and had to have their rate-change proposals reviewed by regulatory bodies to determine whether these changes were reasonable.

In return for fulfilling these public obligations, common carriers were protected from new competition. When a company proposed to expand service to another state, an existing transportation company could argue that it currently serviced the traffic adequately and could oppose entry of a new interstate carrier. Often, the opposition of existing carriers prevented the entry of new carriers.

In the early 1980s, however, Congress passed major legislation changing the government's role. Recent policy changes have essentially replaced the common carrier system with a market-transaction system similar to that of any other private business. The new market approach allows shippers and carriers to actively negotiate for transport services rather than accept one of a few alternatives offered by carrier consortiums. Deregulation increased economic efficiency in the provision of transportation services due to new flexibility on the part of carriers in adjusting to demand. Highways, railways, and airways are the arteries that enable shoppers and tourists to travel between states. Because of this, passenger transportation plays a key role in rural economic development. Many rural industries draw their workers from surrounding communities up to fifty miles away. For these industries, the interstate transportation system is a critical link providing them access to the labor force. Policies and investments that reduce the cost of interstate commerce rural regions are a potential catalyst for rural economic development.

The urgency of finding workable solutions to interstate commerce issues has prompted new ways of thinking. In 1982, the U.S. government appropriated $5 million to provide technical assistance to local agencies through the Rural Technical Assistance Program. The principal delivery system for the program was a network of Technology Transfer Centers. Under the Federal Highway Administration program, the Technology Transfer Centers were designed to provide training and other technology transfer products to local users. One of the primary objectives of the program is to serve as a communications link among the various sources of new technology and the state and local agencies that can apply the technology in daily operations. In 1983 there were ten Technology Transfer Centers. Today, there are more than fifty across the United States.

Today, the Federal Communication Commission (FCC) has come to the forefront because of its responsibility to regulate e-commerce. The FCC sought comment on two rule-making dockets in 2000: the Access Charge Reform rule making docket and the Complete Detariffing for Competitive Access Providers and Competitive Local Exchange Carriers (CLEC detariffing) rulemaking docket, which is involved with the regulatory or market-based approaches that would ensure that competitive local exchange carriers (CLEC) rates for interstate access are reasonable. There are many current proposals being discussed at these proceedings, and the FCC invites all interested parties to comment on whether mandatory detariffing of CLEC interstate access service rates would provide a market-based deterrent to excessive terminating access charges. In addition, the FTC has been sponsoring workshops throughout the country that are intended to educate people about how marketplaces work and explore the anticompetitive scenarios. The FTC will be involved in scrutinizing virtual competition in e-marketplaces.

BIBLIOGRAPHY

Brierty, Edward, and Reeder, Robert. (1991). *Industrial Marketing, Analysis Planning and Control.* Englewoods Cliffs, NJ: Prentice Hall.

Gillis, William. (1989). *Profitability and Mobility in Rural America.* University Park, PA: Pennsylvania State University Press.

MacAvoy, Paul. (1975). *The Economic Effects of Regulation.* Cambridge, MA: The MIT Press.

Miller, Sidney. (1953). *Inland Transportation.* New York: McGraw Hill Publishing.

PATRICIA A. SPIROU

INTERSTATE COMMERCE COMMISSION

The Interstate Commerce Act of 1887 created the Interstate Commerce Commission (ICC), the U.S. government's first regulatory agency. The initial purpose of the ICC was to control railroads and their unfair business practices. The U.S. government had to become a regulator because in 1886 the Supreme Court had ruled in the case of *Wabash Railroad v. Illinois* that states could not control interstate commerce.

Railroads presented some special problems because they were capital-intensive, had high maintenance costs, and had two types of rail lines. This led to unfair pricing practices. For

Police lieutenant Beavers Armstrong places a segregation sign.

major trunk lines, where there was competition, the railroads charged lower rates and even gave rebates. For spur lines, where there was a monopoly, the railroad charged higher rates for the same type of cargo.

Even with the federal government taking charge of regulating railroads, the Interstate Commerce Commission still got off to a rocky start. In its first sixteen court actions, the ICC only won one case; and the Supreme Court had several judgments against the ICC which limited its power. However, later legislation gave the ICC rulings more power. The Elkins Act of 1903 was aimed at unfair competitive methods, and the Hepburn Act of 1906 eliminated the necessity of a court order to make ICC rulings binding and gave the ICC control of gas and water pipelines.

The Motor Carrier Act of 1935 placed the emerging trucking industry under ICC jurisdiction. Typical ICC duties included holding hearings to investigate complaints, approving transportation mergers, and overseeing consumer-protection programs.

By the 1960s, the ICC had grown into a massive bureaucracy, peaking at 2400 employees. Shortly thereafter, the agency came under severe criticism. Some groups argued that, because of regulation, the country's transportation was inefficient and perhaps corrupt. The major criticism—that regulation created artificially high rates—led to pressure for deregulation and signaled the beginning of the demise of the ICC. First, the Railroad Revitalization and Regulatory Reform Act of 1976 curtailed the ICC power to regulate rates unless the railroad had a monopoly on certain routes. In 1977, air cargo deregulation and the reforms taking place in the trucking industry further eroded the power of the ICC. After the early rocky years of deregulation, the transportation industry had become more efficient thanks to innovative technology, thereby reducing costs. The final act of deregulation came in 1994, when the ICC lost most of its control over the trucking industry.

By this time, the ICC had dropped from a high of 2400 employees to 300 and was constrained by a severely reduced budget. The Republicans, who had wanted to eliminate the ICC for a number of years, took control of Congress in 1995. As a first step, the fiscal 1996 spending bill (HR2002-FL 104-50) gave the ICC no budget. Then the House Transportation and Infrastructure Committee approved HR2539, and the debate began. The major objection from the Democratic side was centered on protection for railroad workers who might lose their jobs because of mergers. After ironing out their differences, Congress sent President Clinton legislation to terminate the ICC (HR2539-PL 104-88). On December 29, 1995, the 108-year-old Interstate Commerce Commission was disbanded.

BIBLIOGRAPHY

"End of the Line for ICC." *Nation's Business* 84(3) (March 1996): 32.

"ICC Elimination." (1995—1996). *Congress and the Nation* 9:381-383.

"Interstate Commerce Commission." Archived at: http://www.federalregister.com. 1999.

"Interstate Commerce Commission." *West's Encyclopedia of American Law.* (Vol 6, 1998, 209-210). St. Paul, MN.

"President Signs Bill Terminating ICC." (1996). *Congressional Quarterly Weekly Report* 54(1) (6 January 1996):58.

"R.I.P., ICC." (1996). *American Heritage.* 47(3) (May/June):22.

"Weekly Compilation of Presidential Documents." *Congressional Quarterly Weekly Report* (1996). 32:1 (8 January):1.

MARY JEAN LUSH
VAL HINTON

INTRANET/EXTRANET

The first global electronic network was the Internet. Today there are also new Internet subsystems called an intranet and an extranet. While computer users may use all three systems throughout a single day, there are some similarities and differences among them that are important. To aid in understanding these three systems, let us use the example of a computer-using employee, Sally, in an automobile dealership. Sally might use the Internet to check flight schedules to plan for an upcoming sales meeting. Sally might also use the intranet to check on a shipment of cars for the automobile dealership. Sally could also use the extranet to check the latest wholesale pricing of tires.

DEFINITIONS AND RELATIONSHIPS

Internet Although the Internet has existed for more than a quarter of a century it is now used widely in schools, homes, and workplaces. The *CMP Net Online Encyclopedia* defines *Internet* as:

(1) A large network made up of a number of smaller networks. (2) "The" Internet is made up of more than 100,000 inter-connected networks in over 100 countries, comprised of commercial, academic and government networks. Originally developed for the military, the Internet became widely used for academic and commercial research . . . Today, the Internet has become commercialized into a worldwide

information highway, providing information on every subject known to humankind.

Intranet The same work defines *intranet* as:

An in-house Web site that serves the employees of the enterprise. Although intranet pages may link to the Internet, an intranet is not a site accessed by the general public.

Note the important difference: The *intranet* is information that is available only to those who are "*in*-house," or some type of corporate partner. Some typical uses of an intranet include access to production schedules, inventory, meetings, and training. Thus if you worked for company A you could have ready access to the information posted on the company Website. However, most intranets also include an organization's partners. Let's say that company A manufactures computer monitors using cathode-ray tubes (CRTs) made by company B. Company A no doubt keeps an exact inventory of how many tubes it has in stock; and it is possible that company B is asked to monitor these numbers so that it can automatically ship CRTs to company A when needed. Of course, company B would not be granted access to other online data belonging to company A.

Extranet The *CMP Net Online Encyclopedia* defines *extranet* as:

A Web site for existing customers rather than the general public. It can provide access to paid research, current inventories and internal databases, virtually any information that is private and not published for everyone. An extranet uses the public Internet as its transmission system, but requires passwords to gain access.

While company A allows public access via the Internet to its Website, it does not include highly sensitive information there. It has an intranet that can be accessed only by employees and selected companies having certain partnerships with it. It also has an extranet website that only their customers can access.

APPLICATIONS AND ISSUES

Access Individual employee access to the Internet, intranets, and extranets varies. Today employees in many organizations may use all of the terms interchangeably, although many employees commonly use the term "Internet" (or "Netscape" or "Internet Explorer") for what would technically be located on an intranet or extranet. An important issue for network administrators (or Webmasters) is access. To enforce proper access, they must know *exactly* who has authorization to the Internet, intranet, and/or extranet. Organizational decisions makers also need to be familiar with policy issues to ensure that the "wrong" people do not gain access to sensitive information. This raises an important issue: Do the benefits of "liberal" access outweigh the possible negative consequences? However, as Gibson (1998) noted: "If you can't trust your business partners, you probably shouldn't be doing business with them."

Usage Restrictions An intranet or extranet can technically be set up in several ways. One way is to have only one Web site but to restrict user access, with usage access authorized on an individual basis. With this method, individuals who attempt to gain access to a site for which they do not have proper "rights," whether accidentally or intentionally, will receive a message like the following from their screen:

Not Found. The requested object does not exist on this server. The link you followed is either outdated, inaccurate, or the server has been instructed not to let you have it. Please inform the site administrator of the referring pages.

In this example, the Web page the individual requested actually exists, but it is available only to personnel who have the "clearance" to view the information. Totally separate Web sites are often designed for differing levels of access. Additionally, add-in products to assist in constructing intranets are also available, such IntraNetics and "intranet-in-a-box," which come configured with links to specific electronic commerce sites, such as Staples and American Express Business Travel ("Intranets," 1999).

INTRANET INNOVATIONS

An organizations intranet can be used in many different ways. A typical use is for training, but many unforeseen uses also arise. This section contains examples of intranet uses within organizations.

Employee Training The Dow Chemical Company is implementing a broad training program by employing the intranet to supplant and possibly eliminate much of the one million hours of classroom training they now offer. Schwartz (1999) noted that Dow spends $80 million yearly to train employees and contractors (Dow University Online) in areas from environmental safety to health issues using TopClass presentation software (WBT Systems) on their Webservers.

Online Conferencing Using the intranet to move beyond storing and sharing static information, Bell Atlantic formed a partnership with IBM's Lotus Development to become more competitive in the communication industry (Trager, 1999). One Lotus application allows Bell Atlantic to easily create and customize a meeting-room simulation on-line (on-line conferencing) for use in its intranet or extranet. Trager also pointed out that Bell Atlantic is interested in Lotus's Sametime real-time collaboration and LearningSpace for distance education.

Unexpected Outcomes Sharing information, such as inventories and shipping dates, via intranet with corporate partners has led to efficiencies. Additionally, other unplanned organizational changes have also evolved. According to Shachtman (1998):

> Employees are using intranets to band together in far-flung groups of need and expertise that defy traditional corporate structure. Advanced intranets allow people to organize around information clusters, not hierarchical schemes, says Mike Gotta, program director at research firm the Meta Group. 'It's a move from a highly rigid workplace to a more organic workspace.'

Shachtman further explains that while knowledge has always been associated with power, the intranet is rapidly breaking down rigid organizational structures.

Portals Intranets are continually changing as more uses are found for Web-based information. A recent innovation is a "portal," a search engine that includes easy links to all kinds of resources, from weather to stock pricess to late-breaking news. The search engines Yahoo, Excite, AltaVista, Lycos and many others have evolved into "portals" in their ever-increasing quest to obtain more users. Now corporate portals are being developed so that when employees use their intranet they easily and quickly find relevant information. Guglielmo (1998) described a corporate portal:

> The concept is simple: Corporate employees turn on their computers and, instead of going to Yahoo! or Excite, go to their company's browser-based internal portal, where they receive easy-to-navigate, highly detailed information to help them do their jobs. They also can make travel arrangements and order office supplies.

Some firms have already begun marketing specific software to create corporate portals. For example, Netscape Communications Corporation, the parent company of Yahoo, is licensing a customized version of its Netcenter portal site (Guglielmo, 1998). Marty Cagan, Netcenter's vice president of business-to-business services stated:

> "Our strategy is to leverage our understanding of the portal market by turning our own portal, which during the business day is the busiest site in the world, into a platform that other customers can build on" (quoted in Guglielmo, 1998).

IMPLICATIONS AND IMPACT

Intranet access to information has already drastically altered the way organizations communicate and conduct business. Robert Moon, Chief Information Officer of Micros Systems, says, "In less than three years, we've gone from the Web being a novelty to a critical application. It's now our main focus" (quoted in Booker, 1999, p. 32).

Indeed, the intranet concept will continue to alter the way organizations function both internally and externally in ways that cannot be imagined in the twentieth century.

BIBLIOGRAPHY

Booker, E. (1999). "ERP's Next Frontier." *Internet Week*March 15: 31-32.

CMP Net Online Encyclopedia. (1999). http://www.techweb.com/encyclopedia/.

Gibson, S. (1998). "Extranets' moment has come." *PC Week* 133 (November 16): 31-32.

Guglielmo, C. *Interactive Week Online.* http://www.zdnet.com/. December 14, 1988.

Interactive Week Online. "Intranets." http://www.zdnet.com/. January 27, 1999.

Schwartz, J. (1999). "Dow Intranet Becomes Classroom." *Internet Week* January: 17.

Shachtman, N. (1999). "Group Think: Employees are Shattering the Traditional Corporate Structure with Intranets." *Internet Week* June 1:31-32.

Trager, L. *Interactive Week Online.* http://www.zdnet.com/. January 7, 1999.

ARMAND SEGUIN
CYNTHIA SHELTON SEGUIN

INTRAPRENEURSHIP

(SEE: *Entrepreneurship*)

INVENTORY CONTROL

Inventory control is the implementation of management's inventory policies in a manner that assures that the goals of inventory management are met. Wise control of inventory is often a critical factor in the success of businesses in which inventories are significant. The goal of inventory control is to be sure that optimum levels of inventories are available, that there are minimal stockouts (i.e., running out of stock), and that inventory is maintained in a safe, secure place and is always readily accessible to the proper personnel.

Policies relate to what levels of inventories are to be maintained and which vendors will be supplying the inventory. How and when inventories will be replenished, how inventory records are created, managed, and analyzed, and what aspects of inventory management will be outsourced are also important components of proper inventory management.

IN THE BEGINNING

Prior to the eighteenth century, possessing inventory was considered a sign of wealth. Generally, the more inventory you had, the more prosperous you were. Inventory existed as stores of wheat, herds of cattle, and rooms full of pottery or other manufactured goods.

This phenomenon occurred for good reason. There were a number of concerns for businesspeople then. Communication was difficult and unreliable, easily interrupted, and often took long periods of time to complete. Stocks were difficult to obtain, and supply was uncertain, erratic, and subject to a wide variety of pitfalls. Quality was inconsistent. More often than not, receiving credit for a purchase was not an option and a person had to pay for merchandise before taking possession of it. The financial markets were not as complex or as willing to meet the needs of business as they are today. In addition, the pace of life was a lot slower. Because change occurred gradually, it was relatively easy to forecast market needs, trends, and desires. Businesses were able to maintain large quantities of goods without fear of sudden shifts in the market, and these inventories served as buffers in the supply line. Customers had a sense of security, knowing that there was a ready supply of merchandise in storage, and that comfort often helped to minimize hoarding.

In the eighteenth and early nineteenth centuries, markets were very specialized. There was often one supplier for each market in each area of business. Except for the basic necessities of life, there was much local specialization and distinct specialization by region. For example, although there might be more than one grist-mill in a community, there would often be only one general store. If customers were unhappy with their existing supplier, they had to suffer some incon-

Japan has a trade surplus of autos with the United States.

venience to find an alternate source because of the monopolies that existed. This made it easier for businesses to market their products and allowed them to maintain large stocks if they had the capital to do so.

Inventory management was a concern then, as it is now. Inventories had to be monitored for accuracy and quality. They had to be protected from the elements, from theft, from spoiling, and from changes in the local economy. Tax laws could have an enormous impact on inventory levels.

THE EARLY TWENTY-FIRST CENTURY

Today's business world shares few similarities with yesterday's. Communication is quick, easy, reliable, and available through a host of media. Supply is certain and regular in most environments of merchandising and manufacturing. Tax laws are generally consistent and reliable. However, market changes can be abrupt and difficult to forecast. Global competition exists everywhere

for almost everything. Products are available from anywhere in the world, with delivery possible within in one day in many cases. Competition is driving the price of most products down to minimum profit levels. Inventories are managed for minimum stocking levels and maximum turnover. In the twenty-first century, high inventory is a sign of either mismanagement or a troubled economy. It is expensive and wasteful to hold and maintain high inventory levels. Proper utilization of space is also a critical component in today's business world, whether one is a retailer, wholesaler, or a manufacturer.

Modern retailers and manufacturers are equipped with an array of tools and support mechanisms to enable them to manage inventory. Technology is used in almost every area of inventory management to help control, monitor, and analyze inventory. Computers, especially, play an enormous role in modern inventory management.

INVENTORY MANAGEMENT SYSTEMS

Ongoing analyses of both inventory management and manufacturing processes have led to innovative management systems, such as just-in-time inventory or the economic-order quantity decision model.

Just-in-time inventory is a process developed by the Japanese based on a process invented by Henry Ford. David Wren (1999) descibes how the process started:

> Henry Ford managed to cut his inventory by forty million dollars by changing how he obtained materials to produce automobiles. Through a process called vertical integration, Ford purchased mines and smelting operations to better control the source and supply of material to produce cars. In this way, he was able to reduce his standing inventory and increase turnover. In the 1950's, Taiichi Ohno, a mechanical engineer working for Toyota Motorcar Company, refined this process into what we know today as Just-in-Time inventory (p. 1).

Just-in-time inventory usually requires a dominant face—a major partner that has the resources to start the process and keep it organized and controlled—that organizes the flow and communication so that all the parties in the supply process know exactly how many parts are needed to complete a cycle and how much time is needed in between cycles. By having and sharing this information, companies are able to deliver just the right amount of product or inventory at a given time. This requires a close working relationship between all the parties involved and greatly minimizes the amount of standing or idle inventory.

In the economic-order quantity decision model, an analysis is made to determine the optimum quantity of product needed to minimize total manufacturing or production costs. In other words, through a complex analysis, management attempts to determine the minimum amount of product needed to do the job and still keep the cost of inventory as low as possible. This analysis considers the amount of time needed to generate an order; to process, manufacture, organize, and ship each product; to receive, inventory, store, and consume each product; and to process the paperwork upon receipt through the final payment process. This is a more independent process than just-in-time inventory; by allowing for a variety of suppliers to participate, it ensures competitiveness. Many companies today employ a mixture of both processes in order to maintain independence yet still have a close relationship with suppliers. Retailers, for example, work closely with suppliers to maintain the lowest possible inventories but still have enough products to satisfy customer demand. Often, companies have access to information about each other's inventory levels, allowing management to further analyze inventories to ensure that each is carrying the correct amount of stock to satisfy market needs and maintain minimum levels.

THE INVENTORY PROCESS

Inventory is generally ordered by computer, through a modem, directly from a supplier or manufacturer. The persons ordering the product have an inventory sales or usage history, which enables them to properly forecast short-term needs and also to know which products are not being sold or consumed. The computer helps management with control by tying in with the sales or manufacturing department. Whenever a sale is made or units of a product are consumed in the manufacturing process, the product is deleted from inventory and made part of a history file that can be reviewed manually or automatically, depending on how management wishes to organize that department. The supplier and the buyer often have a close working relationship; the buyer will keep the supplier informed about product changes and developments in the industry in order to maintain proper stock levels, and the supplier will often dedicate equipment and personnel to assist the buyer.

Even though small companies may work closely with larger suppliers, it is still very important that these small companies manage their inventory properly. Goods need to be stored in a suitable warehouse that meets the needs of the products; some products require refrigeration, for example, while others require a warm and dry environment. Space is usually a critical factor in this ever-shrinking world: It is important to have enough space to meet the needs of customers and keep the warehouse from becoming overcrowded. Inventory needs to be monitored to prevent theft and inaccuracies. Taking physical inventory—physically checking each item against a list of items on hand—is a routine that should be performed a number of times a year. At the very least, inventories should always be checked each year just before the end of the fiscal year and compared against " book" or quantities listed as on hand in the computer or manual ledger. Adjustments can then be made to correct any inaccuracies. Taking inventory more than once a year, and thus looking at stocks over shorter periods of time, often results in discovering accounting or processing errors. It also serves as a notice to employees that management is watching the inventory closely, often deterring pilferage.

Alarm systems and closed-circuit television are just a few of the ways inventories can be monitored. Making sure that everyone allowed into inventory management systems has and uses his or her own password is critical to effective inventory control. By having redundant systems, management can also compare the two to make sure there is a balance. If they go too far out of balance, management is alerted.

IN THE END

Maintaining a clean, orderly, properly lighted, and secure warehouse or stockroom is the basic key to maintaining inventory control. Adding computer technology to aid in management and administration creates a system that is current and competitive. Properly training employees in modern techniques and standards results in a system that will be effective and profitable.

(SEE ALSO: *Costs*)

BIBLIOGRAPHY

Burt, John. (1992). "Controlling Inventory in Process Inventories: Integration is the Key." *Production & Inventory Management*, 12 (February): 25,29.

Christensen, David L. (1997). "Inventory reviews: Inventory control may sound easy when you read it in textbooks, but auditors need more than theory to perform successful reviews." *Internal Auditor.* 54 (October): 50-53.

Lines, Anthony. (1992). "Taking Stock of Stock Control." *Malaysian Accountant.* (April): 27-28.

Malburg, Christopher R. (1994). *Controller's and Treasurer's Desk Reference.* New York: McGraw-Hill.

Thomas, Michael F., and Mackey, James T. (1994). "Activity-Based Cost Variances for Just-in-Times." *Management Accounting IMA*, 75 (April): 49-54.

Wren, Daniel A. (1999). "Just-in-Time Inventory." *Knowledge Management Magazine*, September: 1.

MARK LEFEBVRE

J

JAPANESE MANAGEMENT METHODS

(SEE: *Management/Leadership Styles*)

JOB ANALYSIS AND DESIGN

Job analysis is the term used to describe the process of analyzing a job or occupation into its various components, that is, *organizational structure, work activities,* and *informational content*. The process results in a relevant, timely and tailored database of job-related information that can be used in a variety of ways: to develop conventional, individualized, computer-based and/or critical incident (discussed below) education and training programs and materials; to create and classify job titles; to write job descriptions; to prepare organization charts; to conduct time and motion studies; to determine quality assurance standards; and to write both knowledge- and performance-related employee evaluation measures. Also, job analyses are basic to the preparation of such government publications as the *Occupational Information Network (O'Net), Standard Industrial Classification (SIC), Standard Occupational Classification (SOC), Occupational Outlook Handbook,* and other informational resources describing the job situation (See Figure 1).

Two terms often used interchangeably with *job analysis* are *occupational analysis* and *task analysis*. In the literature, job and occupational analysis most often are viewed as the same. The

Figure 1

process focuses on the analysis of a job into its *occupational structure, work activities,* and *informational content*. Later, the data provided by the analysis guides the organization and development of the occupational training program.

In contrast, *task analysis* is an integral part of the job analysis process. More specifically, task analysis addresses the process of analyzing a particular task into its various elements, that is, performance steps; performance step details; technical information topics; career and occupational guidance information topics; standards of performance; frequency, importance, and complexity; and tools, equipment, materials, supplies and technical references. The information resulting from the task analysis provides a basis for developing the knowledge- and performance-based learning activities of the training program.

PROCESS

A number of individual authors and organizations have detailed the process of conducting job analyses (American Society For Quality, 1996; Blank, 1982; Bortz, 1981; DACUM, 1985; Finch and Crunkilton, 1979; Fryklund, 1956; Mager and Beach, 1967; Mager and Piper, 1976; U.S. Department of the Air Force, 1998-99; U.S. Department of the Army 1990; U.S. Department of Labor, 1987; U.S. Department of the Navy, 1997). The analytical approaches of the various authors and groups differ somewhat in organization and procedural logic. Nonetheless, each analyzes a job or occupation with the intent of identifying its components and incorporating the findings into the development of related "products," that is, training programs and materials, job descriptions, job classifications, and so forth.

Three questions seem to be basic to the majority of the authors. These questions address the issues of organization, activity, and informational content:

- What is the *structure* of the occupation?
- What does the worker *do*?
- What does the worker *need to know*?

ORGANIZATIONAL STRUCTURE

The first question concerns the structure or framework of the occupation being analyzed (Bortz, 1981; DACUM, 1985). If the data derived from the job analysis are used in a situation where organizational structure is important to the "product" being developed, then the structure of the occupation can serve as a basis from which the organizational structure of the product is developed. For example, the hierarchical order of occupational titles in a functionally related family of occupations can serve as a basis for ordering and naming the units and courses of the training program resulting from the job analysis.

WORK ACTIVITIES

The second question addresses the activities of the worker in terms of both *tasks* and *performance steps*. Once identified, the tasks,—that is, completed units of work,—serve in various capacities ranging from the writing of learning objectives of a yet-to-be-developed competency-based training program to the classification of job titles and writing of job descriptions.

The performance steps for completing each task also will be used in the development of a variety of related materials. Whenever procedure is an issue, the performance steps of the tasks come into play. To use an example from the training of employees in psychomotor skills, the sequence of performance steps guides the instructor through a *demonstration* of the steps of the learning objective, to the student's *practice* of the procedural steps, to a final determination of the student's ability to perform the process on a *performance test*. In each of the three performance-related learning activities, procedure is fundamental to their identification and development.

INFORMATION CONTENT

The third question involves identifying the knowledge or informational component of the occupation. Depending on the author, the three types of information most often referred to are *technical information, general information,* and *career and occupational guidance information*.

Technical information is that information the worker *must know* to perform a specific task or group of tasks. Technical information gives the worker the judgment-forming, decision-making ability to perform the task(s) in a safe and correct manner. It is the knowledge base from which the worker can make informed decisions affecting and controlling his/her on-the-job performance.

General information, although related to the job itself or to the individual tasks comprising the job, does not have direct bearing on the performance of either the job or its component tasks. General information complements the activities of the workers but is not crucial to their outcome. For example, detailed knowledge about the manufacture of computer chips has no direct bearing on the performance of a computer programmer or systems analyst.

Career and occupational guidance information allows workers to make decisions about themselves and the workplace. It includes information on such topics as the short-, intermediate-, and long-range employment needs of the community; the career interests and abilities of individuals; work, work roles and responsibilities; job-seeking skills; the employment outlook; and local, state, national, and global economic trends.

APPLICATION

Each of the following are specific applications of the information gained from a completed job analysis. In some cases, most or all of the information is used in the development of the final product, in other cases, only a portion of the job analysis data is used. (See Figure 1.)

Training Program Development The organizational structure, work activities, and informational content identified in a job analysis serve as the basis for developing both the structure and content of a training program. The structure of the occupation determines the organization of the curricular components of the training program. The content of the training program depends on the activities and information needed to perform in the occupation. In a competency-based training program, the titles of the tasks become the titles of the corresponding learning objectives. The technical information topics and performance steps of the tasks, respectively, serve as the basis for identifying and organizing the *knowledge-* and *performance-related* learning activities of the learning objectives.

"Critical incident" training is the result of applying the activities and content of a job analysis in a specific training situation. As discussed by Davies (1981), the critical incident method of instruction "focuses upon collecting information on key tasks, particularly on those where prob-

lems occur" (p. 131). For these tasks, special training can be devised using the activities and informational content first identified in the job analysis and later, translated into learning objectives, curricula and instructional materials.

Job Classification A job classification is used to group occupations by *function level* or *ability*. To classify jobs by function means to categorize them by similarity of function or activity. For example, titles such as "marketing," "accounting," "production," "management," and "human resources development" imply that all people working in the one of these defined areas are performing a similar type of activity. Functional job classifications are regularly used in organizational development and in the preparation of organization charts.

In contrast, to classify occupations by ability level involves using terms that designate amount of on-the-job experience, skill level, and types of education and training. Terms such as "apprentice," "journeyman," "master," "entry-level," "technician," and "specialist" all reflect a classification of jobs by ability level. The classification of employees by ability levels also guides organizational management in establishing the wage and salary schedules of employees.

Job Descriptions/Job Titles A job description is a narrative statement defining a job, that is, what the employer expects of the employee in terms of on-the-job performance. As stated by Winning (1996), " A job description [or position description] is a list of responsibilities and functions . . . required in a particular position" (p. 1). A job description categorizes and defines the activities of a worker in more general terms then those used in a job analysis. The description is intended to provide a profile of the job rather than describe the occupation in the detail found in most job analyses. The entries in a well-written job description are introduced by a descriptive verb and closed by a noun defining the activity, for example, "maintains bank records."

Complementing the job description is the job title. Job titles are general in nature, in that they reflect all the activities contained in a job description. In one sense, a job title is more an extension of the job description than of a completed job analysis.

Organization Charts Organization charts visually depict the line/staff relationships and responsibilities of departments/units and individuals working in an organization. The information gleaned from a job description, together with that found in the accompanying job classification, serves as the basis for determining the final configuration and content of a completed organization chart.

Time and Motion Studies Time and motion studies address the issues of industrial production and efficiency, since they attempt to measure time on task, product quality, and worker safety. These studies are conducted in the workplace under normal working conditions. A completed job analysis provides the researcher with the necessary list of tasks and performance steps, that is, work activities performed by employees in the completion of their jobs. The focus of a time and motion study is to eliminate wasted motion and determine the most efficient way of performing a particular task.

Quality Assurance Standards As defined by Peach (1997), "Quality assurance includes all the planned and systematic activities implemented within the quality system" (p. 38). A job description provides the quality assurance professional with the list of tasks performed in a particular job and the performance steps (procedures) required to perform each of the tasks. Also, in a comprehensive job analysis, standards of performance for both the tasks and performance steps are included. The two sets of criteria assist in determining the quality outcomes of both the task (product) and procedural steps (process).

The same two sets of quality standards are also applicable in the education and training of people for the workplace. Again, the content of the completed job analysis would provide instructors with the standards used in preparing students for employment.

BIBLIOGRAPHY

American Society for Quality. (1996). *Training and Education Standards: ANSI/ASQ Z1.11.* Milwaukee, WI: American Society for Quality.

Blank, William E. (1982). *Handbook for Developing Competency-Based Training Programs.* Englewood Cliffs, NJ: Prentice-Hall.

Bortz, Richard F. (1981). *Handbook for Developing Occupational Curricula.* Boston: Allyn & Bacon.

Davies, Ivor K. (1981). *Instructional Technique.* New York: McGraw-Hill.

Finch, Curtis R., and Crunkilton, John R. (1979). *Curriculum Development in Vocational and Technical Education.* Boston: Allyn & Bacon.

Fryklund, Verne C. (1956). *Analysis Technique for Instructors.* Milwaukee, WI: Bruce.

Job Corps. (no date). *Instructional Systems Development Manual.* (Available from the Office of Economic Development, Washington, DC).

Mager, Robert F., and Beach, Kenneth M., Jr. (1967). *Developing Vocational Instruction.* Palo Alto, CA: Fearon.

Mager, Robert F., and Piper, Peter. (1976). *Course Control Documents—Criterion-Referenced Instruction: Analysis, Design and Implementation.* Los Altos Hills, CA: Mager Associates.

Norton, Robert E. (1997). *DACUM Handbook.* Columbus: Ohio State University Press.

Peach, Robert W., ed. (1997). *The ISO9000 Handbook,* 3rd ed. New York: Irwin/McGraw-Hill.

Step 4: Time and Motion Studies. http://www.courses.ncsu.edu/classes/ted430/msd/msd-104.htm.

U.S. Department of the Air Force, Air Force Officer Accession and Training School. (1998–99). *Curriculum Catalog.* Alabama: Maxwell Air Force Base.

U.S. Department of the Army, Combined Arms Center and Fort Leavenworth. (1990). *Training the Force— Battle Focused Training FM 25-101.* Kansas: Fort Leavenworth.

U.S. Department of Labor. (1998). *O*NET—The Occupational Information Network.* http://www.dolta.gov/programs/onet.html.

U.S. Department of Labor, Bureau of Labor Statistics. (1998–99). *Occupational Outlook Handbook.* Washington, DC: U.S. Government Printing Office.

U.S. Department of Labor, Employment and Training Administration. (1998). O*NET 98 *Keeping Pace with Today's Changing Workplace* [CD-ROM].

U.S. Department of Labor, Office of Management and Budget. (1987). *Standard Occupational Classification Manual.* Washington, DC: U.S. Government Printing Office.

U.S. Department of the Navy. (1997). *Instructional Systems Development/Systems Approach to Training and Education*. http://www.ott.navy.mil/refs/icw/guide/1379-2.pdf.

Winnings, Ethan A. (1996). "The Many Uses of the Job Description." http://www.all-biz.com/articles/jd.htm.

RICHARD F. BORTZ

JOB DESCRIPTION

(SEE: *Job Analysis and Design*)

JOB ENRICHMENT

Job enrichment is a way to motivate employees by giving them increased responsibility and variety in their jobs. Many employers traditionally believed that money was the only true motivating factor for employees and that if you wanted to get more work out of employees, offering them more money was the only way to do it. While that may be true for a small group of people, the majority of workers today like to work and to be appreciated for the work they do. Job enrichment—allowing the employees to have more control in planning their work and deciding how the work should be accomplished—is one way to tap into the natural desire most employees have to do a good job, to be appreciated for their contributions to the company, and to feel more a part of the company team.

Job enrichment has its roots in Frederick Herzberg's *two-factor theory*, according to which two separate dimensions contribute to an employee's behavior at work. The first dimension, known as hygiene factors, involves the presence or absence of job dissatisfiers, such as wages, working environment, rules and regulations, and supervisors. When these factors are poor, work is dissatisfying and employees are not motivated. However, having positive hygiene factors does not cause employees to be motivated; it simply keeps them from being dissatisfied. The second dimension of Herzberg's theory refers to motivators, which are factors that satisfy higher-level needs such as recognition for doing a good job, achievement, and the opportunity for growth

and responsibility. These motivators are what actually increase job satisfaction and performance. Job enrichment becomes an important strategy at this point because enriching employees' jobs can help meet some of their motivational needs. There are basically five areas that are believed to affect an individual employee's motivation and job performance: skill variety, task identity, task significance, autonomy, and feedback. Job enrichment seeks to find positive ways to address each of these areas and therefore improve employee motivation and personal satisfaction.

Skill variety involves the number of different types of skills that are used to do a job. This area is important because using only one skill to do the same task repeatedly can be quite boring, typically causing the employee's productivity to decrease after a period of time. However, using a variety of skills in a job will tend to keep the employee more interested in the job and more motivated.

One way businesses are focusing on this area is through *job rotation*, that is, moving employees from job to job within the company, thereby allowing employees a variety of tasks in their work and helping prevent boredom. While this process can be costly to the company because employees must be trained in several different areas, the cost tends to be balanced by the increase in morale and productivity. Job rotation also gives each employee the opportunity to see how the different jobs of a company fit together and gives the company more flexibility in covering tasks when workers are absent. However, while job rotation is a good way to enrich employees' jobs, it can also hinder performance: Having to know several different jobs in order to rotate, can prevent employees from becoming proficient at any of the jobs. Therefore, the advantages and disadvantages of job rotation as an enrichment strategy have to be carefully weighed.

Task identity is a matter of realizing a visible outcome from performing a task. Being able to see the end result of the work they do is an important motivator for employees. One way to make task identity clearer is through *job enlargement*, which means adding more tasks and responsibilities to an existing job. For example, instead of building just one component part of a humidifier, a team of employees builds the entire product from start to finish. When using job enlargement as an enrichment strategy, it is important that enlarging the job gives the employee more responsibility and more variety, not just more work.

Task significance involves how important the task is to others in the company, which is important in showing employees how the work they do fits in with that done in the rest of the organization. If employees can see how their work affects others, it will be a motivator to do the best job they can.

Many companies take new employees on a tour of the company and provide training sessions on how each part of the company works together with the other parts. In order to accept and handle responsibility, it is important that employees know how the various areas of the company work together; without this knowledge, it is very difficult for them to handle decision-making responsibilities. Putting employees from different areas of the company into planning teams can also help them see the significance of the tasks they perform.

Autonomy involves the degree of freedom, independence, and decision-making ability the employee has in completing assigned tasks. Most people like to be given responsibility; it demonstrates trust and helps motivate employees to live up to that trust. Responsibility can also help speed up work processes by enabling the employee to make decisions without having to wait for management approval. Autonomy is a very important part of job enrichment because it gives the employee power and a feeling of importance.

A type of job enrichment that restructures work to best match the employee to the job is *job redesign*. Job redesign can focus on combining existing jobs, forming work groups, and/or allowing closer contact between employees and individual suppliers or customers. The idea behind job redesign is to match employees with a job they like and are best qualified to perform. Self-managed teams are a type of job design whereby

employees are grouped into teams and given certain guidelines to follow as well as goals to accomplish—and then left alone to accomplish those goals. Self-managed teams demonstrate the company's faith in the employees and give employees a feeling of power and pride in the work they accomplish.

Feedback describes how much and what type of information about job performance is received by the employee. It is one of the most important areas for motivation. Without feedback, employees have no way of knowing whether they are doing things correctly or incorrectly. Positive feedback helps to motivate employees by recognizing the efforts they have put into their work. While monetary rewards for doing a good job can be a strong incentive, sometimes saying "you did a really good job on that project" can mean just as much. Corrective feedback is also important because it lets employees know what areas need improvement.

There are many different types of job-enrichment activities and programs that companies can implement to encourage worker participation and enhance motivation. The team atmosphere is one way to enrich jobs. Grouping employees into teams and allowing the team the freedom to plan, make decisions, and accomplish their goals gives employees a feeling of importance and responsibility. It can also help employees come up with creative ideas on ways to improve work activities by giving them the opportunity to work closely with others. Asking for and encouraging employees to give input on company strategies and plans is another way to enrich jobs. Often times employees have the best input because they are the ones actually performing the activity on a daily basis. Holding company award ceremonies can also help to enrich jobs and motivate employees by recognizing individual employees for their contributions to the company.

The purpose of job enrichment is to improve the quality of an employee's job and therefore motivate the employee to accomplish more. However, in order for job enrichment to work, the employee has to desire and accept new ways of accomplishing tasks. Some employees lack the skills and knowledge required to perform enriched jobs, while others are quite happy doing routine jobs because they feel the current work situation is relatively stress-free. It is likely that these types of employees would not like job-enrichment activities and would not accept the new way of doing things. Therefore, asking for employee input and keeping communication lines open is essential to the success of job-enrichment programs.

BIBLIOGRAPHY

Boone, Louis E., and Kurtz, David L. (1999). *Contemporary Business*, 9th ed. Orlando, FL: Harcourt Brace.

Bounds, Gregory M., and Lamb, Charles W., Jr. (1998). *Business*. OH: South-Western College Publishing.

Fletcher, Jerry L. (1993). *Patterns of High Performance: Discovering the Way People Work Best*. San Francisco: Berrett-Koehler.

French, Wendell L. (1998). *Human Resources Management*. New York: Houghton Mifflin.

Ghoshal, Sumantra, and Bartlett, Christopher A. (1997). *The Individualized Corporation: A Fundamentally New Approach to Management*. New York: Harper Business.

Kolberg, William H., and Smith, Foster C. (1992). *Rebuilding America's Workforce*. Homewood, IL: Business One Irwin.

Madura, Jeff. (1998). *Introduction to Business*. Cinncinnati, OH: South-Western College Publishing.

Nickels, William G., McHugh, James M., and McHugh, Susan M. (1999). *Understanding Business*, 5th ed. Boston: Irwin/McGraw-Hill.

Pride, William M., Hughes, Robert J., and Kapoor, Jack R. (1999). *Business*, 6th ed. New York: Houghton Mifflin.

Rosenbaum, Bernard L., ed. (1982). *How to Motivate Today's Workers*. New York: McGraw-Hill.

MARCY SATTERWHITE

JOB SATISFACTION

Job satisfaction, a worker's sense of achievement and success, is generally perceived to be directly linked to productivity as well as to personal well-being. Job satisfaction implies doing a job one enjoys, doing it well, and being suitably rewarded for one's efforts. Job satisfaction further implies enthusiasm and happiness with one's work. The Harvard Professional Group (1998) sees job satisfaction as the key ingredient that leads to recognition, income, promotion, and the achievement of other goals that lead to a general feeling of fulfillment.

IMPORTANCE TO WORKER AND ORGANIZATION

Frequently, work underlies self-esteem and identity while unemployment lowers self-worth and produces anxiety. At the same time, monotonous jobs can erode a worker's initiative and enthusiasm and can lead to absenteeism and unnecessary turnover. Job satisfaction and occupational success are major factors in personal satisfaction, self-respect, self-esteem, and self-development. To the worker, job satisfaction brings a pleasurable emotional state that often leads to a positive work attitude. A satisfied worker is more likely to be creative, flexible, innovative, and loyal.

For the organization, job satisfaction of its workers means a work force that is motivated and committed to high quality performance. Increased productivity—the quantity and quality of output per hour worked—seems to be a by-product of improved quality of working life. It is important to note that the literature on the relationship between job satisfaction and productivity is neither conclusive nor consistent. However, studies dating back to Herzberg's (1957) have shown at least low correlation between high morale and high productivity, and it does seem logical that more satisfied workers will tend to add more value to an organization. Unhappy employees, who are motivated by fear of job loss, will not give 100 percent of their effort for very long. Though fear is a powerful motivator, it is also a temporary one, and as soon as the threat is lifted performance will decline.

Tangible ways in which job satisfaction benefits the organization include reduction in complaints and grievances, absenteeism, turnover, and termination; as well as improved punctuality and worker morale. Job satisfaction is also linked to a more healthy work force and has been found to be a good indicator of longevity. And although only little correlation has been found between job satisfaction and productivity, Brown (1996) notes that some employers have found that satisfying or delighting employees is a prerequisite to satisfying or delighting customers, thus protecting the "bottom line." No wonder Andrew Carnegie is quoted as saying: "Take away my people, but leave my factories, and soon grass will grow on the factory floors. Take away my factories, but leave my people, and soon we will have a new and better factory" (quoted in Brown, 1996, p. 123).

CREATING JOB SATISFACTION

So, how is job satisfaction created? What are the elements of a job that create job satisfaction? Organizations can help to create job satisfaction by putting systems in place that will ensure that workers are challenged and then rewarded for being successful. Organizations that aspire to creating a work environment that enhances job satisfaction need to incorporate the following:

- Flexible work arrangements, possibly including telecommuting
- Training and other professional growth opportunities
- Interesting work that offers variety and challenge and allows the worker opportunities to "put his or her signature" on the finished product
- Opportunities to use one's talents and to be creative
- Opportunities to take responsibility and direct one's own work
- A stable, secure work environment that includes job security/continuity
- An environment in which workers are supported by an accessible supervisor who provides timely feedback as well as congenial team members
- Flexible benefits, such as child-care and exercise facilities
- Up-to-date technology
- Competitive salary and opportunities for promotion

Probably the most important point to bear in mind when considering job satisfaction is that there are many factors that affect job satisfaction and that what makes workers happy with their jobs varies from one worker to another and from day to day. Apart from the factors mentioned above, job satisfaction is also influenced by the employee's personal characteristics, the manager's personal characteristics and management style, and the nature of the work itself. Managers who want to maintain a high level of job satisfaction in the work force must try to understand the needs of each member of the work force. For example, when creating work teams, managers can enhance worker satisfaction by placing people with similar backgrounds, experiences, or needs in the same workgroup. Also, managers can enhance job satisfaction by carefully matching workers with the type of work. For example, a person who does not pay attention to detail would hardly make a good inspector, and a shy worker is unlikely to be a good salesperson. As much as possible, managers should match job tasks to employees' personalities.

Managers who are serious about the job satisfaction of workers can also take other deliberate steps to create a stimulating work environment. One such step is *job enrichment.* Job enrichment is a deliberate upgrading of responsibility, scope, and challenge in the work itself. Job enrichment usually includes increased responsibility, recognition, and opportunities for growth, learning, and achievement. Large companies that have used job-enrichment programs to increase employee motivation and job satisfaction include AT&T, IBM, and General Motors (Daft, 1997).

Good management has the potential for creating high morale, high productivity, and a sense of purpose and meaning for the organization and its employees. Empirical findings by Ting (1997) show that job characteristics such as pay, promotional opportunity, task clarity and significance, and skills utilization, as well as organizational characteristics such as commitment and relationship with supervisors and co-workers, have significant effects on job satisfaction. These job characteristics can be carefully managed to enhance job satisfaction.

Of course, a worker who takes some responsibility for his or her job satisfaction will probably find many more satisfying elements in the work environment. Everett (1995) suggests that employees ask themselves the following questions:

- When have I come closest to expressing my full potential in a work situation?

- What did it look like?

- What aspects of the workplace were most supportive?

- What aspects of the work itself were most satisfying?

- What did I learn from that experience that could be applied to the present situation?

WORKERS' ROLES IN JOB SATISFACTION

If job satisfaction is a worker benefit, surely the worker must be able to contribute to his or her own satisfaction and well-being on the job. The following suggestions can help a worker find personal job satisfaction:

- Seek opportunities to demonstrate skills and talents. This often leads to more challenging work and greater responsibilities, with attendant increases in pay and other recognition.

- Develop excellent communication skills. Employers value and reward excellent reading, listening, writing, and speaking skills.

- Know more. Acquire new job-related knowledge that helps you to perform tasks more efficiently and effectively. This will relieve boredom and often gets one noticed.

- Demonstrate creativity and initiative. Qualities like these are valued by most organizations and often result in recognition as well as in increased responsibilities and rewards.

- Develop teamwork and people skills. A large part of job success is the ability to work well with others to get the job done.

- Accept the diversity in people. Accept people with their differences and their imperfections and learn how to give and receive criticism constructively.

- See the value in your work. Appreciating the significance of what one does can lead to satisfaction with the work itself. This helps to give meaning to one's existence, thus playing a vital role in job satisfaction.

- Learn to de-stress. Plan to avoid burnout by developing healthy stress-management techniques.

ASSURING JOB SATISFACTION

Assuring job satisfaction, over the long term, requires careful planning and effort both by management and by workers. Managers are encouraged to consider such theories as Herzberg's (1957) and Maslow's (1943) Creating a good blend of factors that contribute to a stimulating, challenging, supportive, and rewarding work environment is vital. Because of the relative prominence of pay in the reward system, it is very important that salaries be tied to job responsibilities and that pay increases be tied to performance rather than seniority.

So, in essence, job satisfaction is a product of the events and conditions that people experience on their jobs. Brief (1998) wrote: "If a person's work is interesting, her pay is fair, her promotional opportunities are good, her supervisor is supportive, and her coworkers are friendly, then a situational approach leads one to predict she is satisfied with her job" (p. 91). Very simply put, if the pleasures associated with one's job outweigh the pains, there is some level of job satisfaction.

BIBLIOGRAPHY

Brief, Arthur P. (1998). *Attitudes in and Around Organizations.* Thousand Oaks, CA: Sage.

Brown, Mark G. (1996). *Keeping Score: Using the Right Metrics to Drive World-Class Performance.* New York: Quality Resources.

Cranny, C. J., Smith, P. C., and Stone, E. F. (1992). *Job Satisfaction: How People Feel About Their Jobs and How It Affects Their Performance.* New York: Lexington Books.

Daft, Richard L. (1997). *Management,* 4th ed. New York: Dryden Press, Harcourt Brace College Publishers.

Everett, Melissa. (1995). *Making a Living While Making a Difference: A Guide to Creating Careers with a Conscience.* New York: Bantam Books.

Herzberg, Frederick. (1968). "One More Time: How Do You Motivate Employees?" *Harvard Business Review* 46 (January):53-62.

Herzberg, F., Mausner, B., Peterson, R. O., and Capwell, D. F. (1957). *Job Attitudes: Review of Research and Opinion.* Pittsburgh: Psychological Service of Pittsburgh.

Locke, Edwin A. (1976). "The Nature and Causes of Job Satisfaction." In M. D. Dunnette, ed., *Handbook of Industrial and Organizational Psychology*. Chicago: Rand McNally.

Maslow, Abraham. H. (1943). "A Theory of Human Motivation." *Psychological Review* 50:370-396.

Motowidlo, S. J. (1996). "Orientation Toward the Job and Organization." In K. R. Murphy, ed., *Individual Differences and Behavior in Organizations*. San Francisco: Jossey-Bass.

The Harvard Professional Group. *Three Hallmarks of a Career Position*. http://www.harvardpro.com/careerjobs5a.htm. 1998.

Ting, Yuan. (1997). "Determinants of Job Satisfaction of Federal Government Employees." *Public Personnel Management* Abstract. 26, no. 3: 313. http://www.ipma-hr.org/pubs/ppm/ting.html.

BERYL C. MCEWEN

L

LABOR

(SEE: *Factors of Production*)

LABOR UNIONS

A labor union is defined as "a group of workers who have banded together to achieve common goals in the key areas of wages, hours, and working conditions" (Boone and Kurtz, 1999, p. 414). Originally, labor unions were primarily made up of male, blue-collar workers; but as the economy of the United States evolved from production industries to service industries, union membership has seen a dramatic increase in white-collar and female workers. In addition, one-fifth of all professionals in the United States are union members (Boone and Kurtz, 1999).

HISTORY AND EVOLUTION

Labor unions began to evolve in the United States in the 1700s and 1800s due to the need for safety and security for workers. Workers formed labor unions in response to intolerable working conditions, low wages, and long hours. In the wake of the Industrial Revolution, men, women, and even children worked in unsafe factories from dawn to dark every day of the week for only pennies a day. These oppressive conditions forced workers to look for ways to improve their situation. They gradually learned that by banding together and bargaining as a group, they could pressure employers to respond to their demands.

The progression of the Industrial Revolution and the formation of labor unions go hand in hand. The Industrial Revolution brought about specialization of employees in the workplace and a dramatic increase in production. This new factory system, which developed in the nineteenth and early twentieth centuries, brought to workers both prosperity (steady employment in good economic times) and hardship (bad working conditions and unemployment during depressions). Thus, the Industrial Revolution changed the American class structure, turning skilled tradesmen into the working class, who found it very difficult to escape factory life.

As more and more workers united to improve their situation, two types of labor unions emerged. Craft unions were made up of workers who were skilled in a specific trade. Many craft unions were organized in the 1790s, such as the Philadelphia shoemakers in 1792, the Boston carpenters in 1793, and the New York printers in 1794 (Estey, 1976).

Beginning in 1827, laborers who worked in the same industry, regardless of their specific job, formed industrial unions, such as the United Steel Workers and the Teamsters. The 1837 depression nearly wiped out these unions, but they were reborn shortly before the Civil War and became strong enough to survive recessions.

Members of the NLRB watch a labor vote.

Five major labor organizations emerged between 1866 and 1936. The National Labor Union was organized in 1866. Though it became a political party and collapsed within six years, it did successfully bring together into a national federation both craft unions and reform groups. The Noble Order of the Knights of Labor, founded in 1869, sought to unite all workers, both skilled and unskilled; but in 1886, when its membership had reached more than 700,000, it split into two groups. The revolutionary socialist group wanted the government to take over production; the traditional group wanted to remain focused on the economic well-being of its members. This second group merged with a group of individual craft unions in 1886 to become the American Federation of Labor (AFL). This was the beginning of today's modern union structure. The AFL's first president, Samuel Gompers, kept the improvement of wages, hours, and working conditions as the objectives of the union (Boone and Kurtz, 1999). AFL membership grew rapidly until the 1920s, when there were few skilled craftworkers yet to be organized. By that time, three-fourths of the organized workers in the United States were members of the AFL (Boone and Kurtz, 1999).

In 1905, an organization called the Industrial Workers of the World was established. Though it was short-lived, this union introduced the sit-down strike and mass picketing.

In the early 1920s, workers in the steel, aluminum, auto, and rubber industries formed many individual industrial unions (groups of employees working in the same industry, yet not using the same skills). These unions did not agree with the craft union concept (grouping workers with the same specific skill), which was the organizational structure of the AFL. Therefore, in 1936, they split with the AFL and became a new group of affiliated unions called the Congress of Industrial Organizations (CIO). Organizing complete industries instead of individual crafts proved a successful way to deal with mass-production industries, and the CIO's membership soon grew to nearly that of the AFL.

GROWTH

Even with so much union organization activity going on, there were less than 1 million union members in the United States in 1900. Membership in labor unions grew slowly from 1920 to 1935, but the modern labor movement was born in the decade between 1933 and 1944. The combination of New Deal labor legislation, competition between the AFL and the CIO, and World War II quadrupled union membership, which by 1937 was more than 5 million. Union membership continued to increase from 1943 through 1956, reaching more than 15 million in 1950. One-fourth of the labor force were union members at that time, when the government officially sanctioned unions.

In 1955, the AFL and CIO settled their differences and merged into one extremely large labor organization. All the major national unions in the United States today except the National Education Association are affiliated with the AFL-CIO.

Union membership declined from 1956 to 1961, when white-collar workers outnumbered blue-collar workers for the first time, women were entering the work force in large numbers, and the economy was changing from a production to a service industry orientation. In 1961, growth resumed; from 1964 to 1974, especially during the time of the Vietnam War, unions gained 4 million members, largely public-sector employees and professionals.

DECLINE

The percentage of U.S. workers who are union members has fallen since the 1980s. This decline is largely due to the decrease in the number of blue-collar jobs, labor legislation protecting workers, better employee-management relationships, and the shift from a manufacturing to a service economy (bringing into the work force more women and young people, who are not easily organized). During the 1990s, despite the decline in the percent of workers who were unionized, nearly 17 million U.S. workers, between one-eighth and one-sixth of the labor force, belonged to labor unions. The six largest labor unions and their percentage of the total U.S. union membership are listed in Figure 1.

ORGANIZATION

Labor unions are organized on several different levels. Local unions represent members in a specific geographic area, such as a city, state, or region. These local unions make up the base of a national union, which unites all its affiliated local unions under one constitution. The Teamsters and the United Steel Workers of America are two examples of large national unions, each uniting many local unions. The decision-making process of national unions is decentralized, which allows decisions to be made at the local level, by those best qualified to make them. Thus, the national union recognizes the autonomy of each local union yet unites them under one set of rules and grants each local union its charter. Some unions have an international level. These international

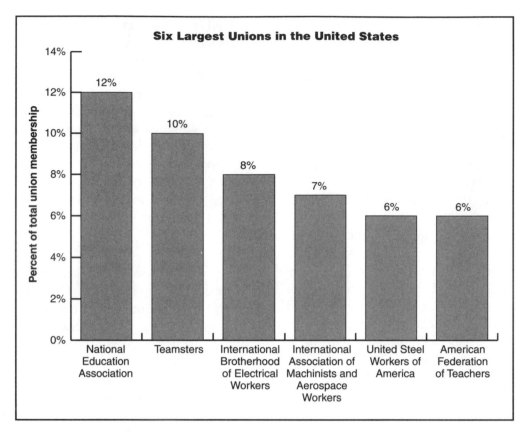

Six Largest Unions in the United States

Figure 1

SOURCE: Boone, Louis E., and Kurtz, David L. (1993). *Contemporary Business.* Fort Worth, TX: Dryden Press.

unions have members both inside and outside the United States, such as in Canada. Their organization is similar to national unions, with local unions being the base of the union structure. The primary emphasis of national unions is economic. Their main function is collective bargaining, though much of the negotiation process occurs at the local union level. Bargaining labor-management contracts, which deal with wages, hours, and working conditions, and settling labor-management disputes are the primary roles of the local and national union leadership (See Collective Bargaining).

The top level of labor union organization is the federation, such as the AFL-CIO. Such a federation is made up of many national and/or international unions. The purpose of the federation level is to coordinate its affiliated unions, settle

disputes between them, and serve as the political representative of the union members.

MEMBERSHIP POLICIES

Various employment policies have been used in business and industry to determine union membership. The closed-shop policy, which was outlawed by the Taft-Hartley Act in 1947, forced workers to join the union in order to be hired at a company and to remain a union member in order to continue employment. The union-shop policy requires all current employees of a company to join the union when it is certified as their bargaining agent (voted in by the majority of the workers). New employees must also join the union under the union-shop policy. However, the Taft-Hartley Act allows individual states to outlaw the union-shop policy. Most union contracts negotiated in the 1990s operate under the union-shop policy. The agency-shop policy allows both union and nonunion workers to be employed by an organization, but the nonunion employees must pay a union fee equal to union dues. This policy requires nonunion workers to pay their "fair share" of the expenses of the union's representing them in negotiations, but none of the cost of the union's political activities. The open-shop policy allows voluntary union membership or nonmembership for all workers. It does not require nonunion workers to pay any union dues or fees.

LABOR LEGISLATION

Both labor unions and management have been affected by federal legislation since 1932, when the Norris-LaGuardia Act was passed. This law protects union activities such as strikes and picketing by making it difficult for management to obtain injunctions against them. In 1935, the Wagner Act (also known as the National Labor Relations Act) made collective bargaining legal and forced employers to negotiate with union officials. The National Labor Relations Board (NLRB) was established by this act. The board oversees union elections and guards against unfair labor practices. The Fair Labor Standards Act of 1938 set a maximum of 40 hours for a basic workweek, outlawed child labor, and set a minimum wage. The Taft-Hartley Act of 1945 limited the power of unions by prohibiting unions from such activities as coercing employees to join unions, charging excessive fees, refusing to bargain collectively with an employer, and using union dues for political contributions. The Taft-Hartley Act was amended in 1959 by the Landrum-Griffin Act, which requires a union to have a constitution and bylaws, secret-ballot elections of officers, and a financial reporting procedure. Management procedures are also regulated by legislation, such as the Plant-Closing Notification Act of 1988, which requires employers to give workers a sixty-day warning of mass layoffs or plant closings.

OUTLOOK

Labor unions were born out of necessity, to protect the health and well-being of American workers. Through the years, they have provided a uni-fied voice for workers and obtained fair treatment of them in the workplace. During the twentieth century, however, laws have been passed that guarantee employees many of the rights that once had to be negotiated in labor-management contracts. An increase in employee-management teamwork and communication has also reduced the need for workers to be represented by labor unions. Thus, labor unions no longer play the vital role they once did in American labor-management relations.

(SEE ALSO: *Collective Bargaining*)

BIBLIOGRAPHY

Boone, Louis E., and Kurtz, David L. (1999). *Contemporary Business*. Fort Worth, TX: Dryden Press.

Estey, Marten. (1976). *The Unions*. New York: Harcourt Brace Jovanovich.

Masters, Marick F. (1997). *Unions at the Crossroads*. Westport, CT: Quorum Books.

Wray, Ralph D., Luft, Roger L., and Highland, Patrick J. (1996). *Fundamentals of Human Relations*. Cincinnati, OH: South-Western Educational Publishing.

PAULA LUFT

LAND

(SEE: *Factors of Production*)

LAW IN BUSINESS

Law governs and regulates virtually all aspects of the business process, from the right to engage in a business or trade, to the legal form of a business, to agreements for buying and selling merchandise or rendering services. Law regulates the quality of products sold and the advertising of products for sale. Law governs the employment relationship, protects business property, and taxes business income. This article explores the relationship of business and law in several of these areas.

BUSINESS LAW AND LAWYERS

Business in the United States is regulated by the federal and state as well as by town and city ordinances. State law regulating forms of business, business agreements, and some taxes is the most important. Federal law regulates such things as advertising, civil rights, and protection of such property as inventions of computer programs. Local law typically regulates business hours, where one can do business (zoning) and some quality control (building codes).

To qualify as a lawyer today, a person usually must earn both a college degree and a three-year law degree and then pass a rigorous examination (the bar exam). Lawyers are certified in only one or possibly two states. Thus a lawyer certified in New York, for example, would not be qualified to answer a question about law in Texas or even a question about local law in a distant city even within the same state.

Lawyers also do not know a business as well as the owner does. All businesses need lawyers from time to time, but it is important for the businessperson to know as much as possible about the law when working with lawyers.

FORMS OF BUSINESS

There are three basic legal forms of business—sole proprietorship, partnership, and corporation.

Sole Proprietorship. Many businesses begin with an idea worked out at the kitchen table, in a garage workshop, or today, on the Internet. There are no legal impediments to or requirements for starting most businesses. One needs only an idea, perhaps inventory, and customers. When one simply starts a business with nothing more, it is called a sole proprietorship. For some business, licenses are necessary. Plumbers, beauticians, and, of course, lawyers and physicians must be licensed by the state, for example, but carpenters, psychologists, tax advisers, and bookkeepers, while they often have professional qualifications, do not need to be legally certified or licensed.

The sole proprietor is responsible for all the debts of the business and in turn receives, after taxes, all of the profits. The sole proprietor may hire employees under an employment agree-

ment. Employees must be of legal age to work, which is normally fourteen or sixteen. A sole proprietorship usually tends to have up to twelve to fifteen employees. If the number of employees increases beyond this, the business normally evolves into another form.

Partnership. The law says that "a partnership is an association of two or more persons to carry on as co-owners a business for profit." [UPA 6(11)]. A number of factors differentiate this form of business from a sole proprietorship. More than one person is involved, and they are co-owners of the business. A partnership, like a sole proprietorship, may employ workers who are not owners.

Business is defined as "every trade, occupation, or profession." A partnership may be made up of members of any occupation. The goal of the partnership is profit; therefore, an organization of persons whose purpose is to, say, encourage recycling or advocate a political cause is not a partnership.

A partnership can be created very easily. If Sam and Mike are mechanics and put on a sign "Sam and Mike's Garage—Open for Business," they have formed a partnership under the law. Any income or losses are split half and half in the absence of an agreement that says otherwise. Normally a partnership is created by written document with the help of a lawyer. Suppose Jill and Joan wanted to start a sporting goods store. Suppose Jill could only work half time but could contribute $50,000 to start the business, while Joan had no money but knew the business and could work full time. With the help of a lawyer, they might agree as follows: The business would operate month to month. If there was income, Joan would draw the first $1500 as salary. Then Jill would draw $750 as salary. Additional income would pay Jill 6 percent per year on the $50,000 she contributed. Finally and hopefully, any additional income would be split evenly between the partners.

If Sam and Mike call their business "Quality Mechanics" or Jill and Joan call their business "Sports Unlimited," the names must be registered with the state and may not be the same as a name previously registered.

A partnership is easy to create, but its drawback is liability. Suppose Joan buys a large inventory that won't sell. Each partner is fully responsible for company debts. It may cost them their life savings. Protection from such liability can be found only in the form of a corporation.

Corporations. A corporation, which is the form of most large businesses and increasingly of small ones, begins when the state issues a charter to a group of promoters. Today, a single person may form a corporation, but normally it is a group. The owners or shareholders contribute money, property, or services for shares of ownership. Shares of larger companies are traded on stock markets, while shares of smaller corporations are held by a few individuals or a single person.

Shareholders elect a board of directors which hires employees. After salaries and other expenses are paid, the profits may be distributed to the shareholders in the form of dividends or reinvested in the corporation to allow it to grow. The corporation insulates the owners from liability. If Jill and Joan's sporting goods store lost money but was a corporation, it might go into bankruptcy, but Jill and Joan would not have to pay any remaining debt from their own money.

Those wishing to start a business would normally consult with a lawyer to determine which legal form the business should take.

BUYING AND SELLING GOODS

Contract law regulates the day-to-day business of buying and selling goods or performing services. A contract is defined in law as an agreement between two parties with an offer, acceptance, and consideration. Jill and Joan now have a corporation—Sports Unlimited, Inc. Ed comes in and decides to buy a tent priced at $225. He offers $225 to Sports Unlimited, which accepts the offer by ringing it up on the cash register. The consideration is what is exchanged; that is, $225 and the tent. When the store accepts the price, there is a binding contract. Suppose a sign clearly

in Ed's view says "All returns must be made within thirty days with cash receipt." This sign becomes part of the agreement. If Ed brings the tent back twenty-nine days later, he can get his money back; if he brings it back thirty-one days later, it would be too late. Even though it is not stated by either party, if Ed used the tent on a camping trip, it would not be returnable. If, however, the tent leaked, it is not "fit for the purposes for which it was intended" and Ed could get his money back within a reasonable time.

Suppose Sam and Mike form Quality Mechanics partnership and Mary comes in and says, "The brakes aren't right, please fix them by 5 P.M." and Mike says, "It will be done!" A contract now exists, even though many terms are missing. Sam and Mike have agreed to fix what is wrong with the brakes, and Mary has agreed to pay a reasonable price. The brakes may need a simple adjustment or a complete overhaul—Sam and Mike agree to do only what is necessary. If they also tune up the engine, Mary need not pay for the tune-up.

WARRANTIES AND PRODUCTS LIABILITY

Warranties and guarantees are of two types—implied and express. If nothing else is said, it is implied that a product is guaranteed to be fit for the purposes for which it is intended. A tent will not leak for a reasonable time and an article of clothing will stand up to reasonable wear and tear. Today, most products come with express (written) warranties. Most common are limited warranties, whereby the manufacturer guarantees all parts and workmanship for a period of one year. If the product breaks down or wears out after that, the customer is responsible, although extended warranties can be purchased on many products, such as cars and appliances. Occasionally products are clearly labeled "Sold as is—no warranty of any kind."

EMPLOYMENT LAW

As a business grows, employees are normally hired, and the legal aspects can become very complicated. Basically, an agreement to employ is a contract of offer and acceptance, and the consideration is an exchange of services for a wage or salary. In the United States, contracts of employment can be quite simple. Bob agrees to work for Sports Unlimited, Inc., for $400 a week. He agrees to work under the direction of Jill and Joan for a set number of hours, doing as he is told. He, in the words of the law, is an "employee at will." He may quit at any time or be fired at any time. Sports Unlimited, Inc., is not required to give a reason if it fires him. Bob may request a raise at any time and has no legal right to health benefits or even vacation. However, if Bob brings special skills, he himself may negotiate a contract for any length of time (most common one or two years) and include features such as health insurance, a retirement plan, and vacation. The agreement is between Sports Unlimited, Inc. and Bob.

The law does make some unlimited requirements. Bob must earn at least minimum wage (in early 1999, $5.25/hour). If Sports Unlimited, Inc., hires a painter to paint the building or a lawyer to draw up the corporation papers, the service is done by an independent contractor. But Bob must follow the orders and direction of Jill and Joan because he is an employee. Sports Unlimited, Inc., must withhold wages for Bob's income tax and Social Security. It must also pay state workmen's compensation and unemployment insurance to compensate Bob if he is injured on the job or laid off. Typically a gardener who cuts the grass and trims the hedges is an independent contractor and is simply paid a sum of money. A cleaning person working inside the house under the direction of the owner is an employee, and thus the law requires additional paperwork and taxes.

Bob was free to negotiate with Sports Unlimited, Inc., as he chose. Federal law allows employees of most larger companies to form unions and make a single employment contract. This is known as collective bargaining. If employees wish, the government will conduct an election; if a majority of workers want a labor union, that union must be recognized by the employer and the employer must work out an employment contract with it. A typical contract spells out wages, benefits such as health insurance and va-

cation, rights to compete for promotions, and the circumstances in which an employee may be fired. Normally, the contract says employees may be fired only if they have committed a serious wrong. In the United States, unions represent a minority of employees.

CIVIL RIGHTS LAWS

It is well known that almost all workers are protected by the Civil Rights Act of 1964 as amended and the Equal Pay Act of 1963. Both apply to companies large and small, unionized and non-unionized. The law says that employees may not be discriminated against in terms of conditions of employment including hiring and promotion because of race, religion, creed, national origin, or sex. In the not too distant past, many companies would not hire members of racial or religious minorities for positions of authority regardless of their ability. Women were discouraged from entering many trades, such as construction, or professions, such as law, because they were thought to be unfeminine or forbidden to work in other areas, such as coal mining because they were dangerous—although they were no less dangerous for men.

Affirmative action is not a federal law but an executive policy (ordered by the president) that requires companies that do business with the government, or institutions such as schools that receive federal funds, to work to increase numbers of workers (or students) from underrepresented classes. This can be tricky because companies are required to seek out and promote members of certain minority groups without discriminating against others. This is not an easy task, but it is part of American policy.

BFOQ stands for "bona fide occupational qualification" and represents an exception to civil rights laws. One may discriminate if there is a good reason to do so. Since people have a right to privacy, an attendant in a restroom can be required to be of the same sex. Models for a line of dresses can be exclusively young, slim females, and casting for a movie or play may discriminate on any basis. In a recent case, guards in a male maximum security prison were required to be male. Some questions remain open. Could a Chinese restaurant wishing to create the atmosphere of China have only Chinese servers? That is an open question.

In the 1970's, Congress added older workers to the list of protected classes. Legal protection is given only to persons over forty. A company may refuse to hire a twenty-five-year old as being "too young" or in an actual case, a thirty-seven-year old as being "too old" for a job.

The most recent category to receive protection from discrimination is persons with disabilities—real or perceived—under the Americans with Disabilities Act (ADA) of 1990.

All businesses need to know a few basics about civil rights law. In interviews, no question may be asked about a person's health history or physical or mental condition except "is there any reason physical or otherwise that would prevent you from doing this job?" Reasonable accommodation must be made for those with disabilities. A simple example would be that a desk would be built a little higher for an employee in a wheelchair. The extent of "reasonable" remains an open question. A person subject to occasional seizures would be qualified to work for Sports Unlimited, Inc., as a clerk but probably not for Quality Mechanics as a test driver.

A business must also make sure it is accessible to customers with disabilities. This includes both access to facilities and equal service as a customer. Many open questions remain. For example, to what extent must an Internet sales company provide access to those with vision or hearing impairments? All companies should consult lawyers or specialists on ADA compliance.

There are exceptions. Someone with a history of drug problems need not be hired as an airline pilot or railroad engineer. If drug or alcohol problems come to light, employees must be given reasonable treatment; if they do not respond, they may be fired.

PROTECTION OF PROPERTY AND INTELLECTUAL PROPERTY

Local authorities, of course, provide police protection from theft of inventory and other company property by customers, employees, or outsiders. Yet there is another property that many businesses have that is at least as valuable which is also protected by law—secrets, patents, copyrights, and trademarks/names.

Business Secrets. Businesses frequently keep secret information that is the heart of this business. Customer lists for an insurance company or a stockbroker are examples. State and federal law severely punishes anyone who steals or makes use of such property. The most famous secret in the world might be the formula for Coca-Cola. If any person or company can duplicate Coca-Cola, they may produce and sell it under their own name. The law protects the secret from theft but not from duplication.

Patents. Patents are a protection given by the federal government for inventions. A patent gives the inventor the exclusive rights for seventeen years to use or license the invention. Anyone infringing on the patented product is subject to fine and imprisonment.

Copyrights. Copyrights give authors protection for their works for their lifetime plus fifty years. Works include literary works, musical compositions, and, very important today, computer programs, which includes software. While there are exceptions for classroom use, it is illegal to copy tapes, CDs, or software. This is theft and is punishable by fines. It is important for business today to set high legal standards for employees for proper business use of copyrighted material.

Trademarks and Trade Names. There has been substantial growth in this area in recent years. Trademarks and trade names can be of enormous value, and businesses work hard to protect their property. Coca-Cola and Coke, both the names and the distinctive script, are among the best known of these. Names and logos are now registered in large numbers, and protection is shown by the ™ by the name. Universities, for example, often make substantial money by licensing use of their name, logo, or other associated symbols on clothing and other items. Trademarks and trade names are registered with the federal government. Exclusive use of them lasts as long as they are used.

BIBILOGRAPHY

Bagley, Constance E. (1999). *Managers and the Legal Environment*, 3rd ed. St. Paul, MN: West Publishing Company.

Charley, Robert N. (1996). *The Legal and Regulatory Environment of Business*, 10th ed. New York: McGraw-Hill

Cheeseman, Henry R. (1997). *Contemporary Business Law*, 2nd ed. Upper Saddle River, NJ: Prentice-Hall.

Mann, Richard A., and Roberts, Barry S. (1999). *Smith and Roberson's Business Law*, 11th ed. St. Paul, MN: West Publishing Company.

McGuire, Charles. (1998). *The Legal Environment of Business*, 3rd ed. Dubuque, IA: Kendall/Hunt Publishing.

CARSON H. VARNER

LEADERSHIP

Leadership is a fascinating subject for many people. The term conjures up a familiar scene of a powerful, heroic, triumphant individual with a group of followers returning home after winning a national championship or a war against the evil enemy. They all march through town surrounded by a crowd waving flags. Or an enthusiastic orator delivers an energetic speech, hands waving in the air, to thousands of people gathered in a plaza.

The widespread fascination with leadership may be because of the impact that leadership has on everyone's life. Stories of heroic leadership go back thousands of years: Moses delivering thousands of Hebrews from Egypt or Alexander the Great building a great empire. Why were certain leaders able to inspire and mobilize so many people, and how did they achieve what they achieved? There are so many questions to which we want answers, but many remain as puzzling as ever. In recent decades, many researchers have undertaken a systematic and scientific study of leadership.

Leadership is defined in so many different ways that it is hard to come up with a single working definition. Leadership is not just a person or group of people in a high position; understanding leadership is not complete without understanding interactions between a leader and his or her followers. Neither is leadership merely the ability or static capacity of a leader. We need to look into the dynamic nature of the relationship between leader and followers. In these unique social dynamics, all the parties involved attempt to influence each other in the pursuit of goals. These goals may or may not coincide: Participants actively engage in defining and redefining the goal for the group and for themselves.

Putting all these into a comprehensive statement: Leadership is a process in which a leader attempts to influence his or her followers to establish and accomplish a goal or goals. In order to accomplish the goal, the leader exercises his or her power to influence people. That power is exercised in earlier stages by motivating followers to get the job done and in later stages by rewarding or punishing those who do or do not perform to the level of expectation. Leadership is a continuous process, with the accomplishment of one goal becoming the beginning of a new goal. The proper reward by the leader is of utmost importance in order to continually motivate followers in the process.

What does leadership do for an organization? If we define leadership as a process involving interactions between a leader and followers, usually subordinate employees of a company, leadership profoundly affects the company: It defines or approves the mission or goal of the organization. This goal setting is a dynamic process for which the leader is ultimately responsible. A strong visionary leader presents and convinces followers that a new course of action is needed for the survival and prosperity of the group in the future. Once a goal is set, the leader assumes the role of ensuring successful accomplishment of the goal. Another vital role of leadership is to represent the group/organization and link it to the external world in order to obtain vital resources to carry out its mission. When necessary, leadership has to defend the organization's integrity.

CHARACTERISTICS OF SUCCESSFUL AND EFFECTIVE LEADERSHIP

What does it take to make leadership successful or effective? Early students of leadership examined great leaders throughout history, attempting to find traits that they shared. Among personality traits that they found were determination, emotional stability, diplomacy, self-confidence, personal integrity, originality, and creativity. Intellectual abilities included judgmental ability, knowledge, and verbal communication ability. In addition, physical traits cannot be ignored, such as age, height, weight, and physical attractiveness.

It is not only inborn personality traits that are important but also styles and behaviors that a person learns. Strong *autocratic* leaders set their goals without considering the opinions of their followers, then command their followers to execute their assigned tasks without question. *Consultative* leaders solicit the opinions and ideas of their followers in the goal-setting process but ultimately determine important goals and task assignments on their own. *Democratic* or *participative* leaders participate equally in the process with their followers and let the group make decisions. Extremely laid-back leaders, so called *laissez-faire* leaders, let the group take whatever action its members feel is necessary.

Inspired and led by Renis Likert, a research team at the University of Michigan studied leadership for several years and identified two distinct styles, which they referred to as *job-centered* and *employee-centered* leadership styles. The *job-centered* leader closely supervises subordinates to make sure they perform their tasks following the specified procedures. This type of leader relies on reward, punishment, and legitimate power to influence the behavior of followers. The *employee-centered* leader believes that creating a supportive work environment ultimately is the road to superior organizational performance. The employee-centered leader shows great concern about the employees' emotional well-being, personal growth and development, and achievement.

A leadership study group at Ohio State University, headed by Harris Fleishman, found similar contrasts in leadership style, which they referred to as *initiating structure* and *consideration*. The leadership style of *initiating structure* is similar to the job-centered leadership style, whereas *consideration* is similar to the employee-centered leadership style. It was the initial expectation of both research groups that a leader who could demonstrate both high initiating structure (job-centered) and high consideration (employee-centered) would be successful and effective in all circumstances.

Many students of leadership today believe that there is no one best way to lead, believing instead that appropriate leadership styles vary depending on situations. Fred Fiedler (1967), for instance, believes that a task-oriented leadership style is appropriate when the situation is either extremely favorable or extremely unfavorable to the leader. A favorable situation exists when the relationship between the leader and followers is good, their tasks are well-defined, and the leader has strong power; when the opposite is true, an unfavorable situation exists. When the situation is moderately favorable, a people-oriented leadership style is appropriate. Some theorists suggest that situational factors—the type of task, nature of work groups, formal authority system, personality and maturity level of followers, experience, and ability of followers—are critical in determining the most effective leadership style. For instance, when followers are inexperienced and lack maturity and responsibility, the directive leadership style is effective; when followers are experienced and willing to take charge, supportive leadership is effective.

LEADERSHIP IN A MULTICULTURAL SETTING

One major situational factor is the cultural values of the followers. People who have different cultural norms and values require different leadership styles. In a highly collective society such as Japan, the Philippines, Guatemala, or Ecuador, where the social bond among members is very strong and people look out for one another, a strong patriarch at the top of the social hierarchy tends to emerge as an effective leader. Such a leader is not only accepted by the followers but is also expected to protect their interests. China's Deng Xiao-Ping, whose influence continues even after his death, is a case in point.

On the other hand, in an extremely individualistic society, such as the United States (Hofstede, 1980), where the social bonds are loose and individuals are expected to take care of themselves, success and achievement are admired, and a competitive and heroic figure is likely to emerge as a leader. It is no surprise that John F. Kennedy became such a charismatic figure in the United States. His energetic and inspirational speeches are still vividly remembered.

CHARISMATIC AND TRANSFORMATIONAL LEADERSHIP

Regardless of culture and time, however, a great leader is remembered for his or her charisma, which means "divinely inspired gift" in Greek. Charismatic leaders have profound effects on followers. Through their exceptional inspirational and verbal ability, they articulate ideological goals and missions, communicate to followers with passion and inspiration, set an example in their own behaviors, and demand hard work and commitment from followers, above and beyond normal expectation.

Building on charismatic leadership, Bernard Bass (1985) proposed a theory of *transformational* leadership. Bass views leadership as a process of social exchange between a leader and his or her followers. In exchange for desired behaviors and task accomplishment, a leader provides rewards to followers. This nominal social exchange process is called transactional leadership. In contrast, a transformational leader places a higher level of trust in his or her followers and demands a much higher level of loyalty and performance beyond normal expectations. With unusual charismatic qualities and inspirational person-to-person interactions, a transformational leader transforms and motivates followers to make extra efforts to turn around ailing organizational situations into success stories. Lee Iacocca, when he took over Chrysler as CEO in 1979 and turned around this financially distressed company, was considered an exemplary transformational leader. He was able to convince many people, including employees and the U.S. Congress, to support the ailing company and to make it a success.

WAYS WOMEN LEAD

Leadership qualities such as aggressiveness, assertiveness, taking charge, and competitiveness are traditionally associated with strong, masculine characters. Even women executives tended to show these characteristics in the traditional corporate world. In fact, many of these women executives were promoted because they were even more competitive and assertive than their male counterparts. These successful women executives often sacrificed a family life, which their male counterparts did not necessarily have to do.

The business world is changing, however. Today, much research has found that women leaders are different from their male counterparts in management style: Women leaders tend to be more concerned with consensus building, participation, and caring. They often are more willing than men to share power and information, to empower employees, and to be concerned about the feelings of their subordinates.

Such an interactive and emotionally involved leadership style is not necessarily negative in today's business environment. Indeed, some researchers find it to be highly effective. Internally, a culturally diverse work force demands more interactive and collaborative coordination. Externally, culturally diverse customers demand more personable and caring attention. A caring and flexible management style serves such diverse employees and customers better than traditional methods of management.

LEADERSHIP AND MANAGEMENT

John Kotter (1988) distinguishes leadership from management. Effective management carefully plans the goal of an organization, recruits the necessary staff, organizes them, and closely supervises them to make sure that the initial plan is executed properly. Successful leadership goes beyond management of plans and tasks. It envisions the future and sets a new direction for the organization. Successful leaders mobilize all possible means and human resources; they inspire all members of the organization to support the new mission and execute it with enthusiasm. When an organization faces an uncertain environment, it demands strong leadership. On the other hand, when an organization faces internal operational complexity, it demands strong management. If an organization faces both an uncertain environment and internal operational complexity, it requires both strong leadership and strong management.

BIBLIOGRAPHY

Bass, Bernard M. (1985). *Leadership and Performance Beyond Expectation.* New York: Free Press.

Bass, Bernard M. and Avolio, Bruce, J. (1994). *Improving Organizational Effectiveness Through Transformational Leadership.* Beverly Hills, CA: Sage.

Bennis, Warren G. (1959). "Leadership Theory and Administrative Behavior: The Problem of Authority." *Administrative Science Quarterly* 4: 259-260.

Conger, Jay A., and Kanungo, Rabindra.(1987). "Toward a Behavioral Theory of Charismatic Leadership in Organizational Settings." *Academy of Management Review* 12: 637-647.

Daft, Richard L. (1999). *Leadership: Theory and Practice.* New York: Dryden Press.

Fiedler, Fred E. (1967). *A Theory of Leadership Effectiveness.* New York: McGraw-Hill.

Graef, C. L. (1993). "The Situational Leadership Theory: A Critical Review." *Academy of Management Review* 8: 285-296.

Hall, Richard H. (1982). *Organizations: Structure and Process.* New York: Prentice Hall.

Hofstede, Geert (1980). *Culture's Consequences: International Differences in Work-Related Values.* Beverly Hills, CA: Sage.

Howell, Jane M. (1988). "Two Faces of Charisma: Socialized and Personalized Leadership in Organizations." In Jay A. Conger and Rabindra N. Kanungo, eds., *Charismatic Leadership: The Elusive Factor in Organizational Effectiveness.* San Francisco: Jossey-Bass.

House, Robert J. (1996). "Path-Goal Theory of Leadership: Lessons, Legacy and a Reformulated Theory." *Leadership Quarterly* 7: 323-352.

Hughes, Richard L., Ginnet, Robert C., and Curphy, Gordon J. (1996). *Leadership: Enhancing the Lessons of Experience.* Chicago: Irwin.

Kirkpatrick, S.A., and Locke, Edwin A. (1996). "Direct and Indirect Effects of Three Core Charismatic Leadership Components on Performance and Attitudes." *Journal of Applied Psychology* 81: 36-51.

Kotter, John P. (1988). *The Leadership Factor.* New York: Free Press.

Meindl, James R. (1990). "On Leadership: An Alternative to the Conventional Wisdom." In B. M Staw and L.L. Cummings, eds., *Research in Organizational Behavior,* vol. 12. Greenwich, CT: JAI Press.

Meindl, James R., Ehrlich, S.B., and Dukerich, J.M. (1985). "The Romance of Leadership." *Administrative Science Quarterly* 30: 78-102.

Trice, Harry M., and Beyer, Janis M. (1991). "Cultural Leadership in Organizations." *Organization Science* 2: 149-169.

Yuke, Gary. (1998). *Leadership in Organizations,* 4th ed. New York: Prentice Hall.

LEE W. LEE

LEMON LAWS

(SEE: *Consumer Protection*)

LIFE CYCLE COSTING

(SEE: *Costs*)

LIFESTYLES

As the twenty-first century begins, consumers are demanding advancements in business operations to help simplify their hectic lifestyles. The progression of lifestyle changes, in combination with technological evolution, will influence the way business and marketing operations function. This article focuses on how family, job, cultural background, social class, social activities, and employment have revolutionized business and marketing operations.

FAMILY INFLUENCES ON BUSINESS OPERATIONS

Family life has changed quite a bit over the years. In the 1950s in the United States, it was not uncommon for children to grow up in large families with several siblings. It was also the norm for the mother to stay home to care for the children while the father worked to support the household.

More recently, family size has gotten drastically smaller, and mothers are not always home for the children: They are out in the work force pursuing careers and helping to support the family. In addition, there are many more single-parent homes. Because of both of these trends, many preschool children stay with day-care providers and many older children are at home alone for two or three hours after school until a parent gets home from work, making today's children more self-reliant than children in the past.

The amount of time that families spend together thus has changed significantly from previous generations. Parents do not have the time to do the errands and housework that were once part of their everyday life and still have time to spend with their children. Now, however, because of technological advances, businesses are providing time-saving services. For example, shopping—from grocery shopping to clothes shopping—can be done on-line and the purchases delivered right to their door. E-commerce businesses, such as Shoplink and Homeruns .com, are providing services that allow working parents to avoid spending time in the grocery and other stores.

JOB INFLUENCES ON BUSINESS OPERATIONS

In the past, businesses were managed very differently than they are today. New technology and its rate of advancement have revolutionized the way job objectives are met in business operations. For example, higher education has changed drastically because of technology. Distance learning is one response to adult learners' need for flexibile class schedules. Because today's students can attend classes from their homes, the jobs of faculty and the business operations of higher education have changed notably.

As discussed earlier, families spend less time together today. To remedy this situation, more and more working parents prefer to work out of

their homes, and many companies are recognizing this reality and reorganizing their business operations to accommodate it. According to the American Home Business Revolution:

> Estimates show that a home-based business starts in the United States every 11 seconds. That's 8,000 Americans starting a home-based business every day. At the beginning of the 1990's 24.3 million Americans worked either full time or part time from their homes. The trend has only gone up from there.

Job structure has clearly affected the way business operations function in the twenty-first century.

CULTURAL INFLUENCES ON BUSINESS OPERATIONS

It is difficult to describe the culture of any country, but this is especially true of the United States because of the many different national and ethnic backgrounds of its citizens. But despite the evident diversity of American culture, there are distinct characteristics that are part of culture.

One significant cultural influence or business operation is the Christian religious calendar. Numerous offices recognize Christmas Day (December 25th) and Good Friday (the Friday before Easter) as two of the ten holidays during the calendar year. Indeed, many school vacations revolve around these same two holidays.

The overall culture of an organization is reflected in behaviors that are considered to be the "norm" as regards both verbal and non-verbal communication. Americans tend to speak directly to one another, maintaining eye contact with the person they are talking to. Hand gestures are commonly used while making presentations or in one-on-one conversation to better explain a point.

Generally, upper management determines any organization's corporate culture. Proper business attire was considered to be suits and ties for men and business suits for women. That is no longer the case in many organizations, where the business environment is more casual and jeans and slacks are now considered to be acceptable.

Then there is the role that gender plays in U.S. culture. Women, once relegated to more administrative and support-staff roles, are now upper-level managers alongside men. Jobs are no longer gender-specific in U.S. culture. For example, men now become nurses and women work on construction sites and as forklift operators. The point here is that gender no longer predetermines a person's role in business as it once did.

SOCIAL CLASS INFLUENCE ON BUSINESS OPERATIONS

What comprises social class? Is it the neighborhood one lives in? The occupation one has? The income one earns? The wealth one has acquired? There is no generally agreed-upon definition of social class, but most people agree that social class does exist. Grouping people together and assigning them a status in society is as old as society itself.

The social class of a particular group of people influences the role of business and marketing operations. The key to success in business and marketing operations is twofold. First, identify the market for your product. Second, identify the social class you are dealing with in that market. Businesses must become familiar with the customs and culture of the particular social class they are trying to do business with.

SOCIAL ACTIVITIES INFLUENCE ON BUSINESS OPERATIONS

Marketing to a particular group often incorporates depictions of social activities as a part of the advertising campaign. For example, Mountain Dew commercials portray young teenagers riding mountain bikes and engaging in extreme sports. A commercial for Grey Poupon mustard portrays high-class adults using the product while being chauffeured in a Mercedes. In both examples, the business first needed to verify who the constituted market was for their product. Second, it had to learn the characteristics of those people.

EMPLOYMENT INFLUENCE ON BUSINESS OPERATIONS

Jobs today have changed significantly because of technological advances and global influences. Many companies do business at an international level, which requires travel abroad for many employees. As virtual conferencing becomes more widespread, travel will most likely decline. Technological developments, such as the Internet and CD-ROMs, and global influences, have major implications for business and marketing procedures.

Business operations must integrate new and different marketing procedures to keep current with the changing job market. These changes in the job market require lifelong learning by both employees and employers. Vice President Al Gore embraced this lifelong learning process through his work on the national summit on twenty-first century skills for twenty-first century jobs. He asked more than three hundred leaders from the fields of training, labor unions, government, and management to establish a set of recommendations that would help ensure a prepared nation in the next century. Lifelong learning has a direct effect on businesses and their employees, particularly on marketing operations.

Workers, whether white-collar or blue-collar, are becoming increasingly technically savvy. Today's leaders recognize that each customer's needs are unique. With the cost of sales increasing and the product life cycle becoming shorter, the Internet will enable better and more economical customer service no matter what job market one is a part of.

Marketing operations must embrace e-commerce, internal links via intranets, and Internet marketing and retailing because these tools can extend operations and create new opportunities for businesses. As technology, lifestyle, and employment change, business and marketing operations must also change in innovative ways—or be left behind. It is a matter of survival.

CONCLUSION

Consumers today are demanding convenience to help simplify their hectic lifestyles. This requires business and marketing operations to be aware of the impact of such demographic variables as family, job, cultural background, social class, social activities, and employment.

All these demographic variables play an essential role in business operations. Lifestyles and technology have both changed radically, and the global marketplace is a reality. The key to business success is to understand the diversity that exists in the global marketplace and to respond innovatively to society's changing needs.

Companies that understand the shrinking amount of time families have to spend together and provide services that modern parents need in order to work at a full time job and still maintain a stable home for their children will succeed in the twenty-first century.

BIBLIOGRAPHY

"An Efficiency Measure for a Sustainable Quality of Life." (1999). *Global Ideas Bank.* http://www.globalideasbank.org/SD/SD-94.HTML.

"The Power of The Internet." (2000). *American Home Business Revolution.* http://www.web-hits.net/ahbr/index.html.

MICHELLE VOTO
GINA MUSTOE

LISTENING SKILLS IN BUSINESS

Expressive skills and receptive skills make up the two skills of communication. Speaking and writing are generally referred to as expressive skills; they provide the means by which we express ourselves to others. The receptive skills, listening and reading, are the ways in which we receive information.

It has been reported that senior officers of major North American corporations spend up to 80 percent of their working time in meetings, discussions, face-to-face conversations, or telephone conversations. Most employees spend about 60 percent of the workday listening. Since such a large percentage of one's waking time is consumed by listening activities, it is clear that we could increase our productivity through listening training.

Listening consumes about half of all communication time, yet people typically listen with only about 25 percent of their attention. Ineffective listening is costly, whether it occurs in families, businesses, government, or international affairs. Most people make numerous listening mistakes every day, but the costs—financial and otherwise—are seldom analyzed. Because of listening mistakes, appointments have to be rescheduled, letters retyped, and shipments rerouted. Any number of catastrophes can arise from a failed communication regardless of the type of industry. Productivity is affected and profits suffer.

Research indicates that we hear only 25 percent of what is said and, after two months, remember only one-half of that. This has not always been the case. In first grade we heard 90 percent of what was said, in second grade 80 percent, in seventh grade 43 percent, and by ninth grade only 25 percent. It is imperative that we strive to improve our listening skills. When having difficulty understanding a document that we're reading, we can *reread* it for clarification. However, we cannot *relisten* to oral messages, unless they are mechanically recorded. The listener may misunderstand, misinterpret, or forget a high percentage of the original message. With proper training, though, listening skills can be improved. It has been proven that with extended, focused training in listening, one can more than double one's listening efficiency and effectiveness.

Communication involves message reception and interpretation. Studies of communication have routinely found that nearly everyone listens more than they talk, reads more than they write, and spends a lot more time receiving messages than sending them. The average person speaks at a rate of one hundred to two hundred words per minute. An average listener, however, can adequately process 400 words per minute. Given this differential between what is normally heard and what potentially can be processed, it is little wonder that people tend to "tune out" at certain times. Mental tangents are the obvious product of this differential, and managers who believe that subordinates are listening intently to every word they utter are deluding themselves.

Listening can be compared to exercising or wearing seat belts: Everybody knows it is desirable, but everybody finds it difficult to do on a regular basis. Most of us yearn to talk; we want to be center stage. If you listen to any casual conversation between friends, you will probably note that most people spend much of the conversation paying maximum attention to what they are going to say next. As we listen to others, we spend much time thinking about the next time *we* will be speaking.

Listening is more than just hearing what a speaker says. Hearing is simply the reception of sounds by your ears; listening is interpreting, or making sense of, the sounds that you hear. Hearing is a physical perception; listening is a mental activity. It requires concentration, cooperation, and an open mind.

Many situations at work demand skilled listening. Conferences, interviews, receiving instructions, handling complaints—all call for alert, sensitive listening. Whether you're listening in order to learn how to do a task, in order to make a decision, or in order to achieve friendly relations with your co-workers, it's important to make a concentrated effort to understand what the speaker is saying.

Three types of listening exist. The first type is casual, or informal. You usually don't need to remember details. The second type of listening is active, or formal. This type of listening takes concentration and requires that the listener absorb details. The last type of listening is nonverbal listening.

Speakers have the responsibility to communicate as effectively as they can, but listeners also have responsibilities. They cannot sit back and contentedly assume they have nothing to do. Like speakers, listeners also need to prepare themselves. As they listen, they must concentrate on both the verbal and nonverbal message of the speaker. Listeners are influenced by the speaker, the message, other listeners, physical conditions, and their emotional state at the time of the listening activity. While the first three cannot be controlled by the listener, the last two can.

To give complete attention to the speaker and the speaker's message, the listener should choose a position that allows a full view of the speaker's gestures. Fifty-five percent of a person's message involves nonverbal communication, 38 percent of the message derives from the speaker's voice inflection, and only 7 percent of the message involves the actual words spoken. In addition to the verbal message, the listener should also concentrate on the speaker's nonverbal messages, communicated through gestures, tone of voice, and physical movements. Do the speaker's gestures seem to reinforce or contradict the words? If the speaker is trying to paint herself as a sincere, dedicated woman, do you detect elements of dishonesty? Is the speaker actually timid even though he's trying to play the role of a man full of confidence? Only by carefully watching and analyzing a presenter's body language and thoughtfully listening to his words can you receive the full impact of the message.

As with the spoken word, body language has its own special pace, rhythm, vocabulary, and grammar. Just as in verbal language, there are "letters" that, when correctly joined, form unspoken "words." Such "words" are then linked to create the "phrases" and "sentences" by which messages are exchanged. Relaxed gesturing on the part of the speaker, for example, is usually associated with confidence, while jerking and abrupt motions display nervousness and discomfort. Putting learned information about nonverbal communication to practical use can spell the difference between success or failure in many business and social encounters.

Whether one is involved in a serious negotiation, a job interview, a company meeting, or a personal interaction, the need to listen more effectively is vital. Active listening is important for the following reasons:

1. Listening enables us to gain important information.

2. Listening enables us to be more effective in interpreting a message.

3. Listening enables us to gather data to make sound decisions.

4. Listening enables us to respond appropriately to the messages we hear.

To become a better listener, you should do the following:

1. *Look the part:* Face the speaker and display feedback that the message is being heard and understood. Lean toward the speaker to show interest. Maintain eye contact at least 80 percent of the time. Do not distract the speaker with strange facial expressions and fidgeting.

2. *Listen for nonverbal messages:* Observe the speaker's body language, gestures, and the physical distance. Observe the speaker's facial expressions, eyes, mouths, and hands for hidden messages.

3. *Listen for the main points:* Filter out the nonessential and look for the principal message of the words.

4. *Be silent before replying:* Be certain that the speaker is completely finished speaking before you attempt to speak. Resist the temptation to interrupt unnecessarily.

5. *Ask questions:* It is appropriate to question the speaker in order to clarify meanings and reinforce messages heard.

6. *Sense how the speaker is feeling:* To receive the complete message, it is important to sift out any feelings the speaker is trying to convey. Determine what the speaker is *not* saying.

7. *Take notes:* Jotting down important ideas allows you to review the message at a later time and reinforces the information heard/learned.

8. *Be available:* To be spoken to, one must be available. Get out from behind your desk and papers. Stop your work and concentrate totally on the speaker.

Encourage others to listen by doing the following:

1. Lower your voice volume. It forces others to listen.

2. Make your talk interesting. Focus on your listener's favorite subject—him- or herself. Encourage others to participate by bringing them into the conversation.

3. Create the right environment. Speak where you can be easily heard and understood.

4. Be human to your listeners. Address people by name whenever possible; it helps to get their attention.

Good listening habits are an important ingredient in your journey to success. If you practice careful listening, you'll become more efficient in your job and more knowledgeable about all topics. Responsible, patient listening is a rare thing, but it is a skill that can be developed with practice.

JAN HARGRAVE

LOSS LEADERS

(SEE: *Promotion*)

M

MACROECONOMICS/ MICROECONOMICS

Economics is a broad subject that can be divided into two areas: macroeconomics and microeconomics. To differentiate between the two, the analogy of the forest and the individual trees can be helpful. Macroeconomics is the study of the behaviors and activities of the economy as a whole; hence, the forest. Microeconomics looks at the behaviors and activities of individual households and firms, the individual components that make up the whole economy; hence, the individual trees. Several examples are given below.

MACROECONOMICS

Macroeconomics, being the study of the behaviors and activities of the economy as a whole, looks at such areas as the Federal Reserve System, unemployment, gross domestic product, and business cycles.

The Federal Reserve System was created by the Federal Reserve Act of 1913, which divided the United States into twelve districts with a Federal Reserve Bank located in each. Each of these banks is owned by the member banks located within that district. The Federal Reserve System's most important function is to control the supply of money in circulation. Monetary policies made by the Federal Reserve System's Board of Governors have a tremendous impact on the total economy. These policies influence such factors as the amount of money member banks have available to loan, interest rates, and the overall price level of the economy. Three ways in which the Federal Reserve Board regulates the economy are by changing reserve requirements, changing the discount rate, and buying and selling government securities.

Macroeconomists also study unemployment, which simply defined is a very large work force and a small job market, to determine methods to control this serious economic problem. The U.S. Department of Labor estimates the level of unemployment in the economy by using results from monthly surveys conducted by the Bureau of the Census.

Unemployment means lost production for the economy and loss of income for the individual. One type of unemployment is frictional unemployment, which includes those people who are not employed because they have been fired or have quit their job. Cyclical unemployment follows the cycles of the economy. For example, during a recession, spending is low and workers are laid off because production needs are reduced. Structural unemployment occurs when a job is left vacant because a worker does not have the necessary skills needed or a worker does not live where there are available jobs. Some unemployment is due to seasonal factors; that is, employees are hired only during certain times of the year. To help lessen the problem of unemployment, the government can use its powers to increase levels of spending by consumers, businesses, and the government itself and by lowering taxes or giving tax incentives, which makes available more money with which to purchase goods and services. This in turn puts more laid-off workers back to work. The Federal Reserve System can also increase spending by lowering interest rates.

Total economic spending, which includes consumer, business, and government spending, determines the level of the gross domestic product (GDP), which is the market value of all final products produced in a year's time. GDP is one of the most commonly used measures of economic performance. An increasing GDP from year to year shows that the economy is growing. The nation's policy makers look at past and present GDPs to formulate policies that will contribute to economic growth, which would result in a steady increase in the production of goods and services. If GDP is too high or growing too rapidly, inflation occurs. If GDP is too low or decreasing, an increase in unemployment occurs.

Fluctuations in total economic activity are known as business cycles, and macroeconomists are concerned with understanding why these cycles occur. Most unemployment and inflation are caused by these fluctuations. There are four phases of the business cycle: prosperity (peak), recession, trough, and recovery. The length and duration of each cycle varies. From its highest point, prosperity, to its lowest point, trough, these phases are marked by increases and decreases in GDP, unemployment, demand for goods and services, and spending.

MICROECONOMICS

Microeconomics looks at the individual components of the economy, such as costs of production, maximizing profits, and the different market structures.

Business firms are the suppliers of goods and services, and most firms want to make a profit; in fact, they want to maximize their profits. Firms must determine the level of output that will result in the greatest profits. Costs of production play a major role in determining this level of output. Costs of production include fixed costs and vari-

able costs. Fixed costs are costs that do not vary with the level of output, such as rent and insurance premiums. Variable costs are costs that change with the level of output, such as wages and raw materials. Therefore, total cost equals total fixed costs plus total variable costs ($TC = TFC + TVC$). Marginal cost, which is the cost of producing one more unit of output, helps determine the level at which profits will be maximized. Marginal cost (MC) measures the change (Δ) in total cost when there is a change in quantity (Q) produced ($MC = \Delta TC/\Delta Q$). Firms must then decide whether they should produce additional quantities.

Revenue, the money a firm receives for the product it sells, is also a part of the profit equation because total revenue minus total costs equal profit ($TR - TC = $ profit). Marginal revenue, which is the additional revenue that results from producing and selling one more unit of output, is also very important. As long as marginal revenue exceeds marginal cost, a firm can continue to maximize profits.

There are four basic categories of market structures in which firms sell their products. Pure competition includes many sellers, a homogeneous product, easy entry and exit, and no artificial restrictions such as price controls. A monopoly is the opposite of pure competition and is characterized by a single firm with a unique product and barriers to entry. An oligopoly has few sellers, a homogeneous or a differentiated product, and barriers to entry such as high start-up costs. Where products are differentiated, nonprice competition occurs; that is, consumers are persuaded to buy products without consideration of price. The fourth market structure is monopolistic competition. It includes many sellers, differentiated products, easy entry and exit, and nonprice competition.

BIBLIOGRAPHY

Gottheil, Fred M., and Wishart, David. (1997). *Principles of Economics with Study Guide.* Cincinnati: South-Western College Publishing.

LISA S. HUDDLESTUN

MANAGEMENT

Throughout the years, the role of a manager has changed. Years ago, managers were thought of as people who were "the boss." While that might still be true today, many managers view themselves as leaders rather than as people who tell subordinates what to do. The role of a manager is comprehensive and often very complex. Not everyone wants to be a manager, nor should everyone consider being a manager.

A DEFINITION OF MANAGEMENT

Some would define management as an art, while others would define it as a science. Whether management is an art or a science isn't what is most important. Management is a process that is used to accomplish organizational goals; that is, a process that is used to achieve what an organization wants to achieve. An organization could be a business, a school, a city, a group of volunteers, or any governmental entity. Managers are the people to whom this management task is assigned, and it is generally thought that they achieve the desired goals through the key functions of (1) planning, (2) organizing, (3) directing, and (4) controlling. Some would include leading as a managing function, but for the purposes of this discussion, leading is included as a part of directing.

The four key functions of management are applied throughout an organization regardless of whether it is a business, a government agency, or a church group. In a business, which will be the focus here, many different activities take place. For example, in a retail store there are people who buy merchandise to sell, people to sell the merchandise, people who prepare the merchandise for display, people who are responsible for advertising and promotion, people who do the accounting work, people who hire and train employees, and several other types of workers. There might be one manager for the entire store, but there are other managers at different levels who are more directly responsible for the people who perform all the other jobs. At each level of management, the four key functions of planning, or-

ganizing, directing, and controlling are included. The emphasis changes with each different level of manager, as will be explained later.

Planning Planning in any organization occurs in different ways and at all levels. A top-level manager, say the manager of a manufacturing plant, plans for different events than does a manager who supervises, say, a group of workers who are responsible for assembling modular homes on an assembly line. The plant manager must be concerned with the overall operations of the plant, while the assembly-line manager or supervisor is only responsible for the line that he or she oversees.

Planning could include setting organizational goals. This is usually done by higher-level managers in an organization. As a part of the planning process, the manager then develops strategies for achieving the goals of the organization. In order to implement the strategies, resources will be needed and must be acquired. The planners must also then determine the standards, or levels of quality, that need to be met in completing the tasks.

In general, planning can be strategic planning, tactical planning, or contingency planning. Strategic planning is long-range planning that is normally completed by top-level managers in an organization. Examples of strategic decisions managers make are who the customer or clientele should be, what products or services should be sold, and where the products and services should be sold.

Short-range or tactical planning is done for the benefit of lower-level managers, since it is the process of developing very detailed strategies about what needs to be done, who should do it, and how it should be done. To return to the previous example of assembling modular homes, as the home is nearing construction on the floor of the plant, plans must be made for the best way to move it through the plant so that each worker can complete assigned tasks in the most efficient manner. These plans can best be developed and implemented by the line managers who oversee the production process rather than managers who sit in an office and plan for the overall operation of the company. The tactical plans fit into the strategic plans and are necessary to implement the strategic plans.

Contingency planning allows for alternative courses of action when the primary plans that have been developed don't achieve the goals of the organization. In today's economic environment, plans may need to be changed very rapidly. Continuing with the example of building modular homes in the plant, what if the plant is using a nearby supplier for all the lumber used in the framing of the homes and the supplier has a major warehouse fire and loses its entire inventory of framing lumber. Contingency plans would make it possible for the modular home builder to continue construction by going to another supplier for the same lumber that it can no longer get from its former supplier.

Organizing Organizing refers to the way the organization allocates resources, assigns tasks, and goes about accomplishing its goals. In the process of organizing, managers arrange a framework that links all workers, tasks, and resources together so the organizational goals can be achieved. The framework is called organizational structure, which is discussed extensively in another article. Organizational structure is shown by an organizational chart, also discussed extensively in another article. The organizational chart that depicts the structure of the organization shows positions in the organization, usually beginning with the top-level manager (normally the president) at the top of the chart. Other managers are shown below the president.

There are many ways to structure an organization, which are discussed extensively in the articles referred to previously. It is important to note that the choice of structure is important for the type of organization, its clientele, and the products or services it provides—all which influence the goals of the organization.

Directing Directing is the process that many people would most relate to managing. It is supervising, or leading workers to accomplish the goals of the organization. In many organizations, directing involves making assignments, assisting

workers to carry out assignments, interpreting organizational policies, and informing workers of how well they are performing. To effectively carry out this function, managers must have leadership skills in order to get workers to perform effectively.

Some managers direct by empowering workers. This means that the manager doesn't stand like a taskmaster over the workers barking out orders and correcting mistakes. Empowered workers usually work in teams and are given the authority to make decisions about what plans will be carried out and how. Empowered workers have the support of managers who will assist them to make sure the goals of the organization are being met. It is generally thought that workers who are involved with the decision-making process feel more of a sense of ownership in their work, take more pride in their work, and are better performers on the job.

By the very nature of directing, it should be obvious that the manager must find a way to get workers to perform their jobs. There are many different ways managers can do this in addition to empowerment, and there are many theories about the best way to get workers to perform effectively and efficiently. Management theories and motivation are important topics and are discussed in detail in other articles.

Controlling The controlling function involves the evaluation activities that managers must perform. It is the process of determining if the company's goals and objectives are being met. This process also includes correcting situations in which the goals and objectives are not being met. There are several activities that are a part of the controlling function.

Managers must first set standards of performance for workers. These standards are levels of performance that should be met. For example, in the modular home assembly process, the standard might be to have a home completed in eight working days as it moves through the construction line. This is a standard that must then be communicated to managers who are supervising workers, and then to the workers so they know what is expected of them.

After the standards have been set and communicated, it is the manager's responsibility to monitor performance to see that the standards are being met. If the manager watches the homes move through the construction process and sees that it takes ten days, something must be done about it. The standards that have been set are not being met. In this example, it should be relatively easy for managers to determine where the delays are occurring. Once the problems are analyzed and compared to expectations, then something must be done to correct the results. Normally, the managers would take corrective action by working with the employees who were causing the delays. There could be many reasons for the delays. Perhaps it isn't the fault of the workers but instead is due to inadequate equipment or an insufficient number of workers. Whatever the problem, corrective action should be taken.

MANAGERIAL SKILLS

To be an effective manager, it is necessary to possess many skills. Not all managers have all the skills that would make them the most effective manager. As technology advances and grows, the skills that are needed by managers are constantly changing. Different levels of management in the organizational structure also require different types of management skills. Generally, however, managers need to have communication skills, human skills, computer skills, time-management skills, and technical skills.

Communication Skills Communication skills fall into the broad categories of oral and written skills, both of which managers use in many different ways. It is necessary for a manager to orally explain processes and give direction to workers. It is also necessary for managers to give verbal praise to workers. Managers are also expected to conduct meetings and give talks to groups of people.

An important part of the oral communication process is listening. Managers are expected to listen to their supervisors *and* to their workers. A manager must hear recommendations and complaints on a regular basis and must be willing to follow through on what is heard. A manager who doesn't listen is not a good communicator.

Managers are also expected to write reports, letters, memos, and policy statements. All of these must be written in such a way that the recipient can interpret and understand what is being said. This means that managers must write clearly and concisely. Good writing requires good grammar and composition skills. This is something that can be learned by those aspiring to a management position.

Human Skills Relating to other people is vital in order to be a good manager. Workers come in about every temperament that can be imagined. It takes a manager with the right human skills to manage this variety of workers effectively. Diversity in the workplace is commonplace. The manager must understand different personality types and cultures to be able to supervise these workers. Human skills cannot be learned in a classroom; they are best learned by working with people. Gaining an understanding of personality types can be learned from books, but practice in dealing with diverse groups is the most meaningful preparation.

Computer Skills Technology changes so rapidly it is often difficult to keep up with the changes. It is necessary for managers to have computer skills in order to keep up with these rapid changes. Many of the processes that occur in offices, manufacturing plants, warehouses, and other work environments depend on computers and thus necessitate managers and workers who can skillfully use the technology. Although computers can cause headaches, at the same time they have simplified many of the tasks that are performed in the workplace.

Time-Management Skills Because the typical manager is a very busy person, it is important that time be managed effectively. This requires an understanding of how to allocate time to different projects and activities. A manager's time is often interrupted by telephone calls, problems with workers, meetings, others who just want to visit, and other seemingly uncontrollable factors. It is up to the manager to learn how to manage time so that work can be completed most efficiently. Good time-management skills can be learned, but managers must be willing to prioritize activities, delegate, deal with interruptions, organize work, and perform other acts that will make them better managers.

Technical Skills Different from computer skills, technical skills are more closely related to the tasks that are performed by workers. A manager must know what the workers who are being supervised are doing on their jobs or assistance cannot be provided to them. For example, a manager who is supervising accountants needs to know the accounting processes; a manager who is supervising a machinist must know how to operate the equipment; and a manager who supervises the construction of a home must know the sequence of operations and how to perform them.

MANAGEMENT THOUGHT

There are many views of management, or schools of management thought, that have evolved over the years. What follows is a brief discussion of some of the theories of management that have greatly affected how managers manage today.

Classical Thought The classical school of management thought emerged throughout the late 1800s and early 1900s as a result of the Industrial Revolution. Since the beginning of time, managers have needed to know how to perform the functions discussed earlier. The Industrial Revolution emphasized the importance of better management as organizations grew larger and more complex. As industry developed, managers had to develop systems for controlling inventory, production, scheduling, and human resources. It was the managers who emerged during the Industrial Revolution, many who had backgrounds in engineering, who discovered that they needed organized methods in order to find solutions to problems in the workplace.

Classical management theorists thought there was one way to solve management problems in the industrial organization. Generally, their theories assumed that people could make

logical and rational decisions while trying to maximize personal gains from their work situations. The classical school of management is based on scientific management which has its roots in Henri Fayol's work in France and the ideas of German sociologist Max Weber. Scientific management is a type of management that bases standards upon facts. The facts are gathered by observation, experimentation, or sound reasoning. In the United States, scientific management was further developed by individuals such as Charles Babbage (1792–1871), Frederick W. Taylor (1856–1915), and Frank (1868–1924) and Lillian (1878–1972) Gilbreth.

Behavioral Management Thought It was because the classical management theorists were so machine-oriented that the behavioralists began to develop their thinking. The behavioral managers began to view management from a social and psychological perspective. These managers were concerned about the well-being of the workers and wanted them to be treated as people, not a part of the machines.

Some of the early behavioral theorists were Robert Owen (1771–1858), a British industrialist who was one of the first to promote management of human resources in an organization; Hugo Munsterberg (1863–1916), the father of industrial psychology; Walter Dill Scott (1869–1955), who believed that managers need to improve workers' attitudes and motivation in order to increase productivity; and Mary Parker Follett (1868–1933), who believed that a manager's influence should come naturally from his or her knowledge, skill, and leadership of others.

In the behavioral management period, there was a human relations movement. Advocates of the human relations movement believed that if managers focused on employees rather than on mechanistic production, then workers would become more satisfied and thus more productive laborers. Human relations management supported the notion that managers should be paternalistic and nurturing in order to build work groups that could be productive and satisfied.

The behavioral science movement was also an important part of the behavioral management

Douglas McGregor.

school. Advocates of this movement stressed the need for scientific studies of the human element of organizations. This model for management emphasized the need for employees to grow and develop in order to maintain a high level of self-respect and remain productive workers. The earliest advocates of the behavioral science movement were Abraham Maslow (1908–1970), who developed Maslow's hierarchy of needs, and Douglas McGregor (1906–1964), who developed Theory X and Theory Y. These theories are discussed in depth in other articles.

Contemporary Management Thought In more recent years, new management thoughts have emerged and influenced organizations. One of these is the sociotechnical system. A system is a set of complementary elements that function as a unit for a specific purpose. Systems theorists believe that all parts of the organization must be related and that managers from each part must work together for the benefit of the organization. Because of this relationship, what happens in one part of the organization influences and affects other parts of the organization.

Another contemporary approach to managing involves contingency theories. This approach states that the manager should use the techniques or styles that are most appropriate for the situation and the people involved. For example, a manager of a group of Ph.D. chemists in a laboratory would have to use different techniques from a manager of a group of teenagers in a fast-food restaurant.

Closed Management Systems Within the classical and behavioral approaches to management, the managers look only within the organization to improve productivity and efficiency. This is a closed system—the organization operates as though it is in its own environment. Outside influence and information are blocked out.

Open Management Systems Another perspective is the open system. As one would expect, here the organization functions in conjunction with its external environment, acting with and relying upon other systems. Advocates of an open system believe that an organization cannot avoid the influence of outside forces.

SUMMARY

Management is a very complex process to which this article is but a brief introduction. Many other articles in this encyclopedia provide extensive insight into the many aspects of management.

BIBLIOGRAPHY

Nickels, William G., McHugh, James M., and McHugh, Susan. (1987). *Understanding Business.* Chicago: Irwin.

Pierce, Jon L., and Dunham, Randall B. (1990). *Managing.* Glenview, IL: Scott, Foresman/Little, Brown Higher Education.

ROGER L. LUFT

MANAGEMENT: AUTHORITY AND RESPONSIBILITY

How can people be influenced to make commitments to the goals of the organization? In part, this question can be answered by how managers define and use power, influence, and authority. Deciding what type of authority system to create is part of the managerial responsibility of organizing. Compare, for example, two managers. One accepts or rejects all ideas generated at lower levels. The other gives the authority for making some decisions to employees at the level where these decisions will most likely affect those employees. How managers use their power, influence, and authority can determine their effectiveness in meeting the goals of the organization.

RESPONSIBILITY

Responsibility is the obligation to accomplish the goals related to the position and the organization. Managers, at no matter what level of the organization, typically have the same basic responsibilities when it comes to managing the work force: Direct employees toward objectives, oversee the work effort of employees, deal with immediate problems, and report on the progress of work to their superiors. Managers' primary responsibilities are to examine tasks, problems, or opportunities in relationship to the company's short- and long-range goals. They must be quick to identify areas of potential problems, continually search for solutions, and be alert to new opportunities and ways to take advantage of the best ones. How effectively goals and objectives are accomplished depends on how well the company goals are broken down into jobs and assignments and how well these are identified and communicated throughout the organization.

INFLUENCE AND POWER

Formal job definitions and coordinating strategies are not enough to get the work done. Managers must somehow use influence to encourage workers to action. If they are to succeed, managers must possess the ability to influence organization members. Influence is the ability to bring about change and produce results; people derive influence from interpersonal power and authority. Interpersonal power allows organization members to exert influence over others.

Power stems from a variety of sources: reward power, coercive power, information power, resource power, expert power, referent power, and legitimate power. *Reward power* exists if managers provide or withhold rewards, such as money or recognition, from those they wish to influence. *Coercive power* depends on the manager's ability to punish others who do not engage in the desired behavior. A few examples of coercion include reprimands, criticisms, and negative performance appraisals. Power can also result from controlling access to important *information* about daily operations and future plans. Also, having access to and deciding to limit or share the *resources* and materials that are critical to accomplishing objectives can provide a manager with a source of power. Managers usually have access to such information and resources and must use discretion over how much or how little is disseminated to employees. *Expert power* is based on the amount of expertise a person possesses that is valued by others. For example, some people may be considered experts with computers if they are able to use several software programs proficiently and can navigate the Internet with ease. Those who do not have the expert knowledge or experience need the expert's help and, therefore, are willing to be influenced by the expert's power. When people are admired or liked by others, *referent power* may result because others feel friendly toward them and are more likely to follow their directions and demonstrate loyalty toward them. People are drawn to others for a variety of reasons, including physical or social attractiveness, charisma, or prestige. Such politicians as John F. Kennedy were able to use their referent power to effectively influence others. *Legitimate power* stems from the belief that a person has the right to influence others by virtue of holding a position of authority, such as the authority of a manager over a subordinate or of a teacher over a student.

In some respects, everyone has power—the power to either push forward or obstruct the goals of the organization by making decisions, delegating decisions, delaying decisions, rejecting decisions, or supporting decisions. However, the effective use of power does not mean control. Power can be detrimental to the goals of the organization if held by those who use it to enhance their own positions and thereby prevent the advancement of the goals of the organization.

Truly successful managers are able to use power ethically, efficiently, and effectively by sharing it. Power can be used to influence people to do things they might not otherwise do. When that influence encourages people to do things that have no or little relationship to the organization's goals, that power is abused. Abuses of power raise ethical questions. For example, asking a subordinate to submit supposed business-trip expenses for reimbursement for what was actually a family vacation or asking a subordinate to run personal errands is an abuse of power. People who acquire power are ethically obligated to consider the impact their actions will have on others and on the organization.

Employees may desire a greater balance of power or a redistribution of authority within the existing formal authority structure. People can share power in a variety of ways: by providing information, by sharing responsibility, by giving authority, by providing resources, by granting access, by giving reasons, and by extending emotional support. The act of sharing information is powerful. When people don't share information, the need to know still exists; therefore, the blanks are filled in with gossip and innuendo. When people are asked to take on more responsibility, they should be provided with tasks that provide a challenge, not just with more things to increase their workload that don't really matter. People need the legitimate power to make decisions without having to clear everything first with someone higher up in the organization. People who have power must also have the necessary range of resources and tools to succeed. Access to people outside as well as inside the organization should be provided and encouraged. People should be told why an assignment is important and why they were chosen to do it. Emotional support can come in the form of mentoring, appreciation, listening, and possibly helping out.

Sharing power or redistributing authority does not necessarily mean moving people into positions of power; instead, it can mean letting people have power over the work they do, which means that people can exercise personal power without moving into a formal leadership role. The ability to influence organization members is an important resource for effective managers. Relying on the title "boss" is seldom powerful enough to achieve adequate influence.

AUTHORITY

Authority is seen as the legitimate right of a person to exercise influence or the legitimate right to make decisions, to carry out actions, and to direct others. For example, managers expect to have the authority to assign work, hire employees, or order merchandise and supplies.

As part of their structure, organizations have a formal authority system that depicts the authority relationships between people and their work. Different types of authority are found in this structure: line, staff, and functional authority. Line authority is represented by the chain of command; an individual positioned above another in the hierarchy has the right to make decisions, issue directives, and expect compliance from lower-level employees. Staff authority is advisory authority; it takes the form of counsel, advice, and recommendation. People with staff authority derive their power from their expert knowledge and the legitimacy established in their relationships with line managers. Functional authority allows managers to direct specific processes, practices, or policies affecting people in other departments; functional authority cuts across the hierarchical structure. For example, the human resources department may create policies and procedures related to promoting and hiring employees throughout the entire organization.

Authority can also be viewed as arising from interpersonal relationships rather than a formal hierarchy. Authority is sometimes equated with legitimate power. Authority and power and how these elements are interrelated can explain the elements of managing and their effectiveness.

What is critical is how subordinates perceive a manager's legitimacy. Legitimate authority occurs when people use power for good and have acquired power by proper and honest means. When people perceive an attempt at influence as legitimate, they recognize it and willingly comply. Power acquired through improper means, such as lying, withholding information, gossip, or manipulation, is seen as illegitimate. When people perceive the authority of others as illegitimate, they are less likely to willingly comply.

DELEGATION

In order for managers to achieve goals in an efficient manner, part of their work may be assigned to others. When work is delegated, tasks and authority are transferred from one position to another within an organization. The key to effective delegation of tasks is the transference of decision-making authority and responsibility from one level of the organization to the level to which the tasks have been delegated. In order to effectively delegate work, some guidelines should be followed: Determine what each worker can most effectively accomplish; decide whether the worker should just identify a problem or also propose a solution; consider whether the person can handle the challenge of the task; be clear in the objectives of the task; encourage questions; explain why the task is important; determine if the person has the appropriate resources—time, budget, data, or equipment—to get the job done on a deadline; create progress reviews as part of the project planning; and be prepared to live with less than perfect results. Authority should be delegated in terms of expected results. Generally, the more specific the goal, the easier it is to determine how much authority someone needs.

Some employees resist delegation for a variety of reasons. Initiative and responsibility involve risk that some people try to avoid. People tend to play it safe if risk results in criticism. Those who feel they already have more work than they can do avoid new assignments. Some people doubt their own abilities and lack the self-confidence to tackle new assignments. Delegation is an excellent professional development tool so long

as it expands a worker's expertise and growth. Delegation can also compensate for a manager's weakness. A successful team is developed by building on the strengths of its members.

People develop most when stimulated to broaden themselves—when challenged. More authority can add challenge; too much challenge, however, can frustrate people and cause them to avoid new responsibilities. Delegation should involve acceptable challenge—enough to motivate but not so much as to frustrate.

In today's workplace, managers are compelled to rely more on persuasion, which is based on expert and referent power rather than reward, coercive, or inappropriate use of power. A manager who shares power and authority will be the one with the greatest ability to influence others to work toward the goals of the organization.

BIBLIOGRAPHY

Bartol, Kathryn M., and Martin, David C. (1994). *Management.* New York: McGraw-Hill.

Hirschhorn, Larry. (1997). *Reworking Authority.* Cambridge, MA: MIT Press.

Lucas, James R. (1998). *Balance of Power.* New York: American Management Association.

Marshall, Don R. (1999). *The Four Elements of Successful Management.* New York: American Management Association.

CHERYL L. NOLL

MANAGEMENT BY OBJECTIVES

(SEE: *Strategic Management*)

MANAGEMENT: HISTORICAL PERSPECTIVES

Since the beginning of time, humans have been managing—managing other people, managing organizations, and managing themselves. Management has been dealt with in this publication as a process that is used to accomplish organizational goals. To some, management is thought of as an art; to others, as a science. Each of those perspectives is grounded in the early writings and teaching of a group of managerial pioneers.

INDUSTRIAL REVOLUTION

While it can be argued that management began well before the Industrial Revolution, it is often felt that what emerged as contemporary management thought was begat with the beginning of industrial development. The Industrial Revolution began in the mid-eighteenth century when factories were first built and laborers were employed to work in them. Prior to this period, most workers were active in an agrarian system of maintaining the land.

Adam Smith (1723–1790), the economist who wrote *The Wealth of Nations*, was an early contributor to management thought during the Industrial Revolution. He was considered a liberal thinker, and his philosophy was the foundation for the laissez-faire management doctrine. His thoughts about division of labor were fundamental to current notions of work simplification and time studies. His emphasis on the relationship between specialization of labor and technology was somewhat similar to the later thinking of Charles Babbage, discussed below.

Another early pioneer of management thought regarding the factory system was *Robert Owen* (1771–1858), an entrepreneur who tried to halt the Industrial Revolution because he saw disorder and evil in what was happening. Owen founded his first factory at the age on 18 in Manchester, England. His approach to managing was to observe everything and to maintain order and regularity throughout the industrial facility.

Owen moved on to a new venture in Scotland, where he encountered a shortage of qualified laborers for his factory. His approach to handling disciplinary problems with his workers was to appeal to their moral sense, not to use corporal punishment. He used silent monitors, a system whereby he awarded four types of marks to superintendents, who in turn awarded workers. The marks were color-coded in order of merit. Blocks of wood were painted with the different colors and placed at each workstation. Workers were rated at the end of each day, and the appropriate color was turned to face the aisle so that anyone passing by could see how the worker had performed the previous day. The system was an attempt to motivate laggards to perform better and good workers to maintain high performance.

Charles Babbage (1792–1871) was noted for his application of technological aids to human effort in the manufacturing process. Babbage invented the first computer, in the form of a mechanical calculator, in 1822; many more modern computers used basic elements of his design. Supervising construction of this invention led Babbage to an interest in management, particularly in the concept of division of labor in the manufacturing process. Babbage invented equipment that could monitor the output of workers, which led to a profit-sharing system in which workers, in addition to being paid a wage, were compensated based on the profits of the company as well as for suggestions that would improve the manufacturing processes.

SCIENTIFIC MANAGEMENT

Scientific principles for the management of workers, materials, money, and capital were introduced roughly during the period from 1785 through 1835. Scientific managers made careful and rational decisions, kept orderly and complete books, and were able to react to events quickly and expertly. Some of the people discussed above were important early contributors to the scientific management movement before others came along to solidify the thinking. Scientific management is with us today as introduced by several more contemporary thinkers.

Frederick Taylor (1856–1915) was an engineer who had a new and different approach to management. His approach was for managers, rather than being taskmasters, to adopt a broader, more comprehensive view of managing and see their job as incorporating the elements of planning, organizing, and controlling. His ideas of management evolved as he worked for different firms. As a result of his experiences as both a worker and a manager, he developed the concept of time and motion studies.

In what became the origin of contemporary scientific management, Taylor set out to scientifically define what workers ought to be able to do with their equipment and resources in a full day of work. In his process of time study, each job was broken into as many simple, elementary movements as possible and useless movements were discarded; the quickest and best methods for each elementary movement were selected by observing and timing the most skilled workers at each. His system evolved into the piece-rate system.

Frank (1868–1924) and *Lillian* (1878–1972) *Gilbreth* refined the field of motion study and laid the foundation for modern applications of job simplification, meaningful work standards, and incentive wage plans. The Gilbreths' were interested in more than just motion studies; they were interested in improving the totality of people and the environment, which they believed could be done through training, better work methods, improved environments and tools, and a healthy psychological outlook. Lillian Gilbreth had a background in psychology and management. Frank Gilbreth's fame did not come until after his death in 1924.

BEHAVIORAL MANAGEMENT

The behavioral school of management grew out of the efforts of some to recognize the importance of the human endeavor in an organization. These people felt that if managers wanted to get things done, it must be through people—the study of workers and their interpersonal relationships.

Henry L. Gantt (1861–1919) was one of the earliest of theses behavioral theorists. Some people would classify him in more than one category, but his passionate concern for the worker as an individual and his pleas for a humanitarian approach to management exemplify the behavioral approach. His early writing called for teaching and instructing workers, rather than driving them.

Mary Parker Follett (1868–1933), although trained in philosophy and political science, shifted her interests to vocational guidance, adult education, and social psychology. These led to her lifetime pursuit of developing a new managerial philosophy that would incorporate an understanding of the motivating desires of the individual and the group. She emphasized that workers on the job were motivated by the same forces that influenced their duties and pleasures away from the job and that the manager's role was to coordinate and facilitate group efforts, not to force and drive workers. Because of her emphasis on the group concept, the words "togetherness" and "group thinking" entered the managerial vocabulary.

Elton Mayo (1880–1949), best known for his Hawthorne experiments, introduced rest pauses in industrial plants and in so doing reduced employee turnover from 250 percent to 5 percent in some cases. He was concerned about human performance and working conditions. The work pauses, better known as breaks, reduced employee pessimism and improved morale and productivity.

MANAGEMENT PROCESS

The father of the management process school of thought was the Frenchman *Henri Fayol* (1841–1925), a mining engineer. He spent his entire working career with the same company, involved with coal mining and iron production. From his experiences as the managing director of the company, Fayol developed his general principles of administration. He thought that the study, analysis, and teaching of management should all be approached from the perspective of its functions, which he defined as forecasting and planning, organizing, commanding, controlling, and coordinating. He thought that planning was the most important and most difficult of these. Much of contemporary management thought revolves around the functions of management.

James D. Mooney (1884–1957) whose writings and research lent credence to the management process school of thinking, is credited with the notion that all great managers use the same principles of management. He emphasized a tight engineering approach to the manager's job of getting work done through others. He gave little

Frank and Lillian Gilbreth refined the field of motion study.

thought to the human element, but instead was exclusively process-oriented. His approach to organizational analysis is now classic.

CONCLUSION

This discussion has been far from exhaustive, and there are diverse opinions about the people who were the earliest developers of management thought. But this discussion has provided thumbnail sketches of some of the primary theorists, leaders, and teachers of management thought. Although there are many other theorists who can be credited with expanding or enhancing their teachings, the basics of each of the schools of thought can be credited to the individuals discussed.

BIBLIOGRAPHY

Duncan, W. Jack. (1989). *Great Ideas in Management.* San Francisco: Jossey-Bass.

George, Claude S. (1972). *The History of Management Thought.* Englewood Cliffs, NJ: Prentice-Hall.

Wren, Daniel A. (1972). *The Evolution of Management Thought.* New York: Ronald Press.

ROGER LUFT

MANAGEMENT INFORMATION SYSTEMS

Before one can explain management information systems, the terms *systems, information,* and *management* must briefly be defined. A *system* is a combination or arrangement of parts to form an integrated whole. A system includes an orderly arrangement according to some common principles or rules. A system is a plan or method of doing something.

The study of systems is not new. The Egyptian architects who built the pyramids relied on a system of measurements for construction of the pyramids. Phoenician astronomers studied the system of the stars and predicted future star positions. The development of a set of standards and procedures, or even a theory of the universe, is as old as history itself. People have always sought to find relationships for what is seen or heard or thought about.

A system is a scientific method of inquiry, that is, observation, the formulation of an idea, the testing of that idea, and the application of the results. The scientific method of problem solving is systems analysis in its broadest sense. Data are facts and figures. However, data have no value until they are compiled into a system and can provide information for decision making.

Information is what is used in the act of informing or the state of being informed. Information includes knowledge acquired by some means. In the 1960s and 70s, it became necessary to formalize an educational approach to systems for business so that individuals and work groups and businesses who crossed boundaries in the various operations of business could have appropriate information. Technical developments in computers and data processing and new theories of systems analysis made it possible to computerize systems. Much of this computerization of systems was an outgrowth of basic research by the federal government.

Management is usually defined as planning, organizing, directing, and controlling the business operation. This definition, which evolved from the work of Henri Fayol in the early 1900s, defines what a manager does, but it is probably more appropriate to define what management is rather than what management does. Management is the process of allocating an organization's inputs, including human and economic resources, by planning, organizing, directing, and controlling for the purpose of producing goods or services desired by customers so that organizational objectives are accomplished. If management has knowledge of the planning, organizing, directing, and controlling of the business, its decisions can be made on the basis of facts, and decisions are more accurate and timely as a result.

Management information systems are those systems that allow managers to make decisions for the successful operation of businesses. Management information systems consist of computer resources, people, and procedures used in the modern business enterprise. The term *MIS* stands for management information systems. MIS also refers to the organization that develops and maintains most or all of the computer systems in the enterprise so that managers can make decisions. The goal of the MIS organization is to deliver information systems to the various levels of corporate managers. MIS professionals create and support the computer system throughout the company. Trained and educated to work with corporate computer systems, these professionals are responsible in some way for nearly all of the computers, from the largest mainframe to the desktop and portable PCs.

BACKGROUND

Management information systems do not have to be computerized, but with today's large, multinational corporations, computerization is a must for a business to be successful. However, management information systems began with simple manual systems such as customer databases on index cards. As early as 1642, the French mathematician and philosopher Blaise Pascal invented the first mechanical adding machine so that figures could be added to provide information. Almost two hundred years later, Charles Babbage, a professor of mathematics at Cambridge University in England, wanted to make a machine that would compute mathematical tables. He attempted to build a computing machine during the 1880s. He failed because his ideas were beyond his technical capabilities, not because the idea was flawed. Babbage is often called the father of the computer. With the advent of the computer, management information systems became automated.

In the late 1890s, because of the efforts of Herman Hollerith, who created a punch-card system to tabulate the data for the 1890 census, it was possible to begin to provide data-processing equipment. The punch card developed by Hollerith was later used to form a company to provide data-processing equipment. This company evolved into International Business Machines (IBM). Mainframe computers were used for management information systems from the

Blaise Pascal.

1940s, 50s, 60s, and up until the 1970s. In the 1970s, personal computers were first built by hobbyists. Then Apple computer developed one of the first practical personal computers. In the early 1980s, IBM developed its PC, and since then, the personal computer industry has mushroomed. Almost every management information system revolves around some kind of computer hardware and software.

Management information systems are becoming more important, and MIS personnel are more visible than in the 1960s and 1970s, when they were hidden away from the rest of the company and performed tasks behind closed doors. So remote were some MIS personnel from the operations of the business that they did not even know what products their companies made. This has changed because the need for an effective management information system is of primary concern to the business organization. Managers use MIS operations for all phases of management, including planning, organizing, directing, and controlling.

THE MIS JOB TODAY

MIS personnel must be technically qualified to work with computer hardware, software, and computer information systems. Currently, colleges and universities cannot produce enough MIS personnel for business needs, and job opportunities are great. MIS managers, once they have risen through their technical ranks of their organization to become managers, must remember that they are no longer doing the technical work. They must cross over from being technicians to become managers. Their job changes from being technicians to being systems managers who manage other people's technical work. They must see themselves as needing to solve the business problems of the user, and not just of the data-processing department.

MIS managers are in charge of the systems development operations for their firm. Systems development requires four stages when developing a system for any phase of the organization:

Phase I is systems planning. The systems team must investigate the initial problem by determining what the problem is and developing a feasibility study for management to review.

Phase II identifies the requirements for the systems. It includes the systems analysis, the user requirements, necessary hardware and software, and a conceptional design for the system. Top management then reviews the systems analysis and design.

Phase III involves the development of the systems. This involves developing technical support and technical specifications, reviewing users' procedures control, designing the system, testing the system, and providing user training for the system. At this time, management again reviews and decides on whether to implement the system.

Phase IV is the implementation of the system. The new system is converted from the old system, and the new system is implemented and then refined. There must then be ongoing maintenance and reevaluation of the system to see if it continues to meet the needs of the business.

TYPES OF SYSTEMS

Management information systems can be used as a support to managers to provide a competitive advantage. The system must support the goals of the organization. Most organizations are structured along functional lines, and the typical systems are identified as follows:

Accounting management information systems: All accounting reports are shared by all levels of accounting managers.

Financial management information systems: The financial management information system provides financial information to all financial managers within an organization including the chief financial officer. The chief financial officer analyzes historical and current financial activity, projects future financial needs, and monitors and controls the use of funds over time using the information developed by the MIS department.

Manufacturing management information systems: More than any functional area, operations have been impacted by great advances in technology. As a result, manufacturing operations have changed. For instance, inventories are provided just in time so that great amounts of money are not spent for warehousing huge inventories. In some instances, raw materials are even processed on railroad cars waiting to be sent directly to the factory. Thus there is no need for warehousing.

Marketing management information systems: A marketing management information system supports managerial activity in the area of product development, distribution, pricing decisions, promotional effectiveness, and sales forecasting. More than any other functional area, marketing systems rely on external sources of data. These sources include competition and customers, for example.

Human resources management information systems: Human resources management information systems are concerned with activities related to workers, managers, and other individuals employed by the organization. Because the personnel function relates to all other areas in business, the human resources management information system plays a valuable role in ensuring organizational success. Activities performed by the human resources management information systems include, work-force analysis and planning, hiring, training, and job assignments.

The above are examples of the major management information systems. There may be other management information systems if the company is identified by different functional areas.

BIBLIOGRAPHY

Rochester, Jack B. (1996). "Tools for Knowledge Workers." I *Using Computers in Information*. Indianapolis, IN: Que Education and Training.

Stair, Ralph M. (1996). *Principles of Information Systems and Managerial Approach*, 2nd ed. Cincinnati, OH: Boyd & Fraser.

LLOYD W. BARTHOLOME

MANAGEMENT/LEADERSHIP STYLES

MANAGEMENT VS. LEADERSHIP

Leading should not be considered the same as managing. Business leaders who do not understand the difference between the functions/roles of leading and managing are quite likely to misinterpret how they should carry out their duties to meet organizational goals. While some managers are high-quality leaders, others only manage resources and don't lead their subordinates. Leadership is one of the four primary activities that are used to influence others. As such, it is a subcategory of the management concept that focuses mainly on behavioral issues and opportunities. Managing is more comprehensive than leading. It involves dealing with resource issues as well as behavioral factors. Generally speaking, not all managers are necessarily leaders, yet the most effective managers, over the long term, are leaders.

Leadership is the process of guiding the behavior of others toward an organization's goals. Guiding, in this context, means causing individuals to behave in a particular manner or to follow a specific set of instructions. Ideally, the behavior exhibited is perfectly aligned with such factors as organizational goals, culture, policies, procedures, and job specifications. The main goal of leadership is to get things done through other people, making it one of the main activities that can enhance the management system. It is accomplished to a great degree through the use of effective communication. Because leadership is a prerequisite for business success, to be a successful business manager one must have a solid understanding of what leadership includes. Indeed, such issues as the increased capabilities afforded by enhanced communication technology and the rise of international business have made leadership even more important in today's business environment. The following sections describe the major theories underlying the most commonly accepted management/leadership practices and the concepts they are based on.

In today's business environment, possessing management skills is no longer sufficient to be successful. Contemporary business practices require that managers have knowledge and experience regarding the differences between management and leading and how both activities must be integrated for business success. Commonly, businesspeople believe that a manager makes sure tasks and duties are completed, while a leader is sensitive to the needs of people and what they need to be exceptional employees. Integrating these concepts allows business managers to apply logic and analytical skills to business activities and tactics while being sensitive to and working with workers as individuals with needs and desires related to their work and careers.

LEADERSHIP BASED ON TRAITS

The trait theory of leadership is based on research which implies that the abilities and dispositions necessary to make a good leader are inborn, not capable of being developed over time. The central thrust of this research is to describe leadership as accurately and analytically as possible. The reasoning is that a description of the full spectrum of managerial leadership traits would make it possible to easily identify individuals who possess them. An organization could then hire only those individuals who possess these traits and thus be assured of always having high-quality leaders.

Current management thoughts, however, suggests that leadership ability cannot be explained by an individual's inherited characteristics. To the contrary, business analysts believe that individuals can learn to be good or even exceptional leaders. Thousands of employees each year complete training to improve their leadership skills. Corporations and not-for-profit organizations continue to do this as an investment, which pays dividends.

IDENTIFYING LEADERSHIP BEHAVIORS

Since trait theory proved not to be aligned with leadership skill, researchers have analyzed other angles to explain leadership success or failure. Rather than looking at the traits successful leaders supposedly should possess, researchers began to investigate what good leaders really do. This behavioral approach was concerned with analyzing how a manager completed a task and whether the manager focused on such interpersonal skills as providing moral support and recognizing employees for their successes. Based on these research efforts, leaders can be accurately described by either their job-centered behavior or their employee-centered behavior, since this research indicated two primary dimensions of leader behavior: a work dimension (structure behavior/job-centered behavior) and a people dimension (consideration behavior/employee-centered behavior).

WHICH LEADERSHIP STYLES ARE MOST EFFECTIVE?

Caution should be exercised when considering what style of leadership is best. Research suggests that no single leadership style can be generalized as being most effective. Organizational situations are so complex that one particular leadership style may be successful in one situation but totally ineffective in another.

CONTINGENCY THEORY

Contingency theory, as applied to management/leadership, focuses on what managers do in practice. Because this theory suggests that how a manager operates and makes decisions depends upon, or is contingent upon, a set of circumstances, it is centered on situational analysis. Using contingency theory, managers read situations with an "if-then" mentality: If this situational attribute is present, then there is an appropriate response that a manager should make. This theory takes into consideration human resources and their interaction with business operations. Managers may take different courses of action to get the same result based on differences in situational characteristics. In general, contingency theory suggests that a business leader needs to outline the conditions or situations in which various management methods have the best chance of success. This theory thus runs directly counter to trait theory, discussed earlier. Some of the challenges to successfully using contingency theory are the need to accurately analyze an actual situation, then to choose the appropriate strategies and tactics, and finally to implement these strategies and tactics.

Managers encounter a variety of leadership situations during the course of their daily activities, each of which may require them to use leadership styles that vary considerably, depending on the situation. In using the contingency model, factors of major concern are leader-member relations, task structure, and the position power of the leader. The leader has to analyze these factors to determine the most appropriate style of response for meeting overall work-unit and organizational goals. Leader-member relations refer to the ongoing degree to which subordinates accept an individual leader or group of leaders. Task structure refers to the degree to which tasks are clearly or poorly defined. Position power is the extent to which a leader or group of leaders has control over the work process, rewards, and punishment. Taking these factors into consideration, leaders can adjust their style to best match the context of their decision making and leadership. For those leaders who have a breadth of leadership styles, knowing when to change styles gives them the tools to successfully deal with the varying nature of business decision making. For those leaders who have a limited repertoire of leadership styles, they and their superiors can use this information to better match work situations with the styles that a specific leader possesses.

Within this continuum, or range, of leadership behaviors, each type of behavior also relates to the degree of authority the manager can display, and inversly, to the level of freedom that is made available to workers. On one end of this continuum, business leaders exert a high level of control and allow little employee autonomy; on the opposite end, leaders exert very little control, instead allowing workers considerable autonomy and self-direction. Thus leadership behavior as it progresses across the continuum reflects a gradual change from autocratic to democratic leadership.

In today's business environment there are more complicated contexts and relationships within which managers and subordinates must work than existed in previous eras. And as contexts and relationships become increasingly complicated, it becomes significantly more difficult for leaders to determine how to lead. In addition, there are major societal and organizational forces that cause confusion about how to lead.

THEORY X AND THEORY Y

Based on the work of psychologists, organizational theorists, and human relations specialists in the 1960s and 1970s, two distinct assumptions, called Theory X and Theory Y, evolved about why and how people work for others. Theory X posits that people do not like to work and will avoid doing so if the opportunity presents itself. Because of this, most people need to be coerced into completing their required job duties and punished if they don't complete the quantity of work assigned at the level of quality required. Again, because of their dislike for work, most people do not want responsibility, prefer to be directed by others, and have little ambition; all they want is job security.

With an almost completely opposite perspective, Theory Y posits that people like to work and see it as a natural event in their lives. Therefore, punishment and threats are not the only means of motivating them to complete work assignments. People are willing to work hard for an organization; indeed, they will use self-direction and control to work toward goals that are understandable and communicated clearly. In this theory of human behavior and motivation, people are seen as seekers of learning and responsibility who are capable of and willing to be engaged with creative problem-solving activities that will help the organization reach its goals. According to Theory Y, leaders need to develop ways to expand the capabilities of their workers so that the organization can benefit from this significant potential resource.

Although Theory Y has much to offer and is widely followed, many organizations still use a variety of policies and practices that are based on Theory X principles. A further development in explaining human work behavior and then adjusting management/leadership practices to it is Theory Z.

THEORY Z

Probably the most prominent of the theories and practices coming from Japan is the Theory Z approach, which combines typical practices from the United States and Japan into a comprehensive system of management/leadership. This system includes the following principles of best management/leadership practice:

- Seek to establish a long-term employment culture within the organization.

- Use collective decision making as much as possible.

- Increase and reinforce the importance of individual responsibility.

- Establish a slow and long-term process for evaluation and promotion.

- Employ implicit, informal control that utilizes explicit, formal measures/tools of performance.

- Institute and use moderately specialized job descriptions and career paths.

- Develop policies and practices that support a holistic concern for and support of the individual both at work and at home (as regards family issues).

Theory Z has had a marked impact on the manner in which companies are led today. Theory Z strategies have been instrumental in building stronger working relationships between subordinates and their leaders because of the increased level of worker participation in decision making as well as leaders' higher level of concern for their subordinates.

MANAGERIAL GRID

Business researchers at the University of Texas have developed a two-dimensional grid theory to explain a leadership style based on a person's (1) concern for production and (2) concern for people. Each axis on the grid is a 9-point scale, with 1 meaning low concern and 9 meaning high concern. "Team" managers, often considered the most effective leaders, have strong concern both for the people who work for them and for the output of the group/unit. "Country club" managers are significantly more concerned about their subordinates than about production output. "Authority-compliance" managers, in contrast, are singularly focused on meeting production goals. "Middle-of-the-road" managers attempt to balance people and production concerns in a moderate fashion. And, finally, "impoverished" managers tend to be virtually bankrupt in both categories, usually not knowing much or caring much about either. Grid analysis can be quite useful in helping to determine managers' strengths, weak points, areas where they might best be utilized, and types of staff development they might need to progress.

PATH-GOAL LEADERSHIP THEORY

In path-goal leadership theory, the key strategy of the leader is to make desirable and achievable rewards available to employees. These rewards are directly related to achieving organizational goals. Basically, the manager articulates the objectives (the goal) to be accomplished and how these can and should be completed (the path) to earn rewards. This theory encourages managers to facilitate job performance by showing employees how their work behaviors directly affect their receiving desired rewards.

SYSTEMS THEORY AND THE LEADERSHIP/ MANAGEMENT FUNCTION

A system is a group of interrelated and dependent components that function holistically to meet common goals. Systems theory suggests that organizations operate much like the human biological system, having to deal with entropy, support synergy, and subsystem interdependence. The law of entropy states that there are limited resources available and that as they are used/consumed, their beneficial features are dispersed and are not available to the same degree as they were originally. The other two considerations in a systems approach are the achievement of synergy, or the creation of a total value greater than the value of separate parts, and of subsystem interdependence or the linkage of components in such a way that synergy can take place.

In the effort to enhance system performance, managers/leaders must consider the openness and responsiveness of their business organization and the external environment in which it operates. In this environment, leaders must consider the four major features of business system theory: inputs, organizational features, outputs, and feedback. The inputs for most systems include human labor, information, hard goods, and financing. Organizational features include the work process, management functions, and production or service technology. Outputs include employee satisfaction, products or services, customer and supplier relationships, and profits/losses. In guiding a unit or the whole organization, business leaders need to consider features of their organization's system as it interacts with and responds to customers, suppliers, competitors, and government agencies.

TRANSFORMATIONAL LEADERSHIP

Transformational leadership inspires organizational success by dramatically affecting workers' attitudes about what an organization should be as well as their basic values, such as trust, fairness, and reliability. Transformational leadership, which is similar to charismatic or inspirational leadership, creates in workers a sense of ownership of the organization, encourages new ways of solving problems and promotes lifelong learning for all members of the organization. Although the topic of transformational leadership is both appealing and exciting, more research is needed to develop insights regarding how one becomes a successful transformational leader.

CONFLICT MANAGEMENT

Of all the skills that a manager/leader needs, none is more important than managing the conflicts that inevitably arise in any organization. Conflicts can arise between members in the same work unit, between the work group and its leader, between group leaders, and between different work groups. Some of the most common causes of conflict are communications breakdowns, personality clashes, power and status differences, goal discrepancies, disputed authority boundaries, and allocation of resources.

The following processes are among those usually suggested to eliminate, reduce, and prevent conflict:

- Focus on the facts of the matter; avoid unsupported assertions and issues of personality.

- Develop a list of all possible resolutions of the conflict that will allow the adversarial parties to view the issue from a different perspective.

- Maintain a balance of power and accessibility while addressing the conflict.

- Seek a realistic resolution; never force a consensus, but don't get bogged down in a never-ending debate to achieve one.

- Focus on the larger goals/mission of the organization.

- Engage in bargaining/negotiating to identify options to address the conflict.

- If needed, use a third party to mediate the differences. Bringing in an outside person can add objectivity and reduce personality issues.

- Facilitate accurate communications to reduce rumors and to increase the common understanding of the facts and issues.

There is a widely accepted model for understanding how individuals approach situations involving conflict resolution. This model is two-dimensional. On one axis is the dimension of cooperativeness; on the other, the dimension of assertiveness. As discussed earlier, effective leaders vary their style to meet the needs of a specific situation. Hence, during a conflict situation in which time is a critical concern, an assertive style is needed to resolve the conflict so that time is not lost during a drawn-out negotiation process. Oppositely, when harmony is critical, especially when relationships are new or in their early stages, a collaborative and cooperative approach to conflict resolution is needed. This model for conflict resolution fits well with and supports the notion of contingency and situational leadership.

JAPANESE MANAGEMENT/LEADERSHIP METHODS

In the decades since the end of World War II, business leaders around the world have marveled at the ability of Japanese managers to motivate and successfully lead their subordinates to levels of outstanding performance in terms of both the quantity and quality of production. Therefore, Japanese approaches to management and leadership have been studied intensely to find similarities and differences between local practices and theirs. Among the approaches that have been cited as contributing to Japanese success are the following:

- Japanese corporations make the effort to hire employees for a lifetime, rather than a shorter period of time. This helps workers to feel a close relationship with the organization and helps build employee ownership of the organization's success.

- Employees are elevated to a level of organizational status equivalent to that of management by leveling the playing field with regard to dress, benefit packages, support services/amenities, restrooms, stock ownership plans, and so forth.

- Employees are shown that they are valued and a critical part of the company. This is done by having ceremonies to honor employees, providing housing at nominal cost to employees, having facilities for social activities that are sponsored by the organization, offering competitive salaries, and so forth.

- A significant effort is made to build positive and strong working relationships between leaders and their subordinates. This includes making sure that leaders take time to get to know their employees and become cognizant of their main concerns. Such a relationship can have a marked impact on the extent to which employees value the organization and their leaders.

- There is collective responsibility for the success of the organization. Individual accountability is downplayed to the climate that prevails in U.S. organizations.

- Implied control mechanisms are based on cultural values and responsibility.

- Nonspecialized career pathways are typical. Employees work in a number of job categories over the course of their tenure so that they can gain a broader sense of the nature of all the work that is done in the organization.

- There is a holistic concern for the welfare of every employee. Organizations and their leaders take the time to assist employees with personal issues and work opportunities.

- The Japanese are generally concerned with how the company performs and how individual work groups perform rather than how an individual performs. Therefore, incentives for individuals are less likely to be effective than incentives associated with the performance of a work group or of a whole unit. In addition, Japanese leaders and workers focus much less on monetary rewards than on esteem and social rewards.

Another major development in the manufacturing and handling of goods was developed in Japan. This development was *kanban*, or what we know as the just-in-time (JIT) inventory and materials handling system. In this system managers/leaders locate high-quality suppliers within a short distance of their operations. They also establish specific quality standards and delivery requirements, as well as materials handling procedures, that these suppliers are contractually obligated to adhere to.

Although these techniques have proven to be successful in Japan, attempts to duplicate them in another culture may have disappointing results. The importance of cultural mores cannot be underestimated. What may work in Japan, France, or the United States may not work anywhere else simply because of cultural factors. Yet Japanese management/leadership principles have taught managers around the world to consider new approaches in order to achieve the higher standards of organizational effectiveness necessary in today's global economy. Business leaders around the world are examining their practices in light of the success that the Japanese and others have had in the areas of strategy building, organizational development, group/team cooperation, and establishing competitive advantage.

(SEE ALSO: *Leadership*)

THOMAS HAYNES

MANAGERIAL GRID

(SEE: *Management/Leadership Styles*)

MANUFACTURING

One can trace the origins of modern manufacturing management to the advent of agricultural production, which meant that humans didn't constantly have to wander to find new sources of food. Since that time, people have been developing better techniques for producing goods to meet human needs and wants. Since they had additional time available because of more efficient food sources, people began to develop techniques to produce items for use and trade. They also began to specialize based on their skills and resources. With the first era of water-based exploration, trade, and conflict, new ideas regarding product development eventually emerged, over the course of the centuries, leading to the beginning of the Industrial Revolution in the mid-eighteenth century. The early twentieth century, however, is generally considered to mark the true beginning of a disciplined effort to study and improve manufacturing and operations management practices. Thus, what we know as modern manufacturing began in the final decades of the twentieth century.

The late 1970s and early 1980s saw the development of the manufacturing strategy paradigm by researchers at the Harvard Business School. This work focused on how manufacturing executives could use their factories' capabilities as strategic competitive weapons, specifically identifying how what we call the five P's of manufacturing management (people, plants, parts, processes, and planning) can be analyzed as strategic and tactical decision variables. Central to this notion is the focus on factory and manufacturing trade-offs. Because a factory cannot excel on all performance measures, its management must devise a focused strategy, creating a focused factory that does a limited set of tasks extremely well. Thus the need arose for making trade-offs among such performance measures as low cost, high quality, and high flexibility in designing and managing factories.

The 1980s saw a revolution in management philosophy and the technologies used in manufacturing. Just-in-time (JIT) production was the primary breakthrough in manufacturing philosophy. Pioneered by the Japanese, JIT is an integrated set of activities designed to achieve high-volume production using minimal inventories of parts that arrive at the workstation "just in time." This philosophy—coupled with total quality control (TQC), which aggressively seeks to eliminate causes of production defects—is now a cornerstone in many manufacturers' practices.

As profound as JIT's impact has been, factory automation in its various forms promises to have an even greater impact on operations management in coming decades. Such terms as "computer-integrated manufacturing" (CIM), "flexible manufacturing systems" (FMS), and "factory of the future" (FOF) are part of the vocabulary of manufacturing leaders.

Another major development of the 1970s and 1980s was the broad application of computers to operations problems. For manufacturers, the big breakthrough was the application of materials requirements planning (MRP) to production control. This approach brings together, in a computer program, all the parts that go into complicated products. This computer program then enables production planners to quickly adjust production schedules and inventory purchases to meet changing demands during the manufacturing process. Clearly, the massive data manipulation required for changing the schedules of products with thousands of parts would be impossible without such programs and the computer capacity to run them. The promotion of this approach by the American Production and Inventory Control Society (APICS) has been termed the MRP Crusade.

The hallmark development in the field of manufacturing management, as well as in management practice in general, is total quality management (TQM). Although practiced by many companies in the 1980s, TQM became truly pervasive in the 1990s. All manufacturing executives are aware of the quality message put forth by the so-called quality gurus—W. Edwards Deming, Joseph M. Juran, and Philip Crosby. Helping the quality movement along was the creation of the Baldrige National Quality Award in 1986 under the direction of the American Society of Quality

Control and the National Institute of Standards and Technology. The Baldrige Award recognizes up to five companies a year for outstanding quality management systems.

The ISO 9000 certification standards, issued by the International Organization for Standardization, now play a major role in setting quality standards, particularly for global manufacturers. Many European companies require that their vendors meet these standards as a condition for obtaining contracts.

The need to become or remain competitive in the global economic recession of the early 1990s pushed companies to seek major innovations in the processes used to run their operations. One major type of business process reengineering (BPR) is conveyed in the title of Michael Hammer's influential article "Reengineering Work: Don't Automate, Obliterate." The approach seeks to make revolutionary, as opposed to evolutionary, changes. It does this by taking a fresh look at what the organization is trying to do, and then eliminating non-value-added steps and computerizing the remaining ones to achieve the desired outcome.

The idea is to apply a total system approach to managing the flow of information, materials, and services from raw material suppliers through factories and warehouses to the end customer. Recent trends, such as outsourcing and mass customization, are forcing companies to find flexible ways to meet customer demand. The focus is on optimizing those core activities in order to maximize the speed of response to changes in customer expectations.

Based on the work of several researchers, a few basic operations priorities have been identified. These priorities include cost, product quality and reliability, delivery speed, delivery reliability, ability to cope with changes in demand, flexibility, and speed of new product introduction. In every industry, there is usually a segment of the market that buys products—typically products that are commodity-like in nature like sugar, iron ore, or coal—strictly on the basis of low cost. Because this segment of the market is frequently very large, many companies

are lured by the potential for significant profits, which they associate with the large unit volumes of the product. As a consequence, competition in this segment is fierce—and so is the failure rate.

Quality can be divided into two categories: product quality and process quality. The level of a product's quality will vary with the market segment to which it is aimed because the goal in establishing the proper level of product quality is to meet the requirements of the customer. Over-designed products with too high a level of quality will be viewed as prohibitively expensive. Underdesigned products, on the other hand, will result in losing customers to products that cost a little more but are perceived as offering greater benefits.

Process quality is critical since it relates directly to the reliability of the product. Regardless of the product, customers want products without defects. Thus, the goal of process quality is to produce error-free products. Adherence to product specifications is essential to ensure the reliability of the product as defined by its intended use.

A company's ability to deliver more quickly than its competitors may be critical. Take, for example, a company that offers a repair service for computer-networking equipment. A company that can offer on-site repair within one or two hours has a significant advantage over a competing firm that only guarantees service only within twenty-four hours.

Delivery reliability relates to a firm's ability to supply the product or service on or before a promised delivery due date. The focus during the 1980s and 1990s on reducing inventory stocks in order to reduce cost has made delivery reliability an increasingly important criterion in evaluating alternative vendors.

A company's ability to respond to increases and decreases in demand is another important factor in its ability to compete. It is well known that a company with increasing demand can do little wrong. When demand is strong and increasing, costs are continuously reduced because of economies of scale, and investments in new technologies can be easily justified. Scaling back when demand decreases may require many difficult decisions regarding laying off employees and related reductions in assets. The ability to deal effectively with dynamic market demand over the long term is an essential element of manufacturing strategy.

Flexibility, from a strategic perspective, refers to a company's ability to offer a wide variety of products to its customers. In the 1990s companies began to adjust their processes and outputs to dynamic and sometimes volatile customer needs. An important component of flexibility is the ability to develop different products and deliver them to market. As new technologies and processes become widespread, a company must be able to respond to market demands more and more quickly if it is to continue to be successful.

Manufacturing strategy must be linked vertically to the customer and horizontally to other parts of the enterprise. Underlying this framework is senior management's strategic vision of the firm. This vision identifies, in general terms, the target market, the firm's product line, and its core enterprise and operations capabilities. The choice of a target market can be difficult, but it must be made. Indeed, it may lead to turning away business—ruling out a customer segment that would simply be unprofitable or too hard to serve given the firm's capabilities. Core capabilities are those skills that differentiate the manufacturing from its competitors.

In general, customers' new-product or current-product requirements set the performance priorities that then become the required priorities for operations. Manufacturing organizations have a linkage of priorities because they cannot satisfy customer needs without the involvement of R&D and distribution and without the direct or indirect support of financial management, human resource management, and information management. Given its performance requirements, a manufacturing division uses its capabilities to achieve these priority goals in order to complete sales. These capabilities include technology, systems, and people. CIM, JIT, and TQM represent fundamental concepts and tools used in each of the three areas.

Suppliers do not become suppliers unless their capabilities in the management of technology, systems, and people reach acceptable levels. In addition, most manufacturing capabilities are now subjected to the "make-or-buy" decision. It is current practice among world-class manufacturers to subject each part of a manufacturing operation to the question: If we are not among the best in the world at, say, metal forming, should we be doing this at all, or should we subcontract to someone who *is* the best?

The main objectives of manufacturing strategy development are (1) to translate required priorities into specific performance requirements for operations and (2) to make the necessary plans to assure that manufacturing capabilities are sufficient to accomplish them. Developing priorities involves the following steps:

1. Segment the market according to the product group.

2. Identify the product requirements, demand patterns, and profit margins of each group.

3. Determine the order winners and order qualifiers for each group.

4. Convert order winners into specific performance requirements.

It has been said that America's resurgence in manufacturing is *not the result of* U.S. firms being better innovators than most foreign competitors. This has been true for a long time. Rather, it is because U.S. firms are proving to be very effective copiers, having spent a decade examining the advantages of foreign rivals in product development, production operations, supply chain management, and corporate governance then putting in place "functional equivalents" that "incrementally improve" on their best techniques. Four main adaptations on the part of U.S. firms underscore this success:

1. New approaches to product-development team structure and management have resulted in getting products to market

faster, with better designs and manu-facturability.

2. Companies have improved their manufac-turing facilities through dramatic reduc-tions of work-in-process, space, tool costs, and human effort, while simulta-neously improving quality and flexibility.

3. New methods of customer-supplier coop-eration, which borrow from the Japanese *keiretsu* (large holding companies) prac-tices of close linkages but maintain the independence of the organizations desired by U.S. companies, have been put in place.

4. Better leadership—through strong, inde-pendent boards of directors that will dis-miss managers who are not doing their jobs effectively—now exists.

In sum, the last few decades of the twentieth century witnessed tremendous change and ad-vancement in the means of producing goods and the manner of managing these operations that have led to higher levels of quality and quantity as well as greater efficiency in the use of resources. In the new millennium, because of global compe-tition and the expansive use of new technologies, including the Internet, a successful firm will be one that is competitive with new products and services that are creatively marketed and effec-tively financed. Yet what is becoming increas-ingly critical is the ability to develop manufactur-ing practices that provide unique benefits to the products. The organization that can develop su-perior products, sell them at lower prices, and deliver them to their customers in a timely man-ner stands to become a formidable presence in the marketplace.

THOMAS HAYNES

MARKDOWNS

(SEE: *Pricing*)

MARKETING

The term *market* is the root word for the word *marketing*. *Market* refers to the location where exchanges between buyers and sellers occur. *Marketing* pertains to the interactive process that requires developing, pricing, placing, and pro-moting goods, ideas, or services in order to facili-tate exchanges between customers and sellers to satisfy the needs and wants of consumers. Thus, at the very center of the marketing process is satisfying the needs and wants of customers.

NEEDS AND WANTS

Needs are the basic items required for human survival. Human needs are an essential concept underlying the marketing process because needs are translated into consumer wants. Human needs are often described as a state of real or perceived deprivation. Basic human needs take one of three forms: physical, social, and individ-ual. Physical needs are basic to survival and in-clude food, clothing, warmth, and safety. Social needs revolve around the desire for belonging and affection. Individual needs include longings for knowledge and self-expression, through items such as clothing choices. Wants are needs that are shaped by both cultural influences and individual preferences. Wants are often described as goods, ideas, and services that fulfill the needs of an individual consumer. The wants of individuals change as both society and technology change. For example, when a computer is released, a con-sumer may want it simply because it is a new and improved technology. Therefore, the purpose of marketing is to convert these generic needs into wants for specific goods, ideas, or services. De-mand is created when wants are supported by an individual consumer's ability to purchase the goods, ideas, or services in question.

Consumers buy products that will best meet their needs, as well as provide the most fulfill-ment resulting from the exchange process. The first step in the exchange process is to provide a product. Products can take a number of forms such as goods, ideas, and services. All products are produced to satisfy the needs, wants, and demands of individual buyers.

The second step in the satisfaction process is exchange. Exchange occurs when an individual receives a product from a seller in return for something called consideration. Consideration usually takes the form of currency. For an exchange to take place, it must meet a number of conditions. (1) There must be at least two participants in the process. (2) Each party must offer something of value to the other. (3) Both parties must want to deal with each other. (4) Both participants have the right to accept or to reject the offer. (5) Both groups must have the ability to communicate and deliver on the mutual agreement. Thus, the transaction process is a core component of marketing. Whenever there is a trade of values between two parties, a transaction has occurred. A transaction is often considered a unit of measurement in marketing. The earliest form of exchange was known as barter.

HISTORICAL ERAS OF MARKETING

Modern marketing began in the early 1900s. In the twentieth century, the marketing process progressed through three distinct eras—production, sales, and marketing. In the 1920s, firms operated under the premise that production was a seller's market. Product choices were nearly nonexistent because firm managers believed that a superior product would sell itself. This philosophy was possible because the demand for products outlasted supply. During this era, firm success was measured totally in terms of production. The second era of marketing, ushered in during 1950s, is known as the sales era. During this era, product supply exceeded demand. Thus, firms assumed that consumers would resist buying goods and services deemed nonessential. To overcome this consumer resistance, sellers had to employ creative advertising and skillful personal selling in order to get consumers to buy. The marketing era emerged after firm managers realized that a better strategy was needed to attract and keep customers because allowing products to sell themselves was not effective. Rather, the marketing concept philosophy was adopted by many

firms in an attempt to meet the specific needs of customers. Proponents of the marketing concept argued that in order for firms to achieve their goals, they had to satisfy the needs and wants of consumers.

MARKETING IN THE OVERALL BUSINESS

There are four areas of operation within all firms: accounting, finance, management, and marketing. Each of these four areas performs specific functions. The accounting department is responsible for keeping track of income and expenditures. The primary responsibility of the finance department is maintaining and tracking assets. The management department is responsible for creating and implementing procedural policies of the firm. The marketing department is responsible for generating revenue through the exchange process. As a means of generating revenue, marketing objectives are established in alignment with the overall objectives of the firm.

Aligning the marketing activities with the objectives of the firm is completed through the process of marketing management. The marketing management process involves developing objectives that promote the long-term competitive advantage of a firm. The first step in the marketing management process is to develop the firm's overall strategic plan. The second step is to establish marketing strategies that support the firm's overall strategic objectives. Lastly, a marketing plan is developed for each product. Each product plan contains an executive summary, an explanation of the current marketing situation, a list of threats and opportunities, proposed sales objectives, possible marketing strategies, action programs, and budget proposals.

The marketing management process includes analyzing marketing opportunities, selecting target markets, developing the marketing mix, and managing the marketing effort. In order to analyze marketing opportunities, firms scan current environmental conditions in order to determine potential opportunities. The aim of the marketing effort is to satisfy the needs and wants of consumers. Thus, it is necessary for marketing managers to determine the particular needs and wants of potential customers. Various quantitative and qualitative techniques of marketing research are used to collect data about potential customers, who are then segmented into markets.

MARKET SEGMENTATION

In order to better manage the marketing effort and to satisfy the needs and wants of customers, many firms place consumers into groups, a process called market segmentation. In this process, potential customers are categorized based on different needs, characteristics, or behaviors. Market segments are evaluated as to their attractiveness or potential for generating revenue for the firm. Four factors are generally reviewed to determine the potential of a particular market segment. Effective segments are measurable, accessible, substantial, and actionable. Measurability is the degree to which a market segment's size and purchasing power can be measured. Accessibility refers to the degree to which a market segment can be reached and served. Substantiality refers to the size of the segment in term of profitability for the firm. Action ability refers to the degree to which a firm can design or develop a product to serve a particular market segment.

Consumer characteristics are used to segment markets into workable groups. Common characteristics used for consumer categorizations include demographic, geographic, psychographic, and behavioral segmentation. Demographic segmentation categorizes consumers based on such characteristics as age, gender, income level, and occupation. It is one of the most popular methods of segmenting potential customers because it makes it relatively easy to identify potential customers. Categorizing consumers according to their locations is called geographic segmentation. Consumers can be segmented geographically according to the nations, states, regions, cities, or neighborhoods in which they live, shop, and/or work. Psychographic segmentation uses consumers' activities, interests, and opinions to sort them into groups. Social class, lifestyle, or personality characteristics are psychographic variables used to categorize con-

sumers into different groups. In behavioral segmentation, marketers divide consumers into groups based on their knowledge, attitudes, uses, or responses to a product.

Once the potential market has been segmented, firms need to station their products relative to similar products of other producers, a process called product positioning. Market positioning is the process of arranging a product so as to engage the minds of target consumers. Firm managers position their products in such a way as to distinguish it from those of competitors in order to gain a competitive advantage in the marketplace. The position of a product in the marketplace must be clear, distinctive, and desirable relative to those of its competitors in order for it to be effective.

COVERAGE STRATEGIES

There are three basic market-coverage strategies used by marketing managers: undifferentiated, differentiated, and concentrated. An undifferentiated marketing strategy occurs when a firm focuses on the common needs of consumers rather than their different needs. When using this strategy, producers design products to appeal to the largest number of potential buyers. The benefit of an undifferentiated strategy is that it is cost-effective because a narrow product focus results in lower production, inventory, and transportation costs. A firm using a differentiated strategy makes a conscious decision to divide and target several different market segments, with a different product geared to each segment. Thus, a different marketing plan is needed for each segment in order to maximize sales and, as a result, increase firm profits. With a differentiated marketing strategy, firms create more total sales because of broader appeal across market segments and stronger position within each segment. The last market coverage strategy is known as the concentrated marketing strategy. The concentrated strategy, which aims to serve a large share of one or a very few markets, is best suited for firms with limited resources. This approach allows firms to obtain a much stronger position in the segments it targets because of the greater emphasis on these targeted segments. This greater emphasis ultimately leads to a better understanding of the needs of the targeted segments.

MARKETING MIX

Once a positioning strategy has been determined, marketing managers seek to control the four basic elements of the marketing mix: product, price, place, and promotion, known as the four P's of marketing. Since these four variables are controllable, the best mix of these elements is determined to reach the selected target market.

Product. The first element in the marketing mix is the product. Products can be either tangible or intangible. Tangible products are products that can be touched; intangible products are those that cannot be touched, such as services. There are three basic levels of a product: core, actual, and augmented. The core product is the most basic level, what consumers really buy in terms of benefits. For example, consumers do not buy food processors, per se; rather, they buy the benefit of being able to process food quickly and efficiently. The next level of the product is the actual product—in the case of the previous example, food processors. Products are typically sorted according to the following five characteristics: quality, features, styling, brand name, and packaging. Finally, the augmented level of a product consists of all the elements that surround both the core and the actual product. The augmented level provides purchasers with additional services and benefits. For example, follow-up technical assistance and warranties and guaranties are augmented product components. When planning new products, firm managers consider a number of issues including product quality, features, options, styles, brand name, packaging, size, service, warranties, and return policies, all in an attempt to meet the needs and wants of consumers.

Price. Price is the cost of the product paid by consumers. This is the only element in the marketing mix that generates revenue for firms. In order to generate revenue, managers must consider factors both internal and external to the organization. Internal factors take the form of marketing objectives, the marketing-mix strategy, and production costs. External factors to consider are the target market, product demand, competition, economic conditions, and government regulations. There are a number of pricing strategies available to marketing managers: skimming, penetration, quantity, and psychological. With a price-skimming strategy, the price is initially set high, allowing firms to generate maximum profits from customers willing to pay the high price. Prices are then gradually lowered until maximum profit is received from each level of consumer. Penetration pricing is used when firms set low prices in order to capture a large share of a market quickly. A quantity-pricing strategy provides lower prices to consumers who purchase larger quantities of a product. Psychological pricing tends to focus on consumer perceptions. For example, odd pricing is a common psychological pricing strategy. With odd pricing, the cost of the product may be a few cents lower than a full-dollar value. Consumers tend to focus on the lower-value full-dollar cost even though it is really priced closer to the next higher full-dollar amount. For example, if a good is priced at $19.95, consumers will focus on $19 rather than $20.

Place. Place refers to where and how the products will be distributed to consumers. There are two basic issues involved in getting the products to consumers: channel management and logistics management. Channel management involves the process of selecting and motivating wholesalers and retailers, sometimes called middlemen, through the use of incentives. Several factors are reviewed by firm management when determining where to sell their products: distribution channels, market-coverage strategy, geographic locations, inventory, and transportation methods. The process of moving products from a manufacturer to the final consumer is often called the *channel of distribution*.

Promotion. The last variable in the marketing mix is promotion. Various promotional tools are used to communicate messages about products, ideas, or services from firms and their customers. The promotional tools available to managers are advertising, personal selling, sales promotion, and publicity. For the promotional program to be effective, managers use a blend of the four promotional tools that best reaches potential customers. This blending of promotional tools is sometimes referred to as the *promotional mix.* The goal of this promotional mix is to communicate to potential customers the features and benefits of products.

INTERNATIONAL MARKETING

International business has been practiced for thousands of years. In modern times, advances in technology have improved transportation and communication methods; as a result, more and more firms have set up shop at various locations around the globe. A natural component of international business is international marketing. International marketing occurs when firms plan and conduct transactions across international borders in order to satisfy the objectives of both consumers and the firm. International marketing is simply a strategy used by firms to improve both market share and profits. While firm managers may try to employ the same basic marketing strategies used in the domestic market when promoting products in international locations, those strategies may not be appropriate or effective. Firm managers must adapt their strategies to fit the unique characteristics of each international market. Unique environmental factors that need to be explored by firm managers before going global include trade systems, economic conditions, political-legal, and cultural conditions.

The first factor to consider in the international marketplace is each country's trading system. All countries have their own trade system regulations and restrictions. Common trade system regulations and restrictions include tariffs, quotas, embargoes, exchange controls, and nontariff trade barriers. The second factor to review is the economic environment. There are two economic factors which reflect how attractive a particular market is in a selected country: industrial structure and income distribution. Industrial structure refers to how well developed a country's infrastructure is while income distributed refers to how income is distributed among its citizens. Political-legal environment is the third factor to investigate. For example, the individual and cultural attitudes regarding purchasing products from foreign countries, political stability, monetary regulations, and government bureaucracy all influence marketing practices and opportunities. Finally, the last factor to be considered before entering a global market is the cultural environment. Since cultural values regarding particular products will vary considerably from one country to another around the world, managers must take into account these differences in the planning process.

Just as with domestic markets, managers must establish their international marketing objectives and policies before going overseas. For example, target countries will need to be identified and evaluated in terms of their potential sales and profits. After selecting a market and establishing marketing objectives, the mode of entry into the market must be determined. There are three major modes of entry into international markets: exporting, joint venture, and direct investment. Exporting is the simplest way to enter an international market. With exporting, firms enter international markets by selling products internationally through the use of middlemen. This use of these middlemen is sometimes called indirect exporting. The second way to enter an international market is by using the joint-venture approach. A joint venture takes place when firms join forces with companies from the international market to produce or market a product. Joint ventures differ from direct investment in that an association is formed between firms and businesses in the international market. Four types of joint venture are licensing, contract manufacturing, management contracting, and joint ownership. Under licensing, firms allow other businesses in the international market to produce products under an agreement called a license. The licensee has the right to use the manufacturing process, trademark, patent, trade secret, or other items of value for a fee or royalty.

Firms also use contract manufacturing, which arranges for the manufacture of products to enter international markets. The third type of joint venture is called management contracting. With this approach, the firms supply the capital to the local international firm in exchange for the management know-how. The last category of joint venture is joint ownership. Firms join with the local international investors to establish a local business. Both groups share joint ownership and control of the newly established business. Finally, direct investment is the last mode used by firms to enter international markets. With direct investment, a firm enters the market by establishing its own base in international locations. Direct investment is advantageous because labor and raw materials may be cheaper in some countries. Firms can also improve their images in international markets because of the employment opportunities they create.

BIBLIOGRAPHY

Boone, Louise E., and Kurtz, David L. (1992). *Contemporary Marketing*, 7th ed. New York: Dryden/Harcourt Brace.

Churchill, Gilbert A., and Peter, Paul J. (1995). *Marketing: Creating Value for Customers*. Boston: Irwin.

Farese, Lois, Kimbrell, Grady, and Woloszyk, Carl (1991). *Marketing Essentials*. Mission Hills, CA: Glencoe/McGraw-Hill.

Kotler, Philip, and Armstrong, Gary (1993). *Marketing, an Introduction*, 3rd ed. Englewood Cliffs, NJ: Prentice-Hall.

Semenik, Richard J., and Bamossy, Gary J. (1995). *Principles of Marketing: A Global Perspective*, 2d ed. Cincinnati, OH: South-Western.

ALLEN D. TRUELL

MARKETING CONCEPT

Business philosophy has experienced three major shifts during the history of commerce in the United States. It has moved from a production orientation to a sales orientation to the current consumer orientation. Each of these philosophies has reflected the economic environment of its time.

From the early years of the country into the late 1920s, businesses had limited production capacity and continuous demand for their products. Under those circumstances, it was inevitable that the prevailing philosophy would be "produce as much as you can and it will sell." Business goals based on that belief naturally focused on production. Marketing concerns were limited to order taking and product distribution.

With the introduction of mass production in the late 1800s, the gap between production and the demand for goods and services began to narrow. By the 1930s, production capacity had caught up with and, in many areas, exceeded demand. In order to maintain or regain production and sales levels, businesses adopted a sales-oriented philosophy. This philosophy held that "if you do enough advertising, promotional activities, and direct selling, you can convince the market to buy all of your output." Initially, companies capitalized on the emergence of the radio as an advertising vehicle and the employment of large sales forces to reach prospective customers in new markets. In the 1940s, the introduction of television enabled them to expand sales efforts even further.

After the end of World War II, two forces combined to create an explosion in demand for goods and services. One was the pent-up demand for products resulting from wartime shortages. The other was the enormous added demand generated by the return of G.I.s who were establishing new homes and families. The spending boom caused by these forces was sustained by the baby boom and the increased standard of living that followed. At the same time, wartime production capacity and technological developments were shifted to civilian applications, production continued to increase, and new ventures were formed to take advantage of the opportunities.

The net result of all this economic activity was heavy competition for the consumer dollar. Businesses quickly came to realize that if they were going to get their share of those dollars, they were going to have to become more consumer-oriented. This change in philosophy became known as the *marketing concept*.

Although this philosophy had been taking shape for nearly seven years, it was not articulated until it appeared in the 1952 annual report of General Electric. One widely used definition evolving from the report's description is "an organization-wide consumer orientation with the objective of achieving long-range profitability." As this definition implies, there are three parts to the marketing concept. They are:

1. *A customer focus:* The marketing concept begins with the premise that the starting point for business decisions is the customer's needs and wants. Those needs and wants are carefully researched and thoroughly analyzed. Then, goods and services are identified and/or developed to satisfy them.

2. *A profit goal:* The marketing concept dictates that goods and services made available by a business must be produced and sold at a profit. The profit objective is integral to the survival and growth of the business. Without it, the business would not be available to serve the needs and wants of customers.

3. *A total company effort:* Effective implementation of the marketing concept requires involvement of employees from all departments at all levels of the business. Training must be provided and employees must be motivated to achieve the common goals of maximum customer satisfaction and profitability.

Businesses that have embraced the marketing concept have found that it has had a strong impact on sales. They have also found that, in many respects, it has changed the way they operate.

Most of the changes in management practice have been related to changes in thinking inherent in the marketing concept. These include making decisions on the basis of customer needs and wants instead of production schedules and sales goals, viewing profit as an objective rather than an accounting outcome, and taking an active interest in *all* aspects of the business. Putting the marketing concept into practice has also forced managers to think through what they are going to do and their reasons for doing it.

Changes in marketing activities that have occurred under the concept involve both marketing strategies and marketing functions. Market research has become a prominent tool. Data gathered to determine customer needs and wants and to provide feedback on company performance has been put to use. Special attention has been paid to product quality and to targeting services, as well as goods, to customer preferences. The customer's interest has been designated as the first priority in all marketing activities. In selling, for example, helping the customer has been given greater emphasis than getting the sale. In addition, the search for innovative ways to reach and serve the customer has become an ongoing enterprise.

Changes in production brought about by use of the marketing concept, such as closely controlled inventories, have centered on efficiency. Changes in operations, such as extended hours and immediate delivery, have focused on convenient product availability. Additional changes in business practice have been aimed at cost control to give customers maximum value for the price they pay.

During the 1990s, attempts were made to improve on the marketing concept by extending it and broadening it. The effort to extend the concept involved combining it with total quality management (TQM). The intent to take customer satisfaction to a higher level and meet customer's exact needs. This initiative met with limited success. Efforts to broaden the marketing concept expanded it to include social concerns. The assumption was that by addressing broader customer concerns (the environment, AIDS, etc.), along with basic needs and wants, customer satisfaction—and profitability—would also be expanded. Some companies have had success with this wider concept.

(SEE ALSO: *Marketing research*; *Market segmentation*; *Quality management*; *Target marketing.*)

BIBLIOGRAPHY

Jackson, Kathy. (1992). "Strategy at Ford: Develop Cars (Aiming New Cars at Specific Market Niches)." *Automotive News* November: 1-11.

Kotler, Phillip. (1998). "A Generic Concept of Marketing." *Marketing Management* April: 48-54.

Nickels, William G., McHugh, James M., and McHugh, Susan M. (1999). *Understanding Business* Burr Ridge, IL: Irwin/McGraw-Hill.

Pellett, Jennifer. (1994). "Men's Wearhouse: Creating a Service-Value Package." *Discount Merchandiser* May: 146-149.

EARL C. MEYER
WINIFRED L. GREEN

MARKETING: HISTORICAL PERSPECTIVES

This article is an introduction to the historical development of marketing, one of the major functional areas of a business firm. First, marketing is described and defined. Then, the evolution of marketing in the United States is described, touching on several major eras, including the simple trade era, the production era, the sales era, the marketing department era, the marketing company era, and the relationship marketing era.

WHAT IS MARKETING?

"Marketing is advertising, like those false or deceptive ads on television that try to get you to buy something that you don't really want."

"Marketing is like those pushy car salespeople, or those salespeople that come to our front doors selling overpriced vacuum cleaners."

"I hate those rude telemarketers calling at all times of the day and night."

Some individuals think that marketing involves deceptive, high-pressure tactics to get people to buy something they don't really want. Those individuals are incorrect. While marketing usually involves advertising or personal selling, marketing (practiced correctly) should not try to get people to buy things they don't want, nor should marketers use deceptive or pushy tactics to get people to buy. In fact, marketing is really the process of developing products to *satisfy* customers through proper pricing, promotion, and distribution.

The basic goal behind marketing is to satisfy the customer. Satisfied customers are much more valuable than customers who have been deceived into buying something. For example, satisfied customers are more likely to buy your product again. Furthermore, satisfied customers are more likely to speak well of the product to friends and acquaintances, which can increase the possibility that they, in turn, will buy the firm's product. Indeed, marketing is really the process of developing and maintaining long-term exchange relationships. However, companies have not always practiced this philosophy. The remainder of this article describes how company beliefs have changed over time.

THE SIX STAGES OF MARKETING EVOLUTION

Marketing as it exists today is a relatively recent phenomenon, even though its roots reach back into the nineteenth century. In the early nineteenth century a woman who wanted a new dress had two choices: to make her own or to hire someone to make one for her. If she decided to hire someone, she would pick out the fabric and get measured, and the dress would be custom-made for her. There were no standard sizes as there are today. Standard sizes are the result of modern mass-manufacturing processes.

The Simple Trade Era Prior to the Industrial Revolution, people made most of what they consumed. Any excess household production could be brought to town and sold or traded for other goods. This type of economy is commonly referred to as a pure subsistence economy. In a pure subsistence economy, there is little need for marketing (to facilitate exchanges), since each household produces what it consumes.

However, with the advent of the Industrial Revolution, businesses rather than households became the producers of many types of goods. When the producers of products are not also the consumers of those products, exchanges must

An early assembly line in Highland Park, Michigan.

take place. Thus serious thinking about the exchange process—that is, marketing—began in the wake of the Industrial Revolution. The evolution of marketing into the most important business function in many firms was first recognized by Robert Keith (1960), an executive at Pillsbury, and was substantiated by other business leaders at other firms. According to Keith, marketing evolved into its present-day prominence within Pillsbury during four distinct periods beginning after the simple trade era in American history. Keith called these periods the production era, the sales era, the marketing era, and the marketing company era.

The Production Era The production era is so named because many companies' main priority was the reduction of the cost of production. Companies felt that exchanges could be facilitated merely by lowering manufacturing costs and, in turn, passing along the cost savings to customers in the form of lower prices.

This focus on production (which lasted from just after the Civil War until the 1920s) was fueled by such milestones as Henry Ford's invention of the assembly line and the more efficient work principles advanced by Fredrick W. Taylor's scientific management movement (Haber, 1964). These two innovations made business managers aware that mass production resulted in steeply declining unit costs of production. In turn, the declining unit costs of production made profit possibilities look fabulous.

The rationale for mass production seemed sound at the time. According to Michael Porter (1980), reduced production costs can lead to reduced selling prices, which appeal to the largest segment of customers. Unfortunately, turbulent economic conditions associated with the late 1920s through the 1940s caused many companies to fail even though they had adopted this *production-oriented* philosophy. As a result, companies looked for other ways to facilitate the exchange process.

The Sales Era The next era of marketing evolution is called the sales era because many companies' main priority was to move their products out of the factory using a variety of selling techniques. During the sales era, companies felt that they could enhance their sales by using a variety of promotional techniques designed to inform potential customers about and/or persuade them to buy their products. This type of thinking was initiated by the economic climate of the time.

When Herbert Hoover was elected president in 1928, the mood of the general public was one of optimism and confidence in the U.S. economy. Few people had any reason to believe that prosperity would not continue. In his acceptance speech for the Republican presidential nomination, Hoover said: "We in America today are nearer to the final triumph over poverty than ever before in the history of any land. The poorhouse is vanishing from among us."

However October 29, 1929—"Black Tuesday"—marked the beginning of the Great Depression. This was the single most devastating financial day in the history of the New York Stock Exchange. Within the first few hours that the stock market was open, prices fell so far as to wipe out all the gains that had been made in the previous year. Since the stock market was viewed as the chief indicator of the American economy, public confidence was shattered. Between October 29 and November 13 (when stock prices hit their lowest point), more than $30 billion disappeared from the American economy—comparable to the total amount the United States had spent on its involvement in World War I (Schultz, 1999).

The amount of disposable and discretionary income that consumers had to spend on necessities and luxuries also decreased dramatically as the unemployment rate approached 25 percent. Companies found that they could no longer sell all the products that they produced, even though prices had been lowered via mass production. Firms now had to get rid of their excess products in order to convert those products into cash. In order to get rid of products, many firms developed sales forces and relied on personal selling, advertising signs, and singing commercials on the radio to "move" the product. Theodore Levitt (1960), a prominent marketing scholar, has noted that these firms were not necessarily concerned with satisfying the customer, but rather with selling the product. This *sales orientation* dominated business practice through the 1930s until World War II, when most firms' manufacturing facilities were adapted to making machinery and equipment for the war effort. Of course, the war dramatically changed the environment within which business was conducted. This also changed companies' philosophies of doing business.

The Marketing Department Era The manufacturing capability of most industrialized countries—except the United States—had been destroyed during World War II. Therefore U.S. firms once again found it relatively easy to sell the products they manufactured because there was little competition from abroad. Armed with sales concepts developed during the sales era, as well as new manufacturing capabilities and large research and development (R & D) departments developed during the war, firms realized that they could produce hundreds of new and different products.

Firms realized that they needed a set of criteria to determine which products would be manufactured and which would not, as well as a new management function that would incorporate many related functions such as procurement, advertising, and sales into one department, the marketing department. It was also at this time that many firms realized that the company's purpose was no longer to manufacture a variety of products, but to satisfy their customers.

The change in company thinking or purpose from that of manufacturing products to that of satisfying customers was truly revolutionary and had many implications. Firms that see themselves as manufacturers of products use selling techniques that are preoccupied with converting products into cash. Firms that see themselves as marketers focus on satisfying the needs of buyers through the products that are sold, as well as all those functions associated with developing the product, delivering the product, and consuming the product. In short, selling focuses on the needs of the seller; marketing focuses on the needs of the buyer.

Theodore Levitt (1960) has pointed out that Henry Ford's development of the assembly line illustrates the difference between firms that focus on production (a production orientation) and those that focus on customers (a customer orientation). Ford is widely known as a production genius for developing the assembly line. Many incorrectly believe that the reduced manufacturing cost made possible by the assembly line allowed Ford to sell millions of $500 cars (a production orientation). However, Ford's thinking was actually the reverse. He invented the assembly line because he concluded that millions of buyers would be willing to pay $500 for an automobile (a customer orientation). His main task was to reduce manufacturing costs (in whatever way possible) so that he could sell cars at $500 and still make a profit. The assembly line was the result, not the cause, of his low price. As Ford himself put it:

> We first reduce the price to the point where we believe that more sales will result. Then we go ahead and try to make the prices. We do not bother about the costs. The new price forces the cost down . . . because what earthly use is it to know the cost if it tells you that you cannot manufacture at a price at which an article can be sold? But more to the point is the fact that, although one may calculate what a cost is, and of course all of our costs are carefully calculated, no one knows what a cost ought to be. One way of discovering . . . is to name a price so low as to force everybody in the place to the highest point of efficiency. (Ford, 1923)

In short, during the marketing department era, many companies changed their thinking or purpose from that of manufacturing products to that of satisfying customers. Firms with a *customer orientation* attempt to create satisfying products that customers will want to buy. Beginning in the 1960's some firms had implemented this customer-oriented philosophy to the point where the marketing department set the agenda for the entire company. These types of firms are referred to as *marketing companies.*

The Marketing Company Era Firms that have moved from simply having a marketing department that follows a customer orientation to having the marketing department guide the company's direction are called marketing companies. In marketing companies, the marketing department sets company operating policy, including technical research, procurement, production, advertising, and sales. A press release from Two-Ten News Network (1998) exemplifies the strategy of a marketing-driven firm:

> *Atlanta—AGCO Corporation, a leading worldwide designer, manufacturer and distributor of agricultural equipment, today announced management appointments to strengthen and expand its global marketing and sales functions. According to Robert J. Ratliff, Chairman of the Board and Chief Executive Officer of AGCO, "These appointments will strengthen AGCO's position as a marketing-driven*

company. Marketing is the key function that has been the basis of AGCO's worldwide profitable growth. AGCO's strategy is to vigorously expand our sales and marketing strength around the world while implementing aggressive reductions to manufacturing costs to adjust to industry conditions. These appointments reflect AGCO's commitment to further expand AGCO's market leadership around the world and to maintain profitability."

As can be seen with AGCO, marketing is the basic motivating force for all activities within the corporation, from finance to sales to production, with the objective of satisfying the needs of the customer. Firms that practice this philosophy of bringing all departments together with the objective of satisfying their customers are practicing the *marketing concept.*

The marketing concept states that if all of the organization's functions are focused on customer needs, profits can be achieved by satisfying those needs. The satisfaction of customer needs can be accomplished through product changes, pricing adjustments, increased customer service, distribution changes, and the like.

Today, some firms take the marketing concept one step further by establishing long-term relationships with their customers, as discussed in the next section.

The Relationship Marketing Era Relationship marketing is the process whereby a firm builds long-term satisfying relations with its customers in order to retain the customers' loyalty in buying the firm's products. Philip Kotler (1997), a noted author of several books on marketing, has pointed out that the need for customer retention is demonstrated by the fact that the cost of attracting a new customer is estimated to be five times the cost of keeping a current customer happy.

One example of a firm that practices relationship marketing to retain customer loyalty is Saturn. Saturn has been able to retain 60 percent of their customers—meaning that 60 percent are repeat buyers. Melissa Herron (1996) explained that Saturn accomplishes relationship marketing by taking a different view of what it sells. Traditionally, car manufacturers have sold cars, but

Saturn expanded its product to include the entire experience—the shopping experience, the buying experience, and the ownership experience. Even if its cars were no better than competitors', the company decided, the entire buying and consumption experience would be better.

This philosophy is made clear in the company's values and mission statement. Saturn's values include commitment to customer enthusiasm, commitment to excel, teamwork, trust and respect to the individual, and continuous improvement. Their mission statement also supports their relationship building philosophy:

"Earn the loyalty of Saturn owners and grow our family by developing and marketing U.S. manufactured vehicles that are world leaders in quality, cost and customer enthusiasm through the integration of people, technology and business systems."

This relationship-oriented strategy is most obvious in the company's advertising and in its pricing philosophy. For example, most car ads highlight the car's features: it's sexy and it's fast or it's comfortable and it's safe. In Saturn ads however, the car is secondary. Greg Martin, a Saturn official, explained that most car companies zero in on the four wheels and the engine, while Saturn's ads tell you you're going to get a good car and you're going to get treated well. The company-customer relationship is enhanced through trust, respect, and quality products (Herron, 1996).

In summary, relationship marketing takes the marketing concept one step further by establishing long-term, trusting, win-win relations with customers in order to satisfy the customer, foster customer loyalty and encourage repeat buying.

CONCLUSION

This article has presented a historical overview of the evolution of marketing in the United States, from just after the Civil War until the present. In general, companies have determined that, in order to be successful, they must become less internally focused and more externally focused (on the customer). This trend in company thought has extended to the point where many firms now see themselves as long-term partners with their customers. As information technology becomes more advanced, marketers will be able to become more acutely aware of their customers' needs and more quickly able to provide goods and services to satisfy those needs.

BIBLIOGRAPHY

Ford, Henry. (1923). *My Life and My Work*. New York: Doubleday, Page and Company.

Haber, Samuel. (1964). *Efficiency and Uplift*. Chicago: University of Chicago Press.

Herron, Melissa. "Masters of Marketing; Saturn: Enthusiasm Sells." *Builder Online*. http://209.143.248.128/monthly/1996/sep/marid.htx. September 1996.

Keith, Robert J. (1960). "The Marketing Revolution." *Journal of Marketing* 24:35-38.

Kinnear, Thomas C., Bernhardt, Kenneth L., and Krentler, Kathleen A. (1995). *Principles of Marketing*, 4th ed. New York: HarperCollins.

Kotler, Philip. (1997). *Marketing Management: Analysis, Planning, Implementation, and Control*, 9th ed. Upper Saddle River, NJ: Prentice-Hall.

Levitt, Theodore. (1960). "Marketing Myopia." *Harvard Business Review* July-August: 45-56.

Porter, Michael. (1980). *Competitive Strategy*. New York: Free Press.

Schultz, Stanley K. *The Crash and the Great Depression*. http://us.history.wisc.edu/hist102/lectures/lecture18.html. 1999.

Two-Ten News Network. http://releases.twoten.press.net/releases/date/1998/09/22/BUSINESS-Agco.html. September 22, 1998.

JAMES E. STODDARD

MARKETING MIX

The term *marketing mix* refers to the four major areas of decision making in the marketing process that are blended to obtain the results desired by the organization. The four elements of the marketing mix are sometimes referred to the four Ps of marketing. The marketing mix shapes the role of marketing within all types of organizations, both profit and nonprofit. Each element in the marketing mix—product, price, promotion, and place—consists of numerous subelements.

Marketing managers make numerous decisions based on the various subelements of the marketing mix, all in an attempt to satisfy the needs and wants of consumers.

PRODUCT

The first element in the marketing mix is the product. A product is any combination of goods and services offered to satisfy the needs and wants of consumers. Thus, a product is anything tangible or intangible that can be offered for purchase or use by consumers. A tangible product is one that consumers can actually touch, such as a computer. An intangible product is a service that cannot be touched, such as computer repair, income tax preparation, or an office call. Other examples of products include places and ideas. For example, the state tourism department in New Hampshire might promote New Hampshire as a great place to visit and by doing so stimulate the economy. Cities also promote themselves as great places to live and work. For example, the slogan touted by the Chamber of Commerce in San Bernardino, California, is "It's a great day in San Bernardino." The idea of wearing seat belts has been promoted as a way of saving lives, as has the idea of recycling to help reduce the amount of garbage placed in landfills.

Typically, a product is divided into three basic levels. The first level is often called the core product, what the consumer actually buys in terms of benefits. For example, consumers don't just buy trucks. Rather, consumers buy the benefit that trucks offer, like being able to get around in deep snow in the winter. Next is the second level, or actual product, that is built around the core product. The actual product consists of the brand name, features, packaging, parts, and styling. These components provided the benefits to consumers that they seek at the first level. The final, or third, level of the product is the augmented component. The augmented component includes additional services and benefits that surround the first two levels of the product. Examples of augmented product components are technical assistance in operating the product and service agreements.

Products are classified by how long they can be used—durability—and their tangibility. Products that can be used repeatedly over a long period of time are called durable goods. Examples of durable goods include automobiles, furniture, and houses. By contrast, goods that are normally used or consumed quickly are called nondurable goods. Some examples of nondurable goods are food, soap, and soft drinks. In addition, services are activities and benefits that are also involved in the exchange process but are intangible because they cannot be held or touched. Examples of intangible services included eye exams and automobile repair.

Another way to categorize products is by their users. Products are classified as either consumer or industrial goods. Consumer goods are purchased by final consumers for their personal consumption. Final consumers are sometimes called end users. The shopping patterns of consumers are also used to classify products. Products sold to the final consumer are arranged as follows: convenience, shopping, specialty, and unsought goods. Convenience goods are products and services that consumers buy frequently and with little effort. Most convenience goods are easily obtainable and low-priced, items such as bread, candy, milk, and shampoo. Convenience goods can be further divided into staple, impulse, and emergency goods. Staple goods are products, such as bread and milk, that consumers buy on a consistent basis. Impulse goods like candy and magazines are products that require little planning or search effort because they are normally available in many places. Emergency goods are bought when consumers have a pressing need. An example of an emergency good would be a shovel during the first snowstorm of the winter.

Shopping goods are those products that consumers compare during the selection and purchase process. Typically, factors such as price, quality, style, and suitability are used as bases of comparison. With shopping goods, consumers usually take considerable time and effort in gathering information and making comparisons among products. Major appliances such as refrigerators and televisions are typical shopping goods. Shopping goods are further divided into uniform and nonuniform categories. Uniform shopping goods are those goods that are similar in quality but differ in price. Consumers will try to justify price differences by focusing on product features. Nonuniform goods are those goods that differ in both quality and price.

Specialty goods are products with distinctive characteristics or brand identification for which consumers expend exceptional buying effort. Specialty goods include specific brands and types of products. Typically, buyers do not compare specialty goods with other similar products because the products are unique. Unsought goods are those products or services that consumers are not readily aware of or do not normally consider buying. Life insurance policies and burial plots are examples of unsought goods. Often, unsought goods require considerable promotional efforts on the part of the seller in order to attract the interest of consumers.

Industrial goods are those products used in the production of other goods. Examples of industrial goods include accessory equipment, component parts, installations, operating supplies, raw materials, and services. Accessory equipment refers to movable items and small office equipment items that never become part of a final product. Office furniture and fax machines are examples of accessory equipment. Component parts are products that are turned into a component of the final product that does not require further processing. Component parts are frequently custom-made for the final product of which they will become a part. For example, a computer chip could be produced by one manufacturer for use in computers of other manufacturers. Installations are capital goods that are usually very expensive but have a long useful life. Trucks, power generators, and mainframe computers are examples of installations. Operating supplies are similar to accessory equipment in that they do not become part of the finished product. Operating supplies include items necessary to maintain and operate the overall firm, such as cleaners, file folders, paper, and pens. Raw materials are goods sold in their original form before being processed for use in other products. Crops, crude oil, iron ore, and logs are examples of raw materials in need of further processing before being used in products. The last category of industrial goods is services. Organizations sometimes require the use of services, just as individuals do. Examples of services sought by organizations include maintenance and repair and legal counsel.

PRICE

The second element in marketing mix is price. Price is simply the amount of money that consumers are willing to pay for a product or service. In earlier times, the price was determined through a barter process between sellers and purchasers. In modern times, pricing methods and strategies have taken a number of forms.

Pricing new products and pricing existing products require the use of different strategies. For example, when pricing a new product, businesses can use either market-penetration pricing or a price-skimming strategy. A market-penetration pricing strategy involves establishing a low product price to attract a large number of customers. By contrast, a price-skimming strategy is used when a high price is established in order to recover the cost of a new product development as quickly as possible. Manufacturers of computers, videocassette recorders, and other technical items with high development costs frequently use a price-skimming strategy.

Pricing objectives are established as a subset of an organization's overall objectives. As a component of the overall business objectives, pricing objectives usually take one of four forms: profitability, volume, meeting the competition, and prestige. Profitability pricing objectives mean that the firm focuses mainly on maximizing its profit. Under profitability objectives, a company increases its prices so that additional revenue equals the increase in product production costs. Using volume pricing objectives, a company aims to maximize sales volume within a given specific profit margin. The focus of volume pricing objectives is on increasing sales rather than on an immediate increase in profits. Meeting the price

level of competitors is another pricing strategy. With a meeting-the-competition pricing strategy, the focus is less on price and more on nonprice competition items such as location and service. With prestige pricing, products are priced high and consumers purchase them as status symbols.

In addition to the four basic pricing strategies, there are five price-adjustment strategies: discount pricing and allowances, discriminatory pricing, geographical pricing, promotional pricing, and psychological pricing. Discount pricing and allowances include cash discounts, functional discounts, seasonal discounts, trade-in allowances, and promotional allowances. Discriminatory pricing occurs when companies sell products or services at two or more prices. These price differences may be based on variables such as age of the customer, location of sale, organization membership, time of day, or season. Geographical pricing is based on the location of the customers. Products may be priced differently in distinct regions of a target area because of demand differences. Promotional pricing happens when a company temporarily prices products below the list price or below cost. Products priced below cost are sometimes called loss leaders. The goal of promotional pricing is to increase short-term sales. Psychological pricing considers prices by looking at the psychological aspects of price. For example, consumers frequently perceive a relationship between product price and product quality.

PROMOTION

Promotion is the third element in the marketing mix. Promotion is a communication process that takes place between a business and its various publics. Publics are those individuals and organizations that have an interest in what the business produces and offers for sale. Thus, in order to be effective, businesses need to plan promotional activities with the communication process in mind. The elements of the communication process are: sender, encoding, message, media, decoding, receiver, feedback, and noise. The sender refers to the business that is sending a promotional message to a potential customer. Encoding involves putting a message or promotional activity into some form. Symbols are formed to represent the message. The sender transmits these symbols through some form of media. Media are methods the sender uses to transmit the message to the receiver. Decoding is the process by which the receiver translates the meaning of the symbols sent by the sender into a form that can be understood. The receiver is the intended recipient of the message. Feedback occurs when the receiver communicates back to the sender. Noise is anything that interferes with the communication process.

There are four basic promotion tools: advertising, sales promotion, public relations, and personal selling. Each promotion tool has its own unique characteristics and function. For instance, advertising is described as paid, nonpersonal communication by an organization using various media to reach its various publics. The purpose of advertising is to inform or persuade a targeted audience to purchase a product or service, visit a location, or adopt an idea. Advertising is also classified as to its intended purpose. The purpose of product advertising is to secure the purchase of the product by consumers. The purpose of institutional advertising is to promote the image or philosophy of a company. Advertising can be further divided into six subcategories: pioneering, competitive, comparative, advocacy, reminder, and cooperative advertising. Pioneering advertising aims to develop primary demand for the product or product category. Competitive advertising seeks to develop demand for a specific product or service. Comparative advertising seeks to contrast one product or service with another. Advocacy advertising is an organizational approach designed to support socially responsible activities, causes, or messages such as helping feed the homeless. Reminder advertising seeks to keep a product or company name in the mind of consumers by its repetitive nature. Cooperative advertising occurs when wholesalers and retailers work with product manufacturers to produce a single advertising campaign and share the costs. Advantages of advertising include the ability to reach a large group or audience at a relatively low cost per individual contacted. Further, advertising allows organizations to control the message, which means the message can be adapted to either a mass or a specific target audience. Disadvantages of advertising include difficulty in measuring results and the inability to close sales because there is no personal contact between the organization and consumers.

The second promotional tool is sales promotion. Sales promotions are short-term incentives used to encourage consumers to purchase a product or service. There are three basic categories of sales promotion: consumer, trade, and business. Consumer promotion tools include such items as free samples, coupons, rebates, price packs, premiums, patronage rewards, point-of-purchase coupons, contests, sweepstakes, and games. Trade-promotion tools include discounts and allowances directed at wholesalers and retailers. Business-promotion tools include conventions and trade shows. Sales promotion has several advantages over other promotional tools in that it can produce a more immediate consumer response, attract more attention and create product awareness, measure the results, and increase short-term sales.

Public relations is the third promotional tool. An organization builds positive public relations with various groups by obtaining favorable publicity, establishing a good corporate image, and handling or heading off unfavorable rumors, stories, and events. Organizations have at their disposal a variety of tools, such as press releases, product publicity, official communications, lobbying, and counseling to develop image. Public relations tools are effective in developing a positive attitude toward the organization and can enhance the credibility of a product. Public relations activities have the drawback that they may not provide an accurate measure of their influence on sales as they are not directly involved with specific marketing goals.

The last promotional tool is personal selling. Personal selling involves an interpersonal influence and information-exchange process. There are seven general steps in the personal selling process: prospecting and qualifying, pre-approach, approach, presentation and demonstration, handling objections, closing, and follow-up. Personal selling does provide a measurement of effectiveness because a more immediate response is received by the salesperson from the customer. Another advantage of personal selling is that salespeople can shape the information presented to fit the needs of the customer. Disadvantages are the high cost per contact and dependence on the ability of the salesperson.

For a promotion to be effective, organizations should blend all four promotion tools together in order to achieve the promotional mix. The promotional mix can be influenced by a number of factors, including the product itself, the product life-cycle stage, and budget. Within the promotional mix there are two promotional strategies: pull and push. Pull strategy occurs when the manufacturer tries to establish final-consumer demand and thus pull the product through the wholesalers and retailers. Advertising and sales promotion are most frequently used in a pulling strategy. Pushing strategy, in contrast, occurs when a seller tries to develop demand through incentives to wholesalers and retailers, who in turn place the product in front of consumers.

PLACE

The fourth element of the marketing mix is place. Place refers to having the right product, in the right location, at the right time to be purchased by consumers. This proper placement of products is done through middle people called the *channel of distribution*. The channel of distribution is comprised of interdependent manufacturers, wholesalers, and retailers. These groups are involved with making a product or service available for use or consumption. Each participant in the channel of distribution is concerned with three basic utilities: time, place, and possession. Time utility refers to having a product available at the time that will satisfy the needs of consumers. Place utility occurs when a firm provides satisfaction by locating products where they can be easily acquired by consumers. The last utility is possession utility, which means that whole-

salers and retailers in the channel of distribution provide services to consumers with as few obstacles as possible.

Channels of distribution operate by one of two methods: conventional distribution or a vertical marketing system. In the conventional distribution channel, there can be one or more independent product manufacturers, wholesalers, and retailers in a channel. The vertical marketing system requires that producers, wholesalers, and retailers to work together to avoid channel conflicts.

How manufacturers store, handle, and move products to customers at the right time and at the right place is referred to as *physical distribution*. In considering physical distribution, manufacturers need to review issues such as distribution objectives, product transportation, and product warehousing. Choosing the mode of transportation requires an understanding of each possible method: rail, truck, water, pipeline, and air. Rail transportation is typically used to ship farm products, minerals, sand, chemicals, and automobiles. Truck transportation is most suitable for transporting clothing, food, books, computers, and paper goods. Water transportation is good for oil, grain, sand, gravel, metallic ores, coal, and other heavy items. Pipeline transportation is best when shipping products such as oil or chemicals. Air transport works best when moving technical instruments, perishable products, and important documents.

Another issue of concern to manufacturers is the level of product distribution. Normally manufacturers select from one of three levels of distribution: intensive, selective, or exclusive. Intensive distribution occurs when manufacturers distribute products through all wholesalers or retailers that want to offer their products. Selective distribution occurs when manufacturers distribute products through a limited, select number of wholesalers and retailers. Under exclusive distribution, only a single wholesaler or retailer is allowed to sell the product in a specific geographic area.

BIBLIOGRAPHY

Boone, Louise E., and Kurtz, David L. (1992). *Contemporary Marketing*, 7th ed. New York, NY: Dryen/Harcourt Brace.

Churchill, Gilbert A., and Peter, Paul J. (1995). *Marketing: Creating Value for Customers*. Boston MA: Irwin.

Farese, Lois, Kimbrell, Grady, and Woloszyk, Carl (1991). *Marketing Essentials*. Mission Hills, CA: Glencoe/McGraw-Hill.

Kotler, Philip, and Armstrong, Gary (1993). *Marketing: An Introduction*, 3d ed. Englewood Cliffs, NJ: Prentice-Hall.

Semenik, Richard J., and Bamossy, Gary J. (1995). *Principles of Marketing: A Global Perspective*, 2d ed. Cincinnati, OH: South-Western.

ALLEN D. TRUELL

MARKETING RESEARCH

Accelerating product cycles, easy access to information on products and services, highly discerning consumers, and fierce competition among companies are all a reality in the world of business. Too many companies are chasing too few consumers. In his book "Kotler on Marketing: How to Creat, Win, and Dominate Markets," Philip Kotler, marketing guru and a professor at Northwestern University's Kellogg Graduate School of Management, discusses what a business has to do to be successful. He wrote, "The premium will go to those companies that invent new ways to create, communicate and deliver value to their target markets" (quoted in Mendenhall, 1999, p. 52).

Knowing, understanding, and responding to your target market is more important than ever. And this requires information—good information. Good information can lead to successful products and services. Good information is the result of market research.

WHAT IS MARKETING RESEARCH?

According to the Marketing Research Association (2000), marketing research is defined as follows:

"Marketing research is the function which links the consumer, customer, and public to the marketer through information—information used to identify and define marketing opportunities and problems; generate, refine, and evaluate marketing actions; monitor marketing performance; and improve understanding of marketing as a process.

"Marketing research specifies the information required to address these issues; designs the method of collecting information; manages and implements the data collection process; analyzes the results; and communicates the findings, recommendations and their implications."

Marketing research is a $1.3-billion-dollar-a-year industry. The industry is growing at over 10 percent a year, with profits running at a similar level (Lee, 1999). Marketing research provides, analyzes, and interprets information for manufacturers on how consumers view their products and services and on how they can better meet consumer needs. The ultimate goal is to please the consumer in order to get, or keep, the consumer's business.

HISTORY OF MARKETING RESEARCH

Pioneers. Marketing research as an organized business activity began between 1910 and 1920. The appointment of Charles Collidge Parlin as manager of the Commercial Research Division of the Advertising Department of the Curtis Publishing Company in 1911 is generally noted to be the beginning of marketing research. Parlin's success led several industrial firms and advertising media to establish research divisions. In 1915, the United States Rubber Company hired Dr. Paul H. Nystrom to manage a newly established Department of Commercial Research. In 1917, Swift and Company hired Dr. Louis D. H. Weld from Yale University to become manager of their Commercial Research Department.

In 1919, Professor C.S. Duncan of the University of Chicago published *Commercial Research: An Outline of Working Principles*, considered to be the first major book on commercial research. In 1921, Percival White's *Market Analysis* was published; the first research book to gain a large readership, it went through several editions. *Market Research and Analysis* by Lyndon O. Brown, published in 1937, became one of the

Phone surveyors are often used to collect marketing data.

most popular college textbooks of the period, reflecting the growing interest in marketing research on the college campus. After 1940, numerous research textbooks were published and the number of business schools offering research courses grew rapidly.

Following World War II, the growth of marketing research increased dramatically. By 1948, more than two hundred marketing research organizations had been created in the United States. An estimated $50 million was spent on marketing research activities in 1947. Over the next three decades this expenditure level increased more than tenfold (Kinnear, 1991).

Methodological Development. Major advances in marketing research methodology were made from 1910 to 1920. Questionnaires, or surveys, became a popular method of data collection. With the growth of survey research came improvements in questionnaire design and question construction. During the 1930s, sampling

became a serious methodological issue. Modern approaches to probability sampling slowly gained acceptance in this period.

From 1950 through the early 1960s, methodological innovations occurred at a fairly steady pace. At this time, a major development occurred: the commercial availability of large-scale digital computers. The computer was responsible for rapidly increasing the pace of methodological innovation, especially in the area of quantitative marketing research. As the field of marketing research attracted increasing interest, two new journals began publication in the 1960s: the *Journal of Marketing Research* and the *Journal of Advertising Research* (Kinnear, 1991).

The many technological advances in computers in the 1990s had a major impact on many aspects of the marketing research profession. These innovations included checkout scanners in supermarkets, computer-assisted telephone interviewing, data analysis by computers, data collection on the Internet, and Web-based surveys.

TYPES OF MARKETING RESEARCH

Marketing research can be classified as exploratory research, conclusive research, and performance-monitoring research. The stage in the decision-making process for which the information is needed determines the type of research required.

Exploratory research is appropriate for the early stages of the decision-making process. This research is usually designed to provide a preliminary investigation of the situation with a minimum expenditure of cost and time. A variety of approaches to this research are used, including use of secondary data sources, observation, interviews with experts, and case histories.

Conclusive research provides information that helps the manager evaluate and select a course of action. This involves clearly defined research objectives and information needs. Some approaches to this research include surveys, experiments, observations, and simulation. Conclusive research can be subclassified into descriptive research and causal research.

Descriptive research, as its name suggests, is designed to describe something—for example, the characteristics of consumers of a certain product; the degree to which the use of a product varies with age, income, or sex; or the number of people who saw a specific TV commercial. A majority of marketing research studies are of this type (Boyd and Westface, 1992).

Causal research is designed to gather evidence regarding the cause-and-effect relationships that exist in the marketing system. For example, if a company reduces the price of a product and then unit sales of the product increase, causal research would show whether this effect was due to the price reduction or some other reason. Causal research must be designed in such a way that the evidence regarding causality is clear. The main sources of data for causal research are interrogating respondents through surveys and conducting experiments.

Performance-monitoring research provides information regarding the status of the marketing system; it signals the presence of potential problems or opportunities. This is an essential element in the control of a business's marketing programs. The data sources for performance-monitoring research include interrogation of respondents, secondary data, and observation.

THE MARKETING RESEARCH PROCESS

The marketing research process is comprised of a series of steps called the research process. To conduct a research project effectively, it is important to anticipate all the steps and recognize their interdependence.

Need for Information. The first step in the research process is establishing the need for marketing research information: The researcher must thoroughly understand why the information is needed. The manager is responsible for explaining the situation surrounding the request for information and establishing that the research information will assist in the decision-making process. Establishing the need for research information is a critical and difficult phase of the research process. Too often the importance of this initial step is overlooked, which results in research findings that are not decision-oriented.

Research Objectives. Once the need for research information has been clearly defined, the researcher must specify the objectives of the proposed research and develop a specific list of information needs. Research objectives answer the question "Why is this project being conducted?" The answer could be as broad as the determination of the amount of effort needed to increase the company's market share by 5 percent or as specific as the determination of the most preferred of five moisturizers by women in southern California. Only when the researcher knows the problem that management wants to solve can the research project be designed to provide the pertinent information.

The difficult part of establishing research objectives is the conflict that often exists between the value of information and the research budget. Since each piece of information has some cost associated with it, whether it is the cost of the account manager's travel expenses or the cost of having an outside agency perform a telephone

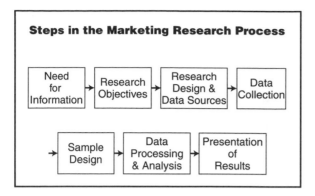

Steps in the Marketing Research Process

Need for Information → Research Objectives → Research Design & Data Sources → Data Collection → Sample Design → Data Processing & Analysis → Presentation of Results

Figure 1

survey, each piece must be evaluated in terms of its value with respect to the needed decision.

Research Design and Data Sources. The next step in the research process is to design the formal research project and identify the appropriate sources of data for the study. A research design is the framework that specifies the type of information to be collected, the sources of the data, and the data-collection procedures. Although there are many different ways to classify designs, one that gives a clear overview of the various procedures is based on three methods of generating primary data: experimentation, observation, and survey.

Experimentation involves establishing a controlled experiment or model that simulates the real-world marketing situation being investigated. In the observation method, the primary data result from observing the respondents doing something. The survey method involves collecting the primary data by questioning a certain number of people. These are the most widely used methods of obtaining primary data (Hisrich, 1990).

To determine the data sources for the research project, an assessment must first be made of the amount and type of data presently available. These data are called secondary data—data already gathered and available, having been accumulated previously for a different purpose. Although these data are assembled quickly and often at a low cost, sometimes they do not satisfy the research objectives.

There are two types of secondary data: internal (data originating within the firm) and external (published data originating outside the firm). Internal secondary data are all the data originating within the firm that were collected for some purpose other than the objective currently being addressed. Two of the most important types of internal data are sales and cost data.

After the internal secondary data have been examined, additional information can be obtained from published external secondary data. The main sources of external data are (1) the Internet, (2) the government, (3) trade, business, and professional associations, (4) the media, (5) trade journals, (6) universities and foundations, (7) corporate annual reports, and (8) commercial data services. Information obtained from any of these sources must be examined carefully to make sure that it fits the particular needs of the researcher.

1. The Internet can provide links to many sources of information, quickly and easily. Searching the Web or visiting a business library's Web site are ways to become familiar with the types of resources available. Two Web sites that are useful in evaluating potential research resources are the New York Public Library's Science, Industry, and Business Library at www.nypl/org/research/-sibl/index.html and the University of Michigan's Document Center at www.lib.umich.edu/libhome/Documents.center/stats.html.

2. The federal government is by far the largest source of marketing data. Although the data are available at a very low price, if any, once they are located, there is often a cost and time commitment in obtaining it. Some government publications are highly specialized, referring to specific studies of products. Other data are more general in nature. State and local governments also provide information. Data such as birth and death records and information on real estate sales and assessed values are public information and

can be obtained from the specific state or local agency.

3. Trade, business, and professional associations also have general data on the various activities and sales of their constituency. For example, the National Kitchen & Bath Association will have general information on kitchen and bath design professionals, research design strategies, and remodeling. Although such data will not be company-specific, they are useful in gaining an overall perspective on the industry. Address and membership information for all associations can be found in the *Encyclopedia of Associations*, updated annually.

4. Most magazines, newspapers, and radio and television stations have marketing data available on their audience. Also, media perform periodic market surveys of buying patterns and demographic information in their market area. For example, the Boston *Globe* does a demographic study of its readers in order to give advertisers a better understanding of the marketing potential of their area.

5. Trade journals also provide a wide variety of marketing and sales data on the areas they cover. For example, if market research were needed in the area of computers, then trade journals such as *Computer World*, *InformationWeek*, and *PC Magazine* should be checked for any pertinent information.

6. Universities and foundations perform a variety of research projects. In addition to special studies supported by grants from the government, universities publish general research findings of interest to the business community through their research bureaus and institutes.

7. Corporate annual and 10-K reports are also useful sources of information on specific companies or general industry trends. These reports may not provide great detail; however, a general picture of the nature and scope of the firms in an industry as well as their general direction can be constructed.

8. There are many firms offering marketing research and commercial data services. Some provide custom research; they design the research project specifically to meet the client's needs. This can be expensive. Others, such as Nielsen Media Research, offer standardized information, compiled regularly and made available to clients on a subscription basis.

After all the secondary data sources have been checked and the needed data have not been found, the third aspect of a research projected begins—the collection of data through primary research. Primary research can be best looked at in terms of three areas: data collection, sample design, and data processing and analysis.

Data Collection. If it has been determined that the required data are not currently available, then the next step is to collect new data. To develop the data-collection procedure, the researcher must establish an effective link between the information needs and the questions to be asked or the observations to be recorded. The process of collecting data is critical, since it typically involves a large proportion of the research budget. The most widely used methods of data collection are focus groups, surveys, or interviews.

Focus groups are often used to collect primary data. A focus group consists of a discussion, usually lasting one and a half to two hours, with eight to twelve individuals and a moderator who is intent on encouraging in-depth discussion of a topic or product. The discussion allows for flexibility and provides broad, in-depth knowledge that cannot be obtained through any other research method.

Surveys, also known as questionnaires, are the most common instrument for data collection. A survey consists of a set of questions presented to respondents for their answers. Surveys need to be carefully developed, tested, and debugged before they are used; they can be administered over the phone, through the mail, via e-mail, or on the Web. Web-based surveys are becoming very common and popular because of their lower cost, convenience, and the increased honesty in responses (Rasmusson, 1999). Web surveys don't replace the traditional techniques, but they can be an effective choice for companies big and small.

Primary research data is often obtained by interviews, either in person or over the telephone. For example, one might personally interview consumers to determine their opinion of a new line of low-fat foods or personally interview a few executives to determine their opinion of a nationally known advertising agency. An advantage of personal interviews is that the interviewer can adapt the question to the specific situation at hand. A limitation to this method is that the interviewer can introduce bias into the process by asking leading questions or by giving some indication of the preferred answer. A lot of time, supervision, and interviewer training are needed to implement personal interviews successfully.

Sample Design. When research is being conducted, it is important to determine the appropriate target population of the research—the group of people possessing characteristics relevant to the research problem from whom information will be obtained. Although this may appear to be easy, it is often one of the most difficult tasks in a marketing research project because of the wide variety of factors entering into the determination. For example, it might be important that only recent users of the product be surveyed. Or perhaps the purchasers of the product, not the users, should be the focus of the research.

Once the target population is determined, a decision is needed on how best to represent this population within the time and cost constraints of the research budget. Because there are many different methods used to draw this *sample*—the group of units composed of nonoverlapping elements that are representative of the population from which it is drawn—the best one needs to be chosen for the specific research project.

Data Processing and Analysis. After the data are collected, the processing begins, which includes the functions of editing and coding. Editing involves reviewing the data forms to ensure legibility, consistency, and completeness. Coding involves establishing categories for responses or groups of responses so that numerals can be used to represent the categories (Kinnear, 1991).

It is important that the data analysis be consistent with the requirements of the information needs identified when the research objectives were defined. Data analysis is usually performed with an appropriate software application. This data analysis, whether done by simple numeric counting or by complex computer-assisted analytical techniques, should provide meaningful information appropriate for managerial decisions.

Presentation of Results After the data have been collected and analyzed, the final aspect of the research project can be generated—the development of the appropriate conclusions and recommendations. This is the most important part of the project, but it does not always receive the proper attention. The research results are typically communicated to the manager through a written report and oral presentation. The research findings should be presented in a clear, simple format and be accompanied by appropriate support material. The best research methodology in the world will be useless to managers if they cannot understand the research report. Some preparation guidelines for the written and oral reports are:

- Consider the audience
- Be concise, yet complete
- Be objective, yet effective

The findings should address the information needs of the decision situation. The final measure of the value of the research project is whether or not the findings are successfully implemented in the company.

THE VALUE OF MARKETING RESEARCH

Marketing research has, in a way, pioneered the move toward the broader view of marketing.

Marketing research serves as a coordinating factor between marketing and the other functions of a business, such as engineering, manufacturing, accounting, and finance. This integration has the effect of enhancing the importance of marketing research to the corporation as a whole.

Marketing research will continue to play a key role in organizations in the twenty-first century. Technology will enable marketing research to take the lead in providing useful information for effective business decisions. The Internet's role in marketing research will continue to grow because it provides a quick, cost-effective way of collecting and disseminating data. Market researchers will continue their evolution from supplying "market and opinion research" to a more strategic position of supplying information, consulting, and exchanging information with consumers (Chadwick, 1998). Companies that take advantage of marketing research and view it as a valuable business component will be the companies that survive and thrive.

BIBLIOGRAPHY

Boyd, Harper W., and Westfall, Ralph. (1972). *Marketing Research: Text and Cases*. Homewood, IL: Irwin.

Chadwick, Simon. (1998). "The Research Industry Grows Up—and Out." *Marketing News*. p. 9.

Hisrich, Robert D. (1990). *Marketing*. New York: Barron's.

Lee, Julian. (1999). "Research Means Business." *Campaign* September 10: 37.

Kinnear, Thomas C., and Taylor, James R. (1991). *Marketing Research: An Applied Approach*. New York: McGraw-Hill.

Marketing Research Association. (2000). May. http://www.mra-net.org/industry/definition_mr.cfm.

Mendenhall, Robert. (1999). "Kotler's Latest Rich in Information." *Business Marketing*, December 1: 52.

Rasmusson, Erika. (1999). "Questions That Get Answers." *Sales & Marketing Management*, February: 71.

CHRISTINE F. LATINO

MARKET SEGMENTATION

Market segmentation is one of two general approaches to marketing; the other is mass-marketing. In the mass-marketing approach, businesses look at the total market as though all of its parts were the same and market accordingly. In the market-segmentation approach, the total market is viewed as being made up of several smaller segments, each different from the other. This approach enables businesses to identify one or more appealing segments to which they can profitably target their products and marketing efforts.

The market-segmentation process involves multiple steps (Figure 1). The first is to define the market in terms of the product's end users and their needs. The second is to divide the market into groups on the basis of their characteristics and buying behaviors.

Possible bases for dividing a total market are different for consumer markets than for industrial markets. The most common elements used to separate consumer markets are demographic factors, psychographic characteristics, geographic location, and perceived product benefits.

Demographic segmentation involves dividing the market on the basis of statistical differences in personal characteristics, such as age, gender, race, income, life stage, occupation, and education level. Clothing manufacturers, for example, segment on the basis of age groups such as teenagers, young adults, and mature adults. Jewelers use gender to divide markets. Cosmetics and hair care companies may use race as a factor; home builders, life stage; professional periodicals, occupation; and so on.

Psychographic segmentation is based on traits, attitudes, interests, or lifestyles of potential customer groups. Companies marketing new products, for instance, seek to identify customer groups that are positively disposed to new ideas. Firms marketing environmentally friendly products would single out segments with environmental concerns. Some financial institutions attempt to isolate and tap into groups with a strong interest in supporting their college, favorite sports team, or professional organization through logoed credit cards. Similarly, marketers of low-fat or low-calorie products try to identify and match their products with portions of the market that are health- or weight-conscious.

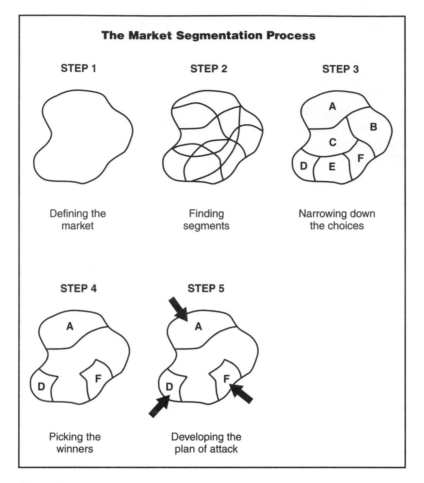

The Market Segmentation Process

STEP 1 — Defining the market

STEP 2 — Finding segments

STEP 3 — Narrowing down the choices

STEP 4 — Picking the winners

STEP 5 — Developing the plan of attack

Figure 1

SOURCE: Croft, Michael J. (1994). *Market Segmentation: A Step-By-Step Guide to Profitable New Business.* London: Routledge.

Geographic segmentation entails dividing the market on the basis of where people live. Divisions may be in terms of neighborhoods, cities, counties, states, regions, or even countries. Considerations related to geographic grouping may include the makeup of the areas, that is, urban, suburban, or rural; size of the area; climate; or population. For example, manufacturers of snow-removal equipment focus on identifying potential user segments in areas of heavy snow accumulation. Because many retail chains are dependent on high-volume traffic, they search for, and will only locate in, areas with a certain number of people per square mile.

Product-benefit segmentation is based on the perceived value or advantage consumers receive from a good or service over alternatives. Thus, markets can be partitioned in terms of the quality, performance, image, service, special features, or other benefits prospective consumers seek. A wide spectrum of businesses—from camera to shampoo to athletic footwear to automobile marketers—rely on this type of segmentation to match up with customers. Many companies even market similar products of different grades or different accompanying services to different groups on the basis of product-benefit preference.

Factors used to segment industrial markets are grouped along different lines than those used for consumer markets. Some are very different; some are similar. Industrial markets are often divided on the basis of *organizational* variables, such as type of business, company size, geographic location, or technological base. In other instances, they are segmented along *operational* lines such as products made or sold, related processes used, volume used, or end-user applications. In still other instances, differences in *purchase practices* provide the segmentation base. These differences include centralized versus decentralized purchasing; policy regarding number of vendors; buyer-seller relationships; and similarity of quality, service, or availability needs.

Although demographic, geographic, and organizational differences enable marketers to narrow their opportunities, they rarely provide enough specific information to make a decision on dividing the market. Psychographic data, operational lines, and, in particular, perceived consumer benefits and preferred business practices are better at pinpointing buyer groupings—but they must be considered against the broader background. Thus, the key is to gather information on and consider *all* pertinent segmentation bases before making a decision.

Once potential market segments are identified, the third step in the process is to reduce the pool to those that are (1) large enough to be worth pursuing, (2) potentially profitable, (3) reachable, and (4) likely to be responsive. The fourth step is to zero in on one or more segments that are the best targets for the company's product(s) or capacity to expand. After the selection is made, the business can then design a separate marketing mix for each market segment to be targeted.

Adopting a market-segmentation approach can benefit a company in several specific areas. First, it can give customer-driven direction to the management of current products. Second, it can result in more efficient use of marketing resources. Third, it can help identify new opportunities for growth and expansion. At the same

time, it can bring a company the broad benefit of a competitive advantage.

Adopting the market-segmentation approach can also be accompanied by some drawbacks. Particularly when multiple segments are targeted, both production and marketing costs can be more expensive than mass marketing. Different product models, for example, are required for each segment. Separate inventories must be maintained for each version. And different promotion may be required for each market. In addition, administrative expenses go up with the planning, implementation, and control of multiple marketing programs.

During the late 1960s, market segmentation moved ahead of mass marketing as the predominant marketing approach. In the following decades, societal changes and wider economic opportunity continually expanded the number of groups with specialized product needs and buying power. In response, businesses increasingly turned to the segmentation approach to capture and/or hold market share.

BIBLIOGRAPHY

Croft, Michael J. (1994). *Market Segmentation: A Step-By-Step Guide to Profitable New Business*. London: Routledge.

Dibb, Sally, and Simkin, Lyndon. (1996). *The Market Segmentation Workbook: Target Marketing for Marketing Managers*. London: Routledge.

Michman, Ronald D. (1991). *Lifestyle Market Segmentation*. New York: Praeger.

Weinstein, Art. (1994). *Market Segmentation: Using Demographics, Psychographics, and Other Niche Marketing Techniques to Predict Model Customer Behavior*. Chicago: Probus Publishing.

EARL C. MEYER
PATRICK M. GRAHAM

MARKET SHARE

(SEE: *Marketing Research*)

MARKUPS

(SEE: *Pricing*)

MASLOW'S HEIRARCHY OF NEEDS

(SEE: *Motivation*)

MASS MARKETING

Mass marketing is a marketing approach in which the marketer addresses all segments of the market as though they are the same. The approach results in a single marketing plan with the same mix of product, price, promotion, and place strategies for the entire market.

The appeal of mass marketing is in the potential for higher total profits. Companies that employ the system expect the larger profit to result from (1) expanded volume through lower prices and (2) reduced costs through economies of scale made possible by the increased volume. In order for the system to work, however, certain conditions must exist. One is that the product must have broad appeal and a few features that distinguish it from competing products. Another is that it must lend itself to mass production. In addition, the opportunity must exist, and the marketer must have the ability to communicate and distribute to the aggregate market.

THE EVOLUTION INTO MASS MARKETING

Mass marketing first emerged as a workable strategy in the 1880s. Prior to that time, local markets in the United States were geographically isolated, few products had brand recognition beyond their local area, and continuous process technology had not yet come into its own. Profits in the fragmented markets were based on a low volume/high price strategy.

Between 1880 and 1890, several things occurred that eliminated the barriers and enhanced the appeal of mass marketing. Both the railroad and telegraph systems were completed, thus providing the potential for nationwide distribution and communication. Mass-production tech-niques and equipment were refined and adapted to a variety of products. Additionally, the population was growing rapidly, the country was recovering from the Civil War, and the largest depression in U.S. history until that time was ending.

These favorable circumstances by themselves did not create mass marketing. Entrepreneurial vision, drive, organization, and resources had to be added to implement the strategy. From 1880 to 1920, early innovators in many different industries stepped forward to seize the opportunity. Although the total number was relatively small—one or a few per industry—the impact on the U.S. economy was enormous. Many of these pioneering marketers built national reputations for their brands and companies that continue today.

Two of the most widely recognized examples are Ford and Coca-Cola. Henry Ford applied the concept in the automobile industry. His Model T was conceived and marketed as a "universal" car—one that would meet the needs of all buyers. By adopting mass-production techniques and eliminating optional features, he was able to reduce costs and sell his product at an affordable price. The combination catapulted the Model T to the top of the market. Asa Candler was equally successful at using mass marketing in the soft-drink industry. Like Ford, he also viewed his product as being the only one that consumers needed. His initial mass-marketing efforts focused on an extensive national advertising campaign. As product recognition grew, he established a network of bottling operations throughout the county to facilitate sales and distribution. No product in history has matched Coca-Cola's total sales.

Other mass marketers of this era achieved success by focusing on one aspect of the approach. Manufacturers such as Quaker Oats, Proctor and Gamble, and Eastman Kodak used refined mass-production techniques to establish consistent product quality. Still other manufacturers, such as Singer Sewing Machine, developed integrated distribution systems to ensure reliable delivery to the market. In general merchandise retailing, Sears and Montgomery Ward developed a mass-marketing niche through mail order. Grocery retailer A&P, on the other hand, established its mass market through private branding and systematic operation of multiple stores.

Mass marketers continued their domination in major industries well into the 1960s. Many of them maintained essentially the same mix, while others expanded their use of the strategy. Sears and Montgomery Ward, for example, added store retailing in the 1920s. In the 1930s, supermarkets appeared with a different emphasis than previous grocery retailers—national brands. Over the next several decades, large discount stores came into prominence with a format similar to the supermarkets.

THE EVOLUTION FROM MASS MARKETING

The successes of mass marketers led to the appearance of an alternate approach to marketing. Potential competitors wanting a share of the large market had two options. One was to replicate the organization, promotion, and distribution systems of the company that had created the mass market. The other was to go after a part of the market that had unique needs by developing products specifically for them. For nearly all of the challengers, building an operation to parallel that of an entrenched industry giant was not profitable or realistic. As a result, most of them gravitated to the more attractive market-segmentation approach. (Figure 1 shows the different demand curves for mass marketing and market segmentation.)

General Motors used market segmentation as early as the 1920s when it produced different models for different groups of customers to compete with Ford. Pepsi made a series of attempts, beginning in the 1930s, to crack into Coca-Cola's market share through changes in product and targeted promotion strategy. In the 1940s, television provided a powerful tool for both new and old companies to reach segmented markets. By the 1960s, market segmentation had surpassed mass marketing as the primary approach.

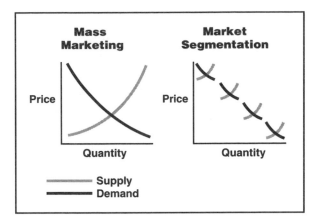

Figure 1

MASS MARKETING NOW AND IN THE FUTURE

In spite of the shift to market segmentation, mass marketing continues to be used in many situations and has potential for others. Products with broad appeal and few distinguishing characteristics—such as household cleaners, potato chips, and pain relievers—lend themselves to mass marketing just as they always have. At the same time, businesses that use mass marketing for their goods and services continue to look for ways to enlarge their markets by designing different appeals for noncustomers. Chewing gum, for example, is presented as an alternative to smoking. Utilities and credit cards offer special rates to entice potential high-volume customers. And discount retailers, such as Wal-Mart, match their mix of mass-marketed products to local customer bases.

Any current or future product that has mass-marketable attributes will likely be marketed by some form of the approach. In addition, the Internet provides a new medium for mass-marketing initiatives, and newly opened international markets offer a possible arena for mass-marketing opportunities.

(SEE ALSO: *Marketing; Marketing mix; Market segmentation; Strategic management*)

BIBLIOGRAPHY

Gardner, Dana. (1998). "E-Mail Status Is Elevated as Mass Marketing Tool." *InfoWorld* June 1:84.

Lakelin, Philip. (1999). "Mass Marketing the Internet." *Telecommunications* (International Edition) April:59-62.

Tedlow, Richard S. (1990). *New and Improved: The Story of Mass Marketing in America.*

Tedlow, Richard S. (1997). "The Beginning of Mass Marketing in America: George Eastman and Photography as a Case Study." *Journal of Macromarketing* Fall:67-81.

EARL C. MEYER

LORI A. DAILEY

MEETING MANAGEMENT

Meetings have been considered very important from time immemorial. In fact, it could be said that virtually all of the great events in history resulted from meetings. Meetings undoubtedly started when the first cave dwellers met to make crude hunting plans. Today, meetings are essential means for achieving the communication necessary for the operation of virtually all organizations, large and small.

Just exactly what is a meeting? A meeting is a number of people assembled together, usually at a prestated date and time, to discuss a topic for the purpose of presenting information, swaying opinion, formulating a decision, practicing a skill, and/or developing a plan of action. Those at the meeting may belong to the same group, to different groups, or perhaps not to any group at all. A meeting might be called by an individual or by an organization. Usually the people meeting convene together physically within a designated area. Sometimes, however, meetings are held by people thousands of miles apart via telephone conference calls or video conferencing.

MAJOR TYPES OF MEETINGS

Many kinds of meetings are held in business. Probably the most common are staff meetings, project team meetings, process and procedure meetings, and quarterly meetings. In most large companies, hundreds of these meetings may oc-cur weekly. Employees of all levels, including many below top-management level, attend them.

Staff meetings. Most supervisors and managers hold weekly or biweekly staff meetings with their "direct reports." In these meetings, they communicate higher-level decisions that have been made, discuss progress of the team toward departmental or company goals, and answer any staff members' questions.

Project team meetings. In most large companies, there are often project teams developed and facilitated by project managers. They are often comprised of people from different departments whose purpose is to design, develop, and/or implement a new product, process, or system. Project team members are assigned certain tasks to complete within stipulated time frames. Many of these people serve as part-time project resources in addition to performing their "regular" jobs.

Process and procedure meetings. These meetings are usually called to communicate new processes and/or procedures to a group of people who are affected. The communication includes an overview of the new process or procedure, the effect on that particular group of people, and steps to follow. A presentation-style format is used, with the presenter serving as the facilitator. At the end, a question-and-answer period usually follows.

Quarterly meetings. Quarterly earnings are announced at these meetings, along with detailed information on the financial status of the entire company and progress made toward strategic and departmental goals. Strategic direction changes are also communicated. A team of high-level executives ordinarily preside, using a presentation-style format.

METHODS OF ACHIEVING EFFECTIVE MEETINGS

In order for meetings to be successful, careful attention must be paid to a myriad of details. Two kinds of details are the most important: (1)

thorough planning of premeeting activities and (2) skillful leadership during the meeting itself.

Premeeting planning. These steps should be taken before the meeting starts:

1. It should be determined whether the meeting really needs to be held or whether the objectives could be achieved through phone calls or written communication.

2. An agenda should be prepared that includes the objective and the desired outcome of the meeting. Date, location, time of meeting, and a list of attendees should be included. A typical agenda includes the following: (a) call the meeting to order; (b) read the minutes of the previous meeting for approval, then correct errors and omissions; (c) hear reports of officers and committees; (d) discuss unfinished business; (e) take up new business; (f) adjourn. Announcements and other business not requiring a vote may come at the beginning or end of the meeting. If possible, the estimated time for each agenda item should be listed.

3. The agenda should be distributed to the participants, providing ample time for them to review the agenda/prework prior to the meeting. Applicable prework should be attached to the agenda. Their roles should be clear to participants: input providers, decision makers, or both. Persons who will be presenting reports should be contacted to ensure that they will be ready.

4. Who will facilitate (preside over) the meeting should be determined. This could be anyone in the company, not necessarily the highest-level attendee. The roles of facilitator and of note-taker may even be rotated. The name and position of this person should be announced before the meeting starts.

5. Attendance should be limited to those with subject-matter knowledge who will make valuable contributions and have decision-making authority.

6. The availability of the necessary materials/equipment to run the meeting effectively should be ensured, such as:

   —extra copies of agenda and prework

   —overhead projector and/or LCD panel/projector

   —easel/flip-chart pads

   —markers, extra pencils

   —name tags

   —extension cords

   —transparencies

7. Light refreshments should be available for people as they arrive; this creates a good feeling and may contribute to the success of the meeting.

Conducting meetings. Once the meeting is underway, following these guidelines will enhance its effectiveness:

1. The facilitator should start the meeting on time. If a gavel is used, it should be rapped once to declare order at the beginning and as necessary throughout the meeting. The facilitator should welcome those present and, if appropriate, have them introduce themselves. After some informal remarks, the facilitator should restate the meeting objectives, establish the ground rules of the meeting, and ask for any additions to the agenda.

2. A quorum (usually a majority of the members) is ordinarily required to conduct business. If the existence of a quorum is questioned, it must be determine that one exists for the meeting to continue.

3. The role of the facilitator is to keep the meeting on track, follow the agenda and time schedule, identify and assign tasks, and listen and ask questions. If the discussion drifts away from the agenda, the facilitator should diplomatically but

firmly declare the errant remarks "out of order" and return discussion to the agenda.

4. Any member recognized by the facilitator may make a motion. Following a second, the group discusses the motion. When discussion ends, the motion is voted on. A majority vote is ordinarily required for a motion to pass. A successful vote approves "immediate action" or "tables" the motion (that is, refers one motion to a committee or postpones discussion until the next meeting).

5. The facilitator must know the degree of formality expected. If informality has prevailed in the past, it should be continued. Informality often permits decision by consensus rather than formal vote. However, if formality prevails, parliamentary procedure must apply. The worldwide reference to this is the publication *Robert's Rules of Order*.

6. Good meeting facilitators try to get as many people as possible to participate in the discussions. It is difficult but necessary to discourage someone who monopolizes the discussion.

7. Special skill is required to manage a meeting if a heated debate breaks out. In such instances, the facilitator must forcefully limit the number and time allotted to those on each side of the issue. Above all, interruptions should not be permitted.

8. There are few things worse than a boring meeting. Good facilitators often find that occasional witty remarks take away humdrum feelings. Another good practice is to laugh heartily at genuinely funny comments.

9. During the meeting, the facilitator must see to that there is agreement on any next steps or assignments and their target completion dates.

10. At the end of the meeting, the facilitator thanks attendees and, if earned, recognizes their good participation. It is often appropriate to get consensus on the date, time, and place of the next meeting.

MEETINGS OF CORPORATION BOARDS OF DIRECTORS

At the top level of corporations are the meetings of the board of directors. Directors generally have authority over all corporate matters. The articles of incorporation, as amended, determine the number of directors.

Boards meet at regularly scheduled times, including during and immediately after shareholder meetings. If special board meetings are called, notice, in most cases, must be given at least ten but not more than sixty days in advance.

Corporation presidents generally preside at board meetings. If the president is unable to do so, the vice president ordinarily presides. Most large corporations use written meeting agendas.

Quorum requirements ordinarily require a majority of the directors to be in attendance. If at least a quorum attends, whatever decisions are made by those present constitute an action by the board. Bylaws seldom permit voting by proxy.

Corporation bylaws ordinarily presume that directors approve of any act passed by the board even if they voted against it unless they file a dissenting statement at or immediately after the meeting.

MEETINGS OF CORPORATE SHAREHOLDERS

State statutes and corporation bylaws require annual shareholder meetings. In addition to topics requested by shareholders, three major agenda items are usually covered:

1. Election of board of directors

2. Financial and competitive "state of the corporation"

3. Plans for the future

Special shareholder meetings can be called if a major corporation change is pending, such as a new line of products or a hostile takeover bid by another corporation. Bylaws usually stipulate that notice of a special meeting must be given at least ten but not more than sixty days in advance.

Every item on the agenda must be checked meticulously for any inaccuracies. The Federal Trade Commission, an independent U.S. governmental agency, has the authority to issue cease-and-desist orders against companies that engage in any misleading practices in any shareholder meetings or publications sent to shareholders.

Unlike at meetings of board of directors, proxies can vote at shareholder meetings. A quorum generally consists of shareholders holding a majority of the voting stock (usually common stock).

BIBLIOGRAPHY

Sniffen, Carl R. J. (1995). *The Essential Corporation Handbook.* ("Directors' Meetings," pp. 6, 227; "Shareholders' Meetings," pp. 161-171.) Grants Pass, OR: Oasis Press/PSI Research.

BRENDA REINSBOROUGH

MERCHANDISE ASSORTMENTS

(SEE: *Product Mix*)

MICROECONOMICS

(SEE: *Microeconomics/Macroeconomics*)

MISSION STATEMENT

(SEE: *Strategic Management*)

MIXED ECONOMY

(SEE: *Economy Systems*)

MONETARY EXCHANGE

(SEE: *Currency Exchange*)

MONETARY POLICY

The central agency that conducts monetary policy in the United States is the Federal Reserve System (the Fed). It was founded by Congress in 1913 under the Federal Reserve Act. The Fed is a highly independent agency that is insulated from day-to-day political pressures, accountable only to the Congress. It is a federal system, consisting of the Board of Governors, twelve regional Federal Reserve Banks (FRBs) and their twenty-five branches, the Federal Open Market Committee (FOMC), the Federal Advisory Council and other advisory and working committees, and more than 4,000 member banks, mostly national banks. By law, all federally chartered banks, i.e., national banks, are automatic members of the system. State-chartered banks may elect to become members.

The seven-member Board of Governors, headquartered in Washington, D.C., is the central agency of the Fed, overseeing the entire operation of U.S. monetary policy. The FRBs are the operating arms of the system and are located in twelve major cities around the nation. The twelve-member FOMC is the most important policy-making entity of the system. The voting members of the committee are the seven members of the board, the president of the FRB of New York, and four of the other eleven FRB presidents, serving one year on a rotating basis. The other seven nonvoting FRB presidents still attend the meetings and participate fully in policy deliberations.

MONETARY POLICY AND THE ECONOMY

Being one of the most influential government policies, monetary policy aims at affecting the economy through the Fed's management of money and interest rates. As generally accepted concepts, the narrowest definition of money is M1, which includes currency, checking account deposits, and traveler's checks. Time deposits, savings deposits, money market deposits, and other financial assets can be added to M1 to define other monetary measures such as M2 and M3. Interest rates are simply the costs of borrowing. The Fed conducts monetary policy through reserves, which are the portion of the deposits that banks and other depository institutions are required to hold either as cash in their vaults, called vault cash, or as deposits with their home FRBs. Excess reserves are the reserves in excess of the amount required. These additional funds can be transacted in the reserves market (the federal funds market) to allow overnight borrowing between depository institutions to meet short-term needs in reserves. The rate at which such private borrowings are charged is the federal funds rate.

Monetary policy is closely linked with the reserves market. With its policy tools, the Fed can control the reserves available in the market, affect the federal funds rate, and subsequently trigger a chain of reactions that influence other short-term interests rates, foreign-exchange rates, long-term interest rates, and the amount of money and credit in the economy. These changes will then bring about adjustments in consumption, affect saving and investment decisions, and eventually influence employment, output, and prices.

GOALS OF MONETARY POLICY

The long-term goals of monetary policy are to promote full employment, stable prices, and moderate long-term interest rates. Most economists think price stability should be the primary objective, since a stable level of prices is key to sustained output and employment, as well as to maintaining moderate long-term interest rates. Relatively speaking, it is easier for central banks to control inflation (i.e., the continual rise in the price level) than to influence employment directly, because the latter is affected by such real factors as technology and consumer tastes. Moreover, historical evidence indicates a strong positive correlation between inflation and the amount of money.

While the financial markets react quickly to changes in monetary policy, it generally takes months or even years for such policy to affect employment and growth, and thus to reach the Fed's long-term goals. The Fed, therefore, needs to be forward-looking and to make timely policy adjustments based on forecasted as well as actual data on such variables as wages and prices, inflation, unemployment, output growth, foreign trade, interest rates, exchange rates, money and credit, conditions in the markets for bonds and stocks, and so on.

IMPLEMENTATION OF MONETARY POLICY

Since the early 1980s, the Fed has been relying on the overnight federal funds rate as the guide to its position in monetary policy. The Fed has at its disposal three major monetary policy tools:

Reserve Requirements Under the Monetary Control Act of 1980, all depository institutions, including commercial banks, savings and loans, and others, are subject to the same reserve requirements, regardless of their Fed member status. As of March 1999, the basic structure of reserve requirements is 3 percent for all checkable deposits up to $46.5 million and 10 percent for the amount above $46.5 million. No reserves are required for time deposits (data from Federal Reserve Bank of Minneapolis, 1999).

Reserve requirement affects the so-called multiple money creation. Suppose, for example, the reserve requirement ratio is 10 percent. A bank that receives a $100 deposit (bank 1) can lend out $90. Bank 1 can then issue a $90 check to a borrower, who deposits it in bank 2, which can then lend out $81. As it continues, the process will eventually involve a total of $1,000 ($100 + $90 + $81 + $72.9 + ... = $1,000) in deposits. The initial deposit of $100 is thus multiplied 10 times. With a lower (higher) ratio, the multiple involved is larger (smaller), and more (less) reserves can be created.

Reserve requirements are not used as often as the other policy tools (discussed below). Since funds grow in multiples, it is difficult to administer small adjustments in reserves with this tool. Also, banks always have the option of entering the federal funds market for reserves, further limiting the role of reserve requirements. As of March 1999, the last change in the reserve requirements was in April 1992, when the upper ratio was reduced from 12 percent to 10 percent.

However, the amount of deposits against which the 3 percent requirement applies does change relatively more often.

The Discount Rate Banks may acquire loans through the "discount window" at their home FRB. The most important credit available through the window is the adjustment credit, which helps depository institutions meet their short-term needs against, for example, unexpected large withdrawals of deposits. The interest rate charged on such loans is the basic discount rate and is the focus of discount policy. A lower rate encourages more borrowing. Through money creation, bank deposits increase and reserves increase. A rate hike works in the opposite direction. However, since it is more efficient to adjust reserves through open-market operations (discussed below), the amount of discount window lending has been unimportant, accounting for only a small fraction of total reserves. Perhaps a more meaningful function served by the discount rate is to signal the Fed's stance on monetary policy, similar to the role of the federal funds rate.

By law, each FRB sets its discount rate every two weeks, subject to the approval of the Board of Governors. However, the gradual nationalization of the credit market over the years has resulted in a uniform discount rate. Its adjustments have been dictated by the cyclical conditions in the economy, and the frequency of adjustments has varied. In the 1990s, for example, the Fed cut the rate seven times—from 7 percent to 3 percent—during the recession from December 1990 to July 1992. Later, from May 1994 to February 1995, the rate was raised four times—from 3 percent to 5.25 percent—to counter possible economic overheating and inflation. In January 1996, the rate was lowered to 5 percent and it stayed there for the next thirty-two months, during which the U.S. economy experienced a solid and consistent growth with only minor inflation. From October to November 1998, the Fed cut the rate twice, first to 4.75 percent and then to 4.5 percent, anticipating the threat from the global financial crisis that had began in Asia in mid-1997 (data from "United States Monetary Policy," 1999).

Open-Market Operations The most important and flexible tool of monetary policy is open-market operations (i.e., trading U.S. government securities in the open market). In 1997, the Fed made $3.62 trillion of purchases and $3.58 trillion of sales of Treasury securities (mostly short-term Treasury bills). As of September 1998, the Fed held $458.13 billion of Treasury securities, roughly 8.25 percent of the total Federal debt outstanding (data from Fisher et al., 1998; *Treasury Bulletin*, 1998).

The FOMC directs open-market operations (and also advises about reserve requirements and discount-rate policies). The day-to-day operations are determined and executed by the Domestic Trading Desk (the Desk) at the FRB of New York. Since 1980, the FOMC has met regularly eight times a year in Washington, D.C. At each of these meetings, it votes on an intermeeting target federal funds rate, based on the current and prospective conditions of the economy. Until the next meeting, the Desk will manage reserve conditions through open-market operations to maintain the federal funds rate around the given target level. When buying securities from a bank, the Fed makes the payment by increasing the bank's reserves at the Fed. More reserves will then be available in the federal funds market and the federal funds rate falls. By selling securities to a bank, the Fed receives payment in reserves from the bank. Supply of reserves falls and the funds rate rises.

The Fed has two basic approaches in running open-market operations. When a shortage or surplus in reserves is likely to persist, the Fed may undertake outright purchases or sales, creating a long-term impact on the supply of reserves. However, many reserve movements are temporary. The Fed can then take a defensive position and engage in transactions that only impose temporary effects on the level of reserves. A repurchase agreement (a repo) allows the Fed to purchase securities with the agreement that the seller will buy back them within a short time period, sometimes overnight and mostly within seven days. The repo creates a temporary increase in reserves, which vanishes when the term expires. If the Fed wishes to drain reserves temporarily from the banking system, it can adopt a matched sale-purchase transaction (a reverse repo), under which the buyer agrees to sell the securities back to the Fed, usually in less than seven days.

BIBLIOGRAPHY

The Federal Reserve System: Purposes and Functions. (1994). Washington, DC: Board of Governors of the Federal Reserve System.

Ferguson, Jr., Roger W. *Remarks by Governor Roger W. Ferguson, Jr.: The Making of Monetary Policy. Federal Reserve Board Speech.* At www.bog.frb.fed.us/boarddocs/speeches/current/19990115.html. 1999.

Fisher, Peter R., Cheng, Virginia, Hilton, Spence, and Tulpan, Ted (1998). "Open Market Operations During 1997." *Federal Reserve Bulletin* July: 517-532.

"Interest Rates and Monetary Policy." San Francisco: Federal Reserve Bank of San Francisco. At www.sf.frb.org/econrsrch/wklylfr/el97-18.html. 1997.

Mishkin, Frederic S. (1998). *The Economics of Money, Banking, and Financial Markets,* 5th ed. New York: Addison-Wesley.

Treasury Bulletin. (1998). December. Washington, DC: U.S. Department of Treasury.

"United States Monetary Policy." Federal Reserve Bank of Minneapolis. At [woodrow.mpls.frb.fed.us/info/policy]. 1999.

EDWARD WEI-TE HSIEH

MONEY

In the modern world we take money for granted. However, pause for a moment and imagine what life would be like without money. Suppose that you want to consume a particular good or service, such as a pair of shoes. If money didn't exist, you would need to barter with the cobbler for the pair of shoes that you want. *Barter* is the process of directly exchanging one good or service for another. In order to purchase the pair of shoes, you would need to have something to trade for the shoes. If you specialized in growing peaches, you would need to bring enough bushels of peaches to the cobbler's shop to purchase the pair of shoes. If the cobbler wanted your peaches and you wanted his shoes, then a *double coincidence of wants* would exist and trade could take place.

But what if the cobbler didn't want your peaches? In that case you would have to find out what he did want, for example, beef. Then you would have to trade your peaches for beef and the beef for shoes. But what if the person selling beef had no desire for peaches, but instead wants a computer? Then you would have to trade your peaches for a computer—and it would take a lot of peaches to buy a computer. Then you would have to trade your computer for beef and the beef for shoes. But what if . . . ? At some point it would become easier to make the shoes yourself or to just do without.

THE EVOLUTION OF MONEY

Money evolved as a way of avoiding the complexities and difficulties of barter. Money is any asset that is recognized by an economic community as having value. Historically, such assets have included, among other things, shells, stone disks (which can be somewhat difficult to carry around), gold, and bank notes.

The modern monetary system has its roots in the gold of medieval Europe. In the Middle Ages, gold and gold coins were the common currency. However, the wealthy found that carrying large quantities of gold around was difficult and made them the target of thieves. To avoid carrying gold coins, people began depositing them for safekeeping with goldsmiths, who often had heavily guarded vaults in which to store their valuable inventories of gold. The goldsmiths charged a fee for their services and issued receipts, or gold notes, in the amount of the deposits. Exchanging these receipts was much simpler and safer than carrying around gold coins. In addition, the depositors could retrieve their gold on demand.

Goldsmiths during this time became aware that few people actually wanted their gold coins back when the gold notes were so easy to use for exchange. They therefore began lending some of the gold on deposit to borrowers who paid a fee, called interest. These goldsmiths were the precursors to our modern fractional reserve banking system.

FUNCTIONS OF MONEY

Regardless of what asset is recognized by an economic community as money, in general it serves three functions:

- Money is a medium of exchange.
- Money is a measure of value.
- Money is a store of value.

Money as a medium of exchange. Used as a medium of exchange, money means that parties to a transaction no longer need to barter one good for another. Because money is accepted as a medium of exchange, you can sell your peaches for money and purchase the desired shoes with the proceeds of the sale. You no longer need to trade peaches—a lot of them—for a computer and then the computer for beef and then the beef for the shoes. As a medium of exchange, money tends to encourage specialization and division of labor, promoting economic efficiency.

Money is a measure of value. As a measure of value, money makes transactions significantly simpler. Instead of markets determining the price of peaches relative to computers and to beef and to shoes, as well as the price of computers relative to beef and to shoes, as well as the price of beef relative to shoes (i.e., a total of six prices for only four goods), the markets only need to determine the price of each of the four goods in terms of money. If we were to add a fifth good to our simple economy, then we would add four more prices to the number of good-for-good prices that the markets must determine. As the number of goods in our economy grew, the number of good-for-good prices would grow rapidly. In an economy with ten goods, there would be forty-five good-for-good prices but only ten money prices. In an economy with twenty goods there would be one hundred and ninety good-for-good prices but only twenty money prices. Imagine all of the good-for-good prices in a more realistic economy with thousands of goods and services available.

Using money as a measure of value reduces the number of prices determined in markets and vastly reduces the cost of collecting price information for market participants. Instead of focusing on such information, market participants can focus their effort on producing the good or service in which they specialize.

Money as a store of value. Money can also serve as a store of value, since it can quickly be exchanged for desired goods and services. Many assets can be used as a store of value, including stocks, bonds, and real estate. However, there are transaction costs associated with converting these assets into money in order to purchase a desired good or service. These transaction costs could include monetary fees as well as time delays involved in the liquidation process.

In contrast, money is a poor store of value during periods of inflation, while the value of real estate tends to appreciate during such periods. Thus, the benefits of holding money must by balanced against the risks of holding money.

SUMMARY

Money simplifies the exchange of goods and services and facilitates specialization and division of labor. It does this by serving as a medium of exchange, as a measure of value, and as a store of value.

DENISE WOODBURY

MONEY SUPPLY

Money is a collection of liquid assets that is generally accepted as a medium of exchange and for repayment of debt. In that role, it serves to economize on the use of scarce resources devoted to exchange, expands resources for production, facilitates trade, promotes specialization, and contributes to a society's welfare (Thornton, 2000). This theoretical definition serves two purposes: It encompasses new forms of money that may arise as a result of financial innovations related to technological change and institutional developments. It also distinguishes money from other assets by emphasizing its general acceptability as a medium of exchange. While all assets serve as a store of wealth, only a few are accepted as a means of payment for goods and services.

While this definition provides a clear picture of what money is, it does not specify exactly what assets should be included in its measurement. There are several liquid assets, such as coins, paper currency, checkable-type deposits, and traveler's checks, which clearly act as a medium of exchange and definitely belong in its measurement. However, several other assets may also serve as a medium of exchange but are not as liquid as currency and checkable-type deposits. For example, money market deposit accounts have check-writing features subject to certain restrictions, and savings accounts can be converted into a medium of exchange with a negligible cost. To what extent such assets should be included in money's measurement is not clear.

As an alternative, economists have proposed defining and measuring money using an empirical approach. This approach emphasizes the role of money as an intermediate target for monetary policy. As Mishkin (1997) points out, an effective intermediate target should have three features: It must be measurable, be controllable by the central bank, and have a predictable and stable relation with ultimate goals. Thus, an asset should be included in the measurement of money if it satisfies the above requirements. Evidence is mixed on which measures of money have a high predictive power. A measure that predicts well in one period might not perform well at other times, and a measure that predicts one goal might not be a good predictor of others.

The Federal Reserve System (the Fed) has incorporated both the theoretical approach and the empirical approach in constructing its measures of the money supply for the United States. The results are four measures of monetary aggregates—M1, M2, M3, and L—that are constructed using simple summations of some liquid assets. M1 is the narrowest measure, corresponding closely to the theoretical definition of money. It consists of six liquid assets—coins, dollar bills, traveler's checks, demand deposits, other checkable deposits, and NOW accounts held at commercial banks and at thrift institutions. These assets are clearly money because they are used directly as a medium of exchange. The M2 aggregate adds to M1 two groups of assets: (1) other assets that have check-writing features, such as money market deposit accounts and money market mutual funds shares, and (2) other extremely liquid assets, such as savings deposits, small-denomination time deposits, overnight repurchase agreements, and overnight Eurodollars. Similarly, the M3 aggregate adds to M2 somewhat less liquid assets, such as large-denomination time deposits, institutional money market funds, term repurchase agreements, and term Eurodollars. Finally, L is a broad measure of highly liquid assets. It consists of M3 plus several highly liquid securities, such as savings bonds, short-term Treasury securities, bankers' acceptances, and commercial paper.

A potential problem with the simple summation procedure, which underlies the construction of the monetary aggregates, is the assumption that all individual components are perfect substitutes. As Barnett, Fisher, and Serletis (1992) point out, this procedure is useful for constructing accounting measures of monetary wealth but does not provide reliable measures of monetary services. As a solution, Friedman and Schwartz (1970) have proposed weighting individual components by their degree of "moneyness," with the weights varying from zero to unity. Another more rigorous solution proposed by Barnett and colleagues (1992) is based on the application of aggregation and index number theory. Evidence along this line of research (Chrystal and McDonald, 1994) suggests that these measures of monetary aggregate are superior to the traditional measures in their predictive contents.

Knowledge of the money-supply process and information about its behavior are important for two interrelated reasons. First, changes in money growth may have significant effects on the economy's performance. Its short-run variations may affect employment, output, and other real economic variables, while its long-run trend determines the course of inflation and other nominal variables. Second, money supply serves as an important intermediate target for the conduct of monetary policy. As a result, changes in money growth may be instrumental in attaining economic growth, price stability, and other economic goals.

Three groups of economic agents play an important role in the process of money-supply determination. The first and most important is the Fed, which sets the supply of the monetary base and imposes certain constraints on the set of admissible assets held by banks and on the banks' supply of their liabilities. Next is the public, which determines the optimum amounts of currency holdings, the supply of financial claims to banks, and the allocation of the claims between transaction and nontransaction accounts. The last is banks, which absorb the financial claims offered by the public, set the supply conditions for their liabilities, and allocate their assets between earning assets and reserves subject to the constraints imposed by the Fed. The interactions among the three groups are shaped by market conditions and jointly determine the stock of money, bank credit, and interest rates (Brunner, 1989).

The level of money stock is the product of two components: the monetary multiplier and the monetary base. The monetary base is the quantity of government-produced money. It consists of currency held by the public and total reserves held by banks. Currency is the total of coins and dollar bills of all denominations. Reserves are the sum of banks' vault cash and their reserve deposits at the Fed. They are the non-interest-bearing components of bank assets, consisting of required reserves on deposit liabilities established by the Fed and additional reserves that banks deem necessary for liquidity purposes.

The Fed exercises its tight control over the monetary base through open-market operations and extension of discount loans. Open-market operations, which are the Fed's authority to trade in government securities, are the most important instrument of monetary policy and the primary source of changes in the monetary base. An open-market purchase expands the monetary base, whereas an open-market sale works in the opposite direction. The Fed's control of the dis-

count loans results from its authority to set the discount rate and limit the level of discount loans through its administration of the discount window.

The money multiplier reflects the joint behavior of the public, banks, and the Fed. The public's decisions about their desired holdings of currency and nontransaction deposits relative to transaction deposits are one set of factors that influence the multiplier. Banks liquidity concerns, and thus their desire to hold excess reserves relative to their deposit liabilities, are another set of factors. The Fed's authority to change the required reserve ratios on bank deposits constitutes the third set of factors. Given the rather infrequent changes in the reserve-requirement ratios, the multiplier primarily reflects the behavior of the public and private banks as well as market and institutional conditions.

For example, a decision by the public to increase its currency holdings relative to transaction deposits results in a switch from a component of money supply that undergoes multiple expansion to one that does not. Thus, the size of the multiplier declines. Similarly, a decision by banks to increase their holdings of excess reserves relative to transaction deposits reduces bank loans, causing a decline in deposits, the multiplier, and the money supply. Finally, a decision by the Fed to raise the reserve-requirement ratio on bank deposits results in a reserve deficiency in the banking system, forcing banks to reduce their loans, deposit liabilities, the money supply, and the multiplier.

Over the 1980-1999 period, the M1 and M2 aggregates grew at average annual rates of 5.5 and 5.7 percent, respectively. However, the growth rates were not stable. They varied between the low of -3.5 percent and the high of 16.9 percent for M1, and between the low of 0.4 percent and the high of 11.4 percent for M2. What factors contributed to the long-run growth and short-run fluctuations in the money supply? During the same time period, the monetary base grew at an average annual rate of 7.5 percent, due primarily to open market operations. Thus changes in the monetary base and open-market operations are the primary source of long-run movements in the money supply. For shorter time periods, however, changes in the money multiplier may also have contributed to the fluctuations in the money supply.

BIBLIOGRAPHY

Barnett, William A., Fisher, Douglas, and Serletis, Apostolos. (1992). "Consumer Theory and the Demand for Money." *Journal of Economic Literature* 4 (December): 2086-2119.

Brunner, Karl (1989). "Money Supply." *In The New Palgrave: Money*, ed. John Eatwell, Murray Milgate, and Peter Newman. New York: W.W. Norton (pp. 263-267).

Chrystal, K. Alec, and McDonald, Ronald. (1994). "Empirical Evidence on Recent Behavior and Usefulness of Simple Sum and Weighted Measures of the Money Stock." *Federal Reserve Bank of St. Louis Review* 76 (March-April): 73-109.

Friedman, Milton, and Schwartz, Anna J. (1970). *Monetary Statistics of the United States: Estimates, Sources, and Methods.* New York: Colombia University Press.

Mishkin, Frederic S. (1997). *The Economics of Money, Banking, and Financial Markets*, 5th ed. Reading, MA: Addison-Wesley.

Thornton, Daniel L. (2000). "Money in a Theory of Exchange." *Federal Reserve Bank of St. Louis Review* 82 (January-February): 35-60.

HASSAN MOHAMMADI

MONOPOLY

A monopoly is a market condition in which a single seller controls the entire output of a particular good or service. A firm is a monopoly if it is the sole seller of its product and if its product has no close substitutes. Close substitutes are those goods that could closely take the place of a particular good; for example, a Pepsi soft drink would be a close substitute for a Coke drink, but a juice drink would not. The fundamental cause of monopoly is barriers to entry; these are technological or economic conditions of a market that raise the cost for firms wanting to enter the market above the cost for firms already in the market or otherwise make new entry difficult. If the barriers to entry prevent others firms from entering the market, there is no competition and the monopoly remains the only seller in its market. The seller is then able to set the price and output of a particular good or service.

A monopoly, in its pure form, is actually quite rare. The majority of large firms operate in a market structure of oligopoly, which means that a few sellers divide the bulk of the market. People often have the impression that the goals of a monopolist are somehow evil and grasping while those of a competitor are wholesome and altruistic. The truth is that the same motives drive the monopolistic firm and the competitive firm: Both strive to maximize profits. A basic proposition in economics is that monopoly control over a good will result in too little of the good being produced at too high a price. Economists have often advocated antitrust policy, public enterprise, or regulation to control the abuse of monopoly power.

BARRIERS TO ENTRY

For a monopoly to persist in the long run, barriers to entry must exist. Although such barriers can take various forms, they have three main sources:

1. A key resource is owned by a single firm.

2. The government gives a single firm the exclusive right to produce a specific good.

3. The cost of production makes a single producer more efficient than a large number of producers.

Monopoly Resources. The first and simplest way for a monopoly to come about is for a single firm to own a key resource. For example, if a small town had many working wells owned by different firms, no firm would have a monopoly on water. If, however, there were only one working well in town, the firm owning that well would be considered a monopoly. Although exclusive ownership of a key resource is one way for a monopoly to arise, monopolies rarely come about for this reason.

Government-Created Monopolies. In many cases, monopolies have arisen because the government has given a firm the exclusive right to sell a particular good or service. For example, when a pharmaceutical company discovers a new drug, it can apply to the government for a patent. If the patent is granted, the firm has the exclusive right to produce and sell the drug for a set number of years. The effects of such a government created monopoly are easy to see. In the case of the pharmaceutical company, the firm is able to charge higher prices for its patented product and, in turn, earn higher profits. With these higher profits, the firm is able to complete further research in its quest for new and better drugs. The government can create a monopoly when, in doing so, it is in the interest of the public good.

Natural Monopolies. A natural monopoly occurs when a single firm can supply a good or service to an entire market at a lesser cost than could two or more firms. An example of a natural monopoly is the distribution of water in a community. To provide water to residents, a firm must first put into place a network of pipes throughout the community. If two or more firms were to compete in providing the water distribution, each would have to pay the fixed cost of building a network. In this case, the average total cost of water is lowest when one firm serves the entire market.

MONOPOLY VERSUS COMPETITION

The major difference between a monopoly and a competitive firm is the monopoly's ability to influence the price of its output. Because a competitive firm is small relative to the market, the price of its product is determined by market conditions. On the other hand, because a monopoly is the sole producer in its market, it can often alter the price of its product by adjusting the quantity it supplies to the market.

An example of a company that garnered monopoly power is the case of Microsoft. In 2000, in an antitrust lawsuit brought against Microsoft, a U.S. federal court judge ruled against the company. Microsoft, a computer company, had established first MS-DOS and later Windows as the

dominating operating system for personal computers. Once it had achieved a position of strength in the market, would-be competitors faced insurmountable hurdles. Software developers face large costs for every additional operating system to which they adapt their applications. Because Microsoft had the dominant operating system, any rival personal computer operating system would have only a handful of applications, compared to tens of thousands of applications for Microsoft's Windows system. This applications barrier to entry gave Microsoft enduring monopoly power.

The judge's ruling in the case made it clear that, besides being illegal, Microsoft's monopoly was not in the public interest and legal measures would be put into place in order to break the monopoly that Microsoft had created.

BIBLIOGRAPHY

Auld, D., Bannock, G., Baxter, R., and Rees, R. (1993). *The American Dictionary of Economics*. New York: Facts on File.

"Busted." (1999). *The Economist*. 353(8145): 21, 23.

Heillbroner, Robert, and Thurow, Lester. (1994). *Economics Explained—Everything You Need to Know About How the Economy Works and Where It Is Going*. Parsippany, NJ: Simon & Shuster.

Mankiw, G. (1998). *Principles of Economics*. New York: Dryden Press.

MICHAEL W. SPAHR

MORALE

(SEE: *Motivation*)

MORTGAGES

(SEE: *Personal Financial Planning*)

MOTIVATION

A simple definition of *motivation* is the ability to change behavior. It is a drive that compels one to act because human behavior is directed toward some goal. Motivation is intrinsic (internal); it comes from within based on personal interests, desires, and need for fulfillment. However, extrinsic (external) factors such as rewards, praise, and promotions also influence motivation. As defined by Daft (1997), motivation refers to "the forces either within or external to a person that arouse enthusiasm and persistence to pursue a certain course of action" (p. 526).

People who are committed to achieving organizational objectives generally outperform those who are not committed. Those who are intrinsically rewarded by accomplishments in the workplace are satisfied with their jobs and are individuals with high self-esteem. Therefore, an important part of management is to help make work more satisfying and rewarding for employees and to keep employee motivation consistent with organizational objectives. With the diversity of contemporary workplaces, this is a complex task. Many factors, including the influences of different cultures, affect what people value and what is rewarding to them.

From a manager's perspective, it is important to understand what prompts people, what influences them, and why they persist in particular actions. Quick (1985) presented these four underlying principles that are important to understanding motivation:

1. People have reasons for everything they do.

2. Whatever people choose as a goal is something they believe is good for them.

3. The goal people choose must be seen as attainable.

4. The conditions under which the work is done can affect its value to the employee and his or her perceptions of attainability or success.

When management was first studied in a scientific way at the turn of the twentieth century, Frederick Winslow Taylor worked to improve productivity in labor situations so important in those days of the developing Industrial Revolution. Taylor developed efficiency measures and

incentive systems. When workers were paid more for meeting a standard higher than their normal production, productivity increased dramatically. Therefore, workers seemed to be economically motivated. At this time in history, social issues involved in human behavior were not yet considered. A more humanistic approach soon developed that has been influencing management ever since.

During the late 1920s and early 1930s, Elton Mayo and other researchers from Harvard University conducted studies at a Western Electric plant in Hawthorne, Illinois, to measure productivity. They studied the effects of fatigue, layout, heating, and lighting on productivity. As might be expected when studying lighting, employee productivity levels increased as the illumination level was increased; however, the same effect was noted when the illumination level was decreased. The researchers concluded that the attention paid to the employees was more of a contributing factor to their productivity level than the environmental conditions. The fact that paying attention to workers could improve their behavior was called the *Hawthorne effect*. As a result of this research, it was evident that employees should be treated in a humane way. These findings started the human relations movement—a change in management thinking and practice that viewed increased worker productivity as grounded in satisfaction of employees' basic needs. [Many years later, it was discovered that the workers in the Hawthorne experimental group had received an increase in income; therefore, money was probably a motivating factor, although it was not recognized as such at the time. (Daft, 1997)].

Motivation theories have continued to evolve and have their roots in behavioral psychology. They provide a way to examine and understand human behavior in a variety of situations. A simple model of motivation is shown in Figure 1.

Ongoing changes in the workplace require that managers give continuous attention to those factors that influence worker behavior and align them with organizational goals. No one theory is appropriate for all people and for all situations. Each individual has his or her own values and

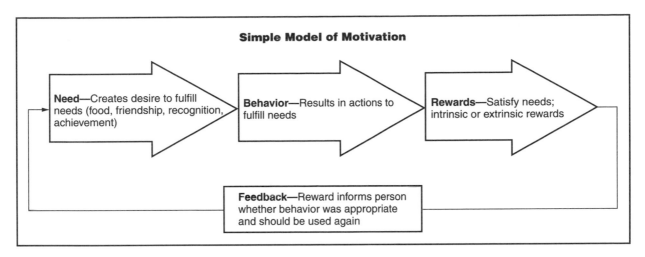

Simple Model of Motivation

Need—Creates desire to fulfill needs (food, friendship, recognition, achievement)

Behavior—Results in actions to fulfill needs

Rewards—Satisfy needs; intrinsic or extrinsic rewards

Feedback—Reward informs person whether behavior was appropriate and should be used again

Figure 1

differing abilities. In business settings, managers apply motivation theories to influence employees, improve morale, and implement incentive and compensation plans.

The following discussion of motivation theories is grouped according to need, process, and reinforcement theories.

NEED THEORIES

Need theories are based on some of the earliest research in the field of human relations. The premise behind need theories is that if managers can understand the needs that motivate people, then reward systems can be implemented that fulfill those needs and reinforce the appropriate behavior.

Hierarchy of Needs Abraham Maslow, a professor at Brandeis University and a practicing psychologist, developed the *hierarchy of needs* theory. He identified a set of needs that he prioritized into a hierarchy based on two conclusions (Daft, 1997; McCoy, 1992; Quick, 1985):

1. Human needs are either of an attraction/ desire nature or of an avoidance nature.

2. Because humans are "wanting" beings, when one desire is satisfied, another desire will take its place.

The five levels of needs are the following (see Table 1):

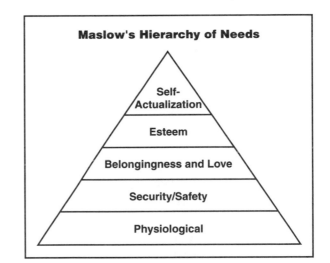

Maslow's Hierarchy of Needs

Self-Actualization

Esteem

Belongingness and Love

Security/Safety

Physiological

Table 1

- *Physiological*: These are basic physical comfort or bodily needs: food, sex, drink, and sleep. In the workplace, these needs translate into a safe, ergonomically designed work environment with an appropriate base salary compensation.

- *Security/safety*: People want to feel safe, secure, and free from fear. They need stability, structure, and order. In the workplace, job security and fringe benefits, along with an environment free of violence, fills these needs.

- *Belongingness and love*: This is a need for friends, family, and intimacy—for social acceptance and affection from one's peers. In the workplace, this need is satisfied by participation in work groups with good relationships among co-workers and between workers and managers.

- *Esteem*: People want the esteem of others and they want to be regarded as useful, competent, and important. People also desire self-esteem and need a good self image. In the workplace, increased responsibility, high status, and recognition for contributions satisfy these needs.

- *Self-actualization*: This highest motivation level involves people striving to actualize their full potential, to become more of what they are capable of being. They seek to attain self-fulfillment. In the workplace, people satisfy this need by being creative, receiving training, or accepting challenging assignments.

Focusing on the needs of retraining for growth and challenge as well as rewards and recognition is important to the quality of work life. Managers can affect the physical, social, and psychological environment in the workplace, and they have a responsibility to help employees fulfill their needs.

ERG Theory In his work, Clayton Alderfer expanded on Maslow's hierarchical theory. He proposed three need categories and suggested that movement between the need levels is not necessarily straightforward. Failure to meet a higher-order need could cause an individual to regress to a lower-order need. These *ERG theory* categories are:

- *Existence needs*: Needs for physical well-being

- *Relatedness needs*: Needs for satisfactory relationships with others

- *Growth needs*: The development of human potential and the desire for personal growth and increased competence (Daft, 1997)

Motivation-Hygiene Theory Frederick Herzberg, a professor of psychology at Case Western Reserve University, studied the attitudes of workers toward their jobs. Herzberg proposed that an individual will be moved to action based on the desire to avoid deprivation. However, this motivation does not provide positive satisfaction because it does not provide a sense of growth. Herzberg's research found that positive job attitudes were associated with a feeling of psychological growth. He thought that people work for two reasons: for financial reasons to avoid physical deprivation, and for achievement because of the happiness and meaning it provides. Herzberg also identified the concept of job enrichment, whereby the responsibilities of a job are changed to provide greater growth and challenge (McCoy, 1992; Quick, 1985 p. 10-12)] 1985. His *motivation-hygiene* theory includes two types of factors:

1. *Motivation* is based on the positive satisfaction that psychological growth provides. The presence of factors such as responsibility, achievement, recognition, and possibility for growth or advancement will motivate and satisfy people. The absence of these factors will not necessarily demotivate or cause dissatisfaction.

2. *Hygiene* is based on an individual's desire to avoid deprivation and the resulting physical and emotional discomfort. Hygiene factors include willingness to supervise; positive working conditions; interpersonal relations with peers, subordinates, and superiors; status; job security; and salary. These factors do not motivate, nor will their presence cause job satisfaction. Their absense, however, will cause dissatisfaction.

Although salary is considered a hygiene factor, it plays an indirect part in motivation as a measure of growth and advancement or as a symbol of recognition of achievement.

Theory X and Theory Y Douglas McGregor, a professor at the Massachusetts Institute of Technology and a social psychologist, was greatly influenced by the work of Maslow. McGregor recognized that people have needs and that those needs are satisfied at work. He described two sets of assumptions about people that he labeled *Theory X* and *Theory Y* (Bruce and Pepitone, 1999; Quick, 1985):

- The assumptions of *Theory X* are that most people will avoid work because they don't like it and must be threatened or persuaded to put forth adequate effort. People have little ambition and don't want responsibility. They want to be directed and are most interested in job security.

- The assumptions of *Theory Y* are that work is very natural to people and that most people are self-directed to achieve objectives to which they are committed. People are ambitious and creative. They desire responsibility and derive a sense of satisfaction from the work itself.

These assumptions were, at one time, applied to management styles, with autocratic managers labeled as adhering to Theory X and democratic managers to Theory Y. Unfortunately, this fostered a tendency to see people as members of a group rather than as individuals. The important contribution of McGregor's theory was to recognize these two perspectives and to recognize that people can achieve personal objectives through helping organizations achieve their objectives. Their work can be a motivator.

Acquired Needs Theory David McClelland developed the *acquired needs theory* because he felt that different needs are acquired throughout an individual's lifetime. He proposed three needs:

1. *Need for achievement*: The desire to accomplish something difficult, attain a high standard of success, master complex tasks, and surpass others

2. *Need for affiliation*: The desire to form close personal relationships, avoid conflict, and establish warm friendships

3. *Need for power*: The desire to influence or control others, be responsible for others, and have authority over others.

McClelland found through his research that early life experiences determine whether people acquire these needs. The need to achieve as an adult is influenced by the reinforcement of behavior received as a child when a child is encouraged to do things independently. If a child is reinforced for warm, human relationships, then the need for affiliation as an adult develops. If a child gains satisfaction from controlling others, then the need for power will be evident as an adult (Daft, 1997).

PROCESS THEORIES

Process theories help to explain how individuals select particular behaviors and how individuals determine if these behaviors meet their needs. Because these theories involve rational selection, concepts of cognition are employed. Cognition, according to Petri (1996), "is generally used to describe those intellectual or perceptual processes occurring within us when we analyze and interpret both the world around us and our own thoughts and actions (p. 236).

Expectancy Theory Victor Vroom developed the *expectancy theory*, which suggests that individuals' expectations about their ability to accomplish something will affect their success in accomplishing it. Therefore, this theory is based on cognition—on thought processes that individuals use.

The expectancy theory is based on an individual's effort and performance, as well as the desirability of outcomes associated with high performance. The value of or preference for a particular outcome is called valence. To determine valence, people will ask themselves whether or not they can accomplish a goal, how important is the goal to them (in the immediate as well as the long term), and what course of action will provide the greatest reward. An individual's expectation of actually achieving the outcome is crucial to success, and many factors influence this (Daft, 1997; Quick, 1985).

The expectancy theory can be applied through incentive systems that identify desired outcomes and give all workers the same opportunities to achieve rewards, such as stock ownership or other recognition for achievement.

Equity Theory The *equity theory* focuses on individuals' perceptions of how fairly they are treated in comparison to others. It was developed by J. Stacy Adams, who found that equity exists when people consider their compensation equal to the compensation of others who perform similar work. People judge equity by comparing inputs (such as education, experience, effort, and ability) to outputs (such as pay, recognition, benefits, and promotion).

When the ratio is out of balance, inequity occurs. And inequitable pay can create an impossible situation when implementing salary and incentive systems. According to Daft (1997), Individuals will work to reduce perceived inequity by doing the following:

- *Change inputs*: Examples include increasing or reducing effort.

- *Change outcomes*: Examples include requesting a salary increase or improved working conditions.

- *Distort perceptions*: This occurs when individuals cannot change their inputs or outcomes; one example is artificially increasing the importance of awards.

- *Leave the job*: Individuals might do this rather than experience what they perceive to be continued inequity.

When administering compensation and incentive programs, managers must be careful to assure that the rewards are equitable; if programs are not perceived as equitable, then they will not contribute to employee motivation.

REINFORCEMENT THEORIES

Theories of reinforcement are based not on need but on the relationship between behavior and its consequences. In the workplace, these theories can be applied to change or modify on-the-job behavior through rewards and punishments.

B. F. Skinner, a professor at Harvard, was a highly controversial behavioral psychologist known for his work in operant conditioning and behavior modification. His *reinforcement theories* take into consideration both motivation and the environment, focusing on stimulus and response relationships. Through his research, Skinner noted that a stimulus will initiate behavior; thus, the stimulus is an antecedent to behavior. The behavior will generate a result; therefore, results are consequences of behavior.

According to McCoy (1992), "The quality of the results will be directly related to the quality and timeliness of the antecedent. The more specific the antecedent is and the closer in time it is to the behavior, the greater will be its effect on the behavior. . . . The consequences provide feedback to the individual" (p. 34).

If the results are considered positive, then the behavior is positively reinforced. When the behavior is positively reinforced, the individual is more likely to repeat the behavior. People tend to have an intrinsic (internal) need for positive reinforcement. And when a behavior is ignored, the behavior tends to go away or become extinct. The four types of reinforcement are the following (Daft, 1997):

- *Positive reinforcement*: The application of a pleasant and rewarding consequence following a desired behavior, such as giving praise.

- *Negative reinforcement*: The removal of an unpleasant consequence following a desired behavior, such as a manager no longer reminding a worker about a weekly deadline when the worker meets the deadline. This reinforcement is also called avoidance.

- *Punishment*: The application of an unpleasant outcome when an undesirable behavior occurs to reduce the likelihood of that behavior happening again. This form of reinforcement does not indicate a correct behavior, so its use in business is not usually appropriate.

- *Extinction*: The withdrawal of a positive reward. If the behavior is no longer positively reinforced, then it is less likely to occur in the future and it will gradually disappear.

Continuous reinforcement can be effective in the early stages of behavior modification, but partial reinforcement is more commonly used. Reinforcement is most powerful when it is administered immediately.

The appropriateness of a reward depends on the situation. But for managers to apply rewards appropriate for work performance, it is necessary to understand what constitutes a reward. And no single reward will be perceived as positive by all employees. Rewards, however, are important in behavior-based incentive plans because they reward employee behavior that is desirable for the company. According to McCoy (1992), both incentives and recognition provide a reward; however, incentives drive performance while recognition is an after-the-fact display of appreciation for a contribution.

Financial rewards are certainly important in compensation programs. Social recognition provides employees with a sense of self-worth by acknowledging the contributions they have made. This recognition could be given in the form of a ceremony that helps to validate and is an important compensation—and one that probably costs a company very little in relationship to the benefit to employees (McCoy, 1992).

SUMMARY

The application of motivation theories can help managers to create work situations and employee recognition systems that help workers fulfill their needs. As Maslow wrote, "man has a higher nature ... and ... this higher nature includes the needs for meaningful work, for responsibility, for creativeness, for being fair and just, for doing what is worthwhile and for preferring to do it well" (pp. 244-245).

Some aspects of all jobs may be routine or mundane, but other aspects can be developed to promote job satisfaction and increased productivity. The sharing of responsibility can provide opportunities for growth, renewal, and achievement. This empowerment of workers can heighten employee motivation and improve morale. Both long-term and short-term incentive programs are needed for the employee commitment and effectiveness necessary to achieve organizational objectives. And in all instances, workers must be treated fairly and equitably.

BIBLIOGRAPHY

Bruce, Anne, and Pepitone, James S. (1999) *Motivating Employees*. New York: McGraw-Hill.

Daft, Richard L. (1997). *Management*, 4th ed. Orlando, Fl.: Harcourt Brace.

Maslow, Abraham H. (1998). *Toward a Psychology of Being*, 3d ed. New York: Wiley.

McCoy, Thomas J. (1992). *Compensation and Motivation: Maximizing Employee Performance with Behavior-Based Incentive Plans*. New York: AMACOM, a division of American Management Association.

Petri, Herbert L. (1996). *Motivation: Theory, Research, and Applications*, 4th ed. Pacific Grove, CA: Brooks/Cole.

Quick, Thomas L. (1985). *The Manager's Motivation Desk Book*. New York: Wiley.

PAT R. GRAVES

MOTIVATION-HYGIENE THEORY

(SEE: *Motivation*)

MULTIMEDIA SYSTEMS

A computer system can be defined as equipment (hardware), processes (software), and people organized to perform a function (Shelly, et al., 1998). Using this definition, a business multimedia system can be defined as hardware, software, and people organized to perform the functions of communication. Businesses use multimedia primarily for communication through presentations and for storage and retrieval of original documents and media files. For years, businesses have used multimedia systems that create, edit, produce, and distribute documents, movies, sound, and videotapes. Multimedia systems are also used to prepare presentations for marketing, cmployee training, public relations, and any other area in which mass communication is needed. Many companies commit resources (specialized personnel, photography and television studios, and other equipment) to mass-produce these forms of communication.

Traditional multimedia systems use specialized equipment that records sounds and graphics in an analog format such as cassette tapes, records, or videocassette tapes. Analog equipment relies on waves to record information such as sounds or video. These analog systems are similar to a traditional temperature gauge or a speedometer in an automobile, which use indicators that point to temperatures or speeds. Specialized analog equipment may include sound tape recorders, video cameras, videotape editing equipment, playback equipment, and projection systems.

COMPUTER-BASED MULTIMEDIA

Technology has changed the hardware used to develop multimedia from the traditional analog equipment to computer-based or digital multimedia systems. Digital systems sample analog waves and convert them into a series of numbers, 0s and 1s (digital), for processing by a computer. Microcomputer-based multimedia systems (Sharda, 1999) provide hardware and software that allow a person to use a computer to combine text, still graphics or pictures, sound, video (motion graphics), and links to Web sites and other software into a presentation. Multimedia presentations should allow users to interact with, navigate, and respond to the presentation (Hofstetter, 1997).

Multimedia applications in business are used in a variety of ways. Companies use multimedia computers in the following applications:

- Accounting and records management
- Compact disks (CDs) for product catalogues and individualized presentations
- Employee interactive training materials
- Internet web pages
- New product development using computer assisted design (CAD) software
- Sales and other types of group presentations
- Self-running presentations for trade show booth or kiosk applications

"Multimedia hierarchy" is a term used to reflect how much computing power is needed to process information. Multimedia systems have different levels of components that handle tasks ranging in difficulty from simple text processing to complex digital motion video. As more powerful computers are developed, more applications can be used by businesses.

TEXT PROCESSING

Text is the first and simplest level in the multimedia hierarchy. Traditionally, text has been keyboarded into the computer. Optical character recognition (OCR) scanners allow text to be scanned into the computer from printed documents using page scanners, or from universal product code (UPC) bar codes on products using wand, or hand-held, scanners. Magnetic ink character recognition (MICR) scanners have been used for processing checks since the 1950s, using the magnetic ink at the bottom of checks. Text may also be put into the computer using sound equipment.

SOUND PROCESSING

Sound in business multimedia applications enables a user to describe products, give instructions, enhance a presentation, or provide cues for some action by the viewer. Hardware for capturing and processing sounds includes a card attached to the main "motherboard" of the computer system. A sound card contains connections for input and output devices. Usually software is included with the card that allows the user to control volume and devices and to create and edit sound files.

Sound cards capture analog audio signals from microphones, music CDs, musical instrument digital interface (MIDI) devices— electronic keyboards similar to piano keyboards—and other sound sources through a line-in jack on the card. Computer users can plug in record turntables, cassette tape players, or any other device from an audio-out jack on those devices and record sounds. Sound cards also have output jacks for speakers, or the audio-out can be plugged into other sound-recording devices. The card contains two computer chips called the analog-to-digital (AD) and digital-to-analog (DA) chips. These chips convert sound waves to digits and digits to sound waves.

Sound-application software is used to mix different sound sources. Users can add effects, such as fade in and fade out or an echo effect, to the digital sound track. Several competing stan-

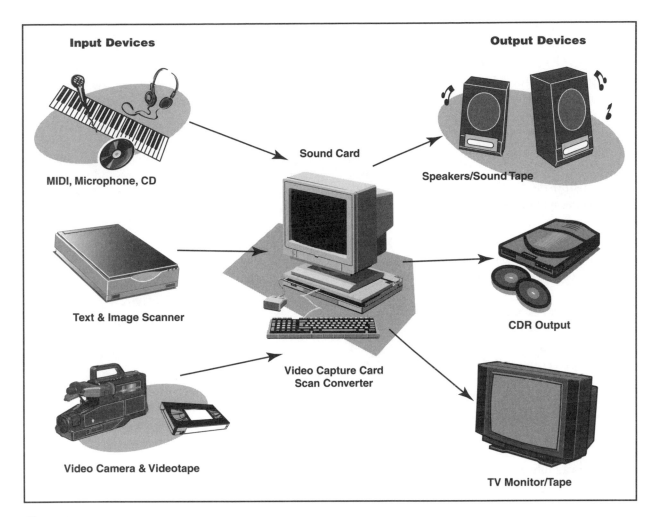

Figure 1

dards exist for computer sound files. These standards depend on the manufacturer of the hardware or developers of the software. The more users of a given standard there are, the more portable the file is to other users and to Internet applications. MIDI files and wave files found on the Internet are common examples.

Voice-pattern-recognition software allows the user to speak through a microphone directly to a word-processing software package. The analog voice of the user is converted to a digital sound file through a sound card on the computer, and the user's voice pattern is converted into text. Whether the text is entered by keyboard, scanner, or voice-recognition hardware

and software, the text can be used for presentations, Web pages, or other media forms to talk with the audience.

STILL-IMAGE PROCESSING

Various specialized forms of multimedia include image-processing systems designed specifically for handling business forms, images, graphics, or pictures. An example may be found in banking systems that use computer output microform (COM) devices to store images of checks and place several images on the customer's bank statement rather than returning the canceled checks. Company reports are often recorded as very small images on microfilm (rolls) or microfiche (cards) rather than paper to save storage space. Accountants and records managers may use multimedia for saving and archiving images in less physical space. Insurance companies may use imaging systems to scan claim forms, scan and store pictures of damages to customers' property, and provide immediate access to this information from a computer during the processing of a claim.

Draw-and-paint computer programs are used to generate graphics and tables for multimedia applications. These programs allow users to draw objects, fill them with colors, add text, and create special effects. The user-made images are saved in files and then incorporated into a multimedia presentation.

Besides text scanning, scanners can also be used in image processing to capture pictures for printed publications, Internet Web sites, and electronic presentations. A scanner can digitize a picture by converting dark and light areas of a graphic to dots, or pixels. A file is then saved in computer format for future use. Photographic-enhancement software lets users add special effects and edit photos or images. Digital cameras are now available that store pictures in digital format on a disk instead of photographic film. Since these pictures are already in digital format, no scanning is needed and the pictures are computer-ready.

Single images can be "captured" with a video capture board from videotape, from a video camera, or directly from broadcast television. Videotapes record moving pictures by using thirty still pictures, or frames, for every second of motion. Broadcasts and videotapes use a standard developed in the 1950s in the United States called the NTSC (National Television Standards Committee) broadcast standard. NTSC specifications are thirty frames per second, with each frame a matrix of dots, or pixels, that is 640 pixels wide by 480 pixels high. This standard is different in other parts of the world. Other countries use twenty-five frames per second and have different image sizes. High-definition television, which is currently being introduced, will change the standards so that pictures

will have better quality by increasing the number of pixels, which increases the resolution. Inexpensive video capture cards allow the user to capture one of these frames and use it as a still picture in multimedia applications.

FULL-MOTION VIDEO PROCESSING

More expensive boards allow for "full-motion" capture by saving all the frames and sound. Because these files can get very large (640 × 480 pixels per frame times 30 frames per second), several methods have been developed for compressing motion video files. Video is compressed to save it as a smaller file and is decompressed during playback. Several CODECS (COmpress/DECompress) systems use hardware, including computer chips, such as Intel's Indeo, and software, such as MPEG (motion picture experts group). Since video files are large, they are usually brief recordings or clips from video. The clips are used in business presentations, on Web pages, as product descriptions, or as other media bytes to emphasize an important point in a brief amount of time.

SUMMARY

When connecting multimedia equipment to a computer system to develop multimedia applications, each device has computer software that allows the user to manipulate the media files. Beyond the software that manipulates individual elements of a media project, programs are also available that bring the various elements together into a presentation. These programs include presentation graphics programs and multimedia authoring programs such as Macromedia Director, Microsoft PowerPoint, Corel Presentations, and Astound.

Multimedia involves several "hierarchies" or levels of media types. The more difficult items for computers to handle include advanced sound applications and the processing of full-motion video. As technology increases, most computers will become multimedia machines and companies will use their power in every functional area of business.

BIBLIOGRAPHY

Hofstetter, F. T. (1997). *Multimedia Literacy.* New York: McGraw-Hill.

Sharda, N. K. (1999). *Multimedia Information Networking.* Upper Saddle River, NJ: Prentice-Hall.

Shelly, G. B., Cashman, T. J., Waggoner, G. A., and Waggoner, W. C. (1998). *Discovering Computers 98.* Cambridge, MA: Course Technology-ITP.

GEORGE A. MUNDRAKE

MUTUAL FUNDS

Mutual funds belong to a group of financial intermediaries known as investment companies, which are in the business of collecting funds from investors and pooling them for the purpose of building a portfolio of securities according to stated objectives. They are also known as open-end investment companies. Other members of the group are closed-end investment companies (also known as closed-end funds) and unit investment trusts. In the United States, investment companies are regulated by the Securities and Exchange Commission under the Investment Company Act of 1940.

Mutual funds are generally organized as corporations or trusts, and, as such, they have a board of directors or trustees elected by the shareholders. Almost all aspects of their operations are externally managed. They engage a management company to manage the investment for a fee, generally based on a percentage of the fund's average net assets during the year. The management company may be an affiliated organization or an independent contractor. They sell their shares to investors either directly or through other firms such as broker-dealers, financial planners, employees of insurance companies, and banks. Even the day-to-day administration of a fund is carried out by an outsider, which may be the management company or an unaffiliated third party.

The management company is responsible for selecting an investment portfolio that is consistent with the objectives of the fund as stated in its prospectus and managing the portfolio in the best interest of the shareholders. The directors of the fund are responsibile for overall governance of the fund; they are expected to establish procedures and review the performance of the management company and others who perform services for the fund.

Mutual funds are known as open-end investment companies because they are required to issue shares and redeem (buy back) outstanding shares upon demand. Closed-end funds, on the other other hand, issue a certain number of shares but do not stand ready to buy back their own shares from investors. Their shares are traded on an exchange or in the over-the-counter market. They cannot increase or decrease their outstanding shares easily. A feature common of both mutual funds and closed-end funds is that they are managed investment companies, because they can change the composition of their portfolios by adding and deleting securities and altering the amount invested in each security. Unit investment trusts are not managed investment companies like the mutual funds because their portfolio consists of a fixed set of securities for life. They stand ready, however, to buy back their shares.

TYPES OF MUTUAL FUNDS

There are four basic types of mutual funds: money market, stock (also called equity), bond, and hybrid. This classification is based on the type and the maturity of the securities selected for investment. Money market funds invest in securities that mature in one year or less, such as Treasury bills, commercial paper, and certificates of deposits. They are often referred to as short-term funds. Stock, bond, and hybrid funds invest in long-term securities; as such, they are known as long-term funds. Hybrid funds invest in a combination of stocks, bonds, and other securities. According to the Investment Company Institute (ICI), the national association of the U.S. investment company industry, there were 7,791 (6,746 long-term and 1,045 short-term) mutual funds in the United States and 35,979 outside the country at the end of 1999. The total investment by U.S mutual funds amounted to $6.8 trillion (stock = $4.04 trillion, bond = $808 billion, hybrid = $383 billion, money market = $1.61 trillion) and by non-U.S. funds to $3.5 trillion at the end of 1999. The total assets of U.S. mutual funds are less than the total assets of U.S. depository institutions, which stood at $7.5 trillion at the end of 1999.

Mutual funds also differ in terms of their investment objectives, as outlined in their prospectuses. The ICI classifies mutual funds into thirty-three investment objective categories. The main investment objectives within the stock funds include capital appreciation, total return, and world equity. Within each of these objectives, there are subcategories. There are two groups of bond funds: taxable bond funds and tax-free bond funds. Main categories in taxable bond funds are corporate bond funds, high-yield funds, world bond funds, government bond funds, and strategic income funds. The main tax-free bond fund categories are state municipal bond funds and national municipal bond funds. Among money market funds, there are also taxable money market funds and tax-exempt money market funds. As in the case of stock funds, many subcategories exist within each main category of bond and money market funds. In addition to these, there are specialty or sector funds, which invest in a particular segment of the securities market. Examples include biotechnology funds, small-company growth funds, technology funds, index funds, and social criteria funds.

MUTUAL FUND SHARE PRICING

By law, mutual funds are required to determine the price of their shares each business day. They release their prices the same day for publication in the next day's newspapers. Daily prices of mutual fund shares can also be obtained directly from the fund's offices or Web sites of commercial venders of financial information.

The share price represents the net asset value (NAV) per share, which is the current market value of a fund's assets net of its liabilities. The liabilities include securities purchased, but not yet paid for, accrued fees, dividends payable, and other accrued expenses. The NAV per share is obtained by dividing the NAV by the number of shares of the fund outstanding at the end of the day. A buyer of mutual fund shares pays the NAV per share plus any applicable sales load (also known as a front-end load). Sometimes, the sales load is collected when shares are redeemed; such a sales load is known as a back-end load. Funds that have a sales load are known as *load funds*; they use a sales organization to sell their shares for a fee. Funds that sell shares directly and do not have a sales load are known as *no-load funds*. The sales load often differs from fund to fund, and it is subject to National Association of Security Dealers (NASD) regulation. When an investor sells a share, it is the NAV that the seller usually receives. Some mutual funds may charge a redemption fee if the shares are held for less than a specified period.

BENEFITS AND COST OF INVESTING IN MUTUAL FUNDS

Mutual funds provide investors with a way to diversify their investment under professional management, which most investors may not be able to obtain on their own. Since the funds operate with a large pool of money, the investors benefit from economies of scale, such as a lower trading cost and a higher yield. Besides delivering attractive yields, many funds provide their investors with such services as check-writing privileges, custody (as a service), and bookkeeping. Investors also benefit from the knowledgeable investment choices of securities and investment objectives that funds offer.

The cost to the shareholder of investing in mutual funds comes in various forms: front-end loads, management fees, cost of maintaining and servicing shareholder accounts (administrative cost), redemption fees, and distribution fees (also known as 12b-1 fees). As mentioned before, a redemption fee is usually levied on shares held for less than a specified period. A distribution fee is a charge on current shareholders to cover the costs of advertising, promotion, selling, and other activities. It is sometimes combined with load charges. All these expenses are aggregated to obtain a single measure of cost to the shareholder. An aggregate measure commonly found in the published data is the *expense ratio* (expenses as a percent of assets). This measure does not include sales load, if there is one. Rea and Reid (1998) discuss the calculation of an alternative measure of total ownership cost that includes the sales load.

REGULATION AND TAXATION

All U.S. mutual funds are subject to strict regulation by the Securities and Exchange Commission. They are also subject to states's notice filing requirements and anti-fraud statutes. They are required to provide investors a full disclosure of their activities in a written prospectus. They also provide their investors a yearly statement of distribution with the details of the federal tax status of their distribution. Mutual funds in the United States are not subject to corporate income tax, if they meet certain Internal Revenue Code requirements. Instead, mutual fund shareholders are taxed on the distribution of fund's income. For tax purpose, mutual funds distribute their net income to the shareholders in two ways: (1) dividend and interest payments and (2) realized capital gains.

PERFORMANCE AND COMPARISON

The rate of return is widely used for comparing the performance of mutual funds. The rate of return on a mutual fund investment for a period of one year, for example, is calculated by adding the change in the NAV ($NAV_t - NAV_{t-1}$) to income and capital gains distributed during the year and dividing the sum by the NAV at the beginning of the year. The following describes the calculation of return for no-load funds:

$$R_t = \frac{[(NAV_t - NAV_{t-1}) + i + c]}{NAV_{t-1}.}$$

where R, i, and c represent rate of return, income, and capital gains, respectively. For load funds, the calculation of return must account for load charges by adding them to the NAV_{t-1}. The performance of a mutual fund is often compared with the performance of a benchmark portfolio that is selected to reflect the investment risk level of the fund's portfolio to see whether the mutual fund had a superior performance.

The rate of return of a mutual fund with a NAV of $15.00 at the beginning of a year and $15.50 at the end of that year, and distributed $0.75 and $0.50 per share as income and capital gain respectively during the year would be:

$$[(\$15.50 - \$15.00) + \$0.75 + \$0.50]/\$15.00 = 11.67\%$$

ANALYSIS AND REPORTING

Key statistics pertaining to a fund—such as the NAV, offer price, sales charges, expense ratio, and performance measure for various categories of funds—are regularly calculated, analyzed, and published. Two firms well known for their analytical service are the Lipper Analytical Services (Lipperweb.com) and the Morning Star Inc. (Morningstar.com). The *Wall Street Journal* and *Barron's* carry the information supplied by Lipper Analytical Services on a regular basis. Investment Company Institute (www.ici.org) also provides a wealth of information on mutual funds, including historical data and Web site addresses of its member funds.

(SEE ALSO: *Financial Institutions*)

BIBLIOGRAPHY

Bogle, John. (1994). *Bogle on Mutual Funds.* Richard D. Irwin. Chicago, IL.

Crane, Peter G. (1997). *Mutual Fund Investing on the Internet.* Ap Professional. Burlington, MA.

Henriques, Diana B. (1995). *Fidelity's World: The Secret Life and Public Power of the Mutual Fund Giant.* New York: Simon and Schuster Trade.

Levine, Alan, Gail Liberman and Christy Heady. (1996). *The Complete Idiot's Guide to Making Money with Mutual Funds.* Hampshire, UK: Macmillan General Reference.

Levy, Haim. (1996). *Introduction to Investments.* Cincinnati, OH: South Western College Publishing.

Mutual Fund Fact Book. (2000). Washington, DC: Investment Company Institute.

Rea, John D., and Reid, Brian K. (1998). "Trends in the Ownership Cost of Equity Mutual Funds." *ICI Perspective,* 41(3), (November): 2-15.

Sharpe, William F., Alexander, Gordon J., and Bailey, Jeffery V. (1999). *Investments.* 6th ed., Upper Saddle River, NJ: Prentice Hall.

ANAND G. SHETTY

N

NATIONAL ASSOCIATION OF STATE BOARDS OF ACCOUNTANCY

More than 100 years ago, in 1896, New York appointed the first board of certified public accountant (CPA) examiners. By 1925 all US jurisdictions were administering CPA examinations. Though all states today administer a single Uniform CPA Examination, there are still fifty-four independent boards of accountancy (for all states, the District of Columbia, Guam, the Virgin Islands, and Puerto Rico) that issue licenses to accountants. These boards set entry requirements for their licensees; enforce measures to support continuing competence, through both professional education and/or peer review requirements for renewal of individual licenses and firm registrations; and insure that technical and ethical standards are upheld via disciplinary proceedings growing out of a complaint-based system. Board-levied penalties for malpractice range from fines, to additional education requirements, to pre-report issuance reviews, to withdrawal of license.

The average CPA is generally more aware of the activities of the professional associations than of those of the state board of accountancy. But the professional path of all CPAs all begins with the board: They had to apply to the state board of accountancy to take the Uniform CPA Examination; then they took the examination under the auspices of a state board and waited to hear the results of that examination issued by the state board. It is the state board that requires renewal forms and fees to be submitted and the state board that allows licensees from other states to begin to practice within its borders. Fortunately, in the vast majority of cases, the licensee will never see the disciplinary side of the state board's operations. However, that is a vital aspect of the board's operations that protects the public from unqualified practitioners. The wronged consumer needs no legal counsel. A complaint can be brought directly to the board by any individual or organization. In fact, government agencies that uncover inferior performance by licensees are encouraged to refer their complaints to the accountancy boards. With the growth of the Internet, several states accept on-line complaints via their Web sites.

BOARD MEMBERSHIP

For a long time, the CPA profession has prided itself on self-regulation, partially because of the discipline enforced by its professional organizations and partially because the state boards are primarily composed of licensees. Typically members of a board of accountancy are appointed by a state's governor and include both licensed CPAs and public members. The CPA members are often selected by the governor after consulting with the state's CPA society. A small daily stipend for meeting attendance and travel is awarded by some states; others do not provide such compensation. Boards vary in size from five members to nineteen, many with only one public member. In some jurisdictions, there is a limited term of service; in others, board members can be re-appointed indefinitely. Many of the boards appoint task forces or committees to handle various activities, such as continuing professional education or investigations, which increases the number of volunteer participants. Legal assistance to the boards may come only from the state's attorney general's office or it may also be available from independent counsel. In some states, boards share their administrative staff with other regulatory boards, yet in one jurisdiction the accountancy board has a dedicated staff of over sixty. Similarly, revenues generated by the boards are not treated uniformly: One state will allow the board to use its revenues directly for its licensees; another will have all revenues go into the state's general fund.

As of 1998, the number of licensees in each jurisdiction ranged from Texas, with more than 74,000, to Guam, with 86. Other states with large numbers of licensees include California, with more than 63,000; Ohio, with more than 36,000; and New York, with more than 33,000.

ABOUT NASBA

While the regulation of certified public accountants (and in some jurisdictions "public accountants" or "licensed public accountants") exists on a state-by-state basis, the boards share many concerns; it is from those mutual concerns that the National Association of State Boards of Accountancy (NASBA) was born. Thanks to the efforts of the New Jersey State Board of Public Accountants, the organization was formed in 1908 as the National Association of CPA Examiners, with seventeen examiners from ten states. At that time the New Jersey Board invited all accountancy board members "to confer in regard to matters of mutual interest."

Today, as in 1908, NASBA provides a forum for the boards to exchange views on professional and regulatory issues and trends affecting regulation. Since 1997 its headquarters have been in Nashville, Tennessee, and a satellite office is maintained in New York City. Committee meetings as well as annual and regional meetings are held at sites throughout the country.

Volunteer leadership includes a chairman, vice chairman, nine directors-at-large, and eight regional directors. The directors-at-large are elected for three-year terms. All others serve one-year terms, and all are elected by the member boards at the annual meeting. Officers are not limited to licensees.

To help NASBA achieve its mission of "enhancing the effectiveness of state boards of accountancy," the association holds an annual meeting and regional meetings as well as special issue conferences (including those on continuing professional education, ethics, and legislation) for representatives of accountancy boards. It has volunteer committees researching and reporting on issues of concern, such as examinations, relations with government agencies, and international recognition. The committees are composed of members of the state boards of accountancy as well as state board administrators. In addition, a state accountancy board administrators' committee and legal counsel committee work to assist these individuals who specifically work for the member boards.

NASBA's communication efforts include a monthly newsletter, a biennial digest of state laws, an annual Uniform CPA Examination candidates' statistics report, and an Internet Web site (www.nasba.org) that is linked to the Web sites of all of the state boards that maintain sites. Some audio- and videotape production is also done.

NASBA promulgates no laws. Its committees develop model statutes and rules; however, it is the state legislatures and accountancy boards that do the final drafting and implementing of the laws that regulate the practice of public accountancy. NASBA's committees consult with professional organizations, including the American Institute of Certified Public Accountants (AICPA), the National Society of Accountants, and the American Accounting Association, as they develop suggestions. A joint NASBA/AICPA committee developed the Uniform Accountancy Act (UAA) and Rules, which are continually reviewed and updated as necessary. Model contracts and handbooks have also been developed by NASBA committees.

The profession's technical standards are developed by the AICPA. Members of the profession can be brought before the AICPA for disciplinary procedures in cases where such standards have not been met; however, while the professional organization can withdraw membership privileges, it is only the state board of accountancy that can withdraw the license to practice. Since a person's livelihood is involved in such a decision, every effort is made by the boards to ensure that due process is followed throughout all disciplinary proceedings. Formal hearings are held with legal counsel present, if the licensee so desires.

ENTRY-LEVEL REQUIREMENTS

Requirements to become a certified public accountant vary slightly from jurisdiction to jurisdiction. As Internet practice increases cross-border engagements, all states are being encouraged to move in the direction of adopting one set of standards, as detailed in the UAA. This model act calls for 150 hours of education, one year of experience as attested to by a CPA, and successful completion of the Uniform CPA Examination. For those licensees signing audit reports, additional experience is required. To find out the specific requirements for each state, a candidate needs to check with the state board of accountancy.

The required 150-semester-hour education includes a baccalaureate degree with a concentration in accounting, though not necessarily an accounting major. Again, it is necessary to check with the appropriate accountancy board.

Each of the state boards is charged with the responsibility of administering the Uniform CPA Examination, which is developed and graded by the AICPA. Grades are released to candidates through the state boards. The examination as given in May 2000, for example, was a four-part test given over a two-day period. The four sections of the examination were: auditing (AUDIT), business law and professional responsibilities (LPR), financial accounting and reporting—business enterprises (FARE), and accounting and reporting—other areas. (ARE).

In November 1997, 20.8 percent of the candidates passed all parts of the exam for which they sat. This does not mean they passed the entire examination, since some candidates retake the examination and consequently only take selected parts. In a few jurisdictions, candidates can choose to take only a limited number of parts at a time. Studies are currently being conducted to transform the Uniform CPA Examination into a computer-based examination rather than paper-and-pencil test. Such a transformation would shorten the time needed to complete the examination and enable candidates to take the examination on additional dates.

Experience is another requirement carefully defined in each state's accountancy rules. At one time only auditing experience in public accounting firms was acceptable. Now, in many states, work in government, industry, and academia that leads to professional competence is also being accepted.

CONTINUING COMPETENCE

Continuing professional education (CPE) is mandatory for license renewal in all jurisdictions except Wisconsin. Some states have course requirements in auditing and accounting, others have course requirements in ethics, and still others allow licensees to select courses to meet CPE requirements. With more than half of CPAs now not working as public accountants, pressure exists for enlarging the scope of CPE to encompass a broader range of programs and experiences that help ensure the licensee's competence.

In many states CPA firms are required to register with the accountancy board. The firms are then required to participate in quality review programs periodically, which bring the firms' attest services under the review of outside professionals.

AREAS OF COMMITTEE ACTIVITY

The focus of NASBA's committees echoes the areas of the boards' mutual concerns. Examination, for entry-level candidates as well as international licensees seeking U.S. recognition, continues to be a primary area of interest. Ensuring that the examination adequately measures competence is an ongoing concern. The Examination Review Board audits the preparation, administration, and grading of the Uniform CPA Examination to ensure the boards' requirements are met.

Many states call for CPAs to give evidence of "good moral character." This has been interpreted to mean having knowledge of professional ethics as well as having no criminal record that could be related to practicing accounting. NASBA's ethics committee and administrators committee both are concerned with these issues.

Committees on public perception, strategic initiatives, new horizons, and so forth demonstrate the association's continuing concern with keeping in touch with the public's and the profession's expectations and goals. Information about NASBA is available from NASBA at 150 Fourth Avenue North, Nashville, TN 37219-2417; (615) 880-4200; or www.nasba.org.

Licensed public accountants and public accountants are also recognized in a limited number of jurisdictions

(SEE ALSO: *American Institute of Certified Public Accountants; Public Oversight Board*)

LOUISE DRATLER HABERMAN

NATIONAL BRANDS

(SEE: *Product Labeling*)

NATIONAL BUSINESS EDUCATION ASSOCIATION

The National Business Education Association (NBEA) is an organization whose efforts are directed primarily toward teachers of business and computer technology on all grade levels. One of its mottoes is "Educating for Success in Business and Life."

The NBEA has an executive office at 1914 Association Drive, Reston VA 20191-1596. Its web site is http://www.nbea.org.

The NBEA is administered by the NBEA executive board whose membership in part includes four officers (president, president-elect, secretary-treasurer, past president) and an executive director. In addition, the executive board consists of two representatives each from the five regions (Eastern, Southern, North Central, Mountain-Plains, and Western) and the president of each of its five regional affiliates. The executive board also has representatives from two organizations: National Association for Business Teacher Education (NABTE) and the International Society for Business Education (ISBE).

The official publication of the NBEA is the *Business Education Forum*, published four times a year (October, December, February, and April). The magazine has a publisher, assistant publisher, and editor housed in the NBEA executive office. The editorial policy of the publication is directed by the NBEA Publications Committee, composed of five business educators. The topic editors are business educators. During a recent school year, the editorial topics were accounting, administration and supervision, basic business and economics, entrepreneurship, communications, international business, keyboarding, marketing, methods, research, student organizations, technology, and NABTE review.

In addition to the *Business Education Forum*, the NBEA publishes a yearbook each year as well as other publications.

The NBEA holds an annual convention that rotates from region to region. The convention program incorporates a combination of general sessions featuring well-known speakers, group meetings on a variety of topics, and workshops that often focus on computer topics. One of the features of the convention is a variety of exhibitions showing the latest publications, computer equipment and software, and teaching aids. Awards are presented to outstanding business educators recognized by the regional associations. In addition, the most prestigious award, the John Robert Gregg Award, is presented at the convention.

The NBEA has four categories for membership dues: professional membership, combination professional and ISBE membership, undergraduate student, and retired.

G. W. MAXWELL

NATIONAL LABOR RELATIONS BOARD

The National Labor Relations Board (NLRB) is an independent federal agency. Its creation in 1935 by Congress was in response to the National Labor Relations Act (the Wagner Act). Later acts, such as the Taft-Hartley Act, have amended the original NLRB.

The NLRB is made up of three principal parts: The board, the general counsel, and the regional offices. The board is made up of five members who serve five-year terms. It acts as a quasi-judicial body in deciding cases on formal records. The general counsel is independent of the board, and is responsible for the investigation and prosecution of unfair labor practice cases, as well as overseeing the regional offices. Members of the general counsel serve four-year terms. Both the board and general counsel are appointed by the president with Senate approval. The regional offices and its subdivisions serve certain geographic areas, and they are dispersed throughout the United States—mainly in or near large cities.

The function of the NLRB is twofold. First, it determines and implements, through secret ballot elections, the choice by employees as to whether or not they wish to be represented by a union (and if so by which union) in dealing with their employers. Secondly, it prevents unlawful acts (unfair labor practices), either by employers or by the unions.

Congress, through the National Labor Relations Act, regulates labor-management relations, thereby giving the NLRB its authority. The NLRB, though, has no independent power to enforce its mandates; instead, enforcement is done through the courts of appeals.

One example of what the NLRB does was provided in 1995, when it helped bring a speedy end to the baseball strike. The NLRB secured a 10(j) injunction requiring the owners to withdraw their one-sided imposed changes to the negotiated system of setting baseball wages.

BIBLIOGRAPHY

Gross, James A. (1974). *The Making of the National Labor Relations Board.* New York: State University of New York Press.

TOD W. REJHOLEC

NATIONAL RETAIL FEDERATION

The National Retail Federation (NRF) strives to protect and advance retail industry interests by providing services and conducting programs in government affairs, information technology, education, training, and research. NRF members represent leading merchandise, independent, specialty, discount, and mass-merchandise stores; key suppliers to the retail industry; and more than a hundred trade organizations across the globe. NRF's interactive boards and committees, comprised of industry experts in their areas of specialization, are designed to represent and reflect industry's diversity and breadth. These boards and committees formulate and implement policies, standards, guidelines, and strategies that are consistent with retail industry objectives.

The NRF believes lobbying is a "necessary tool to ensure that [NRF] interests and ... way of doing business is preserved" (Mullin, 1999). *Fortune* magazine, one of the premier publications in the business world, ranked the NRF among the top thirty lobbying organizations in the nation. Additionally, to assist members financially, NRF's member discount program pools the membership's buying power to negotiate reductions on a variety of services and products.

NRF's information technology component serves as the retail industry's information technology headquarters. NRF's groups (the Information Technology Council and various committees) help configure the retail technology environment. They analyze existing and upcoming technologies, as well as potential regulatory and legislative initiatives, and educate private and government entities about retail technology concerns and needs.

Further, through the NRF's various publications (*STORES* Magazine, *Management of Retail Buying, Small Store Survival, Combined Financial, Merchandising and Operating Results of Retail Stores in 1997*, and many others), valuable information, which can be transformed into best practices, is disseminated. For example, the NRF developed standard color and size codes (used to implement Universal Product Codes) and published them in its *Standard Color and Size Code Handbook*.

More information is available from the NRF at 325 7th St., NW, Suite 100, Washington, D.C. 20004; (202) 783-7971 or (800) NRF-HOW2; or http://www.nrf.com.

BIBLIOGRAPHY

Mullin. T. Archived at: http://www.nrf.com/dir/presletter/. 1999.

National Retail Foundation (NRF). Archived at: http://www.nrf.com/dir/standing/. 1999.

NRF. "Information Technology: The Headquarters of Technology Across the Retail Industry." Archived at: http://www.nrf.com/hot/it/. 1999.

NRF. "Member Discount Program." Archived at: http://www.nrf.com/services/group/. 1999.

NRF. "Mission Statement." Archived at: http://www.nrf.com/about/. 1999.

NRF. "Publications." Archived at: http://www.nrf.com/pubs/. 1999.

MARY JEAN LUSH
VAL HINTON

NATIONAL TRANSPORTATION SAFETY BOARD

When the National Transportation Safety Board (NTSB) was established in 1967, it was considered an independent federal agency. However, NTSB's administrative support and funding were funneled through the Department of Transportation (DOT). Over time, the need for a totally separate, nonreliant agency was recognized, and the 1975 Independent Safety Board Act severed all DOT ties.

Congress charges NTSB with investigating every U.S. civil aviation accident, as well as significant railroad, highway, marine, and pipeline accidents. NTSB, based on investigation findings, then issues safety recommendations in an effort to prevent future accidents.

NTSB's different from other agencies in that it has no official enforcement or regulatory powers, it is a totally independent agency, and its specially trained staff conduct investigations and determine probable cause. Its investigations are broad, looking more for the *big picture*, rather than attempting to focus on a specific detail or category.

With less than 400 employees, NTSB is a small agency. However, it plays a large role in maintaining and/or restoring public confidence in the safety of the nation's transportation systems. NTSB has investigated thousands of surface transportation accidents and more than 100,000 aviation accidents since it began operation in 1967.

The most important outcomes of NTSB investigations are the safety recommendations the agency issues based on investigation findings. NTSB has proven itself to be thorough and impartial and has been able to achieve an admirable (more than 80 percent) acceptance rate of recommendations made to various individuals and organizations in positions to effect change.

NTSB also uses accident investigation findings to identify trends or issues that may otherwise be overlooked. Through proactive outreach efforts (e.g., conferences, symposia, and state advocacy), NTSB makes the public aware of potential safety problem areas, such as child safety seat concerns or accidents related to human fatigue factors.

NTSB also enjoys an international leadership role, specifically in regard to accidents involving cruise ships or foreign-flag vessels in U.S. waters or U.S. planes or U.S.-made aircraft overseas.

Robert Francis, vice chairman of the National Transportation Safety Board.

NTSB has thus contributed significantly to increasing levels of safety for individuals worldwide.

To focus attention on NTSB recommendations with the most potential to save lives, NTSB has created its "Most Wanted List" of improvements in transportation safety, which includes areas where rapid improvement is considered essential. This list includes requiring railroads to install collision avoidance systems, having natural gas distribution companies install excess flow valves in high-pressure residential systems, having voyage and flight data recorders with increased parameters installed on ships and airplanes respectively, and requiring fire detection and suppression equipment in airplane cargo compartments.

NTSB's safety recommendations have resulted in many safety improvements. For instance, recommendations stemming from the ValuJet Flight 92 accident in Florida resulted in a Department of Transportation's Research and Special Programs Administration Agency (RSPA) rule prohibiting passenger-carrying aircraft from transporting oxygen generators as cargo. In the wake of natural gas pipeline accidents in Catskill, New York, and Allentown, Pennsylvania, cast-iron pipe monitoring and replacement programs were implemented by two major gas-distribution companies. The Federal Aviation Association (FAA) has acted to have Boeing 737 rudder systems modified based on NTSB recommendations stemming from the USAir Flight 427 incident in Pittsburgh. In response to an NTSB-issued emergency recommendation based on its 1996 Child Passenger Protection Study, the automobile industry attached labels and sent warning letters to owners about the dangers posed to children by airbags. Information on other actions resulting from NTSB recommendations is available from NTSB at 490 L'Enfant Plaza SW, Washington, D.C. 20594; (202) 314-6000; or http://www.ntsb .gov/.

BIBLIOGRAPHY

Hall, Jim. Testimony of Jim Hall, Chairman NTSB, before the Committee on Appropriations Subcommittee on Transportation and Related Agencies, House of Representatives, Regarding Fiscal Year 1998 Budget Request. March 11, 1997. Archived at: http://www.ntsb.gov/ speeches/jh970311.html.

National Transportation Safety Board (NTSB). Website: http://www.ntab.gov/. 1999.

NTSB. "About the NTSB: History and Mission." Archived at: http://www.ntsb.gov/Abt_NTSB/history.htm. 1999.

NTSB. Strategic Plan. Archived at: http://www.ntsb.gov/ Abt_NTSB/strategic/plan.htm. 1999.

MARY JEAN LUSH
VAL HINTON

NEGOTIATION

Negotiation is the process of two individuals or groups reaching joint agreement about differing needs or ideas. Oliver (1996) described negotiation as "negotiators jointly searching a multidimensional space and then agreeing to a single point in the space."

Negotiation applies knowledge from the fields of communications, sales, marketing, psychology, sociology, politics, and conflict resolution. Whenever an economic transaction takes place or a dispute is settled, negotiation occurs; for example, when consumers purchase automobiles or businesses negotiate salaries with employees.

NEGOTIATION STYLES

Two styles of negotiating, competitive and cooperative, are commonly recognized. No negotiation is purely one type or the other; rather, negotiators typically move back and forth between the two styles based on the situation.

On one end of the negotiation continuum is the competitive style. Competitive negotiation—also called adversarial, noncooperative, distributive bargaining, positional, or hard bargaining—is used to divide limited resources; the assumption is that the pie to be divided is finite.

Competitive strategies assume a "win-lose" situation in which the negotiating parties have opposing interests. Hostile, coercive negotiation tactics are used to force an advantage, and prenegotiation binding agreements are not allowed. Concessions, distorted communication, confrontational tactics, and emotional ploys are used.

Skilled competitive negotiators give away less information while acquiring more information, ask more questions, create strategies to get information, act firm, offer less generous opening offers, are slower to give concessions, use confident body language, and conceal feelings. They are more interested in the bargaining position and bottom line of the other negotiating party, and they prepare for negotiations by developing strategy, planning answers to weak points, and preparing alternate strategies.

A buyer-seller home purchase transaction illustrates competitive negotiating. The buyer gathers information to determine home value, quality, expenses, and title status. The seller gathers information to ensure that the prospective buyer qualifies for the loan. The parties negotiate concessions regarding home repairs, items to remain in the house, closing dates, and price. The negotiations stall as the buyer and seller disagree on a closing date; the seller retaliates by keeping the buyer out of the home for several days after the closing date. As a consequence of the competitive strategies used, the relationship between the buyer and seller suffers; however, the end result (sale and purchase of a home) satisfies both parties.

On the other end of the negotiating style continuum is cooperative negotiating, also called integrative problem solving or soft bargaining. Cooperative-negotiation is based on a win-win mentality and is designed to increase joint gain; the pie to be divided is perceived as expanding. Attributes include reasonable and open communication; an assumption that common interests, benefits, and needs exist; trust building; thorough and accurate exchange of information; exploration of issues presented as problems and solutions; mediated discussion; emphasis on coalition formation; prenegotiation binding agreements; and a search for creative alternative solutions that bring benefits to all players. The risk in cooperative negotiating is vulnerability to a competitive opponent.

Cooperative negotiators require skills in patience; listening; and identification and isolation of cooperative issues, goals, problems, and priorities. Additionally, cooperative negotiators need skills in clarifying similarities and differences in goals and priorities and the ability to trade intelligently, propose many alternatives, and select the best alternative based on quality and mutual acceptability.

Cooperative negotiating might be used, for example, in a hiring situation. An employer contacts a candidate to encourage the candidate to submit his or her credentials for a job opening. Trust is built and common interests are explored as the employer and candidate exchange information about the company and the candidate's qualifications. Creative solutions are explored to accommodate the candidate's and employer's special circumstances, including work at home, flexible scheduling, salary, and benefits. The two parties successfully culminate the negotiations with a signed job contract.

THE NEGOTIATION PROCESS

Stages in the negotiation process are (1) orientation and fact finding, (2) resistance, (3) reformulation of strategies, (4) hard bargaining and decision making, (5) agreement, and (6) follow-up (Acuff, 1997). For example, a consumer purchasing an automobile investigates price and performance, then negotiates with an agent regarding price and delivery date. Resistance surfaces as pricing and delivery expectations are negotiated. Strategies are reformulated as the parties determine motivation and constraints. Key issues surface as hard bargaining begins. Problems surface, and solutions—such as creative financing or dealer trades—are created to counter pricing and delivery problems. After details are negotiated, the agreement is ratified. After the sale, the agent may follow up with the buyer to build a relationship and set the stage for future purchase and negotiation. The six stages of the process would be approached differently depending on where the negotiators reside on the style continuum.

Basic strategies, both cooperative and competitive, that can be applied in the negotiation process are the following:

- Use simple language.
- Ask many questions.
- Observe and practice nonverbal behavior.
- Build solid relationships.
- Maintain personal integrity.
- Be patient.
- Conserve concessions.
- Be aware of the power of time, information, saying no, and walking away.
- Pay attention to who the real decision maker is, how negotiators are rewarded, and information sources.
- Listen actively.
- Educate the other party.
- Concentrate on the issues.
- Control the written contract.
- Be creative.
- Appeal to personal motivations and negotiating styles.
- Pay attention to power tactics.
- Be wary of such unethical tactics as raising phony issues; extorting; planting information; and making phony demands, unilateral assumptions, or deliberate mistakes.

The following summarize strategies that might be used in various stages of negotiations:

INITIAL STAGES

- Plan thoroughly.
- Identify and prioritize issues.
- Establish a settlement range.
- Focus on long-term goals and consequences.
- Focus on mutual principles and concerns.
- Be aware that "no" can be the opening position and the first offer is often above expectations.
- Be aware of the reluctant buyer or seller ploy.

MIDDLE STAGES

- Revise strategies.

- Consider many options.
- Increase power by getting the other side to commit first.
- Add credibility by getting agreements in writing.
- Be wary of splitting the difference.
- To handle an impasse, offer to set it aside momentarily.
- To handle a stalemate, alter one of the negotiating points.
- To handle a deadlock, bring in a third party.
- When asked for a concession, ask for a trade-off.
- Be wary if the other party uses a "higher authority" as a rationale for not meeting negotiating points.
- Be aware of the "vise" tactic ("you'll have to do better than that").

ENDING STAGES

- Counter the other party's asking for more concessions at the end by addressing all details and communicating the fairness of the deal in closure.
- Counter a persistent negotiator by withdrawing an offer.
- Do not expect the other party to follow through on verbal promises.
- Congratulate the other side.

INTERNATIONAL NEGOTIATING

In international negotiations, obstacles arise when negotiating teams possess conflicting perspectives, tactics, and negotiating styles. Negotiators often assume that shared beliefs exist when, in reality, they do not. Examples are different uses of time; individualism versus collectivism; different degrees of role orderliness and conformity; and communication patterns, that differ widely worldwide. These cultural factors affect the pace of negotiations; negotiating strategies; degree of emphasis on personal relationships; emotional aspects; decision making; and contractual and administrative elements (Acuff, 1997). The goal of the negotiator should be to "look legitimately to the other side by their standards" (Fisher, 1984).

COLLECTIVE BARGAINING

Collective bargaining frequently requires a third party to help the parties reach an acceptable solution. In these situations, such strategies as mediation, arbitration, and conflict resolution are used.

SUMMARY

Negotiation is the process of two individuals or groups reaching joint agreement about differing needs or ideas. Two styles of negotiating, competitive and cooperative, are commonly recognized, with most negotiators moving back and forth between the two styles based on the situation. A number of strategies were discussed that negotiators might use in negotiation stages. The effectiveness of various strategies can vary based on cultural differences.

BIBLIOGRAPHY

Acuff, Frank L. (1997). *How to Negotiate Anything with Anyone Anywhere Around the World*. New York: American Management Association.

Fisher, Roger, and Ury, William, with Bruce Patton. (1991). *Getting to Yes: Negotiating Agreement Without Giving In*, 2nd ed. Boston: Houghton Mifflin.

Oliver, Jim R. (1996). "A Machine Learning Approach to Automated Negotiation and Prospects for Electronic Commerce." http://opim.wharton.upenn.edu/-oliver27/papers/jmis.ps. July 31, 1996.

DONNA L. MCALISTER-KIZZIER

NETWORKING

Networking means joining or linking devices such as computers. A local area network (LAN) is a collection of computers and other devices connected through some medium that transmits mostly data. The following characteristics are closely associated with LANs; however, one must be aware that LANs are continually changing.

LAN CHARACTERISTICS

Private ownership: LANs consist of devices such as computers, scanners, printers, and cables that are privately owned. Networks also consist of privately owned lines, wires, hubs, and servers. Lines can be made of twisted-pair or coaxial-cable wires, or they can be wireless (such as radio or infrared waves). Hubs connect LAN segments, which are lengths of wire that have one or several attached devices. Servers are computers that are dedicated to one function, such as managing printers or storing applications or data. In short, businesses create and manage their own networks.

LAN size: The size of a LAN is determined by the type of LAN configuration and specifications that are used. Generally, LANs range from several hundred yards up to several miles, but mostly they reside in an office or classroom, building, or several buildings. On one hand, an Ethernet network using 10Base2 ("Thin Ethernet") can have one segment 200 meters in length or five linked segments up to 1,000 meters in length. The *10* in 10Base2 stands for 10 megabits per second, *Base* means baseband, and *2* means 200 meters. On the other hand, FDDI (Fiber Distributed Data Interface) networks can be up to 200 kilometers (124 miles) in length; however, these are mostly used as backbones that link several LANs.

LAN speed: Another characteristic of a LAN is speed. LAN speed is most often measured in bits per second. For example, a byte (or one character or space) consists of 8 bits. If an average word length is 5 characters and an average double-spaced page is about 200 words, then a page (counting words and spaces) would consist of about 9600 bits — [(200 words × 5 characters) + 199 spaces] × 8 bits. If a network speed is 9600 bits per second (bps), then a normal double-spaced page is transmitted every second. Another LAN could operate at 56 kilobits (kbps)—or 56,000 bits—per second, about 6 pages of information per second. However, LANs are typically faster than 9600 and 56,000 bps. Many LANs are 10, 16, or 100 megabits per second (Mbps). A 100-Mbps LAN can send 100,000,000 bits in one second—or 10,416 pages per second. Some LANs can transmit 2.8 billion bits per second—gigabits (Gbps). At 2 Gbps (2,000,000,000/9600), 208,000 pages flash by every second—more than most people read in a lifetime! Engineers and LAN administrators are finding even faster ways to communicate data. LAN speeds are reaching terabits per second (Tbps). One Tbps equals 1000 gigabits—an almost unthinkable speed.

The medium used to carry signals in a LAN can be conducted or radiated. Electric signals over wire are conducted. Fiber-optic lines, microwaves, infrared waves, and radio waves are examples of radiated media.

Wire can be coaxial cable or shielded (STP) or unshielded (UTP) twisted pair. UTP is cheaper to install than STP or coaxial cable; therefore it is a popular network choice. However, STP or coaxial cable should be used if there is risk that a network might be harmed by electromagnetic interference. Other networks that overcome electromagnetic interference are fiber-optic lines and wireless media. They, too, are more expensive than UTP wiring.

Twisted-pair wires are rated by the American Wire Gauge (AWG) standard. The smaller the number, the thicker the wire. Regular telephone wire is rated a 28, which is too thin for most LANs. LANs use AWG that is between 22 and 26. Another characteristic of twisted-pair wires is the number of twists per foot. More twists may reduce crosstalk, but they also increase wire costs. Crosstalk occurs when one line picks up noise or voices from another line during a conversation or data transmission. Usually 2 twists per foot are minimum, while 4 are preferred.

The EIA (Electronic Industries Association) is another standard for rating wires. The EIA classifies LAN wires for different uses. For example, Category 3, or "Cat 3," must contain 3 twists per foot; it is commonly used in creating 10-Mbps LANs. "Cat 5" is good for 100 Mbps and up to 2 Gbps.

Low error rates: Older LANs had a difficult time eliminating electromagnetic interference, which created errors during data transmission. Therefore, error checking of data frames was necessary and performed by a protocol. On LANs, data are sent in separate frames controlled by protocols. Protocols are rules between sending and receiving LAN devices. Protocols used parity checks or algorithms to determine whether a data frame had transmission errors. As LAN technology has improved, less error checking is necessary. Less error checking converts to higher bit-rate speeds. An example of new LAN technology, with less error checking, is the ATM (asynchronous transfer mode), or cell-relay, LAN.

Currently, most LANs use baseband transmission. Baseband means that there is one signal transmission per line. What this means is that only one device can use the line at a time. The channel is full when one device is sending data. Because baseband LANs are easily monitored, so errors can be detected and reduced. Broadband means that the line can handle several transmissions at one time. This is accomplished using different frequencies that act as separate channels; this is called frequency division multiplexing (FDM). Broadband LANs are more complex than baseband LANs, and they require expensive technology. Additionally, broadband is more susceptible to errors than baseband.

LAN USES

LANs have become an operational necessity for just about every business. Burgeoning information demands make it necessary to link all computers for efficient data sharing and storage. Furthermore, e-mail, electronic commerce, and video conferencing are enhanced services for today's LAN users.

In addition to sharing data and hardware, properly managed networks increase productivity. Things like standardized applications, controlled access, users' rights, companywide backups, and recovery strategies help businesses manage their information more efficiently than at any time in the past.

Standards also help LAN development and allow different devices from many manufacturers to be connected. Standards originate from businesses, organizations, and networking practices that are associated with electronics, communications, and computers.

When LANs are linked to other LANs, a network structure called a wide area network (WAN) is formed. WANs have many configurations and can extend globally. One aspect of a WAN is a gateway to the Internet. Gateways are special switches that allow LANs with different topologies, controls, and protocols to communicate.

LAN CONFIGURATIONS

Three common LAN configurations are bus, ring, and star topologies. All topologies have advantages and limitations.

A bus topology is a physical layout in which microcomputer workstations and other devices are connected to a UTP/STP or cable segment. Data travel in frames through a wire, called a bus, from the sending station to the receiving station. Bus wiring is looped together with terminators at each end. Terminators are used so that signals can recognize the bus end. When this happens, the signal is reflected back to the other end of the bus. This LAN topology is the most widely used configuration due to the popular Ethernet bus protocol.

Ring configurations are used, too. IBM is responsible for developing and promoting ring configurations. On a ring, all computers are connected to a continuous loop wire or cable. Data flow in one direction. Each workstation is a repeater. Repeaters charge up a signal and send it over the next segment to the next workstation; this process is repeated around the ring.

A star topology is a group of workstations connected to a controlling switch. Data packets always flow through the switch to get from one workstation to another. Switches control and manage all data flow. Switches can read the destination address on a data frame and route the frame to the line segment that contains the destination workstation.

LAN DATA FLOW

LANs need flow control to operate at high speeds. Flow control is another protocol function. Two common LAN protocols are CSMA/CD (carrier sense multiple access/collision detection) and token passing.

CSMA/CD is also called contention. CSMA/CD is used by one of the oldest and most used standards—Ethernet. Contention is a LAN term that means that any station can broadcast a data frame on the bus line at any time. A sending station creates a frame by putting a destination address along with its own address around a unit of information called a data unit. This frame is broadcast to every workstation on the bus. All stations check the destination address to see if the frame is for them.

Token-passing protocols can work on a ring or bus, but they are mainly used on a ring. A 3-byte "free" token is always circulating around a ring and stops at every station. When Station A wants to send data to Station B, it waits for the token. When the token stops at Station A, A changes the "free" token to "busy" and attaches a data frame. The data frame contains a header with the destination and source address around a data unit. The combined token and data frame go from one station to another until they get to Station B. Station B recognizes the busy token and checks the destination address. Since the frame has "its" destination address, it copies the data frame and changes a part of the header, acknowledging that it received the data. The token and data frame return to Station A and A deletes the data frame and changes the token back to "free." This process continues when any station wants to send a frame.

CONCLUSION

LANs are efficient and necessary business tools. They began as individual, stand-alone microcomputers that evolved not in any pattern but based on unique business needs. Technology and standards help networking grow. Perhaps someday a worldwide network of linked computers will exist to communicate data, voice, and video to everyone in the world.

DENNIS J. LaBONTY

NORTH AMERICAN INDUSTRY CLASSIFICATION SYSTEM

The North American Industry Classification System (NAICS) groups establishments into industries according to their primary economic activities. It facilitates the collection, calculation, presentation, and analysis of statistical data by industry. The United States, Canada, and Mexico developed the system to provide comparable statistics among North American Free Trade Agreement countries. Statistical agencies in these countries use NAICS to produce information by industry on inputs and outputs, productivity, industrial performance, unit labor cost, and employment. Both government and business use this information to understand industries and the economy.

NAICS is founded on a production-oriented conceptual framework. It groups establishments according to similarity in the processes used to produce services or goods. This supply-based framework delineates differences in production technologies. In this system, an industry is not solely a grouping of products or services.

BACKGROUND

The NAICS replaced the Standard Industrial Classification (SIC) in the United States. Developed in the 1930s, the SIC was periodically revised to reflect economic changes through 1987. The SIC was increasingly criticized as rapid changes affected both the U.S. and world economies. NAICS addresses such changes by developing production-oriented classifications for new industries, high-technology industries, and service industries in general.

In 1992, the Office of Management and Budget (OMB), an Executive Office of the President, established the Economic Classification Policy Committee (ECPC). The ECPC was chartered to provide a "fresh-slate" examination of economic classifications for statistical purposes. The ECPC ultimately joined with Mexico's Instituto Nacional de Estadistica, Geografia e Informatica (INEGI) and Statistics Canada to develop the NAICS. The three countries will rejoin to update the NAICS codes on a regular five-year cycle, in contrast to the sporadic revisions of the SIC codes.

All federal agencies have adopted NAICS United States for statistical use. NAICS commences implementation for reference year 1997 in the United States and Canada, and for 1998 in Mexico. The U.S. Bureau of the Census used NAICS to prepare the 1997 Economic Census, available in 1999. Government-wide implementation of NAICS will continue at least through 2004 in the United States. Updated information about implementation is available from the Census Bureau's NAICS Internet site at www.census.gov/naics.

STRUCTURE OF NAICS

NAICS uses a six-digit code to identify particular industries, in contrast to the four-digit SIC code. The structure of NAICS is hierarchical. The first two digits of each code indicate the sector. The third, fourth, fifth, and sixth digits indicate the subsector, industry group, NAICS industry, and national industry respectively. There are codes for 1170 U.S. industries in NAICS—United States, 1997.

NAICS classifies sectors first. The NAICS—United States, 1997 manual presents the twenty sectors, their two-digit codes, and the distinguishing activities of each, as follows:

11 Agricultural, Forestry, Fishing and Hunting—Activities of this sector are growing crops, raising animals, harvesting timber, and harvesting fish and other animals from farms, ranches, or the animals' natural habitat.

21 Mining—Activities of this sector are extracting naturally occurring mineral solids, such as coal and ore; liquid minerals, such as crude petroleum; and gases, such as natural gas; and beneficiating (e.g., crushing, screening, washing, and flotation) and other preparation at the mine site, or as part of mining activity.

22 Utilities—Activities of this sector are generating, transmitting, and/or distrib-

uting electricity, gas, steam, and water and removing sewage through a permanent infrastructure of lines, mains, and pipe.

23 Construction—Activities of this sector are erecting buildings and other structures (including additions); heavy construction other than buildings; and alterations, reconstruction, installation, and maintenance and repairs.

31-33 Manufacturing—Activities of this sector are the mechanical, physical, or chemical transformation of material, substances, or components.

41-43 Wholesale Trade—Activities of this sector are selling or arranging for the purchase or sale of goods for resale, capital or durable nonconsumer goods, and raw and intermediate materials and supplies used in production, and providing services incidental to the sale of the merchandise.

44-46 Retail Trade—Activities of this sector are retailing merchandise generally in small quantities to the general public and providing services incidental to the sale of the merchandise.

48-49 Transportation and Warehousing— Activities of this sector are providing transportation of passengers and cargo, warehousing and storing goods, scenic and sightseeing transportation, and supporting these activities.

51 Information—Activities of this sector are distributing information and cultural products, providing the means to transmit or distribute these products as data or communications, and processing data.

52 Finance and Insurance— Activities of this sector involve the creation, liquidation, or change in ownership of financial assets (financial transactions) and/or facilitating financial transactions.

53 Real Estate and Rental and Leasing— Activities of this sector are renting, leasing, or otherwise allowing the use of tangible or intangible assets (except copyrighted works), and providing related services.

54 Professional, Scientific, and Technical Services—Activities of this sector are performing professional, scientific, and technical services for the operations of other organizations.

55 Management of Companies and Enterprises— Activities of this sector are the holding of securities of companies and enterprises, for the purpose of owning controlling interest or influencing their management decision, or administering, overseeing, and managing other establishments of the same company or enterprise and normally undertaking the strategic or organizational planning and decision making of the company or enterprise.

56 Administrative and Support and Waste Management and Remediation Services— Activities of this sector are performing routine support activities for the day-to-day operations of other organizations.

61 Educational Services— Activities of this sector are providing instruction and training in a wide variety of subjects.

62 Health Care and Social Assistance— Activities of this sector are providing health care and social assistance for individuals.

71 Arts, Entertainment, and Recreation— Activities of this sector are operating or providing services to meet varied cultural, entertainment, and recreational interests of their patrons.

72 Accommodation and Food Services— Activities of this sector are providing customers with lodging and/or pre-

paring meals, snacks, and beverages for immediate consumption.

81 Other Services (Except Public Administration) — Activities of this sector are providing services not elsewhere specified, including repairs, religious activities, grantmaking, advocacy, laundry, personal care, death care, and other personal services.

91-93 Public Administration—Activities of this sector are administration, management, and oversight of public programs by federal, state, and local governments.

EXAMPLE

NAICS code 711211 identifies the Sports Teams and Clubs industry in the United States and Canada. It belongs to:

Sector 71—Arts, Entertainment and Recreation

Subsector 711—Performing Arts, Spectator Sports, and Related Industries

Industry Group 7112—Spectator Sports

NAICS Industry 71121—Spectator Sports

National Industry 711211—Sports Teams and Clubs

The NAICS—United States, 1997 manual gives a detailed description of the Sports Teams and Clubs industry. It consists of professional or semiprofessional sports teams or clubs engaged in live sporting events (e.g., football, baseball, and soccer games) for a paying audience. These establishments may or may not run their own stadium, arena, or other facility to present sporting events. The United States, Canada, and Mexico collect similar data for NAICS industry 71121, Spectator Sports. The United States and Canada collect more detailed data at the six-digit national industry level for Sports Teams and Clubs. The United States collects data for two additional national industries within the NAICS industry: Spectator Sports: Racetracks (code 711212) and Other Spectator Sports (code 711219).

ASSIGNMENT OF NAICS CODES

NAICS is a classification system for establishments. NAICS—United States, 1997 defines an establishment as "the smallest operating entity for which records provide information on the cost of resources—materials, labor, and capital—employed to produce the units of output" (EOP 1998, p. 16). In the United States the establishment is generally a single physical location using a distinct process to produce goods or services. An enterprise (company) may consist of more than one establishment. Each establishment within the enterprise is assigned a NAICS code. Statistical agencies such as the Census Bureau and the Bureau of Labor Statistics assign NAICS codes based on information reported to them.

INTERNATIONAL COMPARABILITY

Comparable data for the United States, Canada, and Mexico are generally available at the five-digit NAICS industry level. The sixth digit of the NAICS code is used to define national industries, which differ among the three countries due to differences in economic and organizational structures.

Many other countries collect data using the International Standard Industrial Classification (ISIC) system established by the United Nations (UN) in 1948. The UN's Statistical Commission revised the ISIC structure and codes in 1958, 1968, and 1989. Similar to NAICS, ISIC primarily classifies establishments (rather than enterprises and firms). The criteria used to classify ISIC division and groups are: (1) the type of goods and services produced; (2) the uses of goods and services produced; and (3) the inputs, process, and technology of production. The third classification criterion of the ISIC is the conceptual foundation of NAICS. Hence, NAICS is aligned more closely with ISIC than the 1987 SIC system. Statistics compiled on NAICS are comparable with statistics compiled according to ISIC, Revision 3, for some sixty high level groupings.

BIBLIOGRAPHY

Executive Office of the President (EOP), Office of Management and Budget. (1998). *North American Industry Classification System—United States, 1997.* Springfield, VA: National Technical Information Service.

MARY MICHEL

NOT-FOR-PROFIT ACCOUNTING

The terms "not-for-profit," "nonprofit," and even "nonbusiness" have been used to describe organizations that have one basic characteristic in common: Their primary purpose is related to social objectives, not to profit. These organizations may also have other common characteristics, such as nonprofit tax status, an appointed board, and for some, oversight of their operations by a governmental agency. Examples of such not-for-profits (NFPs) include libraries, museums, performing arts organizations, zoological and botanical societies, trade associations, unions, professional associations, fraternal organizations, private and community foundations, voluntary health and welfare organizations, social and country clubs, religious organizations, and public broadcasting stations.

State and local governments are not considered to be part of this group, although the accounting practices for some NFPs may be the same as those used by state and local governments as a number of NFPs are part of a state or local government.

BUSINESS MANAGEMENT OBJECTIVES

These have a broader focus than traditional for-profit company management goals and objectives. The comprehensive management of NFPs incorporates a wide range of goals beyond the generation of profits. Evaluative measures closely related to profits, such as return on investment and earnings per share, are not relevant to the managers of NFP organizations.

Yet, simply meeting annual budget targets does not mean an NFP is successful. In fact, it could mean just the opposite if financial goals have been achieved through the minimization of important social and customer goals. Like for-profit organizations, NFP management methods should begin with a mission statement and incorporate sets of interrelated goals that clearly relate the performance of numerous organizational activities back to the mission. Unfortunately, many times the evaluative focus is largely based on financial measures.

One recognized management method that uses a diverse approach beyond just financial measure for evaluating organizational performance is the balanced scorecard (BSC). BSC ties performance objectives together within the perspectives of the customer/client, financial, learning and growth, and internal business processes. Although traditional financial goals are in the mix, client needs, employee learning and growth, and the analysis of unique internal business processes take on equal importance with financial goals. The BSC links short-term goals to a long-term strategy guided by the organization's mission statement. These four areas are linked with objective performance measures that support one another. The BSC is an example of a management method that uses more than bottom-line or budget criteria in guiding the performance of organizations. Such a method is particularly pertinent to nonprofit organizations with a wide range of objectives beyond traditional financial ones.

Clearly there is an underlying difference in NFP measures of performance when compared with similar for-profit measures. For example, financial concerns for an NFP may be focused on flexibility of resource usage rather than return on investment. Since NFPs may work with client caseloads, a performance measure may be related to the number of documents processed or response time tied to measures of customer satisfaction. Employee growth measures might relate to training levels or measures of expanding growth in job skills. Evaluations of internal business processes might trace the employee training to its innovative effect on older programs and the introduction of successful new programs.

NFP ACCOUNTING STANDARDS

These standards are established by the Financial Accounting Standards Board (FASB) or the Government Accounting Standards Board (GASB). Additionally, the American Institute of Certified Public Accountants (AICPA) influences the accounting for nonprofit organizations with its industry and accounting guides and Statements of Position (SOPs).

It may appear that the accounting methods used by NFPs are the same among all of them. Currently, this is not the case, however, because NFPs can be considered either "governmental" or "nongovernmental" NFPs for accounting purposes. The distinction is important because it affects the generally accepted accounting principles (GAAPs) to be followed—modified accrual for "government" organizations and accrual for "nongovernmental" organizations. Even among organizations classified "governmental" NFPs, the methods of accounting may differ.

A governmental NFP has one or more of the following characteristics (American Institute of Certified Public Accountants, *Not-for-Profit Organization*, par. 1.03, New York: AICPA, 1996):

1. Popular election of officers or appointment (or approval) of a controlling majority of the members of the organization's governing body by officials of one or more state or local governments.

2. The potential for unilateral dissolution by a government with net assets reverting to a government.

3. The power to enact and enforce a tax levy.

One of the most common characteristics that result in an NFP's being classified as a governmental NFP is that a majority of its board is appointed by a state or local government.

There are three different GAAP methods of accounting used to prepare financial statements for a nonprofit organization, depending on how it is classified. The choices are business accrual, nonprofit SOP accrual, and modified accrual.

Governmental NFPs may use nonprofit SOP accrual or modified accrual methods of accounting. They would use nonprofit SOP accrual if they had been previously applying an SOP for nonprofit organizations or health and welfare organizations and decided to continue to use this method. These organizations have a choice of using either modified accrual or nonprofit SOP accrual.

The standard-setting organization that establishes modified accrual accounting standards for NFPs is the GASB. Nongovernmental NFPs follow the business accrual methods that are used by corporations. These accounting standards are set by the FASB. It should be clear that there are both governmental museums and nongovernmental museums, for example. This governmental/nongovernmental division is present among other NFPs, too. Therefore, if resources used in a program, for example, are compared between governmental/nongovernmental NFPs without adjustments for the accounting method in use, there can be serious misinterpretations.

There are other differences. Under accrual accounting for nongovernment NFPs, the Statement of Activities (income statement) uses the term "net assets" in place of "excess" or "deficiency," as is the case under modified accrual. Corporations call this the "net income." Typical revenue and expense items are included in the Statement of Activities, but nongovernmental NFPs also includes increases and decreases in restricted assets. Restricted assets are received grants or donations for which the organization has not completed its obligations under the grant or donation requirements. Thus, changes in restricted grants or donations are included in the calculation of *net assets*, whereas the *excess* or *deficiency* in a modified accrual statement for a governmental NFP does not include these items.

As an example, assume that Nonprofit A, a nongovernmental NFP, receives a restricted grant, and at the same time Nonprofit B, a governmental NFP, gets the same restricted grant. Under modified accrual accounting, the restricted grant is considered to be a liability because the terms of the grant have not been fulfilled. Under accrual accounting, it is not considered a liability; instead it is recorded as a revenue item. Under accrual concepts, the restricted grant is considered to be temporarily restricted, but its restrictions are assumed to be removed when expenditures are made under the grant. Because total revenues are different in the two hypothetical NFPs, the balances transferred to their respective balance sheets are also different.

On the balance sheet, another important difference is that the term "fund balance" is not used on an accrual-based balance sheet for a nongovernment NFP but is used on the balance sheet of a governmental NFP. A fund balance develops as a result of the difference between assets and liabilities. It represents the residual between those account groupings. For most funds, the balance in the Fund Balance is a source of additional appropriations. In the balance sheet for a nongovernmental NFP, the residual is termed "net assets." Net assets are a residual between assets and liabilities, but there is a difference. First, net assets are divided into unrestricted, temporarily restricted, and permanently restricted amounts. Permanently restricted net assets are those with a donor-related stipulation restricting the donated resources from being used and allowing only the income earned on the balance to be used. Temporarily restricted net assets are those donations that can be used for spending after the expiration of specific actions or the occurrence of a specified event. The remaining net assets are classified as unrestricted and include those resources that are typically found in the Fund Balance.

These classifications do not appear in the Fund Balance for a governmental NFP where all reserved amounts in the Fund Balance have been determined by the direct internal actions of managers, not by the external actions of granter or donors. Consequently, the Fund Balance reflects the summation of the appropriation process occurring inside the organization. Under modified accrual, the classifications within the Fund Balance show the restrictions on available *spendable* resources only. Reserve for Encumbrances and

Designated Funds are examples of managerial restrictions of previously received appropriations that remain unexpended. Here, restricted grants are recorded as liabilities rather than as part of the residual, that is, the Fund Balance. This difference in the two methods is related to differing views about the resources that are actually available for spending.

Another difference between the methods is that accrual accounting for NFPs does not strongly support the fund concept whereby assets and related liabilities are grouped into self-balancing funds. Rather, accrual for NFPs views the entity's assets as being part of one entity rather than as separately grouped accounts for each fund. Modified accrual divides the organizational accounting activities into a series of separate funds that are viewed as separate entities within the organization. Separate funds make it easier to ensure that restricted monies and appropriations are being properly expended.

Obviously, the two methods support diverging accounting viewpoints. Accrual methods use a for-profit income measurement perspective that emphasizes proper matching of revenues and expenses within the correct time period. Modified accrual accounting emphasizes showing the amount of funding that is available for spending and clearly identifying that such funding has been properly used for the purpose for which it was intended. Thus, modified accrual does not emphasize profit determination, but rather fund availability and fund flows for expenditure purposes. The two systems do not even use the same terminology to refer to expended resources. Under accrual, the term "expenses" is used; whereas under modified accrual, the term "expenditures" is used.

Although both accrual and modified accrual accounting require a Balance Sheet and Income Statement, nongovernmental NFPs require a third financial report. For these organizations, a Statement of Cash Flows must be prepared. This statement shows how cash flowed into and out of the organization and analyzes the events that caused an increase or decrease in the cash balance from the beginning to the end of the year. Cash changes are shown as cash inflows or outflows from operations, investing activities, and financing activities. Operations are considered to be cash received from normal business operations with adjustments for the effects of depreciation, changes in receivables, payables, gains or loss on the sale of assets, and capital additions, for example. Investing activities refer to cash transactions such as sale of equipment, investments, or the purchase of buildings and equipment. Cash transactions related to obtaining or paying off notes, expired endowment transfers, and cash interest payments are considered financing activities. These three groupings help determine which types of activities are generating the cash inflows or causing cash outflows in the nongovernmental NFP.

With an accrual system, it is necessary to prepare a Statement of Cash Flows, too. Under modified accrual methods, this statement does not have to be prepared because modified accrual methods already closely correspond with cash methods.

Within this accounting framework of accepted accounting practices for NFPs, there are several real-world practices that are common. First, the small NFP of a larger government is usually considered to be a component unit of that larger governmental body. As a component unit, its financial reports may or may not be separately reported outside the larger governmental unit. In fact, the financial report produced for the NFP by the larger governmental unit may be aggregated with other component units. Consequently, the NFP's internal staff may prepare only separate financial reports issued by the NFP. As a result, the cash method of accounting may be in use. Unless these financial reports have been audited, there is little indication that they have followed GAAP.

The cash basis of accounting for NFPs is not considered to be GAAP, but the cash basis should not be ruled out immediately. If there is no significant difference between the cash system and one of the other methods of GAAP reporting, the cash basis may be acceptable to use. As a result, a fourth method of accounting may be acceptable for use.

G. STEVENSON SMITH

O

OCCUPATIONAL SAFETY AND HEALTH ADMINISTRATION (OSHA)

Prior to and during the early 1970s, workplace safety concerns became an issue in the United States. No consistent guidelines required employers to provide safe and healthful working environments. Workers were experiencing job-related injuries, and too often those injuries were fatal. To address these concerns, Congress enacted PL 91-596 (Occupational Safety and Health Act of 1970), which established the Occupational Safety and Health Administration (OSHA), a federal agency headed by an Assistant Secretary of Labor for Occupational Safety and Health. OSHA is functionally structured, with its major programs grouped into eight directorates (Administrative Programs, Construction, Compliance Programs, Federal-State Operations, Health Standards Programs, Policy, Safety Standards Programs, and Technical Support) as well as an Office of Statistics. Senior executive service members head these directorates and offices. Regional offices and subordinate area and district offices or service centers carry out various programs.

OSHA's mission, as set forth in the 1970 legislation, is to "assure . . . every working man and woman in the nation safe and healthful working conditions." Therefore, OSHA developed and implemented certain standards and enforcement procedures, as well as employers'

compliance assistance plans to help employers achieve and maintain healthful and safe workplaces.

Organizations with ten or more employees are subject to OSHA regulation, and those not in compliance may suffer large fines. For instance, OSHA proposed fines of $46,300 against a steel firm where alleged safety violations cost two workers their lives (Kane, 1998). Since OSHA was created, workplace fatalities have decreased by half; but every day, according to Kane (1998), about seventeen Americans die on the job.

OSHA strives to create worker awareness of and commitment to resolving workplace safety and health issues by collecting and studying data to identify workplace safety and health problems, as well as achieving problem resolution through regulation, compliance assistance, and enforcement strategies. To enforce regulations, OSHA conducts unannounced, on-site inspections. Data on the OSHA Facts homepage indicate that 34,264 federal and 56,623 state inspections were conducted by OSHA during Fiscal Year 1997, and 87,710 federal and 147,610 state violations were documented. For both federal and state violations, approximately $147 billion in penalties were assessed.

While businesses agree that workplaces should be safe and healthy, many have experienced difficulty in meeting OSHA standards. Because small business owners have found OSHA standards to be financially constricting and consider OSHA penalties harsh, a reform movement is in progress. The House of Representatives has been considering incremental reform of the OSHA Act. On 17 March 1998, two bills (H.R. 2877 and H.R. 2864) concerning OSHA's consultation program and elimination of inspection and penalty quotas were approved; and on 27 March, the Workforce Protections subcommittee heard bills recommending peer review panels to oversee OSHA's rulemaking process, as well as protection from enforcement proceedings for employers meeting certain criteria. Additionally, the Safety Advancement for Employees (SAFE) Act approved in October 1997 exempts small business owners from OSHA fines for two years and allows third-party inspectors. Even with ongoing OSHA reform initiatives, no comprehensive reform bill requiring substantial change in OSHA's structure, procedures, or standards has been enacted.

More information is available from OSHA at U.S. Department of Labor, OSHA, Office of Public Affairs, Room N3647, 200 Constitution Ave. NW, Washington, DC 20210; (202) 693-1999; or http://www.osha-slc.gov/html/oshdir.html.

BIBLIOGRAPHY

International Personnel Management Association. "Government Affairs/Occupational Safety and Health Act (OSHA)." Archived at: http://www.ipma-hr.org/govtaffairs/osha.html. 1999.

International Personnel Management Association. "Government Affairs/OSHA Reform." Archived at: http://www.ipma-hr.org/govtaffairs/osha498.html. 1999.

Johnson, D. (ed.) "Hot Topics for October 3, 1997." Archived at: http://www.ishn.com/hot/hotarch/971003.htm. 1997.

Kane, Frank. "OSHA Proposes $463,000 in Fines Against Claremont, H. H., Steel Firm Following Investigation of Two Worker Deaths." Archived at: http://www.osha.gov/media/oshnews/may98/osha98227.html. 1998.

National Federation of Independent Business. "OSHA Reform Key Points." Archived at: http://oshrareform.nfibonline.com/keypoints.html. 1999.

Occupational Safety and Health Administration (OSHA). "OSHA Office Directory." Archived at: http://www.osha-slc.gov/html/oshdir.html. 1999.

OSHA. "OSHA Strategic Plan". Archived at: http://www.osha.gov/oshinfo/strategic/pg1.html. 1999.

OSHA. "Success Stories." Archived at: http://www.osha.gov/oshinfo/success.html. 1999.

OSHA. "OSHA Vital Facts 1997." Archived at: http://www.osha-slc.gov/OshDoc/OSHFacts/OSHAFacts.html. 1999.

MARY JEAN LUSH
VAL HINTON

OFFICE LAYOUT

Office productivity is influenced by a number of factors, one of which is office layout. Because office layout influences the entire white-collar-employee segment of the organization, its importance to organizational productivity should never be underestimated. Office layout is based on the interrelationships among three primary factors: employees, flow of work through the various work units, and equipment.

Efficient office layout results in a number of benefits to the organization, including the following:

1. It affects how much satisfaction employees derive from their jobs.

2. It affects the impression individuals get of the organization's work areas.

3. It provides effective allocation and use of the building's floor space.

4. It provides employees with efficient, productive work areas.

5. It facilitates the expansion and/or rearrangement of work areas when the need arises.

6. It facilitates employee supervision.

Planning the layout tends to occur in two steps, a preliminary stage and a final stage.

PRELIMINARY PLANNING

When designing office layout, a number of factors need to be taken into consideration during the preliminary planning stage, which is generally carried out by administrative office managers, employees, or consultants. Among the factors to consider during preliminary planning are these:

Work flow: Studying the flow of work vertically and horizontally between individuals and work units is critical in designing office layout. The goal is to design a layout pattern in which work moves in a straight-line direction with minimal (if any) backtracking or crisscrossing patterns. The major source documents found within the various work areas are often considered in analyzing work flow.

Organization chart: Studying the organization chart, which visually depicts who reports to whom as well as the relationships among and between employees, is also considered in the preliminary planning stages. Generally, the organization chart helps determine which units should be physically located near one another.

Projection of number of employees needed in the future: Having a good understanding of the possibility of expansion helps assure that layout is designed to accommodate future growth. Among the factors to be considered are the potential need for additional work units as well as the number of additional employees likely to be needed in both existing work units and new work units.

Communication network: Studying the organization's communication network identifies who within the organization has considerable contact (either face-to-face or by phone) with whom. The more contact employees have, the greater is the likelihood that they or their work units need to be physically located near one another.

Departmental organization: Studying departmental organization also helps determine which departments should be placed in close proximity to one another. For example, those departments with significant responsibilities for the accounting and financial aspects of the firm should be located near one another; those with frequent contact with outsiders (personnel and sales, for example) should be located near the entrance to the structure; and noise-producing departments (copying/duplicating, loading dock, etc.) should

be located near one another and away from areas where low noise levels are required.

Ratio of private to general offices: Increasingly, many organizations are opting for more general offices and fewer private offices. This trend probably helps reduce the amount of total office space needed, and it certainly facilitates the rearrangement of office areas. A number of advantages result from using general offices rather than with private offices. General offices are more economical to build than private offices; general offices make it easier to accommodate change in office layout; and it is easier to design efficient heating, cooling, and lighting systems for general offices.

Space requirements: The total amount of needed space is determined by the amount of space needed for each employee (including projections for growth) in each work unit as well as the amount of space needed for various specialized areas. The amount of space each employee needs is determined by the employee's furniture/equipment requirements, the location of such structural features as windows and pillars, and the employee's job functions and hierarchical position.

Specialized areas: Many organizations have a number of specialized areas that must be taken into consideration in the preliminary planning of office layout. Included are such needs as a reception area, board or conference rooms, a computer center, a mailroom, a printing/duplicating room, a central records area, and a storage area.

Safety considerations: A number of safety considerations play an important role in the preliminary planning of layout, including aisles/corridors of sufficient width, door openings, stairwells, and exits. Providing for quick evacuation of the premises in case of an emergency is a critical aspect of the preliminary planning of office layout.

Barrier-free construction: A number of federal laws require that office layout accomodate individuals with disabilities. The 1990 Americans with Disabilities Act requires "reasonable accommodation" of individuals with disabilities. Perhaps most significant in office layout is designing office/work areas in which individuals can easily maneuver wheelchairs.

Expansion: To stay abreast of developing space needs, many organizations undertake a yearly space analysis, just as they prepare a yearly budget. Doing so enables these organizations to be proactive rather than reactive in anticipating future space needs.

Equipment and furniture needs: The amount of equipment and furniture that needs to be accommodated in an organization must be taken into consideration during the preliminary planning of office layout. Failure to take these needs into consideration often results in inefficient office layout.

PLANNING OFFICE LAYOUT

Perhaps the most critical decision that will be made in planning office layout is whether private offices only or a combination of private and general office areas will be used. The trend is toward a minimum of private office areas and maximum use of general office areas. Typically, the general office areas make use of the open office concept, which overcomes a number of the disadvantages of conventional private offices. Whereas private offices tend to be based on the hierarchical structure of the organization, open office areas are based on the nature of the relationship between the employee and his or her job duties.

Open office planning takes into account the cybernetics of the organization, meaning that information flows and processes are considered in the design process. Information flows pertain to paper flow, telephone communications, and face-to-face interaction.

Three different alternatives are used in designing space around the open office concept. These include the modular workstation approach, the cluster workstation approach, and the landscape approach. In each case, panels and furniture components comprise work areas. Typically, the panels and furniture components are prewired with both electrical and phone connections, which considerably simplifies their installation. Panels are available in a variety of colors and finishes, including wood, metal, plastic, glass, carpet, and fabric.

Modular workstation approach. A prime characteristic of the modular workstation approach is the use of panel-hung furniture components to create individual work areas. Storage cabinets and files of adjustable height are placed adjacent to desks or tables. The design of modular workstations enables employees to have a complete office in terms of desk space, file space, storage space, and work-area lighting. Modular workstations are designed according to the specific job duties of their occupants.

In certain situations, the modular workstation approach is preferred to either of the other two open-space concepts. It is especially well suited for those situations that require considerable storage space, and the work area can be specifically designed around the specific needs of the user. Also, changes in layout can be made easily and quickly.

Cluster workstation approach. An identifying characteristic of the cluster workstation approach is the clustering of employee work areas around a common core, such as a set of panels that extend from a hub, much like the spokes in a wheel. The panels define each employee's work area, which typically includes a writing surface, storage space, and filing space. As a rule, cluster workstations are not as elaborate as either modular workstations or landscaped alternatives. Cluster workstations work well for situations in which employees spend a portion of their workday away from their work area.

Two distinct advantages of the cluster workstation are economics and the ease with which layout changes can be made. The cluster workstation is less expensive than either of the other two alternatives.

Landscape approach. Originally developed in Germany, office landscaping is now used extensively throughout the United States. In a way, office landscaping is a blend of the modular and cluster workstation approaches. One significant difference, however, is the abundant use of plants and foliage in the decor. Plants and foliage, in addition to being aesthetically pleasing, provide a visual barrier. Whereas both the modular and the cluster approaches tend to align the components in rows, landscaping arranges work areas in clusters and at different angles.

In its original form, landscaping eliminated all private offices. However, most organizations that make use of landscaping use a hybrid approach in which a ratio of 80 percent open office areas to 20 percent private offices is common.

In conventional office layout, status was accorded employees through their assignment of a private office. Because the open-space concept removes a considerable number of private offices, employees are accorded status through such other aspects as their work assignments, their job duties, the location and size of their work area, and the type and amount of furniture they are given.

PREPARING THE LAYOUT

The actual preparation of the layout is carried out using a variety of tools, including templates, cutouts, plastic models, magnetic boards, and computer-aided design (CAD). For more complex layout projects, CAD is most likely the tool of choice. For simple layout projects, any of the others work well. Regardless of which tool is used, a primary concern is making sure every aspect of the layout (perimeter, structural features, equipment and furniture components, etc.) is scaled properly and consistently.

BIBLIOGRAPHY

Daroff, K., ed. (1991). *Office Planning and Design Desk Reference.* New York: Wiley.

Henderson, J. (1998). *Workplaces and Workspaces: Office Designs that Work.* New York: Wiley.

Shumake, M. *Increasing Productivity and Profit in the Workplace: A Guide to Office Planning and Design.* New York: Wiley.

Turner, G., and Myerson, J. (1998). *New Workspace, New Culture: Office Design as a Catalyst for Change.* Hampshire, England: Gower.

ZANE K. QUIBLE

OFFICE TECHNOLOGY

Office technology focuses on the office information functions, including word processing, data processing, graphics, desktop publishing, and communications. The backbone of technology-rich office environments is a local area network (LAN), which is a single-site computer network, or a wide area network (WAN), which can support worldwide work groups. These networks provide tools for users to transmit data, graphics, mail, and voice across a network. All office functions, ranging from correspondence, to multimedia presentations, to videoconferences, to automated records management, to technologies to support distributed work groups, depend on office technologies. Office technologies, such as keyboarding, dictation, filing, copying, fax, Telex, records management, and telephone and switchboard operations, are candidates for integration.

OFFICE SYSTEMS

Office technologies are integral components of office systems. Office systems exist to facilitate and retain communications, including the creation, processing, retention, and distribution of information. Office systems consist of tasks to be performed, procedures for completing tasks, a set of automated technologies designed to enhance productivity, and people working within the framework of an organizational structure. A compatible synergy among these components creates a smoothly functioning office operation that enhances the productivity and efficiency of the overall organization and contributes to the success of the business. Contributing factors to the synergy include integrated hardware components and integrated software applications.

With the advent of the PC (personal computer), office technologies have radically changed the way companies do business. Prior to the use of PCs in business, secretaries or administrative assistants typed letters, created reports, and organized information in files. Now most office workers have a PC and take responsibility for these functions, as well as many more. Employees key their own letters and e-mails, create spreadsheets, graphs, and multimedia presentations, and keep their files on computer networks.

Laptop computers are used by business travelers to make multimedia presentations, send and receive e-mail, do research on the Internet, play games, and create and send reports and spreadsheets. Laptop computers can also be used to take notes in meetings.

Voice-mail technology has also radically changed the way business is conducted. Voice mail has greatly reduced the need to have an employee answer the phone and take messages for others. Because messages are recorded on voice mail, workers can retrieve the communications and process them as time permits. The messages can be forwarded to other employees, saved, or deleted. An option on some messaging systems is sending messages to groups of people.

Caller-identification became available in the mid-1990s as an option on office telephone systems. This innovation allows the caller to be identified by name and number before the telephone is answered. Some office systems have caller-i.d. only for internal telephones, while other companies have systems that identify callers from outside the company as well.

OFFICE TECHNOLOGIES SUPPORT ALL TYPES OF BUSINESSES

So many office systems functions today depend on office technology that it is difficult to imagine accomplishing all the necessary tasks without them. Sophisticated office technologies are available to support a wide range of businesses.

Independent Entrepreneurs and Small Businesses From a desktop computer, a home-based independent entrepreneur may conduct business locally and worldwide using e-commerce via the Internet. Affordable, high-quality office technology for copying, faxing, and printing is available

for small businesses. In fact, some multifunction machines incorporate all these features into one system. Phone, pager, and voice-mail services are provided using cellular telephones via digital network systems.

The most widely used office software packages include word processing, desktop publishing, spreadsheet, database, presentation graphics, personal information management, accounting, project management, e-mail, and Internet browser software. These applications are available as integrated solutions software, rather than independent applications. The integration capabilities lead to increased efficiencies and higher productivity, provided users are trained well to maximize the power and flexibility available using these automated office tools. Integration between applications supports the following features: common documentation, automatic updating, mail merge, multiple open files, networking capability, ease of use and learning, and common error handling.

Large Businesses and Multinational Organizations The range of office technologies available to support large businesses and multinational organizations is vast and continues to grow. WANs and LANs enable distributed work teams to complete projects using groupware and decision support systems. They provide access to large corporate databases and records management systems to support research, reporting, budgeting, and forecasting. Examples of the types of technologies available and their uses are discussed here.

TYPES OF TECHNOLOGIES

The following section describes various types of office technologies.

Intranets and Extranets An intranet is an internal computer network that is basically a small version of the Internet used within a company. Intranets, which are sometimes called enterprise networks, use Web technologies and the Internet to communicate information to the company employees. Users can post and update information on the intranet by creating and posting a Web page, similar to the method used on the

Internet. Examples of information that might be posted include telephone directories, event calendars, procedure manuals, e-mail, job postings, and employee benefits information. Additional uses of an intranet might include group scheduling and videoconferencing.

An extranet is a company's intranet that extends to authorized users outside the company. It is used to facilitate communications among the company's suppliers or customers. An example might be an airline that would allow travelers and their companions to access flight information for on-time arrivals or delays for specific flights.

Groupware and Decision Support Systems Groupware is software that supports the work of a group. The three major functions are document formatting, information management, and wide area communication. An electronic calendar is used to keep a group informed, on schedule, and coordinated. It tracks management objectives and goals, arranges meetings, sends reminders, and warns when a project falls behind schedule. Groupware also runs an electronic mail network that links the work group with remote operations. It also includes an information system to handle all data relevant to the business and to make this data instantly available throughout the organization. Decision support systems facilitate group decision making by providing a formalized process for brainstorming, distilling key concepts, prioritizing or ranking topics, and achieving group consensus. These systems facilitate the work of project teams distributed worldwide.

Videoconferencing and Teleconferencing A videoconference is a meeting between two or more geographically separated individuals who use a network or the Internet to transmit audio and video data. To participate in a videoconference, a microphone, speakers, and a video camera are necessary. Any image in front of the video camera, such as a person's face or visual aid, displays in a window on each participant's video screen. Another window on the screen, called a whiteboard, that displays notes and drawings simultaneously on all the participants' screens provides multiple users with an area on which they can write or draw. This is becoming a cost-effective way to conduct business meetings, corporate training, and educational classes.

Teleconferencing links a number of people from a number of geographical locations to discuss topics via audio contact. For example, telephones with speakers could be used in two or more locations with one or more participants per location to conduct a meeting. Teleconferences are sometimes used for project progress reports or to discuss alternative strategies for problem resolution among team members distributed geographically.

Multimedia Multimedia integrates text, graphics, animation, audio, and video. Multimedia applications are used for business and education in the office environment. Marketing presentations are developed to advertise and sell products using multimedia. Using a computer, a video projector, and a display screen, presentations can be made to large and small audiences. Interactive advertisements as well as job applications and training applications can be published on the Internet or in kiosk displays.

Computerized Records Management Records management involves managing and controlling office information. Typical applications include maintaining a records center, tracking active and inactive records, making note of vital records, creating archives or historical records, and developing a record retention schedule.

The processing capabilities and storage capacity of computers have made electronic storage and retrieval of information a common practice in business. Computer-generated document management, records management software, and imaging systems assist businesses with large volumes of records. Imaging systems convert all types of documents to digitized electronic data that can be stored and retrieved readily.

These systems include a scanner that converts the paper document to a digitized form, a processor that compresses the image, a storage medium to retain the image, a retrieval mechanism to convert the image for viewing on a monitor, and an output device that processes the image to hard-copy format. Laser optical disks are well suited for high-volume record management because of their high capacity and durability.

Micrographics is the process of creating, using, and storing images and data in microform. The most common type of microform is microfilm. Images, reduced in size, are stored on reels, in cartridges, on cassettes, on aperture cards, on microfiche, and in jackets. Information stored in a computer can be converted to microfilm. Computer output microfilm (COM) is imaged directly from magnetic media. The electrical impulses on the media are converted to visual images and stored on microfilm. Computer input microfilm (CIM) can be converted to electrical impulses, stored on magnetic media, and used as input. CIM can be used to introduce information from a large microfilm file, such as census data, into a computer for processing. Computer-assisted retrieval (CAR) systems are used for high-speed microform indexing and retrieval.

For many businesses, manual records management systems are still the norm. Businesses use one or more of the five basic filing methods—alphabetic, subject, numeric, geographic, and chronological—to store records in vertical and lateral files, open-shelf files, and rotary files. Good records management practices include establishing complete archives, developing retention schedules, and using timelines for transferring records to permanent storage.

Reprographics Reprographics is the multiple reproduction of images. Reprographics today involves the use of two primary types of equipment: copiers and duplicators. Copiers use an image-forming process similar to a camera to create copies directly from existing originals. Duplicators make copies from masters on special paper that must be prepared before copies are reproduced.

Telephone Systems PBX (private branch exchange) and PABX (private automatic branch exchange) systems are telephone switching systems used by larger businesses. A PBX requires a full-time operator, whereas a PABX may be attended or unattended. Calls are automatically distributed to the proper extension in the order in which they were received by an unattended, cordless switchboard. Voice mail is usually included with these telephone systems. In addition, voice recognition may also be a feature, which allows a caller to choose among various options within the voice mail by simply saying a number.

Security A firewall is used to restrict the access to data and information on a network. A firewall is composed both of equipment and software. Companies use firewalls to deny access to the network to outsiders and to restrict employees' access to sensitive data such as payroll or personnel records.

A computer virus is a potentially dangerous computer program designed to cause damage to other computer files. Viruses can spread by users sharing files. These files may be on floppy disks, e-mail, or the Internet. Programmers create viruses for specific purposes, sometimes for a harmless prank, such as scrolling a note across a computer screen, but sometimes for the purpose of destroying or corrupting other files. Viruses have become a significant problem in recent years. The increased use of networks, the Internet, and e-mail has increased the opportunity for viruses to spread as users share files more easily.

An anti-virus program protects a computer from viruses. It functions by scanning for programs that attempt to modify operating systems files or other files that normally are not changed.

Swipe cards, cards with magnetic strips similar to those on credit cards, provide security in offices because they limit access to restricted areas. Employees who need to access the office after hours or to enter secure areas, such as those housing the company's server computers, may use swipe cards.

TV surveillance cameras are used to record people as they enter, exit, and move about the office. Unauthorized access to certain offices or areas is recorded on videotape and may be used when documenting the occurrence. Picture badges are used to identify company employees.

COMMUNICATION IN ORGANIZATIONS

All these office technologies facilitate communication among people in organizations. Increasingly, organizations need personnel with good communication skills—interpersonal, written, verbal, listening skills. They also need personnel who exercise good judgment about which method and medium for communication is most appropriate for a given situation, as well as the technical expertise to use the various office technologies available.

BIBLIOGRAPHY

Austin, L. J., and Willis, C. L. (1997). "Future Work." In C.P. Brantley and B. J. Davis, eds., *The Changing Dimensions of Business Education* (1997 NBEA Yearbook, No. 35.) Reston, VA: National Business Education Association.

Blass, Gary D., et al. (1991). "Finding Government Information: The Federal Information Locator System (FILS)," *Government Information Quarterly* 8(1): 11-32.

Boldt, Dennis, and Groneman, Nancy. (1998). "Internet Use in Document Processing and Computer Applications." In Dennis LaBonty, ed., *Integrating the Internet into the Business Curriculum* (1998 NBEA Yearbook, No. 36.) Reston, VA: National Business Education Association.

Jaderstrom, Susan, Kruk, Leonard, and Miller, Joanne. (1992). *Professional Secretaries International Complete Office Handbook: The Secretary's Guide to Today's Electronic Office.* New York: Random House.

Jurist, R. G. (1999). "The Promise of Technology." In Pat A. Gallo Villee and Michael G. Curran, eds., *The 21st Century: Meeting the Challenges to Business Education* (1999 NBEA Yearbook, No. 37.) Reston, VA: National Business Education Association.

Murphy, J. William. (1999). "Educating for Business: Keeping Pace with the Changing Marketplace." In Pat A. Gallo Villee and Michael G. Curran, eds., *The 21st Century: Meeting the Challenges to Business Education* (1999 NBEA Yearbook, No. 37.) Reston, VA: National Business Education Association.

Shelly, Gary, Cashman, Thomas, Vermaat, Misty, and Walker, Tim. (1999). *Discovering Computers 2000: Concepts for a Connected World.* Cambridge, MA: Course Technology.

Stallard, John J., and Terry, George R. (1984). *Office Systems Management, 9th ed.* Homewood, IL: Irwin.

Swanson, Marie L., Reding, Elizabeth Eisner, Beskeen, David W., and Johnson, Steven M. (1997). *Microsoft Office 97, Professional Edition-Illustrated, A First Course.* Cambridge, MA: Course Technology.

Tilton, Rita Sloan, Jackson, J. Howard, and Rigby, Sue Chappell. (1996). *The Electronic Office: Procedures & Administration.* Cincinnati, OH: South-Western Educational Publishing.

LINDA J. AUSTIN
DEBBIE HUGHES

OLIGOPOLY

An oligopoly is an intermediate market structure between the extremes of perfect competition and monopoly. Oligopoly firms might compete (noncooperative oligopoly) or cooperate (cooperative oligopoly) in the marketplace. Whereas firms in an oligopoly are price makers, their control over the price is determined by the level of coordination among them. The distinguishing characteristic of an oligopoly is that there are a few mutually interdependent firms that produce either identical products (homogeneous oligopoly) or heterogeneous products (differentiated oligopoly).

Mutual interdependence means that firms realize the effects of their actions on rivals and the reactions such actions are likely to elicit. For instance, a mutually interdependent firm realizes that its price drops are more likely to be matched by rivals than its price increases. This implies that an oligopolist, especially in the case of a homogeneous oligopoly, will try to maintain current prices, since price changes in either direction can be harmful, or at least nonbeneficial. Consequently, there is a kink in the demand curve because there are asymmetric responses to a firm's price increases and to its price decreases; that is, rivals match price falls but not price increases. This leads to "sticky prices," such that prices in an oligopoly turn out to be more stable than those in monopoly or in competition; that is, they do not change every time costs change. On the flip side, the sticky-price explanation (formally, the kinked demand model of oligopoly) has the significant drawback of not doing a very good job of explaining how the initial price,

McDonald's bases its pricing on its rivals' prices.

which eventually turns out to be sticky, is arrived at.

Airline markets and automobile markets are prime examples of oligopolies. We see that as the new auto model year gets under way in the fall, one car manufacturer's reduced financing rates are quickly matched by the other firms because of recognized mutual interdependence. Airlines also match rivals' fares on competing routes.

In oligopolies, entry of new firms is difficult because of entry barriers. These entry barriers may be structural (natural), such as economies of scale, or artificial, such as limited licenses issued by government. Firms in an oligopoly, known as oligopolists, choose prices and output to maximize profits. However, firms could compete along other dimensions as well, such as advertising, location, research and development (R&D) and so forth. For instance, a firm's research or advertising strategies are influenced by what its rivals are doing. When one restaurant advertises

that it will accept rivals' coupons, others are compelled to follow suit.

The rivals' responses in an oligopoly can be modeled in the form of reaction functions. Sophisticated firms anticipating rivals' behavior might appear to act in concert (conscious parallelism) without any explicit agreement to do so. Such instances pose problems for antitrust regulators. Mutually interdependent firms have a tendency to form cartels, enabling them to coordinate price and quantity actions to increase profits. Besides facing legal obstacles, cartels are difficult to sustain because of free-rider problems. Shared monopolies are extreme cases of cartels that include all the firms in the industry.

Given that mutual interdependence can exist along many dimensions, there is no single model of oligopoly. Rather, there are numerous models based on different behavior, ranging from the naive Cournot models to more sophisticated models of game theory. An equilibrium concept that incorporates mutual interdependence was proposed by John Nash and is referred to as Nash equilibrium. In a Nash equilibrium, firms' decisions (i.e., price-quantity choices) are their best responses, given what their rivals are doing. For example, McDonald's charges $2.99 for a Value Meal based on what Burger King and Wendy's are charging for a similar menu item. McDonald's would reconsider its pricing if its rivals were to change their prices.

The level of information that firms have has a major influence on their behavior in an oligopoly. For instance, when mutually interdependent firms have asymmetric information and are unable to make credible commitments regarding their behavior, a "prisoner's dilemma" type of situation arises where the Nash equilibrium might include choices that are suboptimal. For instance, individual firms in a cartel have an incentive to cheat on the previously agreed-upon price-output levels. Since cartel members have nonbinding commitments on limiting production levels and maintaining prices, this results in widespread cheating, which in turn leads to an eventual breakdown of the cartel. Therefore, while all firms in the cartel could benefit by cooperating, lack of credible commitments results in cheating being a Nash equilibrium strategy—a strategy that is suboptimal from the individual firm's standpoint.

Models of oligopoly could be static or dynamic depending upon whether firms take intertemporal decisions into account. Significant models of oligopoly include Cournot, Bertrand, and Stackelberg. Cournot oligopoly is the simplest model of oligopoly in that firms are assumed to be naive when they think that their actions will not generate any reaction from the rivals. In other words, according to the Cournot model, rival firms choose not to alter their production levels when one firm chooses a different output level. Cournot thus focuses on quantity competition rather than price competition. While the naive behavior suggested by Cournot might seem plausible in a static setting, it is hard to image real-world firms not learning from their mistakes over time. The Bertrand model's significant difference from the Cournot model is that it assumes that firms choose (set) prices rather than quantities. The Stackelberg model deals with the scenario in which there is a leader firm in the market whose actions are imitated by a number of follower firms. The leader is sophisticated in terms of taking into account rivals' reactions, while the followers are naïve, as in the Cournot model. The leader might emerge in a market because of a number of factors, such as historical precedence, size, reputation, innovation, information, and so forth. Examples of Stackelberg leadership include markets where one dominant firm dictates the terms, usually through price leadership. Under price leadership, the leader firm's pricing decisions are consistently followed by rival firms.

Since oligopolies come in various forms, the performance of such markets also varies a great deal. In general, the oligopoly price is below the monopoly price but above the competitive price. The oligopoly output, in turn, is larger than that of a monopolist but falls short of what a competitive market would supply. Some oligopoly markets are competitive, leading to few welfare distortions, while other oligopolies are monopolistic, resulting in deadweight losses. Furthermore, some oligopolies are more innovative than others. Whereas the price-quantity rankings of oligopoly vis-à-vis other markets are relatively well established, how oligopoly fares with regard to R and D and advertising is less clear.

BIBLIOGRAPHY

Cournot, Augustin. (1963). *Researches into the Mathematical Principles of the Theory of Wealth.* Homewood, IL: Irwin.

Friedman, James W. (1983). *Oligopoly Theory.* Cambridge, UK: Cambridge University Press.

Fudenberg, Drew, and Tirole, Jean. (1986). *Dynamic Models of Oligopoly.* London: Harwood.

Goel, Rajeev K. (1999). *Economic Models of Technological Change.* Westport, CT: Quorum Books.

Shapiro, Carl. (1989). "Theories of Oligopoly Behavior." In *Handbook of Industrial Organization*, vol. 1, ed. Richard Schmalensee and Robert D. Willig. Amsterdam: North-Holland.

RAJEEV K. GOEL

OPERATIONAL STRATEGIES

(SEE: *Strategic Management*)

OPERATIONS MANAGEMENT

An important element of any business system is management, whether an individual or a team performs it. In our society, we no longer think of company management in terms of one person acting as the entrepreneur, but rather as a team effort. Each member possesses specialized knowledge and understanding of one functional area of the business system and is by temperament and training able to work cooperatively with other members of the team toward a common goal.

Whatever the system or organization, the functions of management are always the same: (1) designing, (2) planning, (3) organizing, (4) directing, and (5) controlling. Management establishes the goals and objectives of the firm or organization and plans how to attain them. It is management that organizes the system and directs it so that its goals can be reached. Finally, management must be able to analyze the working of the system in order to control it and to correct any variations from the planned procedures in order to reach the predetermined goals. These functions interact with one another and managers must be skilled in these coordinating processes and functions if they are to accomplish their goals through the efforts of other people.

The concepts of managerial functions has some hidden difficulties when one attempts to apply them to a specific managerial job. First, one cannot tell which functions are most important and how much time must be allocated to each. All functions are important parts of a manager's job, but the significance attached to each one may vary at different times, such as at different stages of a product life cycle. Furthermore, the significance of each function varies at different management levels in the same organization. Operations management, for example, is more focused on directing and controlling than on planning or organizing.

All organizations have operations. Operation management, or technical management, is comprised of department managers and persons with professional technical competence. This level is oriented downward to basic operations, such as producing goods and moving them out the door. A manufacturing company may conduct operation in a mill or factory. The driving force in operations management must be an overriding goal of continually improving service to customers, where "customer" means the next process as well as the final, external user. Since there is an operations element in every function of the enterprise, all people in all jobs in every department of the organization should work together for the improvement of their own operations management elements. It is important to note that the technical expert often seeks recognition from peers and colleagues rather than from managers at the administrative level.

INPUT

The *input* of a system depends on its specific objective. What raw materials will yield the desired output? If one were to visually illustrate a system, the input would be shown as the components vital to it. A television repairperson needs a diagram of a TV set in order to repair it, or an auditor might need a flowchart of a company's accounting system to check for possible diversion of funds. If a system is designed to maintain a state, the input is information or feedback concerning the essential variable that must be maintained. If the purpose of a system is to make a decision, the input is relevant information about the problem. In a production system, the input consists of raw material, labor, and other manufacturing costs that are combined in the final product.

TRANSFORMATION

After input is established the input, it is necessary to *transform* it into a desirable output. In business, the transformation operation is extremely important. Manufacturing, marketing, and distribution must be studied and known in detail. However, there are some areas in which little is known. In a business system, for example, one must consider the way people act and react. Often behavior is placed in this gray area because so little is known about what motivates it. Also, for some people in an organization it may not matter how something works, while others may be vitally interested. A manager may not care how a report gets to him or her, but an accountant would be concerned with all the steps in gathering data, preparing the report, and communicating it to the manager. Thus, in studying any transformation operation, it is important to know the reliability of the process and who is interested in it. This system will vary depending on the output.

OUTPUT

In one sense, *output* is the quality and quantity of the services and goods produced. In another sense, output may be thought of as the payments made for all the factors of production used. In the first sense, the entire system of the firm is designed to produce something that is desired in a market. Consumers want and seek out goods and services that will make their lives happier, more comfortable, healthier, longer, and so on. In order to produce those goods and services, the firm needs inputs. What may be output for one business may be input for another.

In the second sense, output is converted into revenue for the firm that is used to compensate the owners for the risks they have taken, management for its role in producing the revenue, and employees for their role in producing the good or service; it is also used to pay interest for the use of borrowed capital and wages for labor. Rent must be paid for the use of land; goods and materials used in production must be paid for; and taxes must be paid to the government. The output is the result of the system and is closely related to its objective. Output will accomplish or help to accomplish the specific objective if the system has been designed correctly.

FEEDBACK

All systems should include *feedback*. When an input is received in the system and undergoes a transformation operation, the result or output is then monitored and transmitted for comparison with a standard. If there is variation between the output and the standard, suitable action can be taken to correct the variation.

A business organization with many systems that range from very simple to very complex requires a much more complicated feedback network. Information must be communicated from person to person and from one part of the organization to another. In fact, the original data may be transformed many times before it reaches its final destination. Each of these transformations is subject to feedback.

Feedback can be defined as knowledge of results. Three basic types of feedback are needed: informational feedback, corrective feedback, and reinforcing feedback. The flow of information in an organization should be two-way—from managers to workers as well as vice versa. In contrast to informational feedback, corrective feedback is evaluative and judgmental. An effective manager will not only point out mistakes but also get the individual worker headed in the right direction by means of corrective feedback. Positive consequences or reinforcements are one key to desired performance. In other words, reinforcing feedback is a prime means of achieving growth in job performance.

PRODUCTION MANAGEMENT

Products can be classified in many ways and their distribution can take many forms. But the essence of *production management* is that the factors of production—land, labor, and capital—are transformed by management from raw materials into something finished, something to be used, or something to be sold profitably in order to keep the business in operation.

Before production can be started, the firm must determine what kind of product it can profitably produce. Management must decide what markets the product will satisfy, what materials it will contain, what processes will be required to form it, by what means it can be transported, and what quality and quantity of labor will be needed to produce it. Knowledge of all this provides direction to the planning and organization of manufacturing.

Once the firm has decided on the basic product or service to produce, design and development can begin. Planning the product involves all parts of the business system. The marketing department may discover the need for a new or improved product, and the production department may then determine whether it can manufacture the product for sale at a given price. The finance department then decides whether the venture will be profitable and whether financing is available to cover the costs of development, manufacturing, and distribution. Such product planning determines whether development and design will go forward.

The process of refining a product to a finished form sheds further light on the problems of manufacture: the equipment, raw materials, and fabricated parts that will be required, as well as the flow of production. Planning for production actually starts as soon as the decision is made to develop and design a product.

Production management makes suggestions for manufacturing that will save time, effort, and money without impairing the design of the product. Production management is very complex. Decisions must be made about labors, money, machinery, and materials. Inventories of parts must be maintained, and proper machinery and equipment must be combined with labor. All these activities, although performed within the production system, must be closely coordinated with the overall system of the firm.

Production managers are involved in many diverse areas. They are concerned with all the peripheral aspects of production and must be able to manage workers, materials, and machines in a changing environment.

Why is productivity so important? The basic reason is that productivity is a measure of the efficiency with which a person, business, or entire economy produces goods and services. It is a key indicator of a nation's economic strength. In general, the concept of productivity refers to a comparison of the output of a production process with one or more of its inputs. Thus, productivity may mean different things in different situations.

Manufacturing is simply a special form of production by which raw and semifinished materials are processed and converted into finished products needed by consumers. In a broader and more basic sense, production is the transformation of inputs from human and physical resources into outputs desired by consumers. These outputs may be either goods or services. The production of services is often called operations management.

We are now entering an era in which production and corporate management are becoming recommitted to one of the basics of business: making a better product faster and cheaper. This effort is important because the great bulk of assets used in manufacturing companies—capital invested, people employed, and management time—are allotted to the production function of the business rather than to marketing or finance. This situation is also true in service firms.

The organization for manufacturing depends on the complexity of the products manufactured and the size of the company. In a large company the manufacturing organization has divisions such as engineering, production control, inspection, and purchasing. The success of a product depends on the proper development and management of the product.

CONCLUSION

Management is universal. When more than one person is concerned with a goal, there is need for a process by which this goal can be attained. Management is active in every part of business and at every level. Its functions are performed in every department and in every function of the business. The practice of operations management is a continuous process of problem solving and decision making. The functions of management are based on the ability to make decisions and then to carry out all the implications of those decisions.

BIBLIOGRAPHY

Kusiak, Andrew. (1999). "Engineering Design: Products, Processes, and Systems." San Diego: Academic Press.

Moody, Patricia E. (1999). "The Technology Machine: How Manufacturing Will Work in the Year 2020." New York: Free Press.

Williams, Blair R. (1996). "Manufacturing for Survival: The How-to Guide for Practitioners and Managers." Reading, MA: Addison-Wesley.

JANEL KUPFERSCHMID

OPPORTUNITY COST

One of the lamentable facts of life is that nobody can have everything that he or she wants. This is due, in part, to scarce resources. Whether a teenager with a part-time job or a wealthy businessperson, no single person owns all of the money in the world. Furthermore, there are only twenty-four hours in a day, and seven days in a week. Time and money are only two of the many resources that are scarce in day-to-day living.

Unfortunately, because of these limits, individuals have to make choices in using scarce resources. One can use his or her time to work, play, sleep, or pursue other options. Or, one can select some combination of possible activities. People can't spend twenty-four hours a day working, twenty-four hours a day playing, and twenty-four hours a day sleeping. People can choose to spend their salary on a nice house, an expensive vacation, or on a yacht, but they probably can't afford all three. They must make choices with their limited resources of money.

In making choices for using limited resources, it is reasonable to evaluate the costs and benefits of all possible options. For instance, suppose one has been trying to decide how to spend the next few years of one's life. He or she has narrowed the options down to two: (1) working at a full-time job, or (2) becoming a full-time student. Going to school will cost approximately $12,000 per year in tuition, books, and room and board at the local state university for the next four years. In addition, he or she will forego the salary of a full-time job, which is $24,000 per year. This makes the total cost of going to school $36,000 per year. In return he or she gets the pleasure, social interaction, and personal fulfillment associated with gaining an education, as well as the expectation of an increase in salary through the remainder of his or her work life.

The question that must be answer is, "do the benefits of education outweigh the costs?" If they do, school should be selected. If the costs are greater than the benefits, the full-time job should be kept.

An "opportunity cost" is the value of the next-best alternative. That is, it is the value of the option that wasn't selected. In the example, if the person had chosen to keep your job, then the opportunity cost is the benefit of going to school, including the intangible benefits of pleasure, social interaction, and personal fulfillment as well as the tangible benefit of an increased future salary for their remaining working life. If the person had chosen to go to school, then the opportunity cost is the $24,000 per year that would have been earned at the full-time job.

One way of visualizing this concept is through the use of a production possibilities curve—a graph that relates the tradeoff between two possible choices, or some combination of the possibilities. Consider a very simple possible economy for a country. This country can produce two goods: guns (i.e., defense) or butter (i.e., consumer goods). If this country has historically used all of its resources to produce guns then it may be willing to consider allocating some of its resources to the production of butter. Initially, the resources that are least effective in producing guns (e.g., farmland) will be reallocated to the production of butter. Thus, the country doesn't forfeit many guns to produce a relatively large amount of butter. However, as the country reallocates more resources to the production of butter they are decreasingly productive. At the extreme, when the country gives up the last of its production of guns, the resource is very good for producing guns and not very useful in the production of butter (e.g., a high-tech armaments production facility). Figure 1 demonstrates this situation graphically in showing an example of the production possibilities curve.

In Figure 1, everything on the curved line or in the gray area is a possible production combination of guns and butter in the simple economy. Any combination on the line uses all of the available resources, while any combination in the gray area is considered inefficient since it does not use all of the available resources. Any combination in the white area is impossible to achieve, given the country's resource limitations.

The idea that the country will initially reallocate its least productive resource to the production of the other good is known as the *law of increasing opportunity cost.* Thus, if the production of the initial ton of butter costs five hundred guns, then the next ton of butter, which uses resources that are better at producing guns, will cost more guns. The next ton of butter will cost still more guns, and so on. This is represented in Figure 1 by the changing slope of the production possibilities curve.

SUMMARY

Because resources are limited, choices must be made. When evaluating choices in this decision-making process, one attempts to select the best option; that is, one selects the option that offers the most benefit for the costs incurred, and which are possible given any constraints. This is true for individuals, businesses, or countries, though the decisions that each entity makes are vastly different. The second best option is called the opportunity cost and is what is given up when decisions are made.

DENISE WOODBERRY

ORGANIZATIONAL BEHAVIOR AND DEVELOPMENT

The discipline of organizational behavior is concerned with identifying and managing the attitudes and actions of individuals and groups, looking particularly at how people can be motivated to join and remain in the organization, how to get people to practice effective teamwork, how

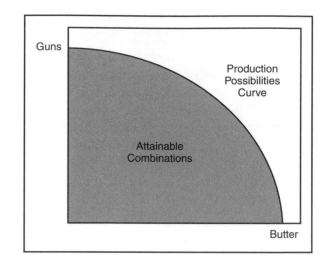

Figure 1

people can accomplish their jobs more efficiently, and how employees can be encouraged to be more flexible and innovative. Attention is brought to these attitudes and actions in order to help managers identify problems, determine how to correct them, and change behavior so that individual performance and ultimately organization effectiveness increase.

As a field of study, organizational behavior is built on a succession of approaches or ways of thinking about people. Since the early 1900s those who studied behavior in organizations have attempted to prescribe ways to effectively manage employees in order to achieve the organization's goals. The early approaches, referred to as the classical view, promoted increased management coordination of tasks, strict specialization and standardization of work tasks, a strict chain of command, and centralized decision making at the manager level. During the 1920s and 1930s the next new school of thought began to emerge, which was referred to as the human relations movement. By and large this movement began with the famous Hawthorne studies at the Western Electric plant that demonstrated how psychological and social processes could affect productivity and work behavior. This new way of thinking looked at organizational behavior by advocating a more people-oriented style of management that was more participative and oriented toward employee needs. Contemporary organizational thought has shifted to a more integrative systems approach, which includes the consideration of external influences; the relationship of the organization with managers and employees; and organizational processes, which are the activities through which work gets accomplished. In other words, the best solution for the situation depends on many factors. The organization is depicted as a number of interrelated, interdependent, and interacting subsystems that are continually changing.

Those who managed by the classical approach emphasized the critical role of control and coordination in helping organizations to achieve goals. Those who managed by the human relations approach considered the risks of high levels of control and coordination, focusing instead on the need for flexibility. So where do today's managers fit in? A contemporary approach to management recognizes that there is no one best way to manage; management approaches need to be tailored to fit the situation.

The manager's role is to effectively predict, explain, and manage behavior that occurs in organizations. Particularly, managers are interested in determining why people are more or less motivated or satisfied. Managers must have a capacity to observe and understand the behavior patterns of individuals, groups, and organizations; to predict what responses will be drawn out by managerial actions; and ultimately to use this understanding and eventual predictions to effectively manage employees. Behavior can be examined on three levels—the individual, the group, and the organization as a whole. Managers seek to learn more about what causes people—individually or collectively—to behave as they do in organizational settings. What motivates people? What makes some employees leaders and others not? How do people communicate and make decisions? How do organizations respond to changes in their external environments?

Although it may be said that the responsibility for studying organizational behavior rests with researchers, assessing and increasing organizational effectiveness is a primary responsibility of managers. They need to collect data about the environment in which people work and describe events, behaviors, and attitudes in order to develop plans for changing and improving behavior and attitudes. Managers can begin to understand organizational behavior by accurately describing events, behaviors, and attitudes. How can this be accomplished?

Data can be gathered by observing situations, surveying and interviewing employees, and looking at written documents. These methods help to objectively describe events, behaviors, and attitudes—a first step in determining their causes and then acting on them.

By direct observation, for example, managers can attend meetings and then describe what is happening, such as who talks most often, what topics are discussed, or how frequently those attending the meeting ask for the managers' viewpoint on the topic. In addition, survey questionnaires could be sent to employees; these might provide concrete data about the situation, proving more useful than relying solely on personal perception of events. Sending the same questionnaire to employees each year could provide some insight into changes in behavior and attitude over time. Employees could also be interviewed in order to examine attitudes in greater depth. Some valuable information about attitudes and opinions may also be gathered by talking informally with employees.

Finally, data could be gathered from organizational documents, including annual reports, department evaluations, memoranda, and other nonconfidential personnel files. An analysis of these documents might provide some insight into the attitudes of employees, the quality of management, group interactions, or other possible reasons behind the problems or situation.

ORGANIZATIONAL DEVELOPMENT

Organizational development (OD) is a planned, ongoing effort by organizations to change in order to become more effective. The need for organizational change becomes apparent when a gap exists between what an organization is trying to do and what is actually being accomplished. OD processes include using a knowledge of behavioral science to encourage an organizational culture of continual examination and readiness for change. In that culture, emphasis is placed on interpersonal and group processes. The fact that OD links human processes such as leadership, decision making, and communication with organizational outcomes such as productivity and efficiency distinguishes it from other change strategies that may rely solely on the principles of accounting or finance.

The fact that OD is planned distinguishes it from the routine changes that occur in the organization, particularly through a more effective and collaborative management or organization culture with special emphasis on forming work teams. The focus on interpersonal and group processes to improve performance recognizes that organizational change affects all members and that their cooperation is necessary to implement change.

The forces compelling an organization to change can be found both inside and outside the organization. Internal forces toward change can affect changes in job technology, composition of the work force, organization structure, organizational culture, and goals of the organization. There are a variety of external forces that may require managerial action: changes in market conditions, changes in manufacturing technology, changes in laws governing current products or practices, and changes in resource availability.

An organization can focus OD change efforts in several areas: changes to structure, technology, and people using a variety of strategies for development. Some of the more common techniques for changing an organization's structure include changes in work design to permit more specialization or enrichment, clarification of job descriptions and job expectations, increase or decrease of the span of control, modification of policies or procedures, and changes in the power or authority structure. Another general approach to planned change involves modifications in the technology used as tools to accomplish work. The assumption behind enhancing technology is that improved technology or work methods will lead to more efficient operations, increased productivity, or improved working conditions. Examples of technological approaches to change include changing processes for doing work, introducing or updating computers or software, and modifying production methods. The third general approach to change focuses on the people in the organization. This approach is intended to improve employee skills, attitudes, or motivation and can take many forms, such as introducing training programs to enhance work skills, increasing communication effectiveness, developing decision-making skills, or modifying attitudes to increase work motivation.

ORGANIZATIONAL DEVELOPMENT STRATEGIES

Choosing the appropriate approach to organizational change depends on the nature of the problem, the objectives of the change, the people implementing the change, the people affected by the change, and the resources available. Several strategies are often thought of as effective techniques for organization development: reengineering, team building, total quality management, job enrichment, and survey feedback.

Reengineering is the sweeping redesign of organizational processes to achieve major improvements in efficiency, productivity, and quality. What makes reengineering so far-reaching is that it goes beyond just modifying and altering existing jobs, structures, technology, or policies. This approach asks fundamental questions, such as: What is the purpose of our business? If this organization were being created today, what would it look like? Jobs, structure, technology, and policies are then redesigned according to the answers to these questions.

As part of the OD process, teams are used as a way of responding quickly to changing work processes and environments; they are encouraged and motivated to take the initiative in making suggestions for improving work processes and products. The term *team* can refer to intact work groups, new work units, or people from different parts of an organization who must work together to achieve a common goal. Often team building begins with a diagnostic session, held away from the workplace, where the team's members examine their strengths and weaknesses. The goal of team building is to improve the effectiveness of work teams by refining interpersonal interactions, improving communication, and clarifying goals and tasks in order to improve overall effectiveness in accomplishing goals. In ideal circumstances, team building is a continual process that includes periodic self-examination and development exercises. Managers must continually develop and maintain strategies for effective team performance by building trust and keeping lines of communication open.

Effective teams are generally attractive to others and cohesive. The extent to which people want to belong to the team makes the team more attractive to others. If others see the team as cooperative and successful, they are more willing to belong. Teams are seen as less appealing if the group's members feel that unreasonable demands are made on them, if the group is dominated by a few members, or if competition exits within the group. A cohesive team exhibits strong interpersonal interaction among its members as well as, increased performance and goal accomplishments.

Reengineering efforts place a strong emphasis on teamwork with the intent of fostering collaboration to accomplish a goal, to resolve problems, and to explore alternatives. These teams can be traditionally managed by an appointed leader or manager or self-managed. Self-managed teams work without an official leader and therefore share responsibility for managing the work team. Managers continue to coach the team, develop strategies for improving performance, and provide resources even though they may not direct the daily activities of the team.

Total quality management (TQM) is the term used to describe comprehensive efforts to monitor and improve all aspects of quality within a firm. Teamwork plays a major role in quality improvement. Total quality management efforts could include employee training, identification and measurement of indicators of quality, increased attention to work processes, and an emphasis on preventing errors in production and service. What is the connection between TQM and OD? Both require a high degree of employee commitment, involvement, and teamwork. Many decisions must be made at the level where the work is accomplished, and managers must be willing to give employees this power. Managers empower employees to make decisions and take responsibility for their outcomes.

Job enrichment is often thought of as a technique of OD. It involves changing a job by adding additional tasks and by adding more responsibility. The widespread use of self-managed teams results in significant job enrichment. By the mere definition of *self-managed teams*, employees are now being asked to perform new tasks and exercise responsibilities within the team that they haven't had to perform before.

Survey feedback involves collecting data from organizational members; these data are then shared with the members during meetings. In these meetings suggestions for formulating change are made based on the trends that emerge from the data. Survey feedback is similar to team building; however, the survey strategy places more emphasis on collecting valid data than on the interpersonal processes of work teams.

OD EFFORTS AND CHANGE

The success or failure of planned change depends not only on the correct identification of the problem but also on recognition of possible resistance to change. It is critical to the successful achievement of organizational development efforts for the manager to recognize the need for change, diagnose the extent of the problems that create this need, and implement the most effective change strategy. Successful OD efforts require an accurate analysis of the needed changes and an identification of the potential resistance to the proposed changes. Two critical points should be addressed concerning the areas in which organizations can introduce change. First, changes made in one area often trigger changes in other areas as well. Managers and those proposing the change must be aware of this systemic nature of change. Second, changes in goals, strategies, technology, structure, process, and job design require that people change. Serious attention must be given to the reactions of employees and possible resistance to changes in these areas.

People may be resistant to change for a number of reasons. They may feel that they will lose status, power, or even their jobs. People react differently to change; even if no obvious threat to their jobs exist, some people's personalities make them more uncomfortable than others with changes in established routines. The reasons for the change or the exact change that will take place may not be understood. However, even if the reasons for the change are understood, employees may not have a high level of trust in the motives of those proposing the change. Also, those who are the targets of the change may genuinely feel that the proposed change is not necessary.

Organizational culture could also influence people's reactions to OD efforts. Organizational culture can be thought of as the organization's personality. The culture is defined by the shared beliefs, values, and patterns behaviors that exist in the organization—in other words, "the way we do things around here." Some organizational cultures may even reward stability and tradition while treating those who advocate change as outsiders. Sometimes the definition and strength of an organization's culture aren't evident until it undergoes change.

How can managers deal with resistance to change? An individual's low tolerance for change is largely a personal matter and can often be overcome with support and patience. Open communication can go a long way toward overcoming resistance to change based on misunderstanding, lack of trust, or different viewpoints. Those who will be affected by the change must be identified, and the reasons for and details about the change must be conveyed accurately to them. Keeping this information "secret" is bound to cause resistance. Also, the people who are the targets of the change should be involved in the change process. This is particularly important when true commitment to, or "ownership" of,

the change is critical and those affected have unique knowledge about the processes or jobs that may be altered.

DOES ORGANIZATION DEVELOPMENT WORK?

Genuine efforts at organizational development require an investment of time, human effort, and money. Do the benefits of OD outweigh these costs? Reviews of a wide variety of OD techniques indicate that they tend to have a positive impact on productivity, job satisfaction, and other work attitudes. These reviews have also pointed out that OD efforts seem to work better for supervisors and managers than for blue-collar workers and that changes that use more than one technique seem to have more impact. There are several factors exist that increase the likelihood of successful OD efforts:

- Recognition of organization problems and influences. Before changes can be proposed, correct identification of the gaps between what an organization is trying to do and what is actually being accomplished must be made.

- Strong support from top-level managers. If managers at the higher levels in the organization do not provide obvious and open support for the OD efforts, the program is likely to fail.

- Action research that provides facts, not opinions, for decision making. Action research includes an identification of the attitudes and behaviors of employees and is part of an ongoing assessment of organizational behavior.

- Communication of what OD is and is not and awareness of why it is being used. The culture of the organization should be such that employees are aware of what organizational development is and is not so that it is not seen as a threat.

To thrive in tomorrow's business environment—characterized by a dynamic work force, rapid changes in technology, and the increasing volatility of the global environment—organizational development must be an ongoing effort; encouraging continual examination and readiness for change must be part of the organization's culture.

BIBLIOGRAPHY

Conner, Daryl R. (1993). *Managing at the Speed of Change: How Resilient Managers Succeed and Prosper Where Others Fail.* New York: Villard Books.

Hammer, Michael, and Champy, James. (1994). *Reengineering the Corporation: A Manifesto for Business Revolution.* New York: HarperBusiness.

Hunt, V. Daniel. (1996). *Process Mapping: How to Reengineer Your Business Processes.* New York: Wiley.

Johns, Gary. (1996). *Organizational Behavior: Understanding and Managing Life at Work,* 4th ed. New York: Harper-Collins.

Kotter, John P. (1996). *Leading Change.* Boston, MA: Harvard Business School Press.

Schein, Edgar H. (1999). *The Corporate Culture Survival Guide: Sense and Nonsense About Culture Change.* San Francisco: Jossey-Bass.

Senge, Peter M. (1999). *The Dance of Change: The Challenges of Sustaining Momentum in Learning Organizations.* New York: Doubleday.

CHERYL L. NOLL

ORGANIZATIONAL EFFECTIVENESS

(SEE: *Organizational Behavior and Development*)

ORGANIZATIONAL STRUCTURE

One of the most challenging tasks of a business may be organizing the people who perform its work. A business may begin with one person doing all the necessary tasks. As the business becomes successful and grows, however, there is generally more work, and more people are needed to perform various tasks. Through this division of work, individuals can become specialists at a specific job. Because there are several people—often in different locations—working toward a common objective, "there must be a plan showing how the work will be organized. The plan for the systematic arrangement of work is the *organization structure*. Organization struc-

ture is comprised of functions, relationships, responsibilities, authorities, and communications of individuals within each department" (Sexton, 1970, p. 23). The typical depiction of structure is the organizational chart. The formalized organizational chart has been around since 1854, when Daniel McCallum became general superintendent of the New York and Erie Railroad—one of the world's longest railroads. According to McCallum, since the railroad was one of the longest, the operating costs per mile should be less than those of shorter railroad lines. However, this was not the case. To remedy management inefficiencies, McCallum designed the first organizational chart in order to create a sense of structure. The organizational chart has been described as looking like a tree, with the roots representing the president and the board of directors, while the branches symbolize the various departments and the leaves depict the staff workers. The result of the organizational chart was a clear line of authority showing where subordinates were accountable to their immediate supervisors (Chandler, 1988, p. 156).

TRADITIONAL STRUCTURES

Traditional organizational structures focus on the functions, or departments, within an organization, closely following the organization's customs and bureaucratic procedures. These structures have clearly defined lines of authority for all levels of management. Two traditional structures are *line* and *line-and-staff.*

LINE STRUCTURE

The line structure is defined by its clear chain of command, with final approval on decisions affecting the operations of the company still coming from the top down (Figure 1). Because the line structure is most often used in small organizations—such as small accounting offices and law firms, hair salons, and "mom-and-pop" stores—the president or CEO can easily provide information and direction to subordinates, thus allowing decisions to be made quickly (Boone and Kurtz, 1993, p. 259).

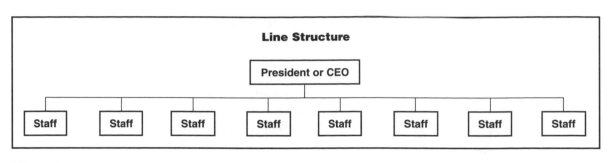

Figure 1

Line structures by nature are fairly informal and involve few departments, making the organizations highly decentralized. Employees are generally on a first-name basis with the president, who is often available throughout the day to answer questions and/or to respond to situations as they arise. It is common to see the president or CEO working alongside the subordinates. Because the president is often responsible for wearing many "hats" and being responsible for many activities, she or he cannot be an expert in all areas (Figure 1).

LINE-AND-STAFF STRUCTURE

While the line structure would not be appropriate for larger companies, the line-and-staff structure is applicable because it helps to identify a set of guidelines for the people directly involved in completing the organization's work. This type of structure combines the flow of information from the line structure with the staff departments that service, advise, and support them (Boone and Kurtz, 1993, p. 259).

Line departments are involved in making decisions regarding the operation of the organization, while staff areas provide specialized support. The line-and-staff organizational structure "is necessary to provide specialized, functional assistance to all managers, to ensure adequate checks and balances, and to maintain accountability for end results" (Allen, 1970, p. 63).

An example of a line department might be the production department because it is directly responsible for producing the product. A staff department, on the other hand, has employees who advise and assist—making sure the product gets advertised or that the customer service representative's computer is working (Boone and Kurtz, 1993, p. 259).

Based on the company's general organization, line-and-staff structures generally have a centralized chain of command. The line-and-staff managers have direct authority over their subordinates, but staff managers have no authority over line managers and their subordinates. Because there are more layers and presumably more guidelines to follow in this type of organization, the decision-making process is slower than in a line organization. The line-and-staff organizational structure is generally more formal in nature and has many departments (Figure 2).

MATRIX STRUCTURE

A variation of the line-and-staff organizational structure is the matrix structure. In today's workplace, employees are hired into a functional department (a department that performs a specific type of work, such as marketing, finance, accounting, and human resources) but may find themselves working on projects managed by members of another department. Organizations arranged according to project are referred to as matrix organizations. Matrix organizations combine both vertical authority relationships (where employees report to their functional manager) and horizontal, or diagonal, work relationships (where employees report to their project supervisor for the length of the project). "Workers are accountable to two supervisors—one functional manger in the department where the employee

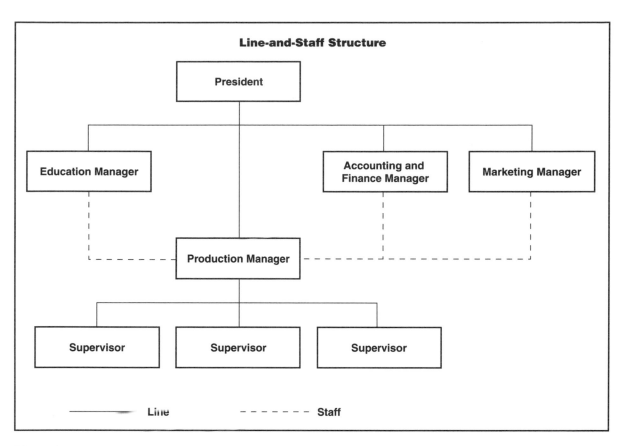

Figure 2

regularly works and one special project manager who uses the employee's services for a varying period of time" (Keeling and Kallaus, 1996, p. 43).

Since employees report to two separate managers, this type of organizational structure is difficult to manage—especially because of conflicting roles and shared authority. Employees' time is often split between departments and they can become easily frustrated if each manager requires extra efforts to complete projects on similar timelines.

Because the matrix structure is often used in organizations using the line-and-staff setup, its also fairly centralized. However, the chain of command is different in that an employee can report to one or more managers, but one manager typically has more authority over the employee than the other manager(s). Within the project or team unit, decision making can occur

faster than in a line-and-staff structure, but probably not as quickly as in a line structure. Typically, the matrix structure is more informal than line-and-staff structures but not as informal as line structures (Figure 3).

CENTRALIZATION

Organizations with a centralized structure have several layers of management that control the company by maintaining a high level of authority, which is the power to make decisions concerning business activities. With a centralized structure, line-and-staff employees have limited authority to carry something out without prior approval. This organizational structure tends to focus on top-down management, whereby executives at the top communicate by telling middle managers, who then tell first-level managers, who then tell the staff what to do and how to do it. Since this organizational structure tends to be

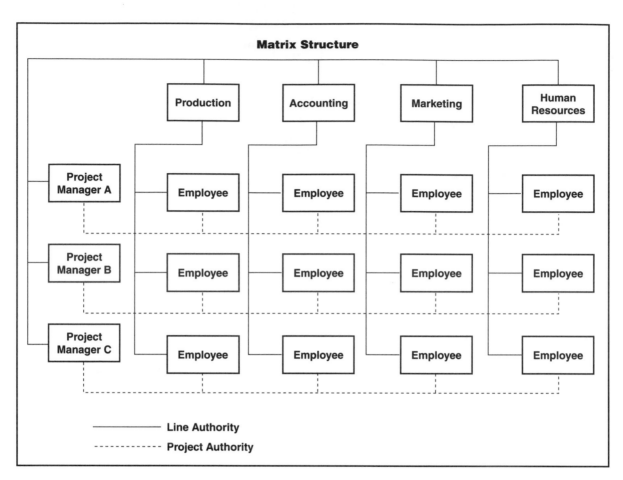

Figure 3

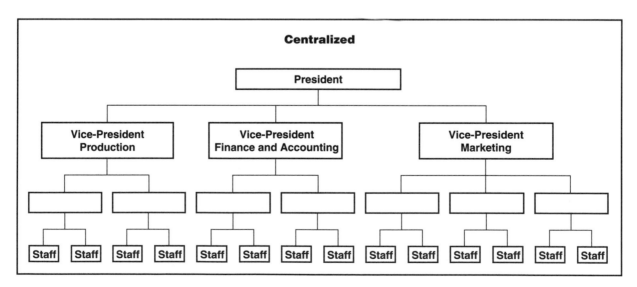

Figure 4

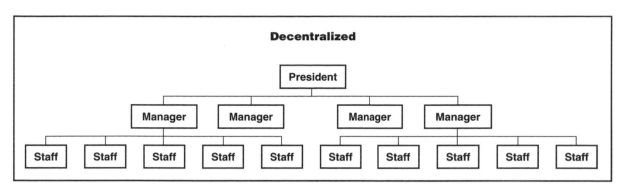

Figure 5

fairly bureaucratic, employees have little free-dom. Centralized organizations are known for decreased span of control—a limited number of employees report to a manager, who then reports to the next management level, and so on up the ladder to the CEO (Figure 4).

DECENTRALIZATION

Because individual creativity can be stifled and management costs can be greater in a centralized organization, many organizations continue to downsize into a more decentralized structure. Decentralization seeks to eliminate the unnecessary levels of management and to place authority in the hands of first-line managers and staff—thus increasing the span of control, with more employees reporting to one manager. Because more employees are reporting to a single manager than before, the managers are forced to delegate more work and to hold the employees more accountable. Downsizing has also helped to change the flow of communication, so that top management hears staff concerns and complaints in a more direct manner and management has a more hands-on approach. The hands-on approach involves less bureaucracy, which means there is a faster response to situations that demand immediate attention. This structure also takes advantage of bottom-up communication, with staff issues being addressed in a timely manner.

The restructuring generally takes place at the mid-management level. Because some middle managers have lost their jobs, been laid off, or simply taken advantage of early retirement and severance packages, their positions have been phased out, thus helping to reduce unnecessary costly salaries and increasing employee span of control. Many middle managers who stayed in their current "positions" found that their jobs have changed to being coaches, or team leaders, who allow their employees greater freedom in completing their work responsibilities (Csoka, 1995, p. 3).

The chain of command is the protocol used for communication within organizations. It provides a clear picture of who reports to whom. Quick decisions can be made in decentralized organizations because approval usually has to come only from the manager one level higher than the person making the decision. The chain of command involves line-and-staff employees, where the staff's job is completing the actual work and the line functions to oversee the staff (Figure 5).

DEPARTMENTALIZATION

Organizations can be divided into various departments, or units, with individuals who specialize in a given area, such as marketing, finance, sales, and so forth. Having each unit perform specialized jobs is known as *departmentalization*. Departmentalization is done according to five major categories (Figure 6): (1) *product*, which requires each department to be responsible for the product being manufactured; (2) *geographic*, which divides the organization based on the location of stores and offices; (3) *customer*, which

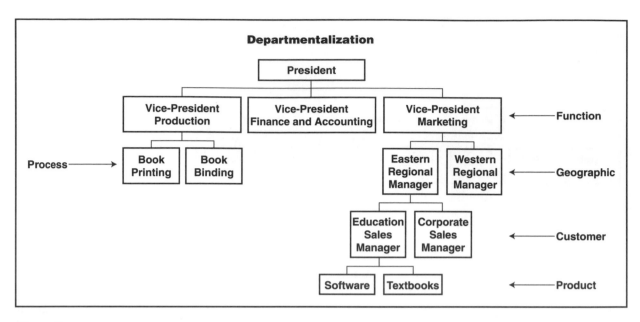

Departmentalization

Figure 6

separates departments by customer type—for example, textbook companies that cater to both grade schools and community colleges; (4) *functional*, which breaks departments into specialty areas; and (5) *process*, which creates departments responsible for various steps in the production process (Boone and Kurtz, 1993).

BIBLIOGRAPHY

Boone, Louis E., and Kurtz, David L. (1993). *Contemporary Business*, 7th ed. Fort Worth, TX: Dryden Press.

Chandler, Alfred D., Jr. (1988). "Origins of the Organization Chart," *Harvard Business Review* 88:2, (March/April): p. 156.

Csoka, Louis. (1995). "Redefining the Middle Manager," *HR Executive Review*, 2(2): 3-5.

Keeling, B. Lewis, and Kallaus, Norman F. (1996). *Administrative Office Management*, 11th ed., Cincinnati, OH: South-Western Educational Publishing.

Litterer, Joseph A. (1980). *Organizations: Structure and Behavior*. New York: Wiley.

Sexton, William P. (1970). "Organization Structure." In William P. Sexton, ed. *Organization Theories*. Columbus, OH: Charles E. Merrill.

CHRISTINE JAHN

OUTPUT

(SEE: *Operations Management*)

OUTSOURCING IN THE BUSINESS ENVIRONMENT

Outsourcing is an option for managing internal tasks. A staffing tool, outsourcing is an arrangement whereby an organization contracts with another organization to perform tasks or functions traditionally handled by internal staff (Boone and Kurtz, 1999).

When an organization decides that more personnel are needed, it must first decide whether to hire more employees, contract workers, or outsource the functions. The focus is on efficiency and cost-effectiveness when deciding whether to outsource. This decision-making process involves internal analysis and evaluation, needs assessment and vendor selection, and implementation and management (Outsourcing Interactive, 1999).

Organizations should remember that outsourcing does not mean abdicating management responsibility. Therefore, companies should

Protestors picket Nike's manufacturing practices of outsourcing.

avoid acting compulsively when deciding on an alternative solution. If the requirements, expectations, and needed resources are not clearly understood, outsourcing does not improve the situation and may even cause it to become worse.

Internal analysis and evaluation involves examining the need for outsourcing and identifying the implementation strategy. Top management of an organization makes these kinds of decisions. People internal and external to the organization provide needs assessment and vendor selection. To assist in identifying qualified vendors, research is focused on the needs of employees and on companies outsourcing the same functions.

Implementation and management allow for administration of the relationship as it evolves between the two—outsourcer and client. Strategy includes ways to monitor and evaluate performance, communicate issues, resolve conflicts, and help employees adapt to change.

ADVANTAGES OF OUTSOURCING

There are several advantages for organizations that choose outsourcing as an alternative to hiring full-time employees. The ten most important reasons for organizations to outsource, as identified in a Survey of Current and Potential Outsourcing End Users in 1998 by the Outsourcing Institute, are:

- *Improved efficiency*: To improve efficiency, a company must aim for dramatic improvements in critical measures of performance such as cost, quality, service, and speed. In some instances, the need to increase efficiency can directly conflict with the need to invest in the primary focus of the business. Outsourcing secondary functions to a specialist allows the organization to realize the benefits of maximizing efficiency.

- *Access to experts and specialists*: Experts and specialists make extensive investments in technology, procedures, and people. Expertise is gained by working with many clients facing similar obstacles.

• *Asset infusion*: Outsourcing often involves the transfer of assets from the customer to the provider. Equipment, facilities, vehicles, and licenses used in the internal operations have value and are sold to the supplier. Certain assets sold to the supplier reveal a win–win approach between outsourcer and client.

• *Freeing of resources for other purposes*: Every organization has limits on the resources available. Outsourcing permits an organization to redirect its resources, most often people, from noncore activities toward activities that serve the customer. Employees whose focus is on internal tasks can now be focused externally toward the customer.

• *Better control over difficult or complex functions*: Outsourcing is a smart option for managing complex tasks. When a function is viewed as difficult to manage or out of control, the organization needs to examine the underlying causes. The organization must understand its own needs in order to communicate those needs to an outside provider.

• *Improved company morale and focus*: Outsourcing lets a company focus on its primary business by having operational functions assumed by an outside expert. In turn, the employees will have increased motivation and morale, since their jobs will be less routine and more meaningful.

• *Reduced capital expenditures*: There is enormous competition within most organizations for capital funds. Deciding where to invest these funds is one of the most important decisions that top management makes. It is often hard to justify secondary capital investments when primary departments compete for the same money. Outsourcing can reduce the need to invest capital funds in these secondary business functions. Instead of acquiring the resources through capital expenditures, they are contracted on an "as-used" basis.

• *Reduced operating costs*: Companies that try to do everything themselves may incur very high research, development, marketing, and deployment expenses, all of which are passed on to the customer. Outsourcing the secondary functions to experts whose only function is

one particular task can be much less expensive in the long run. By outsourcing a task and avoiding hiring full-time employees, a company does not have to pay for insurance, retirement, 401K, or vacation benefits. These benefits can add up to huge expenditures by companies each year.

• *Reduced risk*: Tremendous risks are associated with the investments an organization makes. All aspects of the environment—such as markets, competition, government regulations, financial conditions, and technologies—change rapidly.

• *Utilization of resources that are not available internally*: Outsourcing is a good alternative to adding a new department or creating a costly task force to complete a function. New organizations, spin-offs, or companies expanding into new geographic areas or new technology should consider the benefits of outsourcing from the beginning.

The Survey of Current and Potential Outsourcing End Users (1998) also identified factors leading to successful outsourcing. The most important factors identified were: (1) effective and open communication with the individual and/or groups involved, (2) top-level support and involvement, (3) choice of right vendor, (4) continuous management of the relationships, (5) clarity of company goals and objectives, (6) a visionary plan, (7) availability of external resources, (8) contractual agreement, (9) awareness of personal concerns, and (10) justification of financial involvement.

DISADVANTAGES TO OUTSOURCING

Although there are many advantages to outsourcing, there are also a number of disadvantages. And in some instances, advantages can become disadvantages, depending on the organization and the problems involved.

"Outsourcing is no bed of roses" according to Ed Foster (1996). In order to get the most out of outsourcing, the best in management resources are necessary. The drawbacks to outsourcing include the following:

- *No benefit from a drop in cost of work outsourced*: In some industries, when a long-term contractual agreement ends, a drop in the cost of outsourcing work does not necessarily mean a lowering of the cost to perform the work internally.

- *Problems occurring in the aftermath of layoffs/downsizing*: Morale becomes a concern in the aftermath of some outsourcing deals. Employees are doing more than before for less pay and struggling with problems such as meeting schedules, budget, and quality specifications.

- *Outsourcing impeding the work of the organization*: On rare occasions, organizations have experienced production delays caused by the outsourcing company. John Wyatt, president of James Martin & Company, states, "You rarely hear about the failures of these contracts, but there are many of them" (quoted in Griffin and Ebert, 1999).

- *Managing long-term relationships*: Several factors contribute to a not-so-perfect outsourcing relationship. The factors include (1) pricing and service levels, (2) differing buyer and supplier cultures, (3) lack of flexibility in long-term contracts leading to increased dissatisfaction, (4) both parties failing to make the most of the relationship at the expense of one another, (5) underestimating the time and attention required to manage the relationship or giving management responsibility to the vendor, and (6) lack of management oversight (InfoServer, 1999).

Peter Bendor-Samuel, editor of *InfoServer*, the Journal for Strategic Outsourcing Information, and president of Everest Software Corporation, an outsourcing management company, has definite views regarding outsourcing. He states: "Many companies have been dissatisfied [with outsourcing] and have ranged from being mildly annoyed to extremely unhappy. But there is no question that outsourcing is here to stay, so the question is how to get the most out of it" (quoted in Foster, 1996).

SUMMARY

At one time outsourcing was limited to such services as housekeeping, architectural design, food service, security, and relocation. Today, however, outsourcing has become a popular choice in business and industry. Telemarketing, accounting, travel, data processing, manufacturing, and human resource management are some of the businesses utilizing outsourcing.

Although outsourcing began with small businesses, both large and small organizations are now outsourcing. Griffin and Ebert (1999) reveal that a study by the National Association of Purchasing Management in 1997 projected that at least $121 billion would be spent in the global outsourcing market by the year 2000. However, the Outsourcing Institute in New York projected more than twice that figure.

Outsourcing is no longer solely a domestic concern. Globally, organizations are considering and utilizing outsourcing. With e-commerce playing a significant role in the economy, outsourcing is expected to play a considerable role in the growth of e-commerce.

A number of factors contribute to the decision to outsource, such as improved efficiency, access to experts and specialists, resources available for other purposes, and better control over difficult or complex functions. Organizations utilizing the three-step outsourcing process must perform an internal analysis and evaluation, assess their needs, and select a vendor, and decide on how to implement and manage the function.

There are both advantages and disadvantage to outsourcing. Each must be carefully considered when determining the potential effect on the organization. In order for an organization to successfully outsource, a total commitment by both outsourcer and client is required so that a thriving relationship that benefits both can be formed.

BIBLIOGRAPHY

Bendor-Samuel, Peter. "The Brave New World of Outsourcing." *InfoServe.* http://www.outsourcing-journal.com/issues/may 1998/html. May 1998

Bendor-Samuel, Peter. "A New Way of Doing Business." *InfoServer.* http://www.outsourcing-journal.com/issues/apr1998/html. April 1998.

Bendor-Samuel, Peter. "A World View." *InfoServer*. http://www.outsourcing-journal.com/issues/aug1997/html. August 1997.

Boone, Louis E., and Kurtz, David. (1999). *Contemporary Business*, 9th ed. Fort Worth, TX: Dryden Press.

"Changing Nature of Outsourcing." *InfoServer*. http://www.outsourcing-academics.com/html/acad4.html. 1999.

Foster, Ed. (1996). "Outsource Sense." http://www.infoworld.com/cgi-bin/displayArchive.pl?/96/37/e01-37.1.htm *InfoWorld* 18(37) (September 9):

Griffin, Ricky W., and Ebert, Ronald J. (1999). *Business*, 5th ed. p. 421. Upper Saddle River, NJ: Prentice-Hall.

Horowitz, Alan S. (1999). "Extreme Outsourcing: Does It Work?" *ComputerWorld* 33 (May 10):50-51.

Outsourcing Interactive: An Online Resource of The Outsourcing Institute. http://www.outsourcing.com/howandwhy/main.htm. 1999.

"Outsourcing Relationships: Why Are They Difficult to Manage?" *InfoServer*. http://www.outsourcing-mgmt.com/html/difficult.html. 1999.

Steen, Margaret. (1998). "Thinking Globally." *InfoWorld* 20 (November 20):73-74.

Survey of Current and Potential Outsourcing End-Users, Outsourcing Institute Membership. (1998). http://www.outsourcing.com/howandwhy/research/surveyresults/main.htm.

CAROLYN H. ASHE

P

PACKAGING

(SEE: *Promotion*)

PARTNERSHIP

A *partnership* is an association of two or more persons to carry on as co-owners a business for profit. Partnerships are governed by state law. However, many state legislatures have looked to the Uniform Partnership Act, originally adopted by the National Conference of Commissioners of Uniform State Laws, for guidance. The act was adopted in forty-six states, the District of Columbia, and the U.S. Virgin Islands. The 1990s witnessed major changes to the act, which was originally adopted in the form of the 1992 Uniform Partnership Act. The 1992 act has undergone several amendments, and it currently exists as the Uniform Partnership Act (1997), which had been adopted in approximately half of the states as of the close of the twentieth century. This article will generally follow the Uniform Partnership Act (1997) with an effort to identify those provisions that are less widely accepted, but the reader must keep in mind that state law, not the Uniform Act, will govern in a court of law.

PARTNERSHIP AS DISTINGUISHED FROM OTHER ENTITIES

General partnerships, which are referred to in this article simply as "partnerships," are to be distinguished from other types of entities, including *for-profit* and *nonprofit corporations, nonprofit associations*, and *limited liability companies (LLCs)*. Partnerships are like for-profit corporations and most limited liability companies in that they are intended to operate for profit. However, corporations and limited liability companies are creatures of statute, created and able to exist only by following specific statutory procedures. Partnerships, on the other hand, may exist on a far more informal basis; they can even be based on a handshake agreement. Perhaps the single most significant distinction between corporations and limited liability companies on one hand, and partnerships on the other, is that the former offer liability protection to those who invest in, own, and operate the entities, while general partnerships offer no such protection.

The majority of this article will focus on general partnerships, which are the traditional form of partnerships. However, some discussion will be given below to *limited partnerships* and *limited liability partnerships*, both of which offer at least some liability protection in exchange for conformity with statutory procedures.

PARTNERSHIP ELEMENTS AND FORMATION

As stated earlier, a partnership is an association of two or more persons to carry on as co-owners a business for profit. From this definition, it follows that the essential elements of a partnership are: It is (1) a voluntary agreement (2) to associate for the purpose of sharing profits and losses arising from (3) a common business enterprise and (4) the intention of the principals to form a partnership for those purposes.

The first element of a partnership is a contract among the partners. Any person or entity, so long as that person or entity has the legal capacity to contract, may become a partner. However, because a partnership is a voluntary contractual relationship, no person may become a partner without the consent of all other partners. This contract may be either express or implied and may be written or oral. Of course, the careful planner would favor an express written partnership agreement to provide for the creation, operation, management, and dissolution of the partnership, but this is not a required element. Two individuals who begin making furniture in their garage, selling the furniture to others, and splitting the profits and expenses have formed a partnership, even if neither has ever uttered the word *partnership.*

Unlike the other for-profit entities discussed earlier, there are no organizational documents that must be filed with a public office, and the partnership agreement, even if written, is not a public document. To further illustrate this, to form a corporation the *incorporators* must execute *articles of incorporation* and file those articles with the secretary of state in the state in which the corporation will exist. A corporation is also required to have written *bylaws,* which are the rules of management, operation, and existence of the corporation. Similarly, an LLC does not exist until the *articles of organization* have been filed with the secretary of state, and most state statutes require a limited liability company to have a written *operating agreement* to govern its conduct. There are no such prerequisites to the existence of a partnership. Generally, the only public docu-ments that must be filed by a partnership are those documents necessary to register the business name of the partnership, and this requirement only applies if the partnership is using a name other than the real names of the partners.

PARTNERSHIP AS A DISTINCT ENTITY

An important issue in partnership law is whether the partnership is an entity distinct from the partners in their individual capacity. By way of comparison, it is a fundamental tenet of the law of corporations and of LLCs that those entities are separate and distinct from their shareholders and members, respectively. The issue is not so clear in the case of partnerships. At common law, a partnership was clearly not a legal entity distinct from, or independent of, the partners and had no legal existence apart from the partners themselves. With the adoption of the Uniform Partnership Act (1914), a school of thought emerged a partnership was, at least for some limited purposes, an entity distinct from its partners. However, this issue remained largely unresolved throughout much of the twentieth century. Even the adoption of the 1992 Uniform Partnership Act did not resolve the issue. Finally, the 1997 Uniform Partnership Act stated unequivocally that "[A] partnership is an entity distinct from its partners." [Uniform Partnership Act (1997) (U.L.A.) 201(a).]

The concept of the partnership as a distinct entity remains a difficult issue. In most states, a partnership is a distinct entity for some purposes but not for others. For example, generally a partnership may sue or be sued and may own, hold, or convey real or personal property on its own behalf. The U.S. Bankruptcy code also treats partnerships as distinct entities. However, for purposes of federal income tax, the partnership is not a distinct entity. Although the partnership is required to file a federal tax return, that return is an informational return only, and the partnership has no federal tax liability. All profits and losses of the partnership flow directly to the partners in their individual capacity.

PARTNERSHIP PROPERTY

As mentioned above, a partnership is recognized as a distinct entity for purposes of owning, holding, or conveying real estate. Property contributed to the partnership by the partners, as well as property purchased or otherwise acquired by the partnership, is partnership property, while the property of the partners, such as a partner's personal home and banking account, is not considered partnership property.

LIABILITY OF PARTNERS

Despite the fact that the partnership is an entity distinct from its partners, each partner, in his or her personal capacity, is liable for the debts, obligations, acts, or omissions of the other partners. Therefore, an individual who is owed money by a partnership, is the victim of a breach of contract by the partnership, or is harmed by any act or omission of the partnership, any employee or agent of the partnership, or of any partner acting in his or her capacity as partner has the right to bring suit and collect compensation or damages from the partnership or any of the partners individually. This individual liability is probably the single most important characteristic of a partnership, and it is essential to the consideration of any group of individuals about to embark on a partnership.

The distinction between partnership property and the personal property of partners is of critical importance with regard to creditors of a partnership. In bringing action to collect debts, a partnership creditor must first attach the property of the partnership. Only after all partnership property is exhausted may the partnership creditor become the creditor of the individual partners.

Liability for partnership debts must be distinguished from liability for the personal debts of a partner. A creditor of a partner in his or her individual capacity must collect that debt from the property owned by the partner personally, not from the partnership property. Such a creditor, after exhausting the partner's property, may acquire a *charging order* against the partnership, which entitles the creditor only to the debtor partner's future profits and distributions from the partnership.

PARTNER'S RIGHTS

The partner's right to partnership property is described as a *tenancy in partnership*. The partner is co-owner of this property with his or her partners but has no right to possess, sell, transfer, or assign specific partnership property in any capacity other than on behalf of the partnership. When a partner dies, his or her ownership of specific partnership property automatically *vests* in the surviving partners.

A partner's interest in the partnership itself is a personal property interest in the profits and surplus of the partnership. While a partner is prevented from transferring an interest in individual partnership property, the partner may transfer an interest in the partnership itself. Of course, this right to transfer is subject to the consent of all existing partners to the admission of a new partner, and it may be restricted by a partnership agreement.

Unless a partnership agreement provides otherwise, each partner has the right (1) to be repaid the partner's capital investment in the partnership, (2) to share equally in the profits and losses of the partnership, (3) to share equally in the management and conduct of the partnership business, and (4) to inspect the books and records of the partnership. A partner does not have the right to be compensated for services performed for the partnership. Any dispute among the partners regarding the conduct of the partnership's business is to be decided by a majority of the partners.

DUTIES AND LIABILITY OF PARTNERS

In conduct among partners, each partner owes the other partners an obligation to act with the utmost good faith and loyalty. Partners are not considered to be merely individuals transacting with one another at arm's length, but rather to be fiduciaries of one another. Therefore, the duty among partners involves a very high standard of conduct. A partner may not take advantage of a partnership opportunity, compete with the partnership, or engage in conduct that is detrimental to the best interest of the partnership. In conducting business with individuals who are not partners, every partner is an *agent* of the partnership. Therefore, the acts and words of a partner may be imputed to the partnership.

DISSOLUTION AND WINDING UP

Dissolution is the triggering event that begins the *winding up* of a partnership. Unless the partnership agreement specifically provides otherwise, a dissolution may be caused by the termination of a definite term or the partnership as specified in the partnership agreement, the express will of any partner, the agreement of all partners, the expulsion of a partner, the unlawfulness of the partnership's business, the death or retirement of a partner, or the bankruptcy of any partner or the partnership. These triggering events are further evidence in support of the assertion that a written partnership agreement is essential to a successful partnership. For example, a viable partnership may have many partners, but without an express provision in the partnership agreement to the contrary, the retirement of any one of those partners would trigger the dissolution of the partnership, despite the desires of the remaining partners to continue the partnership. During the winding-up process, the remaining partners may complete unfinished transactions, cease the conduct of the partnership's business, pay the debts of the partnership, and distribute any remaining assets to the partners.

LIMITED PARTNERSHIPS

As opposed to general partnerships, limited partnerships (LPs) are creatures of statute. In most states, it is necessary to file a certificate of limited partnership with the secretary of state to receive approval and to file annual reports. It is also necessary to have a partnership agreement. LPs consist of one *general partner* and one or more *limited partners*. The general partner possesses all management and decision-making power and is afforded no liability protection. The limited partners may not participate in the management of the LP, but in return they receive limited liability protection.

LIMITED LIABILITY PARTNERSHIPS

Like LPs, it is necessary to file a statement of qualification and annual reports to form an LLP. Unlike an LP, all partners in an LLP may participate in the management and control and receive limited liability protection.

KEITH A. BICE

PATENTS

A patent is the grant of a property right for an invention from the United States Patent Office to the inventor. A patent is granted for a twenty-year term beginning with the date on which the patent was filed in the United States, and U.S. patents are only effective in the United States, its territories, and its possessions. The language of the statute gives the inventor the right to exclude others from *making, using, offering for sale,* or *selling* the invention in the United States or *importing* the invention into the United States. Thus, the inventor is guaranteed the right to exclude others from making, using, offering for sale, selling or importing the invention.

The U.S. Constitution gives Congress the power to enact laws relating to patents in Article I, Section 8, which reads "Congress shall have power . . . to promote the progress of science and useful arts, by securing for limited times to authors and inventors the exclusive right to their respective writings and discoveries." Under this power, Congress has from time to time enacted various laws relating to patents. The first patent law was enacted in 1790; the law now in effect is a general revision that was enacted on July 19, 1952, came into effect on January 1, 1953, and is codified in Title 35 of the United States Code. The patent law specifies the subject matter for which a patent may be obtained and the conditions for patentability. The law established the United States Patent Office to administer the law relating to the granting of patents and contains various other provisions relating to patents.

Patent certificates.

In the language of the statute, an individual who "invents or discovers any new and useful process, machine, manufacture, or composition of matter, or any new and useful improvement thereof, may obtain a patent," subject to the conditions and requirements of the law. The term *process*, as defined by law, is a process, act, or method, and primarily includes industrial or technical processes. The term *machine*, as used in the statute, needs no explanation; the term *manufacture* refers to articles that are made and includes all manufactured articles. The term *composition of matter* relates to chemical compositions, which may include mixtures of ingredients as well as new chemical compounds. These classes of subject matter taken together include practically everything that is made by humans and the processes for making them. Consequently, the Atomic Energy Act of 1954 excludes the patenting of inventions useful solely in the utilization of special nuclear material or atomic energy for atomic weapons. The patent law fur-

ther specifies that the subject matter must be *useful*. The term *useful*, in this context, refers to the condition of the subject matter having a useful purpose and also being operable. That is, a machine that will not operate to perform the intended purpose would not be called useful; therefore, the inventor would not be granted a patent. Recent interpretations of the statute by the courts have defined the limits of the field of subject matter that can be patented. Thus the courts have held that the laws of nature, physical phenomena, and abstract ideas are not patentable subject matter.

A patent may only be granted for the creation of a new machine, manufacture, and so on—not for the mere idea or suggestion of the new machine. A complete description of the actual machine or other subject matter for which a patent is sought must be filed with the U.S. Patent Office.

The U.S. Patent Office administers the patent laws as they relate to the granting of patents for inventions and performs other duties relating to patents. Examiners with the office review patent applications to determine if the applicants are entitled to patents under the law. If the inventor is so entitled, the Patent Office approves and issues the patent. Further, the Patent Office publishes not only a list of issued patents but also various other information concerning patents as well as records of assignments of patents. The U.S. Patent Office has no jurisdiction over questions of infringement and the enforcement of patents.

The major purpose of the U.S. Patent Office as an agency of the U.S. Department of Commerce is to grant patents for the protection of inventions and to register trademarks. Further, the Patent Office advises the Department of Commerce and other governmental agencies concerning intellectual property—patents, trademarks, and so on—as well as assisting inventors and businesses in matters concerning their inventions and corporate products. In essence, the United States Patent Office encourages the scientific and technical advancement of the country.

RANDY L. JOYNER

PEER REVIEW

(SEE: *Performance Appraisal*)

PENETRATION PRICING

(SEE: *Pricing*)

PERFORMANCE APPRAISAL

Performance appraisal (PA) is one of the important components in the rational and systemic process of human resource management. The information obtained through performance appraisal provides foundations for recruiting and selecting new hires, training and development of existing staff, and motivating and maintaining a quality work force by adequately and properly rewarding their performance. Without a reliable performance appraisal system, a human resource management system falls apart, resulting in the total waste of the valuable human assets a company has.

There are two primary purposes of performance appraisal: evaluative and developmental. The evaluative purpose is intended to inform people of their performance standing. The collected performance data are frequently used to reward high performance and to punish poor performance. The developmental purpose is intended to identify problems in employees performing the assigned task. The collected performance data are used to provide necessary skill training or professional development.

The purpose of performance appraisal must be clearly communicated both to raters and ratees, because their reactions to the appraisal process are significantly different depending on the intended purpose. Failure to inform about the purpose or misleading information about the purpose may result in inaccurate and biased appraisal reports.

CRITICAL CRITERIA OF DEVELOPING A PA SYSTEM

In order for performance appraisal information to be useful, the PA system must be able to consistently produce reliable and valid results. Measurement items in the performance appraisal system must be designed in such a way that the results of rating are consistent regardless of the raters and the timing of the assessment.

Another critical criterion in developing a PA system is the validity of the measurements. It is important to make sure that the appraisal items are really measuring the intended performance or target behavior. If they are not, the PA system encourages the wrong kind of work behaviors and produces unintended, frequently negative, organizational outcomes. For instance, if the number of traffic violation tickets issued is an item in performance appraisal of police officers, it encourages them to sit on a corner of a street and pull over as many violators as possible during heavy traffic hours. The true purpose of a police force, which is public safety, may become secondary to issuing a large number of tickets for many officers.

WHAT TO EVALUATE

The first important step in developing a PA system is to determine which aspects of performance to evaluate. The most frequently used appraisal criteria are traits, behaviors, and task outcomes.

Traits. Many employees are assessed according to their traits, such as personality, aptitudes, attitudes, skills, and abilities. Traits are relatively easy to assess once a rater gets to know ratees. But traits are not always directly related to job performance. Trait-based assessment lacks validity and thus frequently raises legal questions.

Behaviors. For many jobs, performance is so broadly defined or so conceptual in nature—such as ensuring public safety in the police department—that it is hard to come up with reliable performance measures. In such cases, desirable behaviors can be identified and assessed in the belief that such behaviors lead to successful performance. Such behavior-focused assessment encourages employees to adopt desirable behavioral patterns in the workplace.

Task outcomes. When information about task outcomes is readily available, it is the most appropriate factor to use in evaluating performance. When an organization has a clear and measurable goal as in the case of a sales force, this approach is recommended. However, it has its own pitfalls. There is a problem if employee behaviors are not directly related to the task outcome. Too narrow a focus on measuring outcome only sometimes results in unintended negative consequences. When sales staff narrowly focus on target sales figures to increase their performance measure, for example, they are encouraged to help a few large-volume customers and to ignore many smaller buyers. This may result in poor customer service on the floor.

WHO EVALUATES?

The most common raters of performance are employees' immediate supervisors, who are usually in the best position to know and observe the employees' job performance. They are also responsible for employees' work. Their evaluation is a powerful tool in motivating employees to achieve successful and timely completion of tasks. However, as a result of working together over a long time with the same employees, the immediate supervisor may build up a fixed impression about each employee and use it every time he or she has to evaluate performance.

Some companies find that subordinates are in an excellent position to observe and evaluate their managers' performance, especially when it comes to measuring effective management of their department. While there is merit in asking subordinates to evaluate how they are managed, such evaluation may turn into a popularity contest. Accurate and objective assessment may not be obtained if employees are fearful of possible retaliation from their supervisors. Anonymity of the evaluators is key to the successful use of subordinates for objective evaluation.

Other raters who are frequently used in some companies include peers, customers, and the employees themselves. Peer evaluation is particularly useful when teamwork and collegiality are important to successful task performance. Peer pressure is sometimes a powerful motivator in encouraging teamwork among members. Customer satisfaction is vital to a company's success and can be used in performance appraisal. Many companies systematically collect performance information from customers, typically through anonymous surveys and interviews. Self-assessment is also a useful means, especially when the performance appraisal is intended to identify the training and development needs of potential employees.

Each of these raters contributes to assessing certain aspects of performance. Since job performance is multidimensional in nature, it is important to use different raters or a combination of multiple raters depending on the goal of a performance appraisal system. This multirater

---

Partial Graphic Rating Scale

Instructions: Carefully review employee's work performance during the period indicated above and write in the space an appropriate rating as described below.

1. Unsatisfactory. Performance outcomes are generally unacceptable.
2. Needed Improvement. Performance is deficient in certain areas and improvement is necessary.
3. Average. Performance results consistently meet requirements.
4. Good. Performance outcomes frequently exceed requirements.
5. Excellent. Performance outcomes consistently exceed requirements. Performance is of high quality in every aspect.

Evaluation Factors:

_____ 1. Quantity of work: Considering the volume of work achieved, is he/she at the acceptable level?
_____ 2. Quality of work: Considering accuracy, precision, completeness, and other quality of work, is he/she at the acceptable level?
_____ 3. Job knowledge: Does he/she have adequate skills and knowledge to perform the job?

Figure 1

evaluation, or so-called 360-degree feedback system, is becoming increasingly popular among many American corporations, including General Electric, AT&T, Warner Lambert, and Mobil Oil.

PA METHODS

To ensure the reliability and validity of a PA system, a company must design the evaluation process carefully and develop appropriate measuring scales. Among the many assessment methods developed by human resource management experts, commonly used ones include the Graphic Rating Scale, Behaviorally Anchored Rating Scale, Narrative Technique, Critical-Incident Method, Multiperson Comparison Method, Forced Choice Method, and Forced Distribution Method.

The Graphic Rating Scale is the simplest and most popular method for performance appraisal. As shown on Figure 1, the Graphic Rating Scale offers a list of areas related to job performance. A manager rates each employee on the listed areas according to a numerical score. Although this method is relatively simple and quick to complete, some experts question its validity and reliability. Without elaborate description, appraisal items and scores are subject to various interpretations of raters.

In order to overcome pitfalls of the Graphic Rating Scale, numerous other methods have been developed. The Behaviorally Anchored Rating Scale (BARS), illustrated in Figure 2, offers rating scales for actual behaviors that exemplify various levels of performance. Because raters check off specific behavior patterns of a ratee, PA results of BARS are more reliable and valid than those of the Graphic Rating Scale. Human resource managers must carefully analyze each job and develop behavior patterns pertinent to various levels of performance for the job before they use the BARS.

The Narrative Technique is a written essay about an employee's job performance prepared by a rater. The essay typically describes the rate's job-related behaviors and performance. Without standard performance description, it is a cumbersome task for raters to write an essay for several employees. For example, a rater can be asked to describe the activities, achievements, and level of performance of the employee in a completely open-ended format (unstructured narration). Alternatively, the rater can be provided with some structure to use in the evaluation; for example, "Describe briefly the activities, achievements, and level of performance of the staff member in the following areas: (1) work habits, (2) planning and organizing the tasks, (3) management skills, communications, and development of others."

Behaviorally Anchored Rating Scale

Job: Project Manager

Scale values   Anchors

9	Develops a comprehensive schedule, documents it, obtains required approvals, and distributes it to all concerned.
8	Plans, communicates, and observes target dates and updates the status of operations relative to plans, making schedule modifications as quickly as necessary
7	Experiences minor operational problems but still communicates effectively, laying out all parts of the job and schedules for each
6	Usually satisfies time constraints, with time and cost overruns coming up infrequently
5	Makes list of due dates and revises them but is frequently surprised by unforeseen events.
4	Has a sound plan but neglects to keep track of target dates or to report schedule slippages or other problems as they occur
3	Plans poorly, with ill-defined, unrealistic time schedules
2	Has no plan or schedule of work and no concept of realistic due dates
1	Fails consistently to complete work on time because of no planning. Expresses no interest in how to improve.

Figure 2

The performance review form at a college asks an evaluator to describe the activities, accomplishments, and creative works of the professors in the areas of (1) teaching and (2) research/creative activity. A dean of the college writes about the professor's teaching performance: "Dr. Michael Johnson has been nominated by his students for the Outstanding Teacher Award several times during his service. He introduced many teaching innovations into his classes. His teaching record is exemplary." In the area of creative activity, the dean writes: "Dr. Johnson has a strong and productive research record with a defined focus in organizational leadership. His research has been recognized with several awards given by professional organizations. His creative activity is exemplary."

Similar to the Narrative Technique is the Critical-Incident Method, which involves keeping a running log of effective and ineffective job performance. For example, the PA log of an employee, Mr. Campbell, contains Unsatisfactory Incidents as follows: 1/28/2000: "Refused to try a new work procedure," and 2/15/2000: "Argued

with a customer about the origin of error in the paperwork." The log also contains Satisfactory Incidents as follows: 1/20/2000: "Volunteered to help Charlie complete his assignment in time"; 2/19/2000: "Trained new employees in safety regulations."

The Multiperson Comparison Method asks raters to compare one person's performance with that of one or more others. It is intended to effectively eliminate the possibility of giving the same rating to all employees. In order to separate performance scores among multiple employees, the Forced Choice or Forced Distribution Methods are adopted. Raters must choose one high performer from the list of employees or distribute certain scores to employees at different ranks. For example, only one top person will get 40 percent, two second-rank persons 20 percent, and the bottom one person 10 percent. The Paired Comparison Method is a special case of the Multiperson Comparison Method. Everyone in the evaluation pool is compared against everyone else as a pair and recorded "plus" or "minus" when the target ratee is better or worse,

Paired Comparison Method of Employee Evaluation

For the quality of work: Performance in meeting quality standards

	Employees that are rated:				
	Amy	Barbara	Charlie	Dave	Elaine
As compared to:					
Amy		+	+	−	−
Barbara	−		−	−	−
Charlie	−	+		+	−
Dave	+	+	−		+
Elaine	+	+	+	−	

Note: Barbara ranks the highest.

Figure 3

respectively, than his/her comparison. The final performance ranks are determined by the number of positives. Figure 3 provides for an example.

SUBJECTIVITY AND OBJECTIVITY

Accuracy is critical to performance appraisal. In order to obtain accurate performance information, raters must provide objective and unbiased ratings of employees. But, because it is almost impossible to develop a perfectly accurate performance checklist, managers' subjective opinions are frequently called for. Many companies use some combination of subjective and objective assessment for actual performance appraisal.

Yet there are numerous problems in the actual assessment of employee performance, mainly due to rater bias. Some raters tend to rate all employees at the positive end rather than to spread them throughout the performance scale; this is called "leniency." Alternatively, "central tendency", which places most employees in the middle of the scale, also raises concern about possible appraisal error.

Another common error in performance appraisal is the halo effect. This occurs when a manager's general impression of an employee, after observing one aspect of performance, influences his/her judgment on other aspects of the employee's performance.

Researchers have found that personal preferences, prejudices, appearances, first impressions, race, and gender can influence many performance appraisals. Sometimes raters' personal opinions or political motives creep into the performance appraisal process. They intentionally inflate or deflate performance ratings of certain employees as a way to punish them or promote them out of the department.

Using unreliable and unvalidated performance appraisals may cause a legal problem. A number of court cases have ruled that the performance appraisal systems used by many companies were discriminatory and in violation of Title VII of the Civil Rights Act.

In order to avoid legal problems, companies must develop an appraisal system based on careful job analysis and establish its reliability and validity. They must give clear written instructions to raters for completing evaluations and provide them adequate training if necessary. The company must allow employees to review the results of the appraisals. Human resources departments must play a key role in the development and implementation of an effective performance appraisal system.

BIBLIOGRAPHY

Bernardin, H. J., Kane, J. S., Ross, S., Spina, J. D., and Johnson, D. L. (1996). "Performance Appraisal Design, Development, and Implementation." *In Handbook of Human Resource Management*, Gerald R. Ferris, Sherman D. Rosen, and Darold T. Barnum ed.,Cambridge, Mass: Blackwell, 462-493.

Cascio, W. F. (1998). *Applied Psychology in Human Resource Management*, 5th ed. Upper Saddle River, NJ: Prentice-Hall.

Cawley, B. D., Keeping, L. M., and Levy, P. E. (1998). "Participation in the Performance Appraisal Process and Employee Reactions: A Meta-Analytic Review of Field Investigations," *Journal of Applied Psychology*, 83(4):615-633.

DeNisi, A. S., Robbins, T. L., and Summers, T. P. (1997). "Organization, Processing, and Use of Performance Information: a Cognitive Role for Appraisal Instruments," *Journal of Applied Social Psychology*, 27:1884-1905.

Greller, M. M. (1998). "Participation in the Performance Appraisal Review: Inflexible Manager Behavior and Variable Worker Needs," *Human Relations*, vol. 51, no. 8, pp 1061-1083.

Grote, D. (1996). *The Complete Guide to Performance Appraisal*, New York: AMACOM Book Division.

Illgen, Daniel R., Barnes-Farrell, Janet L., and McKellin, David B. (1993). "Performance Appraisal Process Research in the 1980s: What Has It Contributed to Appraisals in Use?" *Organizational Behavior and Human Decision Processes*, 54:321-368.

Jawahar, I. M., and Stone, T. H. (1997). "Influence of Raters' Self-Consciousness and Appraisal Purpose on Leniency and Accuracy of Performance Ratings" *Psychological Reports*, 80:323-336.

Jourdan, J. L., and Nasis, D. B. (1992). "Preferences for Performance Appraisal Based on Method Used, Type of Rater, and Purpose of Evaluation" *Psychological Report*, 70:963-969.

Kaplan, R. E. (1993). "360-Degree Feedback Plus: Boosting the Power of Co-Worker Ratings for Executives." *Human Resource Management*, 32:299-314.

Kravitz, D. A., and Balzer, W. K. (1992). "Context Effects in Performance Appraisal: a Methodological Critique and Empirical Study" *Journal of Applied Psychology*, 77:24-31.

Maurer, T. J., Raju, N. S., and Collins, W. C. (1998). "Peer and Subordinates Performance Appraisal Measurement Equivalence" *Journal of Applied Psychology*, 83,5:693-902.

Mount, M. K., Judge, J. A., Scullen, S. E., Sytsma, M. R., and Hezlett, S. A. (1998). "Trait, Rater, and Level Effects in 360-Degree Performance," *Personnel Psychology*, 51,3:557.

Peach, E. B., and Buckley, M. R. (1993). Pay for Performance. In H. J. Bernardin and J. Russell (eds.), *Human Resource Management: An Experiential Approach*. New York: McGraw-Hill, 482-515.

Sanches, J. I., De La Torre, P. (1996). "A Second Look at the Relationship Between Rating and Behavioral Accuracy in Performance Appraisal," *Journal of Applied Psychology*, 81:3-10.

Schneier, C. E. and R. W. Beatty, "Developing Behaviorally Anchored Rating Scales (BARS)" *The Personnel Administrator*, August (1979),60.

Smith, H. P. (1997). *Performance Appraisal and Human Development*, Reading, MA: Addison and Wesley Longman Inc.

Wynne, B. (1996). *Performance Appraisal: A Practical Guide*, Philadelphia: Technical Communications, Oct.

LEE W. LEE

PERFORMANCE AUDITS

Performance audits or performance auditing is the public sector version of "Operational Audits" or "Operational Auditing," that are conducted to determine if an entity's operations, programs, or projects are run effectively and efficiently. The Government Accounting Office (GAO) defines a performance audit in its *Government Accounting Standards*, or *Yellow Book*, as:

> An objective and systematic examination of evidence for the purpose of providing an independent assessment of the performance of a government organization, program, activity, or function in order to provide information to improve public accountability and facilitate decision-making by parties with responsibility to oversee or initiate corrective action.

A performance audit has two parts: (1) an economy and efficiency review, and (2) a program review. The economy and efficiency review determines if resources have been used efficiently. The program review, on the other hand, determines whether the resources were used effectively, that is, for the purpose intended by the grantor of resources. Thus, the two reviews complement each other in providing a complete picture of an agency's performance.

The typical performance audit, like all audits, has three phases: planning, fieldwork, and reporting. The planning phase of a performance audit tends to involve more professional judgment and business commonsense than the planning phase of a financial audit, which is limited to a review of financial statements. In planning an audit, the auditor should first determine specific objectives for the audit. *Government Auditing Standards* lists the following specific audit objectives, stated as questions, for the economy and efficiency review:

1. Have sound procurement practices been followed?

2. Have the appropriate type, quality, and amount of resources been acquired at an appropriate cost?

3. Have resources been properly protected and maintained?

4. Has duplication of effort by employees and work that served little or no purpose been avoided?

5. Have idleness and overstaffing been avoided?

6. Have efficient operating procedures been used?

7. Have the optimum amount of resources been used in producing or delivering the appropriate quantity and quality of goods or services in a timely manner?

8. Have laws and regulations been complied with that could significantly affect the acquisition, protection, and use of the entity's resources?

9. Has an adequate management control system for measuring, reporting, and monitoring a program's economy and efficiency been installed and maintained?

10. Have measures of economy and efficiency that are valid and reliable been reported?

Specific objectives, as questions, listed in the *Government Auditing Standards* for the program review include:

1. Have program objectives that are proper, suitable, and relevant been developed?

2. Has the extent to which a program achieves a desired level of program results been determined?

3. Has the effectiveness of the program and/or of individual program components been assessed?

4. Have factors inhibiting satisfactory performance been identified?

5. Has management considered alternatives for carrying out the program that might yield desired results more effectively or at a lower cost?

6. Does the program complement, duplicate, overlap, or conflict with other related programs?

7. Have ways of making programs work better been identified?

8. Has compliance with laws and regulations applicable to the program been ensured?

9. Has the adequacy of the management control system for measuring, reporting, and monitoring a program's effectiveness been assessed?

10. Has management reported measures of program effectiveness that are valid and reliable?

After determining the specific objectives relevant for the audit, the auditor conducts a preliminary survey to obtain information needed to write an audit program and estimate a budget.

The auditor, in completing the preliminary survey, meets with the entity's key employees, reviews relevant documentation such as policy and procedures manuals, and observes the entity's employees as they perform their duties. At the conclusion of the preliminary survey, the auditor is expected to have a thorough understanding of the entity's mission, objectives, goals, operating procedures, and policies. Such knowledge enables the auditor to reach tentative conclusions concerning the audit objectives.

The well-run agency or program will have adopted a well-crafted mission statement, defined a set of goals and objectives that relate to the mission statement, and identified a set of performance measures that accurately reflects entity performance. Thus, the auditor is typically reviewing existing missions, objectives, and goals to determine their reasonableness. Likewise, the entity normally has identified the laws and regulations that its operations or programs must honor. However, an important issue arises if these items are not present or are inadequately prepared. In those cases, the auditor must either stop the performance audit and request that the entity develop the missing items, or the auditor can develop the items and assist the entity in adopting the items recommended by the auditor.

Fieldwork in a performance audit consists of performing the audit tests listed in the audit program. If the preliminary survey was done successfully, then the fieldwork portion of the audit should proceed to confirm the tentative conclusions drawn from the preliminary survey. However, the auditor should fully investigate audit test results that contradict the tentative conclusions and change the audit program accordingly. Once the audit tests are completed, the auditor reaches a final conclusion concerning the entity's performance, which is then presented to interested parties in a draft of the audit report. The draft is then discussed with the entity's management and revised accordingly before it is issued to the appropriate parties. The auditor should return to the entity after giving the entity's management sufficient time to implement any recommendations contained in the audit report. The purpose of this "follow-up" visit is to assess the degree to which management has addressed the findings contained in the audit report.

Management has the responsibility for operating an organization in an effective and efficient manner. In the for-profit sector, this usually means maximizing profit or net income. However, organizations in the not-for-profit sector do not have a measure such as net income or profit to guide the allocation of resources. They adopt alternative performance measure(s) and evaluate them in a manner that fairly reflects performance.

Internal auditors are hired by organizations to assist management in effectively and efficiently operating an organization. Internal auditors do this by reviewing the effectiveness of the organization's internal control process and making sug-

gestions for improving it. In conducting their internal control reviews, the internal auditor should identify the potential risks faced by the organization and then ensure that the most effective and efficient controls are present to address the risks. An internal control review can take many forms, from simply ensuring that controls are present and functioning to an operational audit involving the review of an organization's mission, goals, objectives, and operating procedures.

Up until the 1980s, most internal auditing departments limited the scope of their audits to simply determine whether the organization's policies and procedures were being followed. During the course of these audits, inefficiencies or poor operating procedures were identified and money-savings suggestions generated by the auditors. Concurrently, many organizations have adopted Total Quality Management (TQM) which defines quality in terms of customer satisfaction and measured quality using performance measures that were tracked over time or compared (benchmarked) to other organizations. In addition, organizations faced an increase in legal exposure from laws and regulations enacted beginning in the 1970s and continuing to the present. In the public sector, grantors and constituents demanded accountability in return for the resources provided. Such accountability was to be reported in a document that described efforts and accomplishments. These factors all caused organizations to initially request, and then demand, that their internal auditors downplay compliance with the organization's policies and procedures and emphasize the effective and efficient use of resources and compliance with laws and regulations. This shift in audit scope occurred simultaneously in for-profit and not-for-profit sectors.

The benefits and importance of operational (performance) audits in improving long-term performance is recognized. For example, consider an organization's purchasing function. During the financial audit, an auditor considers only those aspects of the purchasing function that directly affects the financial statements. Thus, the audit would consider whether the terms of purchases are written down in the form of contracts or purchase orders. In addition, the auditor would check to ensure that appropriate officials have been identified who can approve the purchase order. The auditor in a financial audit may go on to check that these two controls were in fact being done, namely that properly approved purchase orders were prepared for all purchases.

The operational auditor, on the other hand, would first identify the purpose of the purchasing function—to get the best terms from vendors for materials and services obtained for the organization. The operational auditor would then obtain the policy and procedures manual for purchasing and review it in the context of the purchasing function's purpose. Additional information may have to be obtained to answer questions raised in the auditor's review. For example, how effective is the bidding process or how much money is actually being saved by obtaining bids? The operational auditor may find that purchasing agents are getting bids for small dollar items, with little return being realized for the effort expended. This type of finding could lead to changes in the policies and procedures followed in the purchasing office with resulting benefits in terms of cost savings accruing to the organization.

BIBLIOGRAPHY

Government Auditing Standards—1994 Revision. (1994). Washington, DC: Comptroller General of the United States.

DOUGLAS E. ZIEGENFUSS

PERSONAL FINANCIAL PLANNING

The best investment a person can make is in himself. Financially, he must have some knowledge about his own affairs because he cannot hand over everything to a financial adviser or broker and expect that person to do it all. If he takes the time to learn about money matters, he will receive a rich reward—dividends in understanding that in the long run will improve his financial position.

HOW DOES ONE BEGIN A FINANCIAL PLAN?

The first step he should take in creating a financial plan is to identify his personal and family financial goals. Goals are based on what is most important to an individual. Short-term goals (up to a year) are things that one desires soon (household appliances, a vacation abroad), while long-term goals identify what one wants later on in life (a home, education for children, sufficient retirement income). Take these short- and long-term goals and establish priorities, making sure an emergency fund is listed as the first item. Then estimate the cost of each goal and set a target date to reach it.

The changing life cycle affects financial planning. A person's goals must be updated as his needs and circumstances change. In one's young adult years, short-term goals may include adequate insurance, establishing good credit, and just getting under way. During a person's middle years, the goals shift from immediate personal spending to education for children and planning for retirement. In one's later years, travel may become a primary goal.

When planning for the future, age is a vital factor. Here are some guidelines to use, depending on one's present age:

Age 20 to 40: When a person is young, growth of financial resources should be a primary goal; a relatively high degree of risk is tolerable. Suggestion: Invest in a diversified portfolio of common stocks or in a mutual fund managed for growth of assets, not income. Speculation (in real estate, coins, metals, etc.) is acceptable.

Age 40 to 60: Stocks are still an attractive choice, but now one needs a more balanced approach. Begin to invest in fixed-rate instruments (bonds) and look into bonds that are tax-free (municipals).

Age 60 and over: By now, the majority of an investor's funds should be in income-producing investments to provide safety and maximum current interest.

There is a rule of thumb that may be appropriate here. It is based on the concept that the percentage of one's portfolio in bonds should approximate one's age, the balance going into equities (stocks). For example at age 40 an investor would keep 40 percent in bonds and 60 percent in equities. At age 60 the reverse would be appropriate; 60 percent bonds and 40 percent equities. Of course, this is a very general idea that may not be appropriate for everyone.

When planning investments for one's age bracket, consider the following:

1. *Security of principal*: This refers to the preservation of one's original capital. Treasury bills are guaranteed by the government, while stocks fluctuate greatly.

2. *Return*: This means the money one earns on investment (interest, dividends, profit).

3. *Liquidity*: This deals with the ease of converting investment into cash.

4. *Convenience*: This refers to the time and energy a person is willing to expend on his investment.

5. *Tax status*: Depending on one's tax bracket, each investment will bear heavily on one's personal situation. Municipal bonds are tax-free, while certificates of deposit (CDs) are fully taxable.

6. *Individual personal circumstances*: Included under this category would be a person's age, income, health, individual circumstances, and ability to tolerate risk.

HOW SHOULD ONE DEAL WITH FINANCIAL RISK IN PLANNING FOR THE FUTURE?

The single most important factor in deciding on the best investments for an individual is the level of risk one can afford to take. Thus the first step in formulating an investment plan is a careful self-examination. How much money does a person have to invest? How great will his financial

needs be for the foreseeable future? How much of his capital can he realistically afford to risk losing, and how great a degree of risk can he and his family handle psychologically? Each of these factors will have a bearing on the degree of risk a person can tolerate in his investment decisions.

The trade-off is simple: To get larger rewards one has to take greater risks.

A person can achieve a balance by investing in a pyramid fashion: Begin with conservative (safe) investments at the foundation (Treasury obligations, insured money markets, CDs) and then gradually build up, accepting a bit more risk at each step. At the very top, you may have high-risk investments (e.g., coins, gold, real estate), but because of the pyramid, these investments will be small compared with the rest of one's holdings. Also, to minimize loss, one should have at least two different types of investments that perform differently during a specific period of time. For example, when interest rates are low, stocks usually gain while money markets do poorly. Diversify!

Every investor must find a comfortable-zone balance of security and risk. This is one of the cardinal rules of financial planning.

Ironically, the goal is to live in comfort, but the key is not to get too "comfortable." Investors don't want to miss out on profitable opportunities.

Here are some guidelines for handling risk that should make an investor more "comfortable"—in both senses of the word.

1. Don't invest in any instrument in which one can lose more that one can potentially gain. This factor is sometimes referred to as *risk-reward balance*.

2. Diversify one's holdings. Spread investment dollars among a variety of instruments, thereby minimizing the potential risk.

3. When investments fail to perform up to expectations (the period to hold them is based upon one's objectives), sell them. "Cutting one's losses" is the only sure way to prevent minor setbacks from turn-

ing into financial nightmares. A rule of thumb is to sell when the value declines by 10 percent of your original cost.

4. Institute a "stop order." Most small market investors have not heard of a "stop order," yet it can "cut one's losses" automatically. When an investor purchases a stock, he gives his broker instructions to sell that stock if it should decline by, say, 10 percent of its original purchase price. The moment the predetermined level is reached, the stock will be sold.

5. Don't discount risk altogether. The rewards may justify "taking a chance." Remember the turtle. It makes progress only when it sticks its neck out.

HOW CAN COMPUTERS HELP WITH FINANCIAL PLANNING?

Financial planning and computers are an ideal match. A person inputs the information; the computer crunches the numbers, makes the projections, and helps keep him on track.

There are software programs designed for personal financial planning and investment. These programs can help one devise a household budget, monitor expenditures in numerous categories, keep meticulous records, and plan for the future. Some programs make year-to-year projections of one's income, expenses, and retirement benefits from now to age 125, and virtually all the programs will import pertinent data into tax-preparation software. Whether an individual prepares his own tax returns or has them done by a professional, having good records is a real boon when that April 15 deadline looms.

If one finds visual data useful, these programs will delight by producing spreadsheets, charts, and graphs. Most programs can even print out checks.

Computer programs make it especially easy to track one's investments. One can enter as many accounts and portfolios as desired, including stocks, mutual funds, bonds, individual retirement accounts (IRAs), and so on. With a link to the Internet, these programs allow an investor to calculate his current net worth with the touch of a key.

HOW DOES ONE CHOOSE A FINANCIAL PLANNER?

Once a person has developed an overall plan, he may want to "go it on his own" or he may use a financial professional, one who shares his sense of values and objectives. Financial planners are paid for their work in one of three ways: fee only, commission only, or fee plus commission. As investors will quickly discover, financial planners do not all charge the same level of fees. Think about how one selects a physician, a school for one's children, a home for one's family. With one's future quality of life hanging in the balance, forgo the "bargain" and choose the best-qualified person available—one whose personal style is compatible. What happens with money in one's life is as intimate as sex—and as central to one's well-being. So choose an adviser one can trust and like.

When considering an individual as one's financial professional, make certain to inquire about his or her education, degrees, certificates, and specializations, if any. However, there are many types of experts, each with a special service and fee schedule. In certain cases, an individual may have more than one title. The following list explains the most frequently encountered titles:

Accredited Estate Planner (AEP): Title awarded by the National Association of Estate Planners to professionals who pass an exam and meet educational requirements.

Chartered Financial Analyst (CFA): Awarded by the Association for Investment Management and Research to securities analysts, money managers, and investment advisers who complete a course and pass an exam.

Certified Financial Planner (CFP): Licensed and certified by the Certified Financial Planner Board after meeting educational, examination, and experience requirements.

Chartered Life Underwriter (CLU): Also awarded by the American College to insurance and financial service professional.

Certified Public Accountant (CPA): Licensed by the state after completing educational courses and passing a uniform national examination administered by the American Institute of Certified Public Accountants.

Registered Investment Adviser (RIA): Indicates registration with the Securities and Exchange Commission; no examination required. (Stockbrokers are exempt from registering as RIAs since they're regulated by the National Association of Securities Dealers [NASD]. They must pass an NASD exam.)

Registered Financial Consultant (RFC): Awarded by the International Association of Registered Financial Consultants to professionals who meet educational and experience requirements and who have earned a securities or insurance license or a certification such as CPA.

When a person has decided on the type of financial professional he wants, he should visit a few and ask them for information on how other clients' investments have performed under their guidance and carefully try to assess how well the planners have been able to achieve for their clients the objectives he is seeking. But it is most important to for him to ask himself whether he would be comfortable with this person handling his financial affairs.

An investor owes it to himself to read (newspapers, magazines, annual reports), learn (seminars, courses), ask (brokers, financial planners), and make certain that he can apply the knowledge gained so that when opportunity does knock, he is not in the backyard looking for four-leaf clovers.

And that is the point. A person must act now so that he can build a firm financial future for himself and his family. Remember that the flowers of all tomorrows are in the seeds of today. The information in this encyclopedia can be the first building block in the creation of a secure and comfortable financial future that only the reader can initiate. There is a saying that sums up finan-cial planning in ten two-letter words: If it is to be, It is up to me.

(SEE ALSO: *Bonds*; *Insurance*; *Mutual Funds*; *Stocks*)

JOEL LERNER

PERSONAL LOANS

(SEE: *Personal Financial Planning*)

PERSONAL SELLING

(SEE: *Promotion*)

PLANNING

(SEE: *Strategic Management*)

POINT OF PURCHASE DISPLAYS

(SEE: *Promotion*)

POLICY DEVELOPMENT

Companies develop policies generally to help them run efficiently in achieving their objectives. They also develop them to comply with the legal and social environment in which they operate as well as to build goodwill with both their employees and their customers. In this way, policies help shape the culture of an organization. They run the gamut from simple parking policies and dress codes to operational policies to complex policies involving benefits and legal rights. To help companies run efficiently, these policies must be appropriate, well written, and easily accessible. Furthermore, as management tools, they must be updated and maintained regularly to work effectively.

DEVELOPMENT METHODOLOGY

To create appropriate policies, companies must decide who is best for the job of creating policy, ensure that they are written clearly, and make them readily available to employees.

Who makes company policy? Depending on the size and management style of a company, the task of creating and writing policy statements varies widely. A small, growing company may start with unwritten policies created by the owners and move to written ones as the need arises. Today, many such companies purchase template policy manuals, adapting them as appropriate to their businesses. As companies grow larger, their need for formal policies grows. These policies help ensure consistency and fairness to all employees.

The management style of the company often determines who sets the policies. Typically, companies with a top-down management style tend to delegate the policy making. Boards of directors often create policies for executives, while executives and managers create them for their subordinates. Very large companies not only have written policies; they often have different policies for different groups of employees. A set of travel policies, for example, may apply only to those employees who travel, or there may even be different policies for international and domestic travelers. The policy may even vary by level in the organization.

As organizational structures have flattened in recent years, companies are moving toward more employee involvement in policy making. A poll of Fortune 500 companies reported that almost half (47 percent) of these companies involve employees in policy decisions. Sometimes policy ideas are solicited from all employees, and sometimes teams of employees create the policies. When policies affect only one department, the department's members contribute substantially to those policies. When policies affect several groups, cross-functional teams are often formed to create those policies.

How should policies be written? One of the most important aspects of effective policies includes communicating them clearly to all affected by them. Two major objectives of well written policy statements are that they be clear and concise. Writers should use words their readers understand; after all, they want statements to be interpreted as they are intended. Also, the tone should be pleasant and the statements should reflect sound practices on such subjects as hiring and firing, pay, and benefits. Many companies also have policies about practices such as giving and receiving gifts, political and charitable contributions, e-mail privacy, Internet use, and health and safety. Some companies even have written policies for activities outside work hours and personal conduct.

Table 1 gives some examples of original and improved policy statements. As you can easily see policy statements need to be specific and precise. A vague policy will not only lead to confusion but could also cause hard feelings, not to mention legal problems. Without the specific detail defining how the three days paid leave could be taken, an employee might expect to have three days tagged on to his or her vacation for the death of a spouse's distant uncle. Or an employee could be under the false impression that vacation days could be accumulated without a cap. That employee might be not only extremely disappointed to learn that the trip to Europe this summer is off because forty days of vacation had not been accumulated but also extremely angry to learn that twenty vacation days were actually lost because they were not taken earlier.

Companies today are extremely sensitive to discriminatory policies. Law requires that women and men be treated uniformly. Most companies with maternity leave have rewritten their policy statements to include paternity leave; others have rewritten their disability policies to include pregnancy. Discriminatory policies relating to age, race, and religion policies are illegal. Policies requiring someone to work on their religious holidays without telling them before they are hired are viewed as discriminatory. Of course, you cannot have a policy that is illegal.

Level of flexibility is another factor to consider in writing policy statements. The objective in writing policy statements is to inform the reader about the content of company policy as clearly as possible. For first-line employees and customers, this usually means being very precise. However, management may want the flexibility to make some decisions on a case-by-case basis.

Original	Improved Revision
If a member of your family dies, you will receive three days off.	If a member of your immediate family dies, you will receive up to three days paid leave for travel to and from the funeral or for funeral and estate business. Your immediate family includes spouse or significant other, parents, grandparents, stepparents, step-grandparents, aunts and uncles, sisters and brothers, stepsisters and stepbrothers, first cousins, sisters-in-law and brothers-in-law, and children and stepchildren.
After you work for the company for six months, you are entitled to one day of vacation for every month worked.	After you successfully complete your probationary period, you may begin accumulating paid vacation days. For each month you work after the probation period, you will earn one day of paid vacation . You can accumulate a maximum of 20 paid vacation days.
Employees may use their accumulated sick leave for childcare or eldercare.	You can use your sick leave to take care of your sick children or stepchildren. You can also use it to attend to special needs of your elder parents, stepparents, grandparents, or step-grandparents.

Table 1

Thus policies written for middle- and top-level management may be purposefully written to allow for flexibility and different interpretations. Also, some types of policies have so many acceptable interpretations that listing them all is both ridiculous and unmanageable. Other times companies will implement a new policy without fully understanding the level of precision it needs. However, there should be a plan to refine the level during rewrites of the policy.

The elder care example above might exemplify a new policy. Initially, an employer might intend that employees use these days to take their elders to doctor and dentist appointments. However, a perfectly acceptable use of this day may be driving elders around to various nursing retirement homes to choose one for their future living. In any case, employers may decide to build in

flexibility at the beginning, recognizing that most of their employees will not abuse this use of their accumulated sick days. However, companies might rewrite this policy later to decrease its flexibility if they find that some employees are testing its reasonable limits.

What technological tools help in policy creation and dissemination? Many technological tools help writers create and disseminate company policies. Most of the full-featured word processors used today include revision features. This tool allows policy writers to share their drafts with others, reviewing changes and suggestions others make and deciding whether or not to accept the change. Companies or groups using intranets can post policy drafts and solicit suggestions directly. Still others prefer to create policies using group software tools that allow users to brainstorm, rank, and create policies anonymously.

Today, many organizations make company policies available on their intranets. In addition to being readily accessible, these policies should be clearly and logically organized. Today's word processors include tools that can generate a table of contents and an index, two components that help make the policies more easily accessible. Another good idea is to create a glossary that includes unfamiliar terms, such as legal definitions, acronyms, and jargon.

Writing or revising policies can be a big project, involving many people and tasks. Project management software is an excellent tool for helping identify the tasks and manage them efficiently.

MAINTENANCE OF POLICY

One final but important aspect of policy development is to review policies periodically and revise them as necessary. Revisions are indicated when companies find they are continually being asked to clarify the statements. Keeping a log of questions as they are asked will help in the revision process. Another indication that updating is needed is frequent employee or customer complaints about a particular policy. While sometimes they do not understand the reason behind the policy, often they are complaining about its fairness or its harshness in comparison with the policy of other businesses.

Other reasons for revising and maintaining policies include both external and internal changes. Changes in the business, work, and social environments often influence needs. Sometimes business mergers, acquisitions, or spin-offs cause companies to revise polices for the new company. Technology such as the Internet, for example, has changed the way many companies do business with both their internal and external customers and suppliers, creating the need to add, delete, and revise policy statements frequently.

Another way to keep current with needed revisions is by keeping up with news items, such as government regulations, health and safety regulations, antitrust laws, morals laws, ethics, etiquette, and much more. Through reading, a company learns what other companies are doing or what problems they have experienced with certain policies. This allows it to take precautionary steps, revising its statements to avoid problems that others have encountered. Of course, keeping up with new laws or interpretations is critical. For example, recently laws have been passed regarding e-mail privacy, and courts have ruled in various ways on the rights of the employer or employee in regard to this issue. Undoubtedly, the courts will be hearing and interpreting more cases on e-mail privacy. Keeping up with current events with an eye to how they might impact your company's policy statements is a good idea.

SUMMARY

Policies are created to help business run more smoothly. Knowing how to develop complete and accurate statements for a specific audience will help organizations succeed in having up-to-date policies that work effectively for them.

BIBLIOGRAPHY

Campbell, Nancy. (1998). *Writing Effective Policies and Procedures: A Step-By-Step Resource for Clear Communication.* New York: American Management Association.

Kuiper, Shirley, and Kohut, Gary F. (1999). "Writing Policies, Procedures, and Instructions." *Contemporary Business Report Writing,* 2nd ed. (pp. 371-392). Cincinnati, OH: South-Western College Publishing.

Peabody, Larry, and Gear, John. (1998). *How to Write Policies, Procedures and Task Outlines: Send Clear Signals in Written Directions.* Ravensdale, WA: Idyll Arbor.

MARIE E. FLATLEY

POWER

(SEE: *Management: Authority and Responsibility*)

PRICE FIXING

Price fixing is the conspiracy by several manufacturers to set prices for goods or services above the normal market rate. The U.S. Justice Department (DOJ) and the Federal Trade Commission (FTC) are the regulatory bodies responsible for determining whether companies are involved in price-fixing tactics. Both bodies have the ability to impose heavy fines on those companies found to be conspiring to fix prices.

The health care industry has been scrutinized many times for price fixing, especially companies that manufacture vitamins. In 1995, the Justice Department fined three vitamin manufacturers a total of $750 million dollars for conspiring to fix vitamin prices. In addition, three vitamin distributors were also found guilty of price fixing that same year; their fines totaled $137 million for fixing the prices for a handful of popular vitamins, and they had to pay just over $1 billion to 1000 corporate buyers of bulk vitamins, an amount reflecting overcharges during the years of the conspiracy.

Roche Holdings AG, which holds forty percent of the global vitamins market, agreed to pay a fined of $500 million and as of 1999 was the object of class-action lawsuits and investigation by the European Commission. Because of the various price-fixing scandals, Roche and other vitamin manufacturers may have trouble raising prices in the future, or even stabilizing them. The price-fixing conspiracy lasted from 1990 through 1999 and affected vitamins A, B2, B5, C, E, and beta carotene. It also included vitamin premixes, which are added to breakfast cereals and other processed foods. The Justice Departments probe of price fixing was expected to continue as the government attempted to build cases against other vitamin manufacturers.

In 1996, the FTC and the DOJ issued a revised Statement of Antitrust Enforcement Policy in Health Care. Under this new enforcement policy, the FTC and the DOJ will not necessarily view joint agreements on price between previously competing providers as unlawful price fixing if the integrated delivery system is sufficiently integrated. The enforcement statement does not, however, provide solid guidance on what constitutes integration sufficient to permit joint negotiations. But, it does offer rules of thumb that will allow those involved in integrated delivery systems to better assess whether their joint pricing activities will raise antitrust concerns.

The securities industry was also closely scrutinized in the 1990s for price-fixing tactics. Investigations of the National Association of Securities Dealers and the NASDAQ market by the Department of Justice and the Securities and Exchange Commission (SEC) during the latter part of the 1990s suggested that market makers colluded to fix prices and widen bid-ask spreads in attempts to increase dealers' profits at investors' expense. At a minimum, market makers appeared to have adopted a quoting convention that could be viewed as anticompetitive behavior.

In understanding the experience of the U.S. securities market, it is important to consider what sorts of behavior are deemed anticompetitive. U.S. law on overt price fixing is clear: Such behavior is illegal. However, in many cases there is no explicit agreement to fix prices. Based on the Sherman Antitrust Act, U.S. courts developed the doctrine of conscious parallelism, which means, according to the Supreme Court, that no formal agreement is necessary to constitute an unlawful conspiracy.

Prior to 1996, market makers were allegedly engaged in many price-fixing scandals. In the late 1990s, the Justice Department found evidence that this practice was still occurring. For example, price quotes on Instinet, a private electronic market, differed from NASDAQ quotes for the same stocks. As of 2000, the SEC was investigating individual traders in connection with price fixing, and there was the possibility that additional civil suits could be filed.

In 1999, a California appeals court unanimously ruled that Arco and eight other oil companies were entitled to summary judgment in a price-fixing suit because there was no evidence of an agreement among them to fix prices or limit the supply of the cleaner-burning gasoline mandated by California. The appeals court agreed with the trial court's original conclusion that the evidence provided by the plaintiffs suggested not a complex tangled web, but nine defendants using all available information sources to determine capacity, supply, and pricing decisions. The court ruled that the companies involved made these pricing decisions because they wanted to maximize their own individual profits and were not concerned about the profits of their competitors.

As of 2000, the Department of Justice was investigating thirty price-fixing cases, many of them involving food additives, feed supplement, and vitamins. Since price fixing occurs when companies conspire to set an artificially high price for a product, the nature of the food additive industry makes it easy to create price-fixing cartels. Because of the small number of companies that are involved in the additive industry, it is easier for them to organize and maintain a price-fixing conspiracy. Price fixing of food additives is also easy because a small number of companies means that prices are negotiated via individual contracts, instead of in an open market.

The establishment in the 1990s of international trade associations, which are facilitated by the European Union, is another major cause of price fixing. These trade associations provide data about their industry to association members, including information on the exact size of the market and the growth rate of the industry. That information can lead to establishment of a cartel, because the companies can extrapolate pricing information.

Archer Daniels Midland was prosecuted in 1996 for illegally fixing the prices of lysine, which is used as a nutritional additive in livestock feed, and citric acid. During the time of the conspiracy, Archer Daniels Midland produced 54 percent of the nation's lysine used in the United States and 95 percent of the world's source. Annual sales of lysine were $330 million in the United States and $600 million worldwide.

The company pleaded guilty to fixing the price of lysine from 1992 to 1996, and the Justice Department fined it $70 million. The higher prices of animal feed resulted in lost income for hog and poultry farmers, as well as feed companies.

BIBLIOGRAPHY

Ackert, Lucy, and Church, Bryan. (1998). "Competitiveness and Price Setting in Dealer Market." *Economic Review* (July): 83(3) 4.

Calderwood, James. (1995). "Antitrust Warning." *Transportation and Distribution* (December): 36(12) 72.

Scheffey, Thomas. (2000). "Westlaw, Lexis Hit with Price-Fixing Claim." *The Connecticut Law Tribune,* (March 6): 20(5) 1.

PATRICIA A. SPIROU

PRICING

Price is perhaps the most important of the four Ps of marketing, since it is the only one that generates revenue for a company. Price is most simply described as the amount of money that is paid for a product or service. When establishing a price for a product or service, a company must first assess several factors regarding its potential impact. Commonly reviewed factors include legal and regulatory guidelines, pricing objectives, pricing strategies, and options for increasing sales.

LEGAL AND REGULATORY GUIDELINES

The first major law influencing the price of a company's product was the Sherman Antitrust Act of 1890, passed by Congress to prevent a company from becoming a monopoly. A monopoly occurs when one company has total control in the production and distribution of a product or service. As a monopoly, a company can charge higher than normal prices for its product or service, since no significant competition exists. The Sherman Antitrust Act empowers the U.S. Attorney General's Office to challenge a perceived monopoly and to petition the federal courts to break up a company in order to promote competition. An example of the successful use of Sherman Antitrust Act regulations occurred when the Attorney General's Office used them to break up the telephone giant, AT&T, in the 1980s. As a result of AT&T's breakup, several new telephone companies, such as MCI and Sprint, were created. The formation of these and other new phone companies during the 1980s resulted in the more competitive pricing of telephone services.

Another significant piece of legislation that has a major effect on determining price is the Clayton Act of 1914, passed by Congress in order to prevent practices such as price discrimination and the exclusive or nearly exclusive dealing between and among only a few companies. Like the Sherman Antitrust Act, this act prevented practices that would reduce competition. The Robinson-Patman Act of 1936, which is technically an extension of the Clayton Act, further prohibits a company from selling its product at an unreasonably low price in order to eliminate its competitors. The purpose of this act was to prohibit national chain stores from unfairly using volume discounts to drive smaller firms out of business. To defend against charges of violating the Robinson-Patman Act, a company would have to prove that price differentials were based on the competitive free market, not an attempt to reduce or eliminate competition. Because regulations of the Robinson-Patman Act do not apply to exported products, a company can offer products for sale at significantly lower prices in foreign markets than in U.S. markets.

Another set of laws influencing the price of a company's product are referred to as the unfair trade laws. Passed in the 1930s, these laws were designed to protect special markets, such as the dairy industry, and their main focus is to set minimum retail prices for a product (e.g., milk), allowing for a slight markup. Theoretically, these laws would protect a specialty business from larger businesses that could sell the same products below cost and drive smaller, specialty stores out of business. Fair trade laws are a different set of statutes that were enacted by many state legislatures in the early 1930s. These laws allow a producer to set a minimum price for its product; hence, retailers signing pricing agreements with manufacturers are required to list the minimum price for which a product can be sold. These acts prevent the use of interstate pricing agreements between manufactures and retailers, grounded in the belief that this would promote more competition and, as a result, lower prices. An important aspect of these acts is that it does not apply to intrastate product prices.

PRICING OBJECTIVES

A critical part of a company's overall strategic planning includes the establishment of pricing objectives for the products it sells. A company has several pricing objectives from which to choose, and the objective chosen will depend on the goals and type of product sold by a company. The four most commonly adopted pricing objectives are (1) competitive, (2) prestige, (3) profitability, and (4) volume pricing.

Competitive Pricing The concept behind this frequently used pricing objective is to simply match the price established by an industry leader for a particular product. Since price difference is minimized with this strategy, a company focuses its efforts on other ways to attract new customers. Some examples of what a company might do in order to obtain new customers include producing high-quality and reliable products, providing superior customer service, and/or engaging in creative marketing.

Prestige Pricing A company may chose to promote, maintain, and enhance the image of its product through the use prestige pricing, which involves pricing a product high so as to limit its availability to the higher-end consumer. This limited availability enhances the product's image, causing it to be viewed as prestigious. Although a company that uses this strategy expects to have limited sales, this is not a problem because a profit is still possible due to the higher markup on each item. Examples of companies that use prestige pricing are Mercedes-Benz and Rolls Royce.

Profitability Pricing The basic idea behind profitability pricing is to maximize profit. The basic formula for this objective is that profits equal revenue minus expenses ($P = R - E$). Revenue is determined by a product's selling price and the number of units sold. A company must be careful not to increase the price of the product too much, or the quantity sold will be reduced and total profits may be lower than desired. Therefore, a company is always monitoring the price of its products in order to make sure it is competitive while at the same time providing for an acceptable profit margin.

Volume Pricing When a company uses a volume-pricing objective, it is seeking sales maximization within predetermined profit guidelines. A company using this objective prices a product lower than normal but expects to make up the difference with a higher sales volume. Volume pricing can be beneficial to a company because its products are being purchased on a large scale, and large-scale product distribution helps to reinforce a company's name as well as to increase its customer loyalty. A subset of volume pricing is the market-share objective, the purpose of which is to obtain a specific percentage of sales for a given product. A company can determine an acceptable profit margin by obtaining a specific percentage of the market with a specific price for a product.

PRICING STRATEGIES

Companies can chose from a variety of pricing strategies, some of the most common being penetration, skimming, and competitive strategies. While each strategy is designed to achieve a different goal, each contributes to a company's ability to earn a profit.

Penetration Pricing Strategy A company that wants to build market share quickly and obtain profits from repeat sales generally selects the penetration pricing strategy, which can be very effective when used correctly. For example, a company may provide consumers with free samples of a product and then offer the product at a slightly reduced price. Alternatively, a company may initially offer significant discounts and then slowly remove the discounts until the full price of the product is listed. Both options allow a company to introduce a new product and to start building customer loyalty and appreciation for it. The idea is that once consumers are familiar with and satisfied with a new product, they will begin to purchase the product on a regular basis at the normal retail price.

Price Skimming Strategy A price-skimming strategy uses different pricing phases over time to generate profits. In the first phase, a company launches the product and targets customers who are more willing to pay the item's high retail price. The profit margin during this phase is extremely high and obviously generates the highest revenue for the company. Since a company realizes that only a small percentage of the market was penetrated in the first phase, it will price the product lower in the second phase. This second-phase pricing will appeal to a broader cross-section of customers, resulting in increased product sales. When sales start to level off during this phase, the company will price the product even lower. This third-phase pricing should appeal to those consumers who were price-sensitive in the first two phases and result in increased sales. The company should now have covered the majority of the market that is willing to purchase its product at the high, medium, and low price ranges. The price-skimming strategy provides an excellent opportunity for the company to maximize profits from the beginning and only slowly lower the price when needed because of reduced sales. Price adjustment with this strategy closely follows the product life cycle, that is, how customers

accept a new product. Price skimming is a frequently used strategy when maximum revenue is needed to pay off high research and development costs associated with some products.

Competitive Pricing Strategy Competitive pricing is yet another major strategy. A company's competitors may either increase or decrease their prices, depending upon their own objectives. Before a company responds to a competitor's price change with one of its own, a thorough analysis as to why the change occurred needs to be conducted. An investigation of price increases or decreases will usually result in one or more of the following reasons for the change: a rise in the price of raw materials, higher labor costs, increasing tax rates, or rising inflation. To maintain an acceptable profit margin for a particular product, a company will usually increase the price. In addition, strong consumer demand for a particular product may cause a shortage and, therefore, allow a company to increase its price without hurting either demand or profit.

When a competitor increases its price, a company has several options from which to chose. The first is to increase its price to approximately the same as that of the competing firm. The second is to wait before raising its price, a strategy known as *price shadowing*. Price shadowing allows the company to attract new customers—those who are price-sensitive—away from the competing firm. If consumers do switch over in large numbers, a company will make up lost profits through higher sales volume. If consumers do not switch over after a period of time, the company can increase its price. Typically, a company will increase its price to a level slightly below that of its competitors in order to maintain a lower-price tactical advantage. The airline industry uses the competitive pricing strategy frequently.

When competitors decrease their prices, a company has numerous options. The first option is to maintain its price, since the company is confident that consumers are loyal and value its unique product qualities. Depending on the price sensitivity of customers in a given market, this might *not* be an appropriate strategy for a company to use. The second is to analyze why a competitor might have decreased its prices. If price decreases are due to a technological innovation, then a price decrease will probably be necessary because the competitor's price reduction is likely to be permanent. Regardless of its competitor's actions, a company may decrease its price. This price reduction option is called *price covering*. This option is most useful when a company has done a good job of differentiating the qualities of its product from those of a competitor's product. On the flip side, the advantage of price covering is reduced when no noticeable difference can be seen between a company's product and that of a competitor.

OPTIONS FOR INCREASING SALES

Companies have several options available when attempting to increase the sales of a product, including coupons, prepayment, price shading, seasonal pricing, term pricing, segment pricing, and volume discounts.

Coupons Almost all companies offer product coupons, reflecting their numerous advantages. First, a company might want to introduce a new product, enhance its market share, increase sales on a mature product, or revive an old product. Second, coupons can be used to generate new customers by getting customers to buy and try a company's product—in the hope that these trial purchases will result in repeat purchases. A variety of coupon distribution methods are available, such as Sunday newspapers and point-of-purchase dispensers.

Prepayment A prepayment plan is typically used with customers who have no or a poor credit history. This prepayment method does not generally provide customers with a price break. There are, however, prepayment methods that do reduce the price of a product. For example, the prepayment strategy is widely used in the magazine industry. A customer who agrees to purchase a magazine subscription for an extended period of time normally receives a discount as compared to the newsstand price. Purchase of gift certificates is another example of how prepayment can

be used to promote sales. For example, a company may offer discounts on a gift certificate whereby the purchaser may only pay 90 to 95 percent of the gift certificate's face value. There are several advantages of using this strategy. First, consumers are encouraged to buy from the company offering the gift certificates rather than from other stores. Second, the revenue is available to a company for reinvestment prior to the product's sale. Finally, receivers will not redeem all gift certificates, and as a result, a company retains all the revenue.

Price Shading One way to increase company sales is to allow salespeople to offer discounts on the product's price. This tactic, known as price shading, is normally used with aggressive buyers in industrial markets who purchase a product on a regular basis and in large volumes. Price shading allows salespeople to offer more favorable terms to preferred industrial buyers in order to encourage repeat sales.

Seasonal Pricing The price for a product can also be adjusted based on seasonal demands. Seasonal pricing will help move products when they are least saleable, such as air conditioners in the winter and snowblowers in the spring. An advantage of seasonal pricing is that the price for a product is set high during periods of high demand and lowered as seasonal demand drops off to clear inventory to make room for the current season's products.

Term Pricing A company has another positive reinforcement strategy for use when establishing product price. For example, a company may offer a discount if the customer pays for the product promptly. The definition of promptly varies depending on company policy, but normally it means the account balance is to be paid in full within a specific period of time; in return, a company may provide a discount to encourage continuation of this early payment behavior by the customer. This term pricing strategy is normally used with large retail or industrial buyers, not with the general public. Occasionally, a company will offer a small discount to customers who pay for a product with cash.

Segment Pricing Segment pricing is another tactic a company can use to modify product price in order to increase sales. Everyday examples of segment pricing discounts are those extended to children, senior citizen, and students. These discounts have several positive benefits. First, the company is appearing to help those individuals who are or are perceived to be economically disadvantaged, a perception that helps create a positive public relations image for a company. Second, members of those groups who ordinarily may not purchase the product are encouraged to do so. Therefore, a company's sales will increase, which will likely result in increased market share and revenue.

Volume Discounts A common method used by a company to price a product is volume discounting. The idea behind this pricing strategy is simple—if a customer purchases a large volume of a product, the product is offered at a lower price. This tactic allows a company to sell large quantities of its product at an acceptable profit margin. Volume pricing is also useful for building customer loyalty.

SUMMARY

Price is an important component of the four Ps of marketing because it generates revenue. Price is often thought of as the money that this paid for a product or service. Several factors need to be examined when setting a product price. Frequently reviewed factors include legal and regulatory guidelines, pricing objectives, pricing strategies, and options for increasing sales, since all of these factors contribute to the price established for a product.

BIBLIOGRAPHY

Boone, L. E., and Kurtz, D. L. (1992). *Contemporary Marketing*, 7th ed. New York: Dryden/Harcourt Brace.

Churchill, G. A., and Peter, J. P. (1998). *Marketing: Creating Value for Customers*, 2d ed. Boston: Irwin/Mcgraw-Hill.

Farese, L., Kimbrell, G., and Woloszyk, C. (1995). *Marketing Essentials*. Mission Hills, CA: Glencoe/McGraw-Hill.

Kotler, P., and Armstrong, G. (1998). *Principles of Marketing*, 8th ed. Englewood Cliffs, NJ: Prentice-Hall.

Semenik, R. J., and Bamossy, G. J. (1995). *Principles of Marketing: A Global Perspective*, 2nd ed. Cincinnati, OH: South-Western.

ALLEN D. TRUELL
MICHAEL MILBIER

PRIVACY AND SECURITY

Personal privacy and security are foundational principles of our society. Yet how much actual privacy do we have? And how secure is the information we believe to be private? The integration of the computer into almost every corner of our lives has greatly affected our personal privacy and security. Databases across the country collect little pieces of data about us every time we use our credit cards, make a telephone call, and send or receive e-mail. In addition, health care records, insurance records, Social Security records, and so forth are all kept in computer files. This computer technology makes records and data easier to compile, combine, and circulate. Therefore, it is important to consider the effects of computerization on individual privacy, corporate security, and legislation.

INDIVIDUAL PRIVACY

Jeffrey Rothfeder's 1992 book, *Privacy for Sale*, illuminates the ways in which computers have changed our lives. Today, most of us depend on technology more than we realize. Although not everyone owns a cellular telephone, global pager, or personal digital assistant (PDA), most people do have credit cards, bank cards, and Social Security numbers. But the piles of files that are maintained when we pay for dinner with a credit card, withdraw cash using an automated teller machine (ATM), and use our Social Security number as identification when cashing a check are just the tip of the iceberg. Health care records, pharmacy databanks, and employment files also provide millions of people with the opportunity to peek into our lives.

Before computerization, most of this information was filed away in dark, musty filing cabinets, never to see the light of day without a

U.S. representative Jay Inslee speaks publicly about banks selling confidential information to telemarketers.

certain amount of physical effort. However, today this information is stored electronically in databases that are interconnected through a wide variety of networks. Your privacy—or the lack thereof—can be just a few mouse clicks away. Privacy advocates assert that electronic record keeping of any information threatens basic American liberties and rights to privacy. Some argue that any machines that have memory—such as answering machines or cellular telephones—are potential privacy concerns.

In addition, computers can be used as vehicles for harassment. The term "spam" was originally used in cyberspace to refer to unrelated or unnecessary (junk) postings to electronic newsgroups and bulletin boards. Eventually, the term was used as a verb to refer to junk e-mail (e.g., "I've been spammed!"). Some states have enacted laws to decrease the amount of on-line harassment. For example, in 1992 Arizona established an antiharassment law that makes it illegal to make threatening or harassing statements via electronic communications. Also in 1992, Michigan passed a stalking law that defined repeated and unwanted electronic messages as harassment. In 1995, Connecticut extended its existing harassment laws to include computer-related communications. Ironically, the corporate and governmental entities that maintain many of the databases that are used to collect information are also vulnerable to their own privacy and security issues.

CORPORATE SECURITY

Today, people in business and industry greatly depend on computer technology for nearly every aspect of their daily activities. From typical desktop applications such as word processing and spreadsheets to fax machines, e-mail, and integrated inventory databases, networks have connected corporations across the world to share information and communicate. It is estimated that 200 million e-mail message are sent each day; that's more than 8 million an hour or nearly 140,000 each second! These messages travel through high-speed Internet connections all across the world, making stops (just for nanoseconds) and leaving a trail of messages along the way. These connections facilitate communication, but they also allow outside access to sensitive computer files.

This vulnerability is expensive; nearly 40 percent of all large corporations and even some governmental agencies have experienced virtual break-ins through network connections. Of these break-ins, 30 percent occurred despite the company's use of a firewall—a software program designed to allow only internal access by authorized personnel. Many corporations and government agencies maintain databases that contain personal information about employees, customers, and clients. Although the legal system has not kept pace with the Information Age, legislation

has been passed to help promote both individual and organizational privacy and security in cyberspace.

LEGISLATION

No one organization, agency, institution, or country owns or maintains the entire Internet; it is a series of linked networks. Collectively, they work together to support the massive amounts of information that are available worldwide. There are also no set rules or regulations or even standards by which Internet communications are evaluated. However, several groups have formed to address the social and legal issues involving cyberspace. The Electronic Frontier Foundation (EFF) was established in 1990 to focus on civil liberties (www.eff.org). The purpose of this group is to protect the First Amendment right to freedom of speech. In 1992, the Internet Society (ISOC) began as an international organization to develop and implement standards for the Internet as well as to maintain historical and statistical databases of Internet usage (www.isoc.org).

The laws related to computer technology are still in their infancy. However, several laws have been enacted to protect privacy and security. For example, the Privacy Protection Act of 1996 (42 U.S.C. 2000) imposes controls on the databanks owned by federal agencies. Any database maintaining personal information cannot be distributed to other federal agencies without going through proper legal channels. In addition, the Family Education Rights and Privacy Act (FERPA) protects the dissemination of student information.

In addition to "taking" information through database access, security issues also include deleting information through database access. Improper use and invasion of privacy through harmful access occurs when people knowingly damage or destroy computer programs by deleting information or installing computer viruses (programs designed to run in the background of a computer's memory, silently destroying data). This improper use is addressed under the Computer Fraud and Abuse Act of 1986 (18 U.S.C. 1030), which prohibits the improper use of "federal interest" computers—computers that communicate and share information across state lines or internationally. Today, any computer that is connected to the Internet (even through a local network provider) is considered a federal interest computer and subject to the Computer Fraud and Abuse Act. In addition, the Electronic Communications Privacy Act (18 U.S.C. 2510) makes it a crime to use a computer system to view or tamper with other people's private messages (e-mail, data files, etc.) stored in an on-line system.

Jurisdictional issues—the power of a court to hear a case—are also a concern, considering the lack of boundaries in cyberspace. For example, if a person living in California uses a computer system based in Nebraska to access information owned by a corporation in Chicago to learn more about an individual living in New York, which court will hear the case? This scenario becomes even more convoluted if we modify the story to take place in countries instead of states. These laws by no means provide total privacy and security protection; they merely define criminal acts and set the parameters for prosecuting those who have violated them. New laws are continually proposed; you can access these bills and keep up to date on the related debates in Congress by accessing the Library of Congress web site at http://lcWeb.loc.gov/.

CONCLUSIONS

In summary, it is apparent that cyberspace has become and will continue to be a major concern to both individual and organizational privacy and security. Although legislation is beginning to become more substantial, it severely lags behind the pace of technology, forcing the burden of responsibility on the individual. To maintain your personal privacy and security, experts suggest following certain guidelines when using credit cards and communication devices (including telephones and computers):

- When subscribing to an Internet service provider (ISP), give them only the necessary information to process your account. Optional information will be kept in a database and po-

tentially connected to your account for identification purposes.

- Do not, under any circumstances, share your password or personal identification number (PIN) with anyone. Also, if given the option to create your own passwords, do not use words or numbers that someone could know (home address, phone number, date of birth, anniversary) or find (Social Security number).

- If you want to surf the Web without leaving behind a personal trail, use an anonymous connection such as an open computer lab at a school, university, or library.

- Never use your credit card to purchase goods or services on-line; avoid similar transactions over the telephone (especially cordless phones and cell phones).

- Don't create your own personal Web page that lists everything about yourself unless you really want everyone to know everything about you.

In conclusion, we can never be sure how much actual privacy we have. The extent of the Internet and interconnected databases is far too great to determine who knows what or how much. However, we do have some control over the security of our private information—if we choose not to share it!

BIBLIOGRAPHY

Ayers, Leslie, Banks, Michael, Hudspeth, Lee, Lee, T. J., and Wendin, Christine Grech. (1998). "Go Deep Undercover." *PC/Computing* November: 154-156.

Behar, Richard. (1997). "Who's Reading Your E-Mail?" *Fortune* February 3:56-70.

Finkelstein, Katherine Eban. (1998). "The Computer Cure." *The New Republic* September 21:28-33.

Miller, L. (1998). "Senders of Junk E-Mail Warned." *USA Today* February 8: D1.

Mitchell, Russ. (1997). "Is the FBI Reading Your E-Mail?" *U.S. News & World Report* October 13:49.

Patterson, B. G. (1998). "Use and Misuse of Computers." In *The Administration of Campus Discipline: Student, Organizational and Community Issues.* Asheville, NC: College Administration Publications.

Pavela, Gary M. (1995). "Sexual Harassment and E-Mail?" *Synfax Weekly Report* November 20:423-424.

Rose, L. (1995). *NetLaw: Your Rights in the Online Community.* Berkeley, CA: Osborne, McGraw-Hill.

Rothfeder, Jeffrey. (1992). *Privacy for Sale.* New York: Simon & Schuster.

Van Horn, Royal. (1998). "Personal Privacy." *Phi Delta Kappan* September: 92-93.

LISA E. GUELDENZOPH

PRIVATE OWNERSHIP

(SEE: *Entrepreneurship*)

PRODUCTION MANAGEMENT

(SEE: *Operations Management*)

PRODUCTIVITY

Productivity is the result or the sum of all effort that it takes to deliver a product or service. Productivity is frequently referred to as output and, to some degree, can be measured. The output generated by a person, organization, or other entity is measured in terms of (the number of) units or items produced and services performed within a specified time frame. Thus, productivity is the economic value of goods and services. It becomes the value or result of the "price" of a product or service minus all "costs" (supplies, materials, human labor, etc., which frequently are monetary) that go into the effort.

PRODUCTIVITY PERFORMANCE MEASURES

Productivity is a performance measure that indicates how effectively an organization converts its resources into its desired products or services. It is a relative measure in that it is used to compare the effectiveness of a country, organization, department, workstation, or individual to itself over time for the same operation, or to other countries, organizations, departments, workstations, or individuals. From a systems perspective, productivity indicates how well an organization transforms its inputs into outputs. In manufacturing, productivity is generally stated as a ratio of output to input. Productivity may be expressed as partial measures, multifactor measures, and total measures. Partial productivity measures are used to analyze activities in terms of a single input (e.g., units produced per worker, units produced per plant, units produced per hour, or units produced per quantity of material). Multifactor productivity measures take into account the utilization of multiple inputs (e.g., units of output per the sum of labor, capital, and energy or units of output per the sum of labor and materials). A total measure of productivity expresses the ratio of all outputs produced to all resources used.

SYSTEM AND SUBSYSTEM PRODUCTIVITY

An important point in seeking productivity improvements in a subsystem of an organization is to link the subsystem improvements to the total system productivity. Optimization of a subsystem operation that does not affect the overall productivity of the organization is a waste of resources. For example, a manufacturer might improve the productivity of its machining operations, as measured by number of units produced per dollar. But if these units cannot be sold and are warehoused, the productivity of the organization has not increased, since the goal of the manufacturer is to generate revenue through the sale of its products. Activities intended to improve productivity must be carefully selected, and the appropriate measures must be developed to ensure that the organization's efforts result in the improvement of its overall productivity.

Numerous specific components are involved in contributing to and measuring productivity. The most important of these are discussed below.

Return on Investment Productivity is closely related to, but not dependent on, profit. It can be measured by return on investment (ROI). ROI is determined after the sale of a product or service minus the deductions for the total amount of effort (resources, etc.) put into its design, development, implementation, evaluation, and marketing. The formula for determining ROI is: "Price" minus "Cost" divided by "Sales."

Productivity Measures for Individuals and Teams An individual's productivity is measured by that person's potential to reach the highest level of productivity possible. That is, a person has certain skills that determine his or her level of capability (an engineer's skills, banker's knowledge, etc.). An individual's experiences and education usually determine his or her skill level regarding a particular job. Other factors, such as a positive environment (working with a good team, having a good boss, liking the physical surroundings in the workplace, being appreciated, etc.) and how motivated one is to do a job, also contribute to productivity. When several individuals come together to work as a team, the team's productivity or the effectiveness of the team is the sum of individual efforts toward achieving a desired goal. Several factors (motivation, expertise, working conditions, team compatibility, potential, etc.) influence the level of productivity achieved.

Productivity Gap A productivity gap (*or capacity gap*) is the difference between what a person can do and what that person actually does. That is, every person has the ability to achieve at a certain level. If a person is not motivated and is not working up to potential, that person's productivity gap is usually quite large. The same principle applies to a work team, organization, and so on. It is desirable to estimate potential (of a person, work unit, company, etc.) to determine where productivity gaps exist (and how large they are) and find ways to close them. By looking at a person's ability in conjunction with other motivational factors, it is possible to estimate a person's (or a group's) potential to achieve desired results. When all factors operate at optimum, the productivity is said to be at its highest level—the productivity gap has been filled or is minimized.

Motivation Productivity is directly related to how motivated a person is to perform a task or activity. Many businesses devote much time and effort to finding ways to motivate employees. Worker enhancement programs (for an individual, team, company, etc.) that are built on ways

to motivate workers (toward self-motivation and long-term motivation) can optimize productivity. Organizations that are most successful in motivating workers provide a variety of programs (formal and informal avenues within and outside the organization) to meet the needs of their employees. Some organizations offer employees sports and recreational activities, fitness and leisure activities, and family-oriented programs (*work-/job-augmented incentives*). Incentive programs may be totally separate from or incorporated into work-team meetings, seminars, and education/training programs. Such a comprehensive approach toward enhancing worker performance may capitalize on quality measures (such as value, total quality management [TQM], quality circles, innovation, etc.) and performance standards (such as profitability, efficiency, customer satisfaction, on-time delivery, etc.) and include a wide range of personal and team rewards and incentives.

Mutual Reward Theory Mutual reward theory (MRT) is based on finding ways for all to benefit. That is, if an organization can assist an employee in reaching some of his or her goals while still meeting the company's production goals, a mutual reward has occurred. When the benefits are at an optimum for all persons involved, the greatest rewards are realized. Productivity is usually directly proportional to the degree of MRT success.

Productivity Benchmarks Factors that enter into productivity benchmarking for an organization include overall operations, worker training, technology, continuous quality improvement, and management philosophy and strategy. Management strategy includes how and at what level decision making takes place—usually greater productivity gains are realized when decision making is pushed to its lowest level possible and is still effective. Also, an organization's efficiency may depend just as much on borrowing and lending strategies (e.g., requiring immediate payment on goods sold while practicing delayed payments to creditors) to maximize resource availability as it does on efficient operations and a safe environment. Thus, there are many important factors included in maximizing ROI—most factors depend on making the right decisions at the right time. What is a good decision for one company may be bad or devastating for another.

Productivity Growth and Economics Productivity growth is defined as a measure of the amount of goods and services that are produced during a specified period of time. Once a standard has been determined, the standard (benchmark or identified level of production) becomes the measure against which all future production can be compared. Since 1950, the U.S. ten-year annual growth rates have been as follows: 1950s: 2.17 percent; 1960s: 2.85 percent; 1970s: 1.71 percent; 1980s, 2.17 percent; 1990s: (estimate) 1.31 percent. The annual growth rate is of particular interest to individuals, since the productivity growth rate is directly proportional to a person's wealth. That is, as productivity levels go up, so does an individual's buying power. In turn, the total economy benefits from the boost.

Productivity Value Added While productivity is more easily measured in manufacturing (products produced) than in services, most productivity researchers agree that people are the world's most valuable resources. Many productivity researchers suggest that education and training are the basic foundation for raising productivity levels. The acquisition of expertise through education and training, coupled with the best equipment and resources within an efficient and safe environment, can be maximized by developing employees into people who want to learn, who want to work at their potential, and who want to continuously improve. These factors are best achieved when an employee is motivated to take pride in the work he or she does. A motivated, self-starting employee is one who adds value to an organization and contributes to the overall productivity of him- or herself, a work group, an organization, and the economy.

BIBLIOGRAPHY

Goodstein, Leonard, Nolan, Timothy, and Pfeiffer, J. William. (1993). *Applied Strategic Planning: How to Develop a Plan That Really Works.* New York: McGraw-Hill.

Hammer, Michael. (1996). *Beyond Reengineering.* New York: HarperBusiness.

Jonash, Ronald S., and Sommerlatte, Tom. (1999). *The Innovation Premium.* Reading, MA: Arthur D. Little.

Langdon, Danny. (2000). *Aligning Performance: Improving People, Systems, and Organizations.* San Francisco: Jossey-Bass/Pfeiffer.

Lewis, James P. (2000). *The Project Manager's Desk Reference.* New York: McGraw-Hill.

Meyer, Marc H., and Lehnerd, Alvin P. (1997). *The Power of Product Platforms: Building Value and Cost Leadership.* New York: Free Press.

Recardo, Ronald J., Wade, David, Mention, Charles A., III, and Jolly, Jennifer A. (1996). *Teams: Who Needs Them and Why?* Houston, TX: Gulf Publishing.

Reinertsen, Donald G. (1997). *Managing the Design Factory: A Product Developer's Toolkit.* New York: Free Press.

Shim, Jae K., and Siegel, Joel G. (1996). *Operations Management.* Hauppage, NY: Barron's Educational Series.

Smith, Elizabeth A. (1995). *The Productivity Manual,* 2d ed. Houston, TX: Gulf Publishing.

Tesoro, Ferdinand, and Tootson, Jack. (2000). *Implementing Global Performance Measurement Systems: A Cookbook Approach.* San Francisco: Jossey-Bass/Pfeiffer.

SHARON LUND O'NEIL
JOHN W. HANSEN

PRODUCT LABELING

An important aspect of marketing and selling a company's product is the product label. The product label is very important not only for selling a product but also for communicating to the consumer information, company image, values, and the perceived value of the product. Therefore, when a company designs a label it must take all of these factors into consideration. In addition to the marketing aspect, certain legal requirements must be met in order for the label to be compliant with federal regulations.

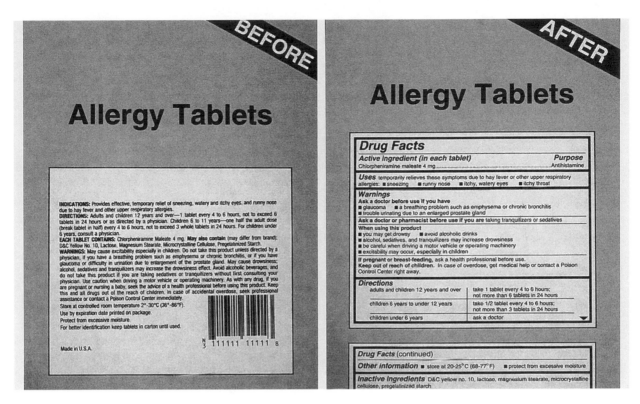

Product labels have changed to meet federal regulations.

SPECIFIC LABEL INFORMATION

Although some products can be identified adequately by brand name alone, many require more complete identification of their nature and use. In short, the purpose of the label is to provide useful and relevant information about the product, as well as to help to market the product. Processed foods, patented drugs, textiles, and numerous other products are required by law to carry a fairly complete list of their ingredients. This specific information is extremely important so that consumers—for example, those who are allergic to certain ingredients—do not use a product that may harm them.

Companies may also provide additional information on their labels that is not legally required. One reason to do so is that consumer groups often publicly protest about the lack of information on labels and request more. A company might decide that it is less expensive to make minor adjustments to its product label than to undergo continued public scrutiny. Furthermore, when a competitor starts including more information or redesigns its label to make it more user-friendly a company might decide to modify its own label to prevent losing sales.

Labels today also include unit pricing, open dating, and nutritional labeling. *Unit pricing* shows the price per unit of standard measure (weight or volume), allowing consumers to compare values among competing products—for example, comparing an expensive brand-name product to a less expensive generic product with similar ingredients. Unit pricing is most often found on the store shelf rather than on the product package. *Open dating* informs consumers about the expected life of the product so they can avoid products that may be spoiled. This information is especially important for such perishable items as milk, eggs, and other products with a short shelf life. *Nutritional labeling* specifies the amount of calories, total fat, cholesterol, dietary fiber, sodium, minerals, vitamins, and protein in processed foods. The label also discloses the percentage daily values per serving for each item based on a 2000-calorie-per-day diet. This information can be useful for consumers who have either special dietary needs or are trying to maintain a healthy balanced daily diet.

Product labels also provide other useful information for consumers. One of the most common features on any label is directions on how the product should be used, or if food, prepared. An example would be directions on clothing indicating how to clean and store the items. Another example would be directions on either prescription or over-the-counter medications that provide information on how many pills should be taken and warn of possible drug interactions. Moreover, most products that could be toxic if ingested have a warning about this on the package as well as instructions on what to do in case of an emergency. This type of label has two main purposes. The first is to help the consumer in case the product is improperly used. The second is to help prevent lawsuits by consumers who misuse products. Generally speaking, more disclosure about the potential hazards of a product provides the company greater legal protection. Nevertheless, no product warning, even a detailed one, can completely prevent all lawsuits.

Most companies also use one or more of three other labels on their products. The first type, known as a *grade label*, identifies the quality of the product by a letter, such as "grade A," or with a word, such as "prime." The second type, an *informative label*, uses phrases such as "Keep refrigerated after opening" to help consumers use the product appropriately. The third type, a *descriptive label*, describes the benefits or positive attributes of the product.

LEGAL ISSUES

The federal government sets forth legal requirements which form a key element of product label design. Federal regulations regarding products and food have become progressively more numerous since the 1960s, due in large part to consumer activism and media attention. The most important of these regulations and laws are discussed here.

At the turn of the twentieth century, responding to consumer pressure, the federal government created two government regulatory bodies: the Food and Drug Administration (FDA), which regulates interstate commerce in foods and drugs, and the Federal Trade Commission (FTC), whose role is to combat deceptive and unfair trade practices. Both agencies have broad powers to interpret and enforce laws and regulations. In addition, each agency has the power to investigate alleged violations of law and to impose significant fines on companies found to be violating the law. The mere publicity that a company is being investigated by either the FDA or FTC for alleged infractions of the law could hurt sales and, in turn, company profits. Therefore, most companies make a strong effort to comply with federal laws that regulate product labels and advertising.

A list of the laws designed to protect consumers follows:

- *Robinson-Patman Act*: This Act prohibits price discrimination.

- *Wheeler-Lea Amendment to the Federal Trade Commission Act*: This amendment controls deceptive and misleading advertising.

- *Federal Hazardous Substance Labeling Act (1960)*: This act requires warnings on the labels of all household-use products that contain potentially hazardous ingredients.

- *Child Protection Act (1966)*: This act strengthens the Federal Hazardous Substance Labeling Act by prohibiting the sale of dangerous toys and other articles that are used by children, especially those items containing electrical, mechanical, or thermal hazards.

- *Fair Packing and Labeling Act (1966)*: The primary purpose of this act is to outlaw deceptive packaging of certain consumer goods. The other intent is to adequately inform consumers of the quantity and composition of product contents and to promote packaging practices that facilitate price comparisons by consumers. In order to comply with the law, companies must include the following information on the label: name of commodity and manufacturer, net quantity of contents expressed in the appropriate category (ounces/grams, pints, liters), and relevant ingredient information.

- *National Traffic and Motor Vehicle Safety Act (1966)*: This act authorizes the federal government to establish and enforce safety standards for all new and used automobiles and tires.

- *Cigarette Labeling Act (1965)*: This act requires that all cigarette packages and ads contain the statement: "Warning: The Surgeon General has determined that cigarette smoking is dangerous to your health."

- *Consumer Product Safety Act (1972)*: This act established the Consumer Product Safety Commission and gave it broad powers to carry out product tests, set safety standards, ban or seize hazardous products, and issue both civil and criminal complaints against business firms that fail to meet product safety requirements.

- *Federal Trade Commission Improvement Act (1975)*: This act expanded the authority of the FTC in various ways; in particular, it gave the FTC the power to set rules concerning warranties on consumer products and empowered it to provide consumers with redress in the form of class-action lawsuits.

- *Nutrition Labeling and Education Act (1990)*: The purpose of this act is to clarify and strengthen the FDA's legal authority to require nutrition labeling on foods and to establish the circumstances under which claims may be made about the nutrients in foods. The act covers only nutrients or substances in food that "nourish"; it does not in any way regulate non-nutrient substances in foods. Moreover, the act requires that labels disclose the amount of specified nutrients in foods. Every covered food would have a uniform nutrition label disclosing the amount of calories, fat, salt, and other nutrients. In order to make this information meaningful, the act requires the FDA to issue standards providing that uniform servings be noted on the food label. Where the full labeling is impractical, the act provides for an exemption or requires that the information be provided in a modified form. An example of who would qualify for this exemption is a restaurant. It would be extremely difficult and expensive for a restaurant to comply with the act; therefore, restaurants are excluded.

BIBLIOGRAPHY

Assel, Henry. (1985). *Marketing Management Strategy and Action*. Boston: Kent Publishing Company.

Bernhardt, Kenneth L., and Kinnear, Thomas C. (1983). *Principles of Marketing*. Scott, Foresman.

Dickson, Peter R. (1994). *Marketing Management*. Harcourt Brace College.

Kotler, Philip. (1980). *Principles of Marketing*. Prentice-Hall.

Myers, James H. (1986). *Marketing*. McGraw-Hill.

Schewe, Charles D., and Smith, Reuben M. (1983). *Marketing Concepts and Applications*. McGraw-Hill.

MICHAEL J. MILBIER

PRODUCT LINES

The product mix of a company is the total composite of products offered by that organization. A product line is a group of products within the product mix that are closely related, either because they function in a similar manner, are sold to the same customer groups, are marketed through the same types of outlets, or fall within given price ranges.

Product-line decisions are concerned with the combination of individual products offered in a given line. The responsibility for a given product line resides with a product-line manager (sometimes called a product-group manager), who supervises several product managers who, in turn, are responsible for individual products within the line. A product is a distinct unit within the product line that is distinguishable by size, price, appearance, or some other attribute. Decisions about a product line are usually incorporated into a divisional-level marketing plan, which specifies changes in the product lines and allocations to products in each line. Product-line managers normally have the following responsibilities: (1) Consider expansion of a given product line; (2) consider products for deletion from the product line; (3) evaluate the effects of product additions and deletions on the profitability of other items in the line; and (4) allocate resources

Tim Allen's line of tools.

to individual products in the line on the basis of marketing strategies recommended by product managers.

One strategy organizations can employ to help sell their products is to use brand-identification strategies. Brand identification is generally defined as creating a brand with positive consumer benefits, resulting in consumer loyalty and repeat purchasing. Other benefits of brand identification include (1) strong in-store recognition, (2) stronger competition against competitors' products, (3) better distribution, and (4) better in-store shelf position. Organizations have four basic types of branding available: individual brand names, family brand names, product-line brand names, and corporate brand names.

Individual brand names can be used to establish brand identification without reference to an integrated product line or to the corporate name. Each brand is sold individually and stands or falls on its own. *Family brand names* involve the opposite strategy—including the firms' total product mix under one family name. The corporate name, rather than the brand name, is emphasized in order to leverage the high-quality name of the organization. This can reduce advertising and marketing costs. *Product-line brand names* involve a strategy midway between an individual brand name and a family brand name strategy. All brands within the product line have a common name. Product-line brand names are used when a company produces diverse product lines that require separate identification. Some companies employ the *corporate brand name* strategy. This strategy associates a strong corporate entity with a brand while maintaining the brand's individuality. If successful, it provides the advantages of both a family brand name and an individual brand name strategy.

An important concept for any product-line manager is the product life cycle, which is defined as the various stages a product goes through (introduction, growth, maturity, and decline). The primary function of the *introduction stage* is to create a solid brand name for the new product. Television, Internet, radio, and print advertisements are coordinated to provide the maximum brand awareness. In the *growth stage*, the company focuses on creating loyalty to the specific product and also attempts to make minor improvements. Advertising emphasizes the benefits of the product, since the name is already known. When the *maturity stage* begins, sales start to level off because of increased competition, changes in consumer behavior, or technological advances that make the product less desirable than that of its competitors. In this stage, a company may decide to put limited resources into an advertising campaign to boost sales or create a new image. In addition, minor adjustments might be made to packaging (e.g., a new label) to reattract consumers. The *decline stage* occurs when sales begin to decline. The company needs to choose between modifying the product to increase sales or discontinuing the product when it finally cannot generate acceptable profits.

The product life cycle is an extremely important element when a company reviews its product line. One of the best ways to extend the life of a product and product line is for a company to use a revitalization strategy. When this tactic is used, the company changes the marketing plan and looks for new markets for the existing product line and the products within it. Here too it is critical that the company is successful in repositioning the product to new market segments. Another method used to extend the life cycle of a product line is a line-modernization strategy, which focuses on either upgrading the entire product line or modernizing specifics products within the line in order to spark new consumer interest in the product or entire product line.

Other general product-line strategies include product-line additions, product-line deletions, and holding strategy. *Product-line additions* involve adding new products to a product line so new market segments can be covered. *Product-line deletions* involve removing a product that has not performed well or is not making enough money. A *holding strategy* involves maintaining the status quo. The product line stays the same and no major modifications or marketing strategy changes are planned. In order to have a profitable product line, the product line manager will need to employ a variety of the strategies.

BIBLIOGRAPHY

Assel, Henry. (1985). *Marketing Management Strategy and Action.* Boston: Kent Publishing Company.

Bernhardt, Kenneth L., and Kinnear, Thomas C. (1983). *Principles of Marketing.* Scott, Foresman.

Dickson, Peter R. (1994). *Marketing Management.* Harcourt Brace.

Kotler, Philip. (1980). *Principles of Marketing.* NJ: Prentice-Hall.

Myers, James H. (1986). *Marketing.* McGraw-Hill.

Schewe, Charles D., and Smith, Reuben M. (1983). *Marketing Concepts and Applications.* McGraw-Hill.

MICHAEL J. MILBIER

PRODUCT MIX

The product mix of a company, which is generally defined as the total composite of products offered by a particular organization, consists of both product lines and individual products. A product line is a group of products within the product mix that are closely related, either because they function in a similar manner, are sold to the same customer groups, are marketed through the same types of outlets, or fall within given price ranges. A product is a distinct unit within the product line that is distinguishable by size, price, appearance, or some other attribute. For example, all the courses a university offers constitute its product mix; courses in the marketing department constitute a product line; and the basic marketing course is a product item. Product decisions at these three levels are generally of two types: those that involve width (variety) and depth (assortment) of the product line and those that involve changes in the product mix occur over time.

The depth (assortment) of the product mix refers to the number of product items offered

Hypothetical State University Product Mix

WIDE WIDTH, AVERAGE DEPTH

Political Science	Education	Mathematics
Political Theory	Elementary Teaching	Calculus I
American Government	Secondary Teaching	Calculus II
International Relations	Teaching Internship	Trigonometry
State Government	Post Secondary Teaching	Math Theory
Nursing	**Engineering**	**English**
Biology	Physics	English Literature
Chemistry	Advanced Math	European Writers
Organic Chemistry	Electrical Concepts	Hemingway Seminar
Statistics	Logic Design	Creative Writing

Table 1

Hypothetical Small College Product Mix

NARROW WIDTH, LARGE DEPTH

Mathematics	Physics
Geometric Concepts	Intermediate Physics
Analytic Geometry and Calculus	Advanced Physics
Calculus II	Topics on Physics and Astronomy
Calculus III	Thermodynamics
Numerical Analysis	Condensed Matter Physics II
Differential Equations	Electromagnetic Theory
Matrix Theory	Quantum Mechanics II

Table 2

within each line; the width (variety) refers to the number of product lines a company carries. For example, Table 1 illustrates the hypothetical product mix of a major state university.

The product lines are defined in terms of academic departments. The depth of each line is shown by the number of different product items—course offerings—offered within each product line. (The examples represent only a partial listing of what a real university would offer.) The state university has made the strategic decision to offer a diverse market mix. Because the university has numerous academic departments, it can appeal to a large cross-section of potential students. This university has decided to offer a wide product line (academic departments), but the depth of each department (course offerings) is only average.

In order to see the difference in product mix, product line, and products, consider a smaller college that focuses on the sciences represented in Table 2. This college has decided to concentrate its resources in a few departments (again, this is only a partial listing); that is, it has chosen a concentrated market strategy (focus on limited markets). This college offers narrow product line (academic departments) with a large product depth (extensive course offerings within each department). This product mix would most likely appeal to a much narrower group of potential students—those students who are interested in pursuing intensive studies in math and science.

PRODUCT-MIX MANAGEMENT AND RESPONSIBILITIES

It is extremely important for any organization to have a well-managed product mix. Most organizations break down managing the product mix, product line, and actual product into three different levels.

Product-mix decisions are concerned with the combination of product lines offered by the company. Management of the companies' product mix is the responsibility of top management. Some basic product-mix decisions include: (1) reviewing the mix of existing product lines; (2) adding new lines to and deleting existing lines from the product mix; (3) determining the relative emphasis on new versus existing product lines in the mix; (4) determining the appropriate emphasis on internal development versus external acquisition in the product mix; (5) gauging the effects of adding or deleting a product line in relationship to other lines in the product mix; and (6) forecasting the effects of future external change on the company's product mix.

Product-line decisions are concerned with the combination of individual products offered within a given line. The product-line manager supervises several product managers who are responsible for individual products in the line. Decisions about a product line are usually incorporated into a marketing plan at the divisional level. Such a plan specifies changes in the product lines and allocations to products in each line. Generally, product-line managers have the following responsibilities: (1) considering expansion of a given product line; (2) considering candidates for deletion from the product line; (3) evaluating the effects of product additions and deletions on the profitability of other items in the line; and (4) allocating resources to individual products in the line on the basis of marketing strategies recommended by product managers.

Decisions at the first level of product management involve the marketing mix for an individual brand/product. These decisions are the responsibility of a brand manager (sometimes called a product manager). Decisions regarding the marketing mix for a brand are represented in the product's marketing plan. The plan for a new brand would specify price level, advertising expenditures for the coming year, coupons, trade discounts, distribution facilities, and a five-year statement of projected sales and earnings. The plan for an existing product would focus on any changes in the marketing strategy. Some of these changes might include the product's target market, advertising and promotional expenditures, product characteristics, price level, and recommended distribution strategy.

GENERAL MANAGEMENT WORKFLOW

Top management formulates corporate objectives that become the basis for planning the product line. Product-line managers formulate objectives for their line to guide brand managers in developing the marketing mix for individual

brands. Brand strategies are then formulated and incorporated into the product-line plan, which is in turn incorporated into the corporate plan. The corporate plan details changes in the firm's product lines and specifies strategies for growth. Once plans have been formulated, financial allocations flow from top management to product line and then to brand management for implementation. Implementation of the plan requires tracking performance and providing data from brand to product line to top management for evaluation and control. Evaluation of the current plan then becomes the first step in the next planning cycle, since it provides a basis for examining the company's current offerings and recommending modifications as a result of past performance.

PRODUCT-MIX ANALYSIS

Since top management is ultimately responsible for the product mix and the resulting profits or losses, they often analyze the company product mix. The first assessment involves the area of opportunity in a particular industry or market. Opportunity is generally defined in terms of current industry growth or potential attractiveness as an investment. The second criterion is the company's ability to exploit opportunity, which is based on its current or potential position in the industry. The company's position can be measured in terms of market share if it is currently in the market, or in terms of its resources if it is considering entering the market. These two factors—opportunity and the company's ability to exploit it—provide four different options for a company to follow.

1. High opportunity and ability to exploit it result in the firm's introducing new products or expanding markets for existing products to ensure future growth.

2. Low opportunity but a strong current market position will generally result in the company's attempting to maintain its position to ensure current profitability.

3. High opportunity but a lack of ability to exploit it results in either (a) attempting to acquire the necessary resources or (b)

deciding not to further pursue opportunity in these markets.

4. Low opportunity and a weak market position will result in either (a) avoiding these markets or (b) divesting existing products in them.

These options provide a basis for the firm to evaluate new and existing products in an attempt to achieve balance between current and future growth. This analysis may cause the product mix to change, depending on what management decides.

The most widely used approach to product portfolio analysis is the model developed by the Boston Consulting Group (BCG). The BCG analysis emphasizes two main criteria in evaluating the firm's product mix: the market growth rate and the product's relative market share. BCG uses these two criteria because they are closely related to profitability, which is why top management often uses the BCG analysis. Proper analysis and conclusions may lead to significant changes to the company's product mix, product line, and product offerings.

The market growth rate represents the products' category position in the product life cycle. Products in the introductory and growth phases require more investment because of research and development and initial marketing costs for advertising, selling, and distribution. This category is also regarded as a high-growth area (e.g., the Internet). Relative market share represents the company's competitive strength (or estimated strength for a new entry). Market share is compared to that of the leading competitor. Once the analysis has been done using the market growth rate and relative market share, products are placed into one of four categories.

- *Stars*: Products with high growth and market share are know as stars. Because these products have high potential for profitability, they should be given top priority in financing, advertising, product positioning, and distribution. As a result, they need significant amounts of cash to finance rapid growth and frequently show an initial negative cash flow.

- *Cash cows*: Products with a high relative market share but in a low growth position are cash cows. These are profitable products that generate more cash than is required to produce and market them. Excess cash should be used to finance high-opportunity areas (stars or problem children). Strategies for cash cows should be designed to sustain current market share rather than to expand it. An expansion strategy would require additional investment, thus decreasing the existing positive cash flow.

- *Problem children*: These products have low relative market share but are in a high-growth situation. They are called "problem children" because their eventual direction is not yet clear. The firm should invest heavily in those that sales forecasts indicate might have a reasonable chance to become stars. Otherwise divestment is the best course, since problem children may become dogs and thereby candidates for deletion.

- *Dogs*: Products in the category are clearly candidates for deletion. Such products have low market shares and unlike problem children, have no real prospect for growth. Eliminating a dog is not always necessary, since there are strategies for dogs that could make them profitable in the short term. These strategies involve "harvesting" these products by eliminating marketing support and selling the product only to intensely loyal consumers who will buy in the absence of advertising. However, over the long term companies will seek to eliminate dogs.

As can be seen from the description of the four BCG alternatives, products are evaluated as producers or users of cash. Products with a positive cash flow will finance high-opportunity products that need cash. The emphasis on cash flow stems from management's belief that it is better to finance new entries and to support existing products with internally produced funds than to increase debt or equity in the company.

Based on this belief, companies will normally take money from cash cows and divert it to stars and to some problem children. The hope is that the stars will turn into cash cows and the problem children will turn into stars. The dogs will continue to receive lower funding and eventually be dropped.

CONCLUSION

Managing the product mix for a company is very demanding and requires constant attention. Top management must provide accurate and timely analysis (BCG) of their company's product mix so the appropriate adjustments can be made to the product line and individual products.

BIBLIOGRAPHY

Assel, Henry. (1985). *Marketing Management Strategy and Action.* Boston: Kent Publishing Company.

Bernhardt, Kenneth L., and Kinnear, Thomas C. (1983). *Principles of Marketing.* Scott, Foresman and Company.

Dickson, Peter R. (1994). *Marketing Management.* Harcourt Brace College Publishers.

Kotler, Philip (1980). *Principles of Marketing.* NJ: Prentice-Hall.

Myers, James H. (1986). *Marketing.* McGraw-Hill.

Schewe, Charles D., and Smith, Reuben M. (1983). *Marketing Concepts and Applications.* McGraw-Hill.

MICHAEL J. MILBIER

PROFESSIONAL EDUCATION

Professional education is a formalized approach to specialized training in a professional school through which participants acquire content knowledge and learn to apply techniques. Although content is what the participant is expected to learn by attending professional school, such an education also helps the participant acquire the competencies needed for proper practice and behavior. Some common goals of professional education include incorporating the knowledge and values basic to a professional discipline; understanding the central concepts, principles, and techniques applied in practice; attaining a level of competence necessary for responsible entry into professional practice; and accepting responsibility for the continued development of competence. It is designed to produce responsible professionals and then to ensure their continuing competence in the profession by

helping them recognize and understand the significance of advancing professional knowledge and improving standards of practice. It involves the translation of learning to practice and is intended to prevent occupations and professionals from becoming obsolete.

ROLE OF PROFESSIONAL EDUCATION

The essence of professionalism is the delivery of a service in response to a social need. Professional education is a response to society's demands for expert help provided by competent people. The growth and development of a profession is a function of specific needs, and the role of the professional changes because of changes in society. Professional education both responds to changing demands and provides impetus to changing the field itself, balancing a forward look with the realities of the present. Professional education is thus both reactive and initiatating. Most problem solving on the job is reactive because decisions need to be made and little time is available for research or consultation with peers.

Special knowledge and skills were once passed on from one professional to others through apprenticeships, were experiential, and came from nonacademic sources. This method became inadequate for preparing competent professionals. Schools were established with the purpose of supplying financial resources and human resources beneficial to society and training the next generation of people. The curriculum attempts to develop discipline and self-awareness in the professional. These schools are charged with planning and delivering a full range of educational services that allow knowledge-based learning through the integration of instruction, research, and technology.

ONGOING AND LIFELONG LEARNING

Professional education determines the quality of services provided. As changes in both practice and theory occur, knowledge increases and beginning levels of competence become insufficient for effective practice. It is not enough merely to collaborate or work closely with peers to find ways to develop new practices and new talents.

One way to improve practices and talents is through formal learning opportunities that allow reflection about what is learned with peers. No profession can effectively deal with the pressing changes of standards and ethics surrounding practice without discussing changes and modifying tasks. Pursuing additional education to satisfy the need for additional information is called lifelong learning.

Lifelong learning is a continuous, seamless effort of training for professionals. Learning occurs through efforts on the part of workers in conjunction with professional schools. It builds on one's current knowledge and understanding and is tailored to reflect interests and goals. Continuing development results in strengthening practices and the development of professionals who assume responsibility for maintaining high standards. Many professionals are self-motivated to learn new competencies required on the job because it enables them to acquire higher degrees of skill and commitment. Training and development creates confident, expert professionals who are motivated to learn and committed to fostering personal growth.

THE INTEGRATION OF TECHNOLOGY EDUCATION

Society has witnessed an explosion in knowledge and technological ability. Changes in job responsibilities and new technologies require specialization in both the profession and the technology. The Internet has changed the nature of professional education by offering an alternative to traditional classroom instruction that delivers the same services as a regular classroom environment.

The Internet is an asset to professional development because of the diversity of resources and ideas it has to offer. In addition, it is readily accessible to most people and user-friendly. The Internet offers a variety of Web-based instructional options, including e-mail, listservs, mailing lists, newsgroups, Web pages, and course management systems.

E-mail is a simple, easy-to-use communication tool used for delivering letters and memos. It usually involves only text and is a fast way to facilitate class interaction and discussion. It allows information such as assignments and announcements to be sent back and forth between instructor and student. Listservs, mailing lists, and newsgroups are simple, convenient, and flexible to use. A listserv is a special-interest discussion group that distributes messages to many users on a mailing list. Users post messages and the listserv software sends the messages to the members. Mailing lists are discussions that allow users to send messages to groups of people as easily as to a single person. Newsgroups are discussion groups organized by topic. Messages are not sent to an e-mail account but are posted to a central location on a network. When users are ready, they select the topics they are interested in and the messages they want to read. Web pages are also an effective tool for exchanging ideas on the Internet. They allow participants to progress through instructional materials to achieve learning outcomes and to participate in electronic discussions during times that are convenient for them, at their own pace, at any time, and from any location. Course management systems are commercially developed software that are designed for classroom management, instructional management, and performance assessment. They allow on-line access, either directly or through Web page links, to course content. These systems monitor participant progress by managing files of participants as they navigate through course content.

Professional development courses on the Internet offer new challenges and new opportunities for professional education. The Internet addresses most professional development needs today. Other innovative opportunities continue to develop that will offer more services to help with research and keep us informed about topics of special interest. By making use of this technology, instruction is extended beyond the physical limitations of traditional classrooms. Internet technology offers an unlimited database of new knowledge that is available at little or no cost. Attention is directed to professional development at all levels. This new vision of professional development requires a new vision of preparation that includes the ability to relate technology to particular professions and to related fields. It is essential that programs access and integrate technology to facilitate participant learning. This type of cooperation continues to build a new educational system that is based on the traditional concept of lifelong learning.

SUMMARY

Professional education educates the new generation of professionals, expanding the frontiers of knowledge and reaching out in service to society. Professional education is increasingly being called upon to play a significant role in the administration of new programs within continuing and new structures. The rapidly changing society in which professionals exist demands that they attempt to maximize work performance. There is no single model that serves as a prototype program. There are many programs that serve the diverse needs of today's professional who are assuming different roles and greater responsibilities. Professional education is a lifelong process and continues to improve, tailoring programs to help shape competent workers for the twenty-first century.

BIBLIOGRAPHY

Abdal-Haqq, Ismat. (1998). *Professional Development Schools: Weighing the Evidence.* Thousand Oaks, CA: Corwin Press.

Evers, Frederick T., and Rush, James Cameron. (1998). *The Bases of Competence: Skills for Lifelong Learning and Employability.* San Francisco: Jossey-Bass.

Guskey, Thomas R., and Huberman, A. M. (1995). *Professional Development in Education: New Paradigms and Practices.* New York: Teachers College Press.

Haworth, Jennifer Grant. (1996). *Assessing Graduate and Professional Education: Current Realities, Future Prospects.* San Francisco: Jossey-Bass.

Maehl, William H. (2000). *Lifelong Learning at Its Best: Innovative Practices in Adult Credit Programs.* San Francisco: Jossey-Bass.

CONNIE ANDERSON

PROFIT SHARING

(SEE: *Employee Compensation*)

PROGRAMMING

Within the context of information systems, the term *programming* is understood to mean computer programming, which is the process of writing computer programs. A computer program is a detailed, step-by-step set of instructions that is executed by a computer in order to perform a specific task or solve a specific problem. A computer can perform a wide variety of tasks, including arithmetic calculations, text formatting, and submission of documents to the printer to be printed. However, the computer *hardware* does not perform these tasks by itself. It needs specific instructions on how to go about performing each specific task. It is these task-specific sets of instructions that are referred to as programs.

PROGRAMMING LANGUAGES

Computer programs are written in a variety of programming languages. These languages fall into two broad categories: low-level programming languages and high-level programming languages. *Low-level programming languages* are so named because they are closer to machine language than to human language; that is, it is easier for the machine (computer) to understand them than it is for humans. *Machine language* is made up of a series of 0's and 1's. Each 0 or 1 is known as a *bit* (short for *bi*nary dig*it*). A group of eight bits, known as a *byte*, represents one character (i.e., a number or a letter). For example, the number 2 is represented as 00000010 and the letter B as 01000010 in the American National Standards Institute (ANSI) code for character representation inside a computer. There are other coding schemes besides the ANSI standard, such as the American Standard Code for Information Interchange (ASCII) and IBM's Extended Binary Coded Decimal Interchange Code (EBCDIC). Each of these standards represents characters in a slightly different way. Such binary representation of characters is the *only* thing that the computer can directly "understand" and execute.

In the early days of computer programming, programmers wrote their programs directly in machine language. The time-consuming and painstaking nature of this process led to the development of *assembly language,* which uses alphabetic mnemonics (rather than binary digits) to write programs. For example, an assembly-language instruction to load the number 5 into a computer's accumulator is: LDA 5. This is more readable than a string of 0's and 1's. A special program called an *assembler* translates assembly-language instructions into machine-language instructions. Assembly language is machine-specific and is used to directly manipulate activity at the hardware level. Therefore, it is still considered low-level.

Further technological advances led to the development of *high-level programming languages* such as COBOL (*CO*mmon *B*usiness *O*riented *L*anguage), FORTRAN (*FOR*mula *TRAN*slator), BASIC (*B*eginners' *A*ll-purpose *S*ymbolic *I*nstruction *C*ode), PASCAL, PL/1, and C. These languages are described high-level because they are closer to human language than to machine language. In these languages, the number 2 and the letter B are coded in the program exactly as they are written. Similarly, the following is a valid line of program code in some high-level languages: SUM = NUM1 + NUM2. A special program, known as a *compiler* or an *interpreter* (depending on the programming language) translates the high-level program code into machine language before it is executed.

CATEGORIES OF PROGRAMMING

There are two main categories of programming, *systems programming* and *applications programming.* Systems programs are more likely to be written in low-level programming languages, while applications programs are written almost exclusively in high-level languages.

Systems Programming Systems programming involves writing programs that enable a computer to carry out its basic internal functions as well as some other specialized functions. Examples of systems programs include operating systems, device drivers, and utility programs.

An *operating system,* which comes as an essential and necessary component of any computer system, is a complex set of programs that coordinates activities inside a computer and ensures the proper and efficient use of all the computer's resources. Among its basic functions are scheduling and running multiple jobs inside the computer, managing storage space, enforcing security (e.g., through password verification), and detecting equipment failure. Through its actions, the operating system enables a user to access the computer's hardware and software components. Examples of operating systems include DOS, Windows 95, Windows 98, Windows NT, Macintosh System 8, UNIX, OS/2, and VAX VMS.

Device drivers are those programs that identify particular devices to a computer and enable the computer to correctly use those devices. For example, a mouse driver program helps a computer identify the mouse attached to it.

Utility programs (or *utilities*) are programs that perform such specialized tasks as reorganizing data on disks, recovering lost data, recovering from system crashes, and detecting and removing computer viruses.

Applications Programming Applications programming refers to the process of developing programs to be used for specific applications, such as a business application (e.g., computing benefits to be paid to different employee classifications) or an academic application (e.g., determining who qualifies for which scholarship, based on specified eligibility criteria). Programming such applications usually requires the programmer to specify the precise logic that would be required to solve the given problem. There are a number of stages in the applications programming process, including problem statement, algorithm development, program coding, program testing, and program documentation.

Problem statement: The programming process begins with a clear, written statement of the problem to be solved by the computer. The im-

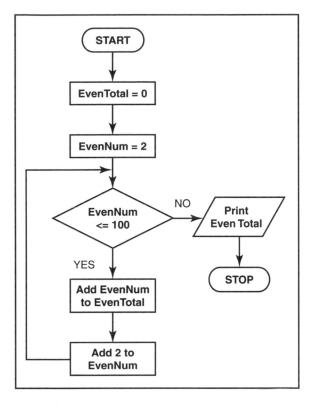

Figure 1
Flowchart to compute the sum of all even numbers from 2 to 100.

portance of this step cannot be overemphasized. A poorly articulated or poorly understood problem statement will result in the wrong solution being developed for the problem at hand. There should also be a statement of the conditions that would determine when the problem has been solved. All known and relevant facts should also be stated at this stage, as well as any necessary assumptions to be made in the program.

Algorithm development: Once the problem has been clearly stated and all the requirements have been understood, the next step is to develop the program logic necessary for accomplishing the task. An algorithm is defined as a logical sequence of steps that must be performed in order to accomplish a given task. There are some tools available to help the programmer develop the algorithm for a given problem. The two best-known and most widely used ones are the *flowchart* and *pseudocode*. Both of these are lan-

guage-independent, focusing primarily on logic flow rather than the syntax of any particular language. A flowchart uses standard flowcharting symbols to visually represent the flow of program logic. Pseudocode, on the other hand, often looks like actual program code, but it is not, since it does not follow any particular language's syntax. The term pseudocode means "false code." Unlike flowcharting, in which standard, universally accepted symbols are used, there are no set standards for writing pseudocode. Figures 1 and 2 illustrate the use of a flowchart and pseudocode, respectively, to depict the logic needed to add up all the even numbers between 2 and 100, inclusive, and print the resulting total.

Program coding: When the programmer is satisfied with the efficacy of the logic developed in the preceding step, it is time to convert that logic (in either flowchart or pseudocode form) to the specific syntax of the programming language that will be used. At this stage, the programmer adheres strictly to all of the syntax requirements for coding the logic as well as other aspects of the program.

Program testing: The coded program is next checked for errors. At least two types of programming errors must be checked for, namely, *syntax errors* and *logic errors*. The presence of *syntax errors* indicates that some syntactic rule(s) of the programming language has (have) been violated. Syntax errors are detected when the program is compiled (the compiler identifies all such errors within the program). They must be corrected before the program can be successfully executed. Even when all the syntax errors have been corrected, there is the possibility of logic errors. *Logic errors* arise when the desired logic is incorrectly specified in the program, thereby resulting in an erroneous output. An example is a program that makes students with failing grades eligible for academic scholarships when, in fact, they should not be. In computer terminology, any error in a program—syntax or logic—is known as a *bug*. The process of correcting these errors is known as *debugging*.

Program documentation: The programming process is complete when the program has been

```
START
  EvenTotal = 0
  EvenNum = 2
  DO WHILE EvenNum <= 100
    Add EvenNum to EvenTotal
    Add 2 to EvenNum
  END DO (loop)
  Print EvenTotal
STOP
```

Figure 2
*Pseudocode to compute the sum
of all even numbers from 2 to
100.*

fully documented. The documentation can be either incorporated into the body of the program itself (*in-line documentation*) or it can be a completely separate document (*external documentation*). Frequently, it is both. Good documentation typically includes the following: a statement of the program's objective(s); descriptions of any input or output records or files needed to run the program; a complete definition of all data names used; and an explanation of the underlying logic, preferably with an accompanying flowchart. Program documentation greatly facilitates *program maintenance*, which is the periodic modification to, or update of, the program in order to keep it current. This is especially important if the person maintaining the program is not the same one who wrote it.

APPLICATIONS PROGRAMS ON THE MARKET

There is a wide array of programs and compilers on the market today, in the form of various software packages. Compilers for all the major programming languages mentioned above are available on virtually all computing platforms. Most of these commercial packages, such as Visual Basic, Visual C++, and Microfocus COBOL, have "visual" front-ends to their programming environments, which makes it easy for programmers to design user-friendly programs for their clients.

BIBLIOGRAPHY

Berlioux, Pierre, and Bizard, Philippe. (1986). *Algorithms: The Construction. Proof, and Analysis of Programs*, trans. Annwyl Williams. New York: Wiley.

Dodd, Kenneth N. (1969). *Computer Programming and Languages*. New York: Plenum.

Flores, Ivan. (1971). *Assemblers and BAL*. Englewood Cliffs, NJ: Prentice-Hall.

Iliffe, J.K. (1972). *Basic Machine Principles*, 2d ed. New York: American Elsevier.

Knuth, Donald E. (1997). *The Art of Computer Programming*, 3d ed. Reading, MA: Addison-Wesley.

McCracken, Daniel, and Golden, Donald. (1990). *Simplified Structured COBOL with Microsoft/Microfocus COBOL*. New York: Wiley.

Parsons, June J., and Oja, Dan. (1998). *Computer Concepts—Comprehensive*, 3d ed. Cambridge, MA: Course Technology.

Washburn, Dale W. (1970). *Computer Programming: A Total Language Approach*. New York: Holt, Reinhart & Winston.

THEOPHILUS B. A. ADDO

PROMOTION

It would be safe to say that most companies engage in some form of promotional activity every day of the year. Promotion is one of the four Ps of marketing—price, product, place, and promotion. Promotion is generally thought of as a sequence of activities designed to inform and convince individuals to purchase a product, subscribe to a belief, or support a cause. All of the various tools available to marketing managers for promotional activities constitute what is known as the promotional mix.

PROMOTIONAL MIX

Marketing managers use different components of the promotional mix as tools for achieving company objectives—advertising, personal selling, public relations, and sales promotion. Each of these elements can be further divided into additional subcomponents or strategies. The majority of a company's promotional resources are usually spent on these four elements for a simple reason: Companies perceive these methods as the most

Sports games are a popular venue for advertising.

effective means to promote their products. Other specialized promotional techniques, however, are also used to enhance promotional objectives.

Advertising Advertising is often thought of as the paid, nonpersonal communication used in the promotion of a cause, idea, product, or service by an identified sponsor. The various advertising delivery methods include banners at sporting events, billboards, Internet Web sites, logos on clothing, magazines, newspapers, radio spots, and television commercials. Among the common forms of advertising are advocacy, comparative, cooperative, informational, institutional, persuasive, product, reminder, point-of-purchase, and specialty.

Personal Selling Personal selling is considered one of the most effective promotional techniques because it facilitates interaction between consumer and seller. With personal selling, a salesperson can listen to and determine a consumer's needs by asking questions and receiving feedback

from the consumer. Furthermore, personal selling activities can generate long-lasting friendships between consumers and sellers that typically generate many repeat purchases. Personal selling can also occur by means of interactive computers, telephone conferences, and interactive videoconferencing. A drawback of personal selling, however, is its high cost. Examples of products promoted through personal selling include automobiles, life insurance, real estate, and many industrial products.

Public Relations Public relations has been described as building goodwill with a company's various publics, including consumers, employees, government officials, stockholders, and suppliers. The overall goal of any public relations effort is to project a positive company image when dealing with such issues as community and government relations, employment practices, and environmental issues.

Consumers. Public relations efforts are extremely important for maintaining a company's consumer base. Consumers must believe that they are buying from a caring, honest, and trustworthy company. Negative media stories about, for example, exploiting workers or producing substandard products can do enormous damage to a company in the eyes of consumers. Erosion of a company's client base is likely to result in both lost sales and lost market share.

Employees. The most valuable asset a company has is its employees. Therefore, it is essential that employees believe in their company. Public relations communications are extremely important in ensuring that employees receive information about the company before outside media receive and report the information. A good example of providing superior public relations would be to inform company employees that a small reduction in the work force is required but that a full severance package will be provided for laid-off employees. Although this news is not positive, the employees are hearing about it first from the company and are also aware that they will be receiving assistance from the company. If employees read or see negative reports about the employer without a credible public relations explanations, they may find other work or reduce their productivity because of low morale.

Government officials. Maintaining a positive public image is also important because government agencies and offices (e.g., Federal Trade Commission, Federal Communication Commission) monitor the media and have regulatory oversight over company activities. Positive stories in the media obviously help promote a positive image to government regulators, which reduces the chance of being investigated and possibly fined. The opposite is also true: Stories about client complaints or other dishonest practices or potentially illegal actions will draw the government's attention and probably some sort of investigation—something that no company wants. An investigation can drag on for months, even years, providing even more negative publicity. Even if the government regulators find no wrongdoing,

the public is still likely to be skeptical because the company was investigated. Therefore, every company must make its best effort to answer any questions that regulators have regarding negative media stories or consumer complaints. A strong, well-organized public relations department will ward off potential trouble by being honest, friendly, positive, and helpful to government regulators and members of the news media.

Stockholders. Another key interest group for any company that offers publicly traded securities are the stockholders. If company stockholders generally receive positive news about a company, they are more likely to maintain investment, which helps keep the stock price up. Negative news that is not countered with positive public relations can create uncertainty about how the company is running and encourage stockholders to sell and to invest in other companies. This action can cause the stock value to decrease, making it difficult to attract new investors.

Suppliers. Positive public relations are essential for a company's relation with its suppliers. Suppliers are most concerned about being paid for the product they are selling to a company. Since most suppliers are generally not paid until ten to twenty days after delivery of their product, they must have faith in the ability of a company to pay its bills. Any negative news regarding a company's financial position in the absence of a full and complete explanation from the public relations department may result in a damaged reputation with suppliers. Suppliers could stop shipping their products or demand that payment is made at the time of delivery. Neither option is appealing to a company, and both could cause critical delays in getting its products to market.

Sales Promotion Sales promotions are marketing practices designed to facilitate the purchase of a product that do not include advertising, personal selling, or public relations. Companies use sales promotion for a variety of reasons; (1) to attract new product users who will hopefully turn into loyal consumers who keep buying the product; (2) to reward existing consumers with a price reduction, thereby maintaining their loyalty; and (3) to encourage repeat sales from occasional consumers.

SPECIAL PROMOTIONAL ACTIVITIES

Companies use a variety of sales promotion tactics to increase sales, including advertising specialties, cash refund offers/rebates, contests and sweepstakes, coupons, patronage rewards, point-of-purchase displays, premiums, price packs/cents-off deals, samples, and trade shows.

Advertising specialties. Companies frequently create and give away everyday items with their names and logos printed on the items such as bottle/can openers, caps, coffee mugs, key rings, and pencils. Companies prefer to use inexpensive handouts that will yield constant free advertising when used by the recipient.

Cash refund offers/rebates. A cash refund or rebate is similar to a coupon except that the price reduction comes after the product is already purchased. In order to receive the cash refund/rebate, the consumer must send in a "proof of purchase" with the company offer in order to obtain the refund. Rebates are often an excellent form of sales promotion for a company to use because a high percentage of consumers will not send in the forms for the refund.

Contests and sweepstakes. Many companies use contests and sweepstakes to increase the sales of a product. As a reward for participating, consumers might win cash, free products, or vacations. With a contest, participants are required to demonstrate a skill; for example, entrants might be asked to suggest a name for a new product, design a company logo, or even suggest a company name change. Contest entries are then reviewed by a panel of judges; the originator of the winning entry receives a prize, usually in the form of cash or a vacation. In contrast to the skill required with contests, a sweepstakes winner is determined by chance. For example, consumers maybe given a scratch card in a fast-food restaurants; if three-of-a-kind or another predetermined criterion is achieved, the consumer would be given a free hamburger or some other selected prize.

Coupons. Coupons are certificates that give consumers a price savings when they purchase a specified product. Coupons are frequently mailed, placed in newspapers, or dispensed at the point of purchase. In addition, some companies have coupons generated when an item is scanned at the register. Companies can promote both new and mature products through the use of coupons.

Patronage rewards. Awards provided by companies to promote and encourage the purchasing of their products are called patronage rewards. Airlines use this strategy by awarding frequent-flyer miles to consumers who use their services often. When a consumer has earned enough frequent-flyer miles, he or she can redeem a free ticket. Credit card companies also use patronage rewards by providing a list of free products a person can order based on the number dollars charged in a specified time period.

Point-of-purchase displays. Point-of-purchase promotions can include displays and demonstrations that take place at the point of purchase. The cardboard cutouts of popular movie stars that are put next to merchandise are excellent examples of this method. One drawback to point-of-purchase displays is that stores do not have time to set up all the ones that are offered, so only a handful of them are used. Companies frequently offer assistance in assembling and removing promotional displays to encourages storeowners to use their point-of-purchase displays.

Premiums. A premium is a good offered free or at a low cost to encourage consumers to buy a particular product. Companies can also offer premiums in the form of reusable containers bearing names and logos in order to help promote other products. In addition, a company may also decide to use a self-liquidating premium. The costs associated with self-liquidating premiums are passed along to consumers through the cost of product.

Price packs/cents-off deals. Price packs provide consumers with a reduced price that is marked directly on the package by the manufacture. Companies can offer price packs in the format of two for the price of one or offer products such as a tube of toothpaste and a toothbrush in one package for a lower price than that of the two items purchased separately. Consumers generally react favorably to price packs because they are perceived as a real bargain.

Samples. Some companies offer free samples of their products. The rationale for offering a free product sample is to achieve immediate consumer introduction to the product. Companies have several ways to introduce potential consumers to product samples. Commonly used delivery methods include mailing the product, passing the product out in stores, or door-to-door delivery of the product. The largest drawback of free samples is their high cost. However, it is expected that the associated sales will offset the initial cost of the free samples.

Trade shows. Most industries hold conventions and trade shows each year to show off new technology, assess consumer trends, and review other issues important to the industry. Trade shows provide firms that sell to a particular industry an excellent opportunity to promote new products, make new contacts, renew existing business relationships, maintain or build a reputation, and distribute promotional materials.

PROMOTIONAL OBJECTIVES

There are a number of promotional objectives, some of the most common being information dissemination, product demand, product differentiation, product highlights, and sales stabilization. Regardless of the promotional objective selected, the company's goal is to inform and convince consumers to buy the product.

Information Dissemination One of the most basic desires of a company is to provide information about a product to potential consumers. Tools available to an organization for informing potential consumers about a product include billboards, flyers, Internet Web sites, magazines, newspapers, radio spots, and television commercials. Normally a variety of these promotional tools are used to communicate a single, coordinated message to potential consumers. These different promotional tools can provide potential consumers with an array of information about a product, such as features, quality, and/or price. The informational focus depends on the makeup of the target audience that the company is trying to reach with its message.

Product Demand Another organizational goal of promotional activities is to create product demand. A company has several promotional options for fostering product demand. For example, a company may focus on using a primary demand strategy that concentrates on trying to increase demand for a general product or service line. Large companies or cooperatives that have well-known and large product lines normally use the primary demand strategy. Advertisements for these companies carry over to all product categories and, as a result, may improve sales in several product areas. Companies also use another marketing strategy, known as selective demand, which concentrates on promoting a specific brand within a company's product line. Selective demand is often used to help promote a new product so that consumers are aware of the new addition to a large company's product line. A company may also utilize a selective demand strategy when it wants to sell a product that has a high profit margin. A good example of this strategy is the active promotion of sport utility vehicles by major automobile companies.

Product Differentiation A common challenge faced by companies is increased competition, which often results in the market being flooded with similar products. Consumers may conclude that no substantial difference exists between the products (homogeneous demand) and, therefore, look for the lowest-priced product to purchase. An industry that has experienced the problem of homogeneous demand is the soft-drink industry. With few exceptions, most consumers do not make a distinction among the numerous beverages that are offered. A company that excels at product differentiation can normally demand a higher price for a product because of its perceived higher quality.

Product Highlights Companies have another tool to employ in order to justify a higher-priced product: A firm can accentuate the product's exceptional quality in detail to convince consumers that the extra cost is worthwhile. Highlighting a product's quality might sound easy, but a company must first develop superior advertisements to promote the product. Moreover, the firm must develop a reputation for making a superior product that is well known to the average consumer. Volvo is one company that has done an excellent job of creating the image of producing only high-quality, safe cars. Thus, Volvo can charge an extra premium for its cars. Caterpillar has also nurtured and promoted a reputation for producing only the best heavy earth-moving equipment in the world. It, too, charges an increased price for its products.

Sales Stabilization A challenge that companies face is inconsistent demand for their products throughout the year. Reasons for this fluctuation can range from seasonal demand to changing economic conditions. Most companies would rather have a consistent demand for their products throughout the year, since this would allow them to have steady production and distribution facility operations. Ice cream manufacturers often face this dilemma because in the summer months demand for ice cream normally reaches its highest levels while sales decrease substantially in the winter. In order to combat these shifts in product demand, ice cream companies might offer coupons to encourage the purchase of their products during slow sales seasons.

SUMMARY

Companies engage in promotional activities virtually every day of the year. The various tools available to marketing managers for such activities are know as the promotional mix. Elements of the promotional mix include advertising, personal selling, public relations, and sales promo-

tion. Each of these promotional mix elements can be further divided into subelements depending upon company objectives.

BIBLIOGRAPHY

Boone, L. E., and Kurtz, D. L. (1992). *Contemporary Marketing*, 7th ed. New York: Dryden/Harcourt Brace.

Churchill, G. A., and Peter, P. J. (1995). *Marketing: Creating Value for Customers*. Boston: Irwin.

Farese, L., Kimbrell, G., and Woloszyk, C. (1991). *Marketing Essentials*. Mission Hills, CA: Glencoe/McGraw-Hill.

Kotler, P., and Armstrong, G. (1993). *Marketing an Introduction*, 3d ed. Englewood Cliffs, NJ: Prentice-Hall.

Semenik, R. J., and Bamossy, G. J. (1995). *Principles of Marketing: A Global Perspective*, 2d ed. Cincinnati, OH: South-Western.

ALLEN D. TRUELL
MICHAEL MILBIER

PSYCHOGRAPHICS

(SEE: *Lifestyles*)

PSYCHOLOGICAL PRICING

(SEE: *Pricing*)

PUBLICITY

Many definitions of *publicity* exist. For example, the *Publicity Handbook* (Yale, 1991), states that "publicity involves supplying information that is factual, interesting, and newsworthy to media not controlled by you, such as radio, television, magazines, newspapers, and trade journals" (p. 2). According to *Effective Public Relations* (Broom et al., 2000), "publicity is information from an outside source that is used by the media because the information has news value. It is an uncontrolled method of placing messages in the media because the source does not pay the media for placement" (p. 10). Finally, *The Random House Handbook of Business Terms* (Nisberg, 1988) defines publicity as "information designed to appear in any medium of communication for the purpose of keeping the name of a person or company before the public or of creating public interest in their activities" (p. 229).

Publicity is typically generated from an organization's public relations department and its goal is to gain media coverage. Examples of newsworthy events that may receive media coverage, or publicity, include ground-breaking ceremonies, press conferences, organized protests, or ceremonial appointments. Successful publicity occurs when an organization has a carefully designed publicity plan, which includes crisis control methods, and when events have real news value. Media gatekeepers (producers, editors, and reporters) favor publicity events that provide opportunities for photos, video or sound recordings, and effectively communicate the source's intended message.

Attempts to gain publicity have typically originated in an organization's public relations department. The goal was, and still is, to gain media coverage, or publicity, including ground-breaking ceremonies, press conferences, organized protests, and ceremonial appointments. Attempts to gain publicity are most often successful when an organization makes the media aware of events that have real news value from the media's point of view.

Ethical performance will help a company prevent or counteract negative publicity and will give a company, organization, or individual a competitive edge in gaining airtime or space in publications. In order to gain publicity, a company or individual must have clearly defined and specific goals. Publicity can help a company accomplish many of its goals. For example, effective publicity can persuade customers to buy a product or service, bring more customers into a store, increase attendance at a special event, and help clarify misconceptions.

A company must carefully pick and choose which events deserve media coverage in order to avoid "overkill." Not everything needs full-scale media attention—only those events that are most newsworthy and important. Advertising, or paid placement, can complement publicity efforts for items that are not truly newsworthy.

CRISIS PREVENTION AND RESPONSE

Negative publicity can be the result of a mishandled crisis. However, anticipating crises and having a solid crisis plan in place can save a company from potentially disastrous situations and enhance its image. A company must first understand the different types of potential crises that exist, avoid common mistakes when handling crises, and act proactively when dealing with a crisis. In the next section we examine four companies that were faced with crises and the way each company dealt with its crisis.

Three major types of potential crises exist. A sudden and unexpected event is an *immediate crisis*. Immediate crises do not allow for research and planning. A fire, bomb scare, or plane crash is an example of immediate crisis. There should be a general consensus among key management on how to react in these situations in order to avoid confusion, delay, or argument. More time for research and planning can be devoted to *emerging crises*, examples of which are employee dissatisfaction, low morale, and sexual harassment in the workplace. Management should take corrective action before these issues become critical. Despite the best efforts by management. *sustained crises* can persist for months or even years. These types of crises can result from media rumors or speculation. An ongoing rumor of company downsizing is an example of a sustained crisis. Once a company or organization has identified the type of crisis, there are specific things that should and should not be done to control unfavorable publicity.

With effective damage-control methods, any type of publicity can be an advantage for an organization. All organizations should have a crisis management team (CMT) whose job is to anticipate crises and be ready to respond to the worst by upholding the image and reputation of the company in times of crisis. Companies can hire external CMTs or develop and train in-house CMTs.

When a crisis arises, certain things should *not* be done. A company or organization should avoid *hesitation* in speaking with the press. Any type of hesitation may be perceived as callousness, incompetence, or a lack of preparation. *Obfuscation*, or being unclear, leads the public to believe that the company is insensitive or is not being honest. *Retaliation* can increase tension and heighten emotions, rather than reduce them. *Prevarication*, or making false statements, is the biggest mistake a company can make because nothing should substitute for the truth. *Pontification*, the use of inflated language, simply avoids the issue at hand. *Confrontation* will keep the issue alive, and *litigation* (a lawsuit) eliminates all other viable solutions to the crisis.

Alternatively, there are certain actions a company *should* take in the event a crisis emerges. First and foremost, communication lines must be opened. Next. a company spokesperson should be selected. All employees should be instructed to send any crisis inquiries directly to the company's spokesperson. The media should be supplied with information as quickly as possible. The company must be open to the media and tell the full story so that reporters do not look to outsiders to fill in the gaps.

The company must express its concern about the crisis and should show empathy for all the people being affected by the problem. Most importantly, the company should tell the public what it is going to do to resolve the crisis and should have a company representative available twenty-four hours a day so long as media interest exists.

Finally, once the crisis is over, the CMT should meet again to summarize the crisis situation, review and evaluate how the plan was implemented, and give open feedback and appropriate recommendations in order to determine where improvements can be made in the crisis-management plan. Now, let's examine the crisis management methods used by four companies: Source Perrier, Exxon, TWA, and Johnson & Johnson.

FOUR CRISES

Source Perrier was unable to overcome negative publicity when top management hesitated in the crisis-solving process. Traces of benzene were found in the company's bottled water in 1990, but top management reassured the public that it was necessary to recall contaminated bottles only in North America. The crisis continued when scientists found benzene in bottled water being sold in Europe. Again, management responded incorrectly by attributing the contamination to a filtering-system problem. The final blow to the company came when the media discovered, and reported, that benzene-tainted products had been sold all over the world for months. The media questioned Perrier's integrity and concern for public safety, and the company lost its dominant position in the marketplace; it has been unable to rebuild its reputation.

Similar to the mistakes Perrier made, Exxon's CEO did not visit Alaska after the tanker *Exxon Valdez* dumped millions of gallons of oil into Prince William Sound in 1989, and TWA's CEO resigned three months after 230 people died in the crash of Flight 800. Arriving to the crash site thirteen hours after the accident, he was criticized for not showing immediate sympathy for the crash victims and their families. Neither Exxon nor TWA has been able to reclaim its market position.

Conversely, Johnson & Johnson handled a disastrous crisis amazingly well in 1982 and the company's reaction remains as a model for effective media relations. After cyanide was discovered in some capsules of Tylenol, a product used by an estimated 100 million people, Johnson & Johnson decided to cooperate fully with the media. It immediately announced a recall of all Tylenol packages in both U.S. and foreign markets. These decisions, which were based on the business principle of being socially responsible, earned Johnson & Johnson praise from the media. The company received additional positive press coverage when it subsequently introduced its new tamper-resistant packaging. Despite not being able to control media coverage of the situation, Johnson & Johnson was able to gain positive publicity because the company had a plan and knew what to do during a crisis.

Publicity is not advertising, public relations, or promotions, because it is not controlled or paid for, but it has many advantages. If used correctly, companies can benefit greatly from publicity. Careful planning, research, and training can reduce negative publicity and can help companies control crises.

BIBLIOGRAPHY

Broom, Glen M., Center, Allen H., and Cutlip, Scott M. (2000). *Effective Public Relations*. ed. by Natalie E. Anderson. 8th ed. Upper Saddle River, NJ: Prentice-Hall.

Carter, Rudeseal Ginger, ed. *Perspectives Public Relations*. St. Paul. MN: Course Wise.

Lesly, Philip, ed. *Lesly's Public Relations Handbook*. 3rd ed. (1983). Englewood Cliffs, NJ: Prentice-Hall.

Nisberg, Jay N. (1988). *The Random House Handbook of Business Terms*. New York: Random House.

Yale, David R. (1991). *The Publicity Handbook: "How to Maximize Publicity for Products, Services, and Organizations"* Lincolnwood, IL: NTC Business Books.

JENNIFER L. JENNESS

PUBLIC OVERSIGHT BOARD

The accounting profession has a unique responsibility in the United States. Regulators, investors, and the general public rely on certified public accountants to assure the integrity and credibility of corporate financial statements. At the same time, the accounting profession has considerable autonomy in regulating itself. To maintain self-regulation, the American Institute of Certified Public Accountants has developed a multilevel system of self-regulation based on exacting quality control standards. The Public Oversight Board plays a critical role within this system. The role of the Public Oversight Board is closely related to the Securities and Exchange Commission Practice Section.

THE SECURITIES AND EXCHANGE COMMISSION PRACTICE SECTION

On September 17, 1977, the American Institute of Certified Public Accountants (AICPA) established the Securities and Exchange Commission Practice Section as a voluntary organization of certified public accountant firms striving for professional excellence in the auditing services they provide to Securities and Exchange Commission registrants. The objectives of the section are (1) to improve the quality of practice by certified public accountant firms, and (2) to establish and maintain mandatory peer reviews for member firms. An executive committee manages the activities of the section. The Public Oversight Board oversees all activities of the section and reports on these activities.

There are three key elements of the self-regulatory program for certified public accountant firms: (1) peer review for the firm's quality control system once every three years, (2) inquiries to determine whether alleged audit failures indicate breakdowns in a firm's quality control system, and (3) oversight of the process by the Public Oversight Board.

The self-regulatory process answers to legislators, regulators, and the general public. Oversight of the process, by the Public Oversight Board and the Security and Exchange Commission, makes the section's self-regulatory system both more effective and more credible.

THE PUBLIC OVERSIGHT BOARD

In 1977, the AICPA created the Public Oversight Board. The board is an independent, private-sector body that monitors and reports on the accounting profession's self-regulatory programs for independent auditors of entities registered with the Securities and Exchange Commission. The board recommends improvements to strengthen the system.

The board's independence is evidenced by its power to select the successors of its members, hire and compensate its staff, set the compensation of its members, and choose its chair. The board consists of five members, primarily non-accountants, who represent a broad spectrum of business, professional, regulatory, and legislative experience. The board, which meets about eight times a year, had its first meeting in March 1978.

Mission and Functions of the Public Oversight Board The primary mission of the Public Oversight Board is to represent the public interest when the Securities and Exchange Commission Practice Section sets, revises, or enforces standards, membership requirements, or rules of procedure. In addition, the board represents the public interest regarding the results of individual peer reviews or the possible quality control implications of litigation alleging audit failure.

The board's main functions are to (1) monitor and evaluate the regulatory and sanction activities of the peer review and executive committees to assure their effectiveness, (2) determine that the peer review committee is ascertaining that firms are taking appropriate action as a result of peer reviews, (3) conduct continuing oversight of all other activities of the section, (4) make recommendations to the executive committee for improvements in the operation of the section, (5) publish an annual report and such other reports as may be deemed necessary with respect to its activities, and (6) attend all meetings of the executive committee.

The Peer Review Program The objectives of the peer review are to determine (1) whether a reviewed firm's system of quality control for its accounting and auditing practice is appropriately comprehensive and suitably designed for the firm, (2) whether its quality control policies and procedures are adequately documented and communicated to professional personnel, and (3) whether such policies and procedures are being complied with so as to provide the firm with reasonable assurance of conforming with professional standards and the membership requirements of the Section.

The board's staff oversees each peer review by evaluating the review teams' qualifications and experience, and by reading the peer review report, letter of comment, and reviewed firm's response letter.

The Quality Control Inquiry Committee In November 1979, the Securities and Exchange Commission Practice Section established the Quality Control Inquiry Committee to consider the implications of allegations of audit failure on a firm's quality control system. Member firms of the section must report to the committee all liti-

gation or regulatory proceeding involving audits of public companies or regulated financial institutions within thirty days of receiving a complaint. The Public Oversight Board oversees the Quality Control Inquiry Committee by reviewing both the plaintiff's allegations and the committee's analysis of them. The board routinely makes recommendations for improvement in the peer review and Quality Control Inquiry Committee programs.

ACTIVITIES OF THE PUBLIC OVERSIGHT BOARD

Since the Public Oversight Board was a brand-new layer in the self-regulatory structure, the first year activities were devoted principally to (1) organizing, defining its role, and recruiting its staff; (2) advising on policy matters during the development of the section's peer review program; (3) monitoring initial peer review; (4) studying the question of the scope of services provided by certified public accountant firms and preparing and publishing a report containing recommendations on the subject; and (5) considering the question of what action should be taken by the section in the event of an alleged or possible audit failure involving one of its member firms.

The board or one or more of its members or staff met on numerous occasions with the members of the Securities and Exchange Commission Practice Section. The board also held public hearings, conferences, and educational sessions on the self-regulatory programs, and received written comments from firms and individuals interested in the scope of service. From the initial efforts, the role of the board became clear.

The board's oversight and monitoring program now consists of (1) post-review of working papers prepared by reviewers, including panels; (2) observation of reviews in process, with emphasis on attendance at exit conferences; and (3) other selected procedures. The board publishes an annual report and other reports as may be deemed necessary with respect to its activities. In addition, the board and its members give speeches, write articles, testify before congressional committees, and conduct special studies on matters bearing directly on the integrity of the audit process. From time to time, special initiatives are undertaken.

In September 1994, the Public Oversight Board formed an Advisory Panel on Auditor Independence to determine whether the Securities and Exchange Practice Section, the accounting profession, or the Securities and Exchange Commission should take steps to better assure the independence of auditors and the integrity and objectivity of their judgments on the appropriate application of generally accepted accounting principles to financial statements. A report was issued, which is discussed later.

In 1998, the board appointed a panel on audit effectiveness, which includes investors, auditors, regulators, audit committee members, and corporate executives, to examine whether audit processes of large-firm members of the Securities and Exchange Commission Practice Section adequately serve and protect the interests of investors.

PUBLICATIONS OF THE PUBLIC OVERSIGHT BOARD

The board publishes an annual report as well as special reports. In 1991, the board published *Evaluation of the Quality Control Inquiry Committee* by Robert K. Mautz and Charles J. Evers. The booklet describes how the profession reconciled two conflicting forces: the protection of the public interest on the one hand and, on the other, the right of a firm to mount a vigorous defense against audit failure litigation.

In 1993, the board published *In the Public Interest: Issues Confronting the Accounting Profession: Litigation, Self-Regulation, Standards, Public Confidence, and Professional Practice*. The report was a result of the board's concerns with the impact of litigation and the influence of publicized allegations on the public perception of the accounting profession's performance.

In 1994, the board published *Strengthening the Professionalism of the Independent Auditor*. The board asked for a more accountable board of directors to strengthen the professionalism of the

outside auditor. In 1995, the board published *Directors, Management, and Auditors: Allies in Protecting Shareholder Interest*. In that report the board urged directors to play an active role in the financial reporting process and urged the auditing profession to look at directors—the shareholders' representatives—as its client.

THE BOARD'S RELATIONSHIP TO THE SECURITIES AND EXCHANGE COMMISSION

The staff of the chief accountant of the Securities and Exchange Commission regularly reviews the Public Oversight Board's files to determine whether the peer review and the Quality Control Inquiry Committee programs are being properly conducted and properly overseen by the board. The commission staff's conclusions are reflected in the commission's annual reports. These reports have stated that the Securities and Exchange Commission Practice Section's programs have increased the reliability of audits.

In addition, the board itself meets from time to time with the Securities and Exchange Commission's staff and commissioner.

(SEE ALSO: *American Institute of Certified Public Accountants; Securities and Exchange Commission*)

BIBLIOGRAPHY

American Institute of Certified Public Accountants. (1991). *Combined Annual Report. SEC Practice Section Division for CPA Firms: American Institute of Certified Public Accountants and Public Oversight Board*. New York: Author.

Public Oversight Board. (1997–1998). *Annual Report*. Stamford, CT: Author.

Public Oversight Board. (1996–1997). *Annual Report*. Stamford, CT: Author.

Public Oversight Board. (1995–1996). *Annual Report*. Stamford, CT: Author.

Public Oversight Board. (1994–1995). *Annual Report*. Stamford, CT: Author.

Public Oversight Board. (1995). *Directors, Management, and Auditors: Allies in Protecting Shareholder Interest*. Stamford, CT: Author.

Public Oversight Board. (1993). *In the Public Interest: Issues Confronting the Accounting Profession. A Special Report*. Stamford, CT: Author.

Public Oversight Board. (1978–1979). *Annual Report.* New York: Author.

Public Oversight Board. (1994). *Strengthening the Professionalism of the Independent Auditor.* (Report to Public Oversight Board of the SEC Practice Section, AICPA from the Advisory Panel on Auditor Independence). Stamford, CT: Author.

Public Oversight Board, Mautz, R., and Evers, C. (1991). "Evaluation of the Quality Control Inquiry Committee." Stamford, CT: Author.

NASHWA GEORGE

PURE CAPITALISM

(SEE: *Economic Systems*)

Q

QUALITY MANAGEMENT

Quality management (QM), also called total quality management (TQM), evolved from many different management practices and improvement processes. Quality management is not specific to managing people, but rather is related to improving the quality of goods and services that are produced in order to satisfy customer demands. Quality management permeates the entire organization as it is being implemented.

TQM has its roots in the quality movement that has made Japan such a strong force in the world economy. The Japanese philosophy of quality initially emphasized product and performance and only later shifted concern to customer satisfaction.

The quality improvement movement began in both the United States and Japan before World War II. Throughout the war, Americans continued to improve concepts related to manufacturing productivity. After the war, the Japanese pursued the idea of quality improvement. It was W. Edwards Deming, an American, who helped the Japanese focus on their fixation with quality.

Rather than trying to inspect the quality of products and services after they have been completed, TQM instills a philosophy of doing the job correctly the first time. It all sounds simple, but implementing the process requires an organizational culture and climate that are often alien and intimidating. Changes that must occur in the organization are so significant that it takes time

and patience to complete the process. Just as the process does not occur overnight, the results may not be seen for a long period of time. Some experts say that it takes up to ten years to fully realize the results of implementing quality management.

THE PROCESS

There are several steps that must be taken in the process of shifting to quality management in an organization:

1. *Provide a QM environment.* A QM environment is one in which the management-driven culture disappears and a participative culture takes its place. The basic tenets of QM are that employees must be involved and that there must be teamwork. Managers must be willing to involve workers in the decision-making process. Workers who function as a team have much more to offer collectively than do individual workers. Pooled resources are more valuable than just one person's contribution.

2. *Modify reward systems.* Reward systems need to be overhauled so as to recognize and encourage teamwork and innovation. The team, not the individual, is the foundation for TQM companies. If a company continues to use traditional compensation plans that create competition between

W. Edwards Deming.

workers, the team concept cannot be implemented. Traditional pay plans are often based on seniority, not on quality and performance. With QM, pay systems focus on team incentives. Each person is paid based on the team's performance. If one person on the team doesn't perform at the level expected, the team members will normally handle the situation. In some cases, payment is based on the performance of the entire company, which requires an even greater team effort.

3. *Prepare workers for TQM.* Workers must constantly be trained with the tools that are needed to upgrade the company's quality. Workers must understand the philosophy of QM before the tools can be used effectively. Managers must be dedicated to transforming their companies into "learning organizations" in which workers want to upgrade their skills and take advantage of the opportunities and

incentives to do so. Companies that are successful with TQM allocate up to about 5 percent of their employees' time on training. Some of this training time might include cross-training, that is, schooling workers in the skills to do a different job in the organization.

4. *Prepare employees to measure quality.* To ensure gains in quality, the results must be measured objectively as the company progresses toward its quality objectives. This requires that employees be trained to use statistical process control techniques. Without knowledgeable workers using quantitative tools, the organization cannot achieve the intended TQM results.

5. *Identify the appropriate starting place.* One of the most difficult tasks in the beginning phases of implementing QM is to determine where to start. One approach to this beginning is to assume that 80 percent of all the company's problems stem from 20 percent of the company's processes (Pareto's Law). By identifying the problematic processes that fall in this 20 percent category, one can begin to focus on what needs attention first. Focusing attention on these problems first will return bigger payoffs and build momentum for the future.

6. *Share information with everyone.* If a team approach is to be used and if employees are expected to be involved in the decision-making process, it is imperative that information be shared with everyone. The decision-making process requires that workers be fully informed.

7. *Include quality as an element of design.* From beginning to end, customer satisfaction should be the focus of the quality management system. That means that the goal of customer satisfaction must be included in the planning processes and then maintained day in and day out.

8. *Make error prevention the norm.* One approach to producing quality products is

to have a group of inspectors who will find the defective items and get rid of them. This is not the QM approach. With QM, the approach is continuous improvement of quality to assure that there are no products that are defective. The quality is built into the manufacturing process, and workers are continually improving products and processes. This approach is more cost-effective for the organization because it eliminates the waste of materials and workers' time.

9. *Encourage cooperation and teamwork.* If mistakes are made, it is the fault of a team of workers, not just one worker. In many organizations that do not use TQM, managers are often on the hunt for someone to blame for problems that are found. This type of environment creates unhealthy stress and discourages innovative thought and practices by workers. The combination of a team approach and QM means seeking to improve the system when problems arise.

10. *Make continuous improvement the goal.* Processes and products should continually be improved. There is no end to the improvement process. This is true for even the best of the best companies. Total quality management never ends.

W. Edwards Deming created fourteen points for management, which are condensed on the Web site of the Deming Institute (http://www .deming.org/deminghtml/teachings/html) and adapted here:

1. Create constancy of purpose toward improvement of product and service, with the aim to become competitive, to stay in business, and to provide jobs.

2. Adopt a new philosophy. We are in a new economic age. Western management must awaken to the challenge, must learn their responsibilities, and must take on leadership for change.

3. Cease dependence on inspection to achieve quality. Eliminate the need for inspection on a mass basis by building quality into the product in the first place.

4. End the practice of awarding business on the basis of the price tag. Instead, minimize total cost. Move toward a single supplier for any one item, based on a long-term relationship of loyalty and trust.

5. Improve constantly and forever the system of production and service, in order to improve quality and productivity, and thus constantly decrease costs.

6. Institute training on the job.

7. Institute leadership. The aim of supervision should be to help people, machines, and gadgets to do a better job. Supervision of management is in need of overhaul, as is supervision of production workers.

8. Drive out fear, so that everyone may work effectively for the company.

9. Break down barriers between departments. People in research, design, sales, and production must work as a team, in order to foresee problems in production and in use that may be encountered with the product or service.

10. Eliminate slogans, exhortations, and targets for the work force asking for zero defects and new levels of productivity. Such exhortations only create adversarial relationships, since the bulk of the causes of low quality and low productivity belong to the system and thus lie beyond the power of the work force. Eliminate work standards (quotas) on the factory floor, substituting leadership. Eliminate management by objective, by numbers, and by numeric goals, also substituting leadership.

11. Remove barriers that rob hourly workers of their right to pride of workmanship.

The goals of supervisors must be changed from sheer numbers to quality.

12. Remove barriers that rob people in management and in engineering of their right to pride of workmanship. This means, inter alia, abolishment of the annual or merit rating and of management by objective.

13. Institute a vigorous program of education and self-improvement.

14. Put everybody in the company to work to accomplish the transformation. The transformation is everybody's job.

It is readily apparent that the process of implementing a quality management system in an organization is closely aligned with the thinking of Deming. A more detailed description of the Deming approach is found in his publication *Out of Crisis* (1986).

RECOGNITION

The importance of quality is emphasized with the awards that are presented to companies that achieve high standards of quality. The Malcolm Baldridge National Quality Award was one of the first given. The 1991 award application identified several categories that companies must address to receive the award. It must be noted that very few awards are presented. Companies are rated on leadership, information and analysis, strategic quality planning, human resources utilization, quality assurance of products and services, qual-ity results, and customer satisfaction. It is a very prestigious honor for a company to be recognized with this award.

Other awards and certifications are also presented. However, they constantly change and new ones are added regularly, so they will not be discussed here. Quality management has become an important philosophy in businesses around the world, and this approach to building better products and services will continue.

BIBLIOGRAPHY

Deming, W. Edwards. (1986). *Out of Crisis.* W. Edwards Deming Institute.

Saylor, James H. (1992). *TQM Field Manual.* New York: McGraw-Hill.

Scarborough, Norman M., and Zimmerer, Thomas W. (2000). *Effective Small Business Management: An Entrepreneurial Approach.* Upper Saddle River. NJ: Prentice Hall.

Svenson, Ray, Wallace, K., Wexler, G., and Wexler, Bruce. (1994). *The Quality Roadmap: How to Get Your Company on the Quality Track And Keep it There.* New York: AMACOM.

Weiss, Alan. (2000). *"Good Enough" Isn't Enough . . . Nine Challenges for Companies That Choose to Be Great.* New York: AMACOM.

ROGER LUFT

QUANTITY DISCOUNTS

(SEE: *Pricing*)

R

READING SKILLS IN BUSINESS

In the business world, workers use special skills to complete their reading tasks. Traditionally, however, business educators have relied on others to develop the job-related reading skills of their students. In 1975, Sticht noted that the overwhelming majority of time in schools is allocated to teaching the reading and interpreting of novels, short stories, dramas, and poetry as opposed to teaching technical reading skills needed in the workplace. More recently, the SCANS (Secretary's Commission on Achieving Necessary Skills) report released in 1991 included the reading of technical material as a foundation skill needed by all workers. Workplace reading includes the ability to understand and interpret various documents including diagrams, directories, correspondence, manuals, records, charts, graphs, tables, and specifications.

In the 1970s, two researchers, Ross and Salzman, studied the reading tasks of randomly selected office workers in the Columbus, Ohio area. Ross completed one-hour observations of one hundred beginning office workers, and Salzman collected 2659 samples of reading, writing, and mathematical activities from thirty-five beginning and thirty-five experienced office workers. Outcomes of these two studies identified three unique reading skills office workers use: proofreading, verifying, and comprehending detail.

Building on the research that Ross and Salzman completed, Schmidt reported, in 1987, the reading levels of office documents collected for the purpose of developing reading materials aimed at building technical reading skills. One hundred and twenty-one documents collected from ten businesses were analyzed for reading level using the FORCAST formula. The FORCAST formula developed in 1975 by Caylor, Sticht, Fox, and Ford uses the percentage of one-syllable words as the basis for determining reading level; hence it eliminates consideration of recurring technical terms, which can artificially raise the reading level of technical materials.

The average reading grade levels for the documents ranged from 11.3 for those collected from a bank to 13.4 for those collected from a university continuing education center office. Other businesses that provided documents and their average reading grade levels included a space industry manufacturer, 11.4; a town administration office, 11.8; a hospital, 12.0; an insurance company, 12.0; a chemical industry manufacturer, 12.1; a railroad, 12.8; a country administration office, 13.1; and a school division office, 13.1. Thus, the reading grade level of typical office documents is considerably higher than general interest reading materials. Further, most reading done by adults is technical, job-related reading and not the type of reading emphasized in schools.

Based on a study of two groups of high school students, in which one group was enrolled in courses required to complete a business program and the other group enrolled in selected elective business courses, Schmidt reported in 1982 that the first group, comprised of 279 students, performed better on a proofreading skills test than the second group, comprised of 1058 students. However, on tests measuring the skills of verifying and comprehending detail, the first group did not score better than the second group. The tests were constructed from actual business documents. From this outcome, Schmidt concluded that reading exercises for developing the skills of verifying and comprehending detail were needed.

The National Business Education Association published the exercises that evolved. In the introduction to the *Office Reading Exercises*, Schmidt describes trial use of the exercises prior to their publication. They were used with experimental and control groups, each with more than two hundred and fifty high school students. After completing a pretest, the experimental group completed the ten exercises, using 15-20 minutes to complete one exercise per day. The students were simply given the exercises and informed of expected outcomes. This group not only scored significantly higher on a post-test administered at the completion of the exercises, but also on a post-test administered after a lapse of three to five weeks. They also scored significantly higher on the post-test than the control group. Thus a research base exists to justify the use of the exercises.

The ten exercises were all developed from actual office documents including a catalog page, a price list, an insurance claim, an enrollment report, a budget allocation form, a meal price schedule, a program confirmation, zoning ordinance information, concentration banking information, and an expense account. Schmidt provides two approaches that can be used for teaching the exercises. One is a holistic approach where the students are simply given the exercises, one day at a time, and told the outcomes desired. This was the approach used in the study described above. They devise, along with their classmates, their own methods for achieving the outcomes. The other approach is instructor-directed and is called a "Guided Approach." It allows the instructor to emphasize the 13 component skills that are subsets of the two main skills, verifying and comprehending detail.

Verifying requires comparing technical information that has been transferred from one place to another to be sure that it has been transferred accurately. *Comprehending detail* is reading printed technical information, then determining if statements about it are accurate. The component skills or sub-skills emphasized in the "Guided Approach" are:

- Following directions
- Perceiving document structure
- Perceiving relationships
- Identifying relevant information
- Locating facts or specifics
- Recognizing comparison/contrasting information
- Interpreting symbols, graphics, or acronyms
- Recognizing sequence of information
- Summarizing or making generalizations
- Selecting relevant information
- Recognizing main idea
- Reading with partner to detect errors
- Recognizing errors: transpositions, typographical and mechanical, additions and omissions

Taylor and Hancock, in a 1993 publication titled "Strategies That Reinforce Academics Across the Business Curriculum," discussed strategies to help introduce, reinforce, and extend students' comprehension, vocabulary, and writing in three reading stages. An overview of the three stages follows.

Pre-Reading Stage. Before students are assigned technical reading, they need to engage in pre-reading strategies to help them in understanding the material. The reading can be broken into smaller segments with a variety of activities that promote student involvement. These might include a graphic organizer, an analogical study guide, or an anticipation/reaction guide. This guide helps focus pre-reading discussion and can also serve for post-reading review.

Reading Stage. At the reading stage, the students need to focus on garnering major ideas as well as important details from the material. A study guide or selective reading guide can help the students achieve this objective. The study guide used should, unlike the text-explicit questions generally supplied by textbook authors, extend the students' thinking beyond mere "parroting" of the text-explicit concepts.

Post-Reading Stage. Once the students have read the material, they need to engage in post-reading activities to assure long-term retention of what they have read. The pre-reading strategies can again be used or students can undertake other activities. These might include vocabulary reinforcement activities, journal writing, or other writing activities that allow the students to apply information from what they have read.

Thus, the reading of technical materials requires the development of unique skills—ones that are not addressed by most teachers. The *Office Reading Exercises* developed by Schmidt and the strategies recommended by Taylor and Hancock provide some approaches that can be used to teach technical reading skills. However, before these approaches are used, instructors should also be concerned with the extent that their students' reading abilities match those required for technical materials. Two methods are available for this purpose: (a) the Cloze procedure developed by Taylor in 1953, which permits the instructor to measure the compatibility of printed materials with the reading ability of students, and (b) a pretest developed from technical terms the material contains.

For classroom use, the following adaptation of the Cloze technique is recommended by Popham, Schrag, and Blockhus.

1. Randomly select reading material in six to nine passages and delete every fifth word in each passage. Stop when 20 words have been deleted.

2. In place of each word deleted, substitute an underscore.

3. Have the material typed, and instruct students to place in each blank a word that makes sense. No guessing or time restrictions permitted.

4. Analyze the answers and give credit for each substitution that approximates the original meaning. Determine a raw score for each student and convert that raw score to a percent by dividing the actual number of correct answers by the possible number of correct answers.

5. Determine the level at which the students comprehend the material by using the following scale. A score of 0-30 percent equals the "Frustration" reading level, a score of 31-49 percent equals the "Instructional" reading level, and a score of 50-100 percent equals the "Independent" reading level.

Some technical materials do not lend themselves to the use of the Cloze test. For these materials a pretest based on technical terms from the material can be developed to provide insight into the extent that students can understand the material. If a student answers less than half of the items on the test correctly, the instructor may assume that the student will have difficulty reading the material.

Students need technical reading skills for the business world. Furthermore, all teachers are expected to reinforce academic competencies in their instruction. The procedures discussed here can help teachers meet the challenge of teaching technical reading skills, those essential for reading in business.

BIBLIOGRAPHY

Caylor, J. S., Sticht, T. G., Fox, L. C., and Ford, J. P. (1975). "Readability of job materials." In Sticht, T. G. ed. *Reading for Working: A Functional Literacy Anthology.* Alexandria, VA: Human Resources Organization.

Popham, E. L., Schrag, A. F., and Blockhus, W. (1975). *A Teaching-Learning System for Business Education.* New York: McGraw-Hill.

Ross, N. (1977). *An Analysis of the Nature and Difficulty of Reading Tasks Associated with Beginning Office Workers.* Doctoral dissertation. Columbus, OH: The Ohio State University.

Salzman, G. G. (1979). *A descriptive study of the reading, writing, and mathematics tasks of beginning office workers.* Doctoral dissertation. Columbus. OH: The Ohio State University.

Schmidt, B. J. (1991). *Office Reading Exercises.* Reston, VA: National Business Education Association, p. 37.

Schmidt, B. J. (1987). "Preparing Business Students to Read Office Documents." *The Delta Pi Epsilon Journal,* (29) 4, 111-124.

Schmidt, B. J. (1982). "Job-related Reading Skills Developed by Business Students." *The Journal of Vocational Education Research,* 7(4), 29-38.

Secretary's Commission on Achieving Necessary Skills. (1992). *Learning A Living: A Blueprint for High Performance.* Washington, D.C.: U.S. Department of Labor.

Taylor, W. L. (1953). "Cloze Procedures: A New Tool for Measuring Readability." *Journalism Quarterly,* 30, 415-433.

Taylor, H. P., and Hancock, D. O. (1993, September). "Strategies That Reinforce Academics across the Business Curriculum." *Delta Pi Epsilon Instructional Strategies,* 9(4).

B. JUNE SCHMIDT

RECESSION

(SEE: *Economic Cycles*)

RECORDS MANAGEMENT

Although records and information management is a crucial function of most companies today, records management at one time was not recognized as being important in the organization. Advancements in technology and the reproduction of electronic documents are steadily causing organizations to change the way they think about records management.

Marcel Robles and Mark Langemo (1999) define records management as:

> The professional management of information in the physical form of records from the time records are received or created through their processing, distribu-
> tion, and placement in a storage and retrieval system until either eventual elimination or identification for permanent archival retention. (p. 30)

This definition is all-inclusive because it notes the significance of the records manager's role in the management of information from the time it is received to either its elimination or its permanent archival retention in the organization. The Emerging Technologies Advisory Group of the Association for Information and Image Management (AIIM) identified the top five emerging technologies as we move into the twenty-first century (Dale, 1999). These technologies have become management concerns and, therefore, concerns of records managers:

1. e-mail management
2. e-mail
3. Knowledge management
4. Records migration
5. Customer relationship management

Hence, as records management takes on a more strategic role in organizations, a very knowledgeable and proficient professional is required in the managerial position.

DEVELOPING AN EFFICIENT SYSTEM

The existence of an increasingly competitive environment along with the rapid pace of business make it essential to have an efficient, economical, and orderly way to collect, process, store, analyze, retrieve, and distribute information (Griffith, 1996). Theodore Vander Noot (1998) suggests ten characteristics of an "ideal information system" that should apply whether the system is a computerized database or a file system or library. (See Table 1)

There are two basic reasons for the increase in information over the years (Hutchens, 1998). The first, *modernity,* has seen the decline in small businesses as larger and more complex businesses begin to dominate. A more *modern democratic government* is seen as the second reason for the growth in information. Both public and private organizations tend to collect more information

Characteristics of an Ideal Information System

1. The information system should minimize elapsed time between a user's query and the response from the system.

2. The more complete the information stored, the more useful the data can be to the end user.

3. The more completely an information system can prevent "lost" files, the more generally useful the system is to users.

4. An information system should provide access to the same document or file by more than one user at one time (multi-user, multi-tasking).

5. The more a retrieval system maximizes pertinence while minimizing redundancy, the more the system services the needs of the user.

6. Retrieval queries should be possible in the official language(s).

7. The information system should make provision for selective security.

8. The simpler a retrieval system is, and the less training required using it, the more acceptable it is to the users.

9. Additions, deletions, and updating of files should be made as efficient as possible.

10. Since work hours, particularly of managers, extend beyond prime shift hours, the ideal system should be able to operate in non-regular hours at reasonable cost.

Table 1

than needed regarding their programs when providing the requested records for the government.

METHODS OF STORING INFORMATION

Four methods are often used for storing information in business and government (Hutchens, 1998):

- a person's brain
- paper
- microfilm
- a computer

Management is relying less and less on intellectual ability and more and more on paper, microfilm, and computers. Electronic document management (EDM) technologies allow for storing, retrieving, and transmitting documents electronically.

Three basic questions should be asked when ridding an organization of outdated files. The guidelines are (Hancock, 1998):

1. Why were the documents created?

2. Why should they be kept?

3. When can they be destroyed?

A records retention schedule should be developed for organizations so as to avoid retention of unnecessary documents. Although we have moved into a digital world, office workers continue to be unable to let go of paper files. The "paperless office" is still a phrase that has not been made reality.

Outsourcing Off-site storage of inactive records is the most common type of records outsourcing (Dykeman, 1996). Records management outsourcing often depends on the quality and cost of the outsourcer. Decision making involves whether to store inactive records off-site or bring in an outsourcing firm to run the entire records management operation.

Electronic Imaging As the growth in documents continues, electronic imaging becomes one preferred means of managing information. Two major advantages of electronic imaging are ease of use and flexibility. Imaging can capture, retrieve, and transmit documents no matter what the form, handwritten or machine-created (Avedon, 1997).

There are three types of documents or images:

- Analog documents—human-readable information on paper or microfilm

- ASCII (American Standard Code for Information Interchange) documents—binary digital-coded representations of information stored on magnetic tape or disks and used with computer, word processing, and OCR (optical character recognition) systems

- Bit-mapped/raster documents—documents scanned via a technique called bit mapping

A computer with a CD-ROM drive is the only equipment needed to benefit from electronic imaging document systems. Most systems convert paper documents or microfilm images to digital form using scanners and electronic images that require a large amount of memory. There are three types of CDs: CD-ROM, DC-R, and CD-RW. In order to determine which type of recorder to use for a particular application, three factors must be considered: speed, buffer, and software.

Bar-Code Technology. More sophisticated automation systems are the driving force behind bar-code technology in records management. Both the quantity and quality of the data input and the use of bar-code labels as miniature data-storage media can enhance the information processed. Enhanced technology, such as high-resolution laser printers and more complex two- and three-dimensional data-recording methodologies, make it possible to store entire pages of information in bar-code format. In turn, these bar codes can be faxed or transmitted electronically between locations. It is imperative that records managers keep abreast of the latest in technology to meet the challenge of storing and retrieving information in the twenty-first century.

Intranets. The computer has opened up multiple possibilities for managing records. The computer with Internet, Web, and e-mail capabilities is now accessible to most, and soon will be accessible to all, employees. Since the Internet and the Web are present in most organizations, the link between people and information is already established, providing a less expensive choice when communicating. An open, information-sharing work environment is provided through an intranet.

Six examples of how an intranet can help achieve the objectives of the records manager are: (1) controlling creation and growth of documents, (2) reducing operating costs, (3) minimizing litigation risks, (4) safeguarding vital information, (5) supporting better management decision-making, and (6) fostering professional-ism in business (Motz, 1998). The global nature of multinational corporations demands easy sharing of information, a demand that has encouraged adoption of the Internet and intranets. All three components of intranets—technical, systemic, and organizational—must be considered in order to be successful.

THE RECORDS MANAGEMENT PROFESSION

The role of the records manager is constantly changing. Advances in technology raise the question of whether the records manager's functions will become automated. It will be important to distinguish between records management business activities that can be: (1) easily automated, (2) partially automated, and (3) never automated (Phillips, 1998). Of course, for job security, records managers should concentrate on technological knowledge and skills required for those activities in the "never automated" category.

Establishing the social relevance of records managers is necessary in order to gain respect as a profession. The Association of Records Managers and Administrators (ARMA) International has provided the foundation for communication with society in general through its Code of Professional Responsibility. The prevailing challenge for records managers involves all of the following: legality, technology awareness, quality assurance, and contingency planning issues (Jones, 1998). In order to meet the challenges, records managers must address potential technology solutions proactively. A major dilemma for records managers is to decide whether to give the organization/customer what they want or what the records manager knows they need.

With the increasing use of technology in the records and information system, it is important for records managers to take a leadership role in organizations and gain a stronger voice in management. ARMA International continues to be a source of help in this area.

BIBLIOGRAPHY

Avedon, Don M. (1997). "Electronic Imaging Management for Beginners." *Office Systems* 14(4) (April): 34, 40.

Dale, Tom. (1999). "Coming Soon to an Office near You: 1999 Trends." *Inform* 13(1) (January): 32-34.

Dykeman, John. (1996). "Managing Office Technology." *Managing Office Technology* 41(7) (July): 34-35.

Griffith, Richard. (1997a). "Critical Issues in Records Management: Part I." *Office Systems* 14(9) (September): 40-44.

Griffith, Richard. (1997b). "Yes, They Can." *Office Systems* 14(4) (April): 41-45.

Hancock, Wayland. (1998). "Scheduling a Way to Get Rid of Your Paper." *American Agent & Broker* 70(5) (May): 12-14.

Hopkins, Kenneth. (1996). "Records Management: The Role Is Changing." *Managing Office Technology* 41(10) (October): 40-41.

Hutchens, Philip H. (1998). "Information Management and the Decisionmaker." *Records Management Quarterly* 32(4) (October): 28-30.

Hyder, Sharon, and Sanders, Robert L. (1997). "Compromise and the Art of Records Management: The Union 76 Example." *Records Management Quarterly* 31(2) (April): 45-48.

Jones, Virginia A. (1997). "Disc and That." *Office Systems* 14(4) (April): 50-52.

Motz, Arlene A. (1998). "Intranets—An Opportunity for Records Managers." *Records Management Quarterly* 32(3) (July): 14-16.

Phillips, John T. (1998). "Can Records Managers Be Automated?" *Records Management Quarterly* 32(1) (January): 63-66.

Phillips, John T., Jr. (1997). "Betting on Bar Codes." *Records Management Quarterly* 31(4) (October): 48-52.

Robles, Marcel, and Langemo, Mark. (1999). "The Funamentals of Records Management." *Office Systems* 16(1) (January): 30-36.

Vander Noot, Theodore J. (1998). "Libraries, Records Management Data Processing: An Information Handling Field." *Records Management Quarterly* 32(4) (October): 22-26.

CAROLYN H. ASHE

REINFORCEMENT THEORIES

(SEE: *Motivation*)

RESPONSIBILITY

(SEE: *Management: Authority and Responsibility*)

RETAILERS

Retailing is a type of business that sells products and services to consumers for their personal or family use. A retailer is the final business in a distribution channel that links manufacturers with consumers. Although a retailer can also be a manufacturer or a wholesaler in the distribution chain, most retailers direct their efforts to satisfying needs of ultimate consumers.

Retailing had its raw beginnings in early America with peddlers, a word that comes from the Old English "ped," which was a pack in which articles to be traded in the streets were stored. One of the earliest records of peddlers in the American colonies is of an itinerant hawker named Richard Graves, who in 1642 shouted his wares from house to house in an attempt to make a deal with whoever would listen to him.

Peddlers traveled throughout America selling their wares, and in the course of this adventure, American peddlers played a part in settling the South and Middle West because of their ability to carry materials to these sparsely populated areas. Although some peddlers had circular routes near home that they serviced each week, most were wanderers, and trips of fifteen hundred miles were not uncommon, often with fifty-pound loads strapped to their back.

Peddlers sold everything from specialized goods to specialized services. Native Americans in New York, for example, hung carved souvenir plates from their horses and traded them from settlement to settlement. Other specialist peddlers were carpenters, preachers, dentists, artists, and even breeders, who offered farmers the services of stallions and bulls for their mares and cows. But the true peddler tended to pack his back or wagon with many items, because it was more profitable to carry a large assortment of goods in anticipation of what people might want or need. Somewhere among all these items would be the famous Yankee notions, which were pins and needles, buttons, razors, brooms, books, window glass, and novelties. Most housewives put aside their "pin money" from the sale of eggs and other products in order to buy these notions, but the peddler would often offer credit or barter

WAL-MART—the largest retailer in the world.

for furs and other valuable goods with those who didn't.

Peddling was a way out of poverty from colonial days onwards, and it is surprising how many notable Americans began their careers as peddlers. Like many other frontiersmen in the nineteenth century, Abe Lincoln's father was a part-time peddler. When he moved his family from Kentucky to Illinois, he took a trunk full of notions to sell from his wagon to help offset the expense of the trip. Inventors John Fitch— inventor of the steamboat—and Thomas Edison both began as peddlers.

Countless American fortunes were amassed by men who started their business on the road across America. B.T. Babbitt, America's first soap millionaire, began by peddling his soap in upstate New York, and the company Stanley Tools was founded by a peddler.

Peddlers probably founded the first real American country stores, which are often described as primitive department stores, in remote backwoods areas during the late 1600s. American country stores enjoyed their heyday between 1820 and 1860, at a time when personal income was rising and the population was growing rapidly. Usually located in the middle of town, the country store was the hub of community activity, and it was characterized by its informality, including bare wood shelves, a hodgepodge of goods, and a porch with rocking chairs where the townspeople could sit and socialize. It has been said that the country storekeeper was all things to all men, and he was usually highly respected and self-educated. His store, with the inevitable flour, cracker. and cookie barrels near the counter, carried what was a wonderland of goods to the civilization-starved settlers; and he usually extended credit liberally. For the kids, penny candy ranging from licorice whips to all-day suckers were prominently displayed in jars atop the counter.

Country stores were far from fashionable. For more than twenty years after paper bags were invented in 1850, clerks were still wrapping most packages in brown wrapping paper, folded over and tied with a string. Trading in the stores was often conducted by barter, or "country pay" as it was called, with customers exchanging corn, wheat, rye, and flax, or articles of household manufacture such as blankets and baskets, for goods on the merchant's shelves. Homemade Indian brooms, maple syrup, barrel staves, skeins of wood, dried apples, blackberries and blueberries, churned butter, potash, and charcoal were usually used as cash crops to barter at the country store.

Abraham Lincoln clerked in a country store as a youth, and the story of young Abe walking several miles to return a penny to a customer is part of American folklore. As for P.T. Barnum, he ran a general store in Bethel, Connecticut, where he claimed he learned many a trick from country people who cheated him as adeptly as any city slicker could.

Among the founders of great modern-day American department store who operated and clerked in country stores Adam Gimbel, L.L. Hudson, Charles A. Stevens, Aaron Montgomery Ward, and Herbert Marcus should be mentioned. Some of the old country stores became grocery stores, and a few evolved into department stores.

As far as anyone knows, the first true department store arose in France in the mid-nineteenth century. The best evidence ascribes its beginnings to Bon Marche of Paris. Founded as a small shop in 1838, Bon Marche had begun to assume the proportions of a department store by the early 1850s. Even at that time, Paris had a long history as a retail and fashion center dating back to 1300, and the city was known for large stores, with up to one hundred people working in stores called The Lame Devil, The Little Sailor, and The Beautiful Farmer's Wife. Aristide Boucicaut is credited with starting Bon Marche as well as the retail concept of allowing people to come into the store and browse, with no obligation to buy. He was also the originator of the money-back guarantee, which at the time was a new concept that built up his trade substantially. In addition, he clearly

marked all his goods with fixed prices and permitted no haggling between customers and clerks.

Although Bon Marche and native country stores provided American merchants with the inspiration for creating department stores, the great majority of these department stores began as dry goods stores. Neither Bon Marche nor any of the world's early department stores would have evolved if economic conditions hadn't been favorable at the time. The American department store is largely a product of the years 1860 to 1910. More available capital during the Industrial Revolution, low taxes, and cheap labor to build and staff stores contributed to the rise of the department store in America. By the late 1860s or early 1870s, the department store had a firm foothold in America. Although the term *department store* isn't recorded in the language until 1887, the idea of separate departments in stores can be found in print at least forty years earlier.

It was also during this time that mail-order retailing began. The earliest colonists, with no manufacturers of their own, first used mail-orders to obtain supplies from the mother country. George Washington ordered goods from England and France, as did Thomas Jefferson. Benjamin Franklin has been called the father of the mail-order catalogue because in 1744 he issued a list of six hundred books he would sell by mail. Aaron Montgomery Ward thought he could eliminate the middleman by selling direct to country people by mail from offices in Chicago. In August 1872 Montgomery Ward, with capital of $1600 in savings, founded what was to become the world's first great mail-order business, soon to be challenged by Sears.

MODERN-DAY RETAILING

Over time, different types of retailers have emerged and prospered because they have attracted and maintained a significant customer base. A retail institution is a group of retailers that provide a similar retail mix designed to satisfy the needs of a specific segment of customers.

The most basic characteristic of a retailer is its retail mix, which include decisions and strategies regarding the type of merchandise sold, the price of the merchandise, the assortment of the merchandise, and the level of customer service.

The traditional general-merchandise retail stores are specialty stores, department stores, and discount stores. Since about 1970, a number of new types of general merchandise retailers have emerged and are becoming increasingly important to consumers. These include category specialists, home-improvement centers, off-price retailers, catalogue showrooms, warehouse clubs, and hypermarkets. A traditional specialty store concentrates on a limited number of complementary merchandise categories and provides a high level of service in an area typically smaller than 8000 square feet.

Department stores are retailers that carry a broad variety and deep assortment, offer considerable customer service, and are organized into separate departments for displaying merchandise. A home-improvement center is a category specialist that combines the traditional hardware store and lumberyard. It focuses on providing material and information that enable do-it-yourselvers to maintain and improve their homes. A warehouse club is a general-merchandise retailer that offers a limited merchandise assortment with little service at low prices to ultimate consumers and small businesses; stores are large and located in low-rent districts, and the goods usually include food and general merchandise. Off-price retailers offer an inconsistent assortment of brand-name, fashion-oriented soft goods at low prices, in exchange for not utilizing the manufacturer's promotional allowances, return privileges, and delayed-payment options.

A catalogue showroom is a retailer whose showroom is adjacent to its warehouse. These retailers typically specialize in hard goods such as housewares, jewelry, sporting goods, garden equipment, and consumer electronics. Catalogue showrooms can offer low prices because they minimize the cost of displaying merchandise, provide minimal service, and are located in lower-rent areas rather than regional malls.

A retail chain is a company operating multiple retail units under common ownership and usually having some centralization of decision making in defining and implementing its strategy. Some retail chains are divisions of larger corporations or holding companies. Due to scale economies and an efficient distribution system, the corporate chains can sell at lower prices. Since about 1990, there has been considerable restructuring of corporate retail chains. These restructuring activities include consolidation and focus, with consolidation of existing retail chains leaving fewer large chains and focus referring to the expertise in managing a specific retail format rather than operating as a holding company for a diverse set of retail formats.

Franchising is a contractual agreement between a franchiser and a franchisee that allows the franchisee to operate a retail outlet using a name and format developed and supported by the franchiser. Approximately one-third of all U.S. retail sales are made by franchisees. Some of the most well known franchises in America are McDonald's, Subway, and Dunkin Donuts.

The mail-order retailing of the late 1800s has developed into two types of nonstore retailing: general-merchandise and specialty catalogue retailers and direct-mail retailers. General-merchandise catalogue retailers offer a broader variety of merchandise in catalogues that are periodically mailed to their customers, while specialty catalogue retailers focus on specific categories of merchandise. Direct-mail retailers typically mail brochures and pamphlets to sell a specific product or service to customers at one point in time. Direct-mail and catalogue retailing are attractive business opportunities because a business can be started with minimal inventory and can use existing mailing lists to tailor its mailings to a targeted market.

U.S. retail sales from 1995 to 2000 exceeded $3 trillion. The total expenditure on goods sold by retailers was greater than expenditures on medical care, housing, and recreation combined. Retailing is also one of the nation's largest industries in terms of employment. More than 20 million people are employed in retailing, which is approximately 20 percent of the U.S. work force.

Wal-Mart is the largest U.S. retailer in terms of merchandise sold through stores. The list of the top twenty-five retailers includes Toys R Us, McDonald's, J.C. Penney, and Dayton Hudson. Many retail entrepreneurs are among the Forbes four hundred wealthiest people in the United States. Examples include Leslie Warner of The Limited; David Thomas, founder and owner of Wendy's; Donald Fisher of The Gap; Gary Comer of Land's End; and Thomas Monaghan of Domino's Pizza.

Currently, retailing is experiencing international expansion, with many retail organizations opening stores and expanding beyond the borders of the United States. The most commonly targeted regions are Mexico, Europe, China, and Japan. U.S. retailers have strong incentives to expand globally, because U.S. markets are saturated in terms of the number of stores, available locations, and competition. Experts believe that some American retailers have a natural advantage when competing globally due to factors including technology and the emulation of American culture abroad. However, like foreign companies entering the United States, American companies entering into these countries face specific government regulations, different cultural traditions, and a variety of languages.

Today, the success of small retailers or major retail corporations depends on how much they embrace the retailing concept. The retailing concept is a management orientation that focuses a retailer on determining its target-market needs and satisfying those needs more effectively and efficiently than its competitors. Three critical environmental factors affect retailing today:

- Competition, because each department store, specialty store, or other type of retail outlet is competing against all others for the consumer's dollar.
- Consumer demographic and lifestyle trends and the impact they will have on retail strategies.
- Needs, wants, and decision-making processes that retail consumers utilize.

Among the list of consumer trends that are greatly affecting retail sales today are the growth of the elderly population, as the baby-boomers age; the rapidly growing minority segments of the U.S. population; the importance of shopping convenience, with consumers wanting one-stop shopping; and the rising number of two-income families.

Examples of retailers using a competitive advantage to maintain their position in the marketplace at the start of the twenty-first century include Autozone, which has convenient neighborhood locations and excellent customer service. Talbot's uses unique synergies between its stores and its catalogue operation and offers private brand clothing. Starbucks, a highly regarded brand name in the coffee industry, has maintained strength and customer loyalty through providing excellent service. Gymboree offers stores with a unique ambiance to enhance their customer's shopping experience, and also offers private label merchandise with strong appeal. Finally, Speigal has developed its competitive advantage and a strong retail hold on consumers through its sophisticated information and distribution system.

BIBLIOGRAPHY

Hatch, Denny. (1998). "Eight Hundred Years Young." *Target Marketing*. (September): 21(9) 5.

Hendrickson, Robert. (1989). *The Grand Emporiums*. New York: Stein & Day/Scarborough House.

Levy, Michael, and Weitz, Barton. (1995). *Retail Management*, Boston: Irwin-McGraw Hill.

PATRICIA A. SPIROU

RETIREMENT PLANNING

(SEE: *Personal Financial Planning*)

REWARD SYSTEMS

(SEE ALSO: *Employee Benefits; Employee Compensation*)

ROBINSON-PATMAN ACT (1936)

The Robinson-Patman Act of 1936 is antitrust legislation that amends Section 2 of the Clayton Act of 1914, which was designed to prevent monopolies by catching early-stage practices leading to corporate mergers. Another provision of the Clayton Act prohibits price discrimination by a seller where the effect is to injure the competition. The Clayton Act was directed at firms that sold goods at higher prices in some areas and at lower prices in others to the detriment of a smaller local seller; it confined the prohibition on price discrimination to the impact on the seller. Thus, competition among buyers could be affected adversely when certain buyers received lower prices. The Robinson-Patman Act is not limited to just price discrimination. It also covers discrimination in the areas of advertising and other promotional programs, as well as in the area of providing services to competing customers.

Price discrimination occurs when a firm charges more than one price for good or services sold to customers and businesses where all other material aspects of the sales are the same (*Encyclopedia Dictionary of Economics*, 1986). The Robinson-Patman Act is commonly referred to as the "chain store act" because it prohibits price cutting of commodities for large buyers (chain stores, department stores, and discount houses) designed to eliminate competition from small buyers (Garman, 1997). The act makes it unlawful for any seller engaged in commerce to discriminate, directly or indirectly, in regard to the price charged to buyers of commodities of like grade and quality sold in interstate commerce for the purpose of resale.

Small businesses implied that their larger competition used their size or market power to gain lower prices from suppliers. This practice enabled the larger competitors to profitably outsell their smaller competitors. The result of this act is that smaller local buyers have restitution against a favored competitor that, because of size, efficiency, or bargaining power, could obtain lower prices from a supplier and, thus, sell products for lower prices. It became illegal for companies engaged in interstate commerce to grant discounts for the same products to large firms without granting similar discounts to smaller independent stores when the selling costs do not vary between the two. The law does permit selling at different prices when costs are based on different methods or quantities involved in the manufacture, sale, or delivery of products (Garman, 1997). The Robinson-Patman Act was intended to protect competitors as well as competition.

According to Meier and colleagues (1998), enforcing the act is a complex task. To prove a price-discrimination case, a market analysis must be conducted which shows that actual competitive injury has occurred or that the seller engaged in significant and sustained price discrimination with the intention of punishing a competitor. However, according to Garman (1997), a discriminatory price may be lawful when it is charged in good faith to meet an equally low price of a competitor.

(SEE ALSO: *Antitrust Legislation*)

BIBLIOGRAPHY

Encyclopedic Dictionary of Economics, The, 3d ed. (1986). Guilford, CT: Dushkin Publishing Group.

Garman, E. T. (1997). *Consumer Economic Issues in America*, 5th ed. Houston, TX: DAME Publications.

Meier, K., Garman, E. T., and Keiser, L. R. (1998). *Regulation and Consumer Protection: Politics, Bureaucracy and Economics*, 3d ed. Houston, TX: DAME Publications.

PHYLLIS BUNN

S

SALES DISCOUNTS

(SEE: *Pricing*)

SCARCITY

(SEE: *Supply and Demand*)

SCHOOL TO CAREER MOVEMENT

One of the purposes of education is to prepare students to become productive workers. Job skills have increased in importance as technology continues to advance. Education and other forms of training have become lifelong enterprises (Straszheim, 1997). The challenge for all levels of education is how to prepare students for a future workplace with technological requirements that may be far different from those that have been predicted. Consideration of school-to-career issues can be found at all levels of education, from elementary through undergraduate and graduate levels. Federal, state, and local governments have been actively involved in identifying and promoting the integration of occupational skills with curricula.

HISTORICAL PERSPECTIVE

The Secretary's Commission on Achieving Necessary Skills (SCANS) was formed in 1990 by the U.S. secretary of labor to investigate the skills needed by young people to succeed in the world of work. Thirty representatives of from the areas education, business, labor, and state government worked for two years to arrive at a definition of workplace know-how. The commission's initial 1991 report, *What Work Requires of Schools*, identified three foundation areas (basic skills, thinking skills, and personal qualities) and five workplace competencies (resources, interpersonal, information, systems, and technology). Successful workers need to be able to acquire and interpret all forms of data. Rote learning is inadequate in a rapidly changing information society. An overabundance of data indicates a need for workers who can efficiently locate and analyze requisite information, determine patterns, and communicate in appropriate formats to the necessary recipients. They will be required to understand and improve social, organizational, and technological systems. Successful workers need to be able to select, apply, and maintain technology. SCANS also found that a high-performance workplace requires workers with solid literacy and computational skills. Successful workers need thinking skills to apply their knowledge as well as such personal qualities as responsibility, self-management, and integrity. The SCANS foundation skills and workplace competencies provide a basis for the development of educational programs designed to foster the development of requisite workplace skills.

Legislators have considered the issue of connecting school-based learning to work-based learning. The objectives of the School-to-Work Opportunities Act of 1994 addressed the following congressional concerns:

- High school students' lack of academic and entry-level occupational skills necessary to succeed in a changing U.S. workplace

- A substantial high school dropout rate

- High youth unemployment

Of necessity, academic standards need to be connected to occupational standards in order to meet the intent of this legislation (Packer and Kane, 1994).

Since the School-to-Work Opportunities Act of 1994 became law, state and local partnerships across the country have worked with the National School-to-Work Office to refine the eight core elements essential to creating school-to-work systems in order to provide guidance to states and local partnerships as they plan and implement school-to-work systems. The eight elements, including opportunities for all youth and a core curriculum that provides a continuum of school-to-work elements, are examined in "Eight Key School-to-Work System Building Elements," (1997).

North Lake College, located in Irving, Texas, addressed curriculum applications of seven of the SCANS workplace skill areas under a grant from a 1994 partnership of the Texas Education Agency, the Texas Department of Commerce, and the Texas Higher Education Coordinating Board. One of the objectives was the application of national occupational standards to the development of technical and occupational programs. This project resulted in a model for instilling workplace skills into academic and occupational programs at the secondary, post-secondary, and apprenticeship levels. The four-phase process included occupational profiling, curriculum enhancement, faculty development, and testing and certification (The National School-To-Work Learning and Information Center, 1997).

David Douglas High School, in Portland, Oregon, has a comprehensive school-to-work sys-

tem known as STARS (Students Taking Authentic Routes to Success). One of ten schools selected in 1996 to be showcased by the U.S. Department of Education as a New American High School, David Douglas is a recognized leader in Oregon. The school has worked in partnership with the Oregon Business Council to redesign its high school program to meet the expectations of the Oregon Education Act for the 21st Century.

INITIATIVES AT ALL LEVELS

In 1993 the SCANS/2000 Program at Johns Hopkins University recognized teachers in grades 4 through 8 who taught workplace know-how through innovative projects that captured the imagination of students. The winning projects reflected five categories: microsocieties (students held jobs and paid bills while participating in a fictional community); school stores (students sold goods and services for profit); media publications (students created multimedia publications, newspapers, or stories); construction and manufacturing enterprises (students designed and assembled a product while learning academic content and work skills); and workplace-based activities (students had contact with employers and the public in actual work environments).

One of these, the Parkland School District University (PSDU) project, grew out of a fifth-grade exploration of geometry and architecture. After students learned about Thomas Jefferson's role as an architect, they designed and built a model university. Students interacted with professionals in numerous fields (architecture, landscaping, real estate, banking, engineering, drafting, law, investment, entrepreneurship, and education), eventually "assuming" these roles. Their initial sketches progressed to scale drawings, blueprints, and the final product—a 400-square-foot model of the university (PSDU). Students successfully accomplished a long-term goal while performing tasks and utilizing skills valued in the work force.

Education cones, school articulation structures to foster the development of career education in grades K-12, are used to group Utah schools. The County School District initiated the school-to-work curriculum with career awareness activities in the cone's seven elementary schools. For instance, second-grade students studying weights and measures visit local grocery stores to experience real-world applications of their learning. Junior high students examine career options and participate in shadowing and mentoring activities. High school students participate in work-based experiences, including internships and apprenticeships. These experiences are integrated with the students' school-based learning.

A growing pool of resources supports the school-to-career movement. For example, the Bureau of Labor Statistics (BLS) has dedicated a portion of the Department of Labor Educational Resources Web Site to career guidance information for elementary students http://stats.bls.gov/k12/html/edu_tch.htm. The information presented—in the format "Jobs for Kids Who Like . . ."—has been culled from *Occupational Outlook Handbook*, the bureau's publication that serves as a resource for high school juniors, seniors, and graduates.

APPRENTICESHIP

The federal government began overseeing apprenticeships after passing the National Apprenticeship Act in 1937. A Michigan program—School to Registred Apprenticeships (STRA)—connects high school students with licensed apprenticeships in skilled trades (Moorlehem, 1998). In its first year, STRA trained individuals in fifty-four schools to set up apprenticeships. The program allows students to begin working in their chosen career while still in high school. Employers pay for college courses and oversee students for four years. Local high school vocational-technical centers provide additional information on apprenticeship programs.

JUNIOR ACHIEVEMENT

Junior Achievement is a nonprofit economic education organization with K-12 programs taught by classroom volunteers from the business community. More than 2.6 million U.S. students are involved each year. Through seven curricula targeted for grades K-6, Junior Achievement programs teach basic business and economic concepts. The middle school programs build on the elementary programs, while the high school programs help students make informed decisions regarding their future ("Junior Achievement," 1998).

JOB SHADOWING

Job shadowing is a way to provide students with an understanding of career requirements and the relationship between school and careers. The Boston Private Industry Council instituted the first Groundhog Job Shadow Day in 1996 as part of its school-to-work initiatives ("Groundhog Shadow Day," 1998). In 1997 it spread throughout the Southeast when sponsored by BellSouth as part of its school-to-work efforts. More than 125,000 students participated in 1998 when national participation was promoted by a coalition of America's Promise, the National School-to-Work Opportunities Office, Junior Achievement, and the American Society of Association Executives. Students have an opportunity to visit a job site, shadow an employee, and become involved in some workplace activities.

The Lehigh Valley [Pennsylvania] Business/Education Partnership (LVBEP), one of whose goals is to promote and facilitate school-to-work learning opportunities, has worked with schools and businesses to arrange hundreds of "Shadow Days" each year ("Student Shadow Program," 1999). These experiences allow students to discuss careers with practicing professionals. It is expected that increased interest in school-to-career activities in area schools will result in shadow days numbering in the thousands. The LVBEP, in collaboration with other organizations, also sponsors an annual Senior High School Leadership Conference. Workshops at the conference address issues pertaining to becoming leaders in the twenty-first century. Other programs offered by LVBEP include:

- Koalaty Kid—students learn about total quality management principles
- Teacher internship programs

- Take N.O.T.E.S.—students learn first-hand about medical careers
- Pathways—business expertise is shared with students

Hamilton and Hamilton (1997) include job shadowing as one of eight major types of work-based learning. They divided job shadowing into three categories: (1) visits to workplaces, which include field trips and actual job shadowing; (2) work-like experiences, which include service learning, unpaid internships, and youth-run enterprises; and (3) employment, which includes youth jobs, subsidized employment training, cooperative education and paid internships, and apprenticeships. Their article. "When Is Learning Work-Based?," offers a range of options for educators to consider in developing school-to-career programs.

MENTORING

Mentoring involves an ongoing relationship between a student and an adult. Project Turn Around, developed by Progressive Learning, is an educational and mentoring program for students who do not perform well in traditional classroom situations ("Inaugural Celebration," 1999). Inaugurated in California in December 1998, this program will provide the computer technology for students in grades 7 through 12 to learn competitive job skills under the supervision of on-line mentors recruited from across the nation.

BIBLIOGRAPHY

"Eight Key School-to-Work System Building Elements." Available at http://www.stw.ed.gov/factsht/bull1197.html.

"Groundhog Shadow Day." (1998). *School To Work News* December: 35.

Hamilton, Stephen F., and Hamilton, Mary Agnes. (1997). "When Is Learning Work-Based?" *Phi Delta Kappan* May: 677-681.

"Inaugural Celebration Launches 'Project Turn Around.'" (1999). *School to Work News.* January: 1, 8.

"Junior Achievement: Teaching Kids How Business Works." (1998). *School To Work News* December 1998: 25-26.

Lehigh Valley Business/Education Partnership. http://www.regiononline.com/lvbep/stc.htm. 1998.

Moorlehem, Tracy. (1998). "Apprenticeship Program Works—Students Get Paid Well as They Learn Skilled Trade." *School To Work News.* September: 8.

National School-to-Work Learning Center. http://www.stw.ed.gov/.

Packer, Arnold. (1993). "Building Workplace Know-How." *Instructor.* September: 67-68.

Packer, Arnold H., Kane, N. (1994). "Report to the Robinson Foundation, The Sydney P. Marland Contest," SCANS/2000 Program Institute for Policy Studies, Johns Hopkins University (available at http://infinia.wpmc.jhu.edu/marland.html).

Packer, Arnold H., Pines, Marion W., Stluka, M. Frank, and Surowiec, Christine. (1996). *School-To-Work.* Princeton, NJ: Eye on Education.

SCANSLink. http://www.dcccd.edu/nlc/misc/scans/nlc.htm. November 15. 1995.

SCANS Report. "Academic Innovations." http://www.academicinnovations.com/report.html. August 14, 1998.

SCANS/2000. http://infinia.wpmc.jhu.edu/. March 21, 1998.

Stinson, Joseph. (1994). "Beyond Shop Talk." *Electronic Learning* February: 18-25.

Straszheim, Donald H. (1997). "How Technology Is Changing Society." June 28. Los Angeles, CA: Milken Institute.

"Student Shadow Program." (1999). *The Lehigh Valley Business Education Partnership In Touch* February: 1.

"Teacher's Guide to BLS Career Information." http://stats.bls.gov/k12/html/edu_tch.htm. 1998.

WINNIFRED G. BOLINSKY

SCIENTIFIC MANAGEMENT

Early attempts to study behavior in organizations came from a desire by industrial efficiency experts to answer this question: What can be done to get workers to do more work in less time? It is not surprising that attempts to answer this question were made at the beginning of the twentieth century, since this was a period of rapid industrialization and technological change in the United States. As engineers attempted to make machines more efficient, it was natural to focus efforts on the human side—making people more productive, too.

Frederick Taylor.

The scientific method of management and job design, which originated with Frederick Winslow Taylor (1856–1915), entails analyzing jobs to determine what the worker does and what the requirements are for the job. After this analysis, the job is designed to ensure that employees will not be asked to perform work beyond their abilities. Another aspect of the scientific method is that jobs are divided into small segments for the worker to perform, a method that works well in establishing expected levels of worker performance. While not as popular as in the past, this method of job design is still used today.

To Taylor, it was obvious that workers were producing below their capacities in the industrial shops of his day. As a foreman in a steel mill, Taylor noticed, for example, that laborers wasted movement when moving pig iron. Believing that productivity could be increased substantially, Taylor carefully analyzed the workers' motions and steps and studied the proper distribution of work and rest. Based on this analysis, he deter-

mined a more appropriate method for performing each aspect of the job. He then carefully selected employees and gave them detailed instructions on how to perform the job using the new method. He required that employees follow the instructions precisely. As an incentive, all workers were told that they would receive a substantial pay increase provided they followed instructions. As a result, worker productivity increased substantially.

However, most of the short-sighted management of that time would set certain standards, often paying by piece-rate for the work. Then, when a worker discovered how to produce more, management cut the rate. In turn, the workers deliberately cut down on output, but management could do nothing about this. Taylor came to realize that the concept of division of labor had to be revamped if greater productivity and efficiency were to be realized. His vision included a superefficient assembly line as part of a management system of operations. He, more than anyone else at the time, understood the inability of management to increase individual productivity, and he understood the reluctance of workers to produce at a high rate.

For more than twenty-five years, Taylor and his associates explored ways to increase productivity. Scientific management has often been described as a series of techniques for increasing production rates by means of better cost-accounting procedures, premium and incentive payments, and time and motion studies (which are designed to classify and streamline the individual movement needed to perform jobs with the intent of finding "the one best way" to do them). But Taylor himself protested this interpretation. In his view, using these techniques did not in itself constitute scientific management, because, as he put it, the main objective of scientific management was "to remove the causes for antagonism between the boss and the men who were under him." Ironically, at times during his experimentation, Taylor achieved the opposite effect by creating antagonism.

As Taylor made his techniques known, others began to contribute to the body of knowledge of scientific management. These theorists included Carl G. L. Barth, a mathematician and statistician who assisted Taylor in analytical work, and Henry L. Gantt, who invented the slide rule and created the Gantt chart. Another associate, Sanford E. Thompson, developed the first decimal stopwatch. Walter Shewhart eventually transformed industry with his statistical concepts and his ability to bridge technical tools with a management system. Frank G. and Lillian Gilbreth, aware of Taylor's work in measurement and analysis, chose the ancient craft of bricklaying for analysis. It was assumed that productivity in bricklaying certainly should have reached its peak thousands of years ago and nothing could be done to increase worker productivity. Yet the Gilbreths were able to show that, by following Taylor's techniques and using proper management planning, productivity could be raised significantly and workers would be less tired than they were under the old system.

By 1912, the efficiency movement had gained momentum. Taylor was even called before a special committee of the House of Representatives that was investigating scientific management and its impact on the railroad industry, whose members regarded it as a way to "speed up" work. Little did Taylor realize how workers would perceive his effort at producing more efficiently. Taylor found out the importance of the cooperative spirit the hard way. He was strictly the engineer at first; only after painful experiences did he realize that the human factor, the social system, and the mental attitude of people in both management and labor had to be adjusted and changed completely before greater productivity could result. He referred to his early experiences in seeking greater output and described the strained feelings between himself and his workers as "miserable." Yet he was determined to improve production. He continued his experiments until three years before his death in 1915, when he found that human motivation, not just engineered improvement, could alone increase output.

Unfortunately, the human factor was ignored by many. Shortly after the railroad hearings, self-proclaimed "efficiency experts" damaged the intent of scientific management. Time studies and the new efficiency techniques were used by incompetent "consultants" who sold managers on the idea of increasing profit by "speeding up" employees. Consequently, many labor unions, just beginning to feel their strength, worked against the new science and all efficiency approaches. With the death of Taylor in 1915, the scientific management acts movement lost, for the moment, any chance of reaching its true potential as the catalyst for the future total quality management system that was to evolve as a key ingredient of organizations of the future.

BIBLIOGRAPHY

Benton, Douglas A. (1998). *Applied Human Relations.* Upper Saddle River, NJ: Prentice-Hall.

Greenberg, Jerald. (1999). *Managing Behavior in Organizations: Science in Service to Practice.* Upper Saddle River, NJ: Prentice-Hall.

Hersey, Paul, Blanchard, Kenneth H., and Johnson, Dewey E. (1996). *Management of Organizational Behavior.* Upper Saddle River, NJ: Prentice-Hall.

Rue, Leslie W., and Byars, Lloyd L. (1990). *Supervision: Key Link to Productivity.* Homewood, IL: Irwin.

Whetten, David A., and Cameron, Kim S. (1995). *Developing Management Skills.* New York: HarperCollins.

Wray, Ralph D., Luft, Roger L., and Highland, Patrick J. (1996). *Fundamentals of Human Relations.* Cincinnati, OH: South-Western Educational Publishing.

Yukl, Gary. (1994). *Leadership in Organizations.* Englewood Cliffs, NJ: Prentice-Hall.

MARCIA ANDERSON

SEASONAL DISCOUNTS

(SEE: *Pricing*)

SECURITIES ACTS: REQUIREMENTS FOR ACCOUNTING

Companies issuing securities to the public are required to file registration reports and statements with the U.S. Securities and Exchange Commission (SEC) in accordance with the 1933 and 1934 Securities Acts. Such reports and statements are intended to provide accounting disclosure to the prospective investors. A company's first offering of securities to the public market is called an Initial Public Offering (IPO).

Registrants rely on specialists in accounting to meet the criteria of the Securities Acts. The chief accountant of the SEC is the principal accounting adviser with respect to difficult or controversial accounting issues. The office of The Chief Accountant is in charge of establishing, coordinating, and expressing SEC policy regarding Accounting and Auditing Standards. Communication is provided through the SEC Accounting Series Releases (Financial Reporting Releases).

The 1933 Securities Act requires that the registration statement be filed and accepted by the SEC before securities are initially offered for sale. The SEC does not evaluate the merit of the securities; it merely determines whether the disclosures provide sufficient information to the investment community.

The registration statement for an IPO consists of two principal components: Part I is the prospectus, an offering document to be distributed to prospective buyers; Part II contains supplemental information that is available for public inspection at the office of the SEC.

The SEC has adopted a revised framework for registration as part of the integrated disclosure system, whereby the form to be used by the registrant depends on the periodic reporting history and the nature of specific transaction events. In the case of an IPO, for example, Form S-L becomes the forepart of the registration statement and outside front cover page of the prospectus.

Disclosures on the inside front and outside back cover pages of the prospectus must provide the following information: summary of the securities offering, risk factors and the ratio of earnings to fixed charges, the use of proceeds, determination of offering price, dilution, plan of securities distribution, description of securities to be registered, and interests of named experts and counsel. The prospectus must also provide information related to the registrant, such as a description of business and property, legal proceedings, market price of equity and dividends, financial statements, supplementary financial information, executive compensation, and Management's Discussion and Analysis (MD&A).

Part II of the IPO covers other information not required in the prospectus, such as issuance- and distribution-related expenses, indemnification of directors and officers, recent sales of unregistered securities, exhibits, and financial statement schedules. An accountant's consent is required for financial information to be included in this part.

The 1934 Securities Act regulates and controls the secondary securities markets and related matters and practices. This legislation also regulates the reporting and registration forms for the financial statements and audit requirements. The principal annual report to be filed by commercial and industrial companies is Form 10-K, which covers financial statements and supplementary data.

Form 10-K also includes information about the business, properties, legal proceedings, security holder voting, Management's Discussion and Analysis regarding financial conditions and operations results, and information about the elective officers of the corporation, their compensation, and their security ownership.

The requirements for Form 10-K are set forth by SEC Regulation S-X. Under this regulation, the balance sheets at the end of each of the two latest fiscal periods, as well as the income statements and cash-flow statements for each of the three latest fiscal years, should be filed within ninety days after the end of the fiscal year. The principal executive officer, the principal financial officer, the principal accounting officer (the controller), and a majority of the board of directors must sign the Form 10-K.

Issuers of securities registered under the 1933 and 1934 Securities Acts are required to file Form 10-Q for each of the first three quarters of the fiscal year within forty-five days after the end of each of the first three fiscal quarters of each year. Form 10-Q calls for financial information, such as a condensed financial statement, and also covers the following: Management's Discussion and Analysis, financial condition and results of operations as required in Regulations S-K and S-X; and special event reports occurring during the quarter, such as legal proceedings, defaults upon senior securities, and matters to be voted by security holders. Form 10-Q may be integrated with the quarterly stockholders' report if the combined report contains full and complete answers to all items required by Part I of Form 10-Q.

The SEC Division of Corporation Finance is in charge of reviewing registration statements as well as annual and periodic reports. It establishes standards for economic and financial disclosure by determining the nature of information required in the registration statements, reports, and other documents to be filed with the SEC. In addition, it enforces provisions with respect to securities offered for sale to the public, listed for trading on securities exchanges, or traded in the over-the-counter market. The Division of Corporation Finance is organized into twelve branches of corporate analysis and examination, covering approximately forty industry groups based on standard classification codes.

Preparation of the registration statements as well as related reports and documents may take three to four months. The lengthy timetable is governed by legal considerations. All parties involved in the preparation, such as the accounting firm, attorneys, and other professionals, may be subject to civil and criminal penalties under the 1933 Securities Act for any misstatements or omissions.

The completed registration statement is submitted to the Division of Corporation Finance, where the statements are reviewed to determine whether the disclosures comply with the 1933 and 1934 Securities Acts. In cases where deficiencies are identified, the Division requests that the registrants complete or explain.

SUMMARY OF INFORMATION DISCLOSURE FORMS

The principal forms identified in this section are intended to provide a convenient point of reference when only a general understanding of their purpose is required. Accountants, after consulting the registrants, should consider whether the company meets the criteria for the use of a particular form.

The forms required by the 1933 Securities Act include: S-1 through S-3, the general forms for registration; S-4, for business combinations; S-11, for estate entities; and SB-1 and SB-2, for small businesses. Form N-1 is used for open-ended investment companies; N-2, for closed-ended investment companies; N-3 and N-4, for insurance companies offering annuity contracts; and N-5 and N-SAR, for registered international investment companies.

Under the 1934 Securities Act, the principal forms required of most registrants are 10-K and 10-KSB, with the latter appropriate for small businesses. Other forms include 11-K, for employee stock purchase or employee option plans; 10-Q, for quarterly reports; 8-K, for certain significant corporate events reported immediately after the month in which event occurred; and 15, to terminate registration.

DISCLOSURES BY FOREIGN CORPORATIONS

As a general rule, a foreign company intending to offer securities in the United States qualifies as a foreign private issuer, unless (1) more than 50 percent of its outstanding voting securities are held by U.S. residents and (2) either the majority of its executive officers are U.S. citizens or residents, or its business is administered or located in the United States.

Under Regulation S-X, foreign issuers are required to provide disclosures under U.S. generally accepted accounting principles (GAAPs). SEC Accounting Bulletin 88 (SAB 88) allows the foreign issuer to include U.S. GAAP disclosures in Management's Discussion and Analysis for information that is not required under its home-country GAAPs.

Form 20-F is the form most commonly used for the registration statement and for annual reporting. Foreign issuers are also required to furnish reports on Form 6-K instead of Forms 10-Q and 8-K, which are applicable to U.S. issuers.

For Canadian companies, Form 40-F has been adapted as part of the Multijurisdictional Disclosure System. Canadian firms may qualify to use Forms F-1, F-2, or F-3 for registering securities under the 1933 Securities Act, instead of the S-1, S-2, and S-3 forms applicable to U.S. companies. The SEC staff allows Canadian issuers to file on U.S. domestic forms (e.g., Form 10-K or 10-Q) prepared in accordance with Canadian GAAP's, as long as the requirements of Form 20-F are satisfied.

All forms described here are subject to change, so be certain to check with the SEC to keep current on reporting requirements.

(SEE ALSO: *Securities and Exchange Commision*)

BIBLIOGRAPHY

Murray, R. J., Decker, Jr., W. E., and Ditmar, Jr., N. W. (1998). *The Coopers & Lybrand SEC Manual*, 6th ed., Englewood Cliffs, NJ: Prentice-Hall.

Strategies for Going Public. (1998). New York: Deloitte Touche Tohmatsu International.

SAMIR FAHMY
LAURENCE MAUER

SECURITIES AND EXCHANGE COMMISSION

The Securities and Exchange Commission (SEC) is a regulatory agency responsible for administering the U.S. laws regarding securities. The purpose of these laws is to ensure fair markets and to provide accurate information to investors. The major securities laws were enacted in the 1930s after the 1929 stock market crash and the anemic performance of the market in the early 1930s.

Congress passed the Securities Act of 1933 to regulate the primary market—the market for new securities. Sometimes called the "truth in issuance act," the 1933 act required a company to submit independently verified financial information, a registration statement, and a prospectus to the Federal Trade Commission.

The Securities and Exchange Act of 1934 created the Securities Exchange Commission, giving it the power to regulate the stock exchanges and the trading practices of the secondary market (a market for currently traded shares). In 1935 the Public Utility Holding Company Act was enacted to regulate all interstate holding companies (a holding company controls other companies by owning their stock) in the utility business.

In 1940 Congress passed two laws covering the people working in the security business. The Investment Company Act of 1940 provided for the regulation of investment companies, including those involved with mutual funds. The Investment Advisers Act of 1940 established regulation of investment advisers and their activities. In 1974 the Employee Retirement Income Security Act gave the SEC jurisdiction over pension funds. Other legislation addressed foreign activities, insider trading, and further clarification of existing legislation.

The SEC consists of five commissioners who are appointed by the president, only three of whom can be from the same political party. Terms are staggered; thus, each June 5, a person rotates off the Commission. To accomplish their duties, the commissioners have office staffs of accountants and lawyers and regional offices in eleven cities.

The organizational structure of the SEC includes eight divisions. The Division of Corporate Finance is responsible for reviewing registration statements, tender offers, and mergers and acquisitions. Overseeing the markets and the market participants is the duty of the Division of Market Regulation. The Division of Investment Management is responsible for the enforcement of three statutes: the Investment Company Act of 1940, the Investment Advisers Act of 1940, and the Public Utility Holding Company Act of 1935. The Division of Enforcement is the investigating arm of the SEC. The Office of Compliance, Inspections, and Examinations determines whether all investment organizations are in compliance with federal securities laws. The remaining divisions' duties are defined by their titles: the Office of General Counsel, the Office of Municipal Securities, and the Office of Investor Education and Assistance.

In enforcing the securities laws, the SEC acts as a guide and adviser whose actions are largely remedial. One common activity of each division is rulemaking. New rules and rule modifications are usually accomplished in open meetings. Those industries or parties affected by rule changes are allowed to present their positions and make comments in an open meeting. Any SEC investigations are conducted by the Division of Enforcement and the field offices. If the evidence indicates a violation, the SEC can take administrative action (such as suspension) or instigate a civil action in an U.S. District Court. If evidence indicates a criminal action, the SEC turns the case over to the Justice Department.

More information is available from the U.S. Securities and Exchange Commission, 450 Fifth St. NW, Washington, D.C. 20549; (202) 942-7114; or www.sec.gov.

BIBLIOGRAPHY

Hirt, Geoggrey A., and Block, Stanley, B. *Fundamentals of Investment Management*, 4th ed. Irwin Publishing.

Levy, Haim. (1996). *Introduction to Investments*. Southwestern College Publishing.

SEC. http://www.sec.gov/asec.

SEC Enforcement Division. http://www.sec.gov/enforce.

Securities and Exchange Commission (SEC). "Current SEC Rulemakers." Archived at: http://www.sec.gov/rulemake.

MARY JEAN LUSH
VAL HINTON

SELF-SERVICE SELLING

(SEE: *Promotion*)

SERVICE INDUSTRIES

From cutting the grass to providing health care to delivering packages, service industries in the United States play an integral part in the daily activities of millions of people and businesses. These services may offer an improved standard of living, professional and technical expertise, or other essential services. The providers of such services involve all sectors of the economy including for-profit private businesses, non-profit organizations and various levels of government.

WHAT ARE SERVICE INDUSTRIES?

The U.S. Department of Commerce's Bureau of Economic Analysis (BEA) measures total national output in terms of Gross National Product (GNP). In measuring output, the BEA also identifies the industry sources of GNP. The BEA broadly defines service industries as those providing products that cannot be stored and are consumed at the place and time of purchase. Generally, these services involve only the performance of actions on behalf of the customer and have little, if any, tangible substance. For example, a theater company staging a play or musical sells customers tickets allowing them to view the theatrical event. Upon completion of the performance, the customers leave with little more than their memory of the actors performing their roles. In some instances, however, the services provided may involve the receipt of a tangible product by the customer. In this instance, the BEA requires that such products contribute minimally to the total cost of the service. An example of this is an automobile service station performing a routine oil change on a car. As part of this service, new oil and an oil filter are provided to the customer.

While some service industry companies such as housekeeping and landscaping contractors sell convenience to their customers, other service industry companies sell professional and technical expertise. Such is the case with tax accountants, who annually complete millions of federal and state tax forms on behalf of their clients. Their clients do not pay for the tax forms that are

U.S. Gross National Product and Service Industry Product

BILLIONS OF DOLLARS

Year	GNP	Service Industry	Service Industry as a Percentage of GNP
1960	$529.8	$206.8	39.0%
1970	$1,042.0	$458.5	44.0%
1980	$2,819.5	$1,274.1	45.2%
1990	$5,764.9	$3,016.9	52.3%
1997	$8,102.9	$4,414.1	54.4%

Table 1

SOURCE: U.S. Department of Commerce, Bureau of Economic Analysis.

Total U.S. Employment, Service Industry Employment, 1986, 1996, and Projections for 2006

THOUSANDS OF JOBS

Year	Total Employment	Service Industry Employment	Service Industry as a Percentage of Total
1986	111,374	74,189	66.6%
1996	132,352	94,300	71.2%
2006	150,927	111,867	74.1%

Table 2

SOURCE: U.S. Department of Labor, Bureau of Labor Statistics.

available at no extra cost from the taxing authorities but for the correct completion of such forms. The tax accountant uses client provided information to complete the forms and to determine the client's taxes, applying knowledge of the ever-changing tax laws.

ECONOMIC IMPORTANCE

The service industries have and continue to play an important role in the U.S. economy. In terms of productivity, the proportion of the U.S. GNP attributed to service industries has consistently trended upward. As illustrated in Table 1, service industries in 1960 accounted for 39 percent of the U.S. GNP. By 1980, this percentage increased to over 45 percent. In 1997, more than 55 percent of the $8.1 trillion U.S. GNP was attributed to productivity in the service industries.

While the vital role of the service industries to the U.S. economy is evident in their proportion of GNP, their importance is magnified by their contribution to the total employment in the U.S. labor market. As illustrated in Table 2, according to data published in 1997 by the U.S. Department of Labor's Bureau of Labor Statistics (BLS). service industries in 1986 were responsible for two-thirds of total U.S. employment. By 1996, the proportion of the total U.S. employment at-

tributed to service industries rose to more than 70 percent. In 1997, the BLS forecasted service industries would be responsible for virtually all job growth between 1996 and 2006 and would account for nearly 75 percent of total U.S. employment by 2006.

As illustrated in Table 3, the BLS projected that between 1996 and 2006 the ten U.S. industries with the greatest percentage increase in employment would be service industries.

SERVICE INDUSTRY PROVIDERS

Services available within the United States are provided by all three sectors of the economy: for-profit businesses; non-profit organizations; and the government. For-profit businesses provide the largest proportion of all services and account for the greatest number of jobs. The government provides the second largest proportion of services and jobs followed by non-profit organizations.

The profitability of the service and the issue of whether the service benefits non-paying third parties or the community are factors that determine which of the three sectors of the economy provide a particular service. By their very nature, for-profit businesses offer those services that can be profitably produced and avoid services that benefit non-paying third parties. The types of services for-profit businesses provide are numerous and cover a broad array of service categories.

The 10 Industries having Highest Projected Employment Growth, 1996 – 2006

EMPLOYMENT IN THOUSANDS OF JOBS

Industry	Employment		Percentage Change, 1996–2006
	1996	2006	
Computer and Data Processing Service	1,208	2,509	108%
Health Services	1,172	1,968	68%
Management and Public Relations	873	1,400	60%
Miscellaneous Transportation Services	204	327	60%
Residential Care	672	1,070	59%
Personnel Supply Services	2,626	4,039	53%
Water and Sanitation	231	349	51%
Individual and Miscellaneous Social Services	846	1,266	50%
Offices of Health Practitioners	2,751	4,046	47%
Amusement and Recreation Services	1,109	1,565	41%

Table 3

SOURCE: U.S. Department of Labor, Bureau of Labor Statistics.

Some examples include residential, amusement and recreational, financial, and professional consulting services.

The government provides services that offer both tax paying and non-tax paying members of society substantial benefits such as national defense and public education. Another example is governmental regulatory agencies such as the Food and Drug Administration, which ensures the quality of products to be consumed by the public. Society has chosen the government to provide such vitally important services rather than risk inadequate provision by businesses or other organizations. In other service areas, for-profit businesses may not always be self-policing.

Non-profit organizations provide services that improve the overall well-being of society that businesses cannot profitably produce or the gov-ernment cannot adequately supply. Examples of this are non-profit organizations that offer educational and recreational programs for inner city youth and non-profit hospitals that provide health-related services to all persons regardless of their ability to pay.

SERVICE INDUSTRY CATEGORIES

Services industries in the United States vary substantially based upon the nature of the service they provide and the customers they serve. In general, the classifications of service industries include business and office, health care, residential care, amusement and recreation, financial, automotive, and educational services.

Within the broad classification of the business and office services industry are those offering services designed to enhance the productivity and profitability of their business clientele. For example, computer and data processing services offer products that improve their clients' processing of paperwork. Management services advise clients on the best management practices. Employment and personnel services assist clients in locating qualified job candidates and provide flexibility without altering their work force. As illustrated in Table 3, several business and office service industries are projected to be among the fastest growing industries beyond the year 2000.

As the life expectancy of Americans continues to grow, so too does the need for health professionals such as physicians and nurses as well as health related services such as nursing homes or in-home health care. During the 1990s, the health care service industry experienced substantial growth, and as Table 3 indicates, the industry is projected to experience substantial growth through the year 2006.

The residential care industry is another area that has experienced substantial growth and is expected, as illustrated in Table 3, to continue to do so beyond the year 2000. The expansion in the residential care industry is caused in part by the growing number of two-income families having limited leisure time. As a result, they employ residential care services to take care of tasks such as lawn-care and house-cleaning.

Amusement and recreation is another service industry that continues to grow at a rapid pace. With disposable income on the rise, Americans are increasing their spending on various forms of amusement such as movies, live theatre, and theme parks. Furthermore, recreational services are expanding as Americans enjoy more active lifestyles, joining health clubs and other sports-related clubs.

The financial services industry includes investment banks, security brokerages, insurance companies, and banking institutions. They provide a broad array of products such as investment counseling. During the 1990s, the financial service industry experienced substantial consolidation as many banks merged with other traditional banks, investment banks, and insurance companies to form multi-function financial institutions.

The automobile service industry maintains and repairs automobiles. It has become increasingly important as the rising cost of new automobiles necessitates maintaining presently owned vehicles for longer periods of time. Furthermore, given the increasing level of technology built into automobiles, even the most basic vehicle maintenance requires work by skilled automotive service technicians.

The educational service industry consists primarily of school based education offered by both public and private institutions. However, increasingly important are also educational institutions that cater to the needs of corporate clientele. These institutions offer corporate training in a variety of areas such as computer technology and foreign languages.

BIBLIOGRAPHY

Boustead, Thomas. (1997). "The U.S. Economy to 2006." *Monthly Labor Review* November: 6-22.

Bowman, Charles. (1997). "BLS Projections to 2006—A Summary." *Monthly Labor Review* November: 3-5.

The Economic Report of the President. (1999). Washington, DC: U.S. Government Printing Office.

Franklin, James C. (1997). "Industry Output and Employment Projections to 2006." *Monthly Labor Review* November: 39-57.

National Income and Product Accounts of the United States, 1929-94. Volume 1. (1998). Washington DC: U.S. Department of Commerce.

Silvestri, George T. (1997). "Occupational Employment Projections to 2006." *Monthly Labor Review* November: 58-83.

Yuskavage, Robert E. (1996). "Improved Estimates of Gross Product by Industry, 1959-94." *Survey of Current Business* August: 133-155.

ALAN G. KRABBENHOFT

SEXUAL HARASSMENT

Sexual harassment is a form of sex discrimination that violates Title VII of the Civil Rights Act of 1964, as amended. It is defined by the Equal Employment Opportunity Commission as unwelcome sexual advances, requests for sexual favors, and other verbal or physical conduct of a sexual nature when submission to or rejection of this conduct (1) explicitly or implicitly affects an individual's employment, (2) unreasonably interferes with an individual's work performance, or (3) creates an intimidating, hostile, or offensive work environment. U.S. law recognizes two types of sexual harassment. The first is termed *quid pro quo*, Latin for "this for that," implying a trade involving sex (e.g., a supervisor offering a subordinate a promotion in exchange for sexual favors or denying a job benefit because of refusal of the supervisor's advances). The second type is "hostile environment" harassment, which is less blatant and harder to define. This occurs when an employee is placed in an uncomfortable or threatening environment due to unwelcome sexual behavior in the workplace. Examples of hostile environment situations include telling jokes or stories of a sexual nature; unwelcome touching, such as patting or hugging; displaying suggestive or sexually explicit photographs, posters, or calendars; or making suggestive facial expressions or gestures.

HISTORY

As a practice, sexual harassment is certainly not new; accounts of women and men placing their

Anita Hill testifies before the Senate.

livelihoods at risk if they did not submit to some sort of sexual activity—from the playful to the criminal—can be found throughout history. However, the term itself is relatively new in American culture, entering the language as recently as 1975. The legal foundation for objecting to sexual harassment was laid in 1964 in Title VII of the Civil Rights Act, which prohibited employment discrimination because of an individual's sex as well as race, color, religion, or national origin. Still, although sex discrimination was illegal, there was no real guidance in existence with regard to sexual harassment. It was not mentioned specifically anywhere in the Civil Rights Act, nor was it found in the fair employment practices statutes enacted in most of the states. When the courts ruled on the issue, they typically saw it as a sort of personal dispute between employee and harasser not covered by law. Largely as a result of the issue's being raised and publicized by women's groups during the early 1970s, the Office of Personnel Management issued guidance in 1980 defining sexual harassment and warning that such conduct was unacceptable in the federal workplace. Still, the new guidelines had no legal enforcement avenues available. Action by the Equal Employment Opportunity Commission in 1980 attempted to remedy this by declaring that it was illegal to sexually harass someone on the job. By this time, sexual harassment had been the subject of several court cases but had not drawn national attention.

KEY EVENTS

The Supreme Court decided its first sexual harassment case in 1986 in *Meritor Savings Bank v. Vinson* with a unanimous landmark ruling that did three important things: confirmed that Title VII outlawed sexual harassment; defined *quid pro quo* harassment; and, finally, added the concept of hostile environmental abuse. The ruling also cautioned that employers have a responsibility for guarding against harassment. *Vinson* was significant in that this was the first time the Court recognized a cause of action for sexual harassment based on creation of the "hostile work environment," in contrast to earlier *quid pro quo* cases in which the demand for sexual favors was at issue. *Vinson* caused employers nationwide to relook at personnel policies and practices with regard to sexual harassment as newly defined.

Many felt that *Vinson* did not go far enough with regard to employer liability, while others felt it criminalized what they saw as harmless humor and friendly flirtation. As this debate continued, largely in the workplaces and courtrooms of the nation, two events occurred: one involving the U.S. military and the other the confirmation of a Supreme Court justice. These events brought the topic of sexual harassment into the national spotlight. In 1991, the Navy's Tailhook scandal captured the nation's attention with reports that female naval officers had been assaulted in a hallway "gauntlet" by their fellow officers during the annual convention of naval aviators held in Las Vegas. Lieutenant Paula Coughlin complained officially to her superiors of her fellow officers' behavior, only to see her complaints initially ignored. She then went public with her story, prompting other female naval officers to do the same. The Tailhook scandal resulted in a number of administrative actions against naval officers, early retirements of some of the Navy's highest officials, and the forced resignation of the Secretary of Navy.

Perhaps the most significant event to make sexual harassment the topic of national debate was the revelation in 1992 that Supreme Court nominee Clarence Thomas had, a decade earlier, allegedly sexually harassed a former employee of his at the Equal Employment Opportunity Commission (EEOC). Anita Hill, a professor at the University of Oklahoma's Law School at the time of Thomas's nomination, had been contacted by Senate staffers regarding a rumor regarding such allegations. Hill indicated that Thomas had repeatedly discussed sexual matters with her in a suggestive and humiliating manner while he was her superior at the EEOC. When the majority of the U.S. Senate appeared ready to confirm Thomas without an airing of the charges, American women protested and effectively stopped the proceedings until the accusations could be examined. The ensuing testimony in Senate hearings by both Hill and Thomas started a firestorm of controversy throughout the nation. Many working women began to speak out of their own experiences and, within days of the hearings, the number of sexual harassment complaints filed with government agencies quadrupled. Ultimately, Thomas was confirmed for the Supreme Court; however, the controversy had the lasting effect of bringing the issue of sexual harassment out of the dark into the light of legal and political debate.

AMENDMENTS TO THE LAW AND COURT DECISIONS

The Civil Rights Act of 1991 expanded the rights of the complainant, allowing individuals who file actions under the law to collect up to $300,000 in compensatory and punitive damages. Also, in the years following the passing of this law, many states tightened sexual harassment laws and added measures to protect victims from reprisal.

In recent years, Supreme Court decisions on sexual harassment have focused more and more on the application of common sense to the particular situation (i.e., looking at the situation as a "reasonable" person would). In 1993, in its decision in *Harris v. Forklift Systems, Inc.*, the Court established the standard and perspective for evaluating whether or not a particular conduct is unlawful harassment. The Court ruled unanimously that while psychological harm may be taken in account in evaluating whether sexual harassment occurred, it is not a requirement in a claim. Conversely, the decision also held that the mere utterance of an offensive statement would not normally constitute a violation of the law.

The following Supreme Court decisions, all issued in 1998, are considered among the most significant in defining sexual harassment law: First, in *Burlington Industries, Inc. v. Ellerth*, the complainant showed that although she was subjected to offensive, vulgar behavior, she had not suffered in any manner relating to her employment situation. In fact, she had been promoted at the company prior to her resignation. The Court ruled that harassment is defined by the behavior of the harasser, not by what subsequently happens to a worker. Another key portion of this decision and that of another case, *Faragher v. Boca Raton*, addressed employer liability with regard to hostile environment harassment and the employee's responsibility to report the offense to someone with decision-making authority. *Faragher* involved a female lifeguard who had claimed she had endured repeated sexual harassment from her male supervisors yet had not formally complained due to her fear of retaliation. During the course of the litigation, it was shown that although Faragher's employer, the city of Boca Raton, Florida, had a sexual harassment policy, it was unknown to both the complainant and her supervisors. The Court indicated that an employer could defend itself successfully if it could prove that it had a known, effective policy against harassment and that the employee had failed to take advantage of it.

In another ruling, *Oncale v. Sundowner Offshore Services, Inc.*, employer liability for sexual harassment between members of the same sex was clearly defined. The case arose out of a suit filed by an oil platform worker who had been subjected to humiliating, sex-related acts by two supervisors and a fellow crew member. The Court unanimously declared that sexual harassment is actionable (i.e., liability can be found) even when the people involved are of the same sex. A key point articulated in the decision was that what mattered was the conduct at issue rather than the sex of the individuals involved or the presence or absence of sexual desire.

POSSIBLE SOLUTIONS

Prior to the *Farragher* and *Ellerth* decisions, the courts decided liability of employers by focusing their attention chiefly on actions taken after an employee complained of harassment. In more recent decisions, the courts are also taking into consideration the steps that employers have taken before claims are filed, including whether or not they have a good sexual harassment policy in place. Such actions by the courts clearly show that prevention remains the best remedy for sexual harassment. The following strategies are recommended by various legal and human resources experts for employers who wish to make their workplaces sexual harassment-free: (1) Have a written state-of-the-art policy on sexual harassment that explains, in easy-to-understand terms, the types of prohibited behavior. Prior to issuance, get a legal review of the policy. Assure that the policy is posted as well as disseminated to all supervisors and employees, preferably at least on an annual basis. (2) Commit to the policy at the highest levels. Assure that employees see this issue as a matter of importance to the company's top managers and all levels of supervision. (3) Develop an internal complaint process that assures confidentiality and has multiple points of access, not just the employee's supervisor. Assure that there are management-level personnel of both sexes available to those who wish to complain. While the Supreme Court did not mandate that employers provide complaint procedures, it did hold that employers may escape liability if they have a complaint process in place and em-

ployees fail to use it. (4) Investigate complaints promptly and thoroughly, maintaining confidentiality as much as possible. Assure swift action to investigate; courts have found companies liable for sexual harassment in part because they took too long to conduct the investigation. Assure that employees complaining or providing information in an investigation are not retaliated against. (5) Conduct high-quality training, including refresher training, for employees, managers, and supervisors on anti-discrimination and anti-sexual harassment policies and practices. Assure that the training covers responsibilities of members of each of these groups regarding the company's sexual harassment policy and complaint procedures. Keep records of such training as tangible evidence of the company's good faith efforts to eliminate sexual harassment. (6) Conduct physical assessments of work areas such as factory floors, warehouses, and remote offices. Often potential problems such as inappropriate posters or cartoon clippings can be identified. (7) Take deliberate, decisive action when the sexual harassment policy is violated. Assure that there is a solid legal basis for the actions proposed. The unjustly accused harasser, as well as the accuser, is a potential plaintiff.

BIBLIOGRAPHY

Barrier, Michael. (1998). "Sexual Harassment." *Nation's Business* December:14-19.

Boo, Katherine. "Universal Soldier: What Paula Coughlin Can Teach American Women." *Washington Monthly*. http://web-cr05.pbs.org/wgbh/pages/frontline/shows/navy/tailhook/debate.html. September 1992.

Cangelosi, Joe, Gatlin-Watts, Rebecca W., and Moore, Herff L. (1998). "Eight Steps to a Sexual Harassment Free Workplace." *Training and Development* April: 12-13.

Debevoise, Kate S., and Tselikis, Penny. (1998). "Sexual Harassment—Still the Hottest Workplace Issue." *Business and Health* May: 19-20.

Eskenazi, Martin, and Gallen, David. (1992). *Sexual Harassment—Know Your Rights*. New York: Carroll & Graf.

Ganzel, Rebecca. (1998). "What Sexual Harassment Training Really Prevents." *Training* October: 86-94.

Heerman, Max, and Raphan, Melissa. (1997). "Eight Steps to Harassment-Proof Your Office." *HRFocus* August: 11-12.

Laabs, Jennifer. (1998). "What You're Liable for Now." *Workforce* October: 34-42.

Lavelle, Marianne. (1998). "The New Rules of Sexual Harassment." *U.S. News and World Report* July 6, 1998: 30-31.

Petrocelli, William, and Repa, Barbara Kate. (1999). *Sexual Harassment on the Job*, rev. ed. Berkeley, CA: Nolo Press.

Phelps, Timothy M., and Winternitz, Helen. (1992). *Capitol Games.* New York: Hyperion.

Segal, Jonathan A. (1998). "Prevent Now or Pay Later." *HRMagazine* October: 145-149.

Van Hyning, Memory. (1993). *Crossed Signals—How to Say No to Sexual Harassment.* Los Angeles: Infotrends Press.

Webb, Susan L. (1991). *Step Forward: Sexual Harassment in the Workplace: What You Need to Know.* New York: MasterMedia.

CLARICE P. BRANTLEY
RITA SHAW RONE

SHERMAN ANTITRUST ACT OF 1890

The Sherman Antitrust Act of 1890, the first and most significant of the U.S. antitrust laws, outlawed trusts and prohibited "illegal" monopolies. The act applies to both domestic companies and foreign companies doing business in the United States. A trust is a relationship between businesses that collaborate through anticompetitive agreements to gain market dominance. Trusts cut prices to drive competitors out of business. "Illegal" monopolies are those that can be shown to use their power to suppress competition. A monopolist has the power to dominate markets—the ability to set the price by altering supply. Anticompetitive techniques include:

- Buying out competitors
- Forcing customers to sign long-term agreements
- Forcing customers to buy unwanted products in order to receive other goods ("Understanding Antitrust Law," 1999)

Through the passage of the Sherman Antitrust Act, Congress provided safeguards to prevent firms from merging with other firms if the effect was to substantially lessen competition and create monopolies.

J.P. Morgan.

The Federal Trade Commission (FTC) and the Antitrust Division of the Department of Justice enforce antitrust laws. The FTC has the power to temporarily stop companies from employing suspected anticompetitive practices, while the Justice Department probes and prosecutes businesses. Blake (1984) wrote that the Supreme Court, as ultimate judicial arbiter of the Sherman Antitrust Act, has interpreted the act as "a comprehensive charter of economic liberty aimed at preserving free and unfettered competition as a rule of trade." It is based on the premise that "the unrestrained interaction of competitive forces will yield the best allocation of our economic resources . . . while at the same time providing an environment conducive to the preservation of our democratic political and social institutions" (p. 253).

The act was passed in response to strong and widespread political pressure to deal with "the trust problem" that reached a peak during the presidential election campaign of 1888. The trusts were corporate holding companies that, by 1888, had consolidated a very large share of U.S. manufacturing and mining industries into nationwide monopolies. Some of the most notorious corporate holding companies were the sugar trust, John D. Rockefeller's oil trust, and J. P. Morgan's steel trust. The original legal form of these organizations had been as business trusts. The Sherman Act made trusts and those who violated the act subject to civil remedies and criminal penalties in actions by the Department of Justice and to treble damages in private suits. The act was broad, providing few standards, which meant the executive branch and federal courts had to resolve the trust issues. The Sherman Antitrust Act of 1890 was revised by the Clayton Antitrust Act of 1914, which was designed to catch early-stage practices that were thought to lead to monopolies, such as corporate mergers and acquisitions, price discrimination, typing agreements, and interlocking directorships. Other antitrust acts followed, including the Federal Trade Commission Act of 1914, the Robinson-Patman Act of 1936, and the Celler-Kefauver Act of 1950.

Consequences of being found guilty of antitrust activity and being a monopoly are a fine not exceeding $10 million if a corporation or $350,000 if person or by imprisonment not exceeding three years, or by both punishments, at the discretion of the court. Furthermore, the court can require breakup of the company and other consequences based on individual cases.

Today in the United States monopolistic power means that a business has the power to raise prices above competitive levels. This typically occurs when an organization has exclusive control over a commercial activity, such as the production or selling of a commodity or service, and thus has the power to fix prices unilaterally because it has no effective competition. Significant antitrust litigation has included the following:

- 1911, American Tobacco—broken up into separate companies

- 1911, Standard Oil—broken up into separate oil-refining and pipeline companies
- 1920, U.S. Steel—no illegal monopoly found
- 1982, IBM—accused of being an illegal monopoly; case dropped
- 1983, AT&T—accused of being an illegal monopoly; broken up into one long-distance and seven "Baby Bell" local phone companies
- 1998, Microsoft—accused of using monopoly power to sell other products; as of February, 2000, penalties had not been set
- 1999, Intel—accused of severing business ties with customers who sue it; penalties varied depending on customers bringing litigation

(SEE ALSO: *Antitrust Legislation*)

BIBLIOGRAPHY

Blake, H. M. (1984). "Sherman Act." *The Guide to American Law*, ed. E. W. Kinter (pp. 251-254). St. Paul: West Publishing Company.

"FTC Approves Intel Deal." *The Washington Post*. www.washingtonpost.com. March 6, 2000.

Garman, E. T. (1997). *Consumer Economics Issues in America*, 5th ed. Houston, TX: DAME Publications.

"Microsoft Judge Focuses on Browser." *The Washington Post*. www.washingtonpost.com. March 6, 2000.

"Understanding Antitrust Law: Sherman Antitrust Act." *The Macon Telegraph*. http://www.maconel.com/special/atrust/html/l.htm. March 11. 1999.

PHYLLIS BUNN

SHOPLIFTING

(SEE: *Crime and Fraud*)

SHOPPING

Shopping involves the purchasing of products by consumers, all of which fall into various shopping product categories that are based on the way consumers think of them and purchase them. The two main categories are convenience goods and shopping goods; two lesser categories are specialty items and unsought goods. Although most shopping products are sold in stores, such as retail, grocery, and specialty stores, some consumer purchases are made through other means, such as catalogue shopping, telemarketing and on-line purchasing (also known as cybershopping). Cybershopping on the Internet is the latest trend in consumer shopping; it is estimated that $300 billion worth of on-line purchases will be made in the first decade of the twenty-first century.

CONVENIENCE GOODS

Convenience goods are goods that consumers purchase frequently, immediately, and with minimal effort. People do not spend a large amount of time shopping for convenience items. They are usually purchases made routinely, such as buying groceries on a weekly basis, or habitually, such as purchasing a daily newspaper. Convenience products include common staples, such as milk and bread. Some convenience goods, however, are not purchased routinely or habitually; they are bought on impulse, such as an ice cream cone on a summer day. Many impulse items are displayed in a manner that encourages quick choice and purchase, such as the candy, magazines, and batteries that are routinely placed near the cash register at check-out counters. Other convenience products may be purchased as emergency items, when the consumers feel there is an urgent need—such as buying candles, water, or shovels when preparing for a storm. Convenience products can be found in stores such as supermarkets, convenience stores, and department stores.

SHOPPING GOODS

Shopping goods are items consumers will conduct a search for in order to find the one that best suits their needs. They usually require an involved selection process. When purchasing a shopping product, consumers will compare a variety of attributes, such as suitability, quality, price, and style. Automobiles are often bought this way. Consumers may also visit a number of shopping places, such as retail stores, before they make a decision. Because of the importance of these types of purchases, consumers usually invest considerable time and energy before making such a purchase.

Shopping products are broken down into two categories: homogeneous and heterogeneous. Homogeneous shopping goods are those that are similar in quality but different in other characteristics. This difference in characteristics is sufficient for the customer to justify a search for the item. Items that are thought of as homogeneous, or the same, would include television sets, various home appliances, or automobiles. Homogeneous shopping goods are also often evaluated on price. After the consumer has decided on desired characteristics, he or she then looks for the most favorable price.

Heterogeneous shopping goods have product features that are often more important to consumers than price; examples include clothing, high-tech equipment, and furniture. The item purchased must meet certain consumer-set criteria, such as size, color, or specific functions performed. When buying heterogeneous shopping goods, consumers often seek out information and advice from salespeople and other experts before purchasing the item. The seller or retailer of heterogeneous shopping goods needs to carry a sufficient variety of the products to suit individual tastes and also needs well-trained salespeople to inform and advise consumers.

SPECIALTY ITEMS

Specialty items have characteristics that impel consumers to make special efforts to find them. Consumers often do not consider price at all when shopping for specialty products, which can include almost any kind of shopping product: Particular types of food, expensive imported cars, or items from a well-known fashion designer or manufacturer can all be considered specialty goods. Usually, specialty goods have a brand name or other type of distinguishing characteristic. Shopping goods are often classified as specialty products based on the location and need of the consumer; for example, some olive oils or wines may be a convenience product in Italy but a specialty product in the United States. Consumers who favor specialty products may travel considerable distances to purchase a particular item. These types of shopping products can often be found in specialty stores, which carry a large assortment within a small line of goods. An example would be a store that carries only candy, but many different types of candy. Other types of specialty stores include bookstores and sporting goods stores.

Unsought Goods. Unsought goods are products that consumers do not want, use, or even think about purchasing. An unsought shopping good could be a product that a consumer may not even know about—or knows about but has never considered purchasing. In addition, consumers often put off purchasing unsought shopping goods because they do not consider them to be important. Unsought shopping goods are frequently brought to customers' attention through advertising, promotions, or chance. Sometimes they are something new on the market, such as digital telephones. At other times they are fairly standard services that some consumers would not bother shopping for, such as life insurance.

BIBLIOGRAPHY

"Council of Better Business Bureau." *Better Business Bureau Online.* http://www.bbb.org. June 2000.

Encyclopedia Britannica.. Britannica.com. May 2000.

Heinzl, John. "Year in Review 1998." (2000). *Internet Retailing.* June.

AUDREY E. LANGILL

SHORTAGES

(SEE: *Supply and Demand*)

SHRINKAGE

(SEE: *Inventory Control*)

SILENT SPRING

(SEE: *Social Responsibility and Organizational Ethics*)

SINGLE AUDIT ACT

The Single Audit Act of 1984 (Public Law 98-502) was passed by Congress to improve auditing and management for federal funds provided to state and local governments. These funds may include grants, contracts, loans, loan guarantees, property, cooperative agreements, interest subsidies, insurance, and direct appropriations from a number of federal agencies. Before the act, each federal agency had the authority to require an audit of each federally funded program or activity; there was no coordination among them, causing audit overlaps and organizational inefficiencies. For example, a state receiving funds from five different federal agencies could have been subjected to five different audits, performed by five different auditors consecutively or simultaneously.

The act created a single organization-wide financial and compliance audit for state and local governments receiving federal funds equal to or greater than $100,000 in any fiscal year (a fiscal year is any twelve-month period). There are four major purposes of the act.

1. To promote the efficient and effective use of audit resources

2. To establish uniform requirements for audits of federal funds provided to state and local governments

3. To ensure that federal funds, to the greatest extent practicable, are audited in accordance with the requirements of the Single Audit Act

4. To improve state and local government's financial management of federally funded programs through more effective auditing

IMPLEMENTATION

The director of the Office of Management and Budget (OMB), a federal agency, is responsible for dictating policies, procedures, and guidelines to carry out the act. These policies, procedures, and guidelines are contained in OMB Circular No. A-128, "Audits of State and Local Govern-

Franklin Raines, Office of Management and Budget director.

ments" (1995). Circular No. A-128 and the act require the following annually.

1. An audit of the state or local government's (entity's) general-purpose or basic financial statements made in accordance with generally accepted government auditing standards covering financial and compliance audits

2. Tests of internal accounting and other control systems to provide reasonable assurance that the entity is managing federal-assisted programs in compliance with applicable laws, regulations, and the specific provisions of contracts or grants

During the course of the audit, the auditor must determine whether the entity's financial statements fairly present its financial position and the results of its financial operations in accordance with generally accepted accounting principles. The auditor must also specifically re-

view transactions (expenditures) to determine whether the amounts were used for allowable services and recipients were eligible to receive them. In addition, the auditor must determine whether the organization has complied with laws and regulations that may have a material effect on its financial statements and on each "major federal-assisted program." ("Major federal assisted program" for state and local governments having federal-assisted expenditures between $100,000 and $100,000,000 is defined in Public Law 98-502 as any program for which federal expenditures during the year exceed the larger of $300,000 or 3 percent of such total expenditures.) Upon completion of the audit, the auditor must prepare a report that includes:

1. Reports on financial statements and schedule of federal funds, the financial statements, and the schedule of total expenditures of federal funds

2. A report on the study and evaluation of internal control systems that identifies the controls evaluated and material weaknesses, if any

3. A report on compliance stating positive assurance for items tested, negative assurance for items not tested, a summary of cases of noncompliance, and identification of the total amount of expenditures questioned

If the auditor discovers fraud or illegal acts, a separate report is required. The state or local government audited must also provide a report containing comments on the findings and recommendations in the auditor's report and details of corrective actions taken or planned if necessary.

The Single Audit Act of 1984 did not include colleges, universities, and other not-for-profit organizations receiving federal funds. These organizations continued to be subjected to audit overlaps and inefficiencies until 1990, when the Office of Management and Budget issued Circular A-133, "Audits of Institutes of Higher Education and Other Non-Profit Institutions," to extend requirements similar to those in the Act and

Circular A-128 to colleges, universities, and other not-for-profit organizations.

SINGLE AUDIT ACT AMENDMENTS OF 1996 (PUBLIC LAW 104-156)

In 1996, Congress amended the Single Audit Act to streamline and improve its effectiveness. The amended act applies to state and local governments, colleges, universities, and not-for-profit organizations that expend (spend) Federal funds equal to or greater than $300,000 in any fiscal year. Major changes to the 1984 act include the following:

1. All state and local governments, colleges, universities, public hospitals, and not-for-profit organizations receiving federal funds are covered under the act.

2. Thousands of entities were exempted from the federally mandated single audit by raising the dollar threshold from $100,000 to $300,000. The Office of Management and Budget is authorized to adjust the threshold amount every two years.

3. Audit requirements are triggered by federal funds "expended" rather than merely "received."

4. The audit report due date is shortened from thirteen months to nine months.

5. Auditors are required to identify major programs for compliance audits based on risk assessment rather than solely on the basis of the total dollar amount of expenditures.

6. The auditor is required to prepare and sign a data-collection form, which is submitted to the federal clearinghouse, instead of sending the full single audit report.

7. A provision is made for pilot projects to test alternative ways of achieving the objectives of the single audit process. For example, the act specifically authorized one creative approach to consider multiple local government entities that operate the same federal programs as a single entity for a single audit.

The Single Audit Act Amendments of 1996 addressed a number of issues that emerged during and after the implementation of the Single Audit Act of 1984. The amendments exempted entities receiving relatively small amount of federal funds, enacted guidelines to ensure that high-risk programs are subject to audit, and simplified reporting requirements.

(SEE ALSO: *Government Accounting*)

BIBLIOGRAPHY

"Audits of State and Local Governments" (Office of Management and Budget Circular No. A-128).

Dyson, Robert A. (1997). "The Revised OMB Circular A-133 and the Single Audit Act Amendments." *The CPA Journal.* January: 46-52.

Foelster, Mary McKnight, and Scott, George A. (1998). "Single Audit Overhaul." *The Journal of Accountancy.* May: 75-78.

Public Law 98-502, "Single Audit Act of 1984." www.hhs .gov/progorg/grantsnet/adminis/law-saud.html.

Public Law 104-156, "Single Audit Act Amendments of 1996." www.ignet.gov/ignet/single/saamend.html.

MARGARET HICKS

SITUATIONAL MANAGEMENT

(SEE: *Management/Leadership Styles*)

SKIMMING PRICES

(SEE: *Pricing*)

SMALL BUSINESS ADMINISTRATION

Today, small businesses generate more than one-third of the gross national product, create the majority of new jobs, and provide arenas for technological innovation. During the early 1950s, the value of small businesses in providing stability for the American economy was realized.

Prior to that time, big business/industry promises of career success too often proved to be empty, and many disillusioned American workers began to embrace the concept of self-employment. As the number of business entrepreneurs increased, it quickly became apparent that such entrepreneurial endeavors needed a protective umbrella if they were to survive normal start-up difficulties common to small business, not to mention competitive pressures generated by larger organizations. In 1953, to address the problem, Congress approved the Small Business Administration Act, which created the Small Business Administration (SBA).

The SBA's administrator directs the delivery of a comprehensive set of financial and business development programs that provide financing worth about $11 billion a year to small businesses across the nation. SBA has 70 district offices across the country and program offices in every state, as well as the District of Columbia, the Virgin Islands, and Puerto Rico.

As an independent federal agency, the SBA aids, counsels, assists, and protects small-business interests based on two principles: quality-focused management and customer-driven outreach.

The SBA provides financial assistance in the form of loan guarantees, rather than direct loans, through 14 specialized programs to help entrepreneurs attain the appropriate financial position to initiate their business and overcome the first few lean years of infancy. It also provides counseling and training assistance to female, minority, veteran, and socially and/or economically disadvantaged business owners. For instance, the Office of Women's Business Ownership has established a women's business owner representative network in every district office, an Online Women's Business Center accessible through the Internet, and nearly 70 women's business centers in 40 states; and the Minority Prequalification Loan Program assists qualified minority-owned, for-profit companies to obtain pre-approval for a 7(a) loan guaranty. The 7(a)

Loan Guaranty Program assists small businesses unable to secure reasonable funding terms through normal lending channels to obtain funding through private-sector lenders on loans guaranteed by the SBA.

While the SBA does not provide grants to start or expand a business, it does coordinate and disseminate information about resources to facilitate awareness of business initiatives, about consulting or mentoring opportunities for managerial novices, and about entrepreneurial success strategies. Further, it provides disaster assistance and has established a unit to coordinate and facilitate technology transfer conferences for small businesses. In an effort to centralize access to a full range of technical and financial assistance for small business owners located in empowerment zones and enterprise communities, in 1994 the SBA developed One-Stop Capital Shops. These partnerships between the SBA and a local community offer comprehensive small-business assistance from a unique, easy-to-access, retail site located in a distressed area, and they generally target underserved communities or the SBA's new markets.

More information is available from the U.S. Small Business Administration Office of Marketing and Customer Service, 409 Third Street SW, Suite 600, Washington, D.C. 20414; (202) 205-6744 or 1-800-8ASK-SBA; or http://www.sba .gov.

BIBLIOGRAPHY

Small Business Administration (SBA). "Mission." Archived at: http://www.sba.gov/intro.html. 1999.

SBA. "SBA Profile." Archived at: http://www.sba.gov/ aboutsba/indexprofile.html. 1999.

SBA. "SBA Office of Women's Business Ownership." Archived at: http://www.sbaonline.sba.gov/ womeninbusiness/. 1999.

SBA. "SBA Online." Archived at: http://www.sbaonline.sba .gov. 1999.

MARY JEAN LUSH
VAL HINTON

SOCIALISM

(SEE: *Economic Systems*)

SOCIAL RESPONSIBILITY AND ORGANIZATIONAL ETHICS

BUSINESS ETHICS

Perhaps the most practical approach is to view ethics as a catalyst that causes managers to take socially responsible actions. The movement toward including ethics as a critical part of management education began in the 1970s, grew significantly in the 1980s, and is expected to continue growing. Hence, business ethics is a critical component of business leadership. Ethics can be defined as our concern for good behavior. We feel an obligation to consider not only our own personal well-being but also that of other human beings. This is similar to the precept of the Golden Rule: Do unto others as you would have them do unto you. In business, ethics can be defined as the ability and willingness to reflect on values in the course of the organization's decision-making process, to determine how values and decisions affect the various stakeholder groups, and to establish how managers can use these precepts in day-to-day company operations. Ethical business leaders strive for fairness and justice within the confines of sound management practices.

Many people ask why ethics is such a vital component of management practice. It has been said that it makes good business sense for managers to be ethical. Without being ethical, companies cannot be competitive at either the national or international levels. While ethical management practices may not necessarily be linked to specific indicators of financial profitability, there is no inevitable conflict between ethical practices and a firm's emphasis on making a profit; our system of competition presumes underlying values of truthfulness and fair dealing.

The employment of ethical business practices can enhance overall corporate health in three important areas. The first area is productivity.

Milton Friedman.

The employees of a corporation are stakeholders who are affected by management practices. When management considers ethics in its actions toward stakeholders, employees can be positively affected. For example, a corporation may decide that business ethics requires a special effort to ensure the health and welfare of employees. Many corporations have established employee advisory programs (EAPs), to help employees with family, work, financial, or legal problems, or with mental illness or chemical dependency. These programs can be a source of enhanced productivity for a corporation.

A second area in which ethical management practices can enhance corporate health is by positively affecting "outside" stakeholders, such as suppliers and customers. A positive public image can attract customers. For example, a manufacturer of baby products carefully guards its public image as a company that puts customer health and well-being ahead of corporate profits, as exemplified in its code of ethics.

The third area in which ethical management practices can enhance corporate health is in minimizing regulation from government agencies. Where companies are believed to be acting unethically, the public is more likely to put pressure on legislators and other government officials to regulate those businesses or to enforce existing regulations. For example, in 1990 hearings were held on the rise in gasoline and home heating oil prices following Iraq's invasion of Kuwait, in part due to the public perception that oil companies were not behaving ethically.

A CODE OF ETHICS

A code of ethics is a formal statement that acts as a guide for how people within a particular organization should act and make decisions in an ethical fashion. Ninety percent of the *Fortune* 500 firms, and almost half of all other firms, have ethical codes. Codes of ethics commonly address issues such as conflict of interest, behavior toward competitors, privacy of information, gift giving, and making and receiving political contributions. According to a recent survey, the development and distribution of a code of ethics within an organization is perceived as an effective and efficient means of encouraging ethical practices within organizations.

Business leaders cannot assume, however, that merely because they have developed and distributed a code of ethics an organization's members have all the guidelines needed to determine what is ethical and will act accordingly. There is no way that all situations that involve decision making in an organization can be addressed in a code. Codes of ethics must be monitored continually to determine whether they are comprehensive and usable guidelines for making ethical business decisions. Managers should view codes of ethics as tools that must be evaluated and refined in order to more effectively encourage ethical practices.

CREATING AN ETHICAL WORKPLACE

Business managers in most organizations commonly strive to encourage ethical practices not only to ensure moral conduct, but also to gain whatever business advantage there may be in having potential consumers and employees regard the company as ethical. Creating, distributing, and continually improving a company's code of ethics is one usual step managers can take to establish an ethical workplace.

Another step managers can take is to create a special office or department with the responsibility of ensuring ethical practices within the organization. For example, management at a major supplier of missile systems and aircraft components has established a corporate ethics office. This ethics office is a tangible sign to all employees that management is serious about encouraging ethical practices within the company.

Another way to promote ethics in the workplace is to provide the work force with appropriate training. Several companies conduct training programs aimed at encouraging ethical practices within their organizations. Such programs do not attempt to teach what is moral or ethical but, rather, to give business managers criteria they can use to help determine how ethical a certain action might be. Managers then can feel confident that a potential action will be considered ethical by the general public if it is consistent with one or more of the following standards:

1. *The Golden Rule:* Act in a way you would want others to act toward you.

2. *The utilitarian principle:* Act in a way that results in the greatest good for the greatest number.

3. *Kant's categorical imperative:* Act in such a way that the action taken under the circumstances could be a universal law, or rule, of behavior.

4. *The professional ethic:* Take actions that would be viewed as proper by a disinterested panel of professional peers.

5. *The TV test:* Always ask, "Would I feel comfortable explaining to a national TV audience why I took this action?"

6. *The legal test:* Ask whether the proposed action or decision is legal. Established

laws are generally considered minimum standards for ethics.

7. *The four-way test:* Ask whether you can answer "yes" to the following questions as they relate to the decision: Is the decision truthful? Is it fair to all concerned? Will it build goodwill and better friendships? Will it be beneficial to all concerned?

Finally, managers can take responsibility for creating and sustaining conditions in which people are likely to behave ethically and for minimizing conditions in which people might be tempted to behave unethically. Two practices that commonly inspire unethical behavior in organizations are giving unusually high rewards for good performance and unusually severe punishments for poor performance. By eliminating such factors, managers can reduce much of the pressure that people feel to perform unethically. They can also promote the social responsibility of the organization.

SOCIAL RESPONSIBILITY

The term *social responsibility* means different things to different people. Generally, corporate social responsibility is the obligation to take action that protects and improves the welfare of society as a whole as well as organizational interests. According to the concept of corporate social responsibility, a manager must strive to achieve both organizational and societal goals.

Current perspectives regarding the fundamentals of social responsibility of businesses are listed and discussed through (1) the Davis model of corporate social responsibility, (2) areas of corporate social responsibility, and (3) varying opinions on social responsibility.

A model of corporate social responsibility that was developed by Keith Davis provides five propositions that describe why and how businesses should adhere to the obligation to take action that protects and improves the welfare of society and the organization:

Proposition 1: Social responsibility arises from social power.

Proposition 2: Business shall operate as an open system, with open receipt of inputs from society and open disclosure of its operation to the public.

Proposition 3: The social costs and benefits of an activity, product, or service shall be thoroughly calculated and considered in deciding whether to proceed with it.

Proposition 4: Social costs related to each activity, product, or service shall be passed on to the consumer.

Proposition 5: Business institutions, as citizens, have the responsibility to become involved in certain social problems that are outside their normal areas of operation.

The areas in which business can become involved to protect and improve the welfare of society are numerous and diverse. Some of the most publicized of these areas are urban affairs, consumer affairs, environmental affairs, and employment practices. Although numerous businesses are involved in socially responsible activities, much controversy persists about whether such involvement is necessary or appropriate. There are several arguments for and against businesses performing socially responsible activities.

The best-known argument supporting such activities by business is that because business is a subset of and exerts a significant impact on society, it has the responsibility to help improve society. Since society asks no more and no less of any of its members, why should business be exempt from such responsibility? Additionally, profitability and growth go hand in hand with responsible treatment of employees. customers, and the community. However, studies have not indicated any clear relationship between corporate social responsibility and profitability.

One of the better known arguments against such activities is advanced by the distinguished economist Milton Friedman. Friedman argues that making business managers simultaneously responsible to business owners for reaching profit objectives and to society for enhancing societal welfare represents a conflict of interest that has the potential to cause the demise of business.

According to Friedman, this demise almost certainly will occur if business continually is forced to perform socially responsible behavior that is in direct conflict with private organizational objectives. He also argues that to require business managers to pursue socially responsible objectives may be unethical, since it requires managers to spend money that really belongs to other individuals.

Regardless of which argument or combination of arguments particular managers might support, they generally should make a concerted effort to perform all legally required socially responsible activities, consider voluntarily performing socially responsible activities beyond those legally required, and inform all relevant individuals of the extent to which their organization will become involved in performing social responsibility activities.

Federal law requires that businesses perform certain socially responsible activities. In fact, several government agencies have been established and are maintained to develop such business-related legislation and to make sure the laws are followed. The Environmental Protection Agency does indeed have the authority to require businesses to adhere to certain socially responsible environmental standards. Adherence to legislated social responsibilities represents the minimum standard of social responsibility performance that business leaders must achieve. Managers must ask themselves, however, how far beyond the minimum they should attempt to go—a difficult and complicated question that entails assessing the positive and negative outcomes of performing socially responsible activities. Only those activities that contribute to the business's success while contributing to the welfare of society should be undertaken.

Social Responsiveness. Social responsiveness is the degree of effectiveness and efficiency an organization displays in pursuing its social responsibilities. The greater the degree of effectiveness and efficiency, the more socially responsive the organization is said to be. The socially responsive organization that is both effective and efficient meets its social responsibilities without

wasting organizational resources in the process. Determining exactly which social responsibilities an organization should pursue and then deciding how to pursue them are perhaps the two most critical decision-making aspects of maintaining a high level of social responsiveness within an organization. That is, managers must decide whether their organization should undertake the activities on its own or acquire the help of outsiders with more expertise in the area.

In addition to decision making, various approaches to meeting social obligations are another determinant of an organization's level of social responsiveness. A desirable and socially responsive approach to meeting social obligations involves the following:

- Incorporating social goals into the annual planning process

- Seeking comparative industry norms for social programs

- Presenting reports to organization members, the board of directors, and stockholders on progress in social responsibility

- Experimenting with different approaches for measuring social performance

- Attempting to measure the cost of social programs as well as the return on social program investments

S. Prakash Sethi presents three management approaches to meeting social obligations: (1) the social obligation approach, (2) the social responsibility approach, and (3) the social responsiveness approach. Each of Sethi's three approaches contains behavior that reflects a somewhat different attitude with regard to businesses performing social responsible activities. The social obligation approach, for example, considers business as having primarily economic purposes and confines social responsibility activity mainly to conformance to existing laws. The socially responsible approach sees business as having both economic and societal goals. The social responsiveness approach considers business as having both societal and economic goals as well as the obligation to anticipate upcoming social problems and to work actively to prevent their appearance.

Organizations characterized by attitudes and behaviors consistent with the social responsiveness approach generally are more socially responsive than organizations characterized by attitudes and behaviors consistent with either the social responsibility approach or the social obligation approach. Also, organizations characterized by the social responsibility approach generally achieve higher levels of social responsiveness than organizations characterized by the social obligation approach. As one moves from the social obligation approach to the social responsiveness approach, management becomes more proactive. Proactive managers will do what is prudent from a business viewpoint to reduce liabilities whether an action is required by law or not.

Areas of Measurement. To be consistent, measurements to gauge organizational progress in reaching socially responsible objectives can be performed. The specific areas in which individual companies actually take such measurements vary, of course, depending on the specific objectives of the companies. All companies, however, probably should take such measurements in at least the following four major areas:

1. *Economic function:* This measurement gives some indication of the economic contribution the organization is making to society.

2. *Quality-of-life:* The measurement of quality of life should focus on whether the organization is improving or degrading the general quality of life in society.

3. *Social investment:* The measurement of social investment deals with the degree to which the organization is investing both money and human resources to solve community social problems.

4. *Problem-solving:* The measurement of problem solving should focus on the degree to which the organization deals with social problems.

The Social Audit: A Progress Report. A social audit is the process of taking measurements of social responsibility to assess organizational performance in this area. The basic steps in conducting a social audit are monitoring, measuring, and appraising all aspects of an organization's socially responsible performance. Probably no two organizations conduct and present the results of a social audit in exactly the same way. The social audit is the process of measuring the socially responsible activities of an organization. It monitors, measures, and appraises socially responsible performance.

Managers in today's business world increasingly need to be aware of two separate but interrelated concerns—business ethics and social responsibility.

BIBLIOGRAPHY

Aupperle, K.E. Caroll, A.B., and Hatfield, J.D. (1985). "An Empirical Examination of the Relationship between Corporate Responsibility and Profitabilty." *Academy of Management Journal* June: 446-63.

Davis, L. (1975). "Five Propositions for Social Responsibility." *Business Horizons June*: 19-24.

Friedman, M. (1989). "Freedom and Philanthropy: An Interview with Milton Friedman." *Business and Society Review* Fall: 11-18.

McGuire, J.B., Sundgren, A., and Schneeweis, T. (1988). "Corporate Social Responsibility and Firm Financial Performance." *Academy of Management Journal* December: 854-72.

Ross, T. (1988). *Ethics in American Business.* New York: Touche Ross & Co.

Sethi, S. P. (1975). "Dimensions of Corporate Social Performance: An Analytical Framework." *California Management Review* Spring: 58-64.

THOMAS HAYNES

SOFTWARE

Computer systems consist in part of hardware that controls the overall activity of the computer. But in order for hardware to function, it must have the necessary instructions. These instructions are supplied by software. There are different kinds of software, each of which serves a specified purpose. Some software is necessary to make the computer operate. Another kind enables the computer to perform specific tasks. Still other software exists solely for entertainment purposes.

OPERATING SYSTEM SOFTWARE

The operating system software makes the computer perform its basic operational functions. Disk operating system (DOS) is one of the earlier types of operating system software used to power IBM-compatible computers. Commands are typed at a prompt to direct the computer to carry out its functions.

Windows is the most common operating system today. It permits several programs to be opened simultaneously and provides ease of movement between the open programs.

Windows NT is used for business networks. Once this operating system is downloaded and running, other kinds of software are opened to perform the desired functions.

The Macintosh Operating System (Mac OS) is designed for use with Apple, Mac, and PowerMac computers. One disadvantage of Mac OS is that fewer programs have been written for it compared to the number written for DOS or Windows.

APPLICATION SOFTWARE

Application software allows performance of specific tasks, such as writing letters, computing formulas, playing games, or carrying out desktop publishing tasks

- *Word-processing software*: Writing tasks previously done on typewriters with considerable effort can now be easily completed with word-processing software. Writing tasks such as keying in reports, letters, and tables, as well as merging documents, can be performed easily. Documents can be easily edited and formatted. Revisions can be made by deleting (cutting), inserting, moving (cutting and pasting), and copying data. Documents can be stored (saved) and opened again for revisions and/or printing. Many styles and sizes of fonts are available to make the document attractive.

- *Spreadsheet software*: Spreadsheet software permits performance of an almost endless variety of quantitative tasks such as budgeting, keeping track of inventory, preparing financial reports, or manipulating numbers in any fashion, such as averaging each of ten departmental monthly sales over a six-month period. A spreadsheet contains cells, the intersection of rows and columns. Each cell contains a value keyed in by the user. Cells also contain formulas with many capabilities, such as adding, multiplying, dividing, subtracting, averaging, or even counting. An outstanding feature is a spreadsheet's ability to recalculate automatically. If one were preparing a budget, for example, and wanted to change a variable such as an increase in salary or a change in amount of car payments, the formulas would automatically recalculate the affected items and the totals.

- *Database software*: A database contains a list of information items that are similar in format and/or nature. An example is a phone book that lists a name, address, and phone number for each entry. Once stored in a database, information can be retrieved in several ways, using reports and queries. For example, all the names listed for a given area code could be printed out and used for a commercial mailing to that area.

- *Desktop publishing software*: This software permits the user to prepare documents by using both word-processing devices and graphics. Desktop publishing software uses word-processing software, with all its ease of entering and revising data, and supplements it with sophisticated visual features that stem from graphics software. For example, one can enhance a printed message with virtually any kind of illustration, such as drawings, paintings, and photographs.

- *Presentation software*: A speaker may use presentation software to organize a slide show for an audience. Text, graphics, sound, and movies can easily be included in the presentation. An added feature is that the slide show may be enhanced by inclusion of handouts with two to six slides printed on a page. The page may be organized to provide space for notes to be written in by the audience as the presentation ensues. An example of this is Power Point. Preparation of the software is simplified by the use of 'wizards' that walk the user through the creation of the presentation.

- *Office suite software*: Office suite software puts together complete programs of software. A typical suite package might include word processing, spreadsheet, databases, and presentation software. Depending on the jobs that need to be done, the suite provides the tools to make professional-looking documents.

Each piece of software works independently as well as with other parts of the suite. Items on the menu bar —such as File, Insert, and Format —work similarly on all the programs in a suite. Thus, familiarity with one program makes it easy to work with the other programs.

A typical example of office suite software is mail sent via bulk rate. It is usually addressed by name to an individual, rather than to "Occupant," with names and addresses accessed from the database memory. Merging those names with the letter in the word processor produces a form letter. A spreadsheet might also have been used to include charts and graphs with the letter. When completed, all forms are inserted into envelopes addressed by means of the database and word processor.

COMMUNICATIONS SOFTWARE

Using telephone lines and working through the computer's modem, communications software makes it possible to communicate to any location in the world using either fax or electronic mail. A fax transmits whatever copy is on an original sheet of paper (text, graphics, or handwriting) to another computer or fax machine. Electronic mail (e-mail) is a text message. It remains in the receiver's computer until retrieved. The message can be stored in either the sender's or the receiver's computer for later processing. Attachments or files can also be sent via e-mail.

UTILITY SOFTWARE

Utility software is used to diagnose computer problems and repair them. A major type is a virus (or "illness") checker. It checks for viruses the

computer may have received from downloading information received from the Internet, e-mail, or another disk. Although some viruses may do little damage, others can cause serious damage to files and/or the computer operating system. It is important for a computer owner to find a virus-check program, install it, use it, and keep it continually updated. New viruses are found continually, and the only way to be safe is to update. Some antivirus software allows easy updating by downloading new files from the Internet.

EDUCATIONAL SOFTWARE

By teaching by means of games, educational software is designed to make learning fun. The approach used in educational software is that of a tutorial in which the learner competes with him or herself. Such software appeals to persons of all ages but particularly to young children, who can learn skills related to reading and arithmetic. Older children and adults can learn or improve on a wide variety of more mature skills.

SPECIAL SOFTWARE ACQUISITION ARRANGEMENTS

Some kinds of software are given away. Another kind permits the potential user to try the software before purchasing it. *Freeware software* is free for those who ask, but the rights remain with the developer. *Public domain software* is free to the user without any copyright or other restrictions. *Shareware software* permits potential buyers to try out the software. A user who likes it may purchase it by sending payment to the developer. The developer in turn may send the buyer supporting materials and information.

SUMMARY

Software is as critical to computers as breathing is to humans. Fortunately, an extremely wide variety of software programs are available that make possible the preparation of virtually any kind of computer product.

BIBLIOGRAPHY

"The Complete Suite: Office 97 Does It All," (1998). *Smart Computing Reference Series: Office 97*, (September): vol. 2(3).

"The Computer's Unsung Hero: Its Operating System," (1995). *Smart Computing*. (February): vol. 6(2).

"Keeping Your Computer Virus-Free", (1999). *Smart Computer Reference Series: Troubleshooting*, 2nd ed. (March): vol. 3(1).

"What You Should Know About Operating Systems", (1998). *Smart Computer Reference Series: Computing for Beginners*, (February): vol. 4(2).

"Where NT Falls in the Windows Family", (1998). *Smart Computer Learning Series: Windows NT*, (August): vol. 4(8).

WANDA SAMSON

SOLE PROPRIETORSHIP

A sole proprietorship is the simplest form of business ownership. Not surprisingly, the vast majority of small businesses begin their existence as sole proprietorships. A sole proprietorship has but one owner. That sole owner may engage in any form of legal business activity any time and anywhere. Other than the various local and state business licenses that every business must purchase regardless of type of ownership, no legal formalities are required to start or operate the business. The owner is responsible for securing and investing the funds for the business. These funds may come from the owner's existing or borrowed financial resources.

The Internal Revenue Service (IRS) permits one exception to the "one sole owner" rule. If the spouse of a married sole proprietor works for the firm but is not classified as either a partner or an independent contractor, the business may still considered to be a sole proprietorship and forgo having to submit a partnership income tax return. Also, the sole proprietorship can avoid self-employment taxes.

If the owner's true name is used, such as "John Smith Auto Repair," there is ordinarily no problem in selecting a name for the sole proprietorship. But care must be taken if a fictitious name is contemplated. The owner must register the name with the county to see whether the name duplicates that of another business. Even if it does not, the owner must submit a "doing business as (dba)" form to the county, or, in a few states, to the secretary of state.

ADVANTAGES

An owner of a sole proprietorship gets to keep all profits derived from the operation but must also bear all losses. The owner may even share any portion of the profits and losses with another person or persons.

The owner has the authority to make all the decisions relating to the business. Since there are no co-owners, there is no need to hold policy-meeting sessions or form any group similar to a board of directors. The owner, of course, must bear the responsibilities that accrue from the decisions made.

The owner may hire employees or work with independent consultants and still retain the sole proprietorship form of ownership. Even if these employees or independent consultants are requested to offer their opinions relating to the firm's business decisions, the opinions are considered to be only recommendations. The owner cannot abdicate any responsibility for the outcomes fostered by these recommendations.

DISADVANTAGES

Unlimited liability is the major disadvantage borne by the sole proprietorship. The owner is financially responsible for satisfying all business debts and/or losses suffered by the firm, even to the point of sacrificing his or her personal or other business interests to pay off any liabilities. For example, assume a lawsuit inflicts a debt of $190,000 on a sole proprietorship that is able to contribute only $85,000 toward settlement of the liability. Further assume that the proprietor owns a home, equipment, and other business investments totaling $365,000.

The following shows the picture of the owner's liability:

Total liability of the proprietorship $190,000

Capability of the proprietorship in settling the liability $85,000

Extent to which the owner's personal assets (totaling $365,000) must be used to settle the debt $105,000

Owners of sole proprietorships have severe potential liabilities from customers, competitors, lenders, employees, and even government. The cost of liability insurance or of defending against a lawsuit is beyond the financial capability of many business firms. For this reason, most individuals holding somewhat extensive personal assets do not ordinarily use the sole proprietorship form of ownership. Instead, an alternative form of ownership is often used, such as corporation or special forms of partnership, that eliminates the unlimited liability.

TERMINATION OF THE BUSINESS

A sole proprietorship legally terminates immediately upon the death of the owner. Even if a spouse, relative, or friend of the deceased owner assumes ownership and keeps the business operating under the same name, legally a new business enterprise has been formed. It is recommended that owners at least make a will, and preferably a revocable trust, to name the beneficiary of the owner's interest in the business.

A sole proprietorship also terminates if the ownership interest is sold to another person or group of persons, if the business is abandoned by the owner, or if the owner becomes personally bankrupt.

These potential risks of sudden termination place sole proprietorships at a serious disadvantage in attracting top-flight employees who may not to wish to tie their future to a business that may suddenly become inoperative.

INCOME TAXES

When filing an income tax return, no legal distinction exists between a person as a sole proprietor and an individual person. The sole proprietor's personal income tax return (Form 1040) must include calculation of the proprietorship's income tax as well as any income or loss that the

owner incurs from any additional entity, such as an employee, investor, or the like.

If, for example, a taxpayer realizes net earnings of $65,000 from a sole proprietorship and $28,000 from investments, the IRS considers the total net income to be $93,000. But, on the other hand, if a sole proprietor suffers a net loss of $42,000 from the business and a $71,000 net income from investments, the IRS would consider the total income to be $29,000.

Sole proprietors use Schedule C of IRS Form 1040 to file their income tax return for the proprietorship section of their income. The details of Schedule C can get very involved; many sole proprietors require professional advice for this phase of their income tax report.

Where applicable, sole proprietors file Form 4562 to report depreciation and amortization, and Form 8829 to report business use of the owner's residence.

TYPES OF BUSINESS

Proprietorships engage in a wide variety of businesses. Using the major categories of the new North American Industry Classification System (NAICS), the types of business activity that small businesses (including sole proprietorships) are likely to be involved an as follows:

Accommodation, food services, and drinking places

Administrative and support and waste management remediation services

Agriculture, forestry, hunting, and fishing

Arts, entertainment, and recreation

Construction

Educational services

Health care and social assistance

Information

Manufacturing

Mining

Professional, scientific, and technical services

Real estate and rental and leasing

Religious, grant making, civic, professional, and similar organizations

Retail trade

Transportation and warehousing

Utilities

Wholesale trade

REQUISITES FOR SUCCESS

Success does not come easily for small business enterprises. To achieve success, authorities have recommended a number of characteristics and activities.

Successful sole proprietors should be strong physically and emotionally. It is very important that they be in good health. Attitudes of business owners are critical; they should possess a positive outlook and enthusiasm. They should be receptive to advice. They need to work very hard, particularly during the first several years.

Sole proprietors should possess considerable business experience, especially in the product or service lines offered by their business. Having an appropriate and sufficient education is very valuable. Other capabilities could be added, such as getting along with different kinds of people, having the ability to plan and organize, knowing how to arrive at and carry out decisions, and being a self-starter.

It is often recommended that sole proprietors select a type of business in which they have both skills and interest. The geographic location should be investigated thoroughly regarding its growth potential. And it may be important for a sole proprietor to consider having a partner.

In setting up a business, a new sole proprietor should do the following:

- Learn as much as possible about the product or service being offered for sale
- Make sure there is enough capital available to meet necessary equipment and building needs as well as to pay for the first year's operating expenses
- Determine the amount to be invested and find the sources of any necessary loans
- Secure the assistance of an accountant, attorney, insurance agent, and banker

- Become familiar with licenses required, zoning laws, and other regulations
- Determine the most desirable types of employees; take steps to locate them and interest them in applying; and learn how to handle all withholdings
- Learn the fundamentals of advertising and, if appropriate, store layout
- Make sure that the appropriate forms of accounting and record keeping are established, and see that balance sheets and income statements are prepared
- Learn all aspects of marketing, including the principles of determining market share

In addition, the new sole proprietor should write a thorough business plan. The Small Business Administration provides the following outline for the elements of a business plan:

I. Cover sheet

II. Statement of purpose

III. Table of contents

    A. The Business

        1. Description of business

        2. Marketing

        3. Competition

        4. Operating procedures

        5. Personnel

        6. Business insurance

        7. Financial data

    B. Financial data

        1. Loan applications

        2. Capital equipment and supply list

        3. Balance sheet

        4. Break-even analysis

        5. Pro-forma income projections (profit and loss statements)

- Three-year summary
- Detail by month, first year
- Detail by quarters, second and third years
- Assumptions upon which projections were based

6. Pro-forma cash flow

C. Supporting documents
- Tax returns of principals for last three years
- Personal financial statement
- Copy of franchise contract and all supporting documents if appropriate

D. Copy of proposed lease or purchase agreement for building space
- Copy of licenses and other legal documents
- Copy of resumes of all principals
- Copies of letters of intent from suppliers, and so forth

SEEKING ADVICE

Sole proprietors find it very helpful to consult with other sole proprietors who successfully operate a business. Many also seek the advice of the Small Business Administration (SBA), an independent government agency.

Organized by Congress in 1953, the SBA now has offices in nearly every major city in the United States. Its toll-free telephone number is 1-800-8-ASK-SBA. Among many other services, SBA sponsors the Service Corps of Retired Executives (SCORE), Business Information Centers (BICS), and Small Business Development Centers (SBDC).

BIBLIOGRAPHY

Bustner, Irving. (1993). *Start and Run Your Own Profitable Service Business.* Englewood Cliffs, NJ: Prentice-Hall.

Davidson, Robert L., III. (1991). *The Small Business Partnership Kit.* New York: Wiley.

Diamond, Michael, and Williams, Julie. (1996). *How to Incorporate, A Handbook for Entrepreneurs and Professionals,* 3d ed. New York: Wiley.

The Small Business Administration. www.sbaonline.sba .gov.

G. W. MAXWELL

SPEAKING SKILLS IN BUSINESS

Studies show that Americans' number-one fear is public speaking. Actors, television personalities, and public speakers all feel it. And so do salespeople, community leaders, and managers who are called on to make seemingly routine presentations.

Experienced speakers, though, know how to combat stage fright. Through careful planning, proper training, and conscious relaxation exercises, these speakers have learned how to channel fear into control and confidence. All people have the actual skills needed for good presentations; using these skills in front of an audience is the area in which training is needed. Good communication and successful speaking skills can be learned.

In defining a presentation, we begin with one end of the spectrum, something that is loosely called a speech. Most speeches have very little impact because they don't ask the speaker to do anything, whereas the very definition of the word *present* is "to bring, to give a gift to." This implies that a giver (a presenter) is tuned in to what the recipient (the audience) wants. What response do we get when we give someone a gift of something he or she really wants? What response do we get when we give someone a gift that he or she really doesn't like? The difference between these two is the difference between sharing a meaningful message and delivering a speech. Audiences dislike being talked to; they eagerly await speakers who drive home a point or idea that they can readily use in their personal or professional lives.

When imparting information, two things are happening simultaneously:

1. The presenter is making a commitment to the audience. The presenter is working to prove a point that will win the support of the audience or that will generate action.
2. The audience is making a judgment on the presenter, asking such questions as, "Do I really trust this person?" "Does this information make any sense?" "Are the facts presented accurate?"

A person who has accepted an invitation to speak should answer three questions before beginning to think about what to say and how to say it:

1. Who is the audience?

2. What does the audience want to know?

3. What is the best way to provide the audience with the information they want?

Most presentations are given for one of five reasons: to entertain, inform, inspire, convince, or persuade. Once the purpose is determined, a talk should be organized around three main parts:

1. *Introduction*: This "hooks" the audience, entices people to listen, and previews what's to come. Effective introductory devices include questions, dramatic or humorous statements, jokes, anecdotes, and personal experiences.

2. *Body*: This is the subject—the meat of the speech. It should relate the who, what, when, where, why, and how of the subject. To keep the talk simple and easy to understand, the speaker should stick to three—no more than four—main points, relying on facts, figures, illustrations, specific examples, and comparisons to support these main points.

3. *Conclusion*: This final section should highlight key points that the audience should remember. It should also make people feel they've gained something by listening. The audience might be challenged to act or react to the message within a specific time frame.

The content of the message should be structured in an orderly and logical manner. This makes it easier for people to follow, digest, and retain the information. If the audience has difficulty following the speaker's train of thought, the message won't get or keep their attention.

The skeletal structure of any presentation should be:

INTRODUCTION
Opener
Objective
Preview
BODY
Key Point 1
Supporting material
Transition statement
Key Point 2
Supporting material
Transition statement
Key Point 3
Supporting material
Transition statement
CLOSING
Summary
To Do

Formulating an achievable and clearly stated objective is crucial. It provides the whole focus for preparation and acts as a guide in determining what to include in the body of the message.

Stating the objective at the beginning of the presentation is equally important. Doing so lets the audience know what to expect. It prepares them for what they are about to hear; therefore, it should always be stated in conversational terms. It might begin this way: "Today we'll explore." or "I'll help you understand."

With the foundation (objective) in place, one can proceed to outline the body of the presentation. Key points are those that "unlock the door" to the subject and let the audience in on the most important content areas of the message.

It is said that every great message contains at least one key point but not more than three. The rule of three forces the speaker to think through the material and distill the most significant points. Having three or fewer points keeps it simple for listeners. Usually information is remembered in groups of threes, fours, or sevens. Telephone numbers, for example, are spoken first with a set of three numbers and then with a second set of four: 123-4567. Elementary school teachers never present material in groups of more than seven items. The way we store and recall information represents the brain's effort to organize and combine data, making it easier to remember.

This same principle applies to the body of a presentation. Simplifying it provides the audience with a message that they will be better able to assimilate and retain.

Supporting material for each key point can be obtained by using:

- Examples
- Stories
- Quotations
- Findings
- Comparisons

Since supporting material accounts for most of the content of a presentation, it generally takes the most time to identify, collect, and develop. Again, though, the rule of three should be applied. Significant points will get lost in the maze of rambling information if too much supporting material is presented. On the other hand, a presentation will not be convincing if too little supporting material to substantiate key points is included.

A transition statement acts as a minisummary or minipreview within the body of the presentation. It announces the end of one point and introduces the next. Transitions help listeners stay with the speaker, making the message easier to follow and remember. Without transitions, a speaker could be halfway into the next point while some of the listeners are still trying to figure out what this has to do with the previous point. A sample transition statement might be: "Now that we have studied . . . ," or "Let's take a look at . . ."

People are most readily persuaded by what they heard frequently and recently; therefore, a summary should include a capsule of the key points in brief sentence form. This review drives the message home to the listener.

Most trainers apply the formula T × 3 (tell them 3 times) when delivering a message:

Preview: Tell them what you're going to tell them.

Body: Tell them.

Summary: Tell them what you told them.

The last point to impress on an audience is how they can use the information presented to bring about meaningful change in their lives. The "To Do" of a message can be accomplished by using statements such as: "I challenge you to . . ." or "I encourage you to . . ."

Memorizing a presentation is a bad idea because stumbling or forgetting one word might cause the whole speech to fall apart. Memorized words also tend to sound cold and lifeless instead of warm and genuine. Reading a speech isn't a good option either, because doing so prevents having eye contact with the audience. Instead, a speaker should write the main points on note cards and rehearse the speech at least five times, striving for spontaneity, variety, and naturalness in delivery.

To assure a successful presentation, follow these suggestions:

1. Practice mental imagery. Imagine yourself triumphantly succeeding. Tell yourself, over and over again, that you have something important to share and that you'll do a great job sharing it.

2. Rehearse privately in front of a mirror and on tape. Critique the pace and tempo of your presentation, as well as your enunciation, articulation, and pronunciation of words. Ask a trusted friend to critique your delivery.

3. Type your talk in large, bold type and number all pages/cards of your presentation. If you drop them, visible numbers will help you put them back together again in the correct order.

4. Conduct extra research. Conducting detailed research on your topic helps you gain a tremendous feeling of mastery and confidence.

5. Dress comfortably, but in good taste, and tuck away a lucky symbol on yourself.

6. Bring along some handouts. Cartoons, objects, or memorabilia that can be passed around the room are very effective "interest grabbers." They're especially useful when you must pause to collect your thoughts or calm your nerves.

7. Talk to someone. Before your talk begins, talk to a friend in your audience. Or talk to several. The more people you have a chance to meet before the talk begins. the more easily you'll be able to treat your audience as a group of friends.

8. Introduce yourself. Talk a bit about your background. Let your audience know something about your interests. Even frightened speakers have the ability to introduce themselves with style.

9. Speak deeply. Let your comments flow from deep within your body. Your voice will sound more forceful as a result.

10. Position yourself firmly at the lectern or table. Rest your hands firmly but comfortably at the edge of the lectern or table. As your hands gently grasp the lectern. you'll boost your sense of command and confidence.

11. Remember that physical action often softens fear. The more you're able to move your body or your major muscle groups, the more likely you'll induce a sense of calm.

12. Modulate your voice. Enunciate carefully, pause when appropriate, and accent important points with a change in volume.

13. State your case. Good presentations are forceful presentations. Don't hesitate to express your viewpoint firmly and don't hesitate to offer provocative ideas to the audience. The more you're able to express strongly held views, the more you'll feel in control of the presentation.

14. Enjoy yourself. You need not be a polished celebrity to deliver a quality talk. Enjoy the experience. To relax yourself and your audience, don't forget to smile!

BIBLIOGRAPHY

Gelf, Michael J. (1988). *Present Yourself.* Rolling Hills Estates, CA.: Jalmar Press.

Ensman, Richard G., Jr. (1993). "Stage Fright Bites the Dust." *Communiqué* Winter:17-22.

Hargrave, Jan L. (1995). *Let Me See Your Body Talk.* Dubuque, IA: Kendall/Hunt.

Lewis, Jan. (1996). "Become a Better Communicator." *Women In Business* July/August:21-24.

Filson, Brent. (1991). *Executive Speeches.* New York, NY: John Wiley.

JAN HARGRAVE

SPECIAL EVENT PRICING

(SEE: *Pricing*)

SPECIALTY GOODS

(SEE: *Shopping*)

SPREADSHEETS

Spreadsheet software is one of the most commonly used technologies for collecting, computing, and displaying data. Spreadsheets were developed as a way of organizing numeric data, by using an electronic table of rows and columns, and of creating business models, graphs and charts, and reports for financial, statistical, or other data.

SPREADSHEET PACKAGES

Spreadsheet packages are available for mainframes, minicomputers, and personal computers. Versions are available for various operating systems, including DOS, Windows (various versions), Macintosh, Unix, Java, Linux, and VMS. Spreadsheet capabilities are included in financial management packages as well as in integrated software packages. Dozens of spreadsheet software packages are available to users. The best-known packages are Microsoft Excel, Lotus 1-2-3, and Corel's Quattro Pro. These three packages are included as parts of integrated packages or suites from Microsoft Corporation, Lotus Development Corporation (owned by IBM Corporation), and Corel Corporation. In addition, dozens of other spreadsheet packages are available, many as "shareware," which offers a user an opportunity to try the product for a limited period and then pay a fee for permission to use the package beyond the evaluation period. Various spreadsheets are listed on the Internet by their developers, either as shareware or for purchase, and some are available for downloading.

SPREADSHEET APPLICATIONS

A spreadsheet is a table representing information in a worksheet form. It can be visualized as a large sheet of paper with rows and columns, and is based on the worksheets used by accountants for manual computations. A spreadsheet can range from a small, simple text table to a large document that can carry out complex computations and statistical analysis of thousands of data entries (Shelly et al., 1998). Simple spreadsheets can be displayed on-screen; more complex spreadsheets extend into vast numbers of cells and can be partially displayed on screen. The power of a spreadsheet is in its ability to store formulas and display their results. A recalculation feature in spreadsheets allows a user to enter new data into the spreadsheet, which can affect other sections of the spreadsheet, and see the results of new calculations. This "what if" feature of spreadsheets is a valuable tool for users.

FORMAT OF A SPREADSHEET

Spreadsheet software packages organize numeric data into table format, vertically in columns and horizontally in rows. Three types of data may be entered into a spreadsheet or worksheet: (1) values or numbers, (2) names or labels, and (3) formulas for calculation. Values may be used for basic arithmetic operations: addition, subtraction, multiplication, or division. Labels identify the information in the worksheet and help to organize it. Formulas perform calculations on data and display and store the resulting values. A cell, the intersection of a row and a column, can contain a label. a value, or a formula for performing calculations.

Only a small part of a spreadsheet is displayed on the screen at one time. Spreadsheets can contain millions of cells in each spreadsheet, and a spreadsheet file can include multiple spreadsheets. For example, the Lotus 1-2-3 (*Lotus 1-2-3 Millennium,* 1999) and Microsoft Excel (*Getting Results with Microsoft Office 97,* 1998) spreadsheets have 256 columns and 65,536 rows. Each spreadsheet thus can contain millions of cells of information. A spreadsheet file also may include multiple worksheets. Spreadsheets are very powerful, extensive electronic worksheets.

A spreadsheet handles such simple functions as adding, subtracting, multiplying and dividing. Arithmetic operators are used to represent the functions: addition ($+$), subtraction ($-$), multiplication ($\times$), and division ($\div$). For example, an entry into cell D3 of "$+$ B3 $+$ C3" would instruct the spreadsheet to sum the contents of cell B3 and C3 and store the sum in cell D3. A symbol at the beginning of a formula identifies the entry as a formula instead of a label. In the example $=$ B3 $+$ C3, the equals sign identifies the entry as a formula.

A simple spreadsheet can be enhanced with tools provided in the spreadsheet. Font styles (e.g., boldface), type sizes, and typefaces can be changed, color can be added to the background of cells or labels, and graphs can be used to illustrate data shown in the spreadsheet.

A spreadsheet is initially set up by default with a given column width, row height, and format for entries. If labels are longer than the column width allowed, the spreadsheet does not "lose" the extra characters; instead they are not displayed if the cell to their right has an entry. The user may change the column width and row height to enhance the appearance of the entries. Values are stored by the spreadsheet in their simplest form initially; an entry of $1050.00, for example, will be stored as 1050. The user then has tools within the spreadsheet for formatting those entries. Numeric data may be formatted as dollars and cents, with commas separating hundreds and thousands, in various formats for different

	A	B	C	D	E
1					
2					
3			Budget for First Quarter		
4					
5	Item	January	February	March	Total
6					
7	Food	200.00	210.00	220.50	630.50
8	Rent	400.00	400.00	400.00	1,200.00
9	Cable Fee	35.00	35.00	35.00	105.00
10	Total	635.00	645.00	655.50	1,935.50
11					
12					
13			Budget for First Quarter		
14					
15	Item	January	February	March	Total
16					
17	Food	200	=B17+B17*.05	=C17+C17*.05	=SUM(B17..D17)
18	Rent	400	400	400	=SUM(B18..D18)
19	Cable Fee	35	35	35	=SUM(B19..D19)
20	Total	=SUM(B17..B19)	=SUM(C17..C19)	=SUM(D17..D19)	=SUM(E17..E19)

Figure 1

countries, with a given number of decimal points, in exponential form, or in other formats. When a formula is entered, the cell displays the result of computations. However, the formula itself is retained. To display the formula itself, not its results, in a cell, a user can choose a format for "text." A formula that is entered as + C3 + D3 − E3, for example, might show a result of 25. If the cell is formatted to the "text" format, the formula will show instead of the computed answer.

A set of data can be described to the spreadsheet by specifying the beginning cell, in the upper-left corner of the data, and the ending cell, in the lower-right corner of the data. For example, to identify a rectangle that begins with cell A1 and extends down to cell D3, the address of the range would be A1 . . . D3. Spreadsheets identify the range with a symbol that means "through." In the example A1 . . . D3, the format used by many spreadsheets, the range would be interpreted as "Cell A1 through Cell D3."

An example of a spreadsheet is shown in Figure 1. Rows 1 through 10 show a spreadsheet; rows 11 through 20 are a duplicate of that spreadsheet, with the text of formulas shown in rows 17 through 20. In row 3, BUDGET FOR FIRST QUARTER, the heading for the entire worksheet, is an example of a label. The column headings and items in column A are labels; columns B through D are values, which are summed in column E with formulas. The formulas in Column E sum the numbers for January, February, and March for each item. Across the bottom of the spreadsheet, the "Total" line is also a result of using formulas to sum the columns.

The heading, "BUDGET FOR FIRST QUARTER," and the column headings show how font changes can enhance the readability and attractiveness of a spreadsheet. Cells can be formatted to boldface, underline, or italicize entries; background color or shading can be added; and typefaces and sizes can be changed. In the sample worksheet, the main and column headings have been boldfaced for emphasis.

Values can be formatted. In the sample spreadsheet, the values in rows 7 through 10 have been formatted to two decimal places with commas. A user can select the desired formatting from a menu.

Spreadsheet data can also be selected for charts, or visual representations of those data. Cells are selected by highlighting them. Spreadsheet packages may chart one set of data in the

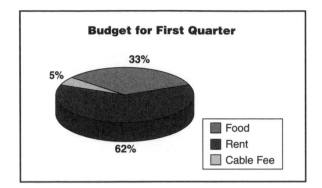

Figure 2

form of a pie chart, or two or more sets of data in bar charts (with vertical bars, horizontal bars, or stacked bars), line charts, area charts, or mixed charts, which combine bars and lines to represent data. They can be displayed in two-dimensional or three-dimensional form. Charts become part of the spreadsheet and may be stored on the same page as the spreadsheet or as a separate page or worksheet. A sample chart for the budget spreadsheet described above is shown in Figure 2.

The chart depicts the total figures from cells E7 through E9 in the spreadsheet, categorized by cells A7 through A9. A pie chart is only one of several choices of charts that could be used. The software provides steps for adding a heading to the chart and a legend, or listing of the labels for the charted data.

MACROS IN SPREADSHEETS

A macro is a series of commands that automate a spreadsheet task, streamline complex procedures, or create applications. For example, a macro to insert the user's name, company name, and date into worksheets can be stored and used repeatedly. A user can enter a macro into a worksheet file or into a macro library, a worksheet file that contains macros. To create a macro, the user enters the commands needed to carry out a task, gives the macro a name, and saves it in a file. To use the macro, the user selects it by name from a menu and asks the spreadsheet to run it. The steps are carried out automatically. For complex tasks that are used often, a macro makes it easier

for a user to avoid mistakes in the task, since the steps are stored as a file and recalled as needed.

SPREADSHEETS IN INTEGRATED PACKAGES

Integrated software packages, which contain several kinds of software within one, usually include a spreadsheet. Information can be copied from a spreadsheet into other software packages, such as a word-processing package. Spreadsheets can be linked to files in other software in the package so that changes made in the spreadsheet are automatically reflected in the linked document. For example, a table from a spreadsheet could be linked to a word-processing document so that any changes in cell entries in the spreadsheet change the contents of the table in the word-processing document. This feature makes the spreadsheet a very powerful tool for analysis and reporting of data in various formats.

BIBLIOGRAPHY

Getting Results with Microsoft Office 97. (1995–1998). Redmond, WA: Microsoft Corporation.

Lotus 1-2-3 Millennium [CD-ROM]. (1999). Cambridge, MA: Lotus Development Corporation.

Shelly, G. B., Cashman, T. J., Waggoner, G. A., and Waggoner, W. C. (1998). *Discovering Computers 98.* Cambridge, MA: Course Technology-ITP.

BETTY J. BROWN

STAGGERS RAIL AND MOTOR CARRIER ACTS OF 1980

Prior to the Staggers Act, the railroad industry was suffering: Many railroads had financial problems, and the conditions of rail facilities had deteriorated. Public demand for a better rail system caused Congress to take action and pass the Staggers Act, which has resulted in rail profits and improved service. The Staggers Rail Act of 1980 marked the most significant change in rail policy since the Interstate Commerce Act of 1887. It eliminated most common-carrier obligations, granted railroads greatly increased commercial freedom, and generally reversed previous policy. The act was an effort to deregulate the

STANDARD AND POOR'S INDEX

nation's railroads. In deregulating the nation's railroads, Congress intended (1) to return the nation's railroads to financial health, (2) to replace government regulation wherever possible with the powers of competition, and (3) to continue to provide captive shippers with protection from "unreasonable" rates. Brennan (1997) reports that since the passage of the Staggers Act, the U.S. freight railroads have been virtually rebuilt. He indicated that economic deregulation has freed up resources such that investor-owned railroads can successfully focus on improved safety and reliability. Thus, the free-market environment has allowed a once-dying industry to recapitalize and make a future for itself.

The regulating agency for the railroads was the Interstate Commerce Commission (ICC). The intent of the Staggers Act was to replace federal regulation with market competition. The ICC was charged by Congress in the Staggers Act to promote rail-to-rail competition. Unfortunately, the ICC did not fully succeed in its charge. The ICC's successor, the Surface Transportation Board (STB) of the U.S. Department of Transportation, was created by Congress in 1995. The STB is responsible for railroad mergers, consolidations, and trackage rights. Railroads are still regulated in terms of entry, exit, and mergers. Railroads largely control their pricing. Changes must be approved by the STB and, if they are, the railroad is not subject to antitrust regulations (Poole, 1997).

The railroad industry is an example of an oligopoly, which is a form of industry structure characterized by a few firms that dominate the market, each large enough to influence market price (Brennan, 1997). In the United States there are nine recognized Class I railroads that form an oligopoly: Burlington, Northern Sante Fe Railway, Conrail, Canadian Pacific Railway, CSX Transportation, Illinois Central, Kansas City Southern Lines, Norfolk Southern, and Union Pacific. Class I rail companies account for 73 percent of the rail mileage operated, 89 percent of freight railroad employees, and 91 percent of freight railroad revenue (Brennan, 1997).

There is not complete agreement, by most measures, that railroad deregulation under the Staggers Act has been a success. The act has lowered rail rates on most commodities, saved shippers money, provided more timely service, and eliminated the necessity for large taxpayer bailouts. Brennan (1997) also agrees that rail profits increased and service improved as a result of the passage of the act. He maintains that the effects of rail deregulation include improvements in service quality and profits, less pressure on rates, and efficiency improvements. The railroad industry has transformed itself from a money-losing business into a much more concentrated and profitable one.

Pete Carpenter, president of CSX Transportation (CSX, 1996), hailed the success of railroads in the sixteen years since the passage deregulation legislation. He cautioned, however, that a challenge to the industry and government today is the need for a passenger commuter rail system that does not denigrate freight services. He indicated that the railroad industry has a good future and is well-poised to take advantage of current market demands.

BIBLIOGRAPHY

Brennan, K. "Railroad Deregulation, Paper #1." *Perspectives on the American Railroad industry: An overview of our industry. http://www.gettysburg.edu/~s368754/group.htm.* 1997.

CSX Transportation. "CSX Transportation President Pete Carpenter Hails Success of Railroad Industry, Cites Challenges Ahead." CSXT Press Release. *http://www.csxt.com/med/press/960917a.htm.* 1996.

Ellig, J. "Railroad Competitive Access: Re-Regulation in Cheap Clothing. Citizens for a Sound Economy foundation, Capitol Comment Number 214." *http://www.csef.org/csefhome/cc214-csef-reg.htm.* 1998.

Poole, K. T. "45-855 Railroads, The First Big Business: Topic 10." *http://k7moa.gsia.cmu.edu/rtopic10.htm.* 1997.

PHYLLIS BUNN

STANDARD AND POOR'S INDEX

(SEE: *Stock and Bond Indexes*)

ENCYCLOPEDIA OF BUSINESS AND FINANCE   793

STANDARD-BASED WORK PERFORMANCE

New forces in the marketplace—including new organizational values, work cultures, and business goals—have reshaped the structures, strategies, and human resource process of most organizations. One change brought about by these marketplace forces is the development of a new set of work standards. These work standards deliver clear and specific goals to employees, so that they understand exactly what is expected of them in order to earn fair and equitable pay for their job performance. These standards also provide employers with a reliable system of performance appraisal. These new compensation processes are referred to as *standard-based work performance.*

Standard-based work performance has also been termed *pay-for-performance, at-risk compensation,* and *merit pay.* It became fashionable in the 1990s, when a large percentage of U.S. organizations began using some form of standard-based work performance. In its purest forms, standard-based work performance also includes *selling on commission* and *piecework,* concepts that have been around much longer.

Standard-based pay is a form of compensation known as *incentive pay.* Under a standard-based pay plan, pay increases are granted to individuals on the basis of their rated performance in a previous time period. Pay increases are granted with the hope of motivating future performance. One philosophy views standard-based work performance compensation as a way to change behavior, while a second philosophy views it as a reward mechanism.

Organizations have moved toward this new form of evaluation related to compensation with the intention of getting the best possible performance from their employees. The main objective of standard-based work performance is to tie pay to performance. Other objectives include maintaining equitable relationships among jobs, attracting job applicants, and keeping payroll costs competitive.

STANDARD-BASED WORK PERFORMANCE PLAN REQUIREMENTS

A key to making standard-based work performance work for an organization is to have the appraisal system backed by a clear sense of corporate purpose. Therefore implementing a new compensation program or appraisal system requires a great deal of planning when deciding what action management wants to elicit from employees. The organizational culture and management styles will determine how to implement changes in compensation. Higher priority should be given to corporate strategy than to industry standards when developing pay plans. If an organization wants to encourage technological change, then linking pay to these measures conveys to employees that the goals of the organization have changed and rewards will be based on reaching the new goals.

Another issue to consider regarding the organizational culture is whether to promote teamwork or individual competition. The goals of each are very different and must be clearly stated. If compensation rewards are to be based on the effectiveness of the team's work rather than on individual performance, the organization needs to train employees to function as members of a team.

An organization must also decide whether performance-based compensation is practiced at executive, middle-management, or all employee levels. This decision is very important, because it will determine the type of training that will be required. All managers using a new appraisal system must have a thorough explanation of the plan and the phasing in process in order to avoid resistance from those employees being evaluated.

Standard-based performance is based on the assumption that performance can be measured. This is not an easy task; it is difficult to objectively measure job performance in many positions. The availability of accurate performance criteria and the ability to accumulate such information will determine the success of linking pay to performance. The key is designing the plan.

Successful performance-based pay plans have three common qualities. They must be clearly communicated to employees, they must include an annual review of the plan, and they need appropriately ambitious goals. The supervisor and employee should jointly develop specific plans on how to reach the goal and how performance in attaining the goal will be measured. This is a time-consuming but necessary task.

STANDARD-BASED WORK PERFORMANCE THEORIES

There are four psychological and three economic theories that address how work standards relate to work performance. The psychological expectancy theory suggests that standard-based work performance is likely to motivate increased performance when performance is necessary to attain an increase in pay. The theory states that in order for the performance-based pay plan to be successful, performance must be accurately measured, pay must be a valued outcome, pay must be made contingent on performance, and the employee must have the opportunity to have an impact on performance.

The psychological reinforcement theory suggests that standard-based performance should motivate increased performance when the outcomes of favorable performance are clearly defined to the employee, the rewards are contingent on a desired performance, and compensation is increased in a timely manner when performance improves.

The psychological equity theory suggests that standard-based pay will increase employee motivation when it leads to perceptions of equity by the employee. It requires an organization to shift from valuing seniority to valuing performance inputs and basing compensation on performance rather than on years of employment.

The psychological goal-setting theory suggests that standard-based performance increases motivation when it is the result of setting more difficult goals and demonstrating a commitment to reach these goals. Goals should be weighted by difficulty, and compensation rewards should be given based on degree of difficulty of the goal achieved.

Marginal productivity theory, an economic theory, suggests that an employee is paid on the basis of performance in order to minimize labor costs and keep the company competitive in the labor market. Although research indicates that pay and performance are not always directly related, reducing fixed compensation costs is a goal toward which most employers strive.

Implicit contract theory, another economic theory, holds that standard-based performance is an implicit contract in which performance is measured by the employer rather than assumed by the employee. Under this theory, an employee can then be paid based on actual contributions that minimize labor costs.

Efficiency wage theory, also an economic theory, suggests that standard-based performance pay should be set high to obligate employees to fully perform rather than shirk duties. When employers pay a premium wage, employees realize that they will encounter personal financial hardship if they lose their jobs. Better performance, reduced turnover, and decreased need to train new employees may offset the initial investment in a premium wage.

Research indicates that when an organization plans on implementing a standard-based performance plan, it must view standards in relation to previous employee performance. It is important for management to be aware of and recognize contributions an employee has made to the organization.

It is equally important to examine performance in terms of measurable outcomes or perceptions of work-related performance. An employee must know what will determine the awarding of increased pay—the manner in which work performed is being measured, the work itself, or the factor to be measured?

There are many examples of work standards in business today. Compensation experts say the key is to design a plan that enforces the goals of the organization and to regularly evaluate the effectiveness of the plan.

The Ford Motor Company, which has a standard-based performance pay plan, measures quality using warranty figures expressed as repairs per thousand vehicles and both short-term and long-term customer satisfaction. The company recognizes there is still a lot more to be done, and it continually challenges itself.

In the late 1990s Sun Microsystems started tracking quality of customer loyalty and customer quality. The results are updated regularly on the company's intranet. Employees understand that the corporation's overall success will affect their compensation. The employees know that their annual bonus is based on a reduction in customer dissatisfiers (late delivery, software defects, poor product quality, etc.) and an increase in customer loyalty.

The original idea for the Sun Microsystems plan resulted from quality benchmarking strategy meetings of chief executive officers of Sun Microsystems, Federal Express, Motorola, and Xerox. The successful standard-based work performance plans of these companies have three main qualities in common: clear communication with employees, annual plan reviews, and appropriately ambitious goals.

Employees must have a clear idea of the organization's specific goals, how their jobs fit into the big picture, and what their rewards will be for doing their part in achieving the goals. The degree to which an employee is accountable for results of the job is the amount of control or opportunity available to the employee. Standard-based performance focuses on the importance of providing accountability for work performance. Goals and compensation should be assessed, reviewed, and updated as part of annual reviews.

Three components in evaluating accountability are the freedom to act, impact, and magnitude. Freedom to act describes the degree to which personal or procedural control exists. Impact is the effect of specific jobs on the objectives of the company. Magnitude is the size of the unit or function affected by the job as related to the big picture of the organization. Magnitude and impact must fit together; neither can be final or meaningful without being related to the other. Accountability is a measurement of the effect of the job on end results.

BIBLIOGRAPHY

Grote, Dick. (1996). *Painless Performance Appraisals Focus on Results, Behaviors*, HR Hay Group. People, Performance, and Pay.

Heneman, Robert L. (1992). *Merit Pay—Linking Pay Increases to Performance Ratings.*

Larson, Melissa. (1998). "Betting Your Bonus on Quality." *Quality Magazine* October:

Quaid, Maeve. (1993). *Job Evaluation—The Myth of Equitable Assessment.*

JAMES E. MILES

STANDARD COSTING

Costing is the identification of the value of resources used for specified goods or services. One purpose of costing is to determine what resources were required to provide the goods or services. A second purpose is to provide a guide to resource usage through the use of budgets that clearly identify managers' responsibility. It is the second purpose that is considered in the following discussion.

METHODS OF COSTING IDENTIFIED IN BUDGETS

Budget figures may be based on *actual, budgeted,* or *standard costs.* These categories are not mutually exclusive. For example, while a standard cost is a budgeted cost, a budgeted cost is not always a standard cost. An actual cost may or may not be the budgeted cost.

Budgets based on actual costs reflect expenditures anticipated for the level of resource use. Budgeted costs are generally described as the best estimate about what should be allowed for forthcoming activity. To establish budgeted costs, actual costs of the previous year, information from supervisors about where resources might be more efficiently used, and subjective judgments about the need to conserve resources are often considered. Standard costs are objectively determined costs that reflect the effective and efficient use of resources.

STANDARD COSTS

Standard costs are costs established through identifying an objective relationship between specified inputs and expected outputs. Therefore, standard costs are generally related to carefully analyzed phenomena both in the laboratory and in the workplace. For example, in the factory of a company that produces high-quality cotton shirts for men, standard costs are used for materials and labor. To establish the standard usage of fabric for a single shirt, the cutting possibilities are analyzed in the laboratory, where attention can be given to how much fabric must be used if the shirt is cut as specified. At this point, the focus is not on how many minutes are needed by an experienced cutter to meticulously cut the fabric so as to minimize usage. Rather, there is experimentation in the ways of cutting and the time required for each way considered. Experimentation continues until the most economical combination of fabric usage and cutting time is established. That combination is likely to be modified to take account of less than perfect conditions in the workplace.

The goal of the personnel responsible for setting standard costs is to provide realistic standards. Workers are to be motivated to achieve output with specified standards. If standards are unreasonable—either too tight or too loose—the level of discipline expected is seriously undermined. If standards cannot be achieved with reasonable effort, workers may become discouraged and become so indifferent that their work quality deteriorates significantly. If standards are too easy to achieve, there may be an unnecessary waste of resources.

Standard costing has applications to any type of business activity. The process described briefly above can be applied, for example, for processing documents in an insurance company or in a financial services business.

MONITORING STANDARD COSTS

Standard costs are monitored as a basis for determining the extent to which expectations are realized. Typically, companies plan for reporting weekly or monthly. A commonly used method is to determine the difference between what the budget allowed and what was actually spent for the output achieved. This difference is called a *variance*. For example, assume that in the factory producing shirts, 12,000 shirts, requiring 30,500 yards of fabric, were cut in a month. The standard usage was 2.5 yards per shirt, for a total of 30,000 yards. The excess usage would indicate an unfavorable usage variance of 500 yards. Variances are generally presented as units × standard cost for the fabric. Therefore, if the standard cost for the fabric was $4.75, the variance would be reported as 500 units × $4.75 = $2,375. A policy must be established about the level of variance that is to be investigated. Some variation from expectations is allowed, and if standards are realistic, much of the variation is eliminated over the period of a year—that is, insignificant favorable variances cancel out insignificant unfavorable variances.

Variances that are determined to be significant are investigated. Careful observation and discussion with those workers involved in producing the output that led to a variance will aid in assessing what circumstances appeared to be the explanation. Wise consideration of what should be done in the future can lead to the elimination of significant variances.

In an objective review of observations and discussions, questions may arise as to the appropriateness of the standards established. There may need to be a reconsideration of the earlier analyses that were the basis for the standards used in the budget followed by operational personnel.

For an organization to gain optimum value from standard costing, all employees involved must understand the motivation for such costing and understand the assessment that will be made. Imposing standard costs without communicating in an honest, candid manner will undermine much of the perceived value of such costing.

RELATED DEVELOPMENTS

Developments such as continuous improvement, target costs, and push-through production have changed to some extent the usefulness of traditional standard costing. However, each of these developments has been implemented in some organizations with aspects of standard costing included. For example, continuous improvement, in a general way, introduces a review of what resources were used this year to identify where fewer resources might be used in the forthcoming year. The task of identifying fewer resources is a standard-setting task. Target costs are calculated by starting with the cost consumers are believed to be willing to pay for the completed good or service, then analyzing the cost in a backward fashion. This process can also involve the basic concept of standard costing. Push-through production, in which groups have responsibility for a number of processes, can profit from standard costing as a basis for monitoring resource usage.

One major barrier to implementation of standard costing in the twenty-first century is the speed of change in how tasks are performed and in the alternative materials available. Frequent change leads to insufficient time for the careful analyses of inputs and outputs. Decisions are based solely on judgments and observations. Such decisions may be close to those established systematically—however, they may not be.

The usefulness of the information provided from analysis of variances related to standard costs has been challenged. Attention to quality, some critics say, is inadequate in this traditional analysis. Others have proposed that quality considerations can be incorporated in standard costing assessment (see Cheatham and Cheatham, 1996).

(SEE ALSO: *Costs*)

BIBLIOGRAPHY

Cheatham, Carole B., and Cheatham, Leo R. (1996). "Redesigning Cost Systems: Is Standard Costing Obsolete?" *Accounting Horizons* 10.4, (December): 23-31.

Drury, Colin. (1999). "Standard Costing: A Technique at Variance with Modern Management?" *Management Accounting* November: 56-58.

Fleischman, Richard K., and Tyson, Thomas N. (1998). "The Evolution of Standard Costing in the U.K. and U.S.: From Decision Making to Control." *Abacus* March: 92-119.

National Association of Accountants (now the Institute of Management Accountants). (1974). *Standard Costs and Variance Analysis.* New Jersey: Montvale.

BERNARD H. NEWMAN
MARY ELLEN OLIVERIO

STANDARD INDUSTRIAL CLASSIFICATION SYSTEM (SIC CODES)

(SEE: *North American Industry Classification System (NAICS)*)

STANDARD METROPOLITAN STATISTICAL AREAS

Over the last half-century, there has been a population movement from rural to urban areas. Because many urban areas cross political boundaries, the Office of Management and Budget has defined three metropolitan statistical areas. A Metropolitan Statistical Area (MSA) is a city of at least fifty thousand people with a surrounding rural population. A Primary Metropolitan Statistical Area (PMSA) is an area of more than a million people with internal and social links. If two or more PMSAs are geographically linked, they are referred to as Consolidated Metropolitan Statistical Areas (CMSA). There are twenty CMSAs in the United States, with New York, northern New Jersey, and Long Island being the largest. This trend toward urbanization has implications for marketing.

In highly industrialized countries, the growth of population has slowed, forcing marketers to adopt segment or target marketing. Segment marketing requires the marketer to break the total market into smaller segments by using certain variables: demographic, geographic, psychographic, and behavioristic.

Demographic variables are objective population characteristics that are easily collected and readily available in the United States. The information marketing people are interested in includes the following: age, gender, race, income, education, occupation, and family size. Demographic variables and geographic variables (such as size, region, and climate) are also important in selecting a market segment.

There are a number of examples of how marketers use some of these demographic variables. In the United States, age is an important variable for market segmentation. For example, since teenagers control a certain spending, certain products are marketed directly to them. The same is true of senior citizens, who constitute a growing segment of the American population.

Gender is another demographic variable. In industrialized countries where people are living longer, women generally outnumber men. The needs and buying habits of women must be factored into any marketing program.

Urbanization and population mobility are two other factors that are considered in marketing programs. Because it is easier to market goods and services in highly urbanized areas, marketing programs are more effective there. Mobility provides opportunities for national advertising for regional brands. For example, some products sold in the northeastern United States have done well in south Florida because many Northeasterners have migrated to Florida

Other variables that affect market segmentation are occupation and education. In 1960 approximately 30 percent of women were working outside the home; today that number has almost doubled. Marketing implications include work clothes for women, more eating out, and easily prepared convenience food. The list of demographic and geographic variables and their marketing implications can go on and on.

However, there are limitations to the use of population data. They may be dated because of the time lag from collecting it to its becoming available; also, census data is collected only every ten years. Some data (for instance, race) may be too broad and thus hide marketing opportunities; for example, the increase in the number of educated and upper-middle-class blacks would suggest a market not normally implied by using data on race. Finally, the use of demographic and geographic variables, which are easily gleaned from data on Metropolitan Statistical Areas, ig-

nores two very important segmentation variables: psychographic and behavioristic variables.

BIBLIOGRAPHY

Evans, Joel R., and Berman, Barry. (1994). *Marketing*, 6th ed. New York: Macmillan.

"Metropolitan Areas." Archived at: http://www.calmis.cahwnet.gov.

"Metropolitan Areas." Archived at:http://www.ntis.gov.fcpc.

Pride, William M., and Ferrell D. C. (1993). *Marketing*. 8th ed. Boston: Houghton Mifflin.

MARY JEAN LUSH
VAL HINTON

STATEMENTS ON MANAGEMENT ACCOUNTING

Statements on Management Accounting (SMA) are promulgated (produced, issued, and implemented) to reflect official positions of the Institute of Management Accountants (IMA), the largest and most prominent management accounting organization in the world. The IMA is an organization of accounting professionals that has a membership of more than 100,000.

HISTORY

One of the chief activities of the IMA is to conduct and sponsor research in management accounting. In 1969 the IMA (at that time operating using the name "National Association of Accountants"—name changed effective July 1, 1991, and is hereafter referred to as the "IMA") created the Management Accounting Practices (MAP) Committee to serve as its senior technical committee. This committee was, and is currently, charged with the task of promulgating statements on management accounting that reflect the views of the IMA. The MAP Committee membership includes twelve representatives appointed by the IMA president from corporate and public accounting as well as education. These representatives are widely considered to be expert authorities in accounting. Past members have included members of other prominent accounting regulatory groups such as the Financial Accounting Standards Board (FASB).

PURPOSE

The purpose of the MAP Committee in issuing SMAs is generally twofold: (1) to express the official position of the IMA on accounting and business reporting issues raised by other standard-setting groups, and (2) to provide broad guidance to IMA members and to the wider business community on management accounting concepts, policies, and practices. Regarding the first stated purpose, other standard-setting groups include those such as the Financial Accounting Standards Board, the Governmental Accounting Standards Board, the International Accounting Standards Committee, and government agencies such as the Securities and Exchange Commission. Regarding the second purpose, the work of the MAP Committee is seen as an effective method of summarizing the wide range of activities that define management accounting.

Some accountants believe that SMAs should be accorded the same considerable authority as generally accepted accounting principles (GAAP) (Schiff and Penino, 1990). As of 1999, such authority has not been granted. There is some support for this position. The American Institute of Certified Public Accountants (AICPA) Statement of Accounting Standards (SAS) No. 5 has defined these issuances as "pronouncements of bodies composed of expert accountants." Also, they are issued only after "a due process procedure, including broad distribution" and SMAs describe existing practices that are "generally accepted" (AICPA, 1982, p. 9).

The usefulness of authoritative statements to guide management accounting practice is apparent given the diversity of industries and accounting practices within industries. In addition, the business environment is becoming increasingly complex as technological advances make practices of the past obsolete. The role of external business reporting is also expanding. In 1994, the AICPA's Special Committee on Financial Reporting (sometimes referred to as the "Jenkins Committee") recommended significant changes in the current financial reporting model to include expanded coverage of both nonfinancial or operating data and more forward-looking or future-oriented data.

The recommendations of the AICPA Special Committee reflect the needs and desires of investors and other business report users to have increasing amounts of information and information of a nontraditional nature. Obtaining nonfinancial and predictive data requires access to previously nondisclosed or proprietary types of data traditionally used by management accountants within their companies. Thus the IMA, through their SMA promulgation mechanism, may be in a good position to produce suggestions in these areas of recommended increased disclosure. While investors and others strive to obtain increased amounts and different types of business information, companies with reporting responsibility are concerned with safeguarding information for which disclosure may affect their competitive position. Recommendations are needed for the control of what information should be released in many cases. This issue is one that will likely be addressed by a convergence of several professional accounting groups. If accounting organizations though SMA promulgation or other means are unable to achieve a satisfactory resolution on demands for increased disclosure, the judicial system may ultimately have to establish these boundaries.

PROCESS

In promulgating statements, the MAP committee uses a "Subcommittee on SMA Promulgation." Generally, each subcommittee member oversees the process of promulgating a particular SMA. After it is drafted, each statement is subjected to a rigorous exposure process whereby input is solicited from other members of the accounting profession in the form of two advisory panels. One panel is composed of a sample of IMA chapter presidents or other individual chapter representatives. (The IMA has more than 400 local chapters organized geographically in cities across America.) The other panel is composed of representatives nominated from other accounting or accounting-related organizations, including the American Institute of Certified Public Accountants, the Financial Executives Institute, the American Accounting Association, and the Society of Management Accountants of Canada.

Once the two advisory panels' comments have been reviewed by the subcommittee and appropriate modifications to a draft have been made, a proposed SMA is submitted to the MAP Committee for approval. The committee will then take one of three possible actions: (1) approve the draft as recommended, (2) further modify and then approve the draft, or (3) return the draft to the subcommittee to be developed further. SMAs are published only after completion of this review process and final approval requiring a two-thirds majority vote by the IMA's Management Accounting Practices Committee.

CONTENT

The SMA subcommittee is guided by a framework for management accounting that considers five broad categories: (1) objectives, (2) terminology, (3) concepts, (4) practices and techniques, and (5) management of accounting activities. All SMAs are classified and numbered based on this five-element framework. For example, SMA No. 1A is included in the objectives classification. Dates of publication are indicated parenthetically after each title.

In addition to following the five-element framework, the IMA's approach to the content of future SMAs, as with past statements, is clearly based on, and fully consistent with, the MAP Committee's definition of management accounting as follows (Institute of Management Accountants, 1981):

Management accounting is the process of identification, measurement, accumulation, analysis, preparation, interpretation, and communication of financial information used by management to plan, evaluate, and control within an organization and to assure appropriate use of and accountability for its resources. Management accounting also comprises the preparation of financial reports for non-manage-

ment groups such as shareholders, creditors, regulatory agencies, and tax authorities.

The majority of issued Statements on Management Accounting are written for use by accounting practitioners. This perspective is consistent with the fact that the greatest number of statements issued to date have been in the Practices and Techniques category. This is also consistent with the stated purpose of an SMA, which is to supply an in-depth understanding of a management accounting subject that would allow a practitioner to implement the concepts and techniques. Often the application of information included in an SMA is illustrated by studies of companies who have implemented the techniques.

The content of issued Statements on Management Accounting ranges from fundamental issues, such as SMA No. 1A, "Definition of Management Accounting," to very specific accounting practice techniques, such as the (1999) SMA No. 4FF, "Implementing Target Costing." The following list comprises all Statements issued to date. [Those marked * are, as of 1999, currently being reviewed for revision.]

1. *Objectives*
   1A* "Definition of Management Accounting" (1981)
   1B* "Objectives of Management Accounting" (1982)
   1C "Standards of Ethical Conduct for Practitioners of Management Accounting and Financial Management" (1997)
   1D* "The Common Body of Knowledge of Management Accountants" (1986)
   1E* "Education for Careers in Management Accounting" (1987)
2. *Terminology*
   2A "Management Accounting Glossary" (1990)
4. *Practices and Techniques*
   4A "Cost of Capital" (1984)

4B "Allocation of Service and Administrative Costs" (1985)

4C "Definition and Measurement of Direct Labor Cost" (1985)

4D "Measuring Entity Performance" (1986)

4E "Definition and Measurement of Direct Material Cost" (1986)

4F "Allocation of Information Systems Costs" (1986)

4G "Accounting for Indirect Production Costs" (1987)

4H "Uses of the Cost of Capital" (1988)

4I "Cost Management for Freight Transportation" (1989)

4J "Accounting for Property, Plant, and Equipment" (1989)

4K "Cost Management for Warehousing" (1989)

4L "Control of Property, Plant, and Equipment" (1990)

4M "Understanding Financial Instruments" (1990)

4N "Management of Working Capital: Cash Resources" (1990)

4O "The Accounting Classification of Real Estate Occupancy Costs" (1991)

4P "Cost Management for Logistics" (1992)

4Q "Use and Control of Financial Instruments by Multinational Companies" (1992)

4R "Managing Quality Improvements" (1993)

4S "Internal Accounting and Classification of Risk Management Costs" (1993)

4T "Implementing Activity-Based Costing" (1993)

4U "Developing Comprehensive Performance Indicators" (1995)

4V "Effective Benchmarking" (1995)

4W "Implementing Corporate Environmental Strategies" (1995)

4X "Value Chain Analysis for Assessing Competitive Advantage" (1996)

4Y "Measuring the Cost of Capacity" (1996)

4Z "Tools and Techniques of Environmental Accounting for Business Decisions" (1996)

4AA "Measuring and Managing Shareholder Value Creation" (1997)

4BB "The Accounting Classification of Workpoint Costs" (1997)

4CC "Implementing Activity-Based Management: Avoiding the Pitfalls" (1998)

4DD "Tools and Techniques for Implementing Integrated Performance Management Systems" (1998)

4EE "Tools and Techniques for Implementing ABC/ABM" (1998)

4FF "Implementing Target Costing" (1999)

4GG "Tools and Techniques for Implementing Target Costing" (1998)

5. *Management of Accounting Activities*

5A "Evaluating Controllership Effectiveness" (1990)

5B "Fundamentals of Reporting Information to Managers" (1992)

5C "Managing Cross-Functional Teams" (1994)

5D "Developing Comprehensive Competitive Intelligence" (1996)

5E "Redesigning the Finance Function" (1997)

(SEE ALSO: *Institute of Management Accountants*)

BIBLIOGRAPHY

Aldridge, C. Richard, and Colbert, Janet L. (1997). "We Need Better Financial Reporting." *Management Accounting* July:32-36.

American Institute of Certified Public Accountants (AICPA). (1982). *Statement on Auditing Standards* No. 31. New York, NY: Author.

"Institute of Management Accountants" (editorial). (1991). *Management Accounting* June:1.

Institute of Management Accountants. www.imanet.org.

Management Accounting Practices Committee. (1981). "Definition of Management Accounting." *Management Accounting Statements* (1A). Montvale, NJ: Institute of Management Accountants.

Schiff, Jonathan B., and Penino, Charles J. (1990). "The Emerging Authority of Statements on Management Accounting." *The Journal of Applied Business Research* Winter:87-91.

Vangermeersch, Richard, and Jordan, Robert. (1996). *The History of Accounting.* (Michael Chatfield and Richard Vangermeersch, eds.). New York: Garland.

B. DOUGLAS CLINTON

STATE SOCIETIES OF CPAS

Independent professional societies for certified public accountants (CPAs) exist in each of the fifty states as well as in Washington, D.C., Puerto Rico, the Virgin Islands, and Guam. CPAs may choose to join their state's professional organization, generally known as (state's name) Society of CPAs or (state's name) Association of CPAs. These organizations consist of CPAs in public practice, in education, and in government and industry. In the larger states, the state societies are divided into chapters by geographic location. The relationships between the state societies and the national organization, the American Institute of Certified Public Accountants (AICPA), and also between the state societies and the state and national Boards of Accountancy, are also examined in this article.

The societies collect dues and are run by full time and/or part-time staff as well as a board of directors with officers elected from the membership. State societies have executive directors; these executive directors belong to an association that maintains an informative Web site: (http://www.cpasea.org). This site has profiles of each of the state societies, including information about their dues, membership, and publications.

SERVICES

State societies sponsor education programs and provide resources for their members as well as opportunities to network with other professionals. They represent the interests of the profession at the state legislative level and have an array of committees that their members can join. While some of the committees are common to most of the states, others may be unique to a state or a region.

Frequently state societies offer additional benefits to their members, such as access to insurance plans for professional liability, life, and health insurance. State society members often list "networking" as an important reason to join; frequently joint meetings/functions are held with other state professionals, such as lawyers, bankers, or educators.

EDUCATION

In many states, practicing CPAs are required to complete continuing professional education (CPE) credits to maintain their license. While licensing is the responsibility of the Board of Accountancy, state societies often offer a variety of CPE courses, usually available to both members and nonmembers. These courses can be taken through attending seminars or through self-study videos and/or workbooks.

ADVOCACY AND PROMULGATION OF PROFESSIONAL STANDARDS

State societies monitor developments in their respective state legislatures that potentially can affect their members. Legislation regarding matters such as regulating the profession, tax issues, and economic issues important to CPAs and their clients is of interest to the members. Depending on the issue, the response of the society may range from making the members aware of proposed legislation, to composing a position paper on a certain issue, to hiring lobbyists to be certain the views of the membership are heard.

COMMITTEES

Some state society committees exist to provide a forum for discussion among members with special interests, such as members in public practice, in business and industry, in government, or in education. Other committees enable members to discuss important topics such as peer reviews, changes or proposed changes in audit standards, or recent changes in tax law. Still others plan social events or fund-raising activities.

AICPA AND STATE SOCIETIES

The American Institute of Certified Public Accountants (AICPA) is a national professional society founded in 1887. It is a membership organization, as are the 54 state societies. As of 1999, AICPA membership numbered 328,000. AICPA members are licensed CPAs, with some limited specialty categories for non-CPA members. The AICPA and the state societies are unaffiliated. CPAs can join the AICPA and/or their state society. Members of state societies often serve on committees at the national level and use the services of the AICPA.

The AICPA employs a variety of professionals who serve as resources for CPAs and assist state societies with problems or initiatives. The AICPA promulgates accounting standards and is responsible for producing the uniform CPA exam. The exam is currently given in May and November in each of the states. Each state's Board of Accountancy is responsible for exam results. The AICPA serves as an advocate for the profession at the national level. Laws that affect CPAs are monitored by employees of the AICPA as well as representatives from the states. The AICPA publishes the monthly *Journal of Accountancy*, a widely read periodical with articles on timely topics affecting CPAs, and maintains a large professional library. Their website (http://www.aicpa.org) contains a wealth of information about the organization as well as the profession.

The AICPA has a Code of Professional Conduct that holds members to certain ethical standards. Most state societies implement the code through a Joint Ethics Enforcement Program. Members who fail to abide by the code may have their membership terminated and their name published. A member's license, however, can only be revoked by a state Board of Accountancy.

BOARDS OF ACCOUNTANCY

Each state has a Board of Accountancy responsible for administering the uniform CPA examination within the state, licensing certified public accountants, and regulating the practice of public accountancy, generally through legislation. State regulations include the requirements for getting a CPA certificate and/or license and rules governing CPE credits—both the number of hours needed and the content areas. State Boards of Accountancy are regulatory agencies with no direct ties to the AICPA or the state societies, although they frequently cooperate on projects that benefit the profession.

The National Association of Boards of Accountancy (NASBA) exists to enhance the effectiveness of the state Boards of Accountancy. It serves as a forum for the nation's state Boards of Accountancy and includes a member from each state's Board of Accountancy. NASBA maintains an informative Web site (http://www.nasba.org).

Although the state's Board of Accountancy is independent of the state's society and the AICPA, they may form joint task forces. Some examples of cooperation include peer review and unifying the requirements for becoming a CPA. Peer review is a method for relicensing mandated by a state's Board of Accountancy. These programs are often monitored by the state society, an arrangement generally accepted by the state Board of Accountancy. Also, an attempt to unify the accountancy laws in the various states has been proposed by NASBA with the AICPA's and several state societies' backing. This effort toward a Uniform Accountancy Act would streamline the regulations for becoming and remaining a CPA in the different states.

CONCLUSION

The state societies and the AICPA are professional organizations that CPAs may join. The state Boards of Accountancy are regulatory agencies. The organizations are independent, with each having a different function. Since the topic of state societies and their relationship to the AICPA and the Boards of Accountancy is not covered in texts or reference material, the best sources of further information are the websites mentioned in this article.

(SEE ALSO: *American Institute of CPAs; National Association of Boards of Accountancy*)

KATHLEEN SIMONS

STOCK EXCHANGES

A stock exchange is a forum for trading in securities representing shares of firms. An exchange provides ways by which financing is raised by the sale of shares to outside investors. It provides a mechanism for the valuation of companies through the process of price discovery and a means by which such information is disseminated.

A formal definition of the term *exchange* is a critical component of law and regulation regarding securities trading markets, discussed by Domowitz (1996) and Lee (1998). In the United States, the New York Stock Exchange (NYSE) is legally an exchange, while the markets operated by the National Association of Securities Dealers (NASDAQ) and Instinet, an electronic communications network (ECN), are not. All three examples nevertheless satisfy the definition of a stock exchange given above. Given differences across countries with respect to legal definitions, a more unified approach is needed to focus the discussion.

The approach taken here is to identify important attributes and functions of institutions satisfying the basic definition in practice. Exchanges provide *trading systems* and may offer more than one. Types of trading systems are sometimes differentiated by the form of *market intermediation* provided by entities with direct access to the system. The nature of *competition* between exchanges is a defining feature, since

exchanges may adopt varying market structures in order to compete in different fashions. A stock exchange is a business entity, and the form of its *governance* arrangements is important in understanding its nature and conduct.

TRADING SYSTEMS

Trading markets may be defined as systems consisting of an order routing system, an information network, and a trade execution mechanism (Stoll, 1992). A trading system is a communications technology for passing allowable messages between traders, together with a set of rules that transform traders' messages into transactions prices and allocations of quantities of stock among market participants.

The nature of allowable messages varies with the exchange's rules and technology. A typical message consists of an offer to buy, or to sell, a given number of shares at a certain price. The NYSE, for example, permits such messages, as well as orders, to buy some amount of stock at current market prices. The OptiMark system of the Pacific Stock Exchange also allows traders to submit a message indicating the strength of the traders' desire to transact an amount of stock at a particular price. Orders for the shares of a company, contingent on the completion of transactions in other companies, are possible. As technology advances, the ability of trading systems to offer more flexible messages increases.

The transformation of messages and information from the system into a price and a set of quantity allocations is governed by another set of rules. In *open outcry auctions*, bids and offers are orally exchanged by traders standing in a single physical location. The acceptance of a bid or offer by another trader generates a transaction. In *dealer systems*, such as NASDAQ, dealers accept orders by telephone or computerized routing, and transact at prices they themselves set. In *batch auctions*, such as that of the Arizona Stock Exchange, price is set by maximizing trading volume, given order submission at the time of the auction. In most computerized markets, traders submit orders to a central *limit order book*, and a mathematical algorithm determines prices and

Floor of New York Stock Exchange.

quantities. Examples include the CAC system of the Paris Bourse and the OM system of the Stockholm Stock Exchange. The range of possibilities here is large, and a taxonomy of rules is given in Domowitz (1993).

MARKET INTERMEDIATION

Investors are generally not given free access to trading systems. Entry into the exchange's systems is intermediated by *brokers*. Brokers may simply route orders to exchanges. They sometimes make decisions as to what exchange, and what system within the exchange, should process various parts of an order. In open outcry markets, brokers also physically represent orders on the floor of the exchange.

Exchanges are differentiated most by a class of intermediaries known as *market makers*. Market makers trade for their own accounts, usually providing an offer to sell and an offer to buy at the same time, but at different prices. In doing so, they both contribute to the pricing process and

supply immediacy to the market by a willingness to be a counterparty to an order for which another investor may not be immediately available.

On some exchanges, most notably the NYSE, there is one primary market maker designated by the exchange, known as the *specialist*. The specialist obtains consideration for the supply of immediacy and the maintenance of an orderly market by having private access to order-flow information through the order book for the stock.

There may be multiple market makers in a given stock, regardless of the precise form of trading system. The prototype example is that of dealer markets, in which the dealers are the market makers. They post bids and offers, and trade out of their own inventory.

Electronic limit order book markets offer the possibility of trading without such financial intermediation. In practice, however, market makers exist on electronic markets as well. Multiple market makers in a security are often designated by an exchange, fulfill obligations not dissimilar to those of a specialist, and receive some consideration for the service. Anyone with direct access to the trading system can function as a market maker, however, simply by continuously offering quotes for stock on both sides of the market.

COMPETITION

Exchanges have two clienteles: companies, which list their shares, and investors, who trade on the exchange. Historically, the product (a listing) offered to companies was a bundle, consisting of (1) liquidity, (2) monitoring of trading against forms of fraud, (3) standard-form rules of trading, (4) a signal that a listing firm's stock is of high quality, and (5) a clearing function to ensure timely payment and delivery of shares (Macey and O'Hara, 1999). The product offered to investors consists of a combination of liquidity and pricing information, as well as any benefits accruing to the investor from the bundle offered to companies.

Government regulation and increased competition from automated trading systems lessen the importance of exchange monitoring and standardized rules. Technological advances in information processing allow better signals about company quality than simple listings, permit wide distribution of pricing information outside exchanges, and enable separation of the clearing function from other exchange operations. The result is that exchanges now compete solely along the dimensions of liquidity and cost of trading (Domowitz and Stell, 1999; Macey and O'Hara 1999).

Competition through liquidity and cost has led to increased automation of the exchange trade execution process. Automated exchanges are less costly to build and operate, and provide lower-cost trade execution. Liquidity is enhanced by the ability to establish wide networks of traders through communications systems with an automated execution system at the nexus. The drive for increased liquidity through computerization has led to new developments in the structure of the exchange services industry, most notably including mergers and alliances between automated exchanges for increased order flow.

Communications technology and the computerization of trade execution have also globalized trading. The physical location and boundaries of an exchange floor are no longer important to traders. A company does not need to be listed, or even traded, on a domestic exchange. Not only are there many possible execution services providers, but electronic exchanges place their own terminals on foreign soil, allowing direct access to overseas listings, regardless of the nationality of the companies involved. An example is the U.K. electronic exchange, Tradepoint, which conducts operations in the United States.

GOVERNANCE

Exchanges historically have been organized as not-for-profit membership cooperatives. Exchange governance is shifting to a for-profit corporate structure. Ten such demutualizations globally are listed in Domowitz and Stell (1999), and such initiatives are under investigation by many traditional exchanges, including NASDAQ and the NYSE. Three rationales for this change have been proposed.

Increased competition between exchanges forces the change in ownership structure (Hart and Moore, 1996). This is the view of the exchange services industry, as well. The industry argument is simply that a corporate structure with a profit motive enables faster initiatives in response to competitive advances than a committee- and voting-oriented membership organization.

Changes in the contractual relationship between exchanges and listing companies might outweigh competition as a force behind the shift from cooperative to corporate ownership arrangements (Macey and O'Hara, 1999). The long-term mutual dependency between companies and exchanges no longer exists, and market makers do not make firm-specific investments that might be fostered under a cooperative umbrella.

The third view is that communications and computerized execution technology permit and encourage the change in governance structure (Domowitz and Stell, 1999). Traditional exchanges are limited by floor space, and access is rationed through the sale of limited memberships. In an automated auction, there are no barriers to providing unlimited direct access, with a transactions-fee pricing structure, which in turn lends itself to corporate for-profit operations. All examples of the change in governance begin with a conversion from floor trading technology to automated trade execution. For trade execution services with no prior history of cooperative governance structure, the mutual structure is routinely avoided in favor of a for-profit joint-stock corporation.

BIBLIOGRAPHY

Domowitz, Ian. (1993). "A Taxonomy of Automated Trade Execution Systems." *Journal of International Money and Finance* 12:607-631.

Domowitz, Ian. (1996). "An Exchange Is a Many Splendored Thing: The Classification and Regulation of Automated Trading Systems." In Andrew Lo, ed., *The Industrial Organization and Regulation of Securities Markets.* Chicago: University of Chicago Press.

Domowitz, Ian, and Stell, Benn. (1999). "Automation, Trading Costs, and the Structure of the Securities Trading Industry." In Robert E. Litan and Anthony M. Santomero, eds., *Brookings-Wharton Papers on Financial Services.* Washington, DC: Brookings Institution.

Hart, Oliver, and Moore, John. (1996). "The Governance of Exchanges: Members' Cooperatives Versus Outside Ownership." *Oxford Review of Economic Policy* 12:53-69.

Lee, Ruben. (1998). *What Is an Exchange? The Automation, Management, and Regulation of Financial Markets.* Oxford: Oxford University Press.

Macey, Jonathan R., and O'Hara, Maureen. (1999). "Globalization, Exchange Governance, and the Future of Exchanges." In Robert E. Litan and Anthony M. Santomero, eds., *Brookings-Wharton Papers on Financial Services.* Washington, DC: Brookings Institution.

Stoll, Hans. (1992). "Principles of Trading Market Structure." *Journal of Financial Services Research* 6:75-107.

IAN DOMOWITZ

STOCK INDEXES

An understanding of the basic characteristics of the different kinds of stocks will be helpful in considering the information in this entry. (See "Stocks")

An investor's most important tool is information: information about stock prices, movement in the market, and business trends. Without sound information, investment decisions are pure guesswork. The first place to look for information about any stock is the financial pages or a newspaper, and the best place to start is with the columns listing the current stock prices on one or more of the major organized exchanges. Figure 1 shows a typical listing for a stock traded on one of the major exchanges, and the following list explains the information in the figure and what it means for prospective investors:

1. *High and low.* These are the highest and lowest prices paid for the stock during the previous fifty-two weeks. This entry shows that the highest price paid for this stock during the previous period was $44 per share; the lowest price, $16 per share.

2. *Stock.* Stocks are listed alphabetically by an abbreviated form of the corporate name.

3. *Dividend.* The rate of annual dividend is shown; it is generally an estimate based on the previous quarterly or semiannual payment. This entry shows that JLJ is paying an annual dividend of $2.50 per share, or about 7 percent yield.

4. *Price/Earnings ratio.* This is the ratio of the market price of the stock to the annual earnings of the company per share of stock. This is an important indicator of corporate success and investor confidence. It cannot be calculated from the information given here. Other data are needed.

5. *Shares traded.*This is the number of shares sold for the day, expressed in hundreds. In the example shown, 3300 shares of JLJ stock were traded. The figure does not

Sample Stock Listing									
High (1)	Low (1)	Stock (2)	Div (3)	P/E (4)	100S (5)	High (6)	Low (6)	Last (7)	Change (8)
44	16	JLJ	2.50	9	33	$35^{1/4}$	34	35	+1/2

Figure 1

include odd-lot sales. *Note:* If the number in this column is preceded by a "z," it signifies the actual number of shares traded, not hundreds.

6. *High and low.* These are the highest and lowest prices paid for JLJ stock during the trading session (that is, the business day). The highest price paid for JLJ stock was $35.25 per share; the lowest price, $34 per share. Stock prices are shown in dollars and fractions of dollars up to 15/16. However, a new system of dollars and cents, implemented in 2000, is now also used.

7. *Closing price.* The final price of JLJ stock for the day. In this case, it was $35 per share.

8. *Change.* The difference between the closing price of the stock for this session and the closing price for the previous close; yesterday's closing price would have been $34.50.

The expectations of future growth and profit are captured through computations that are called market indexes. Such indexes provide, in essence, summaries of expectations. Indexes reflect a variety of assumptions about the factors that influence expectations as assessed by the designers of market indexes. Many market indexes will, at times, provide the same assessments. However, there is considerable difference in the performance of indexes in the long run. The stocks, divisors, and weighting selected for an index lead to long-run difference.

Some of the most popular indexes (as of early 2000) are:

- American Stock Exchange composite index
- Dow Jones Industrial Average index
- Nasdaq composite index
- Nasdaq—100 index
- New York Stock Exchange composite index
- Russell index
- Standard and Poor's 500 index
- 30-Year Treasury bond index

We examine here three of the most widely accepted stock market indexes and the types of stocks they include.

THE DOW JONES INDUSTRIAL AVERAGE

Charles H. Dow introduced the Dow Jones Industrial Average in 1896 when the market was not considered a respectable venture because of unscrupulous dealers, massive speculation, and the lack of information. His average brought about change at a time when people found it quite difficult to understand the ups and downs of fractionalized points. It is called an average because it originally was computed by taking the stock prices, adding them together, and dividing them by the number of stocks. The first figure came out on May 26, 1896, with an average of 40.94. Dow defended his average by comparing it to the placement of sticks in the sand on the beach. His concept was to determine, after each wave, whether the tide was coming in or receding. If the average of his stocks increased progressively, then he was able to call the period a "bull market." If the average dropped lower, then a "bear market" had taken hold.

The Dow provides a comparison of industrial stocks to the direction of the average. In attempts to gauge or predict large-scale trends in stock-market values, the Dow Jones Industrial Average (DJIA) is most often cited. The term "industrial" is a bit misleading. In the late nineteenth century, railroads and steel companies were the important corporations. Today, they do not represent any great hold on the "Dow." The DJIA is the most frequently mentioned of four Dow Jones averages (covering industrial stocks, transportation stocks, utility stocks, and a composite average); it is a barometer of stock market trends based on the stock prices of thirty large U.S. corporations listed on the New York Stock Exchange. Every day, the fluctuations in the prices of these stocks are combined by adding up the prices of the thirty stocks and dividing the result by the designated factor used to compensate for complicating situations, such as stock splits, spin-offs, and periodic substitutions in the list of stocks used.

The current divisor is published every business day in the Money & Investing section of the *Wall Street Journal*. Over the history of the average, the divisor has been changed many times, mostly downward. This explains why the average can be reported as, for example, 10,000, although no single stock in the average approaches that price level. Today, a $1 rise in the price of a component stock would raise the Dow Jones Industrial Average roughly five points, assuming prices of the other twenty-nine stocks were unchanged. The thirty stocks and their symbols that made up the DJIA during 2000 are shown in Figure 2.

THE STANDARD & POOR'S 500

The Standard & Poor's (S&P) index was created (in its present mode) in 1958 in order to make indexes more popular with the investing public. Rather than keeping its previous index, made up of ninety stocks, it moved to a much broader scale of four hundred large capitalization industrial companies, forty utilities, twenty transportation companies, and forty financial firms, making it the S&P 500. In its continuous review, the selection committee replaces about thirty companies annually. The reason for a company's elimination might be its own downsizing (so it can no longer be considered a large-cap stock) or its

acquisition by or merger with a different type of company not represented in the S&P.

The reported number (factor) that one sees in the daily paper or hears about on the financial news report, along with the Dow and the Nasdaq, is determined by the price of the five hundred stocks in the Standard & Poor's index. It is also important to mention that the S&P is market-weighted. This is done so that no single company, or small group of companies, will dominate the index or influence its calculations. Market weighting is determined by taking the number of shares of the outstanding stock of a company and multiplying it by its price. This creates a market situation in which no one company's performance can drastically change the overall performance of this index. The Dow Jones Industrial Average is not calculated in this manner, creating the possibility that the performance of a single stock in the Dow could change the value of the entire index on any given day.

Also, consider the number of businesses involved in the S&P index. With five hundred stocks market-weighted, this index becomes a good indicator of market movements because it mirrors the combined knowledge of thousands of analysts and investors who, through their sales and purchases of stocks, determine the market value of the shares of stocks in the index.

THE NASDAQ COMPOSITE

The Nasdaq (formally known as the National Association of Securities Dealers Automated Quotations) was created in 1971 to compete with the S&P 500 and to measure the entire range of the market. However, with a great proportion of its companies in the high-tech field, the Nasdaq is much more volatile than the stock market in general and the Dow and the S&P in particular. The Nasdaq is not involved only in high-tech stocks; however, the index comprises eight industry subindexes—banking, biotechnology, computers, finance, industrials, insurance, telecommunications, and transportation. The Nasdaq has been called the "index of the new economy," as compared to the "old economy" of the Dow. This composite index includes 5500 companies

Stocks That Make Up the DJIA

Alcoa	(AA)	Exxon	(XON)	McDonald's	(MCD)
Allied Signal	(ALD)	General Electric	(GE)	Merck	(MRK)
American Express	(AXP)	General Motors	(GM)	Microsoft	(MSFT)
AT&T	(T)	Hewlett-Packard	(HWP)	Minnesota Mining	(MMM)
Boeing	(BA)	Home Depot	(HD)	Philip Morris	(MO)
Caterpillar	(CAT)	Intel	(INTC)	Procter & Gamble	(PG)
Citigroup	(C)	Internal Business Machines	(IBM)	SBC Communications	(SBC)
Coca-Cola	(KO)	International Paper	(IP)	United Technologies	(UTX)
Du Pont	(DD)	J.P. Morgan	(JPM)	Wal-Mart	(WMT)
Eastman Kodak	(EK)	Johnson & Johnson	(JNJ)	Walt Disney	(DIS)

Figure 2

and, like the S&P, is market-weighted, thus providing more meaningful numbers. The index's composite figure is computed by measuring the market value of all common stocks listed on the Nasdaq. Any change in any security in any direction will cause the index to change in that direction, but only in proportion to its market value (the last transaction price multiplied by the total shares outstanding). In 1985, Nasdaq introduced the Nasdaq-100 index, which is made up of the largest and most active nonfinancial domestic and international issues on the Nasdaq Stock Market based on market capitalization.

It is true that there is no way to tell where the market will be a year or two from now, but by keeping informed and using indexes as a guide, investors stand a better chance in the roller-coaster market that we have experienced.

JOEL LERNER

STOCKS

There's no doubt that investing in the stock market can be one of the most exciting ways of making money. Nothing quite compares with the thrill of seeing the little-known stock you picked become a hot property, perhaps doubling in price—and then doubling again and again. But as with any investment, the potential risks are equal to the rewards, so investors who want to play the market owe it to themselves to become fully informed before getting involved.

HOW DOES THE STOCK MARKET WORK?

A share of stock represents a unit of ownership in a corporation. When you buy stock, you are becoming a part owner of the business. Therefore, you benefit from any increase in the value of the corporation and you suffer when the corporation performs badly. You're also entitled to share in the profits earned by the corporation.

Stocks are bought and sold in marketplaces known as *stock exchanges*. The exchange itself does not buy or sell stock, nor does it set the price of stock; the exchange is simply a forum in which individuals and institutions may trade in stocks. Stock exchanges play a vital role in a capitalist economy. They provide a way for individuals to purchase shares in thousands of businesses, and they provide businesses with an important source

Japan's electronic stock board.

of capital for expansion, growth, and research and development.

HOW DOES AN INVESTOR PURCHASE STOCK?

Here, in two steps, is what happens when an investor decides to buy or sell a particular stock. First, an account executive at the brokerage house receives the buy or sell order, which may take any of several forms:

- *Round-lot order.* An order to buy or sell 100 shares, considered the standard trading unit

- *Odd-lot order.* An order to buy or sell fewer than 100 shares

- *Market order.* An order to buy or sell at the best available price

- *Limit order.* An order to buy or sell at a specified price

- *Stop order.* An order designated to protect profits or limit losses by calling for sale of the stock when its price falls to a specified level

- *Good till canceled order (GTC).* An order that remains open until it is executed or canceled by the investor

Second, after the order is received, it is sent to the floor of the stock exchange. The brokerage firm's floor broker receives the order and executes it at the appropriate trading post. Confirmation of the transaction is reported back to the account executive at the local office, who notifies the investor. Remarkably, the entire process may take as little as two or three minutes.

WHAT KINDS OF STOCKS ARE AVAILABLE?

There are two kinds of stocks: common and preferred.

Common Stock Each year, hundreds of new issues of stock, known as initial public offerings (IPOs), are sold to the public. Although human life ends at the hands of the *undertaker*, it begins for common stock at the hands of the *underwriter*, who sells the stock, at a fixed price, to a group of initial buyers who in turn "farm out" the investment until it reaches the "street"—which is you, the investor. IPOs have their fans and detractors. If you're anxious to make big money on an IPO, then the letters stand for "immediate profit opportunity." If you're a skeptic, the acronym has only one meaning— "it's probably overpriced."

A share of common stock represents a unit of ownership, or equity, in the issuing corporation. Each share of common stock usually has a par value, which is a more or less arbitrary value established in the corporation's charter and which bears little relation to the stock's actual market value. The market value is influenced by many factors, including the corporation's potential earning power, its financial condition, its earnings record, its record for paying dividends, and general business conditions.

Ownership of a share of common stock carries certain privileges:

1. *A share in earnings.* Each year, the board of directors of the corporation meets to determine the amount of the corporation's earnings that will be distributed to stockholders. This distribution, known as the *dividend*, will vary depending on the company's current profitability. It may be omitted altogether if the company is earning no current profits or if the board elects to plow back profits into growth.

2. *A share in control.* Holders of common stock have the right to vote on matters of corporate policy on the basis of one vote per share held. However, the small investor with only a few shares of stock has little or no practical influence on corporate decisions.

3. *A claim on assets.* In the event of the company's liquidation, holders of common stock have the right to share in the firm's assets after all debts and prior claims have been satisfied.

There are four main categories of common stock, each of which is best for a particular investment strategy and purpose.

1. *Blue-chip stocks.* High-grade, or blue-chip, stocks are issued by well-established corporations with many years of proven success, earnings growth, and consistent dividend payments. Blue-chip stocks tend to be relatively high priced and offer a relatively low-income yield. They are a relatively safe investment.

2. *Income stocks.* Income stocks pay a higher-than-average return on investment. They are generally issued by firms in stable businesses that have no need to reinvest a large percentage of profits each year.

3. *Growth stocks.* Issued by firms expected to grow rapidly during the years to come, growth stocks have a current income that is often low, since the company plows back most of its earnings into research and expansion. However, the value of the stock may rise quickly if the company performs up to expectations.

4. *Speculative stocks.* Speculative stocks are backed by no proven corporate track record or lengthy dividend history. Stocks issued by little-known companies or newly formed corporations, high-flying "glamour" stocks issued by companies in new business areas, and low-priced "penny stocks" may all be considered speculative stocks. As with any speculative investment, there is a possibility of tremendous profit—but a substantial risk of losing all as well.

Preferred Stock Preferred stock, like common stock, represents ownership of a share in a corporation. However, holders of preferred stock have a prior claim on the company's earnings as compared with holders of common stock; hence the name *preferred stock.* Similarly, holders of preferred stock have a prior claim in the company's assets in the event of a liquidation, but they have no voting privileges.

Preferred stock also has certain distinctive features related to dividend payments. A fixed, prespecified annual dividend is usually paid for each share of preferred stock. This fixed dividend may be expressed in dollars (for example, $10 per share) or as a percentage of the stock's par value. It must be paid before dividends are issued to holders of common stock.

However, preferred stock dividends are not considered a debt of the corporation—unlike, for example, the interest due on corporate bonds—because the firm is not obligated to meet its dividend payments. If the corporation is losing money, the board of directors may decide to withhold the dividend payment for a given year. To protect stockholders against undue losses, most preferred stock is issued with a cumulative feature. If a dividend is not paid on cumulative preferred stock, the amount is carried over to the following period, and both current and past unpaid dividends must be paid before holders of common stock can receive any dividend.

WHAT ARE THE ADVANTAGES AND DISADVANTAGES OF STOCKS?

Like any investment, stocks have distinct advantages and disadvantages.

Advantages:

1. *Growth potential.* When a company has the potential for growth in value and earnings, so does its stock. If you pick the right stock or group of stocks, you can profit significantly and relatively quickly. History shows that, as a whole, the stock market has had an upward trend in values, with years of gain outnumbering those of decline by better than three to one.

2. *Liquidity.* Stocks traded on the major exchanges can be bought and sold quickly and easily at readily ascertainable prices.

3. *Possible tax benefits.* Growth stocks, which pay low or no dividends so that company profits can be reinvested, provide an effective tax shelter. As the corporation's value grows, so does the value of the stock, which is a form of tax-deferred income, since no taxes need be paid on these gains until the stock is sold.

Disadvantages

1. *Risk.* There can be no guarantee of making money by investing in stocks. Companies may fail, stock prices may drop, and you may lose your investment. Remember the saying of one concerned investor: "I am not so concerned with the return *on* my investment as I am with the return *of* my investment."

2. *Brokerage commissions.* Most investors need the help and advice of a stockbroker when they become involved in the market. However, high broker commissions can largely erode profits. Since one fee is charged when you buy the stocks and another when you sell them, you are, in effect, forced to pay twice. Unusually well-informed investors should look into the use of a discount broker, who provides little or no investment counseling but charges greatly reduced commissions when trading stocks.

3. *Complexity.* The stock market is complicated, and the amount of knowledge needed to be consistently successful is tremendous. Investors who lack the patience, time, or skill to inform themselves about the market often buy and sell on impulse, thereby minimizing their profits and maximizing their losses.

SUMMARY

Never forget that whenever you buy a stock, there is someone selling it. You may buy the stock because you believe that the investment is good and the price will rise. However, the person selling that same stock believes the opposite, so only one of you will be correct. Think of it in these terms, and you will become a realistic and conservative player.

(SEE ALSO: *Financial Statements; Securities Acts: Requirements for Accounting; Securities and Exchange Commission*)

JOEL LERNER

STRATEGIC MANAGEMENT

Strategic management is the process of developing and executing a series of competitive moves to enhance the success of the organization both in the present and in the future. These competitive moves are derived from the demands of the external environment in which the firm operates as well as the internal capabilities which it has developed or can reasonably hope to build or acquire. While managers may follow somewhat different strategic management routines, a sound process should include an analysis of the current business situation, the formulation of objectives and strategies based on that analysis, and an implementation and evaluation procedure that ensures progress toward each strategy and objective. This article focuses on the formulation of appropriate strategic objectives based on a sound understanding of the internal and external environments faced by the firm. A brief discussion of implementation is included though this topic is covered in greater detail in other entries.

SITUATIONAL ANALYSIS

In order to create appropriate strategic objectives, organizations work to understand their internal capabilities as well as the environment in which they operate. Further, they also seek to clarify their purpose or mission. The situation analysis firmly focuses management's attention on these issues, allowing it to create a fit between its resources and the demands of the competitive situation.

The steps to be taken in a situational analysis are largely agreed upon, though there does exist some debate as to whether one starts with a mission statement or with an analysis of the state of the organization. Those who believe that a mission statement is the logical starting point argue that management must first think carefully and creatively about the future direction of the company if they are to create and implement effective objectives (Thompson and Strickland, 1998). In this way, managers can choose their own vision of what the company ought to be rather than be unduly affected by company history or industry exigencies. On the other hand, managers may want to have a keen understanding of the history and current performance of a company as well as important industry factors so as to craft a strategic vision that is attainable in terms of organizational competencies and industry dynamics. While both sides have merit, this article discusses the state of the organization first.

STATE OF THE ORGANIZATION

In analyzing the state of the organization, managers take a candid measure of its recent performance. Typically, they consider such issues as profitability, stock price performance, market share, revenue growth, customer satisfaction, product innovation, and so forth. These measures can vary from industry to industry. Product innovation, for example, is important to the pharmaceutical industry, while the number of new distributors signed may be a more important measure in the multilevel marketing industry.

In addition to this performance review, managers typically examine a company's (s)trengths, (w)eaknesses, (o)pportunities, and (t)hreats by conducting a (SWOT) analysis. Strengths consist of those things that a company does particularly well relative to its competition and that provide it with some competitive advantage. Strengths can be found in many different areas, including people, such as a particularly competent sales force; systems, such as Federal Express's information systems; locations, like that occupied by a restaurant with sweeping ocean views; and intangible assets, such as a strong brand name. These strengths provide the competitive advantage needed to succeed in the marketplace.

Weaknesses, on the other hand, diminish the competitiveness of a company. They, too, can be found in many different areas, including outdated equipment, a poor understanding of customers, or a high cost structure.

Strengths and weaknesses are typically internal to a company and, therefore, largely under a company's control. Opportunities and threats, on the other hand, are usually derived from the external market situation and require some response from a company if it is to perform well.

Opportunities can arise in many areas, including geographical expansion, new technologies, and changing customer preferences and tastes. Only when a firm has (or can hope to acquire) the specific skills needed to seize upon some option does it become an opportunity for the company.

While opportunities are chances to be seized, threats can be thought of as concerns that are largely outside of the organization's control but have the potential to disrupt its operations. Probably the biggest threat to many companies is their competition. Other sources of threats include foreign economic crises such as the "Asian flu" that began in the latter part of the 1990s, government regulations, natural disasters, and so forth. In creating strategic objectives, management prepares contingency plans to minimize the impact of its most serious threats.

In addition to conducting a SWOT analysis and candid performance review, the executive team may use several other tools to acquire a better understanding of its current situation. They may, for example, identify those forces in the industry that are causing the nature of competition to change for all competitors. One example would be the publicizing of the link between cholesterol and heart disease that made many consumers more aware of the amount of fat in foods. This change made it important for many food manufacturers to either lower the amount of fat in their products or to introduce fat-free or low-fat versions of those products. These forces that change the nature the way companies compete in an industry are known as *driving forces*.

Another tool used by managers in conducting a state-of-the-organization review is an analysis of *key success factors*. In this analysis managers examine those things that all companies within a given industry must do well if they are to survive. These might include rapid service for the fast-food industry, producing large numbers of vehicles so as to offset the high cost of specialized equipment in the automotive industry, or having skilled designers in the fashion industry. By understanding such factors, managers are in a position to better allocate resources so as to perform well in the future.

In addition to these tools, managers may also conduct other types of analyses, including ones focused on customers, economic characteristics of the industry, supplier relationships, and so forth. These analyses constitute a first step in the strategic management process as organizational leaders attempt to understand the organization's current situation so as to later be able to identify those strategic objectives most likely to improve performance.

MISSION STATEMENTS

Having thoroughly understood an organization's internal and external environment, managers establish a mission statement to create a five- to ten-year vision of the company. A mission statement documents the service or product the company provides to the marketplace and the unique way in which it distinguishes itself from other companies. It also indicates the target group of customers that the company serves.

An example of this type of mission statement is provided by *Courtyard by Marriott*. It indicates that *Courtyard by Marriott* is serving economy- and quality-minded frequent business travelers with a premier, moderate-priced lodging facility that is consistently perceived as clean, comfortable, well maintained, attractive, and staffed by friendly, attentive, and efficient people. This mission statement indicates the product and service provided to the target customers and the way in which it will be done.

Mission statements serve several purposes in strategic management. First, they provide direction for the organization. As a firm engages in its strategic planning process it compares its objectives with the path it has set for itself. If any of the goals suggest a deviation from the purpose of the organization, managers must decide if the goal is sufficiently important to warrant a change in the mission statement. Otherwise, the objective might be dropped. With this in mind managers are typically careful to write mission statements that are broad enough to encourage growth but specific enough to give direction.

A second purpose of mission statements is to create a shared sense of purpose and inspiration among employees. In some organizations, employees are required to memorize the mission statement so that they will understand what is appropriate behavior and what is not. For this reason, most mission statements are relatively short so that the purpose of the company remains clearly in the minds of its employees. Further, many companies seek the input of their employees in creating a mission statement so as to create a document that is owned by all.

Finally, mission statements are also external documents. They communicate to the outside world the values and goals of the organization. Unfortunately, some companies create mission statements as a marketing document and then fail to live up to that vision of themselves. For a mission statement to be effective, it must be a living document that motivates behavior.

EXTERNAL ENVIRONMENT REVIEW

Once a company has carefully and frankly understood its situation and has spent time considering the appropriateness of its mission statement, it may choose to do a more thorough review of the external environment. This environment consists of industry, government, competitive, economic, political, and other factors that the organization cannot control but which may have an important impact on the company. For example, the dietary supplements industry in the United States spends large amounts of money to keep abreast of the latest regulations issued by the Food and Drug Administration.

Much of this analysis may be done within the State of the Organization report, but some companies choose to address it as a third step in the strategic planning process so as to assure that they are not caught off guard by these important factors. While the organization cannot control these forces, it can formulate responses that will minimize the potential damage or even put the firm in a better competitive position should the eventuality actually occur.

KEY OBJECTIVES AND STRATEGIES

Having conducted the previous three steps, managers have sufficient information to choose ob-

jectives that are most likely to match the internal capabilities of the firm with the exigencies of the external environment. Thompson and Strickland (1998) state that "objectives represent a managerial commitment to achieving specific performance targets within a specific time frame" (p. 36). While drawing heavily on the previous three steps in the process, objectives rely even more particularly on the SWOT analysis in enhancing certain strengths, overcoming specific weaknesses, capitalizing on opportunities, and addressing the threats. By creating such a fit between the demands of the industry and the skills and competencies of the organization, a firm increases its ability to compete successfully in the marketplace.

Firms may set specific objectives including such things as increasing market share, decreasing customer complaints, cutting costs by 10 percent, or creating a more effective food preparation facility. These broad objectives are then broken down into specific strategies that may, in turn, be broken down into even more specific action steps. It is important that objectives be written in a way that clearly indicates the nature of what is to be achieved, the single individual responsible for the objective, a committee to work on the project, funding assigned, and date to be completed. Based on these requirements, an objective for a rural hospital might take the following form:

Objective 2: Increase revenues from visiting physicians by $500,000.
Person Responsible: Virginia Moody (CEO)
Committee Members: Virginia Moody, Dr. Etta, Erika Boerk (PR director), Sean Ortiz (Facilities Coordinator), and Tristan Roberts (Marketing)
Funding: $125,000
Date Due: June 1, 20XX

Strategies
1. Develop relationship with Dr. Yang (podiatrist).
2. Refurbish existing office space to accommodate visiting physicians.
3. Contract with local newspaper to advertise visits.

4. *Find a dermatologist*
5. *Etc.*

In addition, each of the strategies could also be broken down in similar fashion to include the person(s) responsible, funds required, and due dates.

IMPLEMENTATION

Having created detailed objectives and strategies, an organization may find that some internal adjustments in the way a firm is organized or in the competencies of its workers are required to achieve those objectives. These adjustments may be as simple as sending an employee to a seminar to better understand a new information process software or as complex as creating a new international division to take advantage of overseas opportunities. This process requires the identification of those individual and organization competencies needed to facilitate the accomplishment of the stated objectives.

In addition to serving as a guide to the form of the organization, the objectives also serve as the basis of the year's budgets and performance standards. Having set the funding requirements for each objective, these monies are added to the normal operating budget for each division so that they can fulfill these goals. Further, these objectives and strategies are added to the existing performance standards for each division or department and become an integral part of the performance evaluation of the individuals assigned to each task. In this way the progress of each objective is tracked throughout the year and a specific and agreed-upon measuring stick exists for each employee's performance.

Finally, it should be mentioned that in any strategic management process, but particularly in those taking place in dynamic environments, situations change and strategic plans require modification. While five-year plans may remain relatively unchanged in some industries, other industries may make major modifications monthly. For this reason, most firms consider strategic management to be an ongoing process characterized by periodic progress evaluations and major plan analysis on a yearly basis. Such updates allow a firm to continually reconfigure its internal process and capabilities to create a better fit with the demands of the competitive situation.

BIBLIOGRAPHY

Bourgeios, L. J., III, Duhaime, Irene M., and Stimpert, J. L. (1999). *Strategic Management: A Managerial Perspective,* 2d ed. Fort Worth, TX: Dryden Press.

Hitt, Michael, Ireland, R. Duane, and Hoskisson, Robert E. (1997). *Strategic Management: Competitiveness and Globalization,* 2d ed. Minneapolis/St. Paul, MN: West Publishing Company.

Mintzberg, Henry. (1987). "Crafting Strategy." *Harvard Business Review* July-August: 66-75.

Porter, Michael A. (1980). *Competitive Strategy: Techniques for Analyzing Industries and Competitors.* New York: Free Press.

Porter, Michael A. (1985). *Competitive Advantage: Creating and Sustaining Superior Performance.* New York: Free Press.

Porter, Michael E. (1996). "What Is Strategy?" *Harvard Business Review* November: 61-78.

Prahalad, C. K., and Hamel, Gary. (1990). "The Core Competence of the Corporation." *Harvard Business Review* May-June: 79-83.

Thompson, Arthur A., Jr., and Strickland, A. J. (1998). *Strategic Management,* 10th ed. Boston: Irwin/McGraw-Hill.

NORMAN S. WRIGHT

STRESS, WORK-RELATED

Stress has been defined in a number of ways by a number of different individuals, but everyone agrees that stress is experienced by all workers in the business world no matter what their position. Stress is the body's reaction to any demand placed on it, and health experts agree that some stress is essential for human survival. As demands are placed on a person's body, there will be some kind of automatic reaction. When this reaction is positive, the stress helps individuals perform their jobs better. Positive stress, called eustress, can lead individuals to a new awareness of their abilities and a completely new perspective on their jobs. Negative stress, called distress, upsets individuals and can make them physically sick. It can lead to feelings of distrust, rejection, anger, and depression, which may lead to a number of medical problems, including stroke, heart disease, high blood pressure, cancer, and ulcers.

SYMPTOMS OF STRESS

Because everyone is different, the symptoms of stress are varied and numerous. The symptoms of stress have been placed in different categories, the most common being physical, psychological, behavioral, and mental. Headache, fatigue, grinding teeth, clenched jaws, chest pain, shortness of breath, insomnia, nausea, high blood pressure, muscle aches, constipation or diarrhea, and heart palpitations are all physical symptoms of stress. Anxiety, nervousness, depression, anger, defensiveness, hypersensitivity, apathy, feelings of helplessness, impatience, and short temper are symptoms of psychological stress. Behavioral symptoms include overeating or loss of appetite, procrastination, increased use of alcohol or drugs, pacing, nervous habits (nail-biting, foot-tapping), crying, swearing, poor personal hygiene, and withdrawal or isolation from others. Individuals who experience a decrease in concentration and memory, indecisiveness, confusion, loss of sense of humor, and mind going blank or racing may have mental stress.

Many of these symptoms, when not treated, can lead to serious medical problems as well as loss of time on the job. When individuals experience stress, they often miss work because of illness or arrive late because they dread coming to work. When on the job, they may not performing up to their ability.

REACTION TO STRESS

When individuals perceive or anticipate a threatening or stressful situation, part of the nervous system, the sympathetic nervous system, becomes activated and releases a number of chemicals. One of these chemicals, adrenaline, is a stimulant hormone and is released into the bloodstream. Adrenaline and other hormones, including noradrenaline, produce changes in the body that get the individual geared up for action.

David Posen (1995), who specializes in stress management, indicates that gearing up for action is often called "the fight-or-flight response" because it provides the strength and energy to either fight or run away from danger. These responses increase heart rate and blood pressure in order to get more blood to the muscles, brain, and heart, the organs that are the most important in dealing with danger. This increase in blood flow to the brain, heart, and muscles means that there is a decrease in the blood flow to the skin, digestive tract, kidneys, and liver, where it is least needed in a time of crisis. Individuals will also begin to breathe faster to take in more oxygen, and their muscles will tense so that they are prepared for action. An increased mental alertness and sensitivity of sense organs occurs. As these reactions are taking place, there is also an increase in the blood sugar, fats, and cholesterol and a rise in platelets and blood-clotting factors.

Repeated release of chemicals as a reaction to stress can, over time, cause wear and tear on the heart and blood vessels, eventually leading to heart disease and stroke. Because adrenaline and the other hormones released during stress increase muscle tension, slow digestion, and constrict and dilate arteries, the liver may deliver cholesterol and fat into the bloodstream. The hormone testosterone may increase, which can reduce the levels of high-density lipoproteins (HDL), the good cholesterol.

CAUSES OF STRESS

There are a number of life events, experienced at one time or another by everyone, that cause stress. Some of these are family-related, such as marriage, death of a family member or close friend, divorce or separation, birth or adoption of a child, a personal major illness or illness of a family member, and a major change in a spouse's job or income. An individual's control over the situation will determine the amount of stress these events will cause.

Physical stressors include pollution, excessive noise, physical disability or handicap, weather extremes, smoking, excessive drinking, obesity, overeating, poor nutrition, and lack of rest or relaxation. Many of these physical stressors are beyond an individual's control.

Common workplace stressors include the possibility of dismissal, time pressures, too many responsibilities, unreasonable deadlines, disorganization, adapting to new technology, conflicts with co-workers, information overload, and major changes in job responsibilities.

COMPUTERS AND STRESS

The use of computers in the workplace has introduced new sources of stress. One of the most frequent computer-related stressors is repetitive strain injury (RSI), which occurs when the employee is overworked or when the working environment is not physically conducive to work. Causes of RSI may be repetitious actions such as typing or using a mouse, poor lighting, and poor posture. Another computer-related problem is carpal-tunnel syndrome (CTS), which occurs when the person typing has bad posture and uses incorrect hand movements on the keyboard. Hands and eyes are the main source of communication with the computer. When bad posture and incorrect hand movements are too prevalent, the result is tingling and numbness of the fingers.

Extended time spent working before a computer monitor can produce eye irritation, fatigue, and difficulty focusing, all of which are symptoms associated with eyestrain. Nearsightedness has been associated with eye strain caused by working at a computer monitor.

SOURCES OF JOB STRESS

Job pressures are a major source of stress. Several job conditions have been identified as increasing stress in most employees. Job overload is one such condition. Although some employees may have the ability to do the job, they may not have enough time to do the amount of work necessary. Other employees lack the ability to do the job, being unable to meet the performance standards or expectations set by the employer. Clear job objectives are necessary, and when employees do not know what specific job performance is expected of them, they begin to develop stress.

When jobs are too boring or employees are not challenged to use their abilities, stress occurs. Stress also results from undesirable physical working conditions. Employees experience stress when the work environment is too noisy, too hot, too cold, or too crowded.

A major source of stress involves frequent or significant changes that have a direct effect on the individual's job. These changes can include changes in management, management style, equipment, or job location.

MANAGING STRESS

Just as there are a number of causes for and symptoms of stress, there are a number of ways to manage stress. Individuals vary in their ability to manage stress, and the same techniques do not work for every person. Individuals need to become aware of the stressors they experience and how they react to these stressors.

One stress-management technique that can apply to almost all individuals is learning to manage time more effectively. Managing time more effectively means that individuals learn to prioritize and plan so that they have time for themselves, thus leaving time for listening to music, exercising regularly, mediating, or engaging in whatever type of activity that they find relaxing. Developing an organized time schedule helps ward off tension, which helps reduce stress.

When on the job, employees and managers need to match individual abilities with workload. Managers should be sure that the job objectives are clear so that there is no role ambiguity or role conflict. As employees' work responsibilities change, managers should keep them informed of what is going to happen, why it is going to happen, and when it will happen.

When individuals cannot manage stress on their own or with the help of their managers, medication may be necessary. These medications can, in the short term, moderate physical reactions to stress. Doctors usually prescribe Valium and Xanax for relief from stress. Tranquilizers are suggested for only short periods of time, because individuals can become dependent on them.

BIBLIOGRAPHY

Costley, Dan L., and Todd, Ralph. (1991). *Human Relations in Organizations*, 4th ed. New York: West Publishing Company.

"Ever Thought of Calling in Well?" (1998). *U.S. News & World Report* November 9: 82-83.

GreenTree Nutrition, Inc. "Stress." http://www.greentree .com/condition.html?num = 16. 1999.

Keita, Gwendolyn Puryear, and Hurrell, Joseph J., Jr., eds. (1994). *Job Stress in a Changing Workforce.* Washington, DC: American Psychological Association.

Managing Stress in the Workplace—A Practical Guide for Managers. (1998). Northern Territory Government.

Moore, Jo Ellen. (1999). "Are You Burning Out Valuable Resources?" *HRMagazine* January 1:93-98.

Newton, Tim. (1995). *"Managing" Stress—Emotion and Power at Work.* Thousand Oaks, CA: SAGE Publications.

Posen, David B. (1995). "Stress Management for Patient and Physician." *Canadian Journal of Continuing Medical Education.*

Tim, Paul R., and Peterson, Brent D. (1993). *People at Work—Human Relations in Organizations*, 4th ed. New York: West Publishing Company.

JIM D. RUCKER

SUPPLIERS

(SEE: *Channels of Distribution*)

SUPPLY

(SEE: *Supply and Demand*)

SUPPLY AND DEMAND

The market process is generally modeled using the economic concepts of supply and demand. The plans/desires of consumers are embedded in the concept of demand and the plans/desires of producers in the concept of supply. The plans of these two types of economic actors are brought together in markets, which are the entities in which transactions occur. In a modern economy, markets do not require that the buyers and sellers meet in a geographic place, so markets no longer require actual "marketplaces."

The concept of demand represents the market activity of consumers. Demand is defined as the quantity of a good or service that consumers will be both willing and able to purchase at any given price during a specific period of time, holding all other factors constant. Demand is, therefore, a relationship between price and quantity demanded. Many factors other than price affect the amount consumers choose to purchase, and these factors are what is being held constant within the concept of demand.

Demand can be illustrated in a schedule that shows how many units of a good or service consumers will purchase at several distinct prices. Table 1 shows how many units of a good (widgets) consumers will purchase at a number of different prices. This relationship between price and quantity demanded can also be represented graphically. A demand curve represents the maximum price that consumers would be willing to pay for a particular quantity of the good. Consumers are willing to purchase something because they value that product more than its opportunity cost. The opportunity cost is the value of the best alternative they could purchase with the same money; that is, when a consumer chooses to spend $2 on a hamburger, he or she has decided that the hamburger provides more satisfaction (at that moment in time) than anything else that could be bought with that $2. Thus, the demand curve represents the value of the product to the consumer. The area under the demand curve provides a measure of the total value that consumers receive from consuming that amount of the product.

The nature of this relationship between price and quantity demanded is so consistent that it is called the law of demand. This law states that the relationship defined by the concept of demand is an inverse or indirect one. When prices rise, other factors held constant, consumers will purchase less of the good, and vice versa. The rationale for the law is that when the price of a product changes relative to the price of other products, consumers will change their purchasing patterns by buying less of the now higher-priced good and purchasing more of other goods which are now relatively less expensive that satisfy the same basic wants. Goods that satisfy the same basic wants are called substitutes. For example, if the price of beef rises relative to the price of pork, chicken, and turkey, consumers will shift some of their purchases from beef to pork, chicken, and turkey.

Supply can be defined as the relationship between the price of a good or service and the quantity producers are willing and able to make available for sale in a given period of time, holding other things constant. A supply schedule showing how many widgets producers will make available for sale at several distinct prices is also shown in Table 1. Supply represents graphically the minimum price that consumers are willing to accept in order to make a given amount of the good or service available for sale. As such, it is the opportunity cost to society of producing that particular good.

The law of supply states that this relationship is a direct one. When the price of a good rises, holding other factors constant, producers will be willing to supply more of the product. The rationale for this law is that resource owners will want to use their resources in the most valuable way possible. For example, if the market price of corn rises relative to that of wheat, farmers will choose to plant more of the land available to them in corn and less in wheat.

EQUILIBRIUM

A market is a place where suppliers and demanders meet to conduct an exchange. Modern markets do not require these two parties to be in the same place or even to communicate their desires at the same time. The market process can be thought of as a type of "auction process." Given the supply and demand curves shown in Figure 1, if an auctioneer was to call out a price of $5, consumer would be willing and able to purchase 50 units (the quantity demanded), but producers would be willing and able to supply only 10 units (the quantity supplied). If consumers want to buy 50 units and there are only 10 for sale, there is a shortage of 40 units (quantity demanded minus quantity supplied). Whenever

Widgets

Quantity Supplied	Price	Quantity Demanded
50	$13	10
40	$11	20
30	$ 9	30
20	$ 7	40
10	$ 5	50

Table 1

there is a greater quantity demanded than supplied, there will be a shortage. Consumers will then attempt to compete for the scarce units. This competition will take the form of bidding up the price. To continue with the auction illustration, the auctioneer sees that people want to buy more than is available, and so he calls out a new, higher price of $7 per unit. At $7, the consumers who valued the product more than $5, but less than $7, drop out of the market. That is, the quantity demanded falls from 50 units to 40 units. However, the law of supply tells us that the new, higher price will induce producers to increase the quantity supplied. The quantity supplied rises from 10 to 20 units. Consumers still want to buy more than producers want to sell, so there continues to be a shortage, but the shortage has been reduced from 40 units to 20 units. Consumers still must attempt to out-compete other consumers, and the price is bid up again. Only when our imaginary auctioneer calls out a price of $9 is the quantity consumers demand equal to the quantity that producers supply. This is called the market clearing price. This price "clears" the market because everyone who wants to buy at that price is able to and everyone who wants to sell at that price is able to. This makes the market stable because consumers no longer have a need to bid up the price. Thus, the market is at an equilibrium at the price for which the quantity demanded is equal to the quantity supplied.

If the price is above the market clearing price, consumers will be willing and able to buy less than producers are willing and able to make available for sale. For example, if the price is $13

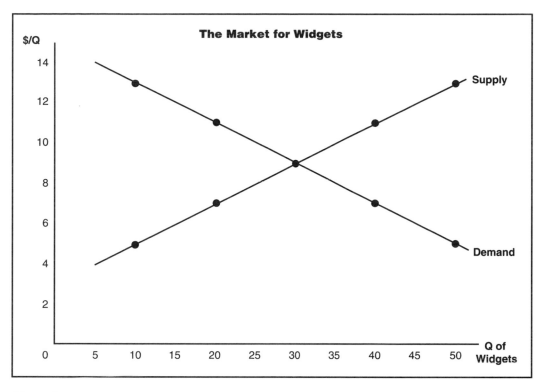

Figure 1

(in Figure 1), quantity demanded will be 10 units and quantity supplied will be 50 units. Whenever quantity supplied is greater than quantity demanded, there will be a surplus. In this case, the surplus is equal to 40 units (quantity supplied minus quantity demanded). If there is a surplus in a market, producers will compete with each other for scarce buyers by bidding down the price. When the price falls to $11, consumers will increase the amount they want to buy to 20 units and producers will reduce the amount they want to sell to 40 units, so that the surplus falls to 20 units. But here, the producers will continue to try to outcompete other producers for the consumers in the market by offering their product for an even lower price. It is not until the price falls to the market clearing level of $9 that the surplus disappears and producers no longer need to bid the price down in order to sell their product.

If the price is below the market clearing price, consumers will up bid the price, and if the price is above the equilibrium price, producers will bid down the price. It is only at the equilibrium price that quantity demanded equals quantity supplied and the market price stabilizes. This is the only price for which consumers have no reason to offer a higher price and producers have no reason to offer a lower price.

NONPRICE DETERMINANTS OF DEMAND

Consumers base their purchasing decisions on several factors other than price. These nonprice determinants of demand are the things that are held constant in the definition of demand. When these factors change, the relationship between price and quantity demanded changes; that is, the demand curve itself shifts. An increase in demand is represented graphically as a shift in the demand curve in a northeasterly direction (for example, from $D0$ to $D1$ in Figure 2), and a decrease in demand is represented as a shift of the demand curve in a southwesterly direction (for example, from $D0$ to $D2$ in Figure 2). The two main nonprice determinants of demand are consumers' incomes and wealth, and the prices of

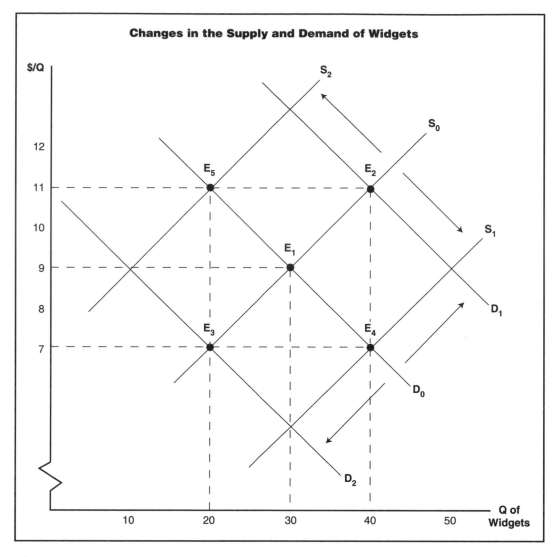

Figure 2

related goods. An increase in income and/or wealth can cause the demand for a good to either increase or decrease. If an increase in income/wealth causes the demand for a good to increase, the good is called a normal good. This increase in demand is illustrated in Figure 2 by a shift from $D0$ to $D1$, causing the market equilibrium to change from $E1$ to $E2$, resulting in an increase in the market price (from $9 to $11) and an increase in quantity bought and sold (from 30 to 40 units). If an increase in income/wealth causes the demand for a good to decrease, the good is called

an inferior good. This is illustrated in Figure 2 by a shift in demand from $D0$ to $D2$. The market then clears at $E3$ with a lower market price ($7) and a smaller quantity (20 units). Likewise, the impact of a change in the price of a related good on a good's demand depends on whether the goods are related as substitute goods or complementary goods. Two goods are substitutes if an increase in the price of one causes the demand for the other to increase, and the goods are complements if an increase in the price of one causes the demand for the other to decrease.

NONPRICE DETERMINANTS OF SUPPLY

Producers base their decisions about what to produce with the productive resources they have at their disposal on more factors than just the prices of the different goods. These other factors are called the nonprice determinants of supply. The major nonprice determinants of supply are the prices of the inputs used to produce the product, the state of technology used to produce the product, and the prices of other goods that are related in production. An increase in supply is represented graphically as a shift in the supply curve in a southeasterly direction and a decrease in supply is shown as a shift in a northwesterly direction (see Figure 2). An increase (decrease) in the price of an input into the production of a good, which would increase (decrease) the cost of production, will cause the supply to fall (rise). For example, an increase in the price of fertilizer will cause the supply of corn to fall, holding other factors constant. If the supply curve were to shift from $S0$ to $S2$, everything else being equal, the market equilibrium would change from point $E1$ to $E5$, causing the market clearing price to rise (from \$9 to \$11) and quantity transacted to fall (from 30 to 20 units). An advancement in technology that lowers the cost of production will also cause supply of the good to rise. For example, the discovery of a new chemical agent that increases the yield of an acre of land planted in corn will increase the supply of corn, holding other factors constant. If the supply curve were to shift from $S0$ to $S1$, the market equilibrium would change from point $E1$ to $E4$, causing the market clearing price to fall (from \$9 to \$7) and the quantity transacted to rise (from 30 to 40 units). An increase (decrease) in the price of a different good that is produced using the same inputs (goods that are related in production) will cause producers to increase their production of the now higher-priced, and hence more profitable, good. In order to do this, resources will need to be reallocated away from the production of other goods. For example, an increase in the price of wheat (relative to the price of corn) will cause producers to shift factors of production toward the production of wheat and away from the production of corn.

John L. Conant

SUPPLY CURVES

(SEE: *Supply and Demand*)

T

TARGET MARKETING

A *target market* is a set of buyers sharing common needs or characteristics that a company decides to serve. A company identifies a target market in order to organize its tasks and cope with the particular demands of the marketplace. Target marketing forms the foundation of a modern marketing strategy because doing it well helps a company be more efficient and effective by focusing on a certain segment of its market that it can best satisfy.

Targeting also benefits consumers because a company can reach specific groups of consumers with offers carefully tailored to satisfy their needs. To do so, a company has to evaluate the various segments and decide how many, and which one, to target. There is no single way to segment a market. A company needs to research different segmentation variables alone, and in combination with others, to find its target market. There are four main variables that can be used in segmenting consumer markets: geographic segmentation, demographic segmentation, psychographic segmentation, and behavioral segmentation.

Geographic segmentation calls for dividing the market into different geographic units, such as nations, regions, states, counties, cities, or neighborhoods. Many companies today are localizing their products—as well as their advertising, promotion, and sales efforts—to fit the needs of individual cities, regions, and neighborhoods.

For example, clothing stores sell clothes targeted to their geographic markets. In January, the Gap clothing store sells winter clothing in Portland, Maine, such as mittens, scarves, and winter jackets. A Gap located in Clearwater, Florida, will sell more T-shirts, shorts, and bathing suits.

Demographic segmentation divides the market into groups based on such variables as age, gender, family size, family life cycle, income, occupation, education, religion, race, and nationality. Demographics is the most popular basis for segmenting customer groups because of consumer needs, wants, and usage rates often closely reflect demographic variables. Even when a market segment is first defined using other factors, such as psychographic or geographic segmentation, demographic characteristics must be known in order to assess the size of the target market and to reach it efficiently. This information is also the easiest and least expensive to retrieve because it is secondary data; that is, it comes from research that has already been conducted. An example of successful demographic target marketing is that of cosmetic companies that have responded to the special needs of minority market segments by adding products specifically designed for black, Hispanic, or Asian women. For example, Maybelline introduced a highly successful line, called Shades of You, targeted to black women, and other companies have followed with their own lines of multicultural products.

Psychographic segmentation is the process of dividing markets into groups based on values, social class, lifestyle, or personality characteristics. Individuals in the same demographic group may fall into very different psychographic segments. Psychographic segmentation involves qualitative aspects—the "why" component of consumer buying patterns. Therefore, a company must conduct its own research, which can become very time-consuming and expensive. Marketers, however, are increasingly focusing on psychographic characteristics. *Redbook* magazine, for example, targets a lifestyle segment it calls "*Redbook* jugglers," defined as 25 to 44-year-old women who must juggle family, husband, and job. According to a *Redbook* ad, "She's the product of the me generation, the thirty-something woman who balances home, family, and career—more than any generation before her, she refuses to put her pleasures aside. She's old enough to know what she wants. And young enough to get it." According to *Redbook*, this consumer makes an ideal target for marketers of health foods and fitness products. She wears out more exercise shoes, swallows more vitamins, drinks more diet soda, and works out more often than do consumers in other groups.

Behavioral segmentation divides a market into groups based on consumer knowledge, attitude, use, or response to a product. Many marketers believe that behavior variables are the best starting points for building market segments. Why does one consumer drink Coke, and another Pepsi, and a third iced tea? Demographics and psychographics can provide many clues, but it is often helpful to consider additional factors as well. Individuals act differently depending on their situation or the occasion for using the product. For example, a woman who shops only at discount stores for clothing may nonetheless think nothing of spending $100 on a bathing suit at a specialty shop for her Caribbean vacation. Some holidays, such as Father's Day and Mother's Day, were originally promoted partly to increase the sale of flowers, candy, cards, and other gifts. Many food marketers prepare special offers and ads for holidays. For example, Beatrice

Foods runs special Thanksgiving and Christmas ads for Reddi-whip in November and December, months that account for 30 percent of all sales of whipped cream.

Companies often begin segmenting their markets by using a single base, then expand by adding other bases. Consider Paging Network, Inc. (PageNet), a small provider of paging services. At first, PageNet used geographic segmentation, targeting easily accessible markets in Ohio and its own state of Texas. Once these markets were secure, the company introduced its product to thirteen additional geographically dispersed markets that represented the most growth potential. The small company next developed profiles of major users of paging services and targeted the most promising user groups, including salespeople, messengers, and service people. Flush with success, PageNet set out to capture more of their targeted markets. They used psychographic segmentation to target parents who leave their children with sitters, commuters who are out of reach of telephones while traveling to and from work or school, and elderly people living alone whose families want to keep an eye on them. Because of its successful use of target marketing, PageNet became the largest and most successful paging systems and services company in the nation. As of 2000, the company was expanding its target base once again with a service called VoiceNow, which transmits voice messages to customers' pagers, targeting customers who want "short bursts of information."

Many variables can be used to segment and select a target market. Practically any variable—such as age, sex, product usage, lifestyle, or desired benefit—can be used to describe a target market. The number of target markets identified also depends on a marketing strategist's ability to be creative in identifying segments. Target marketing is especially important for specialty products and shops. Target marketing rests on the assumption that differences among customers are related to differences in the purchasing behavior.

BIBLIOGRAPHY

Baker, Michael J. (1994). *Dictionary of Marketing and Advertising*, 2nd ed.

Beacham, Walton. (1996). *Beachams Marketing Reference*, vol. 11.

Clemente, Mark N. (1992). *The Marketing Glossary*.

Kotler, Philip, and Armstrong, Gary. (1999). *Principles of Marketing*.

Ostrow, Rona, and Smith, Sweltman R. (1998). *The Dictionary of Marketing*.

Weinstein, Art. (1994). *Marketing Segmentation*.

TATUM TURNER

TARIFFS

(SEE: *International Trade*)

TAXATION

Taxation is the imposition of a mandatory levy on the citizens and/or the businesses of a country by their government. In almost every country, the government derives a majority of its revenues for financing public services from taxation. Most individuals will feel the impact of quite a number of taxes during their lifetimes. In addition, taxes have become a powerful instrument for policy makers around the world to use in attaining economic and social goals. As a result, the system of taxation in the United States and elsewhere has an impact on almost every business and investment decision that is made.

NATURE AND HISTORY OF U.S. TAXATION

In 1936, the U.S. Supreme Court defined a *tax* as "an exaction for the support of the Government." In this regard, there is no direct relationship between the exaction of revenue by the government and any benefit to be received by the taxpayer. As a result, a taxpayer—such as a corporate shareholder—cannot trace his or her tax payment to any particular governmental asset or program. Taxes may be distinguished in a similar fashion from licenses and from fees, which are payments made to the government for some special privilege granted or service rendered (such as a marriage license or a camping fee). They can also be distinguished from regulations and from penalties, which are charges imposed by government to eliminate or control a specific activity.

For taxes to pass constitutional muster, they must be levied on the basis of predetermined criteria. Not only must taxes be determined objectively, but also taxpayers must be able to calculate their tax liability ahead of time. Since most taxes are levied on a recurring or predictable basis, individuals can also engage in tax planning or in tax avoidance. In other words, they are free to conduct their lives in a way that minimizes the amount that must be transferred to the government in taxes.

Despite the adage that nothing is certain in the world but death and taxes, taxation has not always been the chief source of revenue for governments. While the primary goal of taxation is to provide the resources necessary to fund governmental expenditures, any taxing authority that has the power to control the money supply—such as the U.S. federal government—can satisfy its revenue needs merely by creating money. Complete reliance on this governmental power, however, would stimulate excess demand in the economy, which—in turn—would cause price inflation. Taxes, on the other hand, raise revenue with the opposite effect: They drain money from the private sector, causing a reduction in private consumption or investment expenditures.

Reflecting one of the rallying cries of the American Revolution—"No taxation without representation"—the system of taxation in the United States closely parallels the tax regime of England. At the time of its adoption in 1789, the U.S. Constitution gave Congress the power to levy and collect taxes. Promptly exercising this authority, Congress enacted was the Tariff Act of 1789, imposing a system of duties—called excise taxes—on imports. As a result, tariffs became the federal government's principal source of revenue.

As the scope of governmental activities and programs increased, additional sources of revenue were necessary to supplement the tariff system. However, the Constitution required that any direct tax imposed by Congress had to be apportioned among the states on the basis of their relative populations. Because the sizes of the states' populations differed, any tax on income would result in a different tax rate for the citizens of each state. Despite the apportionment requirement, Congress enacted the first federal income tax in 1861 to finance the vastly increased expenditures brought on by the Civil War.

While the original federal income tax was allowed to expire after the Civil War, it did lead to the successful effort to amend the Constitution. The Sixteenth Amendment to the Constitution became effective on February 25, 1913, providing that: "The Congress shall have the power to lay and collect taxes on incomes from whatever source derived, without apportionment among the several States, and without regard to any census or enumeration." Without hesitation, Congress enacted the Revenue Act of 1913, on October 3, 1913 and made it retroactive to March 1, 1913.

As historical conditions changed and the federal government's need for additional revenues increased, Congress exercised its income taxing authority by the passage of many new revenue acts. Since each new piece of legislation simultaneously reenacted previous revenue acts and added new amendments to the law, it became necessary to research over one hundred separate statutory sources to determine what tax law was currently in effect. Eventually, in 1939, Congress resolved the confusion by systematically arranging all of the tax laws into the Internal Revenue Code of 1939, a permanent codification of the law that does not require reenactment.

MAJOR TYPES OF U.S. TAXES

Since its establishment in 1913, the income tax has played the dominant role in providing the funds with which the federal government operates. An income tax is an extraction of some of the taxpayer's economic gain, usually on a periodic basis. The federal government, and almost every state government, imposes a tax on the in-

come of individuals, corporations, estates, and trusts. A final tax reckoning—involving the reporting of income and payment of taxes due—is made at the end of each year. However, in order to ensure tax collections, Congress has created a pay-as-you-go requirement, through a combination of payroll withholdings and estimated tax prepayments during the year.

Income is generally defined as any permanent increment to wealth. It does not include loans or any other temporary increments. As a general rule, Congress considers any incremental wealth to be taxable income, unless specific statutory authority excludes it. These increments to wealth can take many forms, such as cash, property other than cash, and services that are rendered to the taxpayer. While state governments set their own tax rules and rates, a majority of the states use the same definition of gross income as the federal government.

Unlike federal and state income taxes, wealth-transfer taxes are not significant revenue producers. Historically, the primary function of wealth-transfer taxes has been to hinder the accumulation of wealth by family units. Since 1976, the federal estate tax and the federal gift tax have been combined into one tax, known as the unified transfer tax. This unified system eliminates the distinction previously made between taxable lifetime transfers and transfers at death. Under this system, the value of a decedent's taxable estate is treated as his or her final gift.

Like federal income taxes, the tax rates on unified transfers are progressive. This means that an increasing percentage rate is applied to increasing increments of the tax base. Unlike the annual assessment of federal income taxes, the federal transfer tax is computed cumulatively on gifts made during a lifetime as well as on transfers at death. In addition, many states impose an inheritance tax on the right to receive property at death. Unlike an estate tax, which is imposed according to the value of property transferred at death, an inheritance tax is imposed on the recipient of property from an estate, although many wills provide that the estate should pay any inheritance taxes imposed on recipients of property.

In addition to income taxes and wealth transfer taxes, the federal government and most states impose some form of employment tax. The most common form of state employment tax is levied on wages, with the proceeds used to finance that state's unemployment compensation benefits program. In addition to its own unemployment tax, the federal government also imposes a Social Security tax on employers, employees, and self-employed individuals. The federal government uses proceeds from the Federal Insurance Contribution Act (FICA) tax to finance the payment of Social Security benefits as well as Medicare health insurance. If an employee will be eligible for Social Security and Medicare, the FICA tax is paid by both the employee and by his or her employer. Although subject to a different tax rate, self-employed individuals are required to pay FICA taxes on their net earnings from self-employment.

With only a few exceptions, state and local units of government in the United States also use the income tax and wealth transfer taxes as a source of revenue. In addition, these taxing jurisdictions have customarily relied on two other tax sources that generally escape taxation by the federal government:

1. The annual assessment of property tax has traditionally been the backbone of the local revenue system. It is a tax on the value of property—usually only real property, such as land and buildings—owned within a jurisdiction by nonexempt individuals or organizations.

2. In addition, most states and many local units of government impose sales taxes. This is a tax on the gross receipts from the retail sale of tangible personal property—such as automobiles and clothing—and certain services. Each taxing authority determines its own tax rate as well as the services and articles to be taxed. The seller collects the tax at the time of the sale, and then periodically remits the revenue to the appropriate taxing authority.

TAX PLANNING

In the United States and other democracies, a majority of citizens—or their duly elected representatives—vote to impose taxes on themselves in order to finance public services on which they place value but which are not adequately funded by market processes. However, determining which individuals or households or businesses actually reduce their private consumption or wealth as a consequence of a tax is not always a straightforward matter. After all, although taxes affect numerous aspects of our lives, their impact is not uncontrollable.

Tax planning is simply the process of arranging one's actions in light of their potential tax consequences. After all, a character in *Gone with the Wind* improves on the earlier adage by observing, "Death and taxes and childbirth! There's never any convenient time for any of them!" Despite the inconvenience that taxes impose, the average individual will feel the impact of quite a number of taxes during his or her lifetime. As a result, almost any attempt to accumulate or preserve wealth requires diligent tax planning.

The process of minimizing the tax liability—of an individual or of a transaction—is usually referred to as tax avoidance. Not to be confused with tax evasion, tax avoidance is the perfectly legal effort by taxpayers, and by paid tax advisers on behalf of their clients, to take those steps necessary to reduce one's taxes. As a result, anyone interested in minimizing their tax liabilities in the United States should take their cue from a 1947 opinion by Justice Learned Hand: "Over and over again courts have said that there is nothing sinister in so arranging one's affairs so as to keep taxes as low as possible. Everybody does so, rich or poor, and all do right, for nobody owes any public duty to pay more than the law demands: taxes are enforced exactions, not voluntary contributions. To demand more in the name of morals is pure cant."

BIBLIOGRAPHY

Brownlee, W. Elliot. (1996). *Federal Taxation in America: A Short History*. Washington, DC: Woodrow Wilson Center Press.

Graetz, Michael J. (1997). *The Decline (and Fall?) of the Income Tax*. New York: Norton.

Jones, Sally M. (1998). *Principles of Taxation for Business and Investment Planning*. Boston: Irwin/McGraw-Hill.

Richmond, Gail Levin. (1997). *Federal Tax Research: Guide to Materials and Techniques*. New York: Foundation Press.

JEFFREY L. JACOBS

TEAMWORK

(SEE: *Work Groups*)

TELECOMMUNICATIONS

Telecommunications is the transmission of data and information between computers using a communications link such as a standard telephone line. Typically, a basic telecommunications system would consist of a computer or terminal on each end, communication equipment for sending and receiving data, and a communication channel connecting the two users. Appropriate communications software is also necessary to manage the transmission of data between computers. Some applications that rely on this communications technology include the following:

1. Electronic mail (e-mail) is a message transmitted from one person to another through computerized channels. Both the sender and receiver must have access to on-line services if they are not connected to the same network. E-mail is now one of the most frequently used types of tele-communication.

2. Facsimile (fax) equipment transmits a digitized exact image of a document over telephone lines. At the receiving end, the fax machine converts the digitized data back into its original form.

3. Voice mail is similar to an answering machine in that it permits a caller to leave a voice message in a voice mailbox. Messages are digitized so the caller's message can be stored on a disk.

4. Videoconferencing involves the use of computers, television cameras, and communications software and equipment. This equipment makes it possible to conduct electronic meetings while the participants are at different locations.

5. The Internet is a continuously evolving global network of computer networks that facilitates access to information on thousands of topics. The Internet is utilized by millions of people daily.

Actually, telecommunications is not a new concept. It began in the mid-1800s with the telegraph, whereby sounds were translated manually into words; then the telephone, developed in 1876, transmitted voices; and then the teletypewriter, developed in the early 1900s, was able to transmit the written word.

Since the 1960s, telecommunications development has been rapid and wide reaching. The development of dial modem technology accelerated the rate during the 1980s. Facsimile transmission also enjoyed rapid growth during this time. The 1990s have seen the greatest advancement in telecommunications. It is predicted that computing performance will double every eighteen months. In addition, it has been estimated that the power of the computer has doubled thirty-two times since World War II (Withrow, 1997). The rate of advancement in computer technology shows no signs of slowing. To illustrate the computer's rapid growth, Ronald Brown, former U.S. secretary of commerce, reported that only fifty thousand computers existed in the world in 1975, whereas, by 1995, it was estimated that more than fifty thousand computers were sold every ten hours (U.S. Department of Commerce, 1995).

Deregulation and new technology have created increased competition and widened the range of network services available throughout the world. This increase in telecommunication capabilities allows businesses to benefit from the information revolution in numerous ways, such as streamlining their inventories, increasing productivity, and identifying new markets. In the following sections, the technology of modern telecommunications will be discussed.

COMMUNICATIONS NETWORKS

When computers were first invented, they were designed as stand-alone systems. As computers became more widespread, practical, useful, and indispensable, network systems were developed that allowed communication between computers. The term "network" describes computers that are connected for the purpose of sharing data, software, and hardware. The two types of networks include local area networks (LANs) and wide area networks (WANs). As the name suggests, LANs cover a limited geographic area, usually a square mile or less. This limited area can be confined to a room, a building, or a group of buildings. Although a LAN can include one central computer connected to terminals, more commonly it connects a group of personal computers. A WAN covers a much larger geographic area by means of telephone cables and/or other communications channels. WANs are often used to connect a company's branch offices in different cities. Some familiar public wide area networks include AT&T, Sprint, and MCI.

INTERNET, INTRANET, AND EXTRANET

"Internetwork" is the term used to describe two or more networks that are joined together. The term "Internet" describes the collection of connected networks. The Internet has been made accessible by use of the World Wide Web. The Web allows users to navigate the millions of sites found on the Internet using software applications called Web browsers. People make use of the Internet in numerous ways for both personal and business applications. For instance, an investor is able to access a company directly and set up an investment account; a student is able to research an assigned topic for a class report; a shopper can obtain information on new and used cars.

The Internet concept of global access to information transferred to a private corporate network creates an intranet. In conjunction with corporate Internet access, many companies are finding that it is highly practical to have an internal intranet. Because of the increased need for fast and accurate information, an efficient and seamless communications line enabling all members to access a wealth of relevant information instantaneously is vital.

A company intranet in conjunction with the Internet can provide various types of information for internal and/or external use. Uses such as instantaneous transfer of information, reduced printing and reprinting, and elimination of out-of-date information can provide great benefits to geographically dispersed groups. Some examples of information that an intranet might include are company and procedures manuals, a company phonebook and e-mail listings, insurance and benefits information, in-house publications, job postings, expense reports, bulletin boards for employee memoranda, training information, inventory lists, price lists, and inventory control information. Putting such applications on an intranet can serve a large group of users at a substantially reduced cost.

Some companies might want to make some company information accessible to preauthorized people outside the company or even to the general public. This can be done by using an extranet. An extranet is a collaborative network that uses Internet technology to link businesses with their suppliers, customers, or other businesses. An extranet can be viewed as part of a company's intranet. Access by customers would allow entering orders into a company's system. For example, a person may order airline tickets, check the plane schedule, and customize the trip to his or her preferences. In addition to time and labor savings, this type of order entry could also decrease errors made by employees when entering manually prepared orders.

Security and privacy can be an issue in using an extranet. One way to provide this security and privacy would be by using the Internet with access via password authorization. Computer dial-in and Internet access to many financial institutions is now available. This is an example of limited access to information. While bank employees have access to many facets of institutional information, the bank customers are able to access only information that has to do with their own accounts. In addition to their banking account number, they would have to use their password to gain access to the information.

TRANSMISSION MEDIA

The physical devices making up the communications channel are known as the transmission media. These devices include cabling media (such as twisted-pair cable, coaxial cable, and fiber-optic cable) and wireless media (such as microwaves and other radio waves as well as infrared light). Wireless transmission has the advantage of not having to install physical connections at every point. Microwave stations use radio waves to send both voice and digital signals. The principal drawback to this system is that microwave transmission is limited to line-of-sight applications. Relay antennas are usually placed twenty-five to seventy-five miles apart and can have no interfering buildings or mountains between them. Earth-based microwave transmissions, called terrestrial microwaves, send data from one microwave station to another, similar to the method by which cellular telephone signals are transmitted.

Earth stations receive microwave transmissions and transmit them to orbiting communication satellites, which then relay them over great distances to receiving earth stations. Usually, geosynchronous satellites are placed roughly twenty-two thousand miles above the earth. Being geosynchronous allows the satellites to remain in fixed positions above the earth and to be constantly available to a given group of earth stations.

Many businesses either lease or rent satellite and/or microwave communication services through the telephone company or other satellite communication companies. If a business has only a small amount of information to be trans-

mitted each day, it may prefer to use a small satellite dish antenna instead.

TYPES OF SIGNALS AND THEIR CONVERSION BY MODEM

Most telecommunications involving personal computers make use of standard telephone lines at some point in their data transmission. But since computers have been developed to work with digital signals, their transmission presents a noncompatible signal problem. Digital signals are on/off electrical pulses grouped in a manner to represent data. Originally, telephone equipment was designed to carry only voice transmission and operated with a continuous electrical wave called an analog signal. In order for telephone lines to carry digital signals, a special piece of equipment called a modem (MOdulator/DEModulator) is used to convert between digital and analog signals. Modems can be either external to the computer, and thus to be moved from one computer to another, or they can be internally mounted inside the computer. Modems are always used in pairs.

Both the receiving and transmitting modems must operate at the same speed. Multiple transmission speeds allow faster modems to reduce their speed to match that of a slower modem. The transmission rate and direction are determining factors that influence the speed, accuracy, and efficiency of telecommunications systems.

CONCLUSION

Telecommunications is one of the fastest-growing areas of technology in the world. Because of its rapid growth, businesses and individuals can access information at electronic speed from almost anywhere in the world. By including telecommunications in their operations, businesses can provide better services and products to their customers. For individuals, telecommunications provides access to worldwide information and services.

BIBLIOGRAPHY

"A Brief History of Data Communication." http://www .telecom.tbi.net/history1.html. 1999.

"Connecting the Nation: Classrooms, Libraries, and Health Care Organizations in the Information Age." Report prepared by National Telecommunications and Information Administration, Office of Telecommunications and Information Applications, U.S. Department of Commerce. http://www.ntia.doc.gov/connect.html. 1995.

"Extranet and Intranet." http://www.whatis.com/extranet .htm. 1999.

"Geosychronous," "Modem," and "Cabling." (1995). *The Volume Library*, vol. 1. Nashville, TN: Southwestern.

Shelly, Gary B., Cashman, Thomas J., Waggoner, Gloria A., and Waggoner, William C. (1998). *Discovering Computers 98*, brief ed. Cambridge, MA: Course Technology.

Withrow, F. B. (1997). "Technology in Education and the Next Twenty-Five Years." *Technological Horizons in Education Journal*. (T.H.E.), 24(11):59-61.

MARY ALICE GRIFFIN
SUSAN EVANA JENNINGS

TELECOMMUTING.

Telecommuting, the practice of working at home with the aid of computers, modems, and fax machines linked to the office, is becoming more prevalent in the modern business environment for a number of reasons. Environmental standards and car-pool requirements are being imposed on many businesses across the country. Economic factors are causing many employers to consider alternatives to an office facility-based staff. There is also an increasing number of parents who wish to remain at home to care for young children while maintaining their positions at work.

The key to a successful home-based office is to structure it so that customers and business associates sense no difference in work performed in the home and work done in a regular office. Unlike those who run their businesses exclusively from home, the telecommuter must have access to all information and resources required at both locations, and these arrangements must be cost-effective.

For those organizations that balance individual and corporate interests, this new frontier of the alternative workplace offers a profound op-portunity to benefit both the employee and the company (Fisher, 1998). Yet a successful telecommuting program requires the combination of a motivated manager, a motivated employee, and a well-defined task.

DIFFERENT TYPES OF TELECOMMUTING

According to the "Pacific Bell Network Telecommuting Guide," the several different types of telecommuting are:

1. *Working at home*: This is the most popular method, one in which the employee designates workspace at home to conduct business functions.

2. *Satellite offices*: These are remote office locations, usually placed within a large concentration of employee residences, that allow employees at a single company to share common office space and reduce the time and expense of the commute to and from the main office facility.

3. *Neighborhood work centers*: Such a center provides workspace for employees of different companies in one location. Each company housing employees at these locations is usually responsible for the administrative and technical requirements of its employees.

4. *Virtual office mobile workers*: This is the newest form of telecommuting, whereby the telecommuter's office may be an airport, a hotel, or a car. These mobile telecommuters are constantly on the road and use technology to link to the office. ("Pacific Bell Network," 1998).

NUMBER OF TELECOMMUTERS IS GROWING

Today's knowledge workers are ideal candidates for splitting time between a central office and a home office. According to IDC/Link, a research firm in Framingham, Massachusetts, 11 million Americans are telecommuters working at home. In 1997 the advocacy group Telecommuter American counted 11 million at-home corporate workers (Johnson, 1998). Anne Fisher reported

Telecommuting is becoming more widespread.

that the ranks of at-home workers are growing 15 percent a year and that about 7 percent of U.S. white-collar employees now say they tele-commute at least part of the time (Fisher, 1998). Although the telecommuter ranks are growing, only a third of the more than 1800 companies William M. Mercer recently surveyed offer em-ployees the option of telecommuting ("Making Stay-at-Homes," 1998).

William G. Deming, a bureau economist, speculated that the increase in corporate tele-commuting programs may explain much of the increase in the number of telecommuters. *Business Week* stated that one hint that this may be true is that there was not a corresponding increase in unpaid work done at home; indeed, the number of wage and salary workers who do work at home for which they are not paid decreased from 12.2 million to 1.1 million ("Home Sweet Officer," 1998).

Some of the "telecommuting-friendly" employers include Aetna, with 2 percent; Arthur Andersen, with 20 percent; AT&T, with 55 percent; Boeing, with 1 percent; Cisco Systems, with 66 percent; Georgia Power, with 5 percent; Hewlett-Packard, with 8 percent; IBM, with 20 percent; Merrill Lynch, with 5 percent; and The Leisure Company/America West, with 16 percent ("Making Stay-at-Homes," 1998).

WORKPLACE AND WORK FORCE FOR THE NEW MILLENNIUM

The philosophy that people are the most important element of a company has created a new awareness of the necessity to adapt the work facility to the needs of employees. Although telecommuting is one of the fastest-growing business trends, not every line of work is conducive to it. Telecommuting has been common for sales staff who spend most of their time on the road, but this arrangement can work for many other employees involved with office activities.

Technology-driven corporations are in the forefront of telecommuting. Telecommuting is ideal for such individuals as computer programmers, sales representatives, technical writers, public relations individuals, news reporters, clerical assistants, computer systems analysts, engineers, researchers, customer service representatives, pieceworkers, and data-entry clerks.

CHALLENGES

Areas of concern include feelings of isolation, exploitation of workers, working too much, supervision, access to files, and performance evaluation. Union officials fear that telecommuting will lead to "home work" equaling "electronic sweatshops." The implementation of telecommuting in Los Angeles has led to the filing of three notices of alleged unfair labor practices by Local 660 of the Service Employee International Union, which represents half of the county's permanent employees. The fundamental contention was that home workers are less protected from such potential abuses as violations of overtime standards and payment for work on a piecework basis. In Japan, piecework is done by telecommuters, with a truck coming by once a week to pick up the products.

A major stumbling block for companies is created by managers who do not trust that employees will work unless under direct supervision. The adage "While the cat's away, the mouse will play!" applies. The major problem employees face with telecommuting is fear that they won't be remembered when promotion time comes around. To address these concerns, both employers and employees must be involved in the development of the telecommuting program and learn to measure productivity in terms other than office hours.

BENEFITS

Telecommuting benefits both the company and employees in many ways. The most frequently mentioned advantages of telecommuting include greater productivity, improved information turnaround, better communication, reduced office space requirements, greater staffing flexibility, lower employee turnover, and an expanded employee market. Managers state that the key benefit of telecommuting is increased productivity, while employees state the key benefit is greater independence.

Telecommuting provides opportunities for new mothers, physically challenged individuals, the elderly, people living in remote locations, and individuals taking care of housebound persons to join the work force. Telecommuting is seen as a potential means of employing and retaining valuable employees by helping them balance work and home demands as well as reducing commuting costs and time. The major advantages of telecommuting are the reduced time and expense of commuting and the increased flexibility of working hours. Telecommuting is becoming a viable work alternative for many and can attract more individuals into the work force and retain them there. The Information Age brings a myriad of change that can be viewed either as a threat or a treat.

SELECTION OF PERSONNEL

Successful telecommuting requires a cooperative arrangement between managers and employees. Managers must select individuals who are suited to working at home and jobs that can be completed at home. Since it is difficult to monitor the employee and the workplace, the manager must be involved in designing and overseeing the telecommuting program. A trusting relationship between the employer and the employee is essential.

A self-assessment survey and a job description survey developed at the University of Tennessee can assist with the selection of the proper employee and the proper project for telecommuting. The results of such a test should not be used exclusively in determining whether a particular individual should work at home or a particular task should be completed at home; it should be combined with interviews and past evaluations.

Potentially successful employees should be self-directed, self-motivated, productive, well organized, and very knowledgeable about their job. Potentially successfully supervisors should trust employees, have a positive attitude toward telecommuting, be flexible, and be able to communicate well.

EQUIPMENT PROCUREMENT AND SELECTION

Any equipment that works well in the office also works well in the home office. Equipment is needed in two main areas: (1) communication—phone, a fax, and Internet access for e-mail; and (2) information—whether it is a simple calendar and contact database or complex documents, spreadsheets, and presentations. Access software is needed to dial into the office computer or into another machine that has needed files and information.

The American Telecommuting Association (ATA) states that a home office is quick and easy to hook up because of modern technology. Ac-

cording to the ATA, an office could include the following pieces of equipment: a $1000 desktop computer or $2000 notebook computer, fax, printer, copier, and scanner. For less than $2000 one can set up a powerful, complete business system in a spare bedroom or a corner of the kitchen (ATA, 1998).

IMPLICATIONS FOR TRAINING

As economic and demographic changes force telecommuting to become a reality for organizations and employees, there is a tremendous demand for training. A curriculum for a successful telecommuting program should include the following subjects: keyboarding, work environment, office automation, time management, performance-based evaluation, decision making, and ethics.

According to the City of Los Angeles Telecommuting Task Force report, training for home telecommuters should include how to set up a home office, how to start and stop working, how to control interruptions, and how to develop a results orientation to work assignments. The training for supervisors should include establishing performance standards for telecommuters, troubleshooting potential problems, and selecting the right employee and the right task.

SUMMARY

As our global economy in the Information Age evolves, telecommuting will increasingly become a popular work style. Many companies are turning to telecommuting to solve the dilemma of recruiting and retaining quality employees, controlling costs of office space, and meeting environmental standards. The major national advantages for telecommuting include savings in gasoline, a reduction in pollution, a decrease in traffic congestion, and lower highway accident rates.

For a successful telecommuting program, top-down support is vital, employee support is necessary, screening is important, training is essential, and guidelines are required. Major capital investments are not necessary. Telecommuting should be customized for each agency, each employee, and each task.

Peter Drucker sums up telecommuting in the following quotation: "Commuting to office work is obsolete. It is now infinitely easier, cheaper, and faster . . . to move information . . . to where the people are."

BIBLIOGRAPHY

American Telecommuting Association (ATA). http://www.knowledgetree.com/ata.html. 1998.

Apgar M., IV. (1998). "The Alternative Workplace: Changing Where and How People Work." *Harvard Business Review* 76(3):121-136.

Fisher, A. (1998). *Fortune* 138(9):264.

"Home Sweet Office." (1998). *Business Week.* April 6:30.

Johnson, D. (1998). *Home Office Computing* 16(9):63-66.

"Making Stay-at-Homes Feel Welcome." (1998). *Business Week.* October 12:155-156.

"Pacific Bell Network Telecommuting Guide." http://www.pacbell.com/products/business/general/telecommuting/tcguide/tc-0.html. 1998.

CAROL LARSON JONES

TELECONFERENCING

(SEE: *Videoconferencing*)

TELEMARKETING

Telemarketing is the process of selling goods and services over the telephone. It has been used to successfully market a variety of products ranging from insurance to newspapers to industrial equipment, and it has the potential for selling virtually any product.

There are two kinds of telemarketing—outbound and inbound. Outbound telemarketing calls are those placed by salespeople to homes or businesses. Inbound telemarketing occurs when customers call in to businesses to place orders.

Outbound telemarketing is particularly appealing to businesses whose salespeople have traditionally made outside sales calls. It reduces the cost per contact, increases the number of contacts that can be made per day or week, and still retains the human element. Computerized databases of prospects and automated predictive dialers can further extend the potential number of contacts a telemarketer can make. Outbound calls can be used to canvass for new business, follow up former customers, and contact new leads.

Outbound calls present an ideal marketing situation in which the telemarketer has the undivided attention of the prospect and can get immediate feedback. At the same time, the limited window of opportunity requires that the salesperson establish rapport and trust quickly, listen carefully, and provide clear information. Success in outbound sales is related to product knowledge and presentation skills and, thus, can be enhanced by training.

Inbound telemarketing is also a very efficient marketing approach that also retains the element of personal interaction. Calls are generated by catalogues mailed to prospective customers or by radio, television, or print advertisements. These promotional pieces solicit customers to buy by calling a toll-free number. When customers call in, they may either reach a telemarketer directly or receive an electronic message that gives them the option to be connected to a salesperson. Since inbound callers have entered the buying process when they call in, a customer service orientation is more critical to the success of the telemarketer than sales training.

The use of the telephone as a sales tool dates back to the early 1900s. However, the full potential of outbound telemarketing was not recognized by business until WATS (wide area telephone service) lines came into existence in 1960. Likewise, the full potential for inbound sales did not become apparent until the Sheraton motel chain implemented the first toll-free 800 lines in 1967. During the 1970s, telemarketing techniques became more refined and were incorporated into the marketing strategies of business of all sizes. Between 1981 and 1991, spending on telemarketing efforts grew from $1 billion to $60 billion. And in 1997 telemarketing sales, to consumers and businesses, totaled $425.5 billion.

Although telemarketing has experienced continued growth, it has not been without problems. Many consumers have a negative perception of it because of untimely and annoying calls. It has also been the vehicle for a variety of fraudulent schemes, a fact that prompted a crackdown by the U.S. attorney general in 1997. Despite these concerns, the outlook for the industry appears to be positive. Research indicates that businesses are becoming increasingly receptive to doing business with sales representatives by telephone, sales trends are upward, and expansion is indicated by the projection that an additional 5 million telemarketing employees will be hired between 1995 and 2000.

BIBLIOGRAPHY

Goldstein, Linda. (1996). "Reflections on the Past and Predictions for the Future of Telemarketing Legislation." *Telemarketing and Call Center Solutions* February: 48-50.

Kordahl, Eugene B. (1984). "An Overview of the Telemarketing Industry." *ZIP+/Target Marketing* June: 22-26.

McHatton, Robert J. (1988). *Total Telemarketing.* New York: John Wiley.

Romano, Catherine (1998). "Telemarketing Grows Up." *Management Review* June: 31-34.

EARL C. MEYER
WINIFRED L. GREEN

TELEPHONE SKILLS

Telephones are devices that allow the user to communicate messages across lines electronically. One can easily communicate with those both nearby and far away using the telephone by simply dialing a specially designated number. The word *telephone* comes from two Greek words meaning "far" and "sound" ("Telephones," 1990).

Alexander Graham Bell invented the first telephone in 1876 in Boston, an outgrowth of his teaching the deaf and his experimentation with devices to assist in improving the hearing process.

Today it is difficult to estimate the total number of telephones in existence; because of their extreme importance as a communications tool, they are ubiquitous. Telephones come in a wide variety of shapes, sizes, and colors as well as with options that can be configured to accommodate almost any conceivable need.

DEVELOPING EFFECTIVE TELEPHONE SKILLS

Effective telephone skills are predicated on strong communications skills. The four major means of communication are speaking, reading, writing, and listening—with listening being the most important part.

Listening involves sensing, interpreting, evaluating, and responding. The major roadblocks to effective listening include distractions and interruptions. Roadblocks to effective listening can be overcome by practicing the following techniques:

- Being ready to listen actively.
- Keeping your emotions in check.
- Listening for specific information.
- Asking questions when necessary.

PARTS OF AN EFFECTIVE TELEPHONE CALL

Telephone calls may be broken into three major parts—(1) the *introduction*, in which both parties establish their identity and the convenience of the call; (2) the *purpose*, which involves communicating needs by asking well constructed questions; and (3) the *conclusion*, whereby both parties reach a verbal agreement on the points made during the call and any specific action that needs to be taken.

QUESTIONING SKILLS

Questions should be asked in such a way as to obtain the desired information. These are three major types of questions:

- *Open questions*: These questions call for more than a yes/no answer and often begin with *who, what, where, when, why* or *how.*
- *Closed questions*: These questions are used primarily to verify information. Often these

questions begin with *are you, do you, can, could, did, will,* or *would*

- *Forced-choice questions*: These questions call for an either/or response. The listener has the choice of at least two options.

During the call, when both parties are asking questions, it is equally important to listen attentively. Attentive listening can be demonstrated by speaking in such ways that the listener knows you are hearing. It is also an excellent idea to write down any questions you want to ask prior to beginning the call or during the call.

SKILLS FOR MAKING EFFECTIVE TELEPHONE CALLS

Before you make a telephone call, consider *why* you are making the call. Calls could possibly be made to obtain information, return a call, schedule an appointment, or service a customer.

Be ready psychologically to make the call. Have a positive attitude toward making the call at the time you are making it. Place *all* necessary information before you when you make the call.

When making a call, be sure to do the following:

- Identify yourself immediately to get the call off to a positive start.
- Tell the person why you are calling. Be specific.
- Ask well-stated, appropriate questions to obtain the desired action.
- Close the call in a friendly tone with an understanding between both parties of the action(s) that need to be taken.

TOOLS FOR EFFECTIVELY MAKING TELEPHONE CALLS

Telephone numbers may be obtained from your own record, from directories, or from directory assistance.

Have the telephone number directly before you when you get ready to make the call. Developing your own personal telephone list is very helpful.

Telephone directories that contain both White Pages and Yellow Pages can also be sources of excellent information. Use the White Pages when you want to locate a specific name of a person. Use the Yellow Pages when you want to locate a product or service.

Directory assistance provides access to a telephone number by going through a directory assistance operator. Usually there is a fee for obtaining this information.

OPERATOR-ASSISTED CALLS

Operator-assisted calls are the most expensive type of telephone calls. Avoid them if possible. Types of operator-assisted calls include the following:

- *Collect calls*: In collect calls, the person being called must agree to accept the charges for the call.
- *Third-number billing*: Such a call is billed to a third party.
- *Person-to-person*: Such a call involves telling the operator you will speak only to a designated person. If that person is unavailable, you will not have to pay for the call.
- *Cellular calls*: A call made from a cellular phone may require an operator. If this is the case, phone charges can be expensive.

INCOMING TELEPHONE CALLS

Be prepared to answer the telephone when it rings. Keep pens and message pads close by as well as telephone directories and other reference materials. Use an answering machine if you must be away from your desk.

When answering the phone, follow these guidelines:

- Answer the telephone no later than the second ring.
- Identify yourself in a friendly tone.
- Use the caller's name.
- Gather as much information as possible.
- Do not interrupt the caller.
- Give accurate information.

SCREENING CALLS

Screening a call means using judgment to determine whether you should put the caller through to the desired person. By being friendly to the caller without revealing embarrassing or unnecessary information.

TRANSFERRING CALLS

Transferring a call means that, for any number of reasons, it would be best for the caller to speak with someone else. It is important to be thoroughly familiar with the specific procedure for transferring a call.

MESSAGE TAKING

Today, messages may either be left as voice-mail messages for the person being called or written down by someone else. If you are writing down the message, use a telephone message form to fill in the appropriate parts.

HANDLING COMMON TYPES OF SPECIALIZED TELEPHONE CALLS

Handling the wide variety of both incoming and outgoing specialized telephone calls requires in-depth skill. The following are some of the more common types of specialized calls:

- *Information calls*: Calls you make to gather information require careful thought to determine exactly *what* information you are trying to obtain.

- *Scheduling appointment calls*: Know exactly *when* you want an appointment *before* you place the call. Have all information in front of you when you place the call. If you are making calls for another individual, notify that person of the scheduled appointment. Likewise, be certain you have carefully recorded on an appointment calendar the designated scheduled time as well as any special instructions.

- *Complaint calls*: Often a complaint call can become a negative experience by nature of the call's very existence. Be prepared to deal with emotions in as positive a fashion as possible.

- *Collection calls*: Collecting money over the telephone is a challenging experience. Good questioning skills are of paramount importance in handling a collection call.

- *Telemarketing calls*: Selling a product or service over the telephone is done by a skilled salesperson called a telemarketer. Generally, telemarketers have been trained to deal with a wide variety of responses and situations.

It is wise to follow these steps when dealing with specialized calls:

1. Always respond in a courteous and professional manner.

2. Give accurate information.

3. Be prepared to deal with rejection and negative responses.

4. Offer a variety of positive solutions.

5. End all calls courteously.

CUSTOMER SERVICE ON THE TELEPHONE

Customer service is an extremely important aspect of telephone skills. This is the reason most businesses are in existence—to serve the customer. Good customer service via the telephone shows respect for the customer and builds business over time. Good customer service is provided by maintaining an excellent voice quality that is easy to understand and includes a pleasant tone spoken at a reasonable speed. Selecting appropriate vocabulary is also important. If words are used that are not understood, positive communication will not be conveyed. Listen intently when servicing a customer. Be prepared to offer responses that will be delivered in a positive manner.

TELEPHONE EQUIPMENT AND EMERGING TECHNOLOGY

Choosing telephone equipment is a challenge with the wide variety of choices available. Today there are many telephone-related pieces of equipment that can be used with the telephone. Some points to consider when selecting telephone equipment include: size, location, number of phones, special options, and whether to buy or lease. Careful thought should be given to researching your needs before making a decision.

Cellular telephones are the type of mobile phones used, for example, in cars, on planes—or on the street. These phones are serviced through licensed cellular phone companies with a variety of configurations. Check them out carefully. Often bad weather or other types of interference can make communication by cellular phone difficult.

Cordless telephones are portable and very convenient. They come in a wide variety of styles for easy use. Cordless phones can be used only within a certain range of area. Their base must be attached to a telephone line in order to function.

Pagers are devices that can be used to alert the user that someone is trying to call them. Pagers come with various options. The more options that are selected, the more expensive the pager.

TELEPHONE SKILLS AND THE FUTURE

Telephone skills will undoubtedly continue to be increasingly important as the technology and equipment evolve. Strong communication skills will always be highly essential when using the telephone. Evolving technology will enhance the telephone in the future. Telephone skills must be integrated with that technology to make the process work.

BIBLIOGRAPHY

Neal, D. (1998). *Telephone Techniques*, 2d ed. Westerville, OH: Glencoe-McGraw-Hill.

DOROTHY A. MAXWELL

TEMPORARY EMPLOYMENT

Temporary employment is work that is not a permanent job. Rather, temporary employment allows an individual to work for shorter terms in a variety of jobs utilizing many skills. The scope of temporary employment is wide-ranging. In many cases, temporary employment can lead to permanent positions. Temporary employment is an expanding type of work in the twenty-first century. As America joins the global marketplace in seeking qualified employees for its work force, temporary employment is playing a major part in the process.

Since the middle of the twentieth century, temporary employment has expanded greatly and become a viable and effective tool for American businesses. In 1995, it was estimated that the actual size of the "contingent" ("flexible") work force was between 2.2 and 4.9 percent of the work force (Bureau of Labor Statistics, 1995).

The Conference Board estimated in 1997 that by the year 2000, 35 percent of the companies are expected to use contingent workers (U.S. News, 1997).

Clerical workers presently account for approximately 40 percent of the total U.S. temporary payroll. However, the number of contingents includes CEOs, human resources directors, computer systems analysts, accountants, doctors, and nurses ... Approximately 20 percent are professionals ... About 90 percent of short-term temporary workers are supplied by a staffing company (Sunoo, 1998).

When a business can hire temporary help on an "as needed" basis, costs can usually be controlled. In the twenty-first century, temporary employment is playing a major role in expanding jobs in the global marketplace. Employing people on a temporary basis to work in diversified work environments allows businesses worldwide to deal with competition more effectively.

REASONS FOR EXPANSION

There are several major reasons for increased temporary employment. One is *company downsizing*. Many companies are being forced to downsize because of increased costs of operation. When a company is placed in this position, temporary employment often becomes a realistic option. From the standpoint of cost, it is cheaper, as many fringe benefits do not have to be paid to temporary employees. Companies can hire temporary employees for periods of time necessary to accomplish the project or task at hand. Also minimal training is required for temporary employees.

Another reason is *increased global competition.* Today's global marketplace necessitates the use of temporary employment on a worldwide scale. There is a growing acceptance of temporary hiring through Europe. Formerly, many nations did not acknowledge temporary employment; however, governments are beginning to recognize a legitimate need to use all human resources available in dealing with global competition.

Job requirements vary greatly from country to country, thus creating unusual challenges for those considering the use of temporary employees. Benefits also vary greatly. For example, Belgium requires a substantial contribution to health and social security costs for temporaries, a contribution that totals about 35 percent of the gross salary, payable by the temporary help firm. In contrast, the United Kingdom requires very few benefits for temporaries.

In many European countries, temporary employees function as temporary replacements for those on maternity leave. Throughout much of Europe, maternity leaves last much longer than in the United States. For example, in Belgium pregnant employees get four and a half months of leave. In France, employees stop work six weeks before their due date and come back to work eight weeks after the birth of the child. In both countries, the employees' jobs are guaranteed upon return (Messmer, 1994).

VALUES TO FIRMS AND EMPLOYEES

Temporary employment is growing for several reasons. To begin with, technology has provided opportunities for both large and small companies to customize and streamline their tasks. But doing so requires specialized technical competence. Temporary employees can provide state-of-the-art competence.

Professional staffing firms are especially helpful in this area. For example, Manpower has a division called Manpower Technical, whose employees are assigned to many of the world's leading high-technology firms. Specific technology training is provided for them to meet this increasing demand.

In addition, with the workplace constantly undergoing change, temporary employees can "bridge the gap" when a business experiences a shortage of help. Temporary employment gives companies the opportunity to test patterns of employment trends and gives employees the opportunity to explore various careers. The combination creates a unique opportunity for a win-win situation.

Reasons for considering temporary employment are as individual as the individuals who seek temporary employment. The major reasons individuals become temporary employees include the following:

Additional income: With a continuing trend of more family members needing to work, temporary employment provides additional income.

Career-path mobility: Temporary employment can often lead to full-time temporary positions or to permanent positions. Employers who use part-time employees have the opportunity to "try out" an individual to see if perhaps a permanent job match would work. The wide variety of firms using temporary employees provides for ample career exploration.

Temporary employment can alleviate the financial and emotional stress involved in the search for a permanent job, thus resulting in a better permanent job.

Skill improvement: Temporary employment provides employees with an opportunity to gain additional training in specific skills, especially in the area of technology. Most large staffing firms provide training to temporary employees on an ongoing basis.

Flexibility: Temporary employment provides flexibility in a variety of ways. This can be both a plus and a minus. Being assigned a temporary job usually means working with different groups of individuals to get a job done in a short period of time. On the other hand, temporary jobs can provide personal opportunities for acquiring knowledge in various fields of work. Temporary employment demands flexibility in being available for work on short notice with a positive attitude toward whatever the assignment may be.

SOURCES

The most common route to temporary employment is through a professional staffing service. One good approach is to look in the Yellow Pages of the telephone book. Newspapers are also good resources. And the Internet abounds with a wide variety of staffing services. In addition, many companies who have Web sites have a section called "Applying for a Job." Of course, the traditional door-to-door approach can provide opportunities for temporary employment, as can word of mouth.

It is recommended that persons consider these points when seeking a temporary job through use of a staffing service:

1. What is the history of the staffing service?
2. What is its placement record?
3. Do I have to pay a fee if a job is found?
4. What benefits does the temporary staffing service offer?
5. How often am I paid?
6. Is the staffing service affiliated with a national association such as the National Association of Temporary and Staffing Services?
7. What potential is there for growth with the staffing service?
8. What if any job restrictions exist?
9. Will I be kept busy with challenging and interesting assignments?
10. Will I be provided with training?

Getting answers to these questions is important for those considering temporary employment, for they often reflect the quality of the staffing service.

THE FUTURE

The future of temporary employment appears extremely good. Temporary work assignments are becoming more challenging and are lasting for longer periods of time.

Temporary employment will probably continue to be a strong training ground for businesses. The effect of downsizing indicates that no job is stable forever. Because of technology, many jobs have become obsolete, and thus employees without technological skills have been separated from companies for which they had been employed for many years. These displaced workers often turn to temporary employment as an opportunity to improve old skills and learn new ones. Although education can be obtained by returning to a formalized school setting, training can also be obtained at a staffing agency.

Professional temporary employees work for a variety of reasons. Many seek only short-term employment to keep busy. Many are semiretired and looking for a sense of involvement while supplementing their retirement incomes.

Temporary employment offers many interesting opportunities, but it definitely is not for everyone. A staffing agency should be investigated carefully before one signs on. Being flexible and assuming a fair amount of risk taking is recommended. Long- and short-term goals should always be kept in mind.

Temporary employment is almost certainly here to stay and should continue to grow in the years ahead. Learning both the obstacles and the opportunities of temporary employment can provide a sense of focus and direction.

BIBLIOGRAPHY

Bureau of Labor Statistics. (1995). *U.S. Department of Labor, Report 900, Contingent and Alternative Employment Arrangement.*

Sunoo, Brenda P. (1998). "From Santa to CEO—Temps Play All Roles." Archived at: http://www.workforceonly.com/members/research/contingent_staffing/2830.html.

DOROTHY A. MAXWELL

THEORIES X-Y

(SEE: *Management/Leadership Styles; Motivation*)

THEORY Z

(SEE: *Management/Leadership Styles*)

TIME MANAGEMENT

Time is probably the most valuable asset available to people and organizations. Understanding how to manage one's time can contribute mightily to the success of personal and professional lives. However, as with any other asset, it may be wasted if it's not valued.

Unfortunately, it is human nature to waste time. It is true that some people naturally have good time-management skills, having developed good techniques for managing themselves and their time. But others have developed poor habits related to time. Needless to say, most people do not like to proclaim or admit these kinds of weaknesses.

Wasted time cannot be replaced. With increasing demands both in the workplace and at home, a great need exists for time to become more respected, valued, and balanced.

DEFINITION OF TIME MANAGEMENT

Time management may be defined as the discovery and application of the most efficient method(s) of completing assignments of any length in the optimum time and with the highest quality.

This definition of *time management* has widespread applications:

- It applies to the entire spectrum of activities ranging from (1) simple "do-it-this-morning tasks" assigned by individuals to themselves or to others (e.g., prepare several short letters) to (2) large projects developed for a large organization by many people with completion contemplated to take a long period of time (e.g., write a book or open a new branch office).

- It denotes the "best" time, which is usually but not always the shortest time.

- It pertains either to (1) continuing and repetitious activities (e.g., daily logging-in of shipments received) or to (2) occasional activities (e.g., selection of new CEO).

- It includes production of anything, such as manufacture of a tangible product, provision of a service, preparation of a written document, development of a procedure, or arrival at a decision.

- It may include a progress-point assignment (e.g., development of plans for the preliminary testing of a new product) or an end-goal assignment (e.g., a final marketing plan for a new product).

- Development of plans for time management must necessarily presume the existence and application of such desirable personal and work qualities as motivation, discipline, consideration for others, and the desire to succeed.

BENEFITS OF GOOD TIME MANAGEMENT

Many valuable rewards potentially await those willing to develop good time-management practices. In individual careers, increased job performance and promotions may result. In personal lives, individuals may achieve successful marriages, more family time, less debt, and less stress. In addition, all types of organizations—business, civic, school, political, and religious—may receive productive, competitive, and financial benefits from observance of good time-management practices.

ACHIEVEMENT OF GOOD TIME MANAGEMENT

Business firms and other organizations often find it profitable to take tangible steps to learn the best possible time-management strategies. Some or all of the following approaches may be considered:

- Call in an outside person or organization that specializes in time-management consulting and have a detailed evaluative study conducted of the practices being followed.

- Develop task forces within the firm or organization to undertake time-management studies with the goals of finding, analyzing, and "curing" areas experiencing wasteful time procedures.

- Have individuals within the firm or organization engage in educational and research activities related to time management, such as enrolling in college courses, checking the Internet, participating in correspondence courses, and/or attending seminars.

- Check into the possibility of visiting and studying other firms noted for their efficient time-management practices.

ACHIEVING AND APPLYING GOOD TIME-MANAGEMENT PRINCIPLES

In most organizational and personal activities, three areas of endeavor play prominent roles in achieving and applying good time-management principles: (1) development of suitable personal qualities, (2) development of short- and long-range goals, and (3) effective use of computers.

Development of Suitable Personal Qualities Good time management requires the utmost in organizational ability. Answers to questions such as the following must be found: Does the worker have all the necessary tools located conveniently? Can necessary tools be found without wasting time? Is provision made for replacement of items that routinely get used up? Are necessary lists placed in a handy location? Are lighting, temperature, and noise at proper levels? If reference materials are needed to perform the job, are they placed in accessible locations? Where direct contact with other persons is necessary to obtain information, can these persons be quickly contacted? Have procedures been worked out to reduce clutter and confusion? Is complete clean-up of workstations required daily or at other appropriate time intervals? Have job duties been arranged in order of priority?

Planning is necessary to achieve success in time management. Companies find that production moves more efficiently when procedures have been carefully worked out in detail.

Self-discipline and motivation play key roles in this process. Once a commitment is made to improve, an urge to proceed efficiently tends to follow, and it is necessary to apply this urge to the tasks at hand. Motivation grows as workers begin seeing the results of improved production.

Special efforts need to be paid to procrastination, one of the deadliest enemies of good time management. People who suffer from procrastination wait until the last possible moment to do almost anything. Some find it almost impossible to take the first step in any project. It can seriously affect work quality and heighten personal stress. It may create uninvited feelings of panic and chaos.

Perhaps the best cure for procrastination is imposition of strict time limits either upon one's self or upon others in the chain of command.

Development of good time-management practices may require inauguration of a program of self-evaluation. Personal habits may need to be studied carefully to see if any are faulty and need to be improved.

Development of Short- and Long-Range Goals Establishing short- and long-range goals is essential to successful time management in both one's personal life and one's work life.

When establishing goals, it is necessary to determine and specify standards that must be achieved within stated dates and/or times. This involves identifying a series of specific steps designed to bring one closer and closer to a stated goal. A good plan must include amounts of time per day or hour (or other time measurement) that will be devoted to work geared to achievement of the goal. It should include estimated time costs that might result from barriers or obstacles encountered along the way.

Prioritizing—that is, ranking goals in order of importance—is necessary in situations where the most important of the possible goals may not be easily determined. For example, in designing a new refrigerator, there is often a clash between the engineers, who wish it designed to operate at the highest efficiency level, and the marketing people, who wish it to be given a price tag that will maximize its salability. Which is given the highest priority—quality or pricing? A time-management plan may very well be involved in determining the answer.

Effective Use of Computers Computers can provide essential assistance in helping people to manage their time wisely by tracking details, coordinating schedules, facilitating communication, and securing and organizing data.

Computers greatly assist those who work with others at a considerable geographic distance. Written messages can be transmitted instantly through e-mail. Data can be researched comparatively quickly through the Internet.

In and of themselves, however, computers do not provide an automatic solution for time-management problems. They are most helpful to people who are already both knowledgeable and organized—and therefore best able to apply the benefits of computers to time management.

In addition to computers, other technology exists that can contribute to the quality of time-management plans:

- Faxing is the instantaneous transmission of communications from one fax (facsimile) machine to another anywhere in the world.
- Priority mail and overnight-delivery service are offered by the U.S. Post Office.
- Telephones, which once provided only voice-transmission service, now offer voice-mail recording, beepers, cellular service, and other services.

TIME MANAGEMENT AND LARGE PROJECTS

Complications inevitably arise with a large project that involves management and coordination of several organizations and people who are all contributing to its completion. A classic example is a construction project involving a building, dam, bridge, or road.

Suppose, for example, a building is being constructed for XYZ business firm. Often, in cases like this, the role of time is very critical. It may be that XYZ firm has found it necessary to get heavily involved in activities such as selling or leasing its existing location, making the myriad of moving arrangements for its employees and their equipment, and working out contacts with its customers.

XYZ firm very much desires the building under construction to be completed at the agreed-upon time. If not, XYZ firm could encounter large expenses in having to put up with temporary locations and increase the time spent in making large numbers of alternative arrange-

ments. In fact, time in such situations is so critical that contracts often require builders to forfeit fees if the construction is not completed on schedule.

In cases such as this (and in many other applications), extensive use may be made of the Program Evaluation and Review Technique, usually called *PERT*. Developed in the 1950s, PERT groups various activities graphically. Activities in the construction of a large building, for example, might include excavations, various foundation workings, windows, air conditioning, heating, painting, and so on. Each activity requires not only estimates of time but also the costs of labor, material, and money. Some of the activities are sequential—the first activity must be completed before the second can begin. Other activities are concurrent—more than one activity can be worked on at a time. Many valuable rewards await people and organizations who are willing to develop good time management practices.

BIBLIOGRAPHY

Fitzwater, Ivan W. (1997). *Finding Time for Success and Happiness Through Time Management*. Austin, TX: MESA Publications.

Lapin, Lawrence L. (1994). "Project Planning with PERT." *Quantitative Methods for Business Decisions*, 6th ed. Fort Worth, TX: Dryden Press.

Mackenzie, Alec. (1997). *The Time Trap*, 3d ed. New York: AMACOM.

Mayer, Jeffrey J. (1995). *Time Management for Dummies*. Foster City, CA: IDG Books.

Reynolds, Helen, and Tramel, Mary E. (1979). *Executive Time Management*. Englewood Cliffs, NJ: Prentice-Hall.

CARRIE FOLEY

TIME VALUE OF MONEY

Are you indifferent between receiving $1,000 today and receiving $1,000 one year from today? If your intuition prefers receiving the funds today, rather than one year from today, then your intuition recognizes the time value of money. Owners of cash can permit borrowers to rent the use of their cash. *Interest* is payment for the use of cash.

Expenditures for an investment most often precede the receipts produced by that investment. Cash received later has less value than cash received sooner. The difference in timing affects whether making an investment will earn a profit. Amounts of cash received at different times have different values. We use interest calculations to make valid comparisons among amounts of cash paid or received at different times.

CONCEPTS

Businesses typically state interest cost as a percentage of the amount borrowed per unit of time. Examples are 12 percent per year and 1 percent per month. When the statement of interest cost includes no time period, then the rate applies to a year; thus "interest at the rate of 12 percent" means 12 percent per year.

The amount borrowed or loaned is the *principal. Compound interest* means that the amount of interest earned during a period increases the principal, which is then larger for the next interest period.

If you deposit $1,000 in a savings account that pays compound interest at the rate of 6 percent per year, you will earn $60 by the end of one year. If you do not withdraw the $60, then $1,060 will earn interest during the second year. During the second year your principal of $1,060 will earn $63.60 interest; $60 on the initial deposit of $1,000 and $3.60 on the $60 earned the first year. By the end of the second year, you will have $1,123.60. Compounded annually at 8 percent, cash doubles itself in nine years. If a twenty-five-year old invests $2,000 each year which earns 8 percent a year, the retirement fund will grow to more than $425,000 by the time that person reaches age sixty-five.

When only the original principal earns interest during the entire life of the loan, the interest due at the time the borrower repays the loan is *simple interest*. Simple interest calculations ignore interest on previously earned interest. Nearly all economic calculations, however, involve compound interest.

Problems involving the time value of money generally fall into two groups:

1. We want to know the *future value* of cash invested or loaned today.
2. We want to know the *present value*, or today's value, of cash to be received or paid at later dates.

FUTURE VALUE

If you invest $1 today at 12 percent compounded annually, it will grow to $1.12000 at the end of one year, $1.25440 at the end of two years, $1.40493 at the end of three years, and so on, according to the formula:

$$Fn; = P(1 + r)_n$$

where

F_n = accumulation or future value

P = one-time investment today

r = interest rate per period

n = number of periods from today

The amount F_n is the *future value* of the present payment, P, compounded at r percent per period for n periods.

Example. How much will $2,000 deposited today at 8 percent compounded annually be worth 40 years from now?

$2,000 will grow to $2,000 $\times$ $(1.08)^{40}$ = $2000 $\times$ 21.72452 = $434,490 *
*(While you can compute 1.08 can be raised to the 40th power manually, future value tables, calculation, and computers can remove the tedium of such computations.)

PRESENT VALUE

Now, consider how much principal, P, you must invest today in order to have a specified amount, F_n, at the end of n periods. You know the future amount, F_n, the interest rate, r, and the number of periods, n; you want to find P. In order to have $1 one year from today when deposits earn 8 percent, you must invest P of $.92593 today. That is, $F_1 = P(1.08)^1$ "or" $1 = $.92593 $\times$ 1.08.

The number $(1 + r)^{-n}$ [= $1/(1 + r)^n$] equals the present value of $1 to be received after *n* periods when interest accrues at *r* percent per period. The discounted present value of $1 to be received n periods in the future is $(1 + r)^{-n}$ when the discount rate is *r* percent per period for *n* periods.

Example What is the present value of $1 due 10 years from now if the interest rate (equivalently, the discount rate) *r* is 8 percent per year? $(1 + .08)^{-10} \times \$1 = \$.46319\ *$
*(Present value tables and computers simplify such a calculation)

CHANGING THE COMPOUNDING PERIOD: NOMINAL AND EFFECTIVE RATES

"Twelve percent, compounded annually" states the price for a loan; this means that interest increases principal once a year at the rate of 12 percent. Often, however, the price for a loan states that compounding is to take place more than once a year. A savings bank may advertise that it pays 6 percent, compounded quarterly. This means that at the end of each quarter the bank credits savings accounts with interest calculated at the rate 1.5 percent ($= 6\%/4$).

$10,000 invested today at 12 percent, compounded annually, grows to a future value one year later of $11,200. If the rate of interest is 12 percent compounded semiannually, the bank adds 6 percent interest to the principal every six months. At the end of the first six months, $10,000 will have grown to $10,600; that amount will grow to $10,600 $\times$ 1.06 = $11,236 by the end of the year. Notice that 12 percent compounded semiannually is equivalent to 12.36 percent compounded annually. At 12 percent compounded monthly, $1 will grow to $1 $\times$ (1.01)12 = $1.12683 and $10,000 will grow to $11,268. Thus, 12 percent compounded monthly provides the same ending amount as 12.68 percent compounded annually. Common terminology would say that *12 percent compounded monthly has an effective rate of 12.68 percent compounded annually* or *is equivalent to 12.68 percent compounded annually*. If a nominal rate, *r*, compounds *m* times per year, the effective rate equals $(1 + r/m)^m - 1$.

BIBLIOGRAPHY

Stickney, Clyde P., and Weil, Roman L. (2000). *Financial Accounting: An Introduction to Concepts, Methods and Uses*, 9th ed. Ft. Worth, TX: Dryden.

ROMAN L. WEIL

TRADE DISCOUNTS

(SEE: *Pricing*)

TRADEMARKS

Trademarks or *marks* are words, symbols, designs, combinations of letters or numbers, or other devices that identify and distinguish products and services in the marketplace. When trademarks are presented to the public via advertising, marketing, trade shows, or other means, they become one of a company's most valuable assets—potential customers identify a company by its trademark. Because certain trademarks immediately create an image of quality goods and services to potential buyers, they are valuable assets that should be protected.

When trademarks are registered at the state, federal, or international levels, their owners are provided the maximum legal protection for company names and/or company products. Thus, in creating or selecting company names and trademarks, a major concern is to design names and trademarks that may be registered with U.S. Patent Office. Today, the feasibility of designing names for products and services as well as trademarks for them is not likely because millions of trademarks are already registered.

The creation of trademarks involves the development of symbols or other devices to identify products and services in the marketplace. Guidelines exist for creating trademarks. Individuals who are developing trademarks must avoid generically descriptive and misleading terms as well as foreign translations. As soon as a tentative trademark has been developed, its creators should consult a patent attorney for assistance making it sufficiently distinctive to be registrable.

A Chicago Cubs trademark logo.

After the distinctive trademark has been designed, the creators need to ascertain that it is available for use; that is, it should not be currently used by another company. Thus, a trademark search is recommended by a company specializing in trade and service mark law. Once the availability of the proposed trademark has been certified, applications and related artwork are filed with the U.S. Patent Office. On receipt of the application, examiners in the Patent Office conduct a search to validate that the proposed trademark is not confusingly similar to previously registered trademarks and is thus usable. To receive a filing registration date, the owner must provide all of the following: (1) a written application form; (2) a drawing of the mark on a separate piece of paper; (3) the required filing fee; and (4) if the application is filed based on prior use of the mark in commerce, three specimens for each class of goods or services. The specimens must show actual use of the mark with the goods or services. The specimens may be identical or they may be examples of three different uses showing the same mark.

If the Patent Office search does not yield any conflicting trademarks and the proposed trademark is deemed registrable, it is published for opposition in the Patent Office's *Official Gazette.* Anyone who believes that a company may be damaged by the registration of the proposed trademark has an opportunity to challenge its registration. If no objection to the proposed trademark is filed, then the registration is allowed and issued. Thus, the trademark is distinctive and the ® may be used after it. Once the trademark has been issued by the Patent Office, its owners need to watch for inappropriate use of it. In addition, trademark owners need to monitor proposed trademark registrations for similar trademarks.

Trademark maintenance involves periodic filing of documents with the Patent Office to keep the registration active. Unlike copyrights or patents, trademark rights can last indefinitely if the owner continues to use the mark to identify its goods or services. The term of a federal trademark registration is ten years, with ten-year renewal terms. However, between the fifth and sixth year after the date of initial registration, the registrant must file an affidavit setting forth certain information to keep the registration alive. If no affidavit is filed, the registration is canceled. A U.S. registration provides protection only in the United States and its territories. The owner of a mark who wishes to protect it in other countries must seek protection in each country separately under the relevant laws. The U.S. Patent Office cannot provide information or advice concerning protection in other countries. Interested parties may inquire directly in the relevant country or its U.S. offices or through an attorney.

RANDY L. JOYNER

TRADE SHOWS

Trade shows provide a forum for companies to display and demonstrate their products to potential buyers who have a special interest in buying

Displays at the Chicago Auto Show.

these products. The compacted time frame and concentrated location of trade shows are cost-effective for exhibiting companies and convenient for buyers.

Since the 1960s, trade shows have become an increasingly prominent part of the promotional mix. Their relative importance is reflected in the promotional expenditures of U.S. companies: Larger amounts are spent each year on trade exhibitions than on magazine, radio, and outdoor advertising; only newspaper and television advertising receive a larger share of promotional dollars.

The primary role of trade shows in the promotional mix is that of a selling medium. Depending on the type of product being exhibited, selling activities can involve booking orders or developing leads for future sales. If show regulations permit, they can even involve selling products directly at the exhibit. Trade shows also serve as vehicles for advertising and publicity. Exhibits can be very effective three-dimensional ads as

well as collection points for names for direct-mail lists. They can also command the attention of the news media, which regularly cover shows in search of stories on new products and new approaches.

Participating companies can also accomplish nonpromotional marketing objectives at trade shows. Market research data, for example, can be collected from show visitors. Competitors' offerings can be evaluated. And contacts can be made with potential suppliers and sales representatives.

More than 10,000 trade shows are held in the United States each year, and the number is growing. Nearly half of those are large business-to-business shows with 100 or more booths. The smaller exhibitions include both business-to-business and consumer shows.

Business-to-business trade shows focus on goods and services within an industry or a specialized part of an industry. They are targeted to wholesalers and retailers with the intent of pushing products through the channel of distribution. Most attendees at these shows are actively looking for products and have the authority to buy. Examples of business-to-business exhibitions are those in the areas of health care, computer products, electronics, advertising specialties, heavy equipment, agriculture, fashions, furniture, and toys.

Consumer trade shows, like business-to-business expositions, also have an industry focus. They are different, however, in that they target the general public and, accordingly, are designed to stimulate end-user demand. The kinds of products exhibited at these open shows include autos, housewares, boats, antiques, and crafts.

Several trade show organizations provide information and assistance to exhibitors and those considering exhibiting. The Center for Exhibition Industry Research (formerly the Trade Show Bureau) is an umbrella organization that represents the entire exhibition and convention field. It sponsors research on the effectiveness and cost-efficiency of trade shows, has a resource center, and serves as a referral point for more specialized groups. The International Association of Exhibit Managers is the association of individuals within companies who are responsible for exhibit arrangements. Others, like the Healthcare Convention and Exhibitors Association, concentrate on the organization and promotion of shows for specific industries.

(SEE ALSO: *Exhibitors and conventions*; *Promotional mix*; *Promotion strategy*; *Pull strategy*; *Push strategy*; *Sales promotion*; *Trade promotion*.)

BIBLIOGRAPHY

Lamas, Bob. (1999). "Involve Your Staff in Trade Shows for Better Results." *Marketing News*. March: 9-10.

Miller, S. (1991). *How to Get the Most Out of Trade Shows*. Illinois: NTC Business Books.

Sisking, B. (1993). *The Successful Exhibitor's Handbook*. Washington: Self-Counsel Press.

Weisgal, M. (1997). *Show & Sell: 133 Business-Building Ways to Promote Your Trade Shows*. New York: AACOM.

EARL C. MEYER
WINIFRED L. GREEN

TRADING BLOCS

An evolving trend in international economic activity is the formation of multinational trading blocs. These blocs are made up of a group of contiguous countries that decide to have common trading policies for the rest of the world in terms of tariffs and market access but have preferential treatment for one another. Organizational form varies among market regions, but the universal reason for the formation of such groups is to ensure the economic growth and benefit of the participating countries. Regional cooperative agreements have proliferated since after the end of World War II. Among the more well-known ones existing today are the European Union and the North American Free Trade Agreement. Some of the lesser-known ones include the MERCOSUR (Southern Cone Free Trade Area) and the Andean Group in South America, the Gulf Cooperation Council in West Asia (GCC), the South Asian Agreement for Regional Cooperation in South Asia (SAARC), and the Association of South East Asian Nations (ASEAN). The existence and growing influence of these multinational groupings implies that nations need to become part of such groups to remain globally competitive. To an extent, the regional groupings reflect the countervailing force to the increasing integration of the global economy—it is an effort by governments to control the pace of the integration.

Trading blocs take many forms, depending on the degree of cooperation and interrelationships, which lead to different levels of integration among the participating countries. There are five levels of formal cooperation among member countries of these regional groupings, ranging from a free trade area to the ultimate level of integration, which is political union.

Before the formation of a regional group of nations for freer trade, some governments agree to participate jointly in projects that create economic infrastructure (such as dams, pipelines, and roads) and that decrease the levels of barriers from those that allow little or no trade to those that encourage substantial trade. Each country may make a commitment to financing part of the

Representatives from Canada, the United States, and Mexico sign the North American Free Trade Agreement in 1994.

project, such as India and Nepal did for a hydro-electric dam on the Gandak River. Alternatively, they may share expertise on rural development and poverty-alleviation programs as well as lower trade barriers in selected goods, as did SAARC, which is comprised of India, Pakistan, Sri Lanka, Bangladesh, Nepal, Maldives, and Bhutan. These types of loose cooperation are considered a precursor to a more formal trade agreement. The evolutionary path for the development of various forms of trading blocs is shown in Figure 1.

FREE-TRADE AREA

A *free-trade area*, which has a higher level of integration than a loosely formed regional cooperative, involves a formal agreement among two or more countries to reduce or eliminate customs duties and nontariff trade barriers among partner countries. However, member countries are free to maintain individual tariff schedules for countries that do not belong to the group. One fundamental problem with this arrangement is that a

free-trade area can be circumvented by nonmember countries, which can export to the member nation having the lowest external tariff and then transport the goods to the destination member nation without paying the higher tariff that would have been applicable if the goods had gone directly to the destination nation. In order to prevent foreign companies from using this export method to avoid tariffs, method of *local content laws* are usually introduced. These laws require that in order for a product to be considered "domestic"—and thus not subject to import duties—a certain percentage or more of the value of the product should be sourced locally within the free-trade area. Thus, local content laws are designed to encourage foreign exporters to set up their manufacturing locations in the free-trade area.

A free-trade area is not necessarily free of trade barriers, among its member countries. Although it is an attempt by treaty to develop freer trade among the member countries, trade dis-

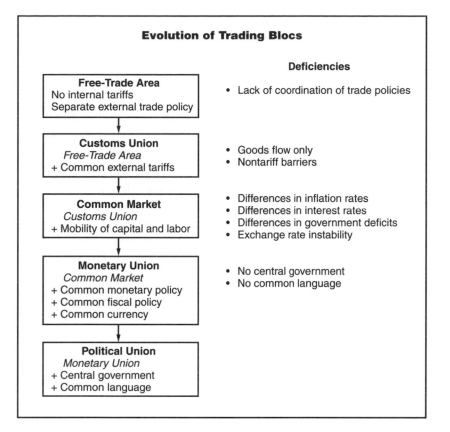

Figure 1

putes and restrictions nonetheless frequently occur.

The *North American Free Trade Agreement (NAFTA)*, a free-trade agreement among Canada, the United States, and Mexico, provides for elimination of all tariffs on industrial products traded among these three countries within ten years from the date of implementation of the NAFTA agreement—January 1, 1994. NAFTA was preceded by a free-trade agreement between Canada and the United States that went into effect in 1989. The United States has a free-trade agreement with Israel as well. Mexico is also negotiating with the European Union about creation of a transatlantic free-trade area without U.S. involvement. Likewise, Canada signed a trade deal with the Andean Group in 1999 as a forerunner to a possible free-trade agreement.

The three NAFTA countries are very different in their economic structure, development, and size. The U.S. economy boasted a gross national product (GNP) of $7.5 trillion and a population of 240 million in 1998. While Canada's per-capita income is similar to that of the United States, its economy is only about 10 percent that of the United States because of its much smaller population of 28 million. On the other hand, Mexico's economy is little more than 5 percent that of the United States, although it has a relatively large population of 92 million. Despite the different sizes of their economies, Canada and Mexico are the largest and second-largest trading partners of the United States. However, trade between Canada and Mexico remains insignificant, while both the Canadian and the Mexican economies are dependent on the U.S. economy as their primary export markets. Two-thirds of Canada's exports and four-fifths of Mexico's exports go to the United States. For both countries, almost half of their trade with the United States takes place on an intrafirm basis, with parent companies and their subsidiaries shipping parts and products among their own corporate units.

The European Free Trade Association (EFTA) EFTA is another well-known free-trade group, consisting of Iceland, Norway, and Switzerland. Although Austria, Finland, and Sweden, used to be EFTA member countries, they have joined the European Union (to be explained later), and Switzerland has applied to become a member. It appears that the EFTA will gradually merge into the European Union.

The Southern Common Market (*Mercado Común del Sur* or MERCOSUR) MERCOSUR is a free-trade area consisting of Brazil, Argentina, Uruguay, and Paraguay, with an automatic schedule for the lowering of internal trade barriers and the ultimate goal of creating a customs union. Chile and Bolivia also became associate members in 1996 and 1997, respectively.

CUSTOMS UNION

The inherent weakness of the free-trade area concept may lead to its gradual disappearance in the future, although it may continue to be an attractive stepping stone to a higher level of integration. When members of a free-trade area add common external tariffs to the provisions of the free-trade agreement, then the free-trade area becomes a *customs union*.

Therefore, members of a customs union not only have reduced or eliminated tariffs among themselves but also have imposed a common external tariff on countries that are not members of the customs union. This prevents nonmember countries from exporting initially to a member country that has a low external tariff with the goal of sending the exports on to a member country that has a higher external tariff. The ASEAN is a good example of a currently functional customs union whose eventual goal is formation of a common market. The Treaty of Rome of 1958, which formed the *European Economic Community*, created a customs union made up of West Germany, France, Italy, Belgium, the Netherlands, and Luxembourg.

COMMON MARKET

As cooperation increases among the countries of a customs union, they can form a *common market*, which eliminates all tariffs and barriers to trade among its members, adopts a common set of external tariffs on nonmembers, and removes all restrictions on the flow of capital and labor among member nations. The 1957 Treaty of Rome that created the European Economic Community had the ultimate goal of creating of a common market—a goal that was substantially achieved by the early 1990s in Western Europe, known as the *European Community* (Austria, Belgium, Denmark, France, Germany, Ireland, Italy, Luxembourg, the Netherlands, Portugal, Spain, and the United Kingdom). German banks can now open branches in Italy, for example, and Portuguese workers can live and work in Luxembourg. Similarly, South American Countries, led by the MERCOSUR and the Andean Group, are actively seeking to create a common market of more than 300 million consumers by 2005.

MONETARY UNION

A monetary union represents the fourth level of integration among politically independent countries. In strict technical terms, a monetary union does not require the existence of a common market or a customs union, a free-trade area or a regional cooperation for development. However, it is the logical next step after a common market, because it requires the next higher level of cooperation among member nations.

In Europe, the *Maastricht Treaty*, which succeeded the Treaty of Rome and called for the creation of a union (and hence the change in name from European Community to European Union), created a *monetary union* and has the ultimate goal of creating a political union, with member countries switch adopting a common currency and a common central bank. A monetary union represents the fourth level of integration among politically independent countries.

The *European Union* (EU) consists of fifteen countries (Austria, Belgium, Denmark, Finland, France, Germany, Greece, Ireland, Italy, Luxembourg, the Netherlands, Portugal, Spain, Sweden, and the United Kingdom). On January 1, 1999, the eleven countries of the so-called euro-zone (excluding EU members Denmark, Greece, Sweden, and the United Kingdom) embarked on a venture that created the world's second-largest economic zone, after the United States. The seeds for the euro were sown three decades ago. In 1969, Pierre Werner, a former prime minister of Luxembourg, was asked to chair a think-tank on how an European monetary union (EMU) could be achieved by 1980. The Werner Report, published in October 1970, outlined a three-phase plan that was very similar to the blueprint ultimately adopted in the Maastricht Treaty, signed on February 7, 1992. Like the Maastricht Treaty, the plan envisioned the replacement of local currencies by a single currency. However, the EMU was put on hold following the monetary chaos created by the first oil crisis. The next step on the path to monetary union was the creation of the European monetary system (EMS) in the late 1970s. Except for the United Kingdom, all member states of the European Union joined the Exchange Rate Mechanism (ERM), which determined bilateral currency exchange rates. Currencies of the, by then, nine member states could still fluctuate, but movements were limited to a margin of 2.25 percent. The EMS also led to the European currency unit (ecu)—in some sense the predecessor of the euro. Note the ecu never became a physical currency.

The foundations for monetary union were laid at the Madrid summit in 1989, when the EU member states undertook steps that would lead to free movement of capital. The Maastricht Treaty, signed shortly afterward, spelled out the guidelines toward creation of the EMU. Monetary union was to be capped by the launch of a single currency by 1999. This treaty also set norms in terms of government deficits, government debt, and inflation that applicants had to meet in order to qualify for EMU membership. All applicants, with the exception of Greece, met the norms, though in some cases (e.g., Belgium, Italy) the rules were bent rather liberally. These eleven countries forming the euro-zone surren-

dered their right to issue their own money starting in January 1999. Monetary policy for this group of countries is now run by the European Central Bank, headquartered in Frankfurt, Germany. Three of the EU member states—namely, the United Kingdom, Sweden, and Denmark—decided to opt out and sit on the fence. Stocks, bonds, and government debt are now denominated in the euro. Companies can use the euro for their transactions and accounting procedures. Until 2002, the euro will be in a "twilight zone"—existing as a virtual currency but is not yet existing physically. The Big Bang in the euro-zone will occur in 2002, when the euro becomes a physical reality and goes into circulation in all EMU member states. During the first half of 2002, local currencies and the euro will coexist. After July 1, 2002, the euro will replace local currencies, which will then no longer be accepted as legal tender.

POLITICAL UNION

The culmination of the process of integration is the creation of a *political union*, which can be another name for a nation when such a union truly achieves the levels of integration described here on a voluntary basis. The ultimate stated goal of the Maastricht Treaty is a political union. Currently, Britain remains the principal opponent of ceding any part of the sovereignty of the nation-state to any envisaged political union. Even the leading proponents of European integration—Germany and France—have reservations about a common defense and foreign policy.

Sometimes countries come together in a loose political union for reasons of common history, as with the British Commonwealth, consisting of nations that were once part of the British Empire. Commonwealth members received preferential tariffs in the early days, but when Britain joined the European Union, this preferential treatment was lost. The group now exists only as a forum for discussion and an expression of common historical ties.

The best-known political union that exists today is the United States, whose individual states went through a process similar to the evolutionary path for the development of various forms of trading blocs in the early years after declaring independence from Great Britain rule in 1776.

BIBLIOGRAPHY

Blecker, Robert A. (1996). *U.S. Trade Policy & Global Growth: New Directions in the International Economy.* Armonk, NY: M. E. Sharpe.

Jacquemin, Alexis, and Pench, Lucio R., ed. (1997). *Europe Competing in the Global Economy.* Lyme, NH: Edward Elgar.

Kotabe, Masaaki, and Coutinho de Arruda, Maria Cecilia. (1998). "South America's Free Trade Gambit." *Marketing Management* 7 (Spring):38-46.

Panagariya, Arvind. (1997). "The Regionalism Debate: An Overview." *World Economy* 2 (June): 477-511.

MASAAKI KOTABE

TRAINING AND DEVELOPMENT

The field of training and development has changed significantly during the past several years, reflecting both its role and importance in achieving higher employee performance and meeting organizational goals. Today, this field has become more important because employees need to learn new skills, advance their knowledge, and meet the challenges of technology in achieving high performance.

BACKGROUND

Training has traditionally been defined as the process by which individuals change their skills, knowledge, attitudes, and/or behavior (Robbins and DeCenzo, 1998). In this context, training involves designing and supporting learning activities that result in a desired level of performance. In contrast, *development* typically refers to long-term growth and learning, directing attention more on what an individual may need to know or do at some future time. While training focuses more on current job duties or responsibilities, development points to future job responsibilities. However, sometimes these terms have been used interchangeably or have been denoted by the single term *performance consulting*, which emphasizes either the product of training and development or how individuals perform as a result of what they have learned (Robinson and Robinson, 1995).

To be effective, training and development must meet a number of goals. First, they must be focused on individual training needs but still reflect organizational goals in terms of desired or expected performance. Second, training and development must reflect learning goals or outcomes, outlining what will be accomplished by this process. Third, they must be based on sound learning principles, be perceived as important by trainees, and be conducted in a manner that maximizes learning. Last, they must be evaluated to determine effectiveness and to help guide change and improvement.

TRENDS IN TRAINING AND DEVELOPMENT

A number of trends have occurred that reflect the common theme of making training more effective. Some of the most significant trends include the following:

- *A greater emphasis on customized training* reflects the needs of trainees, both in terms of the skills and knowledge they currently have and those that they need, along with identifying the unique learning style of each individual. By having this focus, training can better match each individual's learning goals and needs, and thus be perceived as more relevant and appropriate by the trainee.

- *An increased development of personalized learning objectives* relates to present or future job requirements and reflects past performance appraisal information. This information can be gained, in part, by conducting a needs assessment for each trainee and can help in designing learning activities that encompass the critical skills and content areas needed for future performance.

- *A greater use of instructional technologies,* such as distance learning, allows individuals to customize learning to their job situation—such as location, time, access to technology, and so forth. The use of current training technologies can greatly assist individuals in their learning, since training content and delivery can be standardized, quickly updated, and constructed so as to require learners to demonstrate the desired competencies as they engage in learning activities.

- *A greater integration of training and development into the workplace* links learning to job performance. Training outcomes and learning activities are linked to each individual's job requirements so that what trainees learn will be reflected in their job performance. For example, individuals who have participated in a training program on developing teamwork skills would be expected to demonstrate these skills in their future job performance.

- *A greater use of action or performance plans* requires trainees to develop a plan outlining how they will implement what they have learned and how they will determine whether this plan will, in fact, improve performance. The use of this process further links training to job performance; it can also be integrated with the performance appraisal process to measure changes or improvements in an individual's performance.

A MODEL FOR CREATING TRAINING EFFECTIVENESS

With training and development becoming more systematic, models describing the process and activities required to achieve successful training are being used more frequently to explain how training should be designed, delivered, and evaluated. One such model, as shown in Figure 1, outlines the steps that should be completed during the pre-training, training, and post-training stages. This model also presents a brief summary of each of these stages, explaining why each step should be performed carefully and accurately.

During the *pre-training* stage, information is gathered to help determine the need for training. An assessment is made regarding what improvements or changes an organization needs to make, along with an assessment of what trainees need to meet their performance expectations. From this information, a decision can be made regarding the *training gap*, for example, the difference be-

tween the performance that is desired and the performance that currently exists.

After this assessment is complete, a number of *training* activities can be completed, including developing training goals or outcomes, determining the appropriate learning activities and strategies, and achieving an understanding and commitment from the trainees for the program or activities. When these activities are performed effectively, the likelihood that the training will be successful is greatly enhanced.

During the final stage, *post-training*, a number of activities are required to follow up on the training, ensure that it is integrated into the workplace, and measure performance changes and the effectiveness of the training. Although training can be measured through several techniques, the most important and relevant measurement is one that focuses on changes in performance rather than other factors, such as trainees' satisfaction with the training or what they have learned.

IMPACT OF TRAINING AND DEVELOPMENT ON PERFORMANCE AND ORGANIZATIONAL EFFECTIVENESS

One current method of evaluating the impact and importance of training is to examine the potential—or real—benefits to be achieved through training and development. Although not all benefits can be measured on a strict cost-benefit analysis basis, most benefits can be at least informally measured and used to determine effectiveness. The most significant direct benefits of training are the following:

- It clarifies job duties and responsibilities
- It increases an individual's job competence
- It provides the foundation for further development
- It assists in conducting an accurate performance appraisal
- It produces higher levels of performance

In addition, training may also be evaluated in terms of indirect benefits that can add additional value. These indirect benefits could include the following:

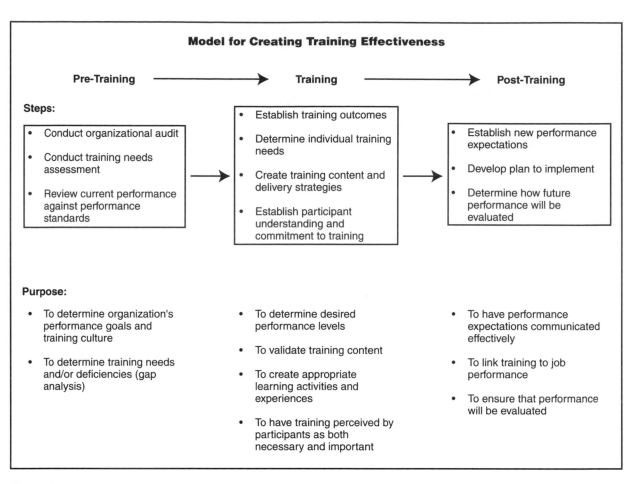

Figure 1

- Enhancing teamwork and team building
- Producing a strong sense of commitment to the organization
- Achieving higher levels of employee motivation
- Assisting in cross-training/job rotation

Although the impact of training can be measured in terms of individual learning and performance, another way to determine its impact is in relation to organizational growth, development, or effectiveness. As organizations have changed in recent times, there has emerged a need to study the critical elements that make organizations prosper and relate these to training and development. It is common today to view organizations in a dynamic sense, noting that they are constantly changing, renewing themselves, and in need of being reflective of current business practices. One current prospective is to view an organization as a "learning culture," reflecting its need to be constantly involved with learning how to become better and to provide significant training opportunities for employees (Senge, 1990). Accordingly, when organizations adopt this learning culture, they create a variety of training opportunities for all employees and develop performance expectations that instill in all employees the need for and value of training and development on a continual basis.

SUMMARY

Training and development have achieved a high degree of recognition for their importance in helping individuals become better performers and assisting organizations in achieving their goals. The field has become more visible, training processes more clearly defined, and the need for training more evident as societal and technological changes have occurred.

Through designing training and development activities as described in the model presented in Figure 1, the benefits outlined in this article—both direct and indirect—can be achieved. Further, when employees learn new skills and acquire new knowledge, they increase their career potential and add extra value to their employers and others whose work is impacted by their performance.

Following a well-structured plan for designing, implementing, and evaluating training and development programs is helpful in ensuring the effectiveness of the program and achieving a return on investment. To be effective, training should reflect the following guidelines:

- It should be tied to the organization's culture and goals. The current mission and goals should guide the development of all training and development activities. Each potential training activity should be reviewed by asking: How will this help achieve the organization's mission or goals?

- It should be perceived as important by trainee. Training should be viewed as important and relevant for achieving personal success and high performance levels.

- It should be relevant to the needs of the trainees. Some form of assessing the needs of the trainees should be completed prior to training to ensure that the program and learning activities are relevant to what the trainees need to learn or do.

- It should be linked to the workplace. Once training is completed, a plan should be completed by all trainees outlining how they will integrate the training results into their job. Some type of action plan—defining what activities will be completed, how they will be done, and when they will be implemented— should be used.

- It should be applied but based on sound learning principles. Current learning and training theories and principles should be used as the foundation for developing and delivering training programs, but the learning activities should stress how these theories and principles can be used in daily job duties.

- It should be supported and reinforced. If training is to be implemented effectively, support should be given by the trainees' supervisor and others who have an impact on the performance of trainees. In addition, policies and performance reward systems should help to support the training efforts and recognize when performance has improved as a result of training.

BIBLIOGRAPHY

DeCenzo, D. A., and Robbins, S. P. (1998). *Supervision Today* Upper Saddle River, NJ: Prentice-Hall, Inc.

Robinson, D. G., and Robinson, J. C. (1995). *Performance Consulting: Moving Beyond Training* San Francisco: Berrett-Koehler Publishers.

Senge, P. M. (1990, Fall). "The Leader's New Work: Building Learning Organizations." *Sloan Management Review* vol. 32(1): 1-17.

DAVID HYSLOP

TRANSFER PAYMENTS

Transfer payments are a form of income to individuals for which no *current* good or service is expected in return. They differ from other payments to individuals for which either a service (including labor services) is performed in return for such payments or a good is exchanged.

Transfer payments can originate from either business or government sources. Business transfer payments include corporate gifts to nonprofit institutions, payments for personal injury, and taxes paid by domestic corporations to foreign governments. Far more important, both in dollar terms and policy significance, are transfer payments originating from government sources. Government transfer payments can be made by any level of government (federal, state, or local) and can take the form of either cash or in-kind benefits. Cash benefits include Social Security; government employee, military, and railroad retirement pensions; unemployment insurance; veterans' benefits; workers' compensation; cash public assistance (including Temporary Assistance for Needy Families [TANF] and Supplemental Security Income [SSI]); and educational assistance. Also included are government payments to nonprofit institutions that do not involve work under research-and-development contracts. Major in-kind government transfer payments include food stamps, medical insurance (Medicaid and Medicare), and housing assistance.

Size and Significance of Transfer Payments.

The size of the U.S. government, measured as public expenditures, increased more than threefold from 1940 to 2000, and much of this increase was due to the growth in transfer payment expenditures, especially on Social Security, Medicare, and Medicaid. In the United States at the end of the twentieth century, transfer payments accounted for 44 percent of government spending by all levels of government (*Economic Report of the President*, 1999).

By their very nature, government transfer payments are excluded from the calculation of a nation's gross domestic product (GDP) since they do not represent compensation for the production of currently produced goods and services. Instead, transfer payments represent a redistribution of income, taking money away from some individuals (taxpayers) and giving it to others who are eligible for the various programs noted above. It is also important to recognize that while a considerable amount of transfer payments represent spending on public assistance—programs to aid the poor—other transfer payments are for social insurance programs (e.g., Social Security, Medicare, unemployment insurance) that bring significant benefits to the middle class. Public assistance programs are typically "means-tested," implying that the recipient must have household income below some threshold level to qualify and that the amount of the benefit decreases as household income increases.

Rationale for Transfer Payments.

Government transfer payments are rationalized in various ways depending on the nature of the programs involved. Public assistance transfer payments are often justified using Richard Musgrave's (1959) "distribution function" of government. Here it is argued the market outcomes may lead to a distribution of income that in the judgment of society is "too unequal." In particular, a government safety net is needed to insure that all members of society, including children and those unable to work, have a minimally adequate standard of living. Most public expenditures on low-income programs involve in-kind benefits, rather than cash assistance, because they allow the public some control over the spending patterns of recipients.

It should be noted that this rationale for government intervention and income redistribution through transfer payments is not without critics. Some would argue that nongovernmental organizations (e.g., churches and other forms of private philanthropy) are better equipped to meet the needs of low-income individuals.

Social insurance transfer-payment programs are rationalized in several ways. One relates to private "market failure" due to the phenomenon of *adverse selection*. Consider a private firm selling unemployment insurance to individuals without knowing the details of their employment status. If the firm were able to offer an insurance policy to a large group, the firm could make a reasonable estimate of the fraction of the group that would become unemployed over some period of time and charge rates accordingly to make a normal profit. But, the firm does not have information on the employment status of any single individual. When selling an unemployment insurance policy to a single individual, the firm must assume that individuals prone to unemployment are the most likely participants in this market. Accordingly, the firm would have to charge higher rates to individuals than for the group as a whole to make a profit. The higher cost of insurance would lead many people to choose not to insure, leading to less than the economically efficient amount of insurance being provided.

Social insurance transfer payments can also be rationalized on the grounds that some individuals lack the foresight to purchase sufficient insurance. For example, in the absence of Social Security some individuals might not save adequately for retirement. Society would then be faced with either letting such individuals retire with less-than-adequate resources or coming to their aid. The possibility of the latter further reduces the incentive for individuals to save during their working years.

Effect on Economic Behavior. Critics sometimes charge that major transfer-payment programs have adverse effects on household decisions to work and save. Regarding work effort, the benefits from means-tested programs are reduced as income from labor increases; in some cases the reduction is dollar-for-dollar, implying an implicit tax of 100 percent on the wages of program participants. In 1996 Congress addressed the work disincentive for the major cash transfer-payment program to low-income persons by changing the name of the program from Aid to Families with Dependent Children (AFDC) to Temporary Assistance for Needy Families (TANF) and mandating work requirements for most program participants.

Many economists believe that Social Security contributes to lower saving rates by individuals and influences their retirement decisions. Individuals view Social Security as an alternative saving vehicle for retirement, leading them to save less than they would in the absence of this program. Nationally, this may depress the level of saving because the Social Security system is financed on a *pay-as-you-go* basis, whereby current workers pay for the benefits of current retirees; benefits are not financed out of any past saving on the part of the retiree. The potential

effect that Social Security has on retirement decisions has been mitigated by legislation passed by Congress in 2000 that eliminated the implicit tax (reduced benefits) of individuals over 65 who choose to continue to work while nonetheless drawing Social Security benefits.

BIBLIOGRAPHY

Council of Economic Advisors. (1999). *Economic Report of the President*, Tables B-82, B-94. Washington, DC: U.S. Government Printing Office.

Feldstein, Martin S. (1996). "Social Security and Saving: New Time Series Estimates." *Journal of Political Economy* June: 151-164.

Moffit, Robert. (1992). "Incentive Effects of the US Welfare System." *Journal of Economic Literature*. March: 1-61.

Musgrave, Richard A. (1959). *The Theory of Public Finance*. New York: McGraw-Hill.

Rosen, Harvey S. (1999). *Public Finance*. Boston: Irwin/McGraw-Hill.

MICHAEL NELSON

TRANSFER PRICING

(SEE: *International Trade*)

TRANSFORMATION

(SEE: *Operations Management*)

TRANSFORMATIONAL LEADERSHIP

(SEE: *Management/Leadership Styles*)

U

UNIFORM CERTIFIED PUBLIC ACCOUNTANT EXAMINATION

Certified public accountant (CPA) is a designation awarded by a state or other governmental jurisdiction to individuals to practice as a licensed certified public accountant. The candidate for the CPA must meet education, examination, and experience requirements.

Examinations were used as early as 1884 to test the qualifications of accountants and to issue certificates of proficiency upon passage of the examination. In the 1880s two competing organizations, the Institute of Accounts and the American Association of Public Accounts [the predecessor to the current American Institute of Certified Public Accountants (AICPA)] were issuing certificates based on satisfactory completion of an examination or years of experience as an accountant. Neither organization was able to effectively control the practice of accounting by nonmembers. Consequently, the two rival organizations cooperated to introduce legislation in New York to regulate the practice of public accounting. In 1896, New York State passed the first accountancy law, which required testing the qualifications of those who wished to practice as public accountants. The first examination was administered in December 1896. This led to the issuance of a state license to practice as a CPA and the emergence of accounting as a profession with education requirements, professional standards, and a code of professional ethics. Other states followed this lead, and eventually fifty-four jurisdictions in the United States (fifty states and four territories) enacted legislation requiring an examination of candidates for licensing as CPAs. The Boards of Accountancy of each jurisdiction are responsible for administering compliance with the public accountancy laws. Efforts are underway to make the requirements more uniform among the various jurisdictions. This would make it easier for a CPA to be licensed in multiple states, an important consideration in the interstate practice of public accounting.

By the 1960s, all the jurisdictions in the United States required CPA candidates to pass a Uniform CPA Examination that is prepared by the AICPA and graded by its Advisory Grading Services, a service it has provided since 1917. The objective of the examination is to provide reasonable assurance to the boards that candidates passing the examination have the level of technical knowledge, skills, and abilities necessary to protect the public interest. The examination insures the public that CPAs entering the profession have met appropriate minimum requirements and that they have passed an examination that has uniform content, coverage, difficulty, and grading methodology.

THE CURRENT EXAMINATION AND REQUIREMENTS

The current examination is a two-day, fifteen-and-one-half-hour examination that is given twice each year-in May and November, on a Wednesday and Thursday-in the jurisdictions using the examination. The examination is a paper-and-pencil linear examination with questions in a predetermined sequence that candidates answer manually on paper answer sheets. The questions include four-option multiple-choice questions, other objective question formats, and essay questions or problems. The examination is given and graded only in English.

The examination covers four sections:

1. *Auditing (AUDIT):* Generally accepted auditing standards and procedures

2. *Accounting and Reporting (ARE):* Federal taxation, managerial accounting, and accounting for governmental and not-for-profit organizations

3. *Financial Accounting and Reporting (FARE):* Generally accepted accounting principles for business enterprises

4. *Business Law and Professional Responsibilities (LPR):* Professional responsibilities and the legal implications of business transactions as they relate to accounting and auditing

The AUDIT, FARE, and LPR sections consist of 50 to 60 percent four-option multiple-choice questions, 20 to 30 percent other objective question formats, and 20 to 30 percent essay questions or problems. The ARE section is completely objective, consisting of 50 to 60 percent four-option multiple choice questions and 40 to 50 percent other objective formats. The candidates' writing skills are evaluated in selected essay questions in the AUDIT, FARE, and LPR sections of the examination. Calculators are provided to the candidates for the ARE and FARE sections, but not the AUDIT and LPR sections, which require minimal calculations.

Since May 1996, the examination has been nondisclosed, meaning that the candidates are no longer allowed to retain or receive their question booklets after taking the examination or to reveal questions on the examination in any manner. Prior to 1996, AICPA published the complete test with the unofficial answers following each examination, and these copies were available for purchase.

In addition to the two-day examination, several jurisdictions require a separate examination in professional ethics, which is given at a different time than the certifying examination.

All jurisdictions use the same examination, but the requirements and procedures for applying to take it differ among the jurisdictions.

Candidates must complete an education requirement, which varies among the jurisdictions. Most require at least a bachelors degree with a concentration in accounting, but a majority of the jurisdictions have legislated an education requirement of at least one hundred and fifty semester hours. Normally this includes a bachelor's degree plus thirty semester hours of advanced coursework. The date when this requirement becomes effective varies among the jurisdictions. Some jurisdictions specify the number of required semester hours or courses in accounting and related business subjects. Candidates may sit for the examination in some jurisdictions before the education requirements are completed.

Other requirements for taking the examination vary among the jurisdictions as to residency, place of employment, and U.S. citizenship.

Candidates should contact the board in the jurisdiction where they plan to sit for the examination or plan to practice for the most current education, residency, and citizenship requirements as such requirements are subject to modification.

EXAMINATION ADMINISTRATION AND PREPARATION

The board of each jurisdiction is responsible for administering an examination as part of the requirements for conferring a CPA certificate. Today, all the jurisdictions use the services provided by the AICPA to prepare and grade the examination.

A Board of Examiners (BOE), a twelve-member senior committee of the AICPA, is responsible for the preparation of the examination and issuance of grades to the boards. The BOE oversees subcommittees that are responsible for each of the four examination sections. The boards, or its appointees, are responsible for administering AICPA-prepared examinations to the candidates in their jurisdiction.

The National Association of State Boards of Accountancy (NASBA), as part of its mission to assist boards in meeting their regulatory responsibilities, provides examination administration and grade-reporting services to its member boards. The CPA Examination Services Division of the NASBA administers the CPA examination for the majority of the jurisdictions. The other boards either administer the examinations or use some other service.

The Advising Grading Services of the BOE grades the examinations for all of the fifty-four boards. The objective is to grade the examination papers fairly and uniformly. Grading bases and guidelines are developed for each examination and approved by the BOE and the section subcommittees.

Each section of the examination is graded separately and reported on a scale ranging from 0 to 100 percent, with a minimum grade of 75 percent required to pass each section. The grading process may include as many as two subsequent reviews of each examination paper. A candidates who receives a passing grade on at least two sections with a minimum grade in the failed sections may receive conditional credit for the sections passed. Candidates are allowed a limited number of additional opportunities to pass the remaining sections. A candidate who does not pass the remaining sections within a specific time must retake the entire examination. Requirements for retaking the examination vary among the jurisdictions.

The grades are mailed by the boards to candidates approximately ninety days after the examination is administered, referred to as the Uniform Mailing Date. The boards may include information on how the candidate performed on each content area of the examination in a Candidate Diagnostic Report. A review of a candidate's examination papers is provided for a board that requests such a review.

The objective of the examination is to test the knowledge and skills that a candidate needs to practice as a CPA in planning and implementing a public accounting engagement. The examination requires candidates to display evaluation, judgment, presentation, and decision-making abilities related to accounting and auditing information.

The content of the four sections of the examination is based on studies of public accounting practice. Each major content area is assigned a percentage that represents the weight assigned to that topic or content area. Candidates' technical knowledge and skills are assessed in the examination's objective sections, and their writing skills are evaluated on the essay questions.

The examination questions are obtained from a number of sources, including members of the BOE, section subcommittees, in-house examination team members, practitioners, and educators. The BOE offers question writing workshops for each examination section to train practitioners and educators interested in writing examination questions.

The AICPA made the examination nondisclosed beginning with the May 1996 exam, thus permitting the BOE to build a large database of examination questions. The nondisclosed nature of the exam also assists the BOE in pretesting and revising exam questions, maintaining a consistent level of difficulty, and enhancing reliability by discouraging the study of prior examinations.

At present the examination is a paper-and-pencil examination, but future examinations may be a computer-based test that a candidate would be able to take by appointment throughout the year rather than only twice a year at a set date.

(SEE ALSO: *American Institute of Certified Public Accountants; Certified Public Accountant.*)

BIBLIOGRAPHY

American Institute of Certified Public Accountants. (1998). *Information for Uniform CPA Examination Candidates*, 14th ed. New York: Author.

Booker, Quinton, Brenner, Vincent C., and Blum, James D. (1998). "Brave New World for the CPA Exam". *Journal of Accountancy* January: 61-64.

Flesher, Dale L., Miranti, Paul J., and Previts, Gary John. (1996). "The First Century of the CPA". *Journal of Accountancy* October: 51-57.

ANTHONY T. KRZYSTOFIK

UNITED STATES GENERAL ACCOUNTING OFFICE

Congress created the U.S. General Accounting Office (GAO) in 1921 as a nonpartisan office to assist with oversight of general government operations by independently auditing federal agencies. As part of the legislative branch, the GAO is independent of the executive branch. Its name is somewhat misleading in that it does not engage primarily in routine accounting activities. Rather it is responsible for overseeing the accountability of government operations to Congress.

The GAO's chief officer is the comptroller general of the United States, who is appointed by the president for a single term of fifteen years with the advice and consent of the Senate. Removal of the comptroller general from office requires the passage of a joint resolution of Congress signed by the president. The protection of office afforded to the comptroller general strengthens the independence of the GAO.

Much of the work that the GAO performs originates as requests from committees of Congress or from individual members of Congress. Other work fulfills GAO mandates or legislative requirements.

HISTORY AND ESTABLISHMENT BY CONGRESS

The GAO was established by the Budget and Accounting Act of 1921, which transferred powers previously held by the Treasury Department to the GAO. The position of comptroller of the Treasury was abolished and that of comptroller general was created. The transfer of powers outside the executive branch represented a substantial change in federal financial management. With the creation of the GAO, an office outside the executive branch had the power to audit the financial affairs of the executive branch. As the presidency became the dominant focus of government in the twentieth century, the GAO became a powerful investigative office of Congress, with authority to examine all matters related to the receipt and disbursement of public funds.

EVOLVING NATURE OF RESPONSIBILITIES

The GAO has broad responsibility for the oversight of financial activities in the executive branch and wide discretion in the application of its responsibilities. Over time the GAO's interpretation of its responsibility has evolved through four phases of dominant orientation: bookkeeping, auditing, evaluation, and systems development. Until the end of World War II, the GAO had a bookkeeping orientation. Its work consisted of checking the accuracy and legality of transactions. Operations were centralized and personnel lacked professional credentials.

Following World War II, responsibility for bookkeeping practices was transferred to executive agencies, and the GAO's orientation shifted to auditing. It began to conduct financial audits of government corporations such as the Tennessee Valley Authority and economy and efficiency audits of particular activities within selected agencies. Additionally, the GAO was aggressive in auditing defense contracts for cost overruns and other abuses. Many of the auditors were military veterans who were educated in accounting.

Starting around 1965 with the adoption of Great Society programs, the GAO's orientation shifted to program evaluation and service to Congress. Personnel with a variety of educational backgrounds were recruited for their expertise.

Since the early 1980s, the GAO's focus has centered on the development of financial and management systems. Resources have been directed to improving internal control systems and financial reporting systems, as well as advancing performance-based management systems.

NATURE OF ACTIVITIES

The GAO has broad responsibilities that include (1) audits and evaluations, (2) accounting and information management policy, (3) legal services, and (4) reporting. Although the GAO has broad powers, the U.S. Supreme Court held in *Bowsher v. Synar* (106 S. Ct. 3181, 1986) that the comptroller general could not exercise executive branch decision-making authority.

GAO audits tend to differ from private-sector financial audits. The scope of GAO audits may be broader or narrower than the scope of nongovernmental audits. To provide the necessary expertise, personnel on GAO audit teams often have academic backgrounds in fields other than accounting. GAO audits tend to be initiated by request and usually are not performed on a routine periodic basis. However, the GAO is responsible for the audit of consolidated government-wide financial statements of the executive branch.

With respect to accounting and information management policy, the GAO participates in the development of accounting principles and standards for the executive branch and advises federal agencies about fiscal policies and procedures. Additionally, it establishes standards for auditing and evaluating government programs, including standards for governmental entities subject to the Single Audit Act of 1984.

The GAO provides legal advice to Congress, reviews legislative proposals, and assists with drafting legislation. Its staff investigates possible civil and criminal misconduct arising out of audits and evaluations. Within its judicial functions, the GAO resolves bid protests that challenge government contract awards, interprets laws governing public expenditure, and adjudicates claims for and against the government.

Findings and recommendations of the GAO are published as reports to Congress, delivered as testimony to Congress, or conveyed in oral briefing. Additionally, the GAO publishes comptroller general decisions. All unclassified reports are available to the public.

To motivate improvements in the performance of federal agencies, the GAO has pursued two important initiatives. These are the High Risk Series and the Performance and Accountability Series. Preliminary work for the High Risk Series began in 1990. High-risk program areas are ones that are vulnerable to waste, fraud, abuse, and mismanagement. These reports identify high-risk program areas, assess causes of risk, recommends ways to reduce risk, and monitor the status of efforts to sustain improvement. Designation as a high-risk program area is a signal of severe weakness. Removal of the designation is recognition of improvement in financial systems and reporting.

The Performance and Accountability Series was introduced in 1999. It includes a general report and separate reports on each cabinet department and most other major independent agencies. The general report discusses the challenges that the federal agency faces in working to improve performance, management, and accountability. This series is oriented to understanding ways performance-based management can be applied to achieve economy, efficiency, and effectiveness in government operations.

The URL for the GAO is http://www.gao.gov. This location provides directions about ways to obtain reports, testimony, decisions, and other information, as well as describing indexes, catalogues, and other means for locating GAO publications.

(SEE ALSO: *Chief Financial Officers Act*; *Government Accounting*)

BIBLIOGRAPHY

Mosher, Frederick C. (1984). *A Tale of Two Agencies: A Comparative Analysis of the General Accounting Office and the Office of Management and Budget.* Baton Rouge, LA: Louisiana State University Press.

Trask, Roger R. (1996). *Defender of the Public Interest: The General Accounting Office. 1921-1966.* Washington, DC: U.S. General Accounting Office.

Trask, Roger R. (1991). *GAO History 1921-1991.* Washington, DC: U.S. General Accounting Office.

U.S. General Accounting Office. (1999). *About the U.S. General Accounting Office*. Washington, DC: Author. The General Accounting Office. (see also: http://www.gao.gov).

U.S. General Accounting Office. (1999). *GAO's Performance and Accountability Series and High Risk Updates*. Washington, DC: Author. (see also: http://www.gao.gov).

Walker, Wallace Earl. (1986). *Changing Organizational Culture: Strategy, Structure and Professionalism in the U.S. General Accounting Office*. Knoxville, TN: The University of Tennessee Press.

JEAN E. HARRIS

UNIVERSAL VENDOR MARKETING

(SEE: *Promotion*)

V

VALUES

(SEE: *Social Responsibility*)

VARIANCE

(SEE: *Costs*)

VIDEOCONFERENCING

George Jetson, a character in the 1970s cartoon, was not terribly futuristic when he used his telephone that enabled him to see the person to whom he was talking. Videoconferencing, as it is known today, has been under development in the research labs at Pacific Bell since the 1920s. The project, referred to as "picturephone," is in the form of a desktop videoconferencing system. Videoconferencing rooms have been in existence at AT&T since the 1960s, where they are used to support large corporate meetings, including the annual shareholder's meeting.

It wasn't until the 1964 World's Fair that the "picturephone" was introduced to the public. AT&T predicted that the "picturephone" would replace the telephone by 1970. Although that prediction was wrong, the recession of the 1970s created a wider acceptance of videoconferencing by corporations that were looking for alternative ways to conduct meetings and conferences while cutting travel costs. Videoconferencing was not successful at that time, however, because the technology needed to attain personalized meetings was lacking.

With technology becoming more affordable and economically justifiable, practical and profitable applications of teleconferencing have gained popularity in the business world. With increasing competition and the need for face-to-face contact with customers, videoconferencing has become more popular because it allows face-to-face interaction without wasting travel time. Teleconferencing also allows for team meetings without the need to travel hundreds of miles.

WHAT IS TELECONFERENCING?

The earliest form of teleconferencing was the telephone conference call, in which several parties in various parts of the world could simultaneously hold a conversation. Businesspeople could talk with each other while sending and receiving faxes to provide a hard copy of the information being discussed. Today computer technology allows for synchronous, or simultaneous, sharing of data through four means: voice, video, digital whiteboard, and data files.

Several parties are able to share not only voice but also a live camera image of themselves while they talk. The size of the image can be shrunk to occupy only a small portion of the computer monitor or large display screen so that a data file can be accessed, displayed, and edited on the monitor at the same time.

Individuals participating in the conference call have the option of sharing and working with data files from either party's computer. While verbally discussing changes within the document and observing each other's body language, either party can edit the document and give immediate feedback. The digital whiteboard provides an electronic version of the dry erase board mounted on the wall. While viewing each other's actions via the computer monitor, individuals can also write on each other's whiteboard with special markers in the color of their choice. This allows professionals to make decisions and solve problems on the spot.

VIDEOCONFERENCING AND BUSINESS

This type of communicating allows people to work from their home via satellite, which increases family and/or personal time while reducing time spent commuting. It is estimated that in 1999, between 8 million and 15 million of the 120 million U.S. employees worked at home and communicated with their offices and customers using a computer and telephone lines. The number of telecommuters in America is expected to double by 2005.

Today's business environment requires most corporate employees to collaborate on a routine basis. Videoconferencing allows for face-to-face planned as well as impromptu meetings of workers who are separated by several thousand miles.

Sales presentations are an example of a profitable and easily justified business use of videoconferencing. When conducting the sales presentation at the customer's location, a sales representative with videoconferencing equipment on a laptop computer can connect the customer with specialists back at the company's offices to answer specific questions about the product being demonstrated. This allows for greater specialization, with the salesperson focusing on closing the sale and the specialists focusing on the technical aspects of the product. The salesperson is able to view the customer's body language and ask the specialist for clarification on customer objections or questions. The customer feels a sense of security by being able to see the individual instead of merely hearing a voice.

Another business application of videoconferencing is the ability to train people without actually traveling to another location. Companies can provide more frequent training to their employees in distant locations for less cost.

The Northrop Grumman Corporation implemented extensive teleconferencing for its 45,000 employees by setting up a hundred Team Communications Centers (TCCs) (teleconferencing rooms) at their offices across the United States. The TCCs are equipped with large digital whiteboards and projector screens. Groups of employees or managers from two or more locations collaborate on, discuss, and edit documents as though they were all in the same room, saving both time and money. The corporation identified airfare savings in 1998 of $150,000. These savings did not include hotels, meals, overtime, or incidentals.

VIDEOCONFERENCING AND EDUCATION

Teleconferencing can bring more educational choice and excellence to remote schools with small student bodies. Specialized courses that individual schools could not offer because of cost or limited student interest can be shared by several schools to provide cost efficiency. Flexibility in scheduling the classes to meet either an individual student's or a group of students' need is another major advantage.

Today, many universities are offering courses over the Internet or by means of other teleconferencing capabilities. This technology enables thousands of students to take college classes without leaving their community or, in many cases, their home. This technology is known as distance learning.

The nature of videoconferencing often requires distance-learning classes to present more class material, use better visuals, and show greater preparation of the teaching materials than traditional classes. These classes also hold students more accountable for their own learning. A major drawback for some students is that they must still attend classes (virtually) at preset times and progress at the pace set for the course.

Internet courses often better meet student needs by allowing them to work within their own time schedules and to progress at their own pace. Students sign into the virtual classroom (chat room) when it is convenient for them and respond to instructor questions and other student responses in much the same manner as they would in a traditional classroom discussion. The major differences are that all students must actively participate and the responses are written rather than oral.

Videoconferencing can present barriers to learning when interpersonal skills such as face-to-face interaction, eye contact, gaze, body language, and voice inflection are not transmitted. Another potential barrier is intercommunication delays when the timing of visual and audio signals, which are known to be effective in communication, are sometimes delayed.

For effective videoconferencing, the design of the room and the training of participants are critical factors. In educational settings, the classroom layout should allow all participants, including the instructor, to see and hear one another clearly. Instructors often need training on how best to project enthusiasm using this medium, how to monitor and adjust the camera and audio components, and how to prepare effective materials. Institutions must have a clear plan of how the system will be used to deliver instruction before they offer classes.

TECHNOLOGY

The three major types of videoconferencing involve conference rooms, roll-around units, and desktop units. The conference room facilities provide the user with a meeting room equipped with the audio and video technology needed to conduct an interactive conference. Roll-around units contain the needed audio and video equipment but are designed to be moveable. They provide a degree of flexibility; however the fact that the units are large often makes them impractical.

Desktop units provide desk or office videoconferencing access at the user's computer. The two essential components in addition to the computer are a small video camera, which usually sits on top of the computer, and a microphone, which can be set on a pedestal or worn as a headset. Telephone network capabilities have limited the quality of the video as well as causing delays in transmission. With the new TV cable hook-ups, however, desktop conferencing is achieving excellent video and audio quality.

Two types of desktop systems are VISIT and TMS. VISIT was an earlier desktop multimedia system integrating desktop videoconferencing, screen sharing, high-speed data transfer, electronic voice-mail access, and voice call management on a desktop computer. It required a plug-in video board; a black-and-white, fixed-focus CCD camera with an electronic auto iris; and application software.

TMS (Telepresence Media Space System), the newer system, is designed to capture the existing physical, cognitive, and social skills of users to support the same confidentiality, intimacy, and trust that develop in people who are engaged in face-to-face interaction. TMS also provides real-time document sharing and editing, video mail, video receptionist, and video recording of meetings. The technology needed for a TMS system includes a Sun workstation as the central server, computer controlled audio-video switch, PictureTel codec, Sony VCR, and camera mounted on the roof.

KEY TO SUCCESSFUL VIDEOCONFERENCING

The key to successful videoconferencing is effective communication skills. The users must be comfortable with the system, so that it appears as transparent as possible. This will allow the receiver to concentrate on the message and the sender to concentrate on making eye contact, so that participants feel included and are not just observers.

Participants in a videoconference should wear solid-colored clothing in dark or neutral colors to enhance the camera's focus. Movements should be slow and smooth, and caution should be taken not to block the camera's line of sight.

Participants should always maintain appropriate on-camera positioning, adhering to the elbows and wrists rule: When you stretch out your arms, the edge of the screen should fall between your elbows and wrists. It is important that participants see each other's facial expressions, but close-up shots should be used judiciously because the camera is sensitive to movement and will exaggerate blinking eyes, moving hands, or shifting in chairs. Videoconferencing participants will find it difficult to pay attention if the subject is not presented in an interesting and enthusiastic manner. Presenters should get beyond the "talking head" model and make the session as interactive as possible.

As in any instructional or corporate setting, the use of images, objects, and audio or video clips will greatly enhance the meeting's effectiveness. Visuals should have large, bold text with simple fonts and concise bulleted information. Time should be allowed for all participants to view the graphics. Participants should always speak in a strong, clear voice and avoid interrupting another speaker because the time delay may cause confusion.

Although videoconferencing has been available for more than seventy years, it is only now that its quality has reached the standards needed in business and educational settings. Its popularity has increased because it is able to save individuals and business both time and money, which are valuable and limited resources. As technology improves, the use of videoconferencing will increase as more businesses and individuals embrace it as an effective means of face-to-face communications.

BIBLIOGRAPHY

"31 Mayors Urge Colorado Businesses to Consider Telework as an Essential Tool to Attract and Retain Highly Skilled Workers." (1998, October 28). http://go.boulder.co.us/news/31mayors.html.

"C/NET Recommends, How Net Phones Work." (1999, February 23). http://www.cnet.com/Content/Reports/Reports/Reviews/NetPhones/ss07.html.

Coventry, L. (1997). *Video Conferencing in Higher Education.* Edinburgh: Institute for Computer Based Learning, Heriot Watt University.

Marrow, Kevin. (1999, January 14). "Exec Surfs to Work From Greek Island." http// www.ivc.ca/part25d.html.

Moore, G., and Schuyler, K. (1996). "Videoconferencing 90's Style: Sharing Faces, Places and Spaces." *PowerGrid Journal.*

"Northrop Grumman Case Study." (1998, December). http://www.microsoft.com/netmeeting/corp/grumman.html.

Reed, J. (1998). "Pacific Bell Knowledge Network Explorer. Communication Skills for Two-Way Video. EMC S23: Article 4." *Pacific Bell Incorporated.* [electrici.com/1.01/sharing-wp.html].

Rosen, Evan. (1996). "Personal Videoconferencing." www.browsebooks.com/Rosen.html.

"Selling the Telecommuting Decision." (1999, January). http//www.telecomute.org/twa_jan99.html.

"Telework Rapidly Growing in Canada." (1999, January 28). http://www.ivc.ca/part12.html.

"Video Teleconferencing." (1998, August 31). http://eagle.emweb.icx.net/video/videocon.html.

JAMES E. MILES

VISUAL MERCHANDISING

(SEE: *Promotion*)

VOICE MESSAGING

Voice messaging is a computerized method of storing and manipulating spoken recorded messages that is accessible to users from any touch-tone phone twenty-four hours a day. A voice-messaging system can be easily accessed by local, remote, or mobile users via land-line or cellular phones. Messages may be created in a user's voice mailbox and then transported to another voice mailbox in a manner similar to the e-mail process.

Voice-messaging systems include such services as voice messages, voice-mail distribution lists, fax-in and fax-on demand in the mailbox, interactive voice response, and voice forms that any user can access anywhere in the world.

HOW VOICE MESSAGING WORKS

Person A calls Person B, who is not available to take the call. Person B's voice mailbox or answering machine takes the call, replaying it when Person B returns and accesses it. The answering machine can be precise to Person B or can be shared with multiple office personnel. If the company has either a precise or shared system, Person B may retrieve the message by using a digitized code assigned to him or her. This code is called a voice-mail number. The voice mail system is designed to transfer a person's call to another telephone automatically by using call forwarding and to prioritize messages so that a specific phone number from Person A—the recipient—is prepared to communicate to Person B—the caller—for feedback.

HOW VOICE MESSAGING RELATES TO THE COMMUNICATION PROCESS

Voice messaging relates to the communication process by increasing productivity, improving internal communication, enhancing customer service, and reducing message-taking costs. The proper implementation of a voice-messaging system could be linked directly to improved public relations in companies.

In companies where a voice system is in place, users can easily change their greeting and the information in it and invite callers to leave their name, number, and any desired information. Voice-messaging systems in some companies permit users to call from any telephone in the world to change their greeting and to retrieve messages at any time of the day or night. Using a voice-message system ensures accurate messages, reduces the need for receptionists to take messages, and frees users from time zone dependence.

Many different types of companies—ranging from investment services to manufacturers, could possibly attain significant benefits in a short period of time, by using a voice-message system for internal communication between remote sites by means of such of integrated features as fax/voice mailboxes and pager notifications. It

appears that the more voice messaging a company uses, the more benefits and revenue savings could be realized.

When using a voice-messaging system, users should especially careful to make their communication clear, concise, complete, and unambiguous. A voice-messaging system can create a "first and lasting" impression for users. Therefore, the following do's and don'ts may should be observed.

THE DO'S

- Communicate with departments to obtain support.
- Consider training classes for company users so they can effectively handle incoming calls to the voice-messaging system.
- Communicate with customer service representatives about proper handling of calls.
- Test and navigate through the various options in the system to improve or streamline the messages.

THE DON'TS . . .

- Be careful not to overlook company customers. Be sure to know how they want their calls handled.
- In communicating, avoid being insular. Consider what your company's competition is doing and how you can apply their success to your company.
- Don't revise the system unnecessarily. Inquire about added features/applications only if you have maximized the use of those in existence.

VOICE-MESSAGING PRIVACY

As voice messaging become more prevalent, the issue of privacy becomes critical. Companies need to be as protective of their voice-mail system as they are of their computer system. Potential abuses of voice-messaging systems include fraudulent long-distance charges, malicious system intrusion, and corporate espionage. Many such abuses can be prevented by establishing certain policies and procedures that can enhance security, such as making it easy for users to change their passwords, establishing a system of automatic random password creation for new mailboxes, and having a flexible password structure. Nine to eighteen digit passwords are advised.

Two components prevalent to voice messaging are a user's outgoing personal greeting recorded in his/her own words and their message left for a receiver's response.

TIPS ON OUTGOING PERSONAL MESSAGES

- When recording a greeting, speak in a slow, clear, and concise fashion.

- Once a greeting has been recorded, call yourself to see how you sound and to determine whether you should re-record the message.

- Keep the recording to eight to twelve seconds.

- With your best voice, speak in a friendly tone of voice.

- If you will be unavailable for an extended period of time, change your message to let your callers know the time of your return and the name and phone number of someone who can help them until then.

TIPS ON LEAVING A MESSAGE

- Be sure to have a message in mind when you place a call in case you have to leave a message.

- Get to the point: Explain who you are and why you have called. Avoid rambling and repeating yourself.

- If you want to speak with someone about a specific topic that could be long and detailed. leave a "subject-matter-only" message; for example, "Allen, I need to speak to you about the XYZ Project at your convenience." Do not leave a long, drawn-out message.

- Do not leave bad-news messages of a personal nature on the voice-mail system. Such messages are inappropriate.

- Be careful of what you say and how you say it, lest you regret the message later. Because most voice-mail systems allow messages to be forwarded to others, you never know who might hear your message. Many voice-messaging systems do not allow you to eliminate a message once it's sent.

- While it may not be necessary to give the date and time of your message, it is wise to leave a date and time when you will be available if you want a callback.

ADVANTAGES AND DISADVANTAGES

With the increasing prevalence of voice messaging, both its advantages and disadvantages have begun to surface.

ADVANTAGES

- It provides twenty-four-hour-a-day answering capability.

- It enhances efficiency and boosts job productivity.

- It saves and generates money for the company.

- It improves the accuracy of message content.

- It enables one to send multiple messages to people.

- It allows messages to be easily updated.

- It reduces the need for administrative/receptionist/secretarial support.

- It serves as an important medium for business communication.

- It makes transferring of phone calls from department to department easier and more efficient.

DISADVANTAGES

- Many people are resistant to technological advancement.

- It can be difficult if users are not trained to use voice-messaging systems.

- A voice-messaging system can be less economical for smaller companies.

- People can "hide behind their mailbox" and not return calls.

- Many people dislike not being able to reach a live person.

- Concern for sender of message "confusing message" and "lack of instructions."

- Too many voice-messaging options may make it difficult for people to recall which options they used previously.

WHEN TO USE VOICE MESSAGING

Voice messaging has become a viable alternative to e-mail and fax systems as a business communicating tool, each of these three methods having specific advantages in different situations. (1) If users need to ensure privacy, deliver information quickly, get a quick response, add a personal touch, or send messages quickly, voice messaging is more desirable than e-mail or fax. (2) If users need to send information to many persons, outside the company, e-mail is most desirable. (3) If users want to edit or attach comments, forward messages to others, send information to many persons outside the company, keep or providing a hard copy, and provide a quick review of information, a combination of voice mail and e-mail is most desirable. (4) If users want to keep or provide hard copies of documents and distribute complex, lengthy information, the fax system is most desirable. (5) If users want to ensure privacy, edit or attach documents, and distribute complex or lengthy information, a combination of voice and fax systems is desirable.

BIBLIOGRAPHY

Anderson, Ronald A., Fox, Ivan, Twomey, David P. (1995). *Business Law & the Regulatory Environment: Principles & Cases.* Ohio: Cincinnati South-Western Educational Publishing Company.

Bandla, Rick. (1998). "VoiceLogiX, Inc. for Telecommunications & Voice Messaging." http://voicelogix.ca/.

Galle, William P., Nelson, Beverly H., Luse, Donna W., and Villere, Maurice. (1996). *Business Communication: A Technology-Based Approach.* Richard D. Irwin. Publishing Toronto, ON.

Norman, Donald A. (1998). "Why Voice Messaging Can't Cut It." *Across the Board* 35(5,17):1.

Okolica, Carol, and Stewart, Concetta M. (1996). "Factors Influencing the Use of Voice Messaging Technology: Voice Mail Implementation in a Corporate Setting." *Central Business Review* 15(1): 55-59.

"Other Messaging Resources." (1998). http://www.vmec.com/pg6.html.

Rood, Clint. (1998). "Advice on Good Voice Messaging." http://voicemessaging.com/advice.htm.

"Six Smart Reasons to Consider Voice Messaging." (1998). http://www.tcentral.com/messaging.html.

Treece, Malra, and Kleen, Betty A. (1998). *Successful Communication for Business and Management.* New Jersey: Prentice Hall.

CHRISTINE M. IRVINE

W

WHOLESALING

Wholesaling refers to all of the transactions in which products are bought for resale, for the making of other products, or for general business operations. A wholesaler is the individual or organization that facilitates these wholesaling activities by buying products and reselling them to yet another reseller, government agency, or an institutional user. As of 1999, there were approximately 512,000 wholesaling companies in the United States (1998), with more than half of all products sold in the country passing through these wholesaling firms. There were approximately 400,000 independent firms that handled close to $2 trillion worth of merchandise and employed close to 6 million workers.

Wholesaling is an important aspect of a company's marketing-channel strategy because it essentially involves the planning associated with industrial customers that need to distribute their products to manufacturers, retailers, government agencies, schools, hospitals, and other wholesalers.

SERVICES PROVIDED BY WHOLESALERS

Because wholesalers are in the business of buying in large quantities and delivering to customers in smaller amounts, they are able to perform physical distribution activities more effectively, including materials handling, warehousing, and inventory management. They often offer quick and frequent pick-up and deliveries, as needed, which allows both the producers of the goods and wholesale customers to avoid the risks associated with holding large inventories.

Wholesalers support retailers by assisting them in their overall integrated market planning through pricing and promotion assistance. In addition, because they enter into sales contracts with a producer and because they can sell different amounts of the product to retailers, wholesalers serve as an extension of the producer's work force. They often provide financial assistance and extend credit as needed.

Keeping producers up to date on market conditions is a critical component of wholesalers' services. Their assessment and analysis of changing market conditions are important for producers that are concentrating on market development and strategies for growth.

Because of their position in the marketing channel, wholesalers have closer contact with retail customers than do producers. Wholesalers can spread their sales costs over more products than can most producers, which results in lower costs per product. Because of this, many producers shift their financing and distribution activities to wholesalers. Because they are often specialists in understanding market conditions and experts at negotiating final purchases, wholesalers are a critical component in retail distribution strategies.

The distinction between services performed by wholesalers and those provided by other busi-

Rice wholesalers.

nesses has changed in recent years. Retailers are discovering that they may be able to deal directly with producers and they may also be able to perform wholesalers' functions themselves. Because of the increased use of computers, retailers have been able to expedite ordering, delivering, and handling of goods more effectively than in the past. However, not all functions of wholesalers can be eliminated; these functions still have to be performed by some member of the marketing channel—producer, retailer, or wholesaler—because they are vital components of supply-chain management.

TYPES OF WHOLESALERS

There are three basic categories of wholesalers: merchant wholesalers; agents, brokers, and commission merchants; and manufacturers' sales branches and offices.

Merchant wholesalers are independent wholesalers that take title to the products they sell. This type of wholesaling accounted for 83 percent of all wholesale establishments in the United States in 1998. Since merchant wholesalers take title to the products that they resell, their earnings are obtained through markup of these goods. Merchant wholesalers are often called distributors and can be categorized as either full-service or limited-function wholesalers (Figure 1).

Full-service wholesalers often provide a wide range of services to the customers for which they purchase products. Customers rely on them for product availability, suitable assortments, breaking of large quantities into smaller ones, financial assistance, and technical advice and service. Although full-service wholesalers often earn higher gross margins than other wholesalers, their operating expenses are also higher because they perform a wide range of functions.

There are four types of full-service wholesalers: general-merchandise wholesalers, limited-line wholesalers, specialty merchandise wholesalers, and rack jobbers. General-merchandise

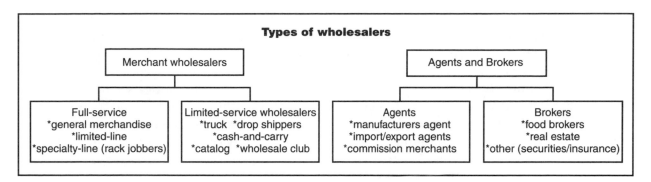

Types of wholesalers

Merchant wholesalers		Agents and Brokers	
Full-service *general merchandise *limited-line *specialty-line (rack jobbers)	Limited-service wholesalers *truck *drop shippers *cash-and-carry *catalog *wholesale club	Agents *manufacturers agent *import/export agents *commission merchants	Brokers *food brokers *real estate *other (securities/insurance)

Figure 1

wholesalers carry an extensive line of products and provide a wide variety of services. Although these wholesalers may carry many different product lines, they do not carry an extensive variety within them. Most general-merchandise wholesalers deal in such products as drugs, non-perishable foods, cosmetics, detergents, and tobacco.

Limited-line wholesalers carry only a few product lines—such as groceries, lighting fixtures, or oil-well drilling equipment—but offer an extensive assortment of products within those lines. They also offer fewer marketing services than general-merchandise wholesalers because they specialize in just a few functions that are associated with the product lines they carry. Limited-line wholesalers often take title to the products, but they may not deliver merchandise, grant credit, provide essential marketing information, or store inventory. This results in smaller profit margins as compared to general-merchandise wholesalers. The decision as to whether a company should use a limited-line wholesaler depends on the structure of the marketing channel and the need to manage the supply chain in order to obtain a competitive advantage i.e. do a "good" job so that competitors don't "steal" the business. Although the number of limited-line wholesalers is relatively small, they are important in the distribution of such products as specialty foods, perishable items, construction materials, and coal.

Specialty-line wholesalers carry the most narrow product assortment, usually consisting of a single product line or part of one. Because specialty-line wholesalers are product experts; they can offer extensive sales and product support.

Rack jobbers, sometimes considered a subcategory of specialty-line wholesalers, concentrate on retail stores. They set up and maintain displays and stock them with goods that are sold on consignment. Retailers depend on rack jobbers for the provision of health and beauty aids, hosiery, books, greeting cards, and magazines.

The five types of limited-function wholesalers are truck jobbers, drop shippers, cash-and-carry wholesalers, catalogue wholesalers, and wholesale clubs. Producers of fast-moving goods, especially those that are perishable and need frequent replenishment, often use truck jobbers because they deliver only within a particular geographic region in order to maintain product freshness. Truck jobbers are often chosen as the wholesaling method because they offer quick and frequent delivery, which is especially crucial for such items as bakery goods, meats, and dairy products.

Drop shippers arrange for shipments directly from the factory to the customer; although they do not physically handle the product, they do take title and responsibility for all the risks associated with the transport of goods. In addition, they offer the necessary sales support for the products they distribute. They operate in a wide variety of industries, including chemicals, industrial packaging, lumber, petroleum, and heating products.

Cash-and-carry wholesalers are intermediaries whose customers are usually small businesses that pay cash and have to arrange the delivery of these products themselves. Cash-and-carry wholesalers usually carry a limited line of products that have a high turnover, such as groceries, building materials, and electrical or office supplies. They do not deliver the products they sell, nor do they extend credit, but they are a vital intermediary for those small businesses that would be unprofitable for larger wholesalers to service.

Catalogue wholesalers are an alternative to cash-and-carry wholesalers that serve both major population centers and remote locations. Prepayment for goods is required, and delivery is arranged through delivery services such as UPS. A wide range of competitively priced products are offered, such as office furniture and equipment, packaging materials, and shelf and storage systems.

Wholesale clubs are organizations that offer customers a fee-based membership that entitles them to make tax-free purchases at below-retail prices. This particular concept is a growing phenomenon in the United States because of the success of such wholesale clubs as Costco and Sam's Club.

The second category of wholesalers is agents and brokers (Figure 1). Agents represent either buyers or sellers on a permanent basis, whereas brokers are middlemen that buyers or sellers employ temporarily. Both agents and brokers perform fewer functions than limited-service wholesalers but they are usually more specific in their product selection, and thus can provide valuable sales expertise. Using agents and brokers allows companies to benefit from the expertise of a trained sales force, which results in a decrease in personal selling costs. Often called functional middleman, agents and brokers perform a limited number of services in exchange for a commission that is based on the selling price.

One type of agent is called a manufacturer's agent; this type accounts for half of all agent wholesalers. They are independent middlemen who represent more than one seller and offer complete product lines. A manufacturer's agent is restricted to a particular territory and sells and takes orders year-round. There is a contractual agreement between the agent and the manufacturer that outlines territories, selling prices, order handling, delivery, service, and warranties. In service-based manufacturer's agent companies, the more services that are offered, the higher the commission. These types of agents are commonly used in the sales of apparel, machinery and equipment, steel, furniture, and automotive products.

Two other types of agents, import and export agents, specialize in international trade. Import agents find products in foreign markets and sell them in their home countries. In many countries, it is extremely difficult and sometimes illegal to try to sell products from another country without going through an import agent. Export agents locate and develop markets abroad for products that are manufactured in their home countries. As of 1998, there were more than five-hundred export agents in the United States who were paid commissions by the companies they represented.

Selling agents are middlemen that market a whole product line or a manufacturer's entire output. They perform all the functions of wholesaling, except that they do not take title of the product. Frequently, companies opt to use selling agents in place of marketing departments. To avoid conflicts of interest, selling agents represent noncompeting product lines and have the authority for pricing, promotion and distribution of those products.

Finally, there are commission merchants. These are agents who receive goods on consignment and negotiate sales in large central markets. Their specialty is securing the best price possible under market conditions. These agents are primarily found in agricultural industries, taking possession of truckloads of commodities and arranging for grading, storage, and transportation. Commission merchants deduct commission and the expense of making the sale, and then turn over the profits to the producer. Although they provide planning and assistance with credit, they do not provide any promotional support.

Since brokers are the intermediaries that bring buyers and sellers together, they are paid a commission on the transaction. Brokers do not enter into contracts for extended time periods; rather they work on a transaction-by-transaction basis. There were approximately 9,000 wholesale brokers in the United States in 1998, and most of them concentrated in food and agricultural industries. Brokers are especially useful to sellers of supermarket products and real estate. Food brokers, for example, sell food and general merchandise to retailer-owned stores and merchant wholesalers, grocery chains, food processors, and organizational buyers. Since brokers perform fewer functions than other intermediaries, they are not involved in financing, physical possession, pricing, or risk taking. What they offer instead is expertise in a particular commodity and a network of established products.

There were more than 35,000 manufacturer-owned wholesalers operating in the United States in 1999. About two-thirds of these were manufacturers' sales branches. These wholesalers maintain inventory and perform a wide variety of functions, such as providing delivery, credit, market feedback, and assistance with promotional planning. Manufacturers sales offices are the other type of producer-owned wholesaler. They do not maintain inventory, but they assist with sales and service, market analysis, and the billing and collection of funds for products sold. Both sales branches and sales offices are located away from the manufacturing plants and closer to customers because the producers are attempting to reach their customers more effectively in an attempt to create a competitive edge in the marketplace.

DEVELOPMENTS IN WHOLESALING

In the early 1990s, wholesaling gross profits declined. Because of the economic recession, a decrease in new store construction, and competition, wholesaling growth declined. Chains, which usually prefer to buy directly from manufacturers, grabbed a larger part of the market in areas such as home-improvement products. But, while tough economic conditions can affect whole-

salers adversely, a booming economy can do the same thing. Retailers, experiencing rapid sales growth, may opt to buy directly from manufacturers, thus cutting wholesalers from the supply chain.

Both retailers and producers are eager to improve their profitability, and the wholesalers are caught in the middle. Industry observers see the power in the channel shifting more toward the retailer, who may choose to reevaluate the current supply-chain members.

Because of these changing market conditions, wholesalers are concentrating on strategies to improve service by adding more value-added concepts. Even though wholesaling has traditionally involved the handling of goods, the activities and functions of wholesalers are being applied more and more in service industries. Access Graphics in Boulder, Colorado, for example, takes an active role in pursuing new business for its vendors by providing them with customer databases that help resellers in identifying sales prospects. In addition, it also provides in-house graphic departments that produce the promotional materials needed by resellers and their customers. Access Graphics believes in adding value to its supply-chain relationships; as a result, it has established a staff of system engineers who help resellers with installation, system design, and computer-memory testing.

Tough market conditions in the United States have forced many wholesalers to adopt a global perspective. Wholesalers have been encouraged by the North American Free Trade Agreement (NAFTA) to expand their operations into Mexico and Canada. It is expected that by 2010, 25 percent of wholesalers' business will come from foreign markets.

International wholesalers will experience stages of growth depending on the economic development of foreign economies. All-purpose wholesale merchants will dominate in simple economic conditions, while an expanding economy will see the emergence of interregional wholesalers. As foreign economic conditions mature, there will be a growth of specialized wholesalers, with product-line and functionally specialized wholesalers dominating the chain. In an advanced economy, channels become controlled by large-scale retailers and manufacturers; thus causing a decline in the need for conventional wholesalers.

Wholesalers that expand through globalization will face the challenge of competition against current wholesalers, new languages, an array of different legal systems and a multitude of cultural differences. However, a decision to stick with domestic markets only could hamper the growth of a wholesaler.

BIBLIOGRAPHY

Bowersox, Donald J., and Cooper, M. Bixby. (1992). *Strategic Marketing Channel Management.* New York: McGraw-Hill.

Lambert, Douglas, and Stock, James R. (1993). *Strategic Logistic Management.* Homewood, IL: Irwin Press.

Pride, William, and Ferrell, O.C. (2000). *Marketing Concepts and Strategies.* Boston, MA: Houghton Mifflin.

U.S. Bureau of the Census. *Statistical Abstract of the United States.* Washington, DC: U.S. Government Printing Office.

Ward, Getahn. (1995). "Firms Tell Suppliers to Trash Paper, Take Orders by Computer," *Commercial Appeal* July 16: C1.

PATRICIA A. SPIROU

WORD PROCESSING

Word processing is the term applied to the computerized production of text-based documents. Documents that are often produced by word-processing systems include memos, letters, mailing labels, reports, proposals, manuals, and basic newsletters. The following sections review the history, components, and features of word processing.

HISTORY OF WORD PROCESSING

Throughout most of the twentieth century, business and government documents were produced with typewriters, first manual and then electric ones. In the mid-1970s, however, computer technology made its way into the typewriter arena,

and computerized typewriters were created. Adapting the term *data processing,* which had been used to refer to computers whose main function was to process data, developers coined the term *word processing* to refer to the new computerized typewriters.

The earliest word processors were very expensive and not financially feasible for most traditional secretarial situations. Because of word-processing systems' expense and limited capability, cost-benefit studies had to be conducted to determine if the investment could be economically justified. Thus many secretarial positions were moved into centralized secretarial pools, called *word-processing centers,* so the word-processing equipment could be used more efficiently.

In the early 1980s, the introduction of the personal computer made it possible to perform multiple functions on the same machine—data processing, word processing, graphic creation, and more. This advancement made systems easier to cost justify, which greatly increased sales. As sales escalated, the cost of computer hardware and software declined, because of competition and economies of scale. With less expensive hardware and more powerful software, businesses and private households purchased personal computers at an even faster pace, and the demand for word-processing software skyrocketed. The increased power and capability, coupled with plummeting costs, largely eliminated the need for many word-processing centers, and many of today's managers and professionals have computers at their own workstations and perform their own word-processing tasks. Keying information directly into a word-processing program, rather than handwriting text, can double or triple the efficiency of document production.

COMPONENTS OF A WORD-PROCESSING SYSTEM

Word-processing (WP) technology requires both hardware and software components. WP hardware consists mainly of a computer and a printer for producing paper documents. However, because electronic mail, or *e-mail,* is such a major means of communication today, systems will benefit from a *modem,* or a link to a network for transmitting word-processing documents electronically.

The computer monitor should be large enough for easy reading of the text. Word-processing software can also enlarge the documents on the screen, which greatly helps those who are visually impaired. Word processors can display text and graphics on the computer screen the same way they will appear when printed on paper. This feature is described by the acronym WYSIWYG (pronounced *wizzie wig*), which stands for *what you see is what you get.* The keyboard and mouse should be situated for comfortable use. *Carpel-tunnel syndrome,* a condition causing discomfort and numbness in the arms and hands, can result from frequent use of a keyboard that is not properly aligned with the operator's body.

Because today's documents often include graphics, which require extra computer power and storage space, computers used for word processing should have fast processors and plenty of hard-disk space. WP systems also should include a laser or ink-jet printer to output professional-looking documents. Color printers are needed in situations requiring color output. Also, for applications involving graphically rich documents, a desktop scanner and digital camera may be added.

Word-processing software usually comes bundled with several other software packages, including *spreadsheet* and *slide show* software. Other parts of the package may include photo-editing and graphics software, plus clip art and photographs.

WORD PROCESSING FEATURES

The following word-processing features can greatly contribute to the processing of documents.

Text composition: Text can be entered into a new document by typing on a keyboard or copying it from other documents. With newer voice-recognition software, you can even speak into a microphone and have the software turn your spoken words into text. Word processors include a thesaurus to assist you in selecting words to use as you compose the message. They also include automatic outliners to assist in organizing the basic structure of the text, as well as counters to calculate the number of words in a document.

Text editing: Once a first draft is created, you can easily add and delete characters. With the cut-and-paste feature, text blocks can also be moved from one part of a document and placed in another location. Further, word processors include spell-checking and grammar-checking features to help identify and fix writing errors. They will not catch all errors, however, so human editing and proofreading are still required. The search-and-replace feature will find all occurrences of selected words or characters and replace them with something else.

Typography: Word processors can print text using any of thousands of different typefaces, commonly called *fonts.* Times Roman, Arial, Century Schoolbook, Garamond, and Helvetica are well-known fonts. In addition to choosing different fonts for text, you can modify the size, color, case, and style of the text. The height of type is measured in units called points, with one point being equal to $\frac{3}{72}$ of an inch. Thus, 72-point type is approximately one inch tall. The type in documents to be read by general audiences should usually be from 10 to 12 points tall. Colored text should be used judiciously, making sure the color complements the message.

Case refers to whether the text is displayed as small letters (lowercase), capital letters (uppercase), or small caps (all letters are capitalized, in a type size slightly smaller than that of the surrounding text, but with the first letter of words that would normally be capital larger, in the type size of the surrounding text). Additionally, changes can be made in the style, such as using italics, boldface, and underlining.

Spacing: The amount of space between words, characters, and lines of text can be modified as needed. Word processors can adjust to any measurement, such as 1.2, 2, or even 5 lines of spacing between lines.

Line formatting: By adjusting left and right margins, you can increase or decrease the length of a line of text (from a readability standpoint, the ideal line length is approximately forty characters). Further, you can create multiple columns of text on a page, such as is common in most newsletters.

Text can also be left justified (all text lines are aligned on the left), right justified (all text lines are aligned on the right), or fully justified (all text lines are aligned on the left and right). Left-justified text is perceived to be less formal; fully-justified text is more formal. Text can also be horizontally centered, which is useful for titles and headings.

Styles: Another feature of word processors is *styles*, which consists of a number of text or formatting specifications that can be automatically applied anytime it is needed. For example, you might create a style called Main Heading, consisting of the following characteristics: Helvetica, 18-point, boldface, italics, and centered. After the style is created, you can apply it to any heading in a document, instead of having to go through the tedious process of selecting the text and then specifying all the characteristics one at a time.

Reference tools: Selected words can be electronically coded for inclusion in a table of contents or index, and the table of contents or index can then be automatically created. Footnotes and endnotes can be created in a similar manner.

Document formatting: Page-layout features are extremely flexible, giving numerous arrangement options for brochures, newsletters, cards, menus, business cards, invitations, and more. By modifying margins, column widths, paper size, and different page subdivisions, you can create a wide variety of documents.

Organizational elements: Word processors provide features to organize information and guide readers through the text. Page-organizing elements can include borders, page numbers, a dropped capital letter at the beginning of a paragraph, and vertical lines between columns. You can also put a colored background behind a block of text to set it off from the rest of the text on a page.

Other layout elements include bulleted lists, numbered lists, and highlighted text, all of which make the associated text more visible and accessible. Further, headers and footers can be typed once and then automatically generated on subsequent pages.

Tables: The tables feature is used for placing text elements in columns and rows, separated by horizontal and vertical lines. Financial information, sales information, telephone lists, and any other similar data can be quickly and effectively organized with the tables feature.

Graphics: Word-processing systems permit the addition of various types of graphics, such as bar charts, line charts, organization charts, clip art, and photographs. Communication can often be greatly enhanced by a combination of text and graphics, instead of just text alone. For example, the last two years' quarterly sales figures are much easier to read and compare in a bar chart than in written text.

Output: In addition to printing word-processed documents in paper form, either in color or black-and-white, these documents can also be output as electronic documents and placed on the Internet as Web documents. The process of creating Internet documents with word-processing software consists of creating the text and graphics in the usual manner and then using the software's Web features to convert the document to a Web-compatible format.

Database tools: Word processors contain tools for creating basic databases, such as address lists, and then generating mailing labels and mass mailings from those lists. The lists can also be searched for text items that match certain criteria, and the text can then be sorted according to various criteria.

Word-processing systems are a critical component of almost any business operation that requires the creation, editing, printing, and mailing of text. Their features will continue to evolve in the years ahead.

BIBLIOGRAPHY

Norton, Peter. (1999). *Word 2000 Tutorial*. Columbus, OH: Glencoe McGraw-Hill.

O'Leary, Timothy J., and O'Leary, Linda I. (1999). *Computing Essentials 1999-2000*, Burr Ridge, IL: Irwin-McGraw-Hill.

Parsons, June Jamrich, and Oja, Dan. (1998). *Computer Concepts*, 3d ed. Cambridge, MA: Course Technology.

Rutkosky, Nita Hewitt. (1999). *Corel WordPerfect 9*. St. Paul, MN: EMCParadigm.

WILLIAM H. BAKER

WORK GROUPS (TEAMS)

Competition in business today has created a desire and need for work groups. The delegation of duties is occurring through this redesign of the work process. The delegation process is in turn creating team environments in organizations. The redesign of the work process is also due to downsizing, a collapsing of the organization's ranks, and the retiring of employees. David Cleland (1996) states that "the traditional model of organizational design is an endangered species" (p. vii). As teams are more readily seen as an effective way to involve employees and solve problems, they have modified the organizational design of many businesses. Consequently, teams are noted as the "common denominator of organizational change" (Cleland, 1996, p. 9).

The team philosophy has become prevalent throughout business. Teams, which began as social-technical-business experiments as part of the total quality management concept, have become an accepted norm in a majority of organizations today (Ozols, 1996). Teams can be categorized as steering teams, project teams, task forces, cross-functional teams, and so forth. Villis Ozols (1996) notes that 51 percent of all employees are on teams of one sort or another.

The role of a team is to improve a situation or solve a problem. Teams were initiated because it was believed that "employees will best respond (be productive) when they have a high feeling of self-worth and of identification with the success of the organization" (Ketchum and Trist, 1992,

p. 18). Reengineering, empowerment, and restructuring strategies can all give employees more control or hands-on involvement in dealing with their changing jobs. Traditional jobs do still exist; however, "jobs are increasingly a patchwork of responsibility fitting into an overall mosaic" (Cleland, 1996, p. 21). Jobs are becoming a collection of responsibilities, and employees need to be more flexible and responsive to changing demands. As individual jobs are changing, so is the manager's role. The manager is not only becoming more of a coach or facilitator but is also charged with developing the self-motivation of employees. These employees should not only set goals for themselves but also evaluate their efforts (Zenger et al., 1992). Employees are still individually important, but they are more important when they contribute to the whole—to the team.

Elisa Mendzela (1997) notes that although groups and teams are not necessarily synonymous, many people refer to almost any work group as a team. Teams have many definitions, including the following:

1. A unified, interdependent, cohesive group of people working together to achieve common objectives (Recardo, 1996, p. 6)

2. People with complementary skills, committed to a common purpose approach, who work together effectively and hold themselves mutually accountable (Mendzela, 1997, p. 62)

3. A number of persons associated together in work or activity (*Merriam-Webster Online Dictionary*, 1999)

Not all individuals necessarily possess team skills. Because American society is an individualistic one, individuals will need to suppress traditional communication methods and learn new ways to function effectively within a team (Pucel and Fruehling, 1997). When team members receive the necessary training to learn needed skills, the team becomes more effective and the individual employee wins as well (Ozols, 1996).

TEAM DEVELOPMENT PROCESS

"Team development is the process of unifying a group of people with a common objective into an effectively functioning unit" (Shonk, 1982, p. 1). The team development process includes defining, analyzing, planning, acting, and evaluating. A combination of these stages will help to produce a productive team.

An organization must first define the team and decide whether the team format is the way to proceed. Analyzing team performance and planning for improvement are essential steps in the team development process. Planning for improvements, implementing actions, evaluation, and follow-up should be designed to work in a circular pattern so as to achieve team improvement and productivity. (See Figure 1.)

ADVANTAGES OF TEAMS

Teams are helpful in dividing and organizing work. Advantages include breaking down departmental or branch barriers, improving service, providing more time for other duties, identifying issues, obtaining feedback from others, and, of course, dividing up work duties and responsibilities. These are all obviously advantageous to any company.

Teams have also been known to decrease error rates, cut order-processing time, increase manufacturing productivity, and decrease theft and absenteeism (Ozols, 1996). However, even with all these benefits, Mendzela (1997) notes that 60 percent of teams fail.

TEAM FAILURE

Reasons for team failure include internal competition, companies' failure to recognize team performance, lack of clear goals or common cause, a team being inappropriate for a situation, and negativity. The team should not be in competition with the individual; the team works through individuals toward a common goal.

When team members are confused about the team's goal or objective, they are basically saying the following three things:

1. *They don't believe in the outcome.*

2. *They don't believe the outcome is reachable.*

3. *They can't figure out what the boss really wants as an outcome.*

(Robbins and Finley, 1995).

Several myths, noted by Harvey Robbins and Michael Finley (1995), lead to unsuccessful teams. The idea that people enjoy working together is not necessarily true. Many people need their own space and feel confined when assigned to a specific group. It is also untrue that a team can solve any problem. This is not the case if the team is not focused on and knowledgeable about the problem. Just because a manager or the company president is overzealous about teams doesn't mean that a team approach can immediately or totally solve a problem. Assigning everything to teams and assuming "the more the merrier" does not work in all situations.

Ozols (1996) states that the major reason for team failure is that teams are set up only to achieve management results, not to answer the employee question "What's in it for me?" Employee job satisfaction, recognition, and so forth are essential in reducing team failure.

SUCCESSFUL TEAMS

Characteristics of successful teams include open-mindedness, involvement, ability to deal with conflict, responsibility, trust, respect for others, effective listening, and full participation. Rob Heselbarth (1997) notes that "a strong team is built by distributing responsibility, authority, and information" (p. 5). The individuals working as a team, as well as the team itself, must possess these characteristics. These characteristics can be evaluated through Pollar's (1997) five categories of team evaluation:

1. Purpose and direction
2. Problem solving and decision making
3. Communication
4. Participation
5. Leadership

A major advantage of the team approach is that employees are happier and more productive when they are grouped and, in turn, have input

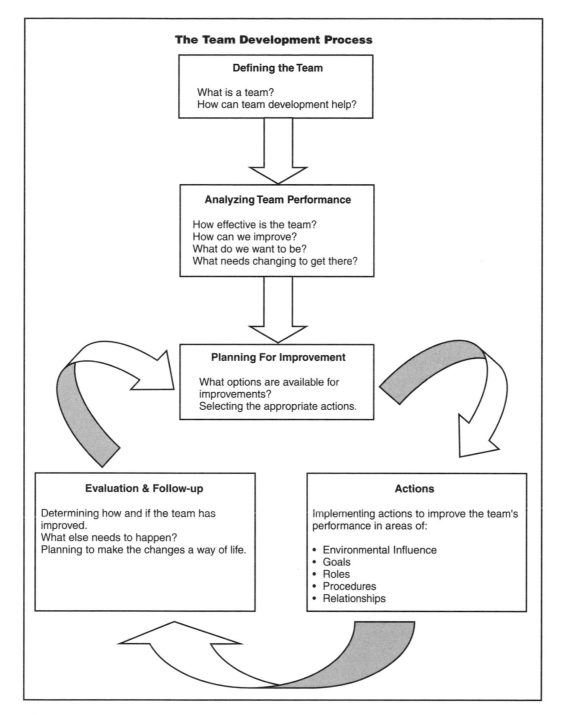

Figure 1

into or control over a certain problem in their organization (Sashkin and Sashkin, 1994). The result of the team's work has a direct impact on the individuals and their jobs; therefore, they are more interested in their work. Teams are suc-

cessful when their individual members are successful.

Many companies have had success with teams. A few examples are noted by Cleland (1996).

- *Federal Express and IDS*: 40 percent boost in production

- *Motorola Corporation*: Teams dedicated to improving quality, cutting costs, and reducing cycle time

- *IBM*: Technology assessment teams to review current and emerging technologies

- *General Electric Company*: Best-practices assessment to determine the basis of the success of competitors

Marilyn Manning and Patricia Haddock (1996) note seven steps to help manage teams:

1. *Communicate the mission of the company.*

2. *Make sure each team member knows what is expected.*

3. *Encourage open communication among team members.*

4. *Resolve conflicts quickly and fairly.*

5. *Encourage interaction among teams.*

6. *Support your teams.*

7. *Motivate and reward.*

(pp. 59-60)

These steps work well in the management of teams and can be incorporated into the team development process.

DISADVANTAGES OF TEAMS

Disadvantages of teams are not always acknowledged. However, when a company is deciding whether to develop teams, the disadvantages, such as potential internal conflict and individual loss, must be weighed against the advantages. (Individual loss refers to individual team members' giving up personal gain; they must share the success.) Power struggles are likely to arise from internal conflict disagreements.

Common problems that may arise include overbearing, dominating, or reluctant participants; floundering; a rush to accomplish goals; digression; acceptance of opinions as facts; and feuding members (Scholtes, 1988). The result will be a lack of focus on the common goal.

PRIOR TO TEAM BUILDING

Because weighing the advantages and disadvantages of teams is important, specific questions must be asked. Certain situations do not call for a team and may be better served by another work mode. Mendzela (1997) offers four specific and demanding questions to help companies determine whether a team approach is best:

1. Why would a team approach be helpful?

2. What is unsatisfactory about the current situation?

3. What are possible causes and solutions?

4. Will your organization really support a team approach?

If a team is deemed beneficial and worth implementing, a mission or purpose statement must be carefully developed. It is important that the team be clear and knowledgeable about its purpose to be able to meet the team goal and, in turn, the objectives and goals of the organization.

CONCLUSION

Teams can be effective or ineffective depending on the team environment. Minda Zetlin (1996) notes the following helpful and hindering habits for teams. Helpful habits include open-mindedness, open and immediately dealing with conflict, respect for others' time, listening, low defensiveness, and full participation. Hindering habits include negative body language, false participation, complaining about other team members rather than discussing problems with them directly (triangling), two-way arguments (crosstalk), accumulating grievances (stamp collecting), speaking at length in too much detail (going deep), and destructive humor.

Whether to use teams is an important organizational decision. Advantages and disadvantages in developing and utilizing teams must be researched. Team outcomes are dependent on an effective design and efficient work with recognition of the teams' efforts.

BIBLIOGRAPHY

Cleland, D. I. (1996). *Strategic Management of Teams.* New York: Wiley.

Heselbarth, R. (1997). "Strong Business Teams Share More Than Matching Hats." *Contractor* 44(3):5, 29.

Ketchum, L. D., and Trist, E. (1992). *All Teams Are Not Created Equal.* Newbury Park, CA: Sage.

Manning, M., and Haddock, P. (1996). *The NAFE Guide to Starting Your Own Business: A Handbook for Entrepreneurial Women.* Chicago: Irwin Professional Publishing.

Mendzela, E. (1997). "Effective teams." *CPA Journal* 67(9):62-63.

Merriam-Webster Online Dictionary. http://www.m-w.com/home.htm. 1999.

Ozols, V. (1996). "Why Teams Don't Work." Rocky Mountain Quality Conference, Denver, CO.

Pollar, O. (1997). "Effective Teams." *Executive Excellence* 14(7):18.

Pucel, D. J., and Fruehling, R. T. (1997). *Working in Teams: Interaction and Communication.* St. Paul, MN: Paradigm.

Recardo, R. (1996). *Teams.* Houston: Gulf.

Robbins, H., and Finley, M. (1995). *Why Teams Don't Work.* Princeton, NJ: Peterson's/Pacesetter Books.

Sashkin, M., and Sashkin, M. G. (1994). *The New Teamwork: Developing and Using Cross-Functional Teams.* New York: American Management Association.

Scholtes, P. R. (1988). *The Team Handbook: How to Use Teams to Improve Quality.* Madison, WI: Joiner Associates.

Shonk, J. H. (1982). *Working in Teams.* New York: AMACOM: A Division of American Management Association.

Zenger, J. H., Musselwhite, E., Hurson, K., and Perrin, C. (1992). "Managing: Leadership in a Team Environment." *Security Management* 36(9):28-33.

Zetlin, M. (1996). "Helps and Hinders: The Habits of Successful Teams." *Getting Results . . . for Hands-on Manager* 41(9):5.

TENA B. CREWS

WORK MEASUREMENT

Work measurement is the careful analysis of a task, its size, the method used in its performance, and its efficiency. The objective is to determine the workload in an operation, the time that is required, and the number of workers needed to perform the work efficiently. Work measurement helps to determine the time spent performing any process and offers a consistent, comparable methodology for establishing labor capacities.

Work measurement can be extremely effective at informing supervisors of the working times and delays inherent in different ways of carrying out work. The purpose of a measurement method is to achieve full coverage of the work to be measured.

A good work measurement system has many benefits. It helps to reduce labor costs, increase productivity, and improve supervision, planning, scheduling, performance appraisal, and decision-making.

WORK MEASUREMENT COMPONENTS

A work measurement system has three components: preferred methods, time values, and reporting. *Preferred methods* are not always the most efficient or fastest way to do a task. They should enhance safety, quality, and productivity. Safety for the employee and for the product should be considered. Quality is equally important; it has been proven that good performance and good quality go hand in hand. People who are trained in the proper method and follow that method will produce high-quality work and perform at an acceptable performance level. *Time values* and *reporting* should also be considered. The time that a job should take is determined not on the basis of speeding up the motions a worker normally makes but on the normal pace of the average worker, taking into consideration allowances for rest periods, coffee breaks, and fatigue. A reporting system is important to the success of any work measurement method. Supervisors and managers must have access to labor-management information that is both timely and complete. Timely information can be used to manage and shift labor hours to areas where they are needed and to correct problems or at least prevent them from becoming a crisis. Personal computers help to apply work measurement more effectively and more cheaply and provide immediate feedback to the workers, supervisors, and managers.

WORK MEASUREMENT METHODS

Work measurement programs involve the use of a number of techniques, each selected to cover an appropriate part of the task. The purpose of measurement is to collect real data about actual events. To obtain time standards, the data are usually converted to target data or data that apply under known conditions. All work measurement systems are based on the same, simple three-stage procedure: analysis, data collection and measurement, and synthesis. They differ in the nature and degree of analysis, the nature and level of data collection and measurement, and the nature of the synthesis process. However, the three-stage procedure remains common.

Before measurement begins, the task to be measured is *analyzed* and broken down into convenient parts that are suitable for the chosen measurement technique. The purpose of the measurement technique is to derive a "basic time" for each of these activities, elements, or motions. At the *measurement* stage, it is necessary to collect descriptive or qualitative data on the nature of the task, the conditions under which it is performed, and other factors, which may have a bearing on the time that the task takes to be complete. When repetitive jobs are measured, data are collected over a number of representative cycles of a job to obtain a "mean" or "typical" value. An analysis of the results can be done using statistical techniques to determine the number of observations that must be made to provide a given level of confidence in the final results.

At the *synthesis* stage, the various parts of the task and their associated basic times are combined together in correct sequence and with the correct frequency to produce the time for a complete job. During this stage, the basic time will be adjusted for allowances to become the standard time for the task.

There are four work measurement methods, each of which has strengths and weaknesses. The *historical data* method shows the time it actually took to complete a task. Such data have the advantages of being easy to collect, understand, and communicate, but they provide no information for future improvement. For the *work sampling* method, a large number of random observations are made of the task to determine the steps in its normal performance. This method is easy to learn and use, and it provides more operational detail than historical data. The disadvantage of work sampling is that it requires thousands of samples to establish an accurate measure for each step.

The *time study* method uses continuous and snapback approaches to record the elapsed time of a task. The snapback approach requires a stopwatch with a reset button that allows the observer to read and record the time at the end of each work element then reset (snapback) the watch to zero. Although popular, the time-study method is subjective and relies heavily on the experience of the time-study analyst. A computerized data collector provides more accurate timing than the stopwatch. However, converting actual time to the expected or normal time remains a problem.

The *predetermined motion/time systems* method is based on the premises that all work consists of basic human motions and that times can be assigned to these motions if they are defined and classified in a systematic way. A film or videotape records what a job entails and how long it takes. This technique is used most frequently in studying high-volume settings such as a workstation or an assembly line. An observer measures a job by watching and analyzing it into its basic constituent motions. This method requires substantial training and practice to acquire and maintain accuracy. It enables all types of tasks to be assigned time/duration values that can then be extended into cost values. The results are not easy to communicate, but when properly executed, this method yields very accurate times.

(SEE ALSO: *Performance Appraisal*)

BIBLIOGRAPHY

Aft, Lawrence S. (1992). *Productivity, Measurement and Improvement*, 2nd ed. Upper Saddle River, NJ: Prentice Hall.

Gagnon, Eugene J. (2000). "How to Measure Work." *Material Handling Management* 55.2 (February). 71-77.

Gowan, C. Bruce. (1999). "Which Work Measurement Tool?" *Manufacturing Engineering* 12.3 (March). 18.

Gregson, Ken. (1993). "Do We Still Need Work Measurement?" *Work Study* 42.5 (July/August). 18-22.

Horngren, Charles, and Foster, George. (1991). *Cost Accounting: A Managerial Emphasis.* 10th ed. Upper Saddle River, NJ: Prentice Hall.

NASHWA GEORGE

WORKPLACE SAFETY

(SEE: *Occupational Safety and Health Administration (OSHA)*)

WRITING SKILLS IN BUSINESS

Business writing has seven purposes:

1. Convey information
2. Explain a situation
3. Request action
4. Seek information
5. Persuade
6. Reply to communication previously received
7. Convey an attitude

The goal of business writing is to have readers understand the message completely, clearly, and accurately. A few recommendations by authorities follow.

EFFECTIVE WRITING

Effective writers use correct grammar, spelling, and punctuation.

Effective Grammar.

1. Use first person personal pronoun (*I*) to indicate who is stating the action: *Sally and I visited the museum.* (not *Me and Sally*)

2. Use parallel construction: *Managers' days are spent completing reports, interviewing personnel, and attending meetings.* (not *in meetings*)

3. Make each sentence complete: *Please read the article; you will find it a truly moving experience.* (not *Please read the article. A truly moving experience.*)

4. Don't run sentences together: *Enter the competition. I think you'll win.* (not *Enter the competition I think you'll win.*)

5. Make the meaning of sentences very clear. Assume you wish to declare limits on your work times. *I work only in the mornings.* (not *I only work in the mornings.*—concentrates not on work times, but on activities.)

6. Use *don't* only with first person (*I*) or second person (*you*). Substitute *doesn't* with third person (*he, she*). *I don't have any quarters. He doesn't have any quarters.*

7. Double negatives are illogical. *I don't want any more carrots.* (not *I don't want no more carrots.*).

8. The use of *lie* and *lay* determines their meaning. *I need to lie down.* (not *lay* down) *She lay in the sun for an hour.* (here *lay* is past tense of *lie*) *Lay the book on the table.* (here *lay* means to set something down)

9. The past tense of know is *known. I have known her for a year.* (not *knowed*)

10. The word *from* usually follows *different. Today is different from yesterday.* (not *than*)

Effective Spelling. Spell all words correctly. Following are correct spellings of words often misspelled:

- accommodation
- judgment
- I dropped the tire off of *its* mounting.
- *It's* Friday.
- E-mail is now *accessible.*
- Will you *accept* my invitation?
- I'm afraid I'll *lose* my notes.
- The nail came *loose.*
- My light is brighter *than* a spotlight.

- I *then* saw my customer.
- I am *grateful* for your assistance.

Effective Punctuation. Use periods to end sentences that:

1. State fact or opinion: *I'm flying United Airlines.*

2. Suggest or order action: *You should visit Dorothy.*

3. Request action in question form: *Will you please go.*

4. Are indirect questions: *She asked when school started.*

5. End with an abbreviation: *She lives on Palm Ave.*

Use question marks to end sentences that:

1. Ask questions of fact or opinion: *Are students admitted?*

2. Close with abbreviations: *Is it 7:00 p.m.?*

Use exclamation points to end sentences showing strong opinions: *Your house is on fire!*

Use commas:

1. After introductory parts of sentences: *After studying, she got an "A" grade.*

2. After prepositional phrases: *During the meeting, everyone talked.*

3. Before and after "interruptors" within sentences: *Please enter, Mrs. Alexander, before guests arrive.*

4. To separate two independent clauses in one sentence joined by a conjunction. *I saw her Friday, but she's home now.*

5. To separate series of three or more words, phrases, or clauses: *Germans, Russians, and Spaniards were there.*

6. Before and after non-essential interruptors, where meanings would be clear without interruptors: *This clock, as you might have guessed, is an antique.*

7. Do not use commas around interruptors that are essential to the meaning: *The automobile parked in Stall C-16 is mine.*

Semicolons join independent clauses not joined by coordinating conjunctions: *Spring is here; it's finally warm!*

Use colons where:

1. Series of items follow: *Four brothers stand before you: Abraham, Benjamin, Charles, and Herman.*

2. Long quotations follow: *The mayor said: ". . . Never before have I experienced the joy of knowing that one of our citizens was elected governor . . ."*

Use quotation marks at beginning and end of:

1. Direct exact quotations: *"Holidays," said one speaker, "are students' friends."*

2. Titles of book chapters, poems, or magazine articles: *The chapter is entitled "Computers and Clocks."*

3. Terms possibly unfamiliar to readers: *An IRA is an "Individual Retirement Account."*

Rules exist for punctuation related to quotation marks:

1. Periods and commas go inside quotation marks: *"I am listening, Father," said Robert, "I am listening."*

2. Colons, semicolons, exclamation points, and question marks go outside quotation marks unless part of the quoted material: *You said, "No one can solve this puzzle"; I found three who could.*

3. Do not use quotation marks around indirect quotations: *He said he'd leave before 3:00 p.m.*

4. Use single quotation marks for quotations within quotations: *Virginia said, "I saw the movie 'Titanic.'"*

5. Use underscore, all capitals, or italics (but not quotation marks) for titles of books; pamphlets, long poems, magazines or newspapers; or performing, musical, literary, or visual art pieces.

Apostrophes have two major rules:

1. To show possession for nouns, not pronouns: *The composer's melody is beautiful.*

2. To substitute for missing letters in "contractions": *You're the winner!*

Some major rules for capitalization are:

1. Capitalize first words in sentences. *Eighty-five books were purchased.*

2. Capitalize names: *Finally Marie visited Portland, Maine.*

3. Capitalize and abbreviate titles: *Here's Mr. Blake.*

EFFECTIVE SENTENCES AND PARAGRAPHS

Writing effectively requires skillfully transforming correct grammar, spelling, and punctuation into sentences and paragraphs.

Effective Sentences Main ideas can be emphasized by placement in independent clauses at ends of sentences: *From shrewd investments, Martin achieved overwhelming success.* Emphasis also comes by comparing or contrasting: *He speaks with the force of a thunderbolt.* Connecting words emphasize ideas: *She's inexperienced; however, look at her sales reports.* Positive attitudes increase sentence effectiveness: *We appreciate your thoughtful reply. We will study it carefully.* (versus *We cannot understand your reply.*)

Effective Paragraphs. Place a central core thought in each paragraph. Central core thoughts may come first followed by supporting sentences:

We're concerned about declines in sales and profits. Two years ago, sales reached $260 million. Last year they dropped to $214 million. Two years ago, our profit rate was 13% on sales. This past year, it dipped to 8%.

Ending paragraphs with central core thoughts are equally effective:

Two years ago, sales reached $260 million. Last year they dropped to $214 million. Two years ago, our profit rate was 13% on sales. This past year, it dipped to 8%. We're concerned about declines in sales and profits.

Skillful repetition makes a paragraph effective:

Bosses forgive occasional tardies. They even overlook mistakes. But they never condone a negative attitude.

Climatic paragraphs can generate excitement by sequencing events in order of occurrence:

On June 14, two girls carrying shopping bags entered our men's furnishings department. While one girl talked to a sales associate, the other slipped around quietly loading her shopping bag. Soon, they left by the front door. However, our security patrol spotted them. When the two girls got outside, security nabbed them and called the police.

VISUAL ASPECTS

Whether transmitted via letter, FAX, e-mail, or inter-office communication, appropriate formats create favorable impressions.

Business Letters. Business letters are mailed to persons outside the writer's company:

- One-inch margins give clean, open appearances.

- Indent first lines of paragraphs five spaces.

- Use 10- or 12-point font sizes for most letters and memos.

- Except for extremely short letters, use single spacing.

- Most business stationery is 8.5 by 10 inches.

- On envelopes, place return address at upper left and addressee's address in approximate vertical and horizontal center.

Business Memos. Memos go to persons within the writer's company. Their format, often informal, is similar to that of business letters.

Facsimilies Business faxes (Facsimiles), business letters, and memos have similar formats. Faxes, however, have attached cover sheets listing name, title, organization, address of company, and fax number of both addressee and writer. Also shown is number of pages, counting cover sheets.

E-Mail Formats for e-mail are less formal than for letters.

- Avoid capitalizing all words. (It's equivalent to shouting.)

- When replying to an earlier e-mail, include a copy of the earlier message you received.

- Always include subject lines.

- Make grammatical structures, typing, numbers, and technical information accurate and clear. Compose lengthy messages off-line.

- Confidentiality cannot be guaranteed with e-mail.

Good Impressions. Always convey a good impression.

- Write sincerely and courteously.

- Avoid big words. Don't try to impress.

- Aim communications to the reader's level

- Have appropriate-length messages. Short messages may be curt; long messages may lose readers.

- Be correct. If the meeting is Wednesday, November 30, don't write Thursday, November 30.

- Messages should flow smoothly from beginning to end and reach logical conclusions.

- Get to the point early.

- Don't pretend to know readers when you actually don't.

- Avoid sex stereotyped communications.

- Correctly convey company policy. Consult with colleagues if necessary.

BIBLIOGRAPHY

Aaron, Jane E. (1998). *The Little, Brown Compact Handbook*, 3rd ed.: 424. New York: Addison-Wesley.

Sabin, William A. (1996). *The Gregg Reference Manual*, 8th ed. Lake Forest, IL: Glencoe/McGraw-Hill.

Voiles, Price R. (1993). *Modern Business English*. 8th ed. Lake Forest, IL: Glencoe/McGraw-Hill.

G. W. MAXWELL

Y

YUPPIES

(SEE: *Lifestyles*)

Index

Numbers in boldface refer to the main entry and the subject. An *f* after a page number notes a figure in the text. A *t* after a page number notes a table in the text.

A

AAA. *See* American Accounting Association
AAAA. *See* American Association for Advertising Agencies
AAPA. *See* American Association of Public Accountants
AARP. *See* American Association of Retired Persons
AAUIP. *See* American Association of University Instructors in Accounting
ABC. *See* Activity-based costing
ABC. *See* Atanasoff-Berry Computer
ABM. *See* Activity-based management
Absolute and comparative advantages. *See* Marketing
Absolute and relative prices. *See* Pricing
Abuse of power, 217
Academic economic professors, 95-96
Acceptance of offer, 185
Access Charge Reform rule (FCC), 514
Accessory equipment goods, 165-166
Accountant profession, advertising and competition in, 5-6
  careers for the, 90-93
  changing genderization of, 11-12
  decision making role by, 4
  documents prepared by, 4
  legal practice associated with, 108
  managerial vs. financial, 4-5
  preparation for, 6
  professional organizations for members of, 10
  public, 1
  during the 21st century, 12
  work performed by, 3-4

See also Certified Public Accountants (CPAs)
Accounting, **1-16**
  careers in, **90-93**
  computerized, 8
  decision making information gathered from, 5
  described, 1
  entity units used in, 3
  ethics in, 316-318
  external and internal regulation of, 11
  FCPA provisions on, 397-398
  government, 417-419
  historical perspectives of, **9-12**
  internal controls provided by, 3-4
  not-for-profit, 645-648
  origins of, 1, 9-10
  profession of, 5
  SEC requirements for, 4, 6, 11, 375, 758-761
  standards of international, 491-493
  during the 21st century, 12
  See also Generally Accepted Accounting Principles (GAAP)
Accounting and Review Services Committee, 155-156
Accounting cycle, **6-8**
Accounting embezzlement, 217
Accounting information systems, **13-16**
  business function context of, 13-14
  implementation of, 15-16
  management information systems (MIS), 13-14
  planning, analysis, design of, 14-15
  technology of, 13
Accounting management information systems, 566
Accounting Principles Board (APB), 2-3, 11
Accounting Research Bulletins, 2-3
Accredited Estate Planner (AEP), 694

ACE Hardware name/logo, 190
Achievement motivation theory. *See* Motivation
Acquired needs theory, 619
Acquisition cost, 205
Acquisitions, 366
  See also Mergers and acquisitions
Activity-based budgeting, 72
Activity-based costing (ABC), 16
Activity-based management (ABM), **16-18**
Acuff, Frank L., 637
ADA. *See* Americans with Disabilities Act
Ad Council, 26, 27
Adjusted trial balance, 8
Administrative services managers, 113
Advanced Research Project Agency (ARPA), 507
Adverse selection, 862
Advertising, **19-24**
  budget for, 22
  career opportunities in, 116
  classic brand, **141-143**
  deceptive, 364-365
  described, 19, 23-24
  ethics and, 330
  evaluation of, 23
  forms of, 19-21
  objectives of, 21
  promotion through, 725
  selecting right approach to, 22-23
  See also Promotion
Advertising agencies, **24-27**
Advertising frequency, 22
Advertising slogans, 26
Advertising specialties, 727
Advisory Grading Services (AICPA), 865
Advisory Panel on Auditor Independence (Public Oversight Board), 734
Advocacy advertising, 19-20

X

Y

Z